Preface

Money magazine's September, 1994, issue proclaimed the Raleigh/Durham, N.C. area "The #1 Best Place To Live in America." The area was rated strongest in the areas of economy, housing, education and health. Since the early 90's The Triangle area has been ranked highly by many publications. Some of the accolades bestowed include: #1 Best City for Business by *FORTUNE* magazine's November, 1993, issue; #4 Best City for International Companies by *World Trade* magazine's October, 1993, issue; Top 20 Hot Spots to Start a Business by *Entrepreneur* magazine's October, 1993, issue; #5 Best Place to Live by *Money* magazine's September, 1993, issue; Top 10 Cities for Economic Growth Between 1965 & 1990 Cato Institute; Washington, D.C., July, 1993; Top 25 Markets Where Homeowners Will Fare Best by *U.S. News & World Report*, April, 1993, issue; *50 Fabulous Places to Raise Your Family*, published in 1993; and the most recent ranking by *Newsweek Japan*, as One of Ten Top Cities Worldwide for Japanese expatriates.

There's no doubt about it, The Triangle area is coming of age, and coming to grips with its emerging metropolitan identity in the process. The Triangle refers to that vast metropolitan area connecting Raleigh, Durham and Chapel Hill. It includes Cary, Garner, Knightdale and Apex, as well as Carrboro, Hillsborough and Pittsboro.

A few years ago, U.S. postal officials in Washington set about trying to determine what postmark should appear on mail originating from the heart of the Triangle. After much discussion and political wrangling, a compromise acceptable to all sides was finally reached. The new postmark would read: "Research Triangle Area" with "Raleigh, Durham and Chapel Hill" listed underneath.

Although the communities are more connected than ever, by Interstate 40 and regional issues, they still retain their distinct identities. There's Raleigh, the state capital, and Cary, its thriving suburb. There's Durham, a one-time tobacco and textile town known today for its high-tech medical research and fine arts programs. Then there's Chapel Hill, home of the first public university to open its doors, and its flourishing small-town neighbor, Carrboro. If you get to know each of these towns, you'll also find that they in turn are made up of distinct, diverse neighborhoods.

Whether you prefer the bustle of an urban neighborhood, the amenities of the suburbs or the tranquility of the countryside, the Triangle has something to offer. And unlike any other area of the state, its population is unusually diverse. The Triangle is a place of pine trees and well as Ph.D.s, of planned unit developments and lively small towns.

iii

We're proud of The Triangle and our Guide attempts to provide a one-stop source of information about this dynamic area. We're including chapters on each of the Triangle's major communities: Cary, Chapel Hill, Durham and Raleigh. Here you'll find detailed information on local history and folklore, neighborhoods and housing prices, schools and child care, parks and recreation, services and utilities and places of worship.

A visitor will appreciate the chapters on Accommodations, Airport, Arts, Attractions, Night Life, Restaurants and Shopping. If you're considering relocating your business, you might be interested in Commercial Development. A newcomer will find Homes (with information on buying, building or renting) especially helpful in making all the decisions associated with moving to a new area. We've also included chapters on Neighbors, Colleges and Universities (some of the best in the country), Hospitals, Media, Spectator Sports, Retirement, and great places to visit on Daytrips and Weekends. For parents, we added a chapter on Kidstuff. Many of our readers recommended a chapter on golf, so we added Golf in the Carolinas.

As a special gift to you, our reader, we have added valuable coupons to the back of the book to assist you in your exploration of the Triangle and the Carolinas. We hope you will enjoy our newest edition and look forward to receiving your comments and suggestions on our More Products Information Card.

ACKNOWLEDGEMENTS

This book includes not only the opinions of the authors, but those of dozens of individuals who offered encouragement, as well as their thoughts and ideas about the Triangle. We thank you all.

ABOUT THE AUTHORS

J. Barlow Herget is a writer who lives happily in Raleigh with his wife and dog. They have two grown children. Barlow received his B.A. in English and history from the University of Arkansas and his M.A. from the University of Virginia. He also was a Neiman Fellow at Harvard University. He has worked for the *Detroit Free Press* and the *News and Observer* as well as the North Carolina Department of Commerce and Data General Corp. His articles have appeared in *The Atlantic*, the *New York Times*, and numerous state and local publications. He has been a resident of the Triangle since 1973 and lives in Raleigh's Cameron Park neighborhood.

Katherine Kopp, a native North Carolinian, has lived in the Triangle since 1973. She is a freelance writer, and has contributed to various local and regional publications, including *The Spectator, Triangle Business, Carolina Parent, Elegant Bride* and others. She received her B.A. in English from the University of North Carolina at Chapel Hill. She lives in Chapel Hill with her husband and three daughters.

THE INSIDERS' GUIDE™

TO THE
TRIANGLE

by

J. Barlow Herget
and
Katherine Kopp

Published and distributed by:

Becklyn Publishing Group, Inc.
P.O. Box 14154
Research Triangle Park, NC
27709

(919) 467-4035

•

Seventh Edition

2nd Printing

•

Copyright 1994
by
Becklyn Publishing Group,
Inc.

•

Printed in the United States
of America

•

This book is produced under a
license granted by:

The Insiders' Guides, Inc.
P.O. box 2057
Manteo, NC 27954
(919) 473-6100

•

ISBN 0-9623690-7-1

BPG
BECKLYN
Publishing Group, Inc.

Publisher/Managing Editor
Carolyn Clifton

President
Barbara C. King

Office Manager
Susan A. Gatens

Editorial Consultant
David McNally

Account Executive
Annabelle Lee Gates

COVER COLOR PHOTOS

Raleigh Skyline:
Courtesy Peter Damroth Photography

Golf in the Carolinas:
Courtesy N.C. Travel and Tourism

Duke Chapel:
Courtesy N.C. Travel and Tourism

ACKNOWLEDGEMENTS

The Capitol:
Courtesy N.C. Travel and Tourism

Brightleaf Square:
Courtesy N.C. Travel and Tourism

Umstead State Park:
Courtesy N.C. Travel and Tourism

NCSU Football:
Courtesy N.C. State University

The Old Well:
Courtesy N.C. Travel and Tourism

Summerfest in Cary:
Courtesy N.C. Symphony

Maps by:
Fraser Van Asch

Bringing You Closer, Taking You Farther.

Whether you're a brand new resident or a Tarheel returning home, one thing's for certain, our Triangle region has gained a national reputation as one of the best places to live and work in the entire country. The Triangle's an easy place to call home, and Cellular One® makes it an easy place to call anywhere. That's because Cellular One's commitment to continued advances in wireless communications technology is bringing the Triangle closer as a region, and taking Triangle residents as far as they want to go. To find out how the first choice in cellular can take you farther, call 800-727-CELL.

CELLULAR**ONE**®

One Of Cablevision's Finest Programs Is A Viewer Call-In Show No One Ever Sees.

ehind the scenes at our Customer Service Center, a dedicated group of very special people answer thousands of Cablevision inquiries each day. One at a time. With enthusiasm. Up-to-the-minute information. And a genuine desire to satisfy every customer.

Everyone at Cablevision knows

Great Service

means more than prompt, cheerful response.

It also means the widest selection of quality programs. A studio-quality picture.

Quick action on requests.

Professional help with VCR-cable connections. And round-the-clock readiness that you can always depend on.

Our ongoing commitment to serving our customers means we take each one of these aspects to heart. Each friendly voice on the telephone, every expert technician in the field wants you to know: we're working hard to make our service the best it can possibly be.

We're Cablevision, serving the Raleigh, Durham, and Chapel Hill areas. Television at its best and the people who keep it coming.

Look At All The Things We Are.™

Table of Contents

Directory of Maps

From the Governor...

The North Carolina State Seal

JAMES B. HUNT JR.
GOVERNOR

Dear Friends:

As Governor of the State of North Carolina, it is indeed my pleasure to welcome you to the Triangle, that vast metropolitan area that connects Raleigh, Cary, Durham, Chapel Hill, and Carrboro.

This area is home to more than 50 corporate, academic and governmental research facilities. What sets it apart from other great research centers, however, is the superior quality of life. Unlike most metro areas, the Triangle consists of medium-sized cities which offer all the amenities of big-city living without the high costs. One can easily go from urban to suburban to rural settings within the area, experiencing Southern Hospitality at its very best all along the way.

Just recently, FORTUNE magazine conducted its fifth annual study of America's best cities for business, and Raleigh/Durham ranked Number One!! Contributing to the area's top ranking was the presence of three top universities-Duke, UNC and NC State-and the 7,000-acre Research Triangle Park. We are extremely proud of this recognition and feel that it is well deserved.

On behalf of all our citizens, I again welcome you and invite you to enjoy all that the Triangle has to offer.

My warmest personal regards.

Sincerely,

James B. Hunt Jr.

The Triangle
Area

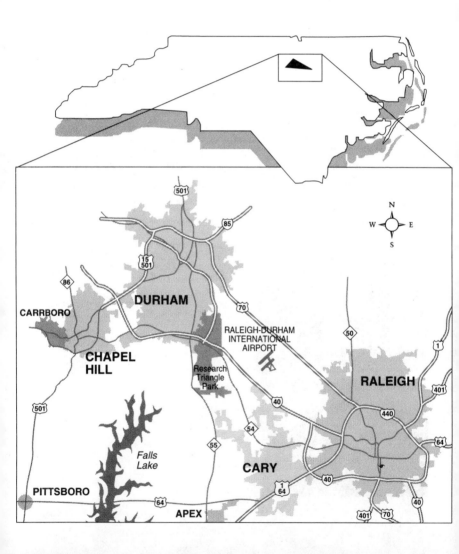

Welcome to the Triangle!

The Triangle area can best be defined as a "community of communities," or as "linked communities." Diversity and livability are the keys to regional success and therefore are fostered.

The term "Research Triangle" comes from the three major research universities in our region: North Carolina State, The University of North Carolina, and Duke University, which form a "triangle." In the early 1950s, our region was losing many of its brightest people. After receiving masters and doctoral degrees, many would leave for other parts of the country or the world. Visionary leaders conceived of the Research Triangle Park to "reverse the brain drain." Its success was not immediate but it gained momentum in the sixties with a key event being the decision of IBM in 1965 to locate in the Park.

FORTUNE magazine recently rated the Raleigh-Durham region as the No. 1 best place in the country to do business. The focus of this year's FORTUNE ranking was innovation and technology. With the research universities and the large companies in the Park, we have a solid base. However, it was noted that we now have many start-up firms related to research in areas including biotechnology, microelectronics, health care, and telecommunications.

Of key importance to the economic success of the region is the RDU International Airport. The Airport is served by all major airlines and is a hub in the American Airlines system. A flight to London's Gatwick Airport will commence on May 26, which will boost the international reputation of the region.

Of course, the region is much more than research universities and high technology. There is the impact of all colleges and universities, with a student population approaching 100,000. Also, Raleigh is the state capital and Durham is properly known as the "City of Medicine." Further, the region serves as a center of commerce for all of eastern North Carolina.

The population and job growth is exceptional and presents a special challenge for continued outstanding land-use planning. Decisions are reached through consensus of many stakeholders including business, government, universities, and neighborhood leaders. The result is a balanced approach that seems to produce excellent results. No one group is dominant.

There are many exciting leisure-time opportunities from cultural, to recreational, to spectator sports. The North Carolina Museum of Art, the North Carolina Symphony, and the American Dance Festival form a solid base for cultural activities. Recreation ranges from athletics of all types to more relaxed activities. The coast and the mountains can be reached in just a few hours. Spectator sports are plentiful and exciting. For example, we are proud that North Carolina State, Duke, and UNC have all won NCAA basketball championships since 1983, including a string of the last three—two by Duke and last year by UNC.

So, welcome to the "community of communities" known as the Triangle area. Expect a lot of give and take, but also expect increased cooperation on key regional goals. The region will work together where it makes sense but will keep its diversity in doing so. You will have a lot of choices and a lot of fun.

Smedes York

In addition to being a prominent local businessman, Smedes York heads the Raleigh-Durham Regional Association, a group dedicated to promoting the economic development of the five-county area encompassing the Triangle.

Inside
Accommodations

The Triangle area has an abundance of accommodations for travelers seeking a comfortable, reasonable place to sleep, thanks in large part to the building of numerous hotels in the Research Triangle Park area. The selection is varied, and room costs range from under $40 for economy motels to over $75 for name chains and considerably more for luxury accommodations. The trend toward pleasant, no-frills motels that cater to budget conscious business people is evident in the Triangle, and one such chain, **The Sundown Inn of America, Inc.,** was started in Raleigh. International chains such as **Holiday Inn, Hilton, Marriott, Sheraton, Quality Inn** and **Radisson** all have locations here as well as many quality local hotels.

You need to know that under North Carolina law, pets are not allowed in hotels and motels, although some places make provisions or allowances for them. You also need to be forewarned that during home college football and basketball and college graduation weekends, it can be rough trying to find a room for the night anywhere in the Triangle without a reserva-tion. In other words, plan ahead if you can.

For the purposes of comparing prices, we have categorized accommodations with one to four dollar signs ($), based on the typical daily rates charged for a standard room with two double beds:

Under $50	$
$51-$75	$$
$76-$100	$$$
$101-up	$$$$

As with the restaurants in town, most accommodations honor major credit cards, except for the properties we've noted. Make sure you find out which cards are honored before you check in if you plan to pay by that method. Keep in mind that this is a guide and rates may change. Weekend rates are almost always less than weeknight rates; for example, the Marriott charges about $103 per night during the week for a double and around $49 on weekends. So, be sure to ask for information on special rates when you make your reservations.

Raleigh

Raleigh's hotels and motels have rotated through a couple of boom and bust cycles. There were stretches when travelers could hardly rent a tent in town; a rush of hotel building would follow until someone hollered "bankruptcy" and then things settled down again.

At present, travelers have little trouble finding rooms, although occupancy rates are creeping over 70 percent again. The following sampling covers most areas of town and we've tried to include landmarks to help you find accommodations conveniently located to your business or other activities.

DAYS INN SOUTH

U.S. Hwy. 70, E.   772-8900
$$

There are few sizeable motels southeast of Raleigh, but this 103-room facility is one that offers a few amenities, such as a pool and 24-hour movies. It is conveniently located near several shopping centers but no decent restaurants. It's a good place to stay if you're looking at Garner real estate. It's a working person's place and truckers are welcome. The Beltline is about two miles away toward Raleigh.

COMFORT SUITES AT CRABTREE

3908 Arrow Dr.   782-6868
$$

Opened in 1990, the Comfort Suites at Crabtree offers 88 suites, all with refrigerators, coffee makers and other amenities to make your stay a comfortable one. Some suites are equipped with whirlpool baths, and a weekday stay in any suite gets you a full breakfast buffet and free van service to and from the airport. Every Monday through Thursday from 5 to 7 p.m., this establishment offers **The Manager's Reception** with complimentary drinks and hors d'oeuvres to all guests and their guests. An outdoor pool provides a means for exercise and relaxation while away from home.

BROWNSTONE HOTEL

1707 Hillsborough St.   828-0811
$$

For years, this was Raleigh's Hilton and, even today, some folks still refer to it as the Hillsborough Street Hilton. But it's the Brownstone now. It is about one mile from the Capitol and downtown, and continues to be a popular gathering place for politicians and legislators when the General Assembly is in session. It is also next to the NCSU campus and has banquet facilities for moderate-sized conventions and meetings. It has a restaurant and pool. A color TV with HBO is in each of its 210 rooms. The **Hillsborough Street YMCA** is right next door.

COURTYARD BY MARRIOTT

1041 Wakestowne Dr.   821-3400
(Wake Forest Road and the Beltline)
$$

This is one of the Marriott chain's three Courtyards in the Triangle area and if you've seen one Courtyard, you know the routine. The location—near Raleigh Community Hospital—gives it excellent access to all parts of the city. It has

153 rooms and is very popular with business travelers who want more than a light left on for them.

ECONO LODGE EAST
3804 New Bern Ave.   231-8818
$

This popular, no-frills, chain operation has a fitness room with workout equipment. It has 123 rooms. It's convenient to Wake Medical Center and points east such as Knightdale, Wendell and Zebulon, if that's where your business takes you.

HILTON CONVENTION CENTER, NORTH RALEIGH
3415 Wake Forest Rd.   872-2323
$$$-$$$$

Built by one of Raleigh's premier hotel-motel building families, Seby and Roddy Jones, this has been a growing hotel, located right off the Beltline and across the road from Raleigh Community Hospital. It is Raleigh's biggest convention center hotel. It has an indoor pool with sun deck, restaurant and one of the better night spots, **Bowties**. Politicians are moving their election-night parties here, where the large convention and meeting facilities accommodate up to 1,500 people—one of the largest such centers on the east coast—and its 338 rooms lodge plenty of guests. This is also a popular place for business seminars.

HOLIDAY INN, STATE CAPITAL
320 Hillsborough St.   832-0501
$$

Part of the downtown Raleigh skyline since the 1970s, this freshly renovated Holiday Inn tower is in the round and one of the more convenient places to downtown and the state government complex, which are within walking distance. From its tower restaurant, you have a grand view of the city and its byways. It has the amenities one expects at a Holiday Inn, including a pool on the second floor. It has 201 rooms.

HOWARD JOHNSON, HIGHWOODS
U.S. Hwy. 1 North & Beltline   872-5000
$

This venerable Howard Johnson is one of Raleigh's best known motels, and it has maintained its clean and efficient service through local ownership, Bryant Lodging. Popular with traveling business people because of its reasonable rates, it is close to a number of good restaurants including the popular **El Dorado** and is near **Highwoods Sportz** racquetball club. It has a pool and 156 rooms, and sits across the highway from the ABB Manufacturing plant.

INNKEEPER MOTOR LODGE, SOUTH
2501 S. Saunders St.   821-0521
$

This economy chain motel was built in 1987 and is located to serve the growing travel trade going south, toward Garner. It is located at the Beltline and South Saunders Street, next to **Sam's Wholesale Club**. It is aimed at the business traveler and has 68 rooms. Fast food restaurants are also nearby, and its location makes it convenient for downtown (five minutes away) and points south, such as Garner, Clayton or Fuquay-Varina.

MARRIOTT AT CRABTREE VALLEY
4500 Marriott Dr.   781-7000
$$$

One of Raleigh's national chain hotels, the Marriott sits off Glenwood Avenue, across from Crabtree Shopping Mall and is the biggest hotel in the city. It quickly established itself as a popular gathering and drinking hole for the party and sports crowd. Its central location to growing northwest Raleigh has made it a popular business meeting place. It's also only 18 minutes from RTP and RDU. When there's a seminar on a big party night, parking can be a problem. It has an indoor-outdoor pool, tennis courts, fitness room and 375 rooms. Also check out the Marriott's less expensive **Courtyard**, at the intersection of the Beltline and Wake Forest Road. Newer still is the **Fairfield Inn**, Marriott's least expensive chain, located at the Beltline and U. S. Highway 1, North.

MEREDITH GUEST HOUSE
2603 Village Ct.   787-2800
$$$

If you need more than a hotel room, you may want to consider a guest house. The Meredith Guest House offers 60 suites that are nothing less than small, well-furnished apartments. They have one-, two- and three-bedroom units and are conveniently located off the Beltline at the Lake Boone Trail exit on Wycliff Road. Included is a 24-hour message center, maid service and room meal service. It even provides a shopping service. The units rent by the day or month, and many Triangle companies lodge employees on temporary assignments here. Also, relocating families with children find the guest house less cramped than a motel room. Pool and fitness center privileges are available.

OAKWOOD BED & BREAKFAST INN
411 N. Bloodworth St.   832-9712
$$$

This bed and breakfast house is located in historic Oakwood, a neighborhood behind the Governor's Mansion in downtown. New management took over in 1993, inheriting an inn that made a name for itself. When it opened, it was selected by one publication as being among the top 10 new B&B accommodations in the country. The house is on the National Register of Historic Homes and has six rooms, all with private baths and telephones. Guests get the "chef's choice" breakfast and afternoon refreshments. They also get quiet—TV on request. FAX and copy machines are also available.

PLANTATION INN RESORT
6401 Capital Blvd.   876-1411
$

This is one of the city's grand old motels, over 35 years old, and **the** place to stay when it first offered travelers the luxuries of a swimming pool, playground for children, putt-putt golf and even a fishing pond! It has seen Raleigh grow out to its doorsteps, yet has retained its green landscape and serene, Southern plantation motif. Its restaurant's buffet has been popular for years, and it offers a number of rooms for meetings and/or private dining. It has 93 rooms.

RADISSON PLAZA
421 S. Salisbury St.   834-9900
$$$

The interior of this 17-story downtown hotel is one of the most elegant of any in the city, and its 350 rooms make it among the largest. It is located next to and is connected through the underground parking lot with the city's Civic Center and the BB&T York-Hannover skyscraper. It is a block away from Memorial Auditorium. The indoor pool features a whirlpool, and the Radisson has business meeting facilities for as many as 700 or as few as 15.

RAMADA INN, CRABTREE
3920 Arrow Dr.   782-7525
$$

This is one of the best Ramada Inns and has the awards to prove it. Locally owned and managed, it was rated one of the five best Ramadas in the world in 1981 and 1983, and its **Colonnade Restaurant** is one of the best in town, with many homemade specialties. Getting to the place is the biggest hurdle, since the entrance is somewhat obscured by the traffic jamming the Beltline and Glenwood Avenue interchange. (The entrance is off the east bound lane of Glenwood Avenue, immediately before the Beltline interchange.) It has 174 rooms, a pool and outdoor exercise stations and satellite access for television.

RESIDENCE INN
1000 Navaho Dr.   878-6100
$$$

Another establishment in the Marriott Hotel group, this one is aimed at the person who wants more than the usual motel room and is planning to stay longer than a night. The rates vary according to stay and it's popular with corporate visitors. There are 144 units, including suites with fireplaces, continental breakfasts, heated pool, whirlpool and sports courts.

SHERATON CRABTREE
4501 Creedmoor Rd.   787-7111
$$$

Opened in 1973, the Sheraton was part of Raleigh's new retail and office hub at Crabtree Valley. It has expanded as the city has grown and office buildings have filled in the woods and slopes nearby; the hotel now has 318 rooms, which makes it one of the largest in the city. It has all the amenities that a Sheraton offers, including a pool and restaurants, and it caters to the business meeting bunch with convention-size facilities.

VELVET CLOAK
1505 Hillsborough St.   828-0333
$$$

Built during the 1960s, the Velvet Cloak—named after Sir Walter Raleigh's gallant gesture with his cloak to cover a puddle for Queen Elizabeth—has been a fixture in the city's hotel life ever since. It set the standard for many years, and its restaurants remain among the best in the city. It has an indoor pool and atrium. It is next to the YMCA, where visiting members can play racquetball and work out. Its location near NCSU and downtown has made it popular both with academics and government leaders, and visiting rock stars at Walnut Creek Amphitheater; it usually is an election eve party site for one of the major candidates. It has 172 rooms.

Cary

Cary has come a long way from the days of the Walker Hotel, built in 1869 by Frank Page and still standing by the Seaboard Railroad next to the Town Hall. Some might argue, however, that the restored Page-Walker hotel now used for civic functions has more charm and elegance than the motels of today. Some will blame the nearness of Raleigh on the dearth of distinctive Cary lodgings, but the town will get its due as more offices and research facilities locate here.

BEST WESTERN

1722 Walnut St.   481-1200
(near South Hills Mall exit
off U.S. Hwys. 1 & 64 south)
$$

Like all units in the Best Western chain, this one is independently owned and the chain gives it a top rating. It is located at one of Cary's busiest exits of I-440, and if you're coming from the airport, you will get off at Exit 293. Almost all of Cary's motels are clustered at this exit. This Best Western has suites, mini-suites, and standard rooms. It has two conference rooms, a satel-lite dish receiver, and a swimming pool. Complimentary breakfast is served daily and complimentary transportation is provided to and from RDU airport and to some local business parks.

COURTYARD BY MARRIOTT

102 Edinburgh Dr.   481-9666
(MacGregor Village)
$$$

This may be Cary's nicest hotel with 149 rooms, and like other Courtyards, it's designed for business travelers. It is conveniently located in southwest Cary, where U.S. Hwy. 1 intersects U.S. Hwy. 64 at MacGregor Village Shopping Center. It opened in 1987 and offers a pool, laundry, exercise room and whirlpool.

EXECUTIVE SUITES

108 Hidden Oaks Dr.   467-6016

This is corporate lodging for those people who need to stay for longer periods of time than a night or two. It offers fully equipped kitchens, maid service and exercise facilities. Check for rates.

HAMPTON INN

201 Asheville Ave.   859-5559
$$

This is one of Cary's newer hotels, another member of a popular chain that caters to the mid-range customer. Like most of the town's other accommodations, the Hampton is located in southwest Cary, near the Western Wake Medical Center and has 131 rooms. Get off U.S. Hwys. 1 and 64 at the exit for U.S. 64. It offers a free continental breakfast, nonsmoking rooms, pool, and exercise room. Children stay free with their parents.

DAYS INN
800 Walnut St.   469-3400
(South Hills Mall exit)
$$

This one opened in August, 1986, and it, too, is located near the South Hills Mall exit off U.S. Highways 1 and 64, but on the east side of the highway. It is a multi-story motel catering to business people who want a clean, comfortable room at a budget price; it has 67 of them. It offers a continental breakfast in its lobby and permits free local phone calls.

Durham

ARROWHEAD INN
106 Mason Rd.   477-8430
$$-$$$$

Retired publisher Jerry Ryan and his wife Barbara, a freelance writer, took one look at this elegant plantation home built in 1774 and knew it would make a perfect bed-and-breakfast inn.

Located on three-and-a-half acres north of town, the inn features eight guest rooms, including six with private baths, all furnished in antiques and country primitives. Downstairs in the parlor, guests can watch television or relax with an assortment of games and puzzles. The Ryans and their daughter who helps run the inn will be happy to direct you to the best local restaurants and interesting sites and activities.

Included in the price of a room is a hearty country breakfast of meat and eggs, homemade breads, preserves and coffee. Children are welcome. The Arrowhead also can accommodate small meetings. As past presidents of the N.C. Bed & Breakfast Association, the Ryans can recommend other B&Bs across the state.

BEST WESTERN SKYLAND INN
I-85 at U.S. Hwy. 70   383-2508
$$

Thirty-one rooms with queen-size beds are offered here, with corporate discounts available. Children under 12 are free when accompanied by an adult. Amenities include a restaurant, swimming pool, color cable TV with HBO, picnic and playground. It is convenient to golf and tennis courts. It's also twelve minutes from the airport (a $25 taxi ride). Call toll-free 1-800-528-1234.

BROWNESTONE MEDCENTER INN
2424 Erwin Rd.   286-7761
NC (800) 872-9009
Outside NC (800) 367-0293
$$-$$$

The Brownestone is conveniently located next to the **Duke Medical Center** and **Duke University**. Complimentary shuttle service to and from the Medical Center is available. The Inn has 140 rooms with double or king-size beds and color cable TV with HBO. There are more expensive rooms on the Executive level, a special floor with its own limited-access elevator, morning newspaper and continental breakfast.

Other services and facilities include an indoor heated pool, Jacuzzi and sauna, handicap rooms, nonsmoking rooms, self-service laundry and same-day dry cleaning, and complimentary afternoon tea in the Williamsburg-style lobby. There is a full-service restaurant and pub that feature daily lunch, dinner and drink specials.

CAMPUS ARMS MOTEL APARTMENTS
501 Elba St.   286-9133
Weekly/Monthly

This place is frequented by people using or visiting nearby **Duke University**, **Durham Regional** or **VA hospitals**, as well as traveling business executives who need to stay in town for more than a week. There are 29 furnished apartments with a living room, kitchen, bedroom and bathroom, including four efficiencies geared for the handicapped. Apartments can be rented by the week or month. All apartments include telephones, color cable TV and weekly maid service.

CAROLINA DUKE MOTOR INN
2517 Guess Rd.   *(919) 286-0771*
(just off I-85)   *NC (800)672-7578*
Outside NC (800) 438-1158
$

This Inn provides a free shuttle to **Duke University Hospital** and the **VA Hospital**. There are 181 rooms with color TV and HBO, and queen- and king-size beds. The **Wabash Restaurant** is open for breakfast and dinner. There's a swimming pool as well as two conference rooms for meetings accommodating up to 30 persons.

CRICKETT INN AT I-85
I-85 at Hillandale Rd.   383-2549
$$

This Cricket Inn offers 120 rooms with color cable TV and there is a swimming pool. It is convenient to several restaurants on Hillandale, Guess and Hillsborough Roads.

CRICKETT INN-MEDICAL CENTER
2306 Elba St.
286-3111
(near Duke Medical Center)
$$

An eight-story high rise near **Duke University and hospitals**, Cricket Inn-Medical Center includes 151 rooms with double or queen-size beds, color satellite TV and a restaurant. Kids stay free.

DAYS INN
I-85 at N. Redwood Rd.   688-4338
(800) 325-2525
$

Located six miles north of Durham off Interstate 85, this popular chain motel includes 119 rooms with double beds. The restaurant is open from 6 a.m. to 10 p.m. Color cable TV, a free kennel for pets and a pool are available.

DURHAM HILTON
3800 Hillsborough Rd. (off I-85) 383-8033
(800) 445-8667
$$$-$$$$

This six-story facility has 154 rooms, 10 suites, an outdoor pool and complete health-club facilities, including sauna, Jacuzzi, a VCR for jazzercise tapes and exercise equipment. **Tipton's** offers regional and New American cuisine, a piano bar, and can accommodate private parties and banquets. **Blue Chips** lounge has two bars and deejay music for late night dancing. With 19 meeting rooms, the Hilton can also accommodate small groups or conferences of more than 500.

HOLIDAY INN WEST

3460 Hillsborough Rd.   383-1551
                         (800) 238-8000
$$

Well-located just off I-85 at the U.S. 15-501 Bypass, the Holiday Inn is convenient to the new Durham Expressway. This property also includes the **Greenery Restaurant** and **Iron Duke Lounge**, meeting rooms holding up to 200 and a closed-circuit TV for teleconferences with other Holiday Inns, along with a swimming pool and rose garden courtyard.

JUNCTION INN

2101 Holloway St.   682-5100
$

This may be the cheapest motel room in town, providing 120 rooms with double beds and color satellite TV with a movie channel. Children under 3 are free and it's within walking distance of several restaurants.

OMNI DURHAM

201 Foster St.   683-6664
$$$

The Omni Durham is in downtown Durham; it also houses the **Durham Civic Center**, which hosts meetings and civic events for the city and its visitors. The Omni has 189 beautifully appointed rooms and three suites. A restaurant and lounge are on the premises. It is a great place to stay if you have business downtown or at Duke University.

SHERATON UNIVERSITY CENTER

2800 Middleton Ave.   383-8578
(US 15-501 at   1-800-325-3535
Morreene Rd.)
$$$

Each of the 322 rooms has cable TV with SpectraVision pay-per-view movies. The VIP floor guests receive complimentary hors d'oeuvres, continental breakfasts and a morning newspaper. Discount rates are available on holidays, during summer months and for extended stays. It also offers special-rate plans for hospital patients and their families.

Praline's Cafe has an all-you-can-eat breakfast and lunch buffet seven days a week plus *a la carte* dining. The **Executive Club** offers the traveling business person a place to work (PC with printer and desks provided) and network, as well as unwind and relax (TV, bumper pool, etc.). The **Varsity Lounge** in the lobby is a convenient place for a drink or a bite to eat.

THE BLOOMING GARDEN INN
A BED AND BREAKFAST

513 Holloway St.   687-0801
$$$-$$$$

Owners Dolly and Frank Pokrass, describe their 1892 yellow Victorian Inn with 20 columns and six gables as a "surprise in the inner city." A 2 1/2-year renovation was completed in the fall of '90.

There are five beautifully appointed rooms, including wonderful suites with Jacuzzis, lace curtains, antiques and artwork set in a

Photo by Veryl Barry.

*The Washington-Duke Inn and Golf Club is located
at the edge of Duke University's West Campus.*

tasteful mix of warm colors. The Inn features leaded, beveled and stained-glass windows, a custom picket fence, a wraparound porch and lots and lots of blooms in season.

The innkeepers' Southern hospitality makes this place a special treat. Guests enjoy full gourmet breakfasts on a relaxed schedule. Convenient to **Duke, Ninth Street, Brightleaf Square**, galleries and antique shops, The Blooming Garden Inn is a comfortable and pleasant place to spend a few days. For the newcomer, Dolly is happy to provide her famous "5 minute tour" of Durham.

TRAVEL TIME INN
4516 Chapel Hill Blvd.   *489-9146*
$

Travel Time is just across the street from **Darryl's Restaurant** (see "Durham" section of **RESTAURANTS**) and adjacent to the Oak Creek Shopping Village (see "Durham" section of **SHOPPING**). There are 80 rooms with color satellite TV, a pool and special discounts for graduation and football weekends.

WASHINGTON DUKE INN AND GOLF CLUB
3001 Cameron Blvd.   *490-0999*
$$$

This 171-room, $16-million luxury hotel is is located at the edge of Duke's west campus. It faces the university's 18-hole golf course, now open to the public, and hotel patrons may use the nearby Duke Forest jogging trails. The inn also offers the **Fairview Restaurant, Bull**

Durham Lounge, suites and meeting facilities.

Research Triangle Park

BEST WESTERN CROWN PARK
4620 South Miami Blvd.   *941-6066*
$$$-$$$$

The Best Western Crown Park features 177 rooms, two suites, and offers many complimentary specials. The Crown Park has an outdoor heated lap pool, weight room, sauna and whirlpool. There is a full-service restaurant on the premises. Other features geared to the business traveler include a library in the hotel and a club room with a large-screen television for relaxing when your business is done.

ECONO LODGE
4433 N.C. Hwy. 55   *544-4579*
(off I-40)   *Outside N.C. (800) 446-6900*
$

This Econo Lodge offers 85 modestly priced rooms with color satellite TV including movie and sports channels. It is adjacent to a 24-hour Waffle House restaurant. There is no pool, but an exercise room, sauna and facilities for the handicapped are available.

GUEST QUARTERS SUITE HOTEL
2515 Meridian Pkwy.   *361-4660*
$$$$

Well situated in the Research Triangle Park, the Guest Quarters Suite Hotel offers travelers the spaciousness of a suite in its 203 rooms, in a conveniently located, first-class hotel. The hotel offers three flexible meeting and banquet rooms, a health club, indoor/outdoor pool, tennis court and jogging trail. The guest library allows you to use an IBM-PC computer or simply catch up with regional and national newspapers and periodicals. The **Piney Point Grill & Seafood Bar** is a comfortable place to enjoy good food. The hotel is located at the intersection of Interstate 40 and N.C. Hwy. 55, very convenient to Raleigh, Durham and Chapel Hill.

HOLIDAY INN/RDU AIRPORT
I-40   *941-6000*
$$$-$$$$

The Holiday Inn in the Research Triangle Park—rated one of the Top 20 in the chain—has 250 rooms, with VCRs in all the rooms.

The hotel has a fine restaurant, **Remington's**, as well as the more casual **Cafe**, and a lobby bar, as well as the popular nightspot, **Horsefeathers**. An upgraded concierge floor on the fifth floor of the hotel offers the business traveler special amenities.

MARRIOTT
South Miami Blvd. at I-40
Vanguard Center(800)228-9290/941-6200
$$$$

This $7-million, six-story Marriott is located in the Vanguard Center office complex off I-40. Features include 224 rooms, nearly 4,000 square feet of meeting and banquet space and a 2,600-sq.-ft.

The Holiday Inn/RDU Airport in Research Triangle Park has been rated one of the Top 20 in the chain.

conference center. The hotel also offers two executive board rooms, the **Garden Court** restaurant and lounge, a lobby bar, gift shop, indoor pool, health club and sauna.

MEREDITH SUITES AT THE PARK
300 Meredith Dr. 361-1234
$$$-$$$$

Luxury accommodations at the Suites include 100 fully furnished and equipped suites geared to business travelers or visitors planning an extended stay. Each suite contains a kitchenette, living room and one or two bedrooms. The hotel also offers use of a health spa and outdoor lap pool. **The Carvery** serves breakfast and lunch featuring homemade soups, sandwiches and specials. Meredith Suites are located at Park Place West, an office complex at the intersection of N.C. Highways 54 and 55, near Research Triangle Park.

RADISSON GOVERNORS INN
N.C. Hwy. 54 549-8631
$$$$

The Radisson Governors Inn is one of the nicer accommodations in the Triangle, adjacent to Research Triangle Park and convenient to RDU International Airport. Recently renovated, it offers 193 rooms with queen-size beds and color satellite TV. The Radisson Governors Inn also features the elegant **Galeria Restaurant**, **Quorum Lounge** and full meeting and banquet facilities. Swimming pool, tennis and exercise trails are on the property.

SHERATON IMPERIAL HOTEL
4700 Emperor Blvd. 941-5050
Page Rd. Exit N.C. (800) 222-6503
off I-40 Outside N.C. (800) 325-3535
$$$-$$$$

This 10-story, 333-room hotel offers luxurious accommodations for tourists and traveling business executives. The 19-acre hotel and convention center complex includes two restaurants (see "Research Triangle Park" section of **RESTAURANTS**) and a nightclub/lounge. Tennis courts, a 2.5-mile area jogging trail, an outdoor pool and a Jacuzzi round out the amenities. The Sheraton's newest addition to the Triangle also offers plenty of space for meetings, conferences, private parties and banquets. Nearby, the 34,000-sq.-ft. **Imperial Athletic Club** offers a gym, 25-meter lap pool, aerobic studios and nautilus equipment for a daily guest fee.

Chapel Hill

The Chapel Hill area offers a variety of accommodations for tourists and business travelers, including luxury hotels, historic inns, bed-and-breakfasts and furnished guest apartment complexes. You should pay special attention here to our advice to plan ahead, because it's tough finding a place to stay near Chapel Hill during UNC home football and basketball weekends unless you have reservations.

CAROLINA INN
W. Cameron Ave. 933-2001
$$$

There's a lot of history behind this building. The old New

Hope Chapel from which Chapel Hill derives its name once stood about where the Carolina Inn's parking lot is today. The Inn itself was built in 1924 by John Sprunt Hill, an industrialist, financier and graduate of the UNC class of 1889. The Hill family deeded it to the university in 1935 and it has been enlarged twice since then.

The financial well-being of the Inn has been constrained in recent years by its need to abide by state personnel wage and benefit guidelines, which are significantly higher than industry wages. A contract to manage the Inn was awarded recently to the Doubletree Corporation, in an effort to restore the inn to profitability. Major renovations are planned for the future.

In the meantime, the Inn continues to be a majestic brick building, with a pillared front porch said to be inspired by the portico of Mount Vernon. Guests may enjoy a quick breakfast or lunch in the **Garden Room** cafeteria, or have lunch, dinner, or a delightful Sunday brunch in the **Hill Room** restaurant (see the "Chapel Hill" section of **RESTAURANTS**).

The Inn also features a full-service bar and a pleasant open-air patio. Expansive conference and banquet facilities are available. And it's all within walking distance of the campus and downtown. There are 140 guest rooms and 14 suites with color televisions.

CHAPEL HILL INNTOWN
609 Hillsborough St.   967-3743
Weekly Rates

Tucked into a cul-de-sac within walking distance of town are

Major renovations are planned for the historic Carolina Inn.

seven townhouses reserved for out-of-town guests needing a place to stay for at least a week. It's perfect for traveling business executives or families visiting for a short time. You can choose between one-bedroom and two-bedroom units, each fully furnished and equipped with washer and dryer, color cable television, central air conditioning, linens, towels, all cooking utensils and appliances. There's even cut firewood for the fireplace.

COLONIAL INN

153 W. King St.   732-2461
Hillsborough
$$

Built in 1759, this is the oldest inn still operating in the United States. It has provided lodging for the likes of Aaron Burr and Lord Cornwallis, to say nothing of the modern-day guests who come from all over the world.

Located in historic Hillsborough, just about 10 miles north of Chapel Hill, the Inn, now operated by Carlton and Sarah McKee, has 10 guest rooms. Throughout the building you'll see many antiques, including a few of the original furnishings.

Guests will enjoy dining on Southern-style food in the Inn's restaurant, antique hunting in downtown Hillsborough or just sitting on rocking chairs on one of the porches or balconies looking out over this historic town (see **NEIGHBORS**).

FEARRINGTON HOUSE COUNTRY INN

Fearrington Village   542-2121
Pittsboro
$$$$

Who says you can't have old-World charm and modern amenities? R.B. and Jenny Fitch, owners of the Fearrington House Country Inn, are offering both with plenty of flair. Their luxurious 15-unit inn evokes images of an 18th-century country retreat, complete with cozy suites, exquisitely landscaped gardens and Belted Galloway cows grazing in the pasture.

Each room is uniquely decorated with antiques gathered from the Fitches' shopping excursions to England. But in addition to the country charm, there are plenty of civilized touches: stereo music, modern baths, afternoon teas in warm sitting rooms, and a complimentary breakfast at the widely acclaimed gourmet **Fearrington House** restaurant right on the premises (see the "Chapel Hill" section of **RESTAURANTS**).

The Country Inn, recipient of the prestigious "Relais & Chateaux" designation, is located at **Fearrington Village**, a 100-acre planned residential development located on a former dairy farm about six miles south of Chapel Hill (see **CHAPEL HILL NEIGHBORHOODS**).

In addition to the Inn and restaurant, there is the **Fearrington Market**, where you'll find fresh bagels and breads, gourmet coffee, wines, cheeses, a wide assortment of gifts and even the latest issues of *The New York Times* and *The Wash-*

ington Post. You can spend your time strolling through the gardens, shopping at **The Fearrington Village Center Shops** (see "Chapel Hill" section of **SHOPPING**) or touring the craft and antique shops in Pittsboro, 10 miles to the south (see **NEIGHBORS**).

HAMPTON INN
1740 U.S. 15-501 Bypass   *968-3000*
$$ *1-800-HAMPTON*

This two-story, 122-room hotel located a stone's throw from the Omni Europa Hotel (see below), is part of a national chain offering comfortable accommodations at lower-than-average prices. How is this done? The Inn eliminates a few "frills" such as restaurants, lounges and meeting spaces—a minor concession to economy given its location near the many eateries and shops at Eastgate (see the "Chapel Hill" section of **SHOPPING**) and along U.S. Hwy. 15-501. You still get a swimming pool, television, movie channels and a phone. And the continental breakfast is on the house.

HOLIDAY INN OF CHAPEL HILL
U.S. 15-501 Bypass   *929-2171*
$$

This Holiday Inn includes 135 comfortable rooms with color cable TV. It is convenient to downtown Chapel Hill, the UNC campus and close to the Interstate 40 interchange. **Teddy's** restaurant (with an adjacent cocktail lounge) features a buffet from 5 to 7:30 p.m., Monday through Friday. There is also an outdoor pool at the hotel.

THE INN AT BINGHAM SCHOOL
Mebane Oaks Rd.   *563-5583*
Orange County
$$-$$$$

Located in the countryside on the site of the old Bingham Preparatory School 11 miles west of Chapel Hill, the Inn offers a convenient and comfortable retreat. Meticulously restored, the former headmaster's home (listed on the National Historic Registry) is now a cozy bed-and-breakfast getaway.

Furnished in 19th-century antiques, the Inn offers six spacious guest rooms with luxurious private baths, including two with whirlpools. One room is located away from the main house in a building called The Milkhouse.

During your stay, you'll be invited to relax by the fire, roam the surrounding farm and woodlands, enjoy complimentary wine and cheese or join in a game of croquet, golf or tennis. A complete Southern breakfast is served in your choice of the formal dining room or an airy sun room. For reservations call or write P.O. Box 267, Chapel Hill, NC 27515.

THE INN AT TEARDROP
175 W. King St.   *732-1120*
Hillsborough
$$-$$$$

Located in the historic district of Hillsborough, this 18th-century inn offers a charming retreat within 15 to 20 minutes of Durham and Chapel Hill. Proprietor Tom Roberts—who opened the Inn in 1987—invites guests to stroll in his gardens and relax in the elegantly furnished parlor or on the back veranda.

For antique hunters, it's a pleasant walk to the shops in downtown Hillsborough and a quick drive to the **Daniel Boone Shopping Village**. It's also convenient to the many outlet stores in nearby Burlington.

This lovely two-and-a-half-story home, which has been occupied alternately as a residence and an inn since 1767, is furnished in antiques as well as reproductions by local craftsman Stephen Jones. Rates include a deluxe continental breakfast.

OMNI EUROPA HOTEL

U.S. 15-501 Bypass   *968-4900*
N.C. (800) 672-4240
Outside N.C. (800) 334-4280
$$$$ *(Variable seasonal special rates)*

As soon as you walk in the door you'll realize this is one of Chapel Hill's most luxurious hotels. Highlighting the well-appointed lobby is a wall-sized bas-relief sculpture called "The Dream," commissioned for this location. The Omni Europa Hotel sits on six rolling acres with lighted tennis courts and a pool.

You can enjoy an elegant dinner in the **Rubens Restaurant** (see "Chapel Hill" section of **RESTAURANTS**) or more casual fare in the **Lobby Lounge**. Take the glass elevator to the **King's Club** lounge on the top floor for late night entertainment, including top-notch jazz performances (see "Chapel Hill" section of **NIGHT LIFE**).

There are 172 rooms and suites. Meeting and banquet space is available for groups of 10 to 700.

THE SIENA

1505 E. Franklin St.   *929-4000*
$$$$

Named for a small Italian city, this luxurious addition to Chapel Hill was designed to recall the intimate hotels of Europe. Rooms range from doubles with king-size beds ($99 double occupancy) to the two-bedroom Presidential Suite ($275), with traditional furnishings, spacious marble-tiled baths (including whirlpools) and nine-foot ceilings.

Il Palio, the Siena's restaurant, features Northern Italian and Mediterranean cuisine and nightly piano entertainment (see "Chapel Hill" section of **RESTAURANTS**).

WINDY OAKS INN
THE PAUL GREEN HOMEPLACE

Old Lystra Church Rd.   *942-1001*
Chatham County
$$

This century-old farmhouse, once occupied by noted playwright Paul Green, has been lovingly renovated. Located on 25 oak-shaded acres about four miles south of Chapel Hill, the Windy Oaks Inn has four guest rooms, including one with a shared bath. Full country breakfasts, featuring delicious homemade biscuits, are included in the price of the room. Guests may take their breakfast on the terrace or in the dining room.

During your stay you may enjoy afternoon teas, strolls to the old log cabin and goldfish pond, or horseback riding expeditions along bridle paths located right on the property. The inn can also accommodate weddings, parties and luncheon meetings.

Photo courtesy Regional Airport Authority.

RDU International is a major north-south connecting hub for American Airlines.

Inside
Airports

The Triangle is served by the ever-growing Raleigh-Durham International Airport (RDU), which offers commercial flights as well as general aviation services, and two small airports for private planes. In this section, we'll tell you about the airlines, commuter services, ground transportation and other facilities available at RDU and we'll give you some basic information about the Horace Williams Airport in Chapel Hill and the Raleigh East Airport between Knightdale and Wendell. Also, a new airport south of Raleigh is in the planning stages.

Raleigh-Durham
International Airport

Located off Interstate 40 between Raleigh and Durham, the Raleigh-Durham International Airport (RDU) is a 15- to 20-minute drive from most points in the Triangle. It wasn't long ago that this location was considered the middle of nowhere. You could drive up, park your car, buy a ticket, check your bags and be off in no time. Thanks to recent expansions, those days are over forever.

RDU has grown dramatically from its beginnings in what was a U.S. Army barracks out in the boonies. In 1993, RDU celebrated its 50th anniversary. More than 10 million passengers pass through its gates, and about 93,000 tons of cargo are shipped through the airport annually. Projections are for those numbers to triple in the next twenty years. Today the airport is served by all major airlines, four commuter lines and 24 air-cargo services.

Anyone who hasn't been to RDU in the last ten years won't recognize it today. In 1982, the airport added the $9.6 million Terminal A. In 1986, another $2.5 million was spent expanding this terminal's passenger waiting areas, gate space and aircraft parking, as well as building a new 10,000-foot runway. Further renovations to Terminal A were completed in the spring of 1991, at a cost of about $2 million.

But while the changes to the rest of the airport have been dramatic, the biggest change of all came several years ago, when American Airlines decided to make RDU one of its major north-south connecting hubs, prompting the construction of the $60 million Terminal C that opened in 1987. American now has over 200 flights per day arriving and departing Terminal C. Just a few years ago, nonstop cross-country flights out of Raleigh-Durham were non-existent.

Today, thanks to continuing expansion of the airport, you can take your pick of a variety of non-stops to most major U.S. metropolitan areas, and direct flights to some international destinations, including London, Paris and Cancun, Mexico. The once-quiet RDU airport is now the 30th-busiest airport in the country, and the 54th-busiest in the world. Here's a list of the major airlines servicing Raleigh-Durham:

American	1-800-433-7300
Delta	1-800-221-1212
Northwest	1-800-225-2525
TWA	1-800-221-2000
United Airlines	1-800-241-6522
U.S. Air	1-800-428-4322

Commuter Airlines

The commuter airlines serving Raleigh-Durham are:

American Eagle	1-800-433-7300
Delta Connection	1-800-221-1212
United Express	1-800-241-6522
USAir Express	1-800-428-4322

General Aviation Services

Here's a list of companies at RDU offering rental, charter and flight-instruction services:

JETCRAFT SERVICES, INC.
1-800-762-7837
Jetcraft offers 24-hour jet and propjet charter service.

AVIATION, INC.
1-800-666-7980
This 24-hour charter service offers both domestic and international flights, as well as aircraft management, sales and brokerage.

NORTH STATE AIR SERVICE, INC.
933-9028
North State offers air-taxi and cargo service. It specializes in trips to the North Carolina Outer Banks, including Portsmouth Island, Hatteras Island and Ocracoke Island. Call for information on chartering a flight.

RALEIGH FLYING SERVICES
840-4400
Raleigh Flying Services offers air charters, aircraft service and flight instruction.

Ground Transportation

AIRPORT PARKING
If you're arriving by car, you can park in the hourly parking lot for 75 cents per hour, up to a maximum of $6.50 a day. For parking for more than 4 hours, you may park in one of the daily lots for 75 cents per hour, with a daily maximum of $3.50.

There is no bus service from the airport to any of the major cities of the Triangle, but there are rental cars, taxis and limousine services. The airport limousine services (usually a van) will charge about $15 per person to get you to downtown Raleigh, Chapel Hill or Carrboro. That's cheaper than local taxis that will charge $20 to $25 for the same trip. But if you are sharing a ride to one location with one or more others, you'll probably do better in a cab, since they charge by the trip and add only moderate surcharges for additional passengers. Many of the hotels and motels offer free shuttle service to and from the airport, so check on that when you make your reservations.

AIRPORT EXPRESS

596-2361

This limousine service charges about $15 per person to downtown Raleigh, Chapel Hill or Durham. Call for details on charges to other locations.

Check the Yellow Pages for rental car companies or for cab companies offering service to and from the RDU Airport.

Horace Williams Airport

The Horace Williams Airport just north of downtown Chapel Hill started out as a grass landing strip in the 1920s. The airport was constructed by the Navy just before World War II. It's now owned by the University of North Carolina. Horace Williams has a 3,500-foot paved and lighted runway. Pilots can give five signals on the 123.0 radio frequency to raise the intensity of the lights for landing. 100

octane, low-lead fuel is available. For more information on the airport, call 962-1337.

Raleigh East Airport

This small airport, with a 3,000-foot asphalt runway, is a nice alternative to RDU if you fly your own airplane. The runway points north-south. It is conveniently located about eight miles east of Raleigh's Beltline on U.S. Highway 64, and you can see the airfield and airplanes from the highway. It is a privately owned airport that is open to the public. Full maintenance and aircraft fuel are available and the lounge has vending machines. It is open seven days a week from 8:30 a.m. until dark. The field is lighted at night and has a rotating beacon. A grass taxiway is available. It doesn't cost to land, and tie-down is available at $35 per month.

Pilots might want to know that the Raleigh East UNICOM is 122.8 and it's 17.2 miles on 109 radial from RDU VOR. A number of King Airs use the field, though most planes are smaller. Available fuel includes 100-octane low-lead and auto gas. Raleigh East specializes in flight training with four full-time instructors. It also provides rental, charter and aerial photography services. For more information, call 266-2209.

RDU Airport serves as a major north-south connecting hub for American Airlines which now has over 200 flights per day arriving and departing Terminal C.

*Raleigh Little Theatre's Youth Series Show,
"The Ice Wolf," was a 1994 hit.*

Inside
Arts

When Sam Shepard needed music for a Broadway play, he turned to The Red Clay Ramblers of Chapel Hill. When Jack Lemmon was to star in Eugene O'Neill's *Long Day's Journey into Night*, the curtain rose first, not in New York, but at Duke University. And when the internationally acclaimed American Dance Festival was looking for a home, it chose Durham. You might say that the Triangle has finally been discovered as a center for the arts.

Natives have long been aware that this corner of North Carolina is home to a string of talented bluegrass and blues musicians, actors and actresses, painters, sculptors, dancers, craftspeople, poets, novelists and playwrights. But now the area is also recognized as a key stop for out-of-town artists on tour.

Since Raleigh, Durham and Chapel Hill are only 20 to 30 minutes apart, Triangle residents don't have to go very far to be inspired or entertained by poetry readings, rock concerts, gallery openings, jazz performers, bluegrass musicians, modern dancers, Broadway plays, community theatre, jugglers, potters, magicians and more.

Here's a guide to The Arts in the Triangle, broken down into the following sections: Theater, Music,

Visual Arts, Dance and Writers. In each section you'll find information on what's available in Raleigh and Cary, Durham, Chapel Hill and Carrboro.

Theater

Thanks to major universities and active community arts groups in Raleigh and Cary, Durham, Chapel Hill and Carrboro, you can find an evening of provocative theater just about any night of the week anywhere in the Triangle. From Broadway-bound Tony Award nominees to one-acts entirely written, directed and acted locally, there's plenty going on in the dramatic arts arena. And if you get really inspired, you may even find yourself climbing on stage through participation in one of several thriving community theatre groups.

Raleigh and Cary

There are several excellent local organizations that span the spectrum of arts in Raleigh and Cary. If you are interested in the arts—dance, music, painting or theater—you may want to become active in these groups. They are the **City of**

Raleigh Arts Commission (831-6234), the **Raleigh Fine Arts Society** (which is more social), the **Cary Cultural Arts Commission** (467-2654), **Wake Visual Arts Association (828-7834)** and the **United Arts Council,** (839-1498) a private, non-profit agency founded in the 1980s to provide financial support to the arts much the way the United Fund supports human services agencies. The Raleigh Arts Commission has published a directory for the area that lists hundreds of organizations and artists. The United Arts Council publishes a quarterly calendar, and the news weeklies, *The Spectator* and *The Independent,* publish weekly calendars; these publications are the best sources for information on the Raleigh and Cary cultural activities. The Wake County Library also maintains a list of clubs, many of which are involved in the arts. The associations and organizations listed here are major and minor groups, but ones that Insiders will know.

NORTH CAROLINA THEATRE
Memorial Auditorium   *831-6916*

The N.C. Theatre is located in the beautifully renovated Memorial Auditorium. It is sponsored in part by the city of Raleigh and produces professional theater for the capital city. Auditions are held for each production in New York and Raleigh. The group traces its roots back to 1972 and Chapel Hill; but in 1983 with partial funding offered

Theatre In The Park

It's Not The Same Old Song And Dance.

Call 919/831-6058 for our season schedule. No dogs allowed.

by the city, it made its home in Memorial Auditorium downtown. Since then, it has produced well known musicals such as *Showboat*, *Sweeney Todd* and *Big River* and hosted several National Tours including *Cats* and *Les Miserables*. Season tickets are available.

RALEIGH ENSEMBLE PLAYERS
201 E. Davie St., Ste. 305   832-9607

The Ensemble Players began in 1980 and is a community theater group—with hopes to become legitimate professional theater—that specializes in contemporary plays and musicals at Artspace in downtown Raleigh, an intimate 90 seat theater. Four to five "Mainstage" productions are performed each season, held at Artspace or other city theaters such as St. Mary's Pittman Theater or NCSU's Stewart Theatre. The 1993/94 show schedule included *The Sum of Us* and *Tales of the Lost Formicans*. The group sponsors acting classes and has plans for voice, technical theater classes and movement. For a schedule, tickets or information, give the Ensemble Players a call.

RALEIGH LITTLE THEATRE
301 Pogue St.   821-3111

This is one of the country's oldest community theaters, born in the Great Depression, and the building is vintage WPA architecture. In 1989, there was a $1 million addition for a youth stage and studio space. The theater, known to Insiders as RLT, is comprised of volunteer performers, with paid artistic director, managing director and technical staff. RLT's productions range from comedies to musicals to dramas. Each season, the Main Stage Series includes five well-known Broadway shows, the City Stage Series presents four contemporary works, and the Youth Series includes five shows for the family audience.

RLT also includes an award winning youth drama program with year-round classes for ages 6 to 18. Its youth theater group in 1991 was selected to represent the USA in Moscow for an international theater camp. RLT's first production, in 1936, was *The Drunkard* and Raleigh theater lovers have been drinking up the shows since. Recent productions have included, *Music Man*, *Big River*, *Me and My Girl*, *Biloxi Blues*, *Ain't Misbehavin'*, *California Suite*, *A Streetcar Named Desire* and *A Walk in the Woods*.

At season's end, there is an awards ceremony in which actors are awarded "Cantey's" for best performances. Membership has risen to over 4,000 in recent years and season tickets are very affordable at $52 for the Main Stage, $35 for the City Stage and $27 for Youth Series. For individual ticket prices at the door, call the box office.

STEWART THEATRE
NCSU Student Center   515-3104

This is perhaps the most active performing arts organization in Raleigh, with its Center Stage series of over 30 professional events each year. You can choose from theater, dance, music and eye opening, ear burning shows such as Los Angeles homeless people's poetry (Like, really wow, dude!).

Stewart is the 800-seat theater in the NCSU Student Center, and every seat is a good one. It opened in 1973 and attracts a wide audience from the Triangle area, although students, faculty and staff get discounts on tickets. You can make up your own series ticket by purchasing four or more shows for a 20% discount, or you can purchase tickets for single events. Discounts are available for children, groups of 10 or more, high school students and senior citizens. Limited reserved seating is available, by advance sale only.

Every season includes music, modern dance, comedy, mime, children's theater, jazz, international events, drama and more from performers such as Bobby McFerrin, North Carolina Shakespeare Festival, National Theatre of the Deaf, Wynton Marsalis and The Boys Choir of Harlem. Ticket prices range from $5 to $22.

THEATRE IN THE PARK
107 Pullen Rd.   *831-6058*

Theatre In The Park and local legend Ira David Wood, the theater's talented executive director, have earned a reputation as one of the state's most exciting and innovative community theater centers since its start in the early '70s.

TIP annually presents a wide range of productions in its intimate and totally flexible performance space. The best in comedy, musicals, Shakespeare, contemporary drama and children's theater are offered not only as mainstage productions, but in its Studio Theatre as well. Over 40 original plays have premiered at TIP, two of which toured off-Broadway. TIP also offers theater classes and workshops for all ages.

A Christmas Carol by Ira David Wood, has been a traditional sellout at Raleigh's Memorial Auditorium. It's Wood's version and he steals the show, every year. Sign up or become a season member of TIP if you want to be guaranteed a seat!

THOMPSON THEATRE
Dunn Street, NCSU   515-2405
The Thompson Theatre is student-oriented, with an emphasis on experimentation. Each production is open to all NCSU students, whether experienced or not, as actors, technicians, crew members and directors. Major productions are directed and produced by the professional theater staff. Experimental productions are completely student-run, and African-American and children's theater are also available for all students.

The two stages—the main theater holds 220 after 1988 renovations, and a smaller, studio stage seats 89—have productions that vary in quality, given casting limitations. After all, NCSU doesn't give a drama degree and engineering is not always the best stepping stone to the stage. But the tickets are among the best value in the Triangle: $7 for adults, and an amazing $3.50 for students. The season usually includes seven performances in the main theater, and eight in the studio.

Durham

ROYALL CENTER FOR THE ARTS
120 Morris St.   560-ARTS
Royall Center for the Arts is actually a plot of land in downtown Durham, bounded by Morris, Chapel Hill, Foster and Morgan streets, on which stands the **Durham Arts Council Building**, the **Carolina Theater** and the **Civic Center Plaza**. One of the best things to happen in downtown Durham in the last several years is the extensive renovation and expansion of The Durham Arts Council building. Thanks to the fund-raising efforts of the Council itself, the persistence of several leaders in the local arts community, and the passage of a bond referendum, the theater and adjoining building were renovated into a vast multipurpose complex.

The Durham Arts Council Building, named for state Senator Kenneth Royall, opened in September 1988. And in early 1994, the restored Carolina Theatre, next to the Arts Council and connected to the civic center complex, reopened after five-plus years of design and construction work. The Carolina Theatre, built in 1926, now holds a 1,016-seat main hall for films and live performances and a 3,500 title video rental shop. Scheduled for 1994 are a musical revue about the building's history, Asian-American and animated film festivals and jazz performances. The reopening of the Carolina Theatre is expected to liven up downtown Durham all year long.

DURHAM ARTS COUNCIL
120 Morris St.   *560-ARTS*

The Durham Arts Council not only makes grants to and houses a number of outstanding local arts organizations, including community theater groups such as the **Durham Theater Guild**, the **Durham Savoyards**, the **Little Big Theatre Company** and the **Young People's Performing Company** (see below), but it also helps with art programs in the Durham Public Schools, produces the annual two-day **CenterFest** and provides classes in the arts for the community. Among the Arts Council's most remarkable recent accomplishments has been the staging of operas, right in the streets of downtown Durham, involving collaboration with virtually every performing arts group in Durham. Call for more information and a schedule of upcoming events.

DURHAM THEATRE GUILD
120 Morris St.   *560-2731*

One of the three community theater groups sponsored by the Durham Arts Council (see others below), the Durham Theatre Guild's mission is to provide quality dramatic productions as well as theatrical opportunities for the local community. The Guild typically stages four plays a year, including one musical. It's done everything from hits such as *A Funny Thing*

Happened on the Way to the Forum and *Godspell* to more obscure alternative theater productions.

DURHAM SAVOYARDS
560-2739

If you like Gilbert and Sullivan, you'll love the Durham Savoyards. Another community theater group under the Durham Arts Council umbrella, the Savoyards have for more than two decades devoted themselves to presenting at least one major G&S production a year. After its collaboration with the Durham Symphony (see the Music section of this chapter) to stage *The Grand Duke*, the Savoyards can say that they have performed each of the 13 existing G & S operettas. In addition to annual G & S performances, the Savoyards frequently sing for special events such as CenterFest (see **ATTRACTIONS**).

MAN BITES DOG THEATER
682-0958

As the name suggests, the establishment of this innovative local group in 1987 was exciting news for downtown arts patrons stalking something different. This offbeat theater laboratory focuses on timely and controversial subjects that otherwise might not be dramatically addressed in our neck of the woods. Recent productions have dealt with AIDS (*The Normal Heart*) and censorship in the arts (*Indecent Materials*). Founders Jeff Storer and Ed Hunt received an "Indie" award from *The Independent* weekly, in recognition of their contributions to the area arts community.

LITTLE BIG THEATRE

120 Morris St.   *383-4931*

The Little Big Theatre does theater for children and adults, sort of like the old "fractured fairy tales" that modify familiar stories and add enough subtle humor and wit to make it really entertaining for all ages. Featuring the talented husband and wife team of Don and Lisa Bridge and several other regular players, the group performs 8 to 10 shows per year. Recent productions have included *The Steadfast Tin Soldier, The Princess and the Pea* and *The Emperor's New Clothes.* The company's productions usually run Wednesday, Thursday and Saturday.

YOUNG PEOPLE'S PERFORMING COMPANY

120 Morris St.   *560-2745*

As the name suggests, this is a community theater group geared specifically for young people from ages 5 to 18. Founded in the spring of 1982, the company offers classes and performance opportunities. It's done *Trojan Women, The Crucible* and *A Midsummer Night's Dream,* as well as its own productions.

DUKE UNIVERSITY

Bryan Center   *684-2306*

A few years ago we got a call from a friend in Washington, D.C., all excited about just having seen Jack Lemmon in *Long Day's Journey into Night* at the Kennedy Center. Imagine how we, the pitied "country cousins," felt telling our friend that we had already seen that same production more than a month ear-

lier, when it opened at Duke University's **Reynolds Theatre**.

Actually that wasn't the first time we one-upped our friends from Washington and New York, and it won't be the last. There's at least one New York producer who is eyeing the Triangle as the ideal place for trying out Broadway-bound plays—sort of a Southern version of New Haven, Connecticut. Triangle audiences have also had the chance to preview Mikhail Baryshnikov in *Metamorphosis* and Julie Harris in *Lucifer's Child.*

Of course we don't always get the big plays before they hit Broadway, but we can always catch them when they come this way on tour, and for usually about half the price, thanks to the Broadway at Duke series. Productions for 1994 will include the world premiere prior to its Broadway opening *City of Angels* and Lynn Redgrave in *Shakespeare for my Father.* One of the nicest places to enjoy that level of theater, as well as music and dance, is at Duke's $16 million **Bryan Center**. Performances take place in the 600-seat **Reynolds Theater** or the 150-seat **Shaefer Laboratory Theater**.

DUKE DRAMA

684-2306

This group of local performers produces educational theater for the university, the community and the state. It stages close to a dozen plays a year in the Bryan Center theaters. Call for more information.

DUKE INSTITUTE OF THE ARTS
109 Bivins Bldg.   *684-6654*

Duke University Institute of the Arts is breaking the boundaries of convention with their new directions in performance art. Call for performance schedules.

TRIANGLE PERFORMANCE ENSEMBLE
St. Joseph's Cultural Center
804 Old Fayetteville St.   *683-1709*

This ensemble focuses on works by black playwrights. Performances are at the **University Theater**, Farrison-Newton Building at N.C. Central University.

HOOF 'N' HORN
683-1210 or 684-4444

Hoof 'N' Horn is a Duke student organization that produces one to three plays a year. Productions scheduled in 1994 include *Working* and *Evita.*

SUMMER FESTIVAL OF ARTS
684-4444

Duke also offers dramatic productions and dance, music and film during its annual summer festival. Call the Duke University Student Union for more information.

NORTH CAROLINA CENTRAL UNIVERSITY
Fayetteville St.   *560-6242*

North Carolina Central University's department of dramatic art sponsors the **Ivan-Dixon Players**, a student group that puts on at least four major productions a year. Central also has featured appearances by guest artists such as James Earl Jones.

Chapel Hill and Carrboro

UNIVERSITY OF NORTH CAROLINA
962-1449

Whether it's a production by the PlayMakers Repertory Company or an experimental piece by the Drama Department, UNC provides Triangle audiences with an array of theatrical possibilities and facilities.

PLAYMAKERS REPERTORY COMPANY
962-7529

Speaking of Broadway, *Agnes of God* was first performed by the PlayMakers Repertory Company, the state's only year-round professional resident theater. Since joining the national League of Resident Theatres in 1976, PlayMakers has been committed to preserving the classics as well as performing more modern works. The 1993-94 season includes *The Grapes of Wrath, Arms and The Man, Marvin's Room, A Winter's Tale,* and our favorite, *Death Of A Salesman,*. The company

PLAYMAKERS REPERTORY COMPANY, THE STATE'S ONLY YEAR-ROUND PROFESSIONAL RESIDENT THEATER, PERFORMS IN THE PAUL GREEN THEATER ON THE CAMPUS OF THE UNIVERSITY OF NORTH CAROLINA IN CHAPEL HILL.

Insiders' Tip

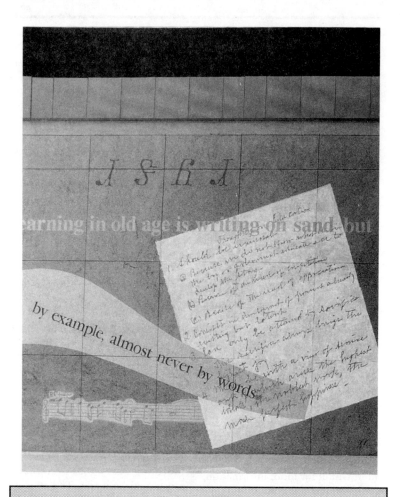

EDUCATION WALL

A 32x96 foot red granite wall. Once it was a vast, empty, rock-hard canvas. Now sandblasted and colored with words and other symbols, the Education Wall celebrates the native wisdom of North Carolina's people.

Artist Vernon Pratt and writer Georgann Eubanks developed the collage with the goal that the Education Wall should not just be *about* education, but that it should provide an educational *experience* to passersby.

As a tribute to education and as a work of public art, the Wall serves as a permanent monument to the continuing process of education which begins in our North Carolina public schools.

YOU ARE

A CHILD

learning in youth is engraving on stone

YOU ARE

When things are at their worst,

SUITABLE

...why do these writers/teachers aim to impart to their students? "I just try to stand out of their light."

TO BE

Love worked where discipline failed.

AWED

ARTWORKS FOR STATE BUILDINGS PROGRAM

Monuments are a visual legacy, inspiring and informing us about our culture. Recognizing that public buildings interpret our society and enrich our experience, the State of North Carolina has set aside 1/2 of 1% of construction or renovation funds for the commissioning of art work for state buildings. This program is administered by the North Carolina Arts Council, Department of Cultural Resources, in conjunction with the Office of State Construction and is limited to buildings with construction costs exceeding $500,000. The Education Wall is the first project created under the 1988 Art Works for State Buildings Act. The State of North Carolina invested $109,975 in this artwork for the Public Education Building. The construction costs of this building are estimated to be $32,346,652.

also presents a special holiday show each year; in 1993, it was a new production of *Beauty and the Beast.* All productions take place in the modern **Paul Green Theater**, named in honor of the late Pulitzer Prize-winning playwright and UNC alumnus. The theatre seats 500 people on three sides of its thrust stage.

LABORATORY THEATER
962-1121

In addition to working with the PlayMakers company, UNC's drama department also stages plays several times a year in its Laboratory Theatre in the basement of Graham Memorial. "The Lab's" productions range from the likes of Edward Albee's *Zoo Story* to original works written and directed by the undergraduate drama students themselves.

ARTSCENTER
300-G E. Main St.   929-ARTS
Carrboro

Formerly known as The ArtSchool, the ArtsCenter for Visual, Performing and Literary Arts started in 1974 as a modest community venture located in a one-room loft in Carrboro. It has since outgrown its second home—in the restored Carr Mill shopping village-and is now located in a much larger, renovated space nearby.

The ArtsCenter has weathered some financial crises in the last few years. But, thanks to the hard work of its board general manager and countless volunteers, the ArtsCenter continues to offer plays, performances, events and classes to area residents. The ArtsCenter's home on East Main Street in Carrboro includes a 300-seat theater, six classrooms, a gallery with skylights, offices, and studios for ceramics, dance, television and recording.

Among many other activities that take place at the ArtsCenter are theatrical events geared to participants of all ages, interests and levels of experience (see below).

In addition to offering performances and events, the ArtsCenter regularly sponsors theater classes for students of all levels and ages. Adults can learn about scenes, play writing and improvisational techniques. There are classes for children from ages 6 to 17 in creative drama, improvisation and fantasy.

Classes and performances are offered to the public at very reasonable prices, with discounts available to Friends of the ArtsCenter.

TRANSACTORS IMPROV COMPANY
The ArtsCenter   929-ARTS
Carrboro

The Transactors Improv Company is made up of four persons, specializing in improvisational theater. Their performances evolve from taking cues from the audience, and are hilariously inspired. Transactors Improv Company performs throughout the Triangle, tours nationally and has won numerous awards.

ACTOR'S CO-OP

The ArtsCenter   929-ARTS
Carrboro

The Actor's Co-op is the ArtsCenter's in-house repertory company, open to aspiring performers, playwrights and directors of all levels. The company meets regularly to study and perform plays of interest to Co-op members. Two to four plays are performed each year, including original pieces as well as those by well-known artists.

NEW PLAYS RISING

The ArtsCenter   929-ARTS
Carrboro

This group sponsors regular readings for new playwrights, as well as several productions each year of original plays by area playwrights.

VILLAGE COMMUNITY THEATRE

P.O. Box 4862
Chapel Hill, NC 27515

This new group is open to interested members of the community, and has positions for both cast and crew members. The group plans to perform classic and well-known productions, as well as original works by area playwrights. The Village Community Theatre also puts on workshops and small productions to help aspiring actors gain experience. Write to the address above for more information.

COMMUNITY YOUTH THEATER

942-6987

Each summer the Community Youth Theater offers four weeks of classes in all phases of drama to talented 9- to 13-year-olds in Orange County. Classes focus on move-

ment, speech, pantomime, acting and technical theater, and culminate in a public performance.

Music

Whether you like the jazz keyboard of Brother Yusef Salim, the rousing folk ballads of troubadour Mike Cross, the sassy lyrics of The Red Clay Ramblers, the rock rhythms of Southern Culture on the Skids or the harmonic strains of the N.C. Symphony, you can hear them and other musical notes regularly in Triangle clubs and music halls. For more information on the night life scene, see **NIGHT LIFE**. Here's a look at what other kinds of live musical presentations are available in Raleigh and Cary, Durham, Chapel Hill and Carrboro.

Raleigh and Cary

CONCERT SINGERS OF CARY

P.O. Box 1921
Cary, NC 27512
Contact: Donna Parker   467-3232

This Cary group of singers, formed in 1991, now has about 150 singers and performs three or four concerts each year. Auditions are held each August. The chorus is directed by Lawrence Speakman and meets at the new Community Center at 404 N. Academy Street, behind the Town Hall Annex on Monday nights from 7:30 until 9:30.

CARY SCHOOL OF MUSIC

127 W. Chatham St.   460-0052

Instructor Pam Mole saw her lifetime dream come true when the doors of the Cary School of Music opened in May of 1993. The school offers private lessons for strings, brass and woodwinds, voice, accordion and percussion. The variety of instruction available is due in large part to the teaching staff (about 15 instructors) she has brought together from such notable organizations as the North Carolina Symphony, the North Carolina School of the Arts and others. Student ensembles perform every other Friday night, accompanied on piano by Dr. Richard McKee of Meredith College. Future plans for the school include performances with the Raleigh Symphony and a series of music camps.

FRIENDS OF THE COLLEGE
Reynolds Coliseum   515-2835
NCSU

Once described as the largest subscription series of its kind, the Friends started in 1959 as a means of bringing first-rate entertainment to eastern North Carolina at an affordable price. On a concert night, buses from all over arrive and traffic going into the campus looks like a Wolfpack basketball crowd. The series has brought many of the world's greats in music and dance to Raleigh, such as the The New York Philharmonic, Van Cliburn, Leontyne Price, Artur Rubenstein, and The Canadian Brass as well as the American Ballet, The New York City National Opera Company and The Royal Winnipeg Ballet. As Raleigh's musical scene has grown, the Friends' series has dwindled—to two in 1993—and concert tickets are sold on a per concert basis.

NORTH CAROLINA SYMPHONY
Memorial Auditorium   831-6060

One of the benefits of being the state's capital city is that it's the logical home for the state's symphony orchestra, and The North Carolina Symphony is one of the state's treasures, dating from 1933. It was the first continuously state-supported symphony in the country and it lives up to that acclaim by performing nearly 200 concerts a year, including 75 in admission-free

127 West Chatham Street, Cary, NC 27511, 919-460-0052

Pam Mole - Director

school performances. It truly is a "people's orchestra" and a special bonus for Triangle residents because many of its evening performances are here. It employs about 65 full-time musicians and is conducted by Gerhardt Zimmermann, former Associate Conductor of the St. Louis Symphony.

Most of its Raleigh performances are in Memorial Auditorium which, with its crystal chandeliers and improved acoustics, rivals any facility in the Southeast. The symphony has performed at Carnegie Hall, the Kennedy Center and Chicago's Orchestra Hall.

The Symphony offers five series: a classical group for longhairs; a pops series for the Chablis and brie bunch; a children's series for the young and restless; a ballet series that features well known ballet companies such as Glasnost's, Pittsburgh and Washington; and an outdoor "summerfest" concert series at Cary's Regency Park. The Durham Series of five concerts takes place in the new Carolina Theater in downtown Durham starting in the fall of 1994 and consists of four classical concerts and a Holiday "Pops" Concert. The Chapel Hill Classical Series of five concerts takes place in Memorial Hall on the UNC Campus. Many of the concerts feature guest performers such as Andre Watts, Henry Mancini, Nadja Salerno Sonnenberg and Doc Severinsen.

You can sign up for season tickets or buy single tickets; call the box office for price ranges for the different series. You'll be surprised at how affordable they are.

RALEIGH BOYCHOIR

Contact: Tom Sibley   881-9259

This choir was started in 1968 by Tom Sibley, who retired in 1988 from the public schools and is organist at Holy Trinity Lutheran Church. Sibley has developed the choir into one of the finest boys' choirs in the region, and this past summer it toured Austria where it gave five performances. It has toured Austria, has sung in Colonial Williamsburg and has performed at the White House—three times. There are 36 boys in the performing choir and 65 total in the larger singing group. Boys range in ages from 8 to 16. There is a monthly membership charge and singers must supply their own concert clothes. In Raleigh, the group perhaps is best known for its annual Hayes Barton Baptist Church concert of carols on the first Sunday in Advent.

RALEIGH CHAMBER MUSIC GUILD

Stewart Theater   515-3104
NCSU

This group started in 1941, and it brings to the Triangle a season of chamber groups, all of them performing at NCSU's Stewart Theater, usually on Sunday evenings at 8, although sometimes in the afternoon. Guest artists have included the Eastman Brass Quintet, Emerson String Quartet, the Guarneri String Quartet, the Boston Camerata, which specializes in music of the Middle Ages, and the Bach Ensemble. Adult season tickets cost about $50.

RALEIGH CIVIC SYMPHONY

Price Music Center   515-7952
NCSU

For those who are not content to sit in their seats and listen, there is the Civic Symphony that is less a city group than an outgrowth of the NCSU Music Department, namely Professor Jonathan Kramer. The orchestra is a combination of "town and gown" performers and meets weekly at NCSU's **Price Music Center**. It is a full symphony with 70 members and it performs two or three times each semester. All are amateurs whether they play that way or not. The orchestra is the parent group for several other orchestras; for more information about where you and your flute might fit in, contact Professor Kramer.

RALEIGH CONCERT BAND

Contact: Carl Van Cott   872-2743

The Concert Band is another nonprofit, all-volunteer group and it receives support from the city's Parks and Recreation Department. In exchange, it is often asked to play at major civic functions where a little horn blowing and a few drum rolls are in order. Many of the 60 members are former high school and college band players who can't put their instruments away. The band performs regularly in the summer at concerts on the state Capitol grounds, free. Toot, toot!

RALEIGH CONSERVATORY OF MUSIC

3636 Capital Blvd.   790-1533

The Raleigh conservatory of Music was established in 1986 as a nonprofit organization dedicated to enriching the lives of individuals

through a lifelong association with music. Programs include "Kindermusik," the initial exposure of infants and preschool children to musical experiences; childhood through adult music instruction; special programs for the handicapped; community performances and accompanying; and outreach programs to expose all segments of the community to the joys of music.

RALEIGH ORATORIO SOCIETY

Contact: 876-2132

The Society is a volunteer organization, but it is by no means an amateur group. These are serious singers, and they can hold a note with the best, including annual performances with the North Carolina Symphony and other visiting orchestras. The Society has been

around for several decades and is considered to be perhaps the best of the Triangle's choral groups. It has performed in some of the city's larger churches, such as Edenton St. Methodist, and a sample of its work includes "Boris Godounov" as well as "The Messiah."

RALEIGH SYMPHONY ORCHESTRA
832-5120

This is not to be confused—although many do—with the Civic Symphony even though some of its members began there and left to form their own orchestra. It is comprised mostly of volunteer musicians with some paid players. It is a full orchestra and sometimes performs with other Triangle musical groups such as the Oratorio Society. It is not afraid to tackle Beethoven or Brahms, Mozart or Mussorgsky. It performs at Meredith College and other places.

NATIONAL OPERA COMPANY
711 Hillsborough St.   *890-6082*

H. L. Mencken's ghost would be surprised to find that, yes, Raleigh does have its own opera com-

pany. Started in 1948, it has survived and prospered, thanks to the largesse of the late lawyer A. J. Fletcher, founder of the WRAL-TV empire and opera lover. The company's mission is threefold: to introduce opera to public school students; to give experience to young singers; and to perform opera in a language the audience understands, namely English. The company has proved to be a good training place, and its alumni include such stars as Samuel Ramey, Jeannette Scovotti and Arlene Saunders. The company makes about 90 to 100 performances a season, and two or three of those are operas in Raleigh. The group usually will make about 20 appearances in Wake County schools in a season. There are 10 full-time singers in the company, a music director and an equipment manager.

YOUTH ORCHESTRAS
Wake County Schools

Raleigh and Cary children have three orchestras with which they can tune their fiddles and other instruments. They all give concerts

and provide young musicians the experience of ensemble playing. The **Raleigh Preparatory String Orchestra** (K-6th grade), the **Capital Area Youth Orchestra** (middle school grades) and the **Raleigh Youth Symphony Orchestra** (high school students) are open to all interested students. They rehearse on a regular schedule and are sponsored by the United Arts Council.

GENERAL ASSEMBLY CHORUS
Contact: Rob Elias   *544-1948*

Hummmmm! This is the Triangle's best barbershop singing group, and it has the trophies to prove it. The chorus has been the Southeast district champions for the last seven years and placed fifth in the national competitions. Numbering 80 men of stout and sweet voice, the chorus has been harmonizing now for 12 years. The group practices on Monday at 7:30 p.m. and holds an annual show at the Civic Center in early spring. You can even hire the chorus for a minimum of $500 a show, and if you can't squeeze all 80 into your living room, you can hire out the traditional barbershop quartet. But these guys are not in it for the money; members vary in vocation from lawyers to salesmen to doctors to plumbers. And unlike their namesakes, these fellows are fun to listen to.

PINECONE
(PIEDMONT COUNCIL FOR
TRADITIONAL MUSIC)
Artspace
Contact: Susan Newberry   *990-1900*

This nonprofit organization, started by a former member of the Apple Chill Cloggers in 1984, has brought to Raleigh and Cary residents a heaping helping of traditional North Carolina, grassroots music, dance and singing. It produces, along with the city's Parks and Recreation Department, monthly concerts of bluegrass music, ballads and authentic folk singing including the old-fashioned shape-note singing. It often performs in the Raleigh Little Theater and, in the spring and summer, in RLT's outdoor amphitheater.

It started the Fiddlers' Convention in 1990 and it performs at Durham's Eno River Park. Admission is charged for some events; others, especially the outdoor shows, are free. The office is downtown on S. Blount St.

LITTLE GERMAN BAND
Contact: Karl Einsle   *847-4282*

Raleigh residents knew the city had attained a cosmopolitan status when the Little German Band began to play in 1971. Many of its members were raised around such ethnic music, and the band members even put on lederhosen and feathered hats when they perform. Members are serious about their oompahs, and can be counted on to have at least one practice session a year, according to one former tuba player. The band has become a featured attraction at Cameron Village's annual Octoberfest and plays, according to one member, "at any opportunity we can."

Durham

In addition to clubs and restaurants (see "Durham" Section of **NIGHT LIFE**), you can regularly find live music at a number of other locations in Durham, including Duke University and North Carolina Central University (see Theater section above).

In the summer, there's **Jazz in the Parks**, a series of concerts in community parks, sponsored by the Durham Recreation Department (call 560-4355 for information). There's always live music at the **July 4th Festival on the Eno**, and at **CenterFest**, the downtown street festival (see **ATTRACTIONS**). And throughout the year, you can attend concerts at **St. Joseph's Performing Arts Center**, a concert auditorium located on Fayetteville Street.

Here's a guide to the musical groups and events you are likely to find in Durham.

DUKE UNIVERSITY

The quantity, quality and diversity of musical offerings on the Duke University campus is enough to keep anyone busy full-time. Here's a quick look at some of what is available. Except where noted, additional information on any of the following may be obtained by writing the Duke University Department of Music, P.O. Box 6695, College Station, Durham, NC 27708.

DUKE ARTISTS' SERIES
684-4444

The Duke University Artists' Series brings to campus a string of nationally and internationally renowned musical artists and performances. The 1993 season included: the Royal New Zealand Ballet, soprano Diane Upshaw, violinist Joshua Bell and the Danish National Radio Symphony Orchestra with pianist Bella Davidovich. Additional information, and individual and season tickets are available by writing: Duke Artists' Series, Box 22146, Durham Station, Durham, NC 27706.

CIOMPI QUARTET
684-4444

Since 1965, this resident chamber music quartet has provided classes and concerts at Duke, as well as worldwide. It emphasizes variety, offering pieces from Mozart to Ward, Brahms to Copeland, in four formal concerts a year. Call for information on season and individual tickets.

DUKE UNIVERSITY CHAMBER ARTS SOCIETY
684-4444

The Chamber Arts Society brings to Duke internationally acclaimed artists, such as the Beaux Arts Trio, the Guarneri String Quartet and the Tokyo String Quartet. Season and individual tickets are available.

DUKE SYMPHONY ORCHESTRA

This 85-piece orchestra is composed of Duke students, faculty and local residents. Led by conductor Lorenzo Muti, it performs about four concerts during the academic year. Individual members often perform with Duke choral groups (see below).

DUKE CHORALE
The chorale performs several concerts each year, including an annual Christmas concert in early December.

DUKE UNIVERSITY COLLEGIUM MUSICUM
Lovers of vocal and instrumental music from the Medieval, Renaissance and Baroque periods will enjoy performances by this select group of Duke students, faculty and local residents. It gives at least one concert each semester.

DUKE JAZZ ENSEMBLE
This 20-member ensemble of students performs several times during the academic year with a repertoire that includes big band, jazz-rock and swing. Conductor Paul Jeffrey leads the ensemble.

DUKE UNIVERSITY WIND SYMPHONY
Each year this select group of about 60 musicians performs two formal concerts and several informal concerts held outdoors in the **Sarah P. Duke Gardens** (see **AT-TRACTIONS**).

NORTH CAROLINA CENTRAL UNIVERSITY
NCCU's Department of Music sponsors several groups and concerts each year. They include New Central Connections, a contempo-

rary jazz ensemble that performs on campus and on tour; the Piano Trio, a faculty chamber group; and the NCCU Choir. For additional information, contact the Department of Music, N.C. Central University, Durham, NC 27707.

NORTH CAROLINA SYMPHONY
Box Office: 919-733-2750
The Durham Series of five concerts is performed in the newly renovated Carolina Theater in downtown Durham and consists of four classical concerts and a **Holiday Pops Concert**. For more information, see "Music"—Raleigh and Cary.

DURHAM SYMPHONY
560-2736
This 65-member, community orchestra annually presents a classical concert series, a **Holiday Pops** concert and a **Lollipops Family Concert** in the spring. The Symphony also sponsors a **Young Artists' Competition** and a concert featuring the winners. And it has collaborated with other Durham Arts Council beneficiaries on such elaborate outdoor street operas as *Carmen* and *Pagliacci*. The Symphony performances are usually at Page and Baldwin Auditoriums on the Duke University campus, and at the Durham Omni Civic Center downtown. The Symphony also performs at the Royall Center For The Arts in the Durham Arts Council Building.

DURHAM CIVIC CHORAL SOCIETY
560-2733
Founded in 1949, the Durham Civic Choral Society gives

local residents an opportunity to perform large and small works accompanied by an orchestra. The Society usually presents at least two concerts a year, including the annual Christmas concert in Duke Chapel. Membership is open to interested individuals; performers must audition.

MALLARME CHAMBER MUSIC SERIES
120 Morris St. 560-2788

This group of local musicians takes its name from the French symbolist poet who held regular Tuesday evening salon gatherings of musicians, poets, painters and actors who wanted to collaborate and share ideas. Last season, the Mallarme Chamber Music Series performed five Tuesday night concerts at the **Peoples Security Insurance Theatre** in the Durham Arts Council Building on Morris Street. The group draws mostly from early 20th century, classical and Romantic pieces not typically performed by other groups in this area. The Mallarme Players also presents two Family Concerts each season.

N.C. BOYS CHOIR
942-5480/489-4974

This choir of 40+ musically talented boys between the ages of 9 and 14 performs about 50 concerts a year, including major Christmas and spring concerts in Duke Chapel, television appearances and programs for local nursing homes, hospitals, schools, churches and groups. It also offers workshops, scholarships and summer camps. The choir features a training choir for beginning singers and a choir of high-school-aged tenors and basses.

COMMON WOMAN CHORUS
489-3368

This chorus, begun in 1983 by 12 women with a desire to sing "women's politically progressive music," has grown to more than 30 members who drive from all over the greater Triangle area to weekly rehearsals in Durham. The chorus has performed for the **War Resistors League** in Raleigh, the annual **Festival on the Eno in Durham** and other events. The chorus is open to all women; no audition is necessary.

Chapel Hill

If you've read the "Chapel Hill" Section of **NIGHT LIFE**, you know that there are lots of clubs and restaurants in this town where you can find great music. But those aren't the only places you should look. There are a variety of musical performances regularly on the UNC campus and at the ArtsCenter in Carrboro. And there are several community groups you may want to join yourself. Here's a guide to what you can expect.

ARTSCENTER
300-G E. Main St.
Carrboro 929-ARTS

Most weekends, the ArtsCenter sponsors one or more musical concerts at reasonable admission prices. Recent concerts have included jazz, folk, country, Irish, big band, rock, reggae and new wave groups. What's more, the ArtsCenter has an ongoing Sunday jazz series, featuring popular local artists like Ed Paolantonio, Rodney Marsh and Steve Wing. Ticket prices are in the $6-$10 range for local performers, more for national performers on tour. Friends of the ArtsCenter receive a discount on ticket prices.

UNIVERSITY OF NORTH CAROLINA

Carolina Union   962-1449

UNC's Student Union sponsors a slew of big and not-so-big name music acts each year. All of them are open to the public. Major concerts are held at Carmichael Auditorium, the Smith Center, Memorial Hall and occasionally outdoors on campus.

During the school year, the Department of Music presents about 60 free concerts by students, faculty and occasional guest artists. Student music groups sponsored by the department include the following: **Carolina Choir, Jazz Lab, Wind Ensembles, Men's and Women's Glee Clubs, Mixed Chorus, Chamber Singers, Symphony and Chamber Orchestra**, and the **Society for the Performance on Original Instruments**. For more information, contact the Department of Music, University of North Carolina, Chapel Hill, NC 27514.

In addition, the Black Student Movement sponsors a **Gospel Choir** that performs on campus. For more information, contact the Black Student Movement, UNC, Chapel Hill, NC 27514.

CHAPEL HILL-CARRBORO COMMUNITY CHORUS
490-5649/542-1602

This group is made up of individuals at all levels of musical achievement who share a common interest in choral music. The Chorus practices at 7:30 p.m. on Tuesdays at Culbreth Middle School. The group performs public concerts twice a year.

PIEDMONT YOUTH ORCHESTRA
967-5076

The Piedmont Youth Orchestra offers experience in playing standard orchestral pieces for students from elementary through high school grades. The orchestra rehearses weekly.

PRO CANTARE ENSEMBLE
929-6381

Founded in 1984, this ensemble of about 35 singers presents two programs a year, one in early June and another in early December. It has a challenging, artistic repertoire; music is chiefly *a cappella*. Past pieces have included masses by Palestrina and Vaughn Williams, jazz choral works, *Magnificat* by Berger, Distler's *The Dance of Death*, *Rejoice in the Lamb* by Britten, and motets by Bach, Victoria, Byrd and Brahms. An audition is required, and the group meets Monday nights in Chapel Hill.

NORTH CAROLINA SYMPHONY

Box Office: 919-733-2750

The Chapel Hill Classical Series of five concerts takes place in Memorial Hall on the UNC Campus. For more information on The

North Carolina Symphony see "Music"—Raleigh and Cary.

VILLAGE SYMPHONY ORCHESTRA

This is a private, nonprofit group for adults who get together to play and further the tradition of community music. The orchestra rehearses Thursdays at 7:30 p.m. at Hill Hall (the music building) on the UNC campus.

HILLTOP HARMONIZERS

This local chapter of barbershop singing enthusiasts meets at 7:30 p.m. every Thursday at University United Methodist Church, 150 E. Franklin Street.

Visual Arts

There must be at least 30 galleries and museums in the Triangle displaying the works of locally and nationally known painters, sculptors, photographers and crafts persons. But you definitely need a guide to help you find them all. Unlike some major urban centers, the cities of the Triangle don't have well-defined art districts. Instead you'll find worthwhile exhibits all over the place: from the N.C. Museum of Art in Raleigh and college campuses in Durham and Chapel Hill, to displays at banks, restaurants and, of course, private galleries tucked into business districts and shopping centers throughout the area. That's where we come in. We hope the following will inspire you to track down the fine art exhibits that await you in Raleigh,

Cary, Durham, Chapel Hill and Carrboro. And in case you want to try your hand at painting, sculpting, photography or crafts, we're including a few places where you can take classes.

Raleigh and Cary

NORTH CAROLINA MUSEUM OF ART
2110 Blue Ridge Rd.   *833-1935*

This is the premier art museum in the state and has become one of North Carolina's treasure houses for the visual arts. It attracts as patrons the state's first families, and its fund raisers draw the rich and famous. Its doors not only open to art works, but for the socially ambitious, the doors often open a way into society. Much of the state's fine art activities are centered here, and Raleigh and Cary residents again can be grateful that they live in or near a capital city that is home to such a museum.

Like the Symphony, this is a tax-supported museum, and it reaches out to its people with a wide variety of free or inexpensive programs. For years, the museum was located downtown and a bitter fight was fought over locating the museum outside the government complex and next to an eyesore prison. Even the design of the building, by Edward Durell Stone's firm, caused controversy. But in 1983, the museum opened at its new address on Blue Ridge Road at a cost of $15.75 million. It has over 181,000 square feet, displaying its permanent collections in American, ancient and European art to maximum advan-

Photo courtesy of N.C. Museum of Art

*A group tours the Greek and Roman collection at the
North Carolina Museum of Art*

tage. The European paintings are considered the museum's finest, particularly in Italian and Dutch and Flemish artists. Its American collection has a number of lush landscapes from the Hudson River School.

The museum organizes between 12 and 15 special exhibitions a year, many from other museums such as the wonderful collection from the Chrysler Museum at Norfolk. Four galleries are set aside for these shows, including the Mary Duke Biddle Gallery, which provides changing educational exhibitions designed particularly for the handicapped. Another gallery is reserved primarily for work by North Carolina artists.

The museum also operates a gift shop and **The Museum Cafe.** The Museum Cafe, operated by the same folks who run the popular, downtown restaurant, Irregardless, is on the premises. Admission to the museum is free; hours are 9 a.m. to 5 p.m. Tuesday through Saturday (Friday, it's 9 to 9) and 11 a.m. to 6 p.m. Sunday. It's closed Mondays.

VISUAL ARTS CENTER
NCSU Student Center   *515-3503*

The Visual Arts Center was added to the University Student Center on Cates Avenue in 1991, and opened in 1992. Exhibitions of contemporary art and design that are related to the University's various curricula are featured in the **Cannon Galleries**. Computer art, textiles, photographs and contemporary North Carolina ceramics, as well as furniture and sculpture, are related to not only the highly technical aspects of the University, but to the College of Humanities and Social Sciences and the School of Design as well. Exhibitions are sometimes derived from the University's substantial research collections, which are also available for study by appointment.

The gallery hours are 12 noon to 8 p.m. Tuesday through Friday, and 2 to 8 p.m. Saturday and Sunday.

SERTOMA ARTS CENTER
1400 W. Millbrook Rd.   *420-2329*

The Sertoma Arts Center is part of Raleigh's Shelley Park, and it has become the center for most of the city-sponsored art activities including a multitude of children's programs. We have listed it under the visual arts because it probably is best known for art classes, programs and shows. But the Sertoma Center is equally a hub of interest for dance, music, pottery, quilt making, photography and literature.

One of its phenomenally successful ventures was the "Dickens Disciples" group that began as a few classes on Charles Dickens by NCSU professor Elliot Engel. The group now claims 1,700 members!

To illustrate the Center's involvement, consider the following sampler: art shows with reception for local artists; Capital City Camera Club's annual competition; workshops in clay portraits, portraits in oil, watercolors, rug hooking; concerts by the Casablanca Orchestra, Broughton High School's acclaimed Carolina Spirit show chorus; a Greensboro tuba ensemble;

readings by local authors every third Sunday at 2:30 p.m.; ballroom dance, square dance, and T'ai Chi Ch'uan; bird carving, bridge, Japanese flower arranging; basic camera use and darkroom orientation. Had enough? Many of the programs are for children.

If you want to learn about the art scene in Raleigh and Cary at the grassroots level, this is a good place to start. Hours are Monday through Thursday, 9 a.m. to 10 p.m.; Friday 9 to 2 and Saturday 10 to 3 p.m. It's open Sunday afternoons, too.

NCSU Craft Center

Lower level, Thompson Theater   515-2457
NCSU

As its name suggests, the NCSU Crafts Center provides opportunities for hands-on experience in beginning through advanced crafts courses such as woodworking, pottery, weaving, and photography. Special interest classes range from flower arranging to telescope making—over 150 multi-session courses in 30 disciplines each year. The Center's Gallery features local and national exhibitions of crafts and is open to the public afternoons and evenings (every day from September through May, and Monday through Thursday during the summer). Call for class brochures and more information.

Arts Together

114 St. Mary's St.   832-9112

Arts Together is a nonprofit community arts school and performance center that has developed a devoted following over the years,

especially among young dancers. It has classes in visual arts, too, and its administrator is on the premises to answer questions. Founder Lemma Mackie believes that just as dance has color and shape, a painting has motion and melody. It has classes for two-year-olds and goes up to adults. (See also under Dance.)

Artspace

210 E. Davie St.   821-2787

Artspace is a very special part of Raleigh's downtown renovation. It was conceived to be a community of artists with studios and performance areas housed under one roof. First broached in 1977, it has become the heart of the city's Art District today in the old Sanders Ford building in the City Market block across from Moore Square. It has a gallery on the first floor and upstairs is a small auditorium, used for lectures, receptions and even political forums! You can walk through the building and see the artisans at work on jewelry or crafts and some, like Kyle Highsmith, whose paintings have been featured in a national magazine, will sell you their wares on the spot. It's a great place to find a bargain.

Artspace is unique in North Carolina and has been a draw for residents as well as visitors who can find a lively hub of art and entertainment, including a comedy club, Playspace for children, antiques and the city's one and only brewery at Greenshields. For a taste of this part of the city, take a Gallery Walk in the spring or fall when seven galleries all near Artspace and Moore Square put on a show.

CITY GALLERY OF
CONTEMPORARY ART
220 S. Blount St.   839-2077

This gallery lives up to its name. It's the local showplace for contemporary artists and receives support from the city. It was established after the state's Art Museum moved from its longtime downtown building to the suburbs, and the City Gallery was intended, in part, to fill the void. Along with Artspace, it has become an anchor to the city's Art District in which seven—count 'em—galleries now have downtown addresses around Moore Square. This is where you can find topical modern photographs on America's homeless or the zaniest gadgets in town. If you have any California cousins, take them here and wait for them to say, "Far out, dude!"

MARITA GILLIAM ART GALLERY
126 Glenwood Ave.   834-5800

Marita Gilliam and Melissa Peden started this contemporary art gallery several years ago. Ms. Gilliam has continued the gallery at this location and represents a number of regional and national artists in her Glenwood Avenue establishment. The gallery always has interesting and unusual works on display. Hours are Monday through Friday 10 a.m. to 5 p.m., and Saturdays, 11 a.m. to 4 p.m. Also, go upstairs and see the other interesting shops in this historic building.

RALEIGH CONTEMPORARY GALLERIES
134 E. Hargett St.   828-6500

No longer new but still very contemporary, this eye-catching gallery started across from the old Art Museum building and has moved one block south to Hargett Street where it is part of "Gallery Row." It shows original paintings, sculpture, fiber art and limited edition graphics, by local and national artists. This gallery also provides consulting services for individuals as well as for corporate clients.

JILL FLINK FINE ART
Cameron Village
2018 Clark Ave.   821-7172

Jill Flink, a printmaker herself, got into picture framing 20 years ago and opened a 5,500-sq.-ft. gallery in 1981. While she no longer owns the business, the gallery continues to maintain quality paintings as well as regional crafts, and items range in price from $4 to $600. It's also a source of art supplies and has a one-hour photo developing service.

LITTLE ART GALLERY
North Hills Mall   787-6317

This is Ruth Green's Little Art Gallery, and it has been a fixture on the Raleigh art scene for two decades. The owner is usually there, and like many of those she buys from, she has definite opinions about art. Don't be afraid to get her advice.

CLARK ART
300 Glenwood Ave.   832-8319

A Raleigh tradition since 1923, Clark Art is one of North Carolina's finest art galleries. Continuously exhibiting both antique and contemporary oil paintings and watercolors by a wide variety of internationally recognized artists, Clark Art also has a unique selection of original engravings, mezzotints, lithographs and prints. Clark Art offers serene landscapes, stirring seascapes, busy marketplaces, Paris street scenes, still lifes, and botanicals. It also specializes in custom framing, with an extensive selection of quality mouldings and frames and assistance from an experienced and helpful staff.

Durham

Thanks to the Durham Arts Council and Art Guild, Duke and N.C. Central universities, and several impressive private galleries, there are plenty of places to explore the visual arts, if you just know where to look. (In addition, you'll discover original works of local artists regularly on display at many restaurants. For information on those establishments, see our "Durham" Section of **RESTAURANTS**.)

DUKE UNIVERSITY MUSEUM OF ART
East Campus   684-5135
Main Street Entrance

This fine museum boasts a permanent collection of Medieval and Renaissance sculpture and decorative arts, Chinese porcelain and jade, Peruvian weavings and other textiles, and African and pre-Columbian works. In addition, there's usually a visiting or temporary exhibit. Recent ones featured the painted and sculpted ceramics of Costa Rica and a series of 17th-century prints from the Nether-

lands. Admission is free. Open 9 a.m. to 5 p.m. Tuesday through Friday, 10 a.m. to 1 p.m. Saturday and 2 to 5 p.m. Sunday.

DUKE CAMPUS GALLERIES
East and West campuses   684-2911

In addition to the Duke Museum of Art, there are two galleries on the east campus and two more on the west (main) campus, featuring rotating exhibits of paintings and photography. They are open to the public free of charge. The **Hanks Gallery** and the **Brown Gallery** are located in the Bryan Center on the West Campus. They are open daily from 8 a.m. to 5 p.m. when school is in session.

The **Bivins Gallery** on the East Campus is open 8 a.m. to 5 p.m. Monday through Friday. Exhibits by area artists change monthly. The **East Campus Gallery** is located in the East Campus Library and is open daily from 8 a.m. to 6 p.m. It features exhibits of artworks by Duke faculty, staff and employees.

N.C. CENTRAL UNIVERSITY MUSEUM OF ART
1801 Fayetteville St.   560-6211

Located on the campus of N.C. Central University, this museum features rotating exhibits of the works of students and of African-American artists. During the school year, it's open to the public free of charge from 9 a.m. to 5 p.m. Tuesday through Friday and 2 to 5 p.m. Sunday. In the summer, it's open from 9 a.m. to 5 p.m. Monday through Friday.

SEMANS GALLERY
120 Morris St.   560-2787

The gallery offers a rotating series of exhibits throughout the year, open to the public free of charge. Exhibitions change monthly. The gallery is in the new Royall Center for the Arts in the Durham Arts Council Building. Hours are Monday through Saturday 9 a.m. to 9 p.m. and Sunday 1 to 9 p.m.

N.C. CENTER FOR CREATIVE PHOTOGRAPHY
560-ARTS

Formerly known as the **Durham Photographic Arts Society**, this Durham Arts Council affiliate offers a variety of classes, workshops, exhibitions, publications and monthly meetings for photographers of all levels of experience. The Center has displayed the works of celebrated photographers such as Ansel Adams, Jerry Yusmann, Olivia Parker, Eron Streetman and Rodney Smith. The Creative Photography Center's exhibits and classes are held at the Royall Center for the Arts. Call for a schedule of events.

CEDAR CREEK POTTERY AND GALLERY OF AMERICAN CRAFTS
Interstate 85 at Creedmoor Rd.   528-1041

If you like pottery and crafts, you'll enjoy the short trek out to Cedar Creek. Drive nine miles north of Durham on I-85 to Exit 186-A (Creedmoor Road and N.C. Hwy. 50) and follow the signs. Featuring the works of more than 200 regularly exhibiting crafts persons, it is open daily from 10 a.m. to 6 p.m.

DURHAM ARTS COUNCIL
560-2787

The Arts Council sponsors classes in painting, graphic design, fiber art, photography and video for students of all ages and experience levels, at various locations in the city. A recent class schedule listed courses in basic drawing and portraiture, graphic design and composition, beginning and advanced photography, quilting, weaving and spinning. Call for a current schedule.

HORIZON GALLERY
Brightleaf Square   688-0313

In its new and expanded gallery space, Horizon offers functional and wearable art: ceramic pieces, pottery by North Carolinian and national craftsmen, jewelry, blown glass, wooden bowls and cutting boards, mirrors and woven items. Hours are 11 a.m. to 7 p.m. Monday through Saturday and 1 to 5 p.m. on Sunday.

TYNDALL GALLERIES
Brightleaf Square   683-8489

Jane Tyndall's gallery showcases painting, sculpture, prints and wearable art, primarily by local and regional artists. The gallery also offers framing and art consultation services for corporate and individual clients.

Chapel Hill and Carrboro

Like other parts of the Triangle, the art exhibits in Chapel Hill and Carrboro are scattered about. But since Chapel Hill and

Carrboro are relatively small towns, it's easy to find the museums and galleries and even tour them all in one day if you are so inclined.

Here's a guide to what you'll find at UNC, the ArtsCenter in Carrboro and several local galleries.

ACKLAND ART MUSEUM

UNC, Columbia St.   *966-5736*

UNC's Ackland Art Museum reopened in 1990, following extensive interior renovation that doubled the existing exhibition space. The museum's permanent collection features Greek and Roman art, Renaissance paintings, works by Flemish masters, and a fine collection of prints. Special exhibits change periodically. Hours are Wednesday through Friday noon to 3 p.m., Saturday 10 a.m. to 5 p.m. and Sunday 1 to 5 p.m.

HANES ART GALLERY

UNC Art Classroom Studio Bldg 962-2015
(next to the Ackland)

The Hanes features rotating exhibits by students and emerging local artists. Admission is free. The gallery is open from 1:30 to 5 p.m. Monday, 9 a.m. to 5 p.m. Tuesday and Thursday, 2 to 5 p.m. Wednesday and 12:30 to 5 p.m. Friday.

CAROLINA UNION GALLERIES

UNC, Carolina Union   *962-1157*

Here in the Student Union building on campus, you'll find rotating exhibits of student artists. Open from 11 a.m. to 7 p.m. when school is in session.

HORACE WILLIAMS HOUSE

610 E. Rosemary St.   *942-7818*

While you're walking around the historic district (see **CHAPEL HILL NEIGHBORHOODS**), don't pass up the Horace Williams House, one of Chapel Hill's oldest homes. Long ago the residence of a professor then known as the "gadfly of Chapel Hill," the house has been maintained by the Chapel Hill Preservation Society. Today the Horace Williams House is a cultural arts center, a place for wedding receptions, private parties, small dance ensembles, concerts and rotating art exhibits. Here you'll find paintings, sculptures and crafts by local and regional artists. Open from 10 a.m. to 5 p.m. weekdays and 1 to 5 p.m. on Sunday.

CAMERON'S

University Mall   *942-5554*

If you're looking for pottery and other functional crafts items, you'll want to check out Cameron's 5,000-sq.-ft. gallery and shop in University Mall (see "Chapel Hill" Section of **SHOPPING**). Danny Cameron chooses works from North Carolina and across the U.S., focusing often on the whimsical or eccentric. Open from 10 a.m. to 9 p.m. Monday through Saturday.

SOMERHILL GALLERY

Eastgate Shopping Center   *968-8868*

Since 1973, Joe Rowand has been bringing together emerging regional artists and enthusiastic collectors in his gallery. Here you'll find the paintings, sculptures and tapestries of American artists, many of them from the Southeast.

Somerhill is located at Chapel Hill's Eastgate Shopping Center, at U.S. 15-501 Business and East Franklin Street. It is open from 10 a.m. to 6 p.m., Monday through Saturday, and other times by appointment.

WOMANCRAFT

Eastgate Shopping Center   929-8362

This shop, recently relocated to Eastgate, offers all kinds of functional items by area craftswomen, including splendid pottery, woven clothing and quilts. Open from 10 a.m. to 5:30 p.m. Monday through Saturday.

ARTSCENTER GALLERIES

300-G E. Main St.   929-ARTS
Carrboro

The ArtsCenter Galleries features rotating exhibits by local and regional artists. It's open from 10 a.m. to 5 p.m. Monday through Friday, Saturday 10 a.m. to 4 p.m.

In addition to providing exhibit space for emerging artists, the ArtsCenter offers a variety of classes in the visual arts for all ages and all levels of experience. A recent class schedule included courses in graphic design, illustration, printmaking, drawing, Chinese painting, photography and video technique. The ArtsCenter also sponsors summer sessions of art classes for kids ages 7 to 12. Call for a current class schedule.

NORTH CAROLINA CRAFTS GALLERY

212 W. Main St.   942-4048
Carrboro

This gallery was opened by Sherri Ontjes as a means to encourage and support N.C. craftsmen.

The gallery sells quilts, pottery, jewelry, stained glass, blown glass, baskets, toys, knitting and weavings, and handmade wooden objects. It is open from 10 a.m. to 6 p.m. Monday through Saturday, with extended hours offered in the holiday season.

Dance

If you think you can only really find dance in the Big Apple, think again. Believe it or not, little ole' Durham is where you'll find what *The New York Post's* Clive Barnes calls "the world's greatest dance festival." After you've seen a performance or two, you'll understand how the annual American Dance Festival won such acclaim.

But the ADF is only part of the Triangle dance scene. If you really want to get a taste of Southern culture, you'll want to see the Apple Chill Cloggers and the Cane Creek Cloggers, both of Chapel Hill. If you get inspired you may want to try a little clogging yourself, or perhaps some international folk dancing. These and other opportunities are all available right here in the Triangle if you know where to look.

Here are some of our suggestions for dance activities you might enjoy in Raleigh and Cary, Durham, Chapel Hill and Carrboro.

Raleigh and Cary

ARTS TOGETHER

114 St. Mary's St.   828-1713

While Durham is the recognized dance mecca in the Triangle,

there are a number of teaching and community dance organizations that serve Raleigh and Cary. Arts Together is one, and it is home to one of the city's better known groups, **The Rainbow Company**. Most of the dance is creative or modern, and the Rainbow Company, which is a multi-age ensemble, has been selected to represent the state on several occasions. The group performs several times a year at area schools and stages. Dance classes also include ballet and director Glenda Mackie, daughter of the founder, Lemma Mackie, has four other choreographers including Betsy Blair and Betsy Hutchinson who start with two-year-olds and keep going. It's a great place for people who gotta dance!

RALEIGH DANCE THEATER
3334 Hillsborough St.   *834-1058*

Ann Vorus, a former soloist with the Atlanta Ballet, is the director of this studio that she established in 1984. She was joined in 1987 by Ruth Spinner Mones, another dance professional, and they offer one of the best schools for classical ballet. This theater presents two performances annually, usually traditional, full-length ballets or repertoire programs of classical and contemporary works. The company has its own guild and board of directors, and Ms. Vorus' husband is the delightful Jackson Parkhurst, conductor of the N. C. Children's Symphony. This group will keep you on your toes.

THE DANCERS STUDIO
6124 St. Giles St.   *782-0622*

Started in 1974 by director Karen Edwards, this 35-member ballet includes apprentice, senior and concert dancers. It is home of the Concert Dancers of Raleigh and a member of Dance Associates. It occasionally performs ballets in Triangle schools; the studio has classes in tap and jazz as well. It offers an annual show for its performance group.

RALEIGH SCHOOL OF DANCE ARTS
North Market Sq.   *833-8440*

This ballet dance school has been in Raleigh since 1961 and moved to north Raleigh in 1993, near the Red Lobster Restaurant off Old Wake Forest Rd. The director is Carole Baxter who trained at the Boston Conservatory of Music and is a former member of the N.C. Civic Ballet Co. She takes students from age three to middle age and teaches tap and jazz along with ballet. Her students perform in the Raleigh Civic Ballet and the company typically conducts two major performances a year.

PINECONE
Artspace   *990-1900*

Traditional North Carolina folk dancing such as clogging, is featured and celebrated by this group. (See the Pinecone listing in Music.)

SERTOMA ARTS CENTER
1400 W. Millbrook Rd.   *420-2329*

Dance also is one of the center's interests, especially for children, and it hosts dancercise classes for ages 15 and up. (See the Sertoma listing in Visual Arts.)

STEWART THEATER

NCSU Student Center   515-3104

The Stewart hosts some of the best professional dance companies in its Center Stage events during the academic year. Performers have included Chuck Davis' African-American Dance Ensemble, Hubbard Street Dance Company, ISO, MOMIX and Bill T. Jones/Arnie Zane & Co. (Also see listing in Theater.)

Durham

AMERICAN DANCE FESTIVAL

Duke University   684-6402

You could spend six weeks in New York City and still not catch as many internationally renowned modern dance performances as you can get right here in Durham every June and July as part of the six-week American Dance Festival.

Established in 1932 in Bennington, Vt., the ADF chose Durham as its home in 1978, and has been thrilling local audiences ever since with the best modern dancers from the world over. In its 59-year history, the ADF has featured such dance greats as Merce Cunningham and Martha Graham, and notable companies including those of Alvin Ailey, Paul Taylor, Twyla Tharp, Lar Lubovitch and Chuck Davis.

Each summer, the Festival draws more than 500 dancers, choreographers, teachers, students and critics to Duke University to study and perform modern dance. *The Wall Street Journal* calls it "artistically the most important gathering of modern dance professionals and students in America."

For six weeks, the ADF offers classes, workshops and nightly performances, many to sellout audiences. Performances are in Page Auditorium and Reynolds Theatre.

The American Dance Festival brings internationally renowned modern dance performances to Durham each summer.

Single tickets range from $10 to $20, with a few less expensive ones for special performances. Season tickets covering more than a dozen events range from about $60 to over $100.

The ADF's presence is felt all year long, through community outreach programs, seminars, lectures and special performances.

NEW PERFORMING DANCE COMPANY
560-7232

This Durham Arts Council affiliate is considered one of the best modern dance ensembles in the area. In addition to performing locally and out of state, the company offers special classes and workshops for students of all ages. Performances are held in the Royall Center for Performing Arts in the Durham Arts Council Building.

ENGLISH COUNTRY DANCE
W. Durham Community Center 683-4355

A few years ago, a group of Durhamites became interested in international folk dancing. After much experimentation with different styles and classes, that interest has evolved into English Country dances that are open to the public at 7:30 p.m. every Thursday. Novices can pick up some instruction at the dance and join right in. English Country dancing, like square dancing, involves the use of callers; once you learn the lingo, all you have to do is follow the caller's instructions.

Occasionally, larger English or Scottish dances are held at another location that is publicized in advance in the local newspapers. If

you really get interested, there's even more going on in Chapel Hill, where people get together regularly to engage in Scottish and contra dancing (similar to Scottish or English country dancing), as well as clogging (see "Chapel Hill" Section below).

Chapel Hill and Carrboro

We once asked some square dancers to define the difference between square dancing and clogging. We knew that both involved rather traditional steps, performed in routines passed down for generations.

Square dancers, we were told, are a good-natured lot who operate under a set of rules that includes the following: only couples may join in, you must bathe before all dances and refrain from drinking and cussing. Cloggers, on the other hand, are considered a much rowdier bunch: they encourage the participation of singles; they are known to imbibe gleefully; and, they frequently hoot and holler as they kick up their heels. You can clog all by yourself, or you can clog with one or more members of the same or opposite sex; nobody much cares what you do as long as you're having a good time.

That said, perhaps it's understandable that Chapel Hill has become a mecca for cloggers. Clogging, and more recently international folk dancing, seem to be the most popular dance activities taking place here.

THE APPLE CHILL CLOGGERS

P.O. Box 119   929-6210
Carrboro, NC 27510

The Apple Chill Cloggers is a nonprofit group, dedicated to preserving and promoting the art of clogging. This group performs and holds workshops all over the south, and occasionally abroad. If you'd like to learn how to clog, you may catch the Apple Chill Cloggers when it occasionally offers instruction at the square dances sponsored regularly at the Presbyterian Student Center on Henderson Street in Chapel Hill. Call the Student Center (967-2311) for a schedule of dances and appearances, or write the Cloggers at the above address.

THE CANE CREEK CLOGGERS

942-5784

Like The Apple Chill Cloggers (see above), this is a troupe specializing in the preservation and performance of traditional Appalachian folk dance. The Cane Creek Cloggers appears regularly at square dances throughout the Triangle at which it always encourages beginners to learn the art of clogging and buck dancing.

CAROLINA SONG & DANCE ASSOCIATION

Carolina Friends School   967-2761
Mt. Sinai Rd.

The Carolina Song & Dance Association sponsors dances and instructions in contra dance regularly at the Carolina Friends School. These popular dances are usually held once a month on a Friday night. They feature newcomer's instruction at 7:30 p.m. and dancing (with live music) at 8 p.m.

THE CHAPEL HILL BALLET CO.

P.O. Box 3233   942-1339
Chapel Hill, NC 27514

The Chapel Hill Ballet Company is committed to developing the potential of area dance students through classes, while bringing an appreciation of ballet to the community through dance concerts and demonstrations. Chapel Hill Ballet Co. sponsors two performances a year that are open to the public.

CHILDREN'S TAP CO.

The ArtsCenter   942-2041
Carrboro

Founded in 1983, the Children's Tap Co. was created to offer young dancers an opportunity to perform and refine their skills, and to offer audiences a chance to enjoy tap dancing entertainment. The company includes a dozen young dancers, ages 14 and younger.

THE ARTSCENTER FOR VISUAL, PERFORMING AND LITERARY ARTS

300-G E. Main St.   942-2041
Carrboro   or 929-ARTS

The ArtsCenter periodically offers classes in both the appreciation and performance of a variety of dance styles.

Writing

Writing sometimes rises above guidebook levels and becomes literature, the artistry of the printed word. The Triangle is home to a number of such artists, some of them among the best in the land. They are often available for personal inspection, as when they are serving as classroom instructors and cannot escape, or appearing at a book signing or attending a writers' meeting.

An Insider, for example, knows that you can meet Doris Betts, the author of *The Ugliest Pilgrim* and other stories, at the University of North Carolina at Chapel Hill where she teaches in the English Department. Lee Smith, named as one of the South's best writers and author of *Fair and Tender Ladies*, teaches writing at NCSU. Kaye Gibbons, whose books *Ellen Foster* and *A Virtuous Woman* got rave reviews, lives in Raleigh, and Tim McLaurin, author of two novels, lives in Chapel Hill. Perhaps the dean of Triangle fiction writers, Reynolds Price, teaches at Duke University, and Clyde Edgerton, the floatplane pilot and author of *Killer Diller*, lives in Durham, too.

Outside of the college campuses and places such as the Sertoma Arts Center, you can pursue the art of writing—or at least a friendly beer—through the **North Carolina Writers Network**. And to use vulgar, yuppie coinage, the Network networks. Contact information for the Network is below, along with some Triangle publishers.

RALEIGH LITERARY ARTS DIRECTORY
Raleigh Arts Commission   831-6234
This handy guide appeared in 1993 and lists—literally—Raleigh area writers and what they write, e.g., prose, poetry. These are people who write stories, essays, novels, poetry, scripts, even greeting cards! Hello!

Also, it's the best directory in the Triangle for writing groups, classes and organizations such as Carolina Crime Writers, Fiction Writers and Horror Writers. Leave it on your coffee table and impress your literary neighbors.

N.C. WRITER'S NETWORK
Box 954   967-9540
Carrboro, NC 27510
This statewide organization publishes a bimonthly newsletter, has an annual conference and offers a wide variety of information and support for fledgling and established writers.

CAROLINA WRENN PRESS
Durham Arts Council   560-2738
Durham, NC 27701
This press, now supported by the Durham Arts Council, publishes fiction, poetry and drama of writers, says the brochure, "who are working at the cultural edge." It is nonprofit and dedicated to the cause of "meaningful contemporary literature."

ALGONQUIN/WORKMAN PUBLISHERS
307 W. Weaver St.   933-2113
Carrboro, NC 27510
This publishing house, founded by UNC professor Louis Rubin, is affiliated with New York's Workman Publishers. This house has published some notable books, such as North Carolina native Vermont Royster's memoirs and several novels by acclaimed Southern contemporary novelists such as Clyde Edgerton and Jill McCorkle. The press is now headed by editor Shannon Ravenal.

Courtesy N.C. Travel and Tourism Division. Photo by Clay Nolen.

Fireworks fill the sky at the North Carolina State Fair held each October in Raleigh.

Inside
Attractions

Here we'll describe the special places and events you won't want to miss in Raleigh, Cary, Durham, Chapel Hill and Carrboro. For some of the sporting attractions, such as the world famous Durham Bulls, see our **SPORTS** section. As you will see, there's something for every month of the year, so mark your calendar now.

Raleigh

THE GENERAL ASSEMBLY
Jones St., Downtown   *733-4111*

Some consider this the best attraction in town; there's nothing like it anywhere else in the state, and it's been running since the 18th century. The General Assembly officially meets on a biannual basis, once every odd year in January. That, however, has become fiction in recent years as state government has become bigger and legislative oversight critical. So, legislators come to town every year now, in odd years for a long session that may last six months and a short session in even years, usually starting in June and lasting a month. Committee meetings usually occur in the morning on the first floor or in the Legislative Office Building across the street. Sessions of the House and Senate begin at 1:30 p.m. with the ringing of bells to alert stray legislators.

Sitting in the comfortable, red plush seats in the galleries, you can watch legislation being made, which some have compared to the manufacture of sausage. Outside the Senate and House chambers, you can see highly paid lobbyists in expensive business suits waiting to whisper advice and counsel in a legislator's ear. The harried, more raggedly dressed crew who huddles in the corners of the chambers and whose members chase legislators down the hall with pad and pencil usually are members of the Fourth Estate, the press. The ones dressed in Goodwill fashions and looking like they slept in the street are the photographers or TV-camera people.

There is drama; there is comedy; there is tragedy; there is intrigue; and there is oratory, vintage Southern style. You can hear the Elizabethan accents of the state's Outer Banks, the rounded drawls of the coastal plains and the twangs of the mountains. Over there, you may see the state's next governor and over here, you may see the next subject of an FBI investigation. Where else in the state can you see a show that costs millions and spends billions and charges no admission? The General Assembly, up close and personal in Raleigh.

ACC TOURNAMENT

Okay, we're cheating. This is neither in Raleigh nor Durham nor Chapel Hill. But it is still very much a Triangle attraction because when tournament time arrives in March, the Atlantic Coast Conference basketball tournament is THE event. As Tournament week begins, the local media will run stories and features on the parties, the players, the spectators, what scalpers will get for tickets, and the fever that takes hold of normally rational business and government leaders. There will be private parties to watch the games; bars and clubs will host special ACC TV nights; and it becomes difficult to get your business phone calls returned during game times.

In the olden days, the Tournament winner was the only team from the ACC admitted to the NCAA Tournament, hence the contest took on a special, frenzied significance as the season's hopes for a chance to compete for the national championship were suddenly compressed into three days of do-or-die basketball. It's different now, but the passions still run high, and winning the ACC title has given NCSU, UNC and Duke momentum in recent years that they've carried into the NCAA finals. The Tournament used to be held at NCSU's Reynolds Coliseum but, in recent years, the playing sites—supposedly neutral arenas—have been in larger coliseums, such as the Greensboro Coliseum, Atlanta's Omni and the Charlotte Coliseum. The tournament was expanded to four days with the addition of Florida State to the ACC. Tickets are almost impossible to come by, unless you're willing to pay scalper's prices or part with an arm or a leg.

ARTSPLOSURE

112 S. Blount St.   832-8699

Artsplosure is Raleigh's celebration for the arts, usually at the end of April and beginning of May, and like a moveable feast, it takes place throughout the city. Sponsored by the city's Arts Office and a number of citizen art organizations, the festival began in 1980 and has continued to grow. The festival stretches over a week and features dance, music, opera, jazz, paintings, concerts, exhibitions and outdoor sculpture. In 1993, the annual **fall Jazz and Blues Music Festival** was merged with the Spring Festival. The new **Spring Jazz & Art Festival** brings a vibrant unifying jazz theme that is reflected in every art form. Jazz programming is extended into the night with a special jam session scheduled over the weekend. Most of the events are free, and you don't have to be content to be a spectator; most of the festival is organized and administered by volunteers. Artsplosure added **First Night** in 1990. Held in downtown Raleigh, First Night is an artistic and alcohol-free celebration of New Year's Eve which keeps getting bigger each year.

CAROLINA NATIONAL STEEPLECHASE
4020 West Chase Blvd.   *832-2768*

Billed as the Triangle's answer to Stonybrook, this race draws over 10,000 people. The steeplechase is held at Wakefield in north Wake County on a course specially constructed for the event. This is a great opportunity to have a fun day watching great horse racing and enjoying the outdoors.

WALNUT CREEK AMPHITHEATRE
Sunnybrook and Rock Quarry rds.834-4000

This 1991 addition to the Triangle's entertainment profile will put superstars in your eyes and leave you gasping "ooohs and aaahhs." It is the latest in multimillion dollar outdoor amphitheaters built with public and private funds, namely by the city of Raleigh and the entertainment giant, Sony/

PACE of Houston, Texas. The $13.5 million amphitheater holds about 20,000 people, 7,000 under the roof. The rest are seated on a great, green sloping hill from which they can view and hear the stage via giant video screens and a state-of-the-art digital sound system.

The amphitheater is part of the city's 240-acre Walnut Creek Park that also features the city's largest softball complex. Walnut Creek has seen tremendous sell-out performances over the past three years including Jimmy Buffet, Elton John, Reba McEntire, Rod Stewart and the Lollapalooza festival among many others. The amphitheatre has proven itself as an important stop on almost all national tours.

You can't bring food or drink, so bring money when you come; parking, too, is extra. Be sure

Artsplosure, Raleigh's celebration of the arts, has been held each Spring since 1980.

Photo courtesy N.C. Travel and Tourism Division.

to take a moment and stand on the top of the hill and soak up the glittering scene below you—it's where the stars come to ground!

JULY FOURTH

State Fairgrounds   *890-3285*
Raleigh Parks and Recreation

Wave the flag and shout huzzah! Raleigh celebrates the Fourth in a big way, starting about 9 a.m. at the State Fairgrounds at the intersection of Hillsborough Street and Blue Ridge Road. Admission is free, and it's a relaxed day in which you can toss horseshoes, test your basketball free throws or football passes in contests sponsored by the city's Parks and Recreation Department, WRAL radio and the State Fairgrounds. The finale, of course, is the fireworks show about 9:15 p.m. The day usually begins with morning horseshoes in the Fairground arenas. Entertainment begins later and has featured popular bands such as Celebration, Casablanca, the Breeze, and some country and bluegrass music from Windy Creek. Cloggers and square dancers perform. Games and rides are held throughout, and concession stands sell Fourth of July specials such as hot dogs and soda pop. Cold watermelon usually is free. One year, there was a hot air balloon ride.

But the big show—and the one that draws 20,000 people to the Fairgrounds, another 100,000 spectators parked all along Interstate 40, Meredith College and any street, road or highway within sight of the Fairgrounds—is the fireworks display. The city spends over $7,500 to

light up the sky with rockets' red glare, and it's a sight and sound show that would make Francis Scott Key proud.

LABOR DAY WEEKEND POPS IN THE PARK

N.C. Symphony   *733-9536*

After Cary's Lazy Daze in August (see "Cary" section of this chapter), the next big event to put on your calendar is the Pops in the Park, Labor Day Weekend Concert that is the Triangle's unofficial-official end to summer. It started several years ago with a late Sunday afternoon concert by the North Carolina Symphony in Pullen Park, and the happy, clapping, well-mannered crowd swamped the accommodations. Thanks to the graciousness of Meredith College, the concert now is held on the college's beautiful front campus and is televised by WRAL-TV.

Families and friends start gathering about 4 p.m. Sunday to spread their blankets, set up tables and celebrate perhaps the biggest community picnic of the summer. It's a great time for people who have been away on vacations or off to summer camp to get back together and swap news or gossip and listen to beautiful music. You will see some of the best picnic meals of the year out here and you might even see someone sipping a little white wine on the grounds of a Baptist college. Meanwhile, you can watch the orchestra set up, tune its instruments and, if you're close enough, you can even hear light classical, Broadway show and movie melodies, with a rousing finale of the "1812 Overture," punctuated with booming fireworks. What follows is Raleigh's most mellow traffic jam of the year as thousands patiently load up their cars and station wagons and slip into the night and into the start of another autumn. If you want to spend the day alone, this is not the place to go; over 25,000 have come in the past.

NORTH CAROLINA STATE FAIR

State Fairgrounds   *733-2145*

If you skip all other attractions, don't miss this October fair; it's been judged one of the best in the country. It lasts 10 days, starting on the third Friday and ending the next Sunday; attendance exceeds 700,000.

It truly is a state fair with all the magic and music of a Rogers and Hammerstein production. For first timers, it's a great place to taste, touch, see and smell all those things that make up North Carolina. Check at fair time for admission, which is under $10 for adults, less for children 6 to 12 and free for children under six and adults over 65. The ticket is good for the entire day, including the Dorton Arena live entertainment which in the past has featured country-western stars Dolly Parton, Charlie Pride, Tammy Wynette, Charlie Daniels and Ronnie Milsap, as well as comedians Jerry Clower and Bob Hope, and rockers like Chubby Checker. It's the kind of fair where judges still hand out blue ribbons for the best cakes, pies, preserves, pigs and cows. For many city kids, it's a chance to see how you grow a hamburger and why a hog is a hog when he eats.

For the frugal, you can go to the Kerr Scott building and get lunch or supper by sampling the free wares, from eggs to sausage to hushpuppies.

The big attractions, of course, are the rides and tents on the Midway, supplied by James E. Straits Shows, that arrive by rail car. Here, you can see the Reptile Lady, the Gorilla Man or lose your supper on the Tilt-A-Whirl or Himalaya. And to close up the nightly entertainment, there is a fireworks display.

Gates open at 9 a.m. and expect a crowd, even with rain which never fails to pour at least one day during fair week. On weekends, the crowd can top 100,000 a day and all seem to be going the opposite way from you on the Midway. Avoid the traffic jam if you can by taking a CAT bus; dozens run regularly down Hillsborough Street every 15 minutes.

CHRISTMAS PARADE

Raleigh Merchants Assn.   *833-5521*
1 Exchange Plaza

Once you've recovered from the State Fair, get ready for the annual Christmas Parade that falls on the Saturday before Thanksgiving and serves to remind you that it's the season to spend money. It's been around for decades now, and it's the city's biggest parade of the year by far. Starting at the intersection of Hillsborough and St. Mary's Streets, forty floats, 20 bands and a cast of thousands march down Hillsborough St. toward the Capitol. The parade turns onto Salisbury Street and goes south to Lenoir

Street where it ends, conveniently, near what's left of the downtown shopping district. If you're used to attending Thanksgiving parades in New York City or Detroit, you're in for a Sunbelt treat—no mittens, woolen underwear, thermal socks or pocket handwarmers are needed down here. Just a good place along the street before the 10 a.m. starting time.

Several traditions keep the crowds—estimated at 150,000—coming back, and one of them is the competition between children marchers in costume. Another competition is held for children with costumed pets. (Eat your heart out, David Letterman!) Reflecting the city's more cosmopolitan makeup, recent years have seen floats from differing nationalities, including Scandinavian, Indian and Latin American entries. You'll see some of the country's best baton twirlers and in the last float, guess who? Santa Clause himself, who always gets the biggest cheer of the day.

OAKWOOD CHRISTMAS TOUR
Historic Oakwood Association   834-0887

The Christmas season in Raleigh is noted for several attractions, one of which is Ira David Wood's production of Charles Dickens' *A Christmas Carol* and another, the Historic Oakwood Christmas Tour. The two-day tour usually begins in the first or second week of December, starting at 1 p.m. and ending at 7 p.m. each day. In 1993, the dates were Dec. 11 and 12. Oakwood is the Victorian neighborhood behind the Governor's Mansion downtown that lifted itself by its own bootstraps and elbow

Christmas time in Historic Oakwood.

Courtesy N.C. Travel and Tourism Division. Photo by William Russ.

grease during the 1970s (see **RA-LEIGH NEIGHBORHOODS**). It has become one of the capital city's showplaces to out-of-towners, and a walking garden tour is offered in September.

The Christmas Tour began in 1972 as a fund-raiser for the struggling Oakwood Association, and it continues to be the group's biggest moneymaker. Tour tickets cost about $8 for adults; it's free for children under 12. Group discounts are available, and tickets can be purchased at the Oakwood Inn on Bloodworth Street.

The Christmas Tour lets you inside the wonderful old homes, many of them decorated in period greenery. There are six to seven homes on the tour and the homeowners are usually there to greet you and give you an intimate history of the house. Refreshments, tea and homemade cookies, are at the final stop on the tour, the Tucker Mansion on Person Street. The hosts and hostesses will, no doubt, need stronger stuff since 1,500 to 2,000 people usually make the tour. On recent tours, the Association has used the city's Raleigh Trolley to help transport tourists. A great entertainment for your visiting grandmother or mother-in-law, or the cousin who is renovating an older home.

MADRIGAL DINNER
NCSU Student Center   515-3775
This is one attraction that has sold out almost as soon as the tickets go on sale each year since it was started in the mid-70s. The Music Department helps stage a holi-

day dinner the way it might have been during the Middle Ages with period songs, instruments and entertainment. The menu comes right off King Arthur's Round Table and the waitstaff, of course, are dressed in costume. The dinner is served several nights, usually during the last week in November or the first week in December. Tickets usually go on sale in mid-October and are priced around $20.

DICKENS FAIR
Raleigh Civic Center   832 1231
The brainchild of former City Councilor Mary Cates, the fair began in 1992 and expanded in 1993, in celebration of Charles Dickens' version of Christmas. A costume competition and reading by Dickens' scholar Elliott Engel is part of the fair. Of course, there is authentic Victorian England food, music and games. The fees in 1993 were $4 for adults, $3 for children.

NEW YEAR'S EVE CONCERT
N.C. Symphony   733-2750
There may be some better ways to end the old year and start a new one, but in the Triangle, the North Carolina Symphony's New Year's Eve concert is one of the more pleasant ways to ring in the new year, and it's safer than many other things. The concert is billed as a "Viennese evening" of light music and waltzes. For those who want the full treatment (about $110 per ticket), they begin with a pre-concert sip of champagne at a local hotel and end with a post-concert dinner and dancing. The concert begins about 8 p.m. and Conductor

Gerhardt Zimmerman leads the fun with commentary along with the music. The concert ends about 10 p.m. Then, the crowd is safely bused to the hotel and dines sumptuously while a dance band picks up the beat and continues the mood with waltzes and other rhythms. Many merrymakers will go with friends, and others spend the night at the hotel, thus avoiding both drunk drivers and the chance of a DWI ticket. Check with the Symphony's box office for ticket prices.

COLLEGE ATTRACTIONS

With all the colleges in Raleigh, there are a number of attractions throughout the year that bring big name entertainment and speakers to the Triangle. NCSU's Reynold's Coliseum is the place where the big entertainers show up during the winter months, depending on when there's an open date and who's on tour. The Coliseum has two to five big shows a year by entertainers such as Dolly Parton, Alabama, Kenny Rogers, Billy Joel, Olivia Newton-John, Van Halen, Barry Manilow, Hank Williams, Jr. and Wayne Newton. Local radio stations and newspapers provide ticket information and prices, but expect to pay as much as $17 to $20.

The colleges themselves, through their various student unions and other organizations, also bring in groups or speakers such as former-President Jimmy Carter. NCSU in 1986 even had a visit from President Reagan, who sat down with students for a sandwich pre-

pared and flown in special by the White House chef. President Bill Clinton made a campaign stop here in 1992. You can usually find out who's coming by checking the weekly calendar of events in the local newspapers.

THE CIVIC CENTER
Fayetteville Street Mall   831-6011

The $18 million Civic Center, which offers 100,000 square feet of interior space and can seat up to 4,000 concert goers, is home to a number of special shows each year. There are three in particular you may want to note on your calendars. One is the **Home and Garden Show**, that appropriately is scheduled in the spring. Also around the same time of year is the popular **Outdoor and Sports Show**, where you can see the latest in camping, hunting and hiking gear. The third show, which stays a week, is the **Carolina Christmas Show** in December, featuring many of the state's crafts people and their wares. It's a great place to do your shopping for unusual, handmade gifts. A new and growing event is the three-day **International Festival** in October. A modest admission is charged for all the events.

The Civic Center also has become the home of the Raleigh Edge, the city's professional tennis team, in the summer months.

N.C. MUSEUM OF ART
(See "Visual Arts" Section of **ARTS**)

FALLS LAKE

12700 Bay Leaf Rd.   *846-9991*

The 22-mile long Falls Lake is one of Raleigh's reservoirs, formed when the Neuse River was dammed at the tiny village of Falls, north of the city. Since it opened in 1983, Triangle residents have streamed to its shores and waters for swimming, picnicking, fishing, water skiing and camping. It has to be one of the area's biggest attractions with 12,490 acres of water and 230 miles of shoreline. The Lake is administered by state and federal agencies and was built by the U.S. Army Corps of Engineers. Judd Burns at the state's park office is the one to call about campsites and access ramps. Estimates of visitors have grown steadily and stand at over two million visitations in the '90s. There are five boat ramps with free access. And one of the park's impoundments, Beaver Lake, is restricted to non-motor-driven boats and preserved for hunting and fishing. Those in boats go after bass and pan fish while some just bring along a cane pole, go below the dam's spillway and catch catfish.

POE CENTER

224 Sunnybrook Rd.   *231-4006*

This health education center opened in 1992 and brings to the Triangle and state a place where children and adults can learn about all aspects of health care, from nutrition to birth control. Wake County Public Schools use the facility for teacher education and the city's Substance Abuse Commission has held meetings here, too. Classrooms have displays on the body and how it works. There are free tours on Tuesdays and interested groups should call for reservations.

CITY MARKET

Management Office
300/200 Parham St.   *828-4555*

Like the ads say, "Raleigh's newest attraction is actually one of its oldest." The 1914 City Market, located on the south side of Moore Square in downtown, began an exciting rebirth in 1989. Today the cobblestone streets are home to a tantalizing array of restaurants, shops and art galleries. Try the homemade brew at **Greenshields**, visit galleries displaying crafts by artisans whose art has been has been shown by major museums, shop for fresh produce at **Big Ed's** or enjoy a Saturday afternoon chamber music concert at the **Queen of Hearts Tea Room**. Mounted police and old fashioned trolley cars, complete with bells and finished with brass and mahogany, recall the elegance of days gone by.

Gardens

There are some beautiful gardens in and around Raleigh and some consider Fayetteville Street Mall and the adjoining Government Mall some of the best landscapes in the state. But there are two gardens of special interest, the **Raleigh Rose Garden** and **WRAL-TV's gardens** surrounding its Western Boulevard offices. Both are popular scenes for spring and summer weddings.

ROSE GARDEN

The Rose Garden is on Pogue Street, two blocks off Hillsborough Street. The garden is maintained by some of the city's garden clubs and it includes an outdoor amphitheater, too. The garden itself sits in what used to be the old State Fairgrounds race track, hence its arena shape.

WRAL GARDENS
WRAL-TV Building, Western Blvd.

On the other side of the NCSU campus are the WRAL gardens. They are maintained by the company and are open to the public most of the year. For information on use of the gardens or the best times for blooms, call the station's public affairs office at 821-8651.

Historic Homes

There are three historic homes in Raleigh that are on any Insider's list: The **Joel Lane House** (he's the fellow who sold the land that became Raleigh), the **Mordecai House and Park**, and the **Governor's Mansion**.

JOEL LANE HOUSE
Hargett and St. Mary's sts.   *733-3456*

This renovated small home and grounds was once part of a 1,000-acre plantation and considered the finest house within a 100-mile radius in the late 18th century. Built in 1760 by the man who later sold the state the property on which the capital city grew, the house is now maintained by volunteers and private grants. It is open to the public on Sunday afternoons, 2:30 to 5, and is available for receptions and meetings. For details, call the Capital Area Visitor Center, which can provide you with contact information.

MORDECAI HOUSE
1 Mimosa St.   *834-4844*

Part of the city's parks system, the Mordecai House and grounds is a quiet spot downtown that is unique for several reasons.

First, the house remained in the same family since its beginnings in 1785 until the 1960s. Its furnishings belonged to the family and span two centuries of styles. When the city acquired the home, officials were amazed at the treasure trove of antiques found in the dilapidated barn out back. The country's Bicentennial Celebration spurred interest and contributions, and with the city's acquisition, the home has been preserved for future generations.

The grounds also contain the birthplace of Andrew Johnson, 17th president of the U.S., as well as six other period buildings, including a charming plantation chapel that can be reserved for small weddings. Hours are 9 a.m. to 5 p.m. Tuesday through Friday, and tours are available on weekends, 1:30 to 3:30 p.m. Moses Mordecai, an early Raleigh lawyer, married one of the owner's daughters and five generations of the family lived there.

GOVERNOR'S MANSION

200 N. Blount St. 733-3456

No, that's not the governor's home phone number. We won't tell you that. It's the number for the Visitors' Center that can arrange a tour for you. The Mansion, officially called the Executive Mansion, is where the governor and his family live. The ground floors are open to the public, one of the most popular times being in the holiday season in December.

The Mansion is a classic example of Queen Anne Cottage-Style Victorian architecture, known among *hoi polloi* as gingerbread style. The building was started in 1883

and completed in 1891, using mostly North Carolina materials. The handmade bricks on the sidewalks often show the initials of the men who made them. The 40,000 square foot house is filled with antiques and crystal chandeliers, many made in North Carolina. It is a "working" mansion in that Governor Jim Hunt's family not only lives there but conducts much of the state's business and entertaining there. Tours take about 30 minutes and usually are arranged in the fall and spring.

Government Buildings

As the capital city, Raleigh's most enduring attractions, perhaps, are its capital buildings on the Government Mall. Below are several that you can see in a day's walking tour, and all are deserving of closer inspection. They are not only attractions; they're the state's heritage.

THE CAPITOL

Capitol Square, Downtown 733-3456

This building is the center of downtown, a landmark from the day it was built in 1840. The current structure is considered one of the best-preserved examples of Greek Revival architecture in the country, with its columns, moldings, and the honeysuckle crown atop the dome carefully patterned after certain Greek temples. It cost $532,682 to build which, at the time, was three times the state's annual income. The granite was quarried in southeast Raleigh and the interior walls

The Executive Mansion in Raleigh is the official residence of the governor and considered one of the country's outstanding examples of Queen Anne Cottage Style Victorian architecture.

are stone and brick. The building's massive wooden truss system still holds up the roof.

Looking around the Government Mall today, it's hard to believe that until the 1880s, the Capitol housed all of state government! The General Assembly continued to meet in the Capitol's cramped chambers until 1963 when it moved to the legislative building on Jones Street. The Capitol is not simply for looks; the governor and his press office work here as does the lieutenant governor. There are several legends about the building, including one involving an escape tunnel and secret rooms. You can walk through between 8 a.m. and 5 p.m. during the week, and tours may be scheduled through the Visitors' Center.

THE LEGISLATIVE BUILDING
Jones St. 733-4111

When the General Assembly outgrew the Capitol, the state employed famed Arkansas architect Edward Durrell Stone to design a new home for the legislators. The 206,000-sq.-ft. building that resulted is every bit as classic as the Capitol and looks as new and contemporary today as it did in 1963 when it opened. It has Stone's trademark colonnade of columns outside and soothing garden fountains inside. The calming effect of the plants and water is often in demand, given the passion of legislative debates. The building's native granite and its marble facing give it a sense of public majesty, and inside, the House and Senate chambers are within view of public galleries overhead. Underneath is parking for

legislators; the first floor is devoted to committee rooms and legislators' offices on the outside walls. The second floor has more offices plus the two chambers and the third floor has the public galleries and a 250-seat auditorium. During weekdays, the building is open to the public; children must be accompanied by an adult.

N.C. MUSEUM OF HISTORY
109 E. Jones St. 733-3456

This building serves several purposes: it has offices for the Secretary of Cultural Resources; it holds the state's archives and library; and three floors are a history museum. The museum moved into its new, gleaming quarters across Edenton Street from the Capitol in 1993. The museum displays the original Carolina Charter of 1663 and exhibits on everyday life in the state, such as displays on period clothing. "Bustles, Bangles and Flappers" shows how the state's First Ladies dressed during their times, and its "On the Job" show presents home, medical, education and farm implements used in the state over the past 200 years. Boys like the exhibits on guns. The Museum has a busy schedule of events, seminars and tours making it a capital attraction for Triangle residents.

N.C. NATURAL SCIENCES MUSEUM
Bicentennial Plaza 733-3456

Probably the most popular capital place among North Carolina's children, this aging museum also is scheduled to be replaced shortly. It sits between the Capitol and the Legislative Build-

ATTRACTIONS

ing. This is where you can see snakes and other live creatures native to the state, many of which have been given names by museum staff and are as well known as some legislators. The emphasis is on environment and what has lived in North Carolina, and the Museum has a long list of classes for children and adults such as "The Killer Bees," "Indians of Eastern North America," and "Meet the Mammals." The Museum is open Monday through Saturday, 9 a.m. to 5 p.m., and Sunday, 1 to 5 p.m.

THE SUPREME COURT
Justice Building
Corner of Morgan and Fayetteville sts.

This is not one of your tourist hot spots, but as the third branch of state government and standing quietly across Morgan Street from the Capitol, it's worth notice. Ask the security guard at the entrance for instructions and go take a look at the court chambers where even the most obnoxious lawyers mind their manners when arguing before the seven-member court.

Cary

LAZY DAZE
Town Hall
316 N. Academy St.   *469-4064*

Cary has several special events during the year, but none of them match the annual Lazy Daze Arts and Crafts Festival, which has become a real Triangle attraction. Usually held in the depths of summer's dog days, the fourth Saturday in August, most of the action takes place in the city's old down-

town area around the intersection of Academy and Chatham streets. The festival draws craftsmen and artisans from all over the region, and they show their wares and paintings from booths set up along Academy Street. It's a great place to look for handmade items, many of them at bargain prices. Live entertainment is featured on a bandstand set up near the intersection and, like the crafts, the music and dancing has a down-home flavor, from mountain cloggers to bluegrass. Over 300 booths have been taken in recent years; and there are plenty of food concessions available.

SUMMERFEST AT REGENCY PARK

The North Carolina Symphony's Summerfest at Regency Park in Cary has become the informal, fun, family event all the Triangle looks forward to every Saturday night in June and the Fourth of July. If you don't have time to bring your own picnic, you can buy light fare at the concert. There are even seats under a tent where you can sit at a table with six friends and enjoy the concert in comfort if you're not a grass and blanket fan. Past series have included Don McLean (American Pie), The Four Freshmen, the jazz guitarist, Charlie Byrd, Michael Murphey and Flash Cadillac.

Everything about the free Fourth of July Concert & Fireworks Extravaganza is Americana at its best—American pops favorites, flags waving, families and friends together, and a sky exploding with spectacular sights and sounds. Tickets in 1993 were $8 for everyone over th age of 12 (children under

12 are free) and $10 for tent seats (all ages). Single tickets are available at the gate and also at the Memorial Auditorium Box office (831-6060), Ticketmaster outlets or the Ticketmaster phone center (834-4000).

Durham

AMERICAN DANCE FESTIVAL
(See "Dance" section in **ARTS**)

BENNETT PLACE
4409 Bennett Memorial Rd.   383-4345
You don't have to be a Civil War buff to appreciate the significance of what occurred on the farm of James and Nancy Bennett in April 1865. It was in the Bennett's home that two battle-fatigued adversaries—Generals Joseph E. Johnston and William T. Sherman—met to work out a peaceful settlement. Their original agreement was nixed in the wake of hostilities surrounding Abraham Lincoln's assassination, but their talks continued and eventually resulted in Johnston's surrender. It was the largest troop surrender of the Civil War, ending the fighting in the Carolinas, Georgia and Florida. The talks at the Bennett farm had two lasting effects. First, they spared North Carolina the destruction experienced by other southern states. And, coincidentally, they contributed to the development of a form of smoking tobacco that would eventually become the economic base for the city of Durham. While Johnston and Sherman were meeting at the Bennett farm, their troops had broken into a tobacco warehouse down-

town and discovered what both sides agreed was the best smoke they had ever had. After the war ended, orders for more tobacco poured into Durham from all over the eastern seaboard (see **INSIDE DURHAM**).

The Bennett grandchildren lived on the farm until 1890. A fire destroyed the farmhouse and kitchen in 1921. The present buildings were reconstructed in the 1960s from Civil War sketches and early photos. To get to Bennett Place, take the Hillsborough Road exit off U.S. 15-501 Bypass or Interstate 85, and follow the signs. It's open from 9 a.m. to 5 p.m. Monday through Saturday, and from 1 p.m. to 5 p.m. Sunday. Admission is free and you can picnic on the grounds.

CENTERFEST
Downtown   682-1141
Every September, the Durham Arts Council and the City Parks and Recreation Department co-sponsor this two-day street festival to draw thousands of participants downtown for food, beuatiful arts-and-crafts exhibits, games, theatre, dancing and music. It's fun for all ages.

DOWNTOWN HISTORIC DISTRICT

Thanks to the **Historic Preservation Society of Durham**, downtown Durham became in 1977 the first solely commercial district to be placed on the prestigious National Register of Historic Places. Take a walk in and around the downtown loop and just look up: You'll be amazed at the exquisite facades and cornices of buildings dating back to the late 19th century. Begin your tour at the NationsBank building at the intersection of Main and Corcoran streets; the 1914 building sits on the property once owned by the city's founder, Dr. Bartlett Snipes Durham. Proceeding up Main Street you'll take in the Kress Building, a 1932 art deco jewel featuring a facade of polychromed terra cotta ornaments. Further up the street, you'll see the arched pedimented doorway of the white marble, Beaux Arts-era Citizens National Bank. The district also includes the Carolina Theatre (formerly the Durham Auditorium) and the old Durham High School, which has been converted into a new Durham Arts Center (see the "Durham" section of ARTS). A detailed brochure and map of the district is available from the Greater Durham Chamber of Commerce by calling 682-2133.

DUKE HOMESTEAD AND TOBACCO MUSEUM
2828 Duke Homestead Rd.   *477-5498*

You can't fully appreciate Durham until you understand how much tobacco played a part in its growth and development (see **INSIDE DURHAM**). The Duke Homestead and Tobacco Museum is where you go for a quick course in how it all began. You'll see a 20-minute film, tour Washington Duke's old two-story factory, take in the old Duke family farm, and, depending on the season, see tobacco planted, harvested or prepared for market. You may also get a chance to beat, sift or pack smoking tobacco just as the Dukes did over a century ago.

Duke's old homeplace was owned by the university until 1974, when it was given to the state. Every year on the last weekend in July, you can attend a tobacco-barn party and see how tobacco was tied on sticks and cured over wood fires. And on the first Sunday in October, you can see a mock tobacco auction and hear the current world-champion auctioneer in action. And in early December, Duke Homestead hosts two special seasonal programs, "Home for the Holidays" and a Christmas candlelight tour of the house. The museum is open free of charge from 9 a.m. to 5 p.m. Tuesday through Saturday, and 1 to 5 p.m. Sunday.

JORDAN LAKE
U.S. Hwy. 64 and Farrington Rd.
(S.R. 1008)   362-0586

On summer weekends, rural Chatham County south of Durham draws thousands of visitors from all over the Triangle to the 14,000-acre lake and recreation area built by the U.S. Army Corps of Engineers. Jordan Lake offers hiking, boating, windsurfing, fishing, hunting, swimming, picnicking and camping opportunities. There are several beaches, boat ramps and campgrounds available to users for a modest fee. Backcountry camping is not permitted. Call for a detailed map and more information. Boat ramps and beaches are located at Wilsonville, near the intersection of the Farrington Road (S.R. 1008) and U.S. Hwy. 64, between Raleigh and Durham. The Chatham Trails Committee of Pittsboro, a group of volunteer hiking enthusiasts, is building a network of hiking trails

Photo courtesy Durham Convention and Visitors Bureau.

Centerfest draws thousands of visitors to downtown Durham every September.

around Jordan Lake. If you are interested in trail building or hiking, write The Chatham Trails Committee, P.O. Box 217, Pittsboro, NC 27312.

JULY 4 FESTIVAL FOR THE ENO
West Point on the Eno 471-1623

Every year local preservationist Margaret Nygard and the Eno River Association sponsor a Fourth of July extravaganza at the West Point on the Eno city park (see **DURHAM PARKS AND RECREATION**). It's usually about three days of crafts exhibits, food, fun and most of all music, including big-name gospel, folk and bluegrass performers. There's a charge for admission and proceeds go to preservation of the park and the Eno River. A detailed schedule of events is always published in the local newspapers in advance.

LAKE MICHIE
Roxboro Road
Boating and fishing: 477-3906
Spruce Pine Lodge: 477-2058
Camping: 683-4355

This small lake located 10 miles north of Durham on Roxboro Road is a great getaway spot. Here you can rent boats, fish, or just spend the day hiking or picnicking. There's also a lodge available for private parties, weddings and meetings.

N.C. MUSEUM OF LIFE AND SCIENCE
433 Murray Ave. 220-5429

Visitors interact with a wide variety of science exhibits at this 70-acre facility. Hands-on science, technology and nature exhibits feature a 15-foot tornado in the Weather exhibit, body mechanics in **BodyTech: the Science Behind Medicine**, native animals in **Carolina Wildlife**, the **Science Arcade**, the **Tree House** discovery room, **Loblolly Park** for kids, **WaterPlay**, **MegaMaze** and the **Ellerbee Creek Railroad** through **Nature Park**. Five new exhibits opened in a new wing in 1993, including **Aerospace**, **Small Science** (especially for young children), **Data Earth**, **Scientifica** and **Life's Devices**. Some exhibits originating here have traveled nationally. Annual community events include Halloween Adventure and the **Santa Train**. School Programs, community classes, summer camps and teacher workshops are also in the Museum's schedule. Admission is $5 for adults, and $3.50 for children aged 3-12 and seniors. Members of the Museum are free, and there are group rates available with reservations. Hours are 10 a.m. to 5 p.m. Monday through Saturday, and 1 to 5 p.m. on Sunday. The museum is open until 6 p.m. during the summer and is wheelchair-accessible.

PATTERSON'S MILL COUNTRY STORE
Farrington Rd.

Amidst a new crop of housing developments and office parks where corn and tobacco once grew, John and Elsie Booker have built a tribute to a simpler time. Elsie, a pharmacist with a fascination for old-timey medicines, and John, a retired tobacco company employee, have scoured the state, collecting the paraphernalia they might have encountered in their respective professions if they had lived in an ear-

Courtesy N.C. Museum of Life and Science. Photo by Alan Weed.

At the N.C. Museum of Life and Science visitors interact with a variety of hands-on science, technology and nature exhibits.

lier era. The result is a replica of a mom-and-pop country store, drug store, doctor's office and tobacco shop all rolled into one. While the Bookers also sell antiques and North Carolina crafts from the store, 90 percent of what you'll see there is not for sale for any price. (If there's not a price tag on it, don't even ask.)

Among Mrs. Booker's collection of more than 10,000 old-fashioned patent medicines, pills, tonics and potions are some rather curious items. Take a close look at the bottle of powdered extract of "psychologically tested" *Cannabis Sativa*, otherwise known as marijuana. Elsie says it was once used as an ingredient for hair tonics to invigorate the scalp. Then there are the unexplainables: desiccated pituitary, male-fern fluid extract and wonder oil. Upstairs you'll find John's collection of tobacco-industry memorabilia, from old advertisements and cigarette packs to cigar store Indians. Considered one of the best collections of mercantile Americana, the Patterson's Mill Country Store is open from 10 a.m. to 5:30 p.m. Monday through Saturday and from 2 to 5:30 p.m. Sunday. It's located on Farrington Road, about two miles north of N.C. 54 between Durham and Chapel Hill.

SARAH P. DUKE MEMORIAL GARDENS
Duke University West Campus
You'll want to keep going back to this spectacular spot on the edge of Duke's west campus to catch each dazzling display of flowers and shrubs in season. Twenty acres of

landscaped gardens and 35 acres of pine forest are open daily to the public. Seasonal blooms include pansies, tulips, daffodils, azaleas, wisteria, roses, daylilies and chrysanthemums as well as flowering dogwood, magnolia, redbud, crab apple and cherry trees. Sunday afternoon concerts are sometimes held in the spring and summer. This is a great place to picnic and spend a lazy afternoon.

STAGVILLE CENTER FOR PRESERVATION
Old Oxford Hwy.   477-9835
Several historic 18th and 19th century plantation buildings set on 71 acres make up the Stagville Center. This is the nation's first state-owned research center for the study of historic and archaeological preservation. Workshops and demonstrations are scheduled throughout the year. The center is located seven miles northeast of Durham on the Old Oxford Highway (S.R. 1004). It's open from 9 a.m. to 4 p.m. Monday through Friday.

Chapel Hill and Carrboro

ACKLAND ART MUSEUM
Columbia St. at Franklin St.   966-5736
The Ackland Art Museum is a small jewel of a museum on the edge of the UNC campus. Named for its benefactor, William Hayes Ackland, the museum is particularly unusual in that a marble sarcophagus containing Mr. Ackland's remains is housed within the building. (Mr. Ackland, a Washington lawyer bequeathed the money to

build an art museum with the stipu-
lation that it contain his mauso-
leum.) A recent addition to the
Ackland has significantly increased
its space, and allowed many paintings and prints from its fine collection to be displayed for the first
time. The museum contains paintings and sculpture from ancient
Greek and Roman times to contemporary works. Hours are Wednesday to Friday, noon to 3 p.m., Saturday 10 a.m. to 5 p.m. and Sunday 1
to 5 p.m.

APPLE CHILL AND FESTIFALL

Franklin St. 968-2784

Twice a year, thousands of
residents from all over the Triangle
converge on Chapel Hill for its famous street fairs. Apple Chill takes
place in the spring, usually about
the third weekend in April, and
Festifall occurs in early October.
Sponsored by the Chapel Hill Parks
and Recreation Department, these
two street fairs offer a variety of arts
and crafts, music, clogging, magicians, puppet shows, jugglers, potters, incredible edibles and more.

FAMILY FOURTH AT KENAN STADIUM

UNC, Kenan Stadium 967-7075

If you like fireworks, live music and big crowds, this is where it's
at on the Fourth of July in Chapel
Hill. In recent years, it has been co-
sponsored by the towns of Chapel
Hill and Carrboro and Orange
County.

HILLSBOROUGH HOG DAY

732-8156

A street festival for pigs and
people, this unusual event takes
place every June in Hillsborough,
north of Chapel Hill and Carrboro.
If you like to eat pork and admire
the pig family, you'll feel at home
here. Hog Day features a highly
competetive barbecue cook-off, with
the results to be enjoyed by those
attending this event. Even if a big
plate of Carolina barbecue is not
your idea of hog heaven, there are
lots of other foods to enjoy, as well
as arts and crafts, music and dance,
and games and activities for kids.

MOREHEAD PLANETARIUM AND SUNDIAL GARDEN

UNC, E. Franklin St. 962-1236 or 549-6863

From watching the universe
spin above your head to visiting the
rare walk-in Copernican Orrery, to
enjoying the beautifully cultivated
sundial rose gardens and Coker Arboretum, the Morehead Planetarium offers a day full of activities
for the whole family. A triangle treasure for family learning and fun,
the Morehead Planetarium presents
both traveling and original shows
about moon landings, space voy-
ages, UFOs and more, along with
special children's shows about a
curious cat who finds himself on a
trip to the moon and a litterbug
who explores the solar system to
learn the unique livability of planet
Earth. Friday evenings, catch Sky
Rambles, a live sky show narrated by
a Morehead Planetarium staff member, or make a special trip to view a
rare wide-angle film stretched across

the Planetarium's 60-foot dome.

The Planetarium is open every day, except December 24 and 25, and there is an evening sky show at least once each day. Admission for adults is $3; seniors, kids and students pay $2.50. Classes and memberships are available for the whole family. Call 549-6863 (toll-free from most of the Triangle) for more information about show times and prices.

N.C. BOTANICAL GARDEN
U.S. Hwy. 15-501   967-2246

Located on 330 acres, this is the largest natural botanical garden in the southeast. As part of UNC's Totten Center, the Botanical Garden is set up for research and conservation of plants native to the southeastern U.S. The main visitor area features displays of native plants arranged by habitats and more than two miles of trails through the woods. Throughout the year, there are special programs and workshops in the Totten Center. The Botanical Garden also hosts a Labor Day Open House featuring free entertainment, educational exhibits and a scavenger hunt. It is open from 8 a.m. to 5 p.m. Monday through Friday. From mid-March through mid-November, it is also open from 10 a.m. to 5 p.m. on Saturday, and 2 to 5 p.m. on Sunday.

OLD FASHIONED JULY 4TH FAMILY DAY
Carrboro   968-7703

An alternative to the extravaganza over at Kenan is this old-

Visitors view the universe at the Morehead Planetarium in Chapel Hill.

Photo courtesy Morehead Planetarium.

fashioned July 4th celebration put on every year by the Carrboro Recreation and Parks Department. It offers arts and crafts exhibits, rides, old films, food, music, dancing, a horseshoe tournament and activities for kids.

UNC WALKING TOUR
962-1630

You can take a half-hour Walkman cassette-guided tour of the historic University of North Carolina, the nation's first university to open its doors. You'll see and hear about the Old Well, the Davie Poplar and the five-acre Coker Arboretum among other sights. The tours begin at the Rotunda of the Morehead Building, Monday through Friday at 2:15 p.m. and on Saturday at 11:30 a.m., March 1 through November 30. A small deposit ensures return of the equipment used on this free tour. In the Visitors' Center of the Rotunda is a new interactive touch-screen computer of information about the campus, and this spring, an outdoor kiosk—the graduation gift of a recent University class—will project this information into the highly-trafficked campus area as well. The Rotunda is well-supplied with informational brochures and pamphlets, but is not always staffed. Call to arrange special tours.

TRIANGLE TRAINING CENTER
Pittsboro   *542-1332*

Triangle Training Center, a 48-acre facility in Chatham County, offers The Ropes Course, an outdoor physical-challenge course designed to assist individuals in developing their full potential through experiential learning. The Ropes Course is designed to develop individual skills and emphasizes effective communication, decision-making, trust-building and leadership skills. The course is open to business, corporate, church and civic groups, as well as student and athletic groups, families and individuals. Call the Training Center for information or a brochure.

The Wilson Library on the campus of the
University of North Carolina at Chapel Hill.

Inside

Colleges and Universities

They don't call this area the Research Triangle for nothing. With four major universities and five colleges, it's no wonder there are more PhDs per capita here than just about anywhere else on the planet. Tremendous educational opportunities await you in the Triangle, whether you are thinking of enrolling full-time in a professional, graduate or undergraduate program, or you're just interested in keeping informed on the latest developments in your own field. If you've got college-bound kids, don't forget that as North Carolina residents you can take advantage of one of the best educational bargains in the country: 1993 tuition for local residents at our state schools—including one that is ranked among the top 20 colleges and universities in the U.S.—was about $1,600 for the academic year. The state also offers a $1,150 grant for residents who attend private, in-state colleges.

But you and your family don't have to enroll in any of these institutions to benefit from their presence. You can use their libraries and take advantage of their varied cultural and sports programs anytime. (For more information on

these opportunities, see our sections on **ARTS, ATTRACTIONS** and **SPORTS**.) In this section, we'll briefly describe the colleges, universities and technical schools in Raleigh, Durham and Chapel Hill. For more information, write to each school for catalogs and brochures.

Raleigh

NORTH CAROLINA STATE UNIVERSITY
Admissions: 112 Peele Hall   515-2011
Box 7103, Raleigh, NC 27695

One of the three corners of the Research Triangle, NCSU is probably the state's premier research institution and one of the best in the country. Its campus lies about one and a half miles from the Capitol on Hillsborough Street in Raleigh. With a 1,563 acre campus and nearby research stations and recreational facilities covering another 2,700 acres, it comprises a big chunk not only of Raleigh's real estate, but of much of the area's economic, social and artistic life. There are several other schools in the city, but "State," as it's often called, commands the most attention.

Founded in 1887 as a land-grant school for agriculture and the mechanic arts, it was long derided as a "cow college" by fans of arch-rival UNC-Chapel Hill. But NCSU is now known as far more than an "ag and tech school". It is among the nation's leaders in engineering, textiles, forestry, architecture, wood and paper science and biotechnology. It also is now the largest school in North Carolina, with about 27,000 students who average 1070 on their SAT scores and earned about a 3.5 GPA in high school.

But first, the basics: tuition, room, board and expenses for an in-state student at NCSU will cost about $7,048 a year; out-of state, $14,574. Considering the school's reputation, that's a bargain. The school maintains dorm rooms or housing for about 7,000 students and tries to place all freshmen who are not commuting in campus housing. The school has about 19,000 undergraduates; it receives about 11,000 applications a year, from which it accepts 3,400 freshmen. Average class size is 35 students. Most of the students come from North Carolina, about 85 percent; the student body is composed of about 40 percent women and 60 percent men.

The university is divided into colleges, with the largest in terms of enrollment being Engineering and the newest being Management. The others are Agriculture and Life Sciences, Education and Psychology,

Photo courtesy N.C. State University.

N.C. State University's sprawling campus serves as a backdrop for the McKimmon Center for extension and continuing education.

Courtesy N.C. Travel and Tourism Division.

The Bell Tower serves as a landmark on the campus of N.C. State University.

Forest Resources, Humanities and Social Sciences, Textiles, Physical and Mathematical Sciences, and Veterinary Medicine as well as the School of Design and Graduate School.

NCSU offers 89 undergraduate, 80 master's and 51 doctoral degree programs. Chancellor Larry K. Montieth, has put new emphasis on undergraduate programs. The result being that undergrads at NCSU have access to world-class research facilities. In engineering, the school maintains a close relationship with a number of Research Triangle companies—over 150 Park employees hold adjunct professorships at NCSU—and its work in signal processing, communication and microchip technology is at the forefront in national research. One of the nation's premier software companies, SAS in Cary, was started by an NCSU professor in the statistics department of mathematical sciences.

Among public universities, NCSU is ranked eighth nationally in terms of industry-sponsored research, and 24th in terms of research expenditures. Its School of Textiles is not only the largest in the country but is considered the best by many in the industry. Departments at NCSU ranked among the top 10 of their kind in the nation include: plant pathology; entomology; horticulture; wood and paper science; forestry; parks, recreation and tourism management; statistics; architecture; mathematics and science education; community college and adult education; food science and nuclear engineering.

The main library, D.H. Hill, is especially strong in biological and physical science, engineering, agriculture and forestry. Its Libraries Information System has been selected as one of the nation's six "Libraries of the Future".

What's surprising is NCSU's record in the non-science areas. Its design school is also ranked among the top 10 in the country. In the humanities, NCSU's faculty includes writer Lee Smith, one of the South's best-known authors.

Outreach and continuing education play a major role at NCSU, too. The Jane S. McKimmon Center is one of the largest continuing education centers in the nation serving more than 110,000 people in about 1,600 different programs annually.

The Japan Center, one of NCSU's institutes, conducts Japanese language programs for business people, as well as courses about Japanese customs for businesses interested in doing business in Japan. It also helped establish the Saturday Japanese School at Effie Green Elementary School in Raleigh for Japanese children whose parents are on assignment with Japanese affiliates here. It permits the children to continue their education in native Japanese.

Life at NCSU is not all books; there are 35 social fraternities and sororities, and an active intramural program. Plus, there are hundreds of student organizations, including a radio station, newspaper and Thompson Theatre. Being in the center of Raleigh gives the school access to the capital city's cultural life, too. But it becomes one big party when the Wolfpack teams are winning—like in '74 and '83 when the basketball teams captured the national championship. Victory celebrations center around the Brickyard, the historic gathering place for students in the heart of the campus, but often spread out into surrounding streets and neighborhoods.

Moreover, there's an unpretentiousness about State students that's refreshing. Some are the first in their families to go to college and they tend to be diligent and hard working. NCSU is big, it's a bargain and it's among the best research universities in the nation. A "cow college" no more.

MEREDITH COLLEGE

3800 Hillsborough St.   *829-8600*
Raleigh, NC 27607

Meredith College, founded in 1891, is a private, comprehensive college for women and one of the Triangle's best kept secrets as a place for a good education at a good price. With an enrollment of over 2,000 students in both undergraduate and graduate programs, Meredith is the largest, private four-year women's college in the Southeast. In a survey by the business magazine, *Barrons*, Meredith was rated as one of the best college bargains in the nation, and the John Templeton Foundation listed the school as among the country's best in building character.

The school's 225-acre campus in west Raleigh is near the beltline and Interstate 40. It provides the city with one of its loveliest architectural settings, complete with a tree-lined drive, columned brick buildings, and flowering trees and shrubs and a new master plan for future growth. Meredith's beautiful campus is the site of many community events, such as the Labor Day concert by the North Carolina Symphony, weddings, and civic and educational meetings.

Tuition, room and board cost about $9,440 per year. Tuition only for non-resident students is about $6,340 per year. The faculty-student ratio is 1 to 17. In the past decade, the college has strengthened its reputation as a resource center for many non-traditional students (over age 23) through the Meredith ReEntry program. The continuing Education Enrichment Program offers short courses on a wide variety of topics such as computers, creative writing and financial planning. The college also offers two postgraduate certification programs: one for legal assistants and the other in the area of cultural management.

With over 30 majors and 12 concentrations, Meredith offers bachelors of arts, music and science degrees. Admissions officials consider both SAT and high school records when admitting students. Over 65 percent of incoming freshmen rank in at least the top 25 percent of their class. The John E. Weems Graduate School (named after Meredith President Weems) offers master's degrees in business administration, music and education. Over 175 women are currently enrolled in the graduate programs. The MBA program features evening classes year-round and is tailored for the demanding schedules of professional women.

With five other colleges and universities in the Triangle area, Meredith students enjoy bountiful cultural, social and educational opportunities. Meredith also offers students opportunities to participate in International Programs and in cooperative education and internships in and around Research Triangle Park.

PEACE COLLEGE
15 E. Peace St.   832-2881
Raleigh, NC 27604

This is another of Raleigh's scenic college campuses, located downtown close to the state government complex. It is the second oldest of the city's colleges, founded in 1857 and named for William Peace, who gave the land and $10,000 to help build Main Hall. It is a two-year, liberal arts college for women with an enrollment of 450, but it is changing to a four-year school, a transition that is expected to be completed by 1995. As a two-year school, Peace has one of the best transfer records in the state, with over 97% of its liberal arts graduates transferring to four-year institutions.

Peace College is affiliated with the Presbyterian Church (USA) and enjoys a good relationship with the First Presbyterian Church of Raleigh. However, women of all denominations find challenging academic programs aimed at three degrees: an associate of arts, associate of science in business, and associate of fine arts in music. According to the director of admissions at Peace College, "We choose to put all of our energy into the lives of freshmen and sophomores, because we think a first-rate beginning in college can make a major positive difference for the rest of a student's life."

With an enrollment that is expected to grow to 600 students, Peace offers a faculty-student ratio of 1 to 15. Peace's size allows young women to become involved in college and community activities. The students often assume leadership positions not generally available to them at larger schools. According to a study produced by the Women's College Coalition, "many of today's women leaders in politics and business attended women's colleges. They credit their school experience for their success."

The cost of attending Peace is lower than at many comparable colleges. Tuition, room and board for the 1992-93 academic year is approximately $9,660; for day students, tuition is $5,220. If you're a state resident, you can subtract from that the $1,150 tuition grant from the state. Many Peace students also receive assistance through scholarships and need-based financial aid. The fiscal strength of the college is based on a $22 million endowment, with no indebtedness (after all, it is a Presbyterian college!).

The college considers both high school rank and SAT scores when admitting students. According to the admissions brochure, an applicant should rank in the top half of her graduating class, and SAT scores should be average or

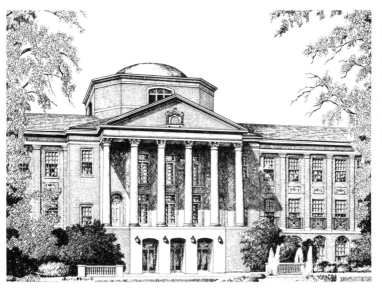

Line drawings by Jerry Miller.

Meredith College's Johnson Hall

Peace College

above-average when compared to the scores of all college-bound students. The college does not release SAT scores. Peace will also offer early admission to exceptional students.

In addition to its regular programs, Peace is a member of Cooperating Raleigh Colleges, a consortium that allows students from member colleges to take classes at other member colleges. Peace students thereby have the opportunity to attend a larger university while still enrolled at Peace. Students are also offered a summer foreign-study program in England each year.

Peace is known for the tradition of graduating its students in long, white dresses, carrying red roses, but as many graduates themselves will say, the oldest tradition at Peace is the lasting friendships that develop among students.

St. Augustine's College

1315 Oakwood Ave.   *516-4000*
Raleigh, NC 27611

St. Augustine's was founded two years after the Civil War by the Episcopal Church to educate freed slaves, and in 1868, it opened its doors to its first four students. Today, it continues its affiliation with the Episcopal Church and its commitment to educate its predominately black student body.

The school's green, wooded campus is located in east Raleigh, not far from the Governor's Mansion, and adjacent to historic Oakwood Cemetery. St. Aug, as it is called, adds a grace and energy to its 125 acres of the capital city.

Tuition, room and board, and books cost about $9,775 a year; for commuting students, it's about $6,175. There are about 1,900 male and female students—with more men than women—enrolled, drawn from 37 states and 24 countries. Many students board in one of the seven dormitories or 24 duplex apartments.

Although it was established to produce educators and a number of its students continue to pursue teaching careers, St. Aug offers bachelor's degrees in 38 majors. In January 1992, the College established a sixth academic division, the Division of Allied Health. This division has had great success with its Medical Technology and Phlebotomy program and plans to institute a nursing degree program shortly.

The school is accredited by the Southern Association of Colleges and Secondary Schools, and its faculty consists of 120 highly skilled men and women, 72% of whom hold the Doctoral degree. The faculty to student ratio is 1 to 16. While average SAT scores for incoming freshmen have improved, they remain between 750 and 850.

St. Augustine's is considered to be among the top five percent of black institutions in the country. It maintains cooperative programs with other Raleigh colleges including NCSU, where students interested in technical degrees can take engineering courses. There is an Army ROTC program and a co-op program that permits students to work in their field while attending college during alternate semesters.

The school considers its small size an advantage, especially to black students who may be the first in their family going to college. Its size doesn't keep the students from having an active social life in clubs, fraternities, sororities and intramurals. Its lecture program has brought numerous national and international speakers to the school, including the Rev. Jesse Jackson and Virginia Gov. Douglas Wilder. President Robert Mugabe of Zimbabwe, entertainers Ossie Davis and Ruby Dee, and the late Arthur Ashe have spoken here, too. The school has an envious athletic record and boasts over 250 world-class athletes among its alumni. It has won several national CIAA championships in cross country, track, tennis and volleyball, and its basketball teams are usually ranked at the top in their leagues.

SAINT MARY'S COLLEGE
900 Hillsborough St.   *828-2521*
Raleigh, NC 27603

This is the city's oldest college, founded in 1842 by the good Rev. Aldert Smedes, whose name still courses through old Raleigh families such as that of former mayor and St. Mary's Trustee G. Smedes York. With an enrollment of about 400 girls and young women, St. Mary's is unique in several other ways, too. It is, for example, the only private Episcopal women's college in the U.S.

It also has been considered "a four-year intermediate college," a hybrid between high school and college—offering the junior and senior years of high school and the

first two years of college. But beginning with the 1994-95 school year, it will also offer grades 9 and 10 for day students. The student mix is about 225 college students and 175 high school. Come commencement, two graduation ceremonies are held, one for the high school students and the other for associate degree holders. The students come mostly from Raleigh, eastern North Carolina and other Southern states. They represent some of the region's socially prominent families.

The school is located at the intersection of Hillsborough and St. Mary's streets, seven blocks west of the Capitol building. Smedes Hall is a red brick and white-columned historic site with a circular, tree-lined driveway leading up to worn, stone steps. The campus is marked by a brick wall along Hillsborough Street and shaded by oaks and magnolias. To the west of Smedes Hall is the small, white chapel, first built in 1856, where students attend required weekly services.

President Clauston L. Jenkins, Jr., presides over a faculty of 43, which gives its students an average 1 to 10 faculty student ratio. Tuition for resident students for the 1994-95 school year is $14,910 for high school and $13,195 for college. For day students, costs are $7,595 a year for high school and $7,125 for the college. A number of scholarships are available. A personal interview is required for students interested in St. Mary's High School. Class rank and special achievements are considered. For the college program, students should have at least a 2.0 GPA and

800 SAT score. Almost all of the two-year college graduates—98 percent—go on to get bachelor's degrees.

This record, say school officials, is proof that its unusual combination of high school and college years prepares its students well for higher academic life. St. Mary's high school students, for example, can take 22 academic credits in accelerated courses, which is six more than required by state public high schools. Its accelerated junior program permits qualified students to skip their 12th grade and go into St. Mary's first college year. The school extended the concept to some 10th grade students who will be placed in 11th grade courses. Also, there are not many high schools whose faculty have a large number of Ph.D.s, as is the case at St. Mary's, where more than a third hold doctorates and all have master's degrees. It has always been respected for its liberal arts courses such as art, languages, history, drama and English.

In a school with St. Mary's history, traditions comprise an important part of scholastic life. Its small size means students can take leadership positions in a number of the school's clubs and organizations. Its tennis team probably is

Line Drawing by Jerry Miller.

Estey Hall at Shaw University.

the biggest athletic threat the school commands, although it competes in basketball and soccer, too. In fact, the new soccer field produced a team ranked 4th in the state.

SHAW UNIVERSITY
118 E. South St. 546-8200
Raleigh, NC 27601

Shaw is one of the country's oldest black four-year colleges, dating back to 1865 when a former Union Army chaplain began teaching theology classes to young blacks with the financial backing of Massachusetts industrialist Elijah Shaw. Its enrollment is about 3,200 men and women and enjoys a faculty to student ratio of 1 to 15. Black Baptist churches helped the University after financial difficulties in the 1980s. Under the leadership of President Talbert Shaw and alumni such as Willie Gary of Florida, who made a $10 million gift to Shaw, the school has survived and progressed and has added many new programs including the Institute for the Study of Ethics and Values.

The campus is located downtown, just east of Memorial Auditorium. Shaw's landmark building, beautiful Estey Hall, is a national historic landmark named after Vermont philanthropist Jacob Estey, and is believed to be one of the first buildings in America built to house women on a coed campus. It has been restored as a community building and reopened in 1993. The school became a source of civil rights activity during the 1960s when Dr. King visited the campus. And several current local black leaders got their start at Shaw, including Wake

County Commissioners Board Chairman Vernon Malone, gospel singer Shirley Caesar, former heavyweight champion James "Bonecrusher" Smith, and Register of Deeds Ken Wilkins. The school offers majors in 21 areas of study in the arts and sciences. Tuition, room and board is about $9,192 a year.

WAKE TECHNICAL COLLEGE
9101 Fayetteville Rd. 772-0551
Raleigh, NC 27603

Wake Tech is part of the state's heralded technical and community college system established in the 1960s. It is located south of Raleigh, beyond Garner, on the highway to Fayetteville, and a new campus is planned north of the city after approval of a 1993 bond issue. The school's mission is to serve those students and citizens who do not attend a four-year institution; it offers a variety of vocational and technical courses.

The Tech campus has grown steadily over the years, with many area residents seeking to upgrade skills in fields such as computer programming and nursing, among others. The college has been unable to accommodate all comers. Enrollment including part-time students is about 7,200.

An associate's degree is offered in a number of programs, and graduates in such fields as electronic and computer technology and chemical technology have been vigorously recruited in the past by Research Triangle companies. It also offers more traditional vocational programs such as auto mechanics and heating and air conditioning.

The business administration curriculum is popular with clerical employees anxious to improve their job skills and prepare for supervisory roles, and the newest course is one in office automation.

Its offerings are lifesavers to some; it's where the high school dropout can prepare for the GED test (high school equivalency) or adults who border on illiterate can learn to read. For foreigners, there is an "English as a Second Language" course. It also has driver education classes. It's the best bargain in the Triangle; courses are about $13.25 per credit hour, with an additional fee if the course is taught off campus at one of the participating Wake County public schools.

Durham

DUKE UNIVERSITY
684-8111

Duke University has long been considered one of the finest private colleges in the nation. In a 1993 nationwide survey by *U.S. News & World Report*, Duke was ranked the seventh-best national university (public or private) in the country. No wonder the *New York Times Magazine* called it one of the nation's "hot" colleges.

It all began back in 1892 when Trinity College, a Methodist school located in rural Randolph County, was moved to Durham with the help of tobacco magnate Washington Duke. In 1924, James Buchanan Duke endowed the institution and it was renamed in the family's honor.

Today Duke encompasses 575 tree-shaded acres in Durham, including the Georgian architecture of the East campus off Broad Street, and the Gothic towers of the Duke Chapel on the West campus a mile and a half away. Here you'll find about 11,000 students working toward a variety of graduate and undergraduate degrees.

Duke's admissions criteria is tough—only 12 percent of those who apply eventually enroll. And its tuition is steep: about $18,500 a year. But students who make it leave with a prestigious credential from one of Duke's eight highly acclaimed schools: Trinity College of Arts and Sciences, School of Engineering, Graduate School, School of Law, School of Medicine, Divinity School, School of The Environment and Fuqua School of Business.

Many students choose interdisciplinary programs such as Women's Studies, the Institute of the Arts, or Technology and Liberal Arts. The Terry Sanford Institute of Public Policy offers graduates and undergraduates a chance to prepare for their chosen careers by studying under federal government officials and nationally respected journalists.

Duke is known for its specialized research in science and medicine. The Duke University Medical Center is engaged in highly sophisticated cancer research, among other things, drawing its patients from all over the country (see **HOSPITALS**). The Center for the Study of Aging and Human Development is the first such facility in the coun-

Photo courtesy Duke University Photo Department.

Baldwin Auditorium on Duke University's East Campus.

try to study what happens biologically, psychologically and socially—as people grow old. And Duke's Primate Center is an active teaching facility devoted to the preservation and study of humanity's most primitive relatives.

The 12,500-sq.-ft. Botany Greenhouse holds the most diverse collection of plants under glass in the Southeast, including over 2,500 different species. (Visitors may tour the facilities from 10 a.m. to 4:30 p.m. daily.)

Finally, there is the F.G. Hall Laboratory for Environmental Research, containing special high-pressure chambers for simulating deep-sea diving experiments. A recent research dive to 2,250 feet set a new world's record.

You don't have to be a research scientist or student to enjoy having Duke University in the neighborhood. Anyone can take advantage of the resources available at the Perkins Library, considered among the top 10 university libraries in the nation, with 4.2 million books and 22,000 periodicals.

You can also enroll in one of dozens of stimulating courses offered through Duke's Continuing Education program. A recent schedule included classes in foreign studies, writing, computers, business skills and career counseling. For a schedule, call 684-6259. If you are age 50 or older, you might sign up for Duke's Institute for Learning in Retirement, a program of classes taught by peers and professionals, including history, language, literature, religion, science, current affairs, business and fitness.

Even if you don't want to study anything at all, Duke has something for you. You can hike, jog or picnic in Duke Forest, the 8,300-acre preserve that serves as a labora-

Photo courtesy Durham Chamber of Commerce.

North Carolina Central University

tory for Duke's School of The Environment.

Other attractions open to the public include: the **Bryan University Center** and **Page Auditorium**, where more than 500 events are presented each year; the **Art Museum** and galleries on both the East and West campuses; and the 20-acre **Sarah P. Duke Gardens**. And of course, there's always Atlantic Coast Conference basketball, football and soccer brought to you by the Duke Blue Devils. For more information on these, see our sections on **ARTS, ATTRACTIONS** and **SPORTS**.

N.C. CENTRAL UNIVERSITY

1801 Fayetteville St.   560-6100
Durham, NC 27707

Founded in 1910 by educator Dr. James E. Shephard, N.C. Central University later became the first state-supported liberal arts college for blacks in the United States. Today, Central is part of the University of North Carolina system and continues to provide educational opportunities to students of all races: about 12 percent of the undergraduates, 28 percent of the graduates and 50 percent of the school's law students are white.

The campus is set on 104 acres southeast of downtown Durham. About 5,700 undergraduate and graduate students are enrolled in 60 programs leading to degrees in 17 fields. Students enroll in one of five schools: the Undergraduate and Graduate Schools of the Arts and Sciences, the School of Business, School of Law, and School of Library and Information Science.

Recent graduate programs have been established for careers in criminal justice and public administration.

NCCU's law school is the only one in the state that offers working adults an opportunity to earn their degree through an evening program. Central also offers an extensive continuing education program, including courses of study available to many workers at their place of employment.

DURHAM TECHNICAL COMMUNITY COLLEGE

P.O. Box 11307   598-9224
Durham, NC 27703

As a member of the N.C. Community College System, Durham Tech is a two-year institution offering vocational and technical training to residents of Durham and Orange counties, as well as fully transferable credit to four-year colleges and universities. Durham Tech features 37 programs of study, 20 of them leading to an associate's degree. Courses of study include accounting, architectural drafting, automotive mechanics, business administration, computer programming, criminal justice, dental laboratory technology, early childhood development, electonics, general education, light construction, occupational therapy assistant, opticianry, paralegal training, pharmacy technology, practical nursing, respiratory therapy, secretarial science and more.

Day, evening and weekend classes are available. Durham Tech also offers short courses, workshops and seminars for continuing career development, as well as customized training programs for businesses and industries in the area. In addition Durham Tech provides programs in adult basic education, high school completion and English as a Second Language.

Chapel Hill

UNIVERSITY OF NORTH CAROLINA AT CHAPEL HILL

Visitor's Services   962-1630
Undergraduate Admissions   966-3621

The University of North Carolina began the celebration of its bicentennial year on October 12, 1993, the 200th anniversary of the laying of the cornerstone for Old East, the oldest building on the campus. The highlight of the University Day ceremony was the keynote address by President Bill Clinton who said, "The idea of the public univeristy, born here in North Carolina played a major role in revolutionizing opportunity for millions and millions of Americans who never even came into this state, but got the opportunity in other states because of the example set here."

The nation's oldest state university has been a leader in higher education since it opened its doors in 1795. The first student to register, Hinton James, was the University's only student for several weeks. "Carolina," as it is known around here, is consistently ranked as one of the top state universities in the country. It has also been named by *US News & World Report*

and *Money* magazine as one of the best bargains in the nation because it offers excellent programs at some of the lowest tuitions. 1994-95 tuition for state residents is about $1,480 per academic year; for out-of-staters, it's about $9,006.

What started in one building with less than 50 students and two professors has mushroomed into a major university with 162 buildings, 24,000 students and nearly 2,400 faculty.

For 200 years now, UNC has been nationally acclaimed for its teaching, research and public service programs. The National Academy of Sciences rated UNC as one of the foremost graduate and research institutions in the U.S., and its faculty as the most outstanding in the Southeast.

With 13 colleges and schools and more than 70 departments and related centers and programs, Carolina offers students a wide choice of curriculums leading to 218 different undergraduate, graduate or professional degrees. You can study in one of eight colleges in the Division of Academic Affairs (General, Arts and Sciences, Business Administration, Education, Journalism, Law, Library Science and Social Work), or one of five schools in the Division of Health Affairs (Dentistry, Medicine, Nursing, Pharmacy and Public Health). In addition, more than 1,500 courses are offered to the general public through special institutes, seminars and workshops.

Even if you don't want to enroll in a class, UNC is a fantastic resource to have in the neighborhood. With more than four million volumes, Carolina's libraries are among the best in the Southeast. You'll enjoy the Rare Book Collection, the North Carolina Collection and the Southern Historical Collection housed in the Wilson library, as well as the resources in the newer Davis graduate library. They are open to the public; North Carolina residents can even get library cards by calling 966-3260.

UNC is also the site of the UNC Hospital complex, the state's principal referral, diagnostic and treatment center (see **HOSPITALS**). UNC and the hospital are the largest employers in Chapel Hill.

What's more, Carolina's 729-acre main campus, known as "The

Noble Grove," is rich in history (see **ATTRACTIONS**), as well as just a nice place to stroll. Among the major attractions offered by UNC are the **Coker Arboretum, Morehead Planetarium, Ackland Art Museum, N.C. Botanical Garden, Playmakers Repertory Company, Dean E. Smith Center** (the "Dean Dome"), **Memorial Hall** and, of course, **Atlantic Coast Conference Basketball** (the Tar Heel men were the national champs in 1993 and the Lady Tar Heels won the title in 1994), football and soccer. For more information on these attractions, see our sections on **ARTS, ATTRACTIONS** and **SPORTS**.

N.C. Travel and Tourism Division photo by William Russ.

The Old Well, which was given its present decorative form in 1897, has become the unofficial symbol of the University of North Carolina at Chapel Hill.

Photo courtesy AAC Management Inc.

*Two Hannover Square, a 29-story skyscraper, greets visitors
to downtown Raleigh with a grand, towering welcome.*

Inside

Commercial Development

The Triangle enjoyed a building boom like much of the country during the mid-80s, but by 1985, the market began to approach saturation and the Triangle became a renters' market. In 1993-94, demand in housing and commercial office space has returned and the apartment market has recovered. The average vacancy rate for commercial office space was below nine percent at the beginning of 1994, according to Carlton Midyette whose Carolantic Realty Company publishes the best market survey in the Triangle. In Raleigh and northwest Raleigh and RTP, the rate dropped to six percent and it was the same for Cary. Durham and Chapel Hill are about eight and ten percent average vacancy rate.

Rent rates vary, of course, but the high range per square foot is from $20.50 a square foot for a floor in Raleigh's new First Union Capital Center to $16.50 a square foot in suburban Smoketree Towers in Highways Office Park. Many are negotiating even better deals, and good suburban Class A office space can be rented for $15.50 a square foot. Some prime Raleigh and Cary commercial land will sell for up to $250,000 per acre, and land around the Park continues to draw high prices, as much as $100,000 an acre, while industrial property will go for $55,000 per acre. Commercial property in a development such as Durham's Treyburn, by contrast, sells for approximately $50,000 an acre.

Here's an Insiders' guide to some of the Triangle's commercial projects and some of the players in the Triangle. They're listed alphabetically, by city. Some of the developments are completed; others are looking for customers like you.

Raleigh

CAROLANTIC REALTY CO.
224 Fayetteville St. Mall   832-0594

Carolantic is an exclusively commercial development firm, established in Raleigh since 1972. It specializes in industrial development and brokerage, sales, property management and leasing, and commercial development investment counseling. Carolantic has been involved in a number of major commercial real estate transactions in the Triangle area, such as the assembly of land around the RDU

Airport, a 2500-acre development now in the planning stages. Its *Annual Great Raleigh Commercial Real Estate Conference* is the best and most accurate survey of market conditions and usually comes out in February. The principals of Carolantic are committed to the city of Raleigh and to the state of North Carolina; they serve on such boards as the North Carolina Nature Conservancy and the N.C. Railroad Commission.

First Union Capital Center
100 Fayetteville St. Mall   832-0768

This 29-story tower opened in 1991 and changed the skyline of Raleigh's downtown. Built by an irrepressible South Carolinian, Ed Bagwell of Southwind, Ltd., the building has 525,000 square feet of space, most of which is rented by its anchor tenant, First Union Bank. The dark granite-and-glass skyscraper is a block away from the Capitol and has an impressive fountain and plaza in front on the Fayetteville Street Mall. There is some parking underneath the building and on top is the elegant Cardinal Club, a private dining club that occupies the top two floors. Bagwell makes decisions quickly, which has enabled him to fill the building with other familiar names such as Deloitte & Touche, the national accounting firm, and two of the city's best-known law firms.

Capital Club Building
16 W. Martin St.   688-8006

This graceful 12-story building, erected in 1930, was renovated in 1990 by Durham developer Andy Widmark. It has become home for small law firms, including that of former U.S. Senator Robert Morgan and City Councillor Eric Reeves and architect Andy Leager, a member of the Triangle Transit Authority. It contains 60,000 sq. ft. and is nicknamed the WTVD building because of that television station's logo and offices at the top.

The Forum
8601 Six Forks Rd.   846-7666

One of the fanciest projects in north Raleigh, the Forum has fountains, pavers in the street, a granite exterior and a location convenient to the fastest-growing quadrant of the city. It opened in 1987, and in 1989, added Forum II, which has 100,000 square feet. It is not far from Strickland Road, which connects arterial thoroughfares, Falls of the Neuse, Six Forks, and Creedmoor roads, and is adjacent to the Six Forks Station shopping center. Taking Strickland Road, you can get to RDU from the Forum in about 15 minutes; to RTP in about 20 to 25 minutes. Forum I is a seven-story building with 132,000 square feet, and when the complex is built out, it will have 400,000 square feet on the project's 12.5 wooded acres.

Gingko Square
Dale and Jefferson sts.   782-9090

This small development is hidden close to downtown Raleigh and sits perched on a bluff overlooking the Seaboard Railroad tracks and Downtown Boulevard near Wade Avenue. The several acres are bordered by aging Chinese gingko trees with their fan-shaped leaves. It includes an eclectic collection of three period buildings that have been restored and a new brick 20,000-square-foot two-story building, occupied mostly by Spectator Publications. Total space is 35,000 square feet. Some of the buildings date back to 1916; restoration began in 1984 and the project was nominated for the city's Sir Walter Raleigh Award for its appearance.

TWO HANNOVER SQUARE

Two Hannover Sq.   *821-2700*

This complex is at the other end of the Fayetteville Street Mall and BB&T is the anchor tenant. The 29-story skyscraper, completed in 1991, greets visitors with a grand, towering welcome as they drive into downtown on South Saunders Street and the Dawson-McDowell Connector. The building was recently acquired by Phonix Limited Partnership of Raleigh.

The classic, 1930s-style tower has about 430,000 square feet. Two Hannover Square joins the 17-story One Hannover Square building and together they comprise one of the biggest pieces of Raleigh's downtown development. The two buildings stand over an underground parking facility with 600 spaces that serve the city's Civic Center. The building is equipped with high-speed elevators and retail space on the ground floor. Its proximity to the Civic Center and the Radisson Plaza Hotel are strong selling points. Two Hannover Square is currently managed and leased by AAC Management, Inc.

HIGHWOODS OFFICE CENTER

U.S. Hwy. 1 and Beltline   *872-4924*

Highwoods, located in the northwest quadrant of the intersection of U.S. Highway 1 and the Beltline, began development in the late 1970s by Raleigh's largest builder, Seby Jones of Davidson and Jones Construction. Today, it's one of the city's best-known office parks and home to Highwoods Properties, one of the Triangle's major

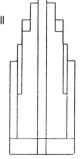

commercial leasing companies. The park includes a hotel and has both a Howard Johnson's and Holiday Inn within walking distance as well as the Raleigh Sportz Health and Fitness Center.

The 200-acre project contains Smoketree Tower, a 170,000-square-foot, 11-story glass and polished-aluminum office building, which is its showpiece. It has a three-story atrium, outdoor fountains, lush landscaping and four high-speed elevators. A larger, 193,000-square-foot, 10-story building was completed in 1992 and contains the national accounting firm Ernst and Young as its anchor tenant.

HILLSBOROUGH PLACE
225 Hillsborough St. 872-8100

When this building opened in 1985, one local newspaper headline proclaimed, "A star is built." Hillsborough Place is located downtown, two blocks from the Capitol building, and contains 105,000 square feet. Inside, it has Art Deco colors, a peaked skylight and four-story atrium. The building includes an underground and ground-level parking deck and sits on a 2-acre lot. Despite its newness and modern touches, it fits nicely with the historic buildings around it.

LANDMARK CENTER
4601 Six Forks Rd. 872-4924

Another example of the striking '80s architecture in the Triangle's commercial development, Landmark Center opened its first building in 1984 and completed Phase 2 in 1987. It is located on Six

Forks Road, a few blocks from **North Hills Shopping Center** and shows post-modern style in its architecture. It has a total of 151,062 square feet in both buildings, which sit on seven acres. It has high speed elevators servicing its five stories and over 600 parking spaces. Between the two buildings is a landscaped plaza with a water feature that is a pleasant meeting or lunch place on pretty days.

NORTH BOULEVARD CENTER
2809 Millbrook Rd. 872-9000

More popularly known as Mini-City, NBC was the city's first large, 1,200-acre planned community when first announced in 1971. It has stuck to its plans, and today constitutes a city within north Raleigh, with residential neighborhoods, shopping centers and 4,000 people working there. It was one of the first to develop showroom-display office space. While 850 acres of the project have been developed, future plans call for a regional shopping mall and a 300,000-square-foot office complex and hotel.

NORTHPARK
Falls of the Neuse & Millbrook rds.
876-2802

The first building in this north Raleigh office park opened in 1980, and it was built and is managed by two local builders, Dan Austin and Bill Mullins. Mullins served with distinction on the city's Planning Commission and is proud of the park's award-winning landscaping. Northpark is located at a key intersection, Falls of the Neuse and Millbrook roads, and it has a cluster of buildings, all with different architecture.

The largest, 4800 NorthPark, is a six-story, polished-granite beauty that opened in 1988, while 4900 NorthPark uses multi-storied brick arches as its trademark. A third building, 5000 NorthPark, is more contemporary in its linear lines and glass. Total space in the three buildings is almost 300,000 square feet. There is plenty of parking and a number of amenities including 24-hour security and day porter service.

CAPITAL CENTER
5511 Capital Center Dr.   *859-1744*

This is one of the elegant, '80s office complexes that have been positioned around the city and feature Spanish marble, fountains and pools. The first two of three 169,000-square-foot buildings are up and well located between Raleigh and Cary, off the new Interstate 440 circumferential highway. The larger building is a seven-story, stainless-steel-and-glass structure. The center is one of developer Harold Lichtin's projects.

WESTCHASE
4000 Westchase Blvd.   *821-2183*

Westchase opened its first building in 1986 and its third in 1990. Combined, the executive centers contain about 300,000 sq. ft. and are located off Blue Ridge Rd. and Wade Ave. near the State Fairgrounds complex. The location has been attractive for tenants who want to be minutes from RDU but close to Raleigh's downtown.

The Associated Press has its offices here as well as Cable Ad-Net.

Cary

HUNTINGTON
N.C. Hwy. 54   *821-7177*
Morrisville

This project actually is located in Morrisville, which bumps up against Cary's northwest town limits. Former Raleigh Mayor G. Smedes York's companies developed the 640-acre property, which is only minutes from RDU Airport and Interstate 40. The development includes apartments and residential neighborhoods, as well as a section for industrial and commercial buildings. Dillard Paper Company located a major warehouse and office facility here. An athletic club opened in 1988 and Morrisville Elementary School in 1991.

MACGREGOR PARK
125 Edinburgh S.   *467-6997*

This 300-acre research and office park across U.S. Highway 64 west from MacGregor Downs residential development has quickly filled with some of the Triangle's best-looking buildings for companies such as Hewlett-Packard, Borg-Warner, Buehler Products, Lord Corporation, and Union Carbide. American Airlines put a large training center here. MacGregor Park is one of the reasons why Cary is changing its image from a bedroom community to a bustling city with its own workplaces. It is minutes from the Raleigh Beltline and 15 to 20 minutes from RDU and RTP. One of the original owners included Gregory Poole, member of an old Raleigh family and developer of MacGregor Downs. Frank Baird's Capital Associates manages the property.

REGENCY PARK
8000 Regency Pkwy. 467-6900

If you want a showpiece commercial development in the Triangle, this is one. The 600-acre office park is being developed by three Canadians, two of them brothers, Eric and Leland Salomon. It is located near MacGregor Downs, but east of U.S. Highways 1 and 64, near the intersection where Highway 64 separates and turns west. IBM was one of the first major tenants and occupies one entire 275,000-square-foot building with one of its software research groups. Regency Park's 10-year plan calls for building about 2.8 million square feet total. The sylvan setting, around a small lake with jogging trails and well-tended grounds, makes this Park one of the best-dressed addresses in the Triangle. It also is home during the summer to the N.C. Symphony's outdoor concerts. It has space available.

WESTON
Off Harrison Ave. at I-40 677-1001

This 982-acre planned unit development (PUD) is one of the classiest in the Triangle and probably the hotest in the 1993-94 market. It is located right off Interstate 40 in northwest Cary. It opened in 1988, and its Weston One building is a spectacular 237,000-square-foot office building designed for the electronic office of tomorrow with raised flooring that permits installation of any communication system available. It features granite and marble, a two-story open lobby with elegant staircases and it overlooks a 520-acre lake. Weston eventually will include light industrial and residential development and already includes some prime Cary tenants such as Bahlsen Incorporated (the cookie company), and MCI. It is only 10 minutes from RDU and, going the other way, about 12 minutes from downtown Raleigh. Julian Ford of North Hills Incorporated, and also a former member of the Raleigh City Council, is the man to call.

Research Triangle Park Vicinity

IMPERIAL CENTER
Page Rd. and I-40 941-5745

This 280-acre complex is one of the showplace developments located on the periphery of the Research Triangle Park. It has a big advantage over the competition in that it has been designated a Foreign Trade Zone, one of three in the state. The FTZ classification allows qualifying companies to import, export and warehouse items used in manufacturing, duty free. Imperial Center is also home to the Research Triangle World Trade Center. Its tenants include GE, Glaxo, IBM, Northen Telecom, Quintiles Inc. and Bristol-Myers.

Located at the intersection of Page Road and Interstate 40, it's five minutes from RDU and almost equidistant from Raleigh and

Durham on Interstate 40; one entrance opens onto state Highway 54, which takes you to Chapel Hill in about 20 minutes. The Sheraton Imperial Hotel, with accompanying conference facilities, adds a touch of elegance to the complex and hosts a number of national and international meetings each year.

ONE COPLEY PARKWAY
Copley Pkwy.   *469-8014*
Morrisville

Its location adjacent to Interstate 40 and its proximity to the airport have made this 1986 project an attractive site for a number of well-known companies. Eastman Kodak, AMEX Life Assurance, Paychex and Moore Business forms, among others, have offices here. One Copley Parkway has about 132,000 square feet of space. Build-to-suit space is also available.

PERIMETER PARK
Airport Rd.   *469-1300*
Morrisville

Perimeter Park and Perimeter Park West were developed by Raleigh builder Harold Lichtin. The buildings on the site offer almost 600,000 square feet of flex space, close to RDU and RTP.

Durham

For many developers, the next best thing to an address inside of Research Triangle Park is a location along the new Interstate 40 corridor or along U.S. Hwy. 70. Both locations provide linkage to Raleigh and Durham, with easy access to Raleigh-Durham Airport, and de-velopment possibilities in both areas continue to emerge.

Meanwhile, downtown Durham has experienced a revitalization in commercial development with the construction of the Omni Durham Hotel and Civic Center, the Durham Centre office towers and the opening of the Royall Center for the Arts in the last few years.

The largest new development in Durham County—although not along either Interstate 40 or U.S. Hwy. 70—is Treyburn, a 5,300-acre industrial-commercial-residential complex north of Durham. A number of corporations have moved or are considering a move to the Treyburn vicinity. You can read about Treyburn's residential development in our section on **DURHAM NEIGHBORHOODS**.

In these pages we'll briefly describe some of the major industrial-office complexes popping up in Durham. More information is available from Durham's City/County Planning Department by calling 560-4137.

ALSTON TECHNICAL PARK
100 Capitola Dr.   *361-4699*

This three-story, class-A office building adjacent to Research Triangle Park provides over 60,000 square feet of office and research and development space, with a very reasonable base rent of $7.75 per square foot. Highwoods Properties (872-4924) is the leasing agent.

DURHAM CENTRE
300 W. Morgan St.   *688-2222*

Durham Centre is a vital component in the rejuvenation of this city's once-ailing downtown. The Peoples Security Building, a 207,000-square-foot tower, houses Peoples Security Insurance and some small businesses. The current rental rate is $18.00 per square foot. Webb Companies is the leasing agent.

ERWIN SQUARE/FIRST UNION PLAZA
2200 W. Main St. 286-7000

The former site of Burlington Mills in West Durham was transformed a few years back into a 48-acre, 1.75-million square-foot complex offering retail, office and residential space. The office tower's 65,000 square feet houses the Durham First Union bank headquarters and the Duke Management Company. Retail space includes Jewelsmith, K. Peterson and the restaurants Parizade and The Market Place Cafe.

MERIDIAN BUSINESS CAMPUS
2525 Meridian Pkwy. 544-2000

This 270-acre business park located at the intersection of Interstate 40 and N.C. Hwy. 55 has just over 100,000 square feet of space, renting for about $18.00 per square foot. The leasing agent is CMD Southeast.

PARK FORTY PLAZA
N.C. Hwy 55 at I-40 477-7777

Located at the edge of Research Triangle Park along the I-40-N.C. Hwy. 55 interchange is Park Forty Plaza, an office complex that contains 121,000 square feet of office space. Commercial Carolina handles leasing for the complex.

PARK PLACE WEST 100 & 200
Intersection of N.C. Hwy. 54 544-6400
and N.C. Hwy. 55 *or* 493-6905

This $11-million business and professional center is located on a 22-acre campus adjacent to Research Triangle Park. The site includes the 100-suite Meredith Guest House, the Garden Terrace Restaurant (see "Durham" Section of **ACCOMODATIONS**), and six two-story office buildings providing almost 23,000 square feet of space. Kenan Development handles leasing for Park Place West 100; Vanguard is the agent for Park Place West 200.

QUADRANGLE OFFICE PARK
N.C. Hwy. 54 at I-40 872-8100

This $16-million office development is situated on N.C. 54 near the Interstate 40 interchange. There are about 88,0000 square feet of office space in Quadrangle I and Quadrangle III, both located at this site. LCOR Inc. handles leasing for the buildings.

SOUTH SQUARE CORPORATE CENTER II
3708 Mayfair St. 361-5800

This 52,000-square-foot office building is located off University Drive near the South Square shopping mall, convenient to retail shops and offices and a short drive from Interstate 40. Highwoods Properties (872-4924) is the leasing agent for this complex and South Square Corporate Center.

UNIVERSITY TOWER
3015 Petty Rd. 361-5800

This 17-story, $20-million tower built by Dallas developer Tom

Stone is the tallest building in Durham, and its visiblity has brought it a lot of attention. Its 100,000 square feet of office space house a number of businesses and law firms, and it is also home to the prestigious University Club, which sits at the top of the tower.

WESTPARK CORPORATE CENTER
N.C. Hwy. 55 and I-40   361-5800
Westpark is located at the intersection of N.C. Hwy. 55 and Interstate 40, near Research Triangle Park. It has 50,000 square feet of space; the leasing agent is Highwoods Properties (872-4924).

Chapel Hill

Most of Chapel Hill's recent growth surge involves residential development. But with the extension of Interstate 40 from Raleigh through Orange County, the pressure is on to allow commercial and industrial development along the highway corridor, through land that is now rolling countryside. Because the Interstate 40 corridor north of Chapel Hill runs through a critical watershed and is near part of the Duke Forest preserve, planners have recommended that high-density development be restricted from much of that area. So far, most of the commercial space in Orange county is along Franklin Street and Fordham Boulevard (U.S. Hwy. 15-501 Bypass) in Chapel Hill.

EUROPA CENTER
100 Europa Dr.   781-8180
The twin towers of the Europa Center went up in two phases and now offer almost 185,000 square feet of office space. The Europa Center's tenants include medical and dental offices, accountants, several law firms, investment advisors and The Center Cafe, a restaurant and catering service.

Inside
Day Trips and Weekend Vacations

Whatever your idea of a fun getaway may be, chances are you can find it within reasonable driving time of the Triangle. If you dream of leisurely walks along sun-drenched beaches, deep-sea fishing or over-dosing on seafood, the beaches are two and one-half to three hours east. If snow-skiing, hiking or white water rafting are more to your liking, the mountains are a three to four hour drive west. The golfer's paradise of Pinehurst is an hour away. Nearby lakes provide water sports of any variety, and if your interests run more to the intellectual than the physical, the Triangle is surrounded by historical sites, museums and other educational opportunities. Here's a guide to some of our favorite places to visit within a few hours of the Triangle.

The latest state road map can be obtained from the N.C. Department of Transportation, P.O. Box 25201, Raleigh 27611. If you are a cyclist, ask for the map of the state's network of bicycle paths. For information on other places to visit, overnight accommodations, bike routes and campgrounds, write: **The North Carolina Travel and Tourism Division**, 430 N. Salisbury St., Raleigh 27611, or call 919-733-4171.

Beaches and Ports

North Carolina has some of the best beaches on the East Coast, and when Triangle people talk about the beach, they usually are talking about the area known as the Crystal Coast, the Cape Fear Coast or Wrightsville Beach at Wilmington. The port cities of Wilmington, Morehead City, Beaufort and New Bern offer a unique blend of history and modern-day commerce.

WILMINGTON

Wilmington, the state's largest port city on the Cape Fear River, is really worth more than a day trip. Home to the UNC-Wilmington Seahawks and their beautiful Williamsburg-style campus, this historical city is now an easy two hours away. It is the east coast terminus for I-40, which now stretches all the way from California, non-stop.

Wilmington is the permanent home to the **Battleship *North Carolina***, a 35,000-ton battleship that is a war memorial to the men and women who served in World War II. Children enjoy climbing aboard to examine the guns and quarters. In town, Wilmington has a historic homes tour and **Chandler's Wharf**, which shows the city as it was in the 19th century. The restored **Cotton Exchange** building is a warren of shops and restaurants near the Hilton Hotel.

Along the Cape Fear Coast, **Carolina Beach** offers good accommodations and a wide variety of shopping and dining experiences along with the more traditional beach activities of fishing and water sports. At **Kure Beach** is **Fort Fisher**, site of one of the country's largest land-sea battles in 1865, and a museum of items from Confederate blockade runners. The **North Carolina Aquarium** is less than two miles away, where you can view live marine life and participate in special aquatic programs.

Orton Plantation near Wilmington (910-371-6851) is one of North Carolina's best-known Southern plantations and rivals those in Virginia. It was an 18th-century rice plantation and the gardens are open to the public today. The stately mansion is private. It is beyond Wilmington off N.C. Highway 133, near the mouth of the Cape Fear River. The best time to visit is in the spring when Orton's dazzling azaleas are in full bloom.

Courtesy N.C. Travel and Tourism. Photo by William Russ.

Wilmington is the permanent home to the Battleship North Carolina, a memorial to the men and women who served in World War II.

WRIGHTSVILLE BEACH

Wrightsville Beach, just over the bridge from Wilmington, is on what are called barrier islands, which protect the state's Atlantic coastlands. Wrightsville is a great little beach town, with charm and character just oozing from its salty seams. And the friendly locals are sensitive about trying to keep it that way. This is a family spot, with miles of beautiful sandy beaches just perfect for long walks, swimming, surf fishing or most any water sport you may enjoy. Accommodations include quality hotels and motels, apartments and cottages and there is a variety of eating establishments featuring, naturally, seafood.

Cape Fear Coast Convention & Visitors Bureau

* INFORMATION CENTER
* VIDEO PRESENTATION
* CONFERENCES
* MEETINGS
* CONVENTIONS

*Wilmington
Wrightsville Beach
Carolina Beach
Kure Beach*

CAPE FEAR COAST CONVENTION & VISITORS BUREAU

24 North Third Street
Wilmington, North Carolina 28401
800-222-4757
910-341-4030

ACCOMMODATIONS AND DINING

Don't miss **The Trolley Stop** for the best hot dogs on the beach—any way you like them! For hardier fare, try **Oceanic** at the pier or **Wally's** or **The Bridgetender** on the Intracoastal Waterway.

And for accommodations, Wrightsville offers the usual choices of beach house rentals, national chains, and independently owned hotels and motels, as well as luxurious resorts. **Shell Island Resort** (800-522-8575) at the north end of the beach is an all-suite hotel with miles of picturesque beach. The **Blockade Runner Resort Hotel and Conference Center** (800-541-1161) is truly elegant with oceanfront dining, entertainment and conference facilities. The amenities are great, but it's the wide beach that lures Insiders who like nothing more challenging than long evening walks watching the sun take a gentle nose-dive. The **Coastline Inn** is also worth checking out (910-763-2800).

THE CRYSTAL COAST

The name "The Crystal Coast" was coined within the last 15 years to describe the area around Beaufort, Morehead City and the beaches of Bogue Banks. Today, the area is unified by a convention center in Morehead City, a Crystal Coast Tourism Development Board and a new awareness of the diversity of the area, part of what makes the Crystal Coast such a great place to vacation or hold a convention.

From the Triangle, the Crystal Coast is an easy three and one-half hours down U.S. Hwy. 70. Choose between the preserved historic area of Beaufort, Morehead City's famous seafood boardwalk, golf courses and shopping, or the Beaches.

BEAUFORT

This quaint seaport from a bygone era, with a wide boardwalk along the waterfront and narrow streets lined with white frame houses in the down-east style, is a favorite dockage for sea-going motor and sailing yachts. Many of the town's beautiful historic homes have been restored and are nestled between grocery stores, gift shops, a wide variety of restaurants and several of North Carolina's most popular bed and breakfast inns. Insiders should know that many of Beaufort's privately owned restored homes are only open to the public during the last weekend of June, when the **Beaufort Historical Society** sponsors its "Old Homes Tour."

Beaufort's **North Carolina Maritime Museum** delights over 200,000 visitors a year with its habitat exhibits, historical displays, aquariums, photographs, films and guided field trips. Insiders usually plan a trip in September to see the Wooden Boat Show, which features, among other events, a sailing regatta of handmade craft. And everyone should spend some time in Beaufort's **Old Burying Ground**. A soldier buried standing up, a girl buried in a keg of rum and some very unusual inscriptions on the ancient graves offer an afternoon walk that will put MTV in perspective.

ACCOMMODATIONS AND DINING

The Cedars Inn at 305 Front St. (919-728-7036) has been watching over the harbor for more than 200 years. Owners Bill and Pat Kwaak have lovingly restored this beautiful home and furnished it with fine American antiques. It also has a superb restaurant. Also on Front Street.

The Inlet Inn looks as though it has been a waterfront fixture since the last century, but it was built within the last decade. The 37-room wooden inn offers harbor-front rooms, each with seating area, bar with refrigerator/ice maker, ceiling fans and cable TV. In many rooms, French doors open onto private porches with rocking chairs. Others offer cozy fireplaces or window seats with vistas of Cape Lookout. Insiders will particularly enjoy the **Widow's Walk lounge** and the courtyard garden. The Inlet Inn can accommodate small conferences, with an on-site meeting room for 25 people and a conference room and dining facility nearby that can handle up to 100. Call 919-728-3600 for reservations.

The **Langdon House**, 135 Craven St. (919-728-5499), is a beautifully restored home built in 1733. Innkeeper Jimm Prest believes it is the little things that make your stay enjoyable and brings this philosophy to every aspect of the inn.

The **Beaufort Grocery** on Queen Street is a bakery, delicatessen and popular gourmet restaurant. The chef is a graduate of the Culinary Institute of America, and everything served here shows the confident touch of people who know good food.

If you like your food with a view, you will love the **Beaufort House**, sitting right on the Beaufort Dock, with splendid views of both the sailboats lining Beaufort's waterway and the wild ponies on Carrot Island.

Harpoon Willies, Front Street on the waterfront, offers barbecue, burgers, specialty sandwiches, and salads, in addition to a fine seafood menu. Insiders love the **Net House Restaurant and Oyster Bar** on Turner Street—the hangout for Beaufort locals. The **Spouter Inn** on Front Street is famous for its unusual sandwiches (trout and provolone, soft shell crab in pita, mushrooms and cukes with swiss), but it offers a full dinner menu as well. Don't ignore the desserts!

MOREHEAD CITY

Morehead City ("Morehead" to everyone at the coast) is an easy town to like. You have to smile at a town that sponsors events like the **Blue Crab Derby** (a race between crabs ... the losers are served at the event—steamed or in crab cakes), **Old Quawk's Day** (a celebration of crankiness, featuring scallop-skipping, the **Old Quawk Look-Alike Contest** and flounder-flinging... how far can you throw a slimy dead flounder?) and the **Bald-Headed Men of America Convention**.

Fill the town with blocks and blocks of seafood restaurants, internationally renowned sport fish-

Staff photo.

The Sanitary Fish Market and Restaurant is a "must visit" attraction on the Morehead City waterfront.

ing fleets and scuba diving charters that explore the "Graveyard of the Atlantic," and you have half the story. In addition to a booming trade in tourism and conventions, Morehead City is one of North Carolina's busiest commercial ports and home to important research facilities operated by Duke, UNC and the State of North Carolina.

The Morehead Waterfront is devoted to commercial fishing, sport fishing, preparing fish and eating fish. Unlike most coastal waterfronts, the **Morehead Wharf** is not devoted entirely to tourism. Shipping and fishing related commercial activities keep the area bustling. These commercial activities in the "ungentrified" areas of the wharf lend an air of authenticity to the whole waterfront. The connections between the fishing boats and the restaurants or the sport fishing boats and the fish markets are right before your eyes.

In addition, the waterfront offers scuba diving charters (**Olympus Dive Shop** is world famous), sport fishing charters, boat rentals, sailboat excursions, party boat tours, day trips to Cape Lookout and seafood sold fresh off the boats.

ACCOMMODATIONS AND DINING

If you stay overnight, the **Hampton Inn** on Bogue Sound at 4035 Arendell St. (919-240-2300) is a fairly new, moderately priced hotel. Nice views of the Sound and Bogue Banks are visible from the beautifully furnished rooms. The Inn has a fresh, nautical theme and offers guests an outside pool and

deck area, a free continental breakfast served in the sunroom, an exercise room and free accommodations for children. There is also a medium-sized meeting room and plenty of parking.

The restaurant everyone must visit is the **Sanitary Fish Market**, located on the waterfront.

BOGUE BANKS (ATLANTIC BEACH, PINE KNOLL SHORES, SALTER PATH, EMERALD ISLE)

Bogue Banks is one of 23 barrier islands off the N.C. coast. Unlike most of the "outer banks," the 27-mile-long Bogue Banks runs from east to west. The Atlantic Ocean drums its southern shore, while Bogue Sound laps its beaches to the north. This unusual orientation leads to one of the island's most vigorously advertised features: its relationship to the sun. As seen from Bogue Banks, the sun both rises and sets over the ocean. Insiders will know not to spend too much time staring at the sun, and will look to their feet instead, because the real significance of an island's orientation is found on the beach.

In the relatively short distance from Hatteras Island to Cape Lookout, the character of the Atlantic Ocean changes dramatically. Off N.C.'s northern banks like Hatteras, the sea is colder and wilder. The beach fades into deep water quickly, occasional rip tides can be treacherous, and few weeks go by without a day or two of waves rough enough to challenge experienced swimmers. Off Bogue Banks, the Atlantic seems to be on vacation. The beach slopes out very gradually. Fifty yards out, the water is only four feet deep. The summer sun warms this shallow water quickly, and it is not uncommon for afternoon swimming to be very comfortable right through October and into early November—weeks after most bathers have abandoned the deeper and colder water around the islands to the North. Atlantic Beach is only three and one-half hours from the Triangle. Its surf is mild enough for a two-year-old to enjoy, the beach is very wide and the sun-warmed shallow water is the most enjoyable of the state's beaches.

This incredible combination has lead to exactly what you would expect—a lot of summer visitors, and a booming tourism industry. Of the Bogue Banks beaches, Atlantic Beach is the most highly developed.

ACCOMMODATIONS AND DINING

The **Day's Inn Suites** on Atlantic Beach (919-247-6400 or 800-325-2525) are truly nice accommodations: a hallway entrance accesses sleeping and bath areas on the main level, and two steps down is a sitting area that looks onto a private porch and, further out, a wonderful view of Bogue Sound. Some rooms are equipped with refrigerators, microwaves and wet bars. Complimentary continental breakfast and dock usage are amenities.

The **Holiday Inn at Atlantic Beach** (919-726-2544) is on the oceanfront, and offers 115 rooms, a private beach, a swimming pool and a full service restaurant. With seven acres on the ocean, **The John Yancey Motor Hotel** (919-726-5188) has been a long-time favorite with many N.C. families. It has rooms and efficiencies, a great pool and the friendliest staff on the beach.

If you want to be pampered, try **The Sands Villa Resort** or **A Place at the Beach** (919-247-2636). The rooms are beautifully furnished one-, two- and three-bedroom, two-bath villas that are complete with washer/dryer, microwave, private balcony and whirlpool bath in the master bedroom. On its 25-acre site, the resort offers indoor and outdoor swimming pools, whirlpool, sauna, tennis courts and a completely equipped exercise room.

DJ Shooters in Atlantic Beach is the restaurant you always hoped you would find at the beach. Its breakfast menu is huge, and on many mornings every seat in the house is full. The atmosphere is friendly and casual. The **New York Deli** on Atlantic Beach Causeway has the area's largest selection of imported beers, and the staff is always happy to make a box lunch for boat or beach. **Mama Rosa's Pizza** on the Causeway in Atlantic Beach will deliver the island's best pizza to your door. Candlelight-casual **Turtle Reef** overlooks the boats on the Causeway. It's the best Caribbean bar on the island.

FORT MACON STATE PARK

More people visit Fort Macon than any other state park. Fort Macon was erected between 1828 and 1835, then restored in 1936. Commanding Beaufort Inlet, it rests on the foundation of an earlier fort built in the 1740s to protect Beaufort against the Spanish. Fort Macon State Park is very well maintained; it is settled in the midst of a maritime forest at the northern tip of Atlantic Beach.

The park offers an interpretive video program, some dramatic views of Beaufort Inlet and some great rooms to explore. Roughly pentagonal, the Fort's open middle court offers doors and windows that open onto chambers constructed under the rampart of the inner fort. A deep moat separates the inner structure from the outer defenses. A few gun emplacements remain. Domed rooms, arches, vaulted stairways and the ambitious scale of the Fort remind us of the skills of our early military engineers. The surrounding maritime forest is thickly grown with myrtle, cedar and yaupon, concealing many dramatic and unusual species of birds. Early morning visitors can usually spot Painted Buntings among the many varieties of warblers.

SALTER PATH/EMERALD ISLE

Development at the eastern end of Bogue Banks tends toward multi-family units—hotels, motels, condominiums and timeshare. Salter Path is still a residential community making the transition to a tourist community with new restaurants, motels and campgrounds. And west of Salter Path, in Emerald Isle, the pattern of development changes again. Emerald Isle was incorporated as a resort town in the mid-50s. Emerald Isle knew what it

wanted to accomplish and has been serving North Carolina's sunlovers ever since.

Emerald Isle features houses for rent—beachfront, soundside, modern, rustic, casual, elegant and in every price range. The housing density in all parts of Emerald Isle is low; in some places, very low. The feeling is casual, with an emphasis placed on the beauty of the island and the ocean, not on the grandeur of the hotels.

If you're looking for a place to spend the night or for something more permanent, call **Emerald Isle Realty (919-354-3315)**. It has been a tradition on the N.C. coast for over 30 years. Strictly a "family affair" from the start, this firm provides a computerized on-line reservation system, in-house maintenance and housekeeping departments, and has hosted thousands of vacationing families from all over the United States every year. In 1993, it moved to a larger office at 7501 Emerald Drive.

Realty World—Clark Realty is a full-service realty company, but it handles many Emerald Isle vacation rentals. With both condos and cottages on its list, this well-established business stands a very good chance of finding exactly the accommodations you seek. For information on rooms and rates, call 919-354-3313 or 800-722-3006.

Look Realty is also a full-service real estate operation. Located on Coast Guard Road (the first stop after crossing the bridge into Emerald Isle), it offers a large inventory of accommodations, from condos to ocean-front homes, for sale or rent. If you are interested in new construction, Look also offers on-site contracting and home design services, as well as a variety of building lots on or near the water.

OUTER BANKS

To go to the state's unique Outer Banks requires more than a day trip. It's a 3 1/2-hour drive from Raleigh, and if you're going to the eastern-most point of the state, Cape Hatteras and its fabled lighthouse, you'll drive even longer. To get to the isolated banks village of Ocracoke, you also will have to take a ferry. But the Outer Banks deserve mention, and when you've got a long weekend or a week at the

beach, put them on your schedule. They are filled with the names of history—Kitty Hawk, Kill Devil Hills, Roanoke Island, Blackbeard the Pirate—and the longest stretch of undeveloped beach in the country. If you're interested in learning more about North Carolina's Outer Banks, pick up a copy of *The Insiders' Guide To The Outer Banks*.

NEW BERN

Ideally juxtaposed between the sea and one of North Carolina's most beautiful national forests— the Croatan—makes this historic little town of lacy crepe myrtle trees appealing to both history buffs and rugged naturalists. At one time, the 157,000-acre Croatan National Forest was home to the Tuscarora Indians who used the forest for hunting and fishing. Today, you can take nature trails through a forest of tall pines and ancient hardwoods for an upclose examination of insect sniping and eating plants. You may be lucky enough to see a deer or alligator, but bears are seldom visible.

The town of New Bern sits at the confluence of the Neuse and Trent Rivers, which is now known as **Union Point Park**, and where most of the waterfront activity buzzes. It was New Bern's linkage to Pamlico Sound and the Atlantic that made this another ideal shipping port for the sought-after naval stores (tar, pitch and turpentine from the loblolly pine) to Europe, the West Indies and up the coast. The town was founded in 1710 and named for Baron Christopher DeGraffenried's

home of Bern, Switzerland. It became the first colonial capital of North Carolina.

When Royal Governor William Tryon began building his residence/government capitol offices, they took on more the appearance of a palace than a modest government home with offices. The original palace burned in 1798, only 28 years after its completion, but was completely rebuilt from architect John Hawks' blueprints. It has been refurbished to its former splendor with a crystal chandelier, a spinet piano like the one Margaret Tryon used to entertain and furnishings authentic to the period. You can take a tour with costume guided hosts (admission is charged) daily throughout the year, but Insiders' vote for spring as the best time to visit as the Royal English gardens are abloom with tulips.

During the summer months, historical drama tours are conducted. Actors portray Governor Tryon, cabinet members, his wife and their servants talking about the everyday happenings in the 1700s. This may give you a better feel for those early years. The restoration includes the **Tryon Palace**, the **John Wright Stanly House** (another handsome house thought to have been designed by Hawks as well), the **Dixon-Stevenson House** that was occupied by Union troops during the Civil War and the new **Academy Museum**.

ACCOMMODATIONS AND DINING

There are two rustic campsites for an economical stay in the area. The **Yogi Bear Jellystone Park** on N.C. Highway 17 N. (919-638-2556) is located on the Neuse River. **Fisher's Landing** on N.C. 70 E. in Riverdale (919-638-5628) is more rustic, but affords you the opportunity to walk along the crescent-shaped beach and do some special communing with wildlife.

In New Bern, you'll find the **Ziegler Motel** at 1914 Trent Boulevard (919-637-4498). This small, older motel is set among azaleas and dogwoods in a residential community. If you are thinking B & B's, the beautifully restored historic ones in town are all excellent selections. The **New Bern House Inn** at 709 Broad St. (800-842-7688) is one block from Tryon Palace and you can walk or use the Inn's tandem bicycles to get around. **King's Arms Inn** at 212 Pollock St. (919-638-4409), built in 1847 as a tavern, once hosted members of the First Continental Congress.

Next door is the 1799 **Henderson House Restaurant (919-637-4784)**, which is our Insiders' tip for lunch or dinner. The food and history of this beautifully restored, award-winning restaurant tie in excellence. The home is reputed to have ghosts and a secret floor where it is thought British loyalists hid when the colonists got the upper hand. The home was later requisitioned by the Union Army during the Civil War. Try Chef Weaver's seafood casserole or carpet-bagger steak.

The **Bagel Cottage** at 712 Pollack St. (919-636-1775) is another that combines unique food in an old-fashioned setting. It's located at the back of an old cottage and you can sit inside or outside at a table that overlooks **the Tryon Palace Cutting Gardens**. Bagel lovers appreciate the daily baked variety of bagels with great soups and salads.

The **Harvey Mansion**, circa 1791, at 221 Tryon Palace Drive (919-638-3205) was the home and offices of John Harvey. The commanding old home on the Trent River is a romantic place for an elegant dinner of "Scallops a la Menthe" or "Flounder Captain Harvey," deliciously prepared by Chef Beat Zutter of Bern, Switzerland.

The **SheratonHotel and Marina** at 1 Bicentennial Park (800-325-3535) offers 165 lavishly appointed rooms and suites, each with a spectacular view. Within easy walking distance from the hotel and its marina are antique and specialty shops, the Tryon Palace and Gardens, a variety of restaurants and museums, plus the historic homes and churches of North Carolina's first state capital.

Piedmont and Sandhills

FAYETTEVILLE

When many people think of Fayetteville, they think "military town"—and that's where they stop. Yes, Fayetteville is the home of Fort Bragg and Pope Air Force Base, and the local economy and character are tightly linked to these institutions and the men and women who

Tryon Palace at New Bern is a restoration of elegant Georgian buildings completed in 1770 as the residence of the colonial governor.

Courtesy N.C. Travel and Tourism. Photo by Clay Nolen.

serve there. But Fayetteville also boasts a variety of other attractions, such as some wonderful architecture, several colorful festivals and two outstanding theater groups.

For those who are interested in learning more about Fayetteville's place in military history, Fort Bragg is open for individual and group tours. One of the best times to go is during CAPEX (capabilities exercises) in June. Call 910-396-5620 or 396-2920 for information. The **82nd Airborne War Memorial Museum** (at Ardennes and Gela streets at Fort Bragg) is a great place to take a military-history buff. You'll learn plenty about the 82nd's role in all U.S. wars since World War I. The grounds are covered with vintage tanks, planes and helicopters from wars gone by. The museum is open Tuesday through Saturday 10 a.m. to 4:30 p.m. and Sunday 11:30 a.m. to 4 p.m. Admission is free. Call 910-432-5307.

Pope Air Force Base is closed to the general public, but group tours can be arranged. Pope AFB holds an annual open house with Fort Bragg during the **Dogwood Festival** in April. It's a great chance to see demonstrations of aircraft and other equipment. Call 910-396-5620, 396-2920 or 394-4183.

Anyone curious about historic architecture will want to view Fayetteville's **Market House** in the center of the downtown area. When Union General William Sherman and his men passed through Fayetteville in 1865, they destroyed the Confederate Arsenal and many other buildings. Sherman left the

Market House intact, it is said, because of its beauty.

There are many other beautiful old buildings in Fayetteville, and you can see 12 or more of the oldest homes, churches and other historic places during the **Olde Fayetteville by Candlelight Tour** held each December. There's probably not a better way to take in the city's architectural heritage. Call 910-483-5311 or 800-255-8217 for information.

The **Dogwood Festival** is Fayetteville's welcome to Spring. Held over 10 days starting the first weekend in April, this event allows Fayetteville to show off its more than 100,000 dogwood trees and thousands of blooming flowers. There are many activities scheduled, including parades, tours, street dancing and the Fort Bragg/Pope AFB Open House. Call 910-483-5311 or 800-255-8217.

The **International Folk Festival** is held in honor of Fayetteville's ethnic diversity. Held on the last Sunday in September, the festival centers around the Market House downtown. It features a big parade, international foods and musical entertainment. Call 910-483-5311 or 800-255-8217.

Maybe some people will be surprised to find the **Cape Fear Regional Theatre** in Fayetteville. Well it's here, and it should not be missed. Located on the corner of Hay Street and Highland Avenue, CFRT is housed in a beautifully renovated old movie house that seats 327 people. Try to find a bad seat—it can't be done. CFRT consistently receives rave reviews from theatre critics across the state for its innovative productions. Insiders know that Cape Fear Regional Theatre is worth the drive to Fayetteville all by itself. Call 910-323-4233 or 323-4234 for the current schedule and ticket information.

If that's not enough, there's yet another venue for high-quality drama in Fayetteville. The **Fort Bragg Playhouse** on Knox Street at Fort Bragg utilizes military personnel and Fayetteville civilians to help staff its casts and crews. Touring professional actors and a few big-name stars usually take the major roles. Fort Bragg's theatre seats slightly over 500. The production schedule is somewhat irregular, depending on availability of military personnel. Call 910-396-7555 for information.

For information on Fayetteville, contact the **Fayetteville Area Convention and Visitors Bureau**, 515 Ramsey Street, Fayetteville, NC 28301, or call 910-483-5311 or 800-255-8217.

BENTONVILLE BATTLEGROUND
Newton Grove, N.C. 594-0789

Civil War and military history buffs must visit this historic site, which is less than an hour's drive from the Triangle. The **Battle of Bentonville** was the last full-scale action in the Civil War, fought over three days, March 19 through 21, in 1865. There were over 4,000 casualties in the armies fighting under Union Gen. William T. Sherman and Confederate Gen. Joseph E. Johnston, who surrendered on April 26 at the Bennett Place near Durham. The battleground today maintains a picnic area and visitors' center. The **Harper House**, where a field hospital was established, still stands and is outfitted as it might have appeared during those bloody three days. Maps inside the center and a film presentation tell the history of the battle, the largest ever fought in North Carolina. On occasion, as was the case in 1990, the battle's anniversary is observed by re-enactments that give visitors a more realistic idea of conditions of the times.

CAPEL RUG MILL OUTLET
121 E. Main St.
Troy, N.C. 910-576-3211

While you're at Jugtown or the Zoo (see below), you may want to go a little bit out of your way and stop in Troy, along N.C. Highway 134. Here you'll find Capel, the oldest and largest manufacturer of braided rugs in the world and the largest importer/manufacturer in the United States. What that means is that the selection of braided as well as oriental rugs is huge, and the prices are unbelievably low. It's well worth the trip.

JUGTOWN AND THE POTTERY MUSEUM
910-625-6121

One of our favorite day trips is a trek through pottery country in Randolph and Moore counties. Here, just about two hours from the Triangle, you'll find pottery being made from native clays, just as it was in the 18th century. In fact, some of the local potters belong to the same families that were shaping their native clay two centuries ago, including the Cravens, Coles, Owens and Teagues.

Stop first at the **Seagrove Potters Museum** in Seagrove along N.C. Highway 220, south of Asheboro and the N.C. Zoo. Here you'll be able to see samples of the area's world famous pottery from its earliest days to the present. At the museum, which is open free to the public Monday through Saturday 10 a.m. to 4 p.m., you can also pick up a map to the shops of some 20 local potters. Our personal favorites are **Cole Pottery** and **Jugtown**.

KERR LAKE, LAKE GASTON

These two man-made lakes are within an hour's drive of the Triangle and provide excellent fishing, boating, picnicking and camping. Both are north of the Triangle near the Virginia state line. Kerr Lake has a shoreline of 800 miles and over 1,000 family campsites and three commercial marinas. For information on Kerr Lake, call Kerr Reservoir at 919-438-7791.

Lake Gaston has at least three access areas at Summit, Henrico and Stonehouse Creek. For more information on Gaston, call the N.C. Wildlife Resources Commission in Raleigh at 733-3633.

MORROW MOUNTAIN STATE PARK
910-982-4402

Just on the other side of Badin Lake from the **Uwharrie National Forest** is this scenic, 4,600-acre state park in Stanly County, a pleasant retreat for swimming, camping, boating, hiking or picnicking. For information on vacation cabins and tent/trailer campsites, call or write: Morrow Mountain State Park, Rt. 2, Box 430, Albemarle, NC 28001.

N.C. ZOOLOGICAL PARK
Route 4, Box 83   *910-879-7200*
Asheboro, NC 27203

Like the famous San Diego Zoo in California, North Carolina's zoological park gives visitors the chance to observe animals while they roam in areas similar to their native habitats. Animals and their admirers are safely kept apart by ditches, waterways and other physical barriers worked into the landscape. This is a perfect outing for the whole family. Here you can observe more than 625 wild animals and over 10,000 exotic plants. By the year 2000, this ever-expanding facility is expected to be the largest natural habitat zoo in the world, and the freshest import is a London zookeeper who plans to make the N.C. Zoo a rival to the best anywhere.

You won't want to miss the **R.J. Reynolds Forest Aviary**, the only one of its kind anywhere. A 55-foot-high glass dome houses exotic plants and birds from all over the world. Walking through the aviary is like exploring a tropical forest, complete with all the sights, sounds and smells. While you're gawking at the African snake plants, don't be surprised if an Indian thrush lands at your feet.

The zoo is located off of N.C. Highway 220, south of Asheboro. From April 1 through October 15, the zoo is open from 9 a.m. to 5 p.m.

Monday through Friday and 10 a.m. to 6 p.m. weekends and holidays. From November 1 through March 31, the hours are 9 a.m. to 4 p.m. daily. Admission is $4 for senior citizens and children ages 2 to 15, and $6 for adults. For more information, call or write.

CHARLOTTE

CAROLINA RENAISSANCE FESTIVAL
Chartolle, N.C.   *704-896-5544*

The annual Carolina Renaissance Festival will be held on weekends in October. Although 1994, marks the first festival, it promises to be a wonderful addition to our list of must see day trips. Admission is charged. Call for information.

DISCOVERY PLACE
301 N. Tryon St.   *704-332-4140*
Charlotte, N.C.

Discovery Place is one of America's top science museums. This hands-on science and technology museum in uptown Charlotte welcomes over 400,000 visitors annually and is open every day of the year except Thanksgiving and Christmas. Awarded "Travel Attraction of the Year" in 1992 by the Southeast Tourism Society, the museum offers an OMNIMAX theatre and planetarium combination which is unique to the United States. With a 79-foot dome, the Planetarium is the largest in the nation.

Among the permanent exhibits are the Collections Gallery, the Aquarium and the Knight Rain Forest. "Hands-on" exhibits are also featured with a collection of experiments designed to teach basic principles of science through color, motion and perception.

The Challenger Learning Center, opened in May of 1992, simulates a rendezvous with Comet Halley in the year 2061. Kid's Place, an early childhood learning area, features the Puppet Place stage with shows that delight visitors of all ages. The museum has hosted outstanding traveling exhibits such as Dinosaurs, The Muppets, India, Bionics and Transplants, Science in Toyland and 1492: Two Worlds of Science.

Open seven days a week, the Exhibit Hall hours are 9 a.m. until 5 p.m. Monday through Wednesday, 9 a.m. until 6 p.m. Thursday through Saturday and 1 to 6 p.m. on Sundays. Reservations for regularly scheduled OMNIMAX and Planetarium shows can be made by calling Scheduling at (704) 372-0471 or 1-800-935-0553.

Admission is $5.50 for adults, $4.50 for students 6–18 years old and senior citizens 60 and over. When accompanied by a parent, admission for children ages 3 to 5 is $2.75, and children under 3 get in free. Admission is free on "Wonderful Wednesday,", the first Wednesday of each month after 2 p.m. Annual family memberships entitle holders to unlimited visits and special benefits.

PARAMOUNT'S CAROWINDS
Exit 90 off I-77 South   *704-588-2600*

Paramount's Carowinds is a world-class theme park with 91 acres of excitement and glamour. Guests can roam in WAYNE'S WORLD, eight new acres that are themed after the *Wayne's World* motion pictures and feature a rock music shop, a replica of Wayne's basement studio and the Scream Weaver ride. You add that to its heart-pounding roller coasters such as the *Hurler*, located in WAYNE'S WORLD, **Thunder Road, Frenzoid** and **VORTEX**, then cool off with **Rip Roarin' Rapids** and **White Water Falls** or the **wave pool** and you're off to a thrilling start.

Walking around the park you'll see such characters as Star Trek Klingons, Romulans, and Vulcans, along with Wayne and Garth. You'll also find scads of movie paraphernalia to buy in the stores. Look for the **Paramount Walk of Fame** that lists prominent movies and their stars. The park's new motto is: "The only place thrills are paramount!"

Paramount's Carowinds' popular one-price ticket covers all rides and park shows. Paladium concerts, featuring big-name entertainers, are extra. In 1994, general admission to Paramount's Carowinds for ages 7 to 59 is $24.95 and $13.50 for children ages 4 to 6 and senior citizens 60 and older. Children 3 and younger are admitted free. Groups, family and individual season passes are available, as are camp sites. Call (704) 588-2606.

WINSTON-SALEM

OLD SALEM
Winston-Salem, N.C.   910-721-7300
About an hour and a half west of the Triangle via I–40 is Winston-Salem's restored 18th century Moravian village. There are almost 100 restored and reconstructed buildings; 12 are open to the public, including Winkler Bakery (where you can buy Moravian sugar cake), the Salem Tavern, the Single Brothers House and several other shops and restored homes. There are many special events during the Christmas season, including the "Lovefeast" and a traditional Moravian candle tea. There are also special services and events at Easter and on July 4th. Old Salem is open Monday through Saturday 9:30 a.m. to 4:30 p.m., and on Sunday from 1:30 to 4:30 p.m. Admission is charged.

MUSEUM OF EARLY SOUTHERN DECORATIVE ARTS (MESDA)
Winston-Salem, N.C.   910-721-7360
MESDA is adjacent to Old Salem, and features 19 furnished rooms, demonstrating the varied styles of Southern furnishings. Many rooms have been reassembled here, just as they were in their original locations. Admission is charged.

REYNOLDA HOUSE
Reynolda Rd.   910-725-5325
Winston-Salem, N.C.
Reynolda House, former home of R.J. Reynolds of tobacco fame, is now a museum of American art. The collection features paintings by diverse artists ranging from 19th century landscape painter Frederic Church to Thomas Eakin and Mary Cassatt. The house contains many of its original furnishings, and is interesting in its own right. Admission is charged for the house and gardens. It is open Monday through Saturday from 9:30 a.m. to 4:30 p.m., and from 1:30 to 4:30 p.m. on Sunday.

SOUTHEASTERN CENTER FOR CONTEMPORARY ART (SECCA)

750 Marguerite Dr.   910-725-1904
off Reynolda Rd.
Winston-Salem, N.C.

SECCA is just down the road from Reynolda House, and well worth a stop. It is a complex of galleries with rotating exhibits by contemporary Southern artists. It is located on the former estate of the Hanes family, and many of the galleries are in the Hanes home. It is open Tuesday through Saturday 10:00 a.m. to 5 p.m., and Sunday 1:00 to 5:00 p.m. Admission is free.

HANGING ROCK STATE PARK

593-8480

This nearly 6,000-acre state park in Stokes County (north of Winston-Salem) is a great getaway for camping, hiking, swimming, fishing and picnicking. For information on vacation cabins and tent/trailer campsites, call or write: P.O. Box 186, Danbury, N.C. 27016.

GUILFORD COURTHOUSE

National Military Park   910-288-8259
New Garden Rd. (off U.S. Hwy. 220)
Greensboro, N.C.

This is the site of a Revolutionary War battle, which pitted Gen. Nathaniel Greene (for whom the city of Greensboro is named) against Gen. Lord Charles Cornwallis, commander of the British troops. Though the American troops eventually withdrew, Cornwallis' losses were heavy, and led to his surrender at Yorktown seven months later. In mid-March each year, a mock battle is staged by Redcoats and soldiers of the Revolution in uniform. The battlefield is now a national park, with a number of monuments (including one of Nathaniel Greene) and a visitor's center. It is open daily from 8:30 a.m. to 5 p.m., and admission is free.

THE NATURAL SCIENCE CENTER

Country Park   910-288-3769
(off Lawndale Dr.)
Greensboro, N.C.

Behind the Guilford Battleground is Country Park, site of this fine museum for children. There are reproductions of dinosaur skeletons, rock and mineral exhibits, a planetarium and a small zoo. It is open Monday through Saturday from 9 a.m. to 5 p.m. and Sunday 1 to 5 p.m. There is a small admission fee.

PINEHURST

910-295-6651

If you like golf, you'll love Pinehurst, once the home of the **World Golf Hall of Fame**, and site of the **1999 U.S. Open** on famed Pinehurst No. 2. (See **GOLFING IN THE CAROLINAS**.)

If that's not enough to entertain you, there are also the four regulation-size croquet courts at the **Pinehurst Hotel and Country Club**, the largest croquet center in the United States. Pinehurst is located off U.S. Highway 15-501 in Moore County.

RAVEN ROCK STATE PARK

Northwest of Lillington, N.C. 910-893-4888

Raven Rock is a 2,731-acre state park that makes a pleasant picnic outing for the family. Located on the Cape Fear River, it's about a one and a half hours' drive from the Triangle and has hiking trails that aren't too taxing. The trails leading to the river are downhill, so keep enough energy to hike back uphill. The rocks along the river are huge, and in winter, giant icicles, 15 to 20 feet in length, hang from them. A good time to go is spring or fall when it's not so hot. Take water or something to drink because there's no fountain down by the river.

SNOW CAMP
910-376-6948

You'll want to visit this historic Quaker landmark in southwest Alamance County during the summer months when there are plenty of activities. Named by Cornwallis' soldiers following the snowy **Battle of Guilford Courthouse**, Snow Camp is most famous today as the site of *The Sword of Peace*, one of North Carolina's most popular outdoor dramas. From late June through July, *The Sword of Peace* re-enacts the conflict experienced by peace-loving Quakers confronted by the American Revolution. Other summer activities at Snow Camp include a traditional Fourth of July celebration complete with a parade and crafts fair and a mid-August molasses festival that has demonstrations of pioneer cooking and crafts. Call for a current schedule. Snow Camp is about a 30-minute drive south and west of Chapel Hill.

UWHARRIE NATIONAL FOREST

The Uwharrie National Forest is proof that you don't have to drive four hours to reach the mountains. Located on Badin Lake in Montgomery County, this wilderness includes 46,000 acres. Write Uwharrie National Forest, District Ranger, U.S. Forest Service, Rt. 1, Box 237, Troy, NC 27371 for information.

Mountains

CASHIERS

Beautiful Cashiers, high in the Blue Ridge Mountains, is a resort town, famous for its many beautiful waterfalls, including **Toxaway Falls** (123 feet), **High Falls** (135 feet) and the beautiful **Rainbow Falls,** which plunges some 200 feet. The **High Hampton Inn** (704-743-2411) in Cashiers, offers a wonderful weekend getaway. Once the 2,300-acre estate of Confederate General and state Governor Wade Hampton, it is now a rustic resort that truly offers something for everyone. There is an impressive 18-hole, par 71 golf course, excellent hiking trails with many dramatic mountain views, and a private fishing lake where you may choose a canoe, fishing boat, sail boat, or, for the landlubbers, a gentle paddle boat. Guest rooms are in the main inn and also in the surrounding guest houses. For dining, the High Hampton offers three country-style meals a day.

BREVARD

Surrounded by the Pisgah National Forest, Brevard offers a variety of activities from rugged outdoor activities to communing quietly with nature or delving into the magical mountain lore through music, drama or local crafts.

Courtesy N. C. Travel and Tourism. Photo by William Russ.

Chimney Rock is a unique rock formation overlooking Hickory Nut Gorge and Lake Lure in Western North Carolina.

TAKE A TRIP TO
WILD WONDERFUL
WEST VIRGINIA

AMERICA'S BEST WHITEWATER

RESORT COMPLEX
CALL 1-800-TRY RIVERS

ISLAND FEVER

**oceanfront
beaches
sailing
golf
tennis
dining
spa
romance
and
sandcastles**

BLOCKADE RUNNER

Blockade Runner Beach Resort • Wrightsville Beach Island, NC

1-800-541-1161  910-256-2251

You can spend the day locating a few of the 250 waterfalls in Transylvania County or Brevard. The best way is to take the scenic 79-mile drive that loops through the **Pisgah National Forest** past camera-demanding shots. You could also hike through the designated trails, (trail maps are available at U.S. Forestry Service office on U.S. Highway 276), and then you could make this a truly frugal weekend by fishing in one of the trout-filled streams for your dinner. There are horseback riding trails to give you one more way to explore the forest.

If you've had enough of communing with nature, check out the **Brevard Music Center**. There is an annual summer **Brevard Music Festival** with international stars. Call the Chamber of Commerce (800-648-4523) for dates or spend a Thursday evening listening to original mountain music and bluegrass at **Silvermont** on East Main Street in Brevard. Drive back down U.S. Highway 64 to Flat Rock and you can take in a play at the **Flat Rock Playhouse**, which is the state theater of North Carolina.

Throughout the mountains you'll find handmade quilts, mountain furniture and toys. Insiders like the **Curb Market** (Farmers' Market) in downtown Hendersonville on Tuesday and Saturday mornings. You'll find reasonable to downright cheap handmade articles, jellies, fresh vegetables and the like.

ACCOMMODATIONS AND DINING

For a cheapy, but fun family weekend near Brevard, call ahead to the **Davidson River Campground** (800-283-2267) for a campsite in the Pisgah National Forest, just off the parkway near Asheville.

In case you had in mind a more pampered "getaway," the area is spilling over with motels and great Bed and Breakfasts in every price range. The **Penrose Motel** (704-884-2691) in Penrose, boasts the best rates in the area and is conveniently located 4 minutes from Pisgah National Forest and 5 minutes from the **Etowah Valley Golf Club**. The **Womble Inn** in Brevard (704-884-4770) serves your breakfast on a silver tray in your room—which will make going home hard to get used to. The 1851 **Red House** (704-884-9349) was here before Brevard of Transylvania County was established. It has been restored with period antiques to its former elegance and is well located in Brevard. For a stay in a 1862 Victorian farmhouse on the edge of the Pisgah National Forest, **Key Falls Inn** (704-884-7559) will fit the bill with a full breakfast.

Now maybe you were thinking—mountains=log cabin. You can bring the family and stay in a log cabin at **The Pines Country Inn** (704-877-3131).

Most folks go to the mountains to rest, but there is a special place that emphasizes some unusual exercise. It is **Earthshine Mountain Lodge** in **Lake Toxaway** (704-862-4207). It offers a program that allows you to invest in empowerment. One of the adventures is known as **High Ropes**, a sensitivity-type exercise that is dependent on inner rather than physical strength. This beautiful lodge also has horseback riding through the Pisgah National Forest, mountain music evenings and good, made-from-scratch food.

If you opt not to cook out, the next least expensive dining bet is **Berry's Restaurant** (935 Asheville Highway), where you'll enjoy country food and Bluegrass music on Fridays. The **Carriage House Restaurant** on Country Club Road in Brevard is another good choice, as is **Oh Susanna's** on West Main Street in Brevard. The Inn at Brevard has great food, and **The Raintree** is positively exceptional.

If you are looking for a deluxe lakeside resort with a full complement of outdoor activities, try the **Greystone Inn**. This refurbished 1915 Swiss-style mansion situated on the banks of Lake Toxaway, has 19 luxurious accommodations located on six levels.

In the mansion, you can choose various sized rooms, some with balconies, fireplaces, oversize Jucuzzis and spectacular views. The Presidential suite, created from the former library, is the ultimate. The king-size bed, set in front of the wall of windows overlooking the lake, is dwarfed by the expanse of this enormous room, which has a 25-foot ceiling with exposed oak beams, massive stone fireplace, matching upholstered chintz-covered chaise lounge, couch, easy chairs and draperies. There is a double marble Jacuzzi and a separate room with a full bath.

In addition, the Inn offers golf, tennis, water sports, hiking and fine dining. You would have difficulty finding a more romantic setting for your getaway.

CHIMNEY ROCK, LAKE LURE

Three movies have been made in this picturesque area in the past few years. Remember "Dirty Dancing?" It was shot at Lake Lure.

The town of Chimney Rock, with a river running beside it, gives a nice rural atmosphere, but it is a touch on the touristy side. You can forgive a lot though as you climb up to the spectacular Chimney Rock Park, or ride in a 26-story elevator inside the mountain. It deposits you at the top of the chimney-shaped rock rendering a panoramic view that is worth the trip all by itself. Below is Hickory Nut Gorge, which includes the Rocky Broad River and Lake Lure. Pack a picnic lunch or grab some take-out food to enjoy at one of the park's many picnic areas.

ACCOMMODATIONS

You can stay at the refurbished art decoesque **Lake Lure Inn** for a truly restful weekend. Or, a favorite stay in Chimney Rock (not touristy) is the **Ginger Bread Inn** right on Main Street, with every room looking like a page out of Country magazine.

CHEROKEE

Who has grown up in America without hearing about the great Cherokee Indians? It is a story of intelligence, skill, hardship, betrayal, sadness and more recently— success, which you can discover by stopping at the **Cherokee Historical Association**. Across the street on Drama Road is the **Museum of the Cherokee Indian**. This is a modern museum displaying over 10,000-year-old artifacts and with explanatory audio/visual programs that chronicle the events of the Cherokee.

The not-to-be-missed **Oconoluftee Indian Village** is a reproduction of how the Eastern Band of the Cherokees lived 200 years ago. And the **Qualla Arts and Crafts Mutual** in the village is a shop that looks more like a museum. This shop of artisans' works is responsible for keeping alive the authentic arts and crafts of the Cherokee. It is also the only place that you'll find these distinct crafts.

Of course, no trip to Cherokee would be complete without attending *Unto These Hills*, now in its 44th season at the newly renovated **Mountainside Theatre**. The outdoor drama professionally blends drama, music and dance to unfold the tragic story of how the proud and misunderstood Cherokees were driven west on the "Trail of Tears" from their Smoky Mountain homeland. It also shows how a few remained and with the help of sympathetic settlers were able to rebuild into a race of productive American citizens.

ACCOMMODATIONS AND DINING

A principal reason that the Cherokee Reservation is such a success is that the businesses are tribal-owned. That includes motels, campgrounds and restaurants. For camping enthusiasts, there are many options. You could try the **Cherokee KOA Campground** (800-825-8352), or for camping in the **Great Smoky National Park** call 615-436-5615. Inside Cherokee, the **Holiday Inn-Cherokee** (800-465-4329) on U.S.

Highway 19 south is a good bet with its North American Indian motif and other convenient services. Holiday Inn's **Chestnut Tree Restaurant** is also a good option for dinner. For those who really want to immerse themselves into the Indian culture, the **Spirits of the River Restaurant** serves authentic Indian food.

MAGGIE VALLEY

If you like gunfights in a mile-high **Ghost Town** theme park and warm mountain hospitality, go to Maggie Valley. There isn't a friendlier place anywhere, thanks in part to octogenarian Miss Jennie Reninger, the town's goodwill ambassador who dresses as "Miss Maggie" and waves to passing tourists. There's also a firstrate zoo in town called **Soco Gardens Zoo**. Maggie Valley is abuzz with activity from May through October.

ACCOMMODATIONS AND DINING

Rustic but elegant lodges can be found next to the Great Smoky Mountains National Park at the 5,000-ft.-plus elevation. If you want to stay in town, **Twin Brook Resort** is ideal.

Maggie Valley Resort has an 18-hole, championship golf course that is a scenically beautiful course with the Blue Ridge and Great Smoky Mountains as a backdrop for streams, lakes, rock formations and ancient trees. The resort also has tennis courts and a swimming pool, but, for the non-golfer, its greatest attraction may well be the food. The resort's international cuisine is prepared by a highly skilled and respected staff, and there is frequently entertainment in the restaurant. For reservations, call 704-926-1616 or 800-438-3861.

ASHEVILLE

Called the "Land of the Sky," this mountain city, where wealthy 1900s vacationers once came for relief from the summer heat, is still compelling vacationers to visit, but now it's throughout the year. Golfers and tennis players have been coming to **Grove Park Inn and Country Club** (704-252-2700), at the foot of Sunset Mountain, since it was hewn out of the mountain in 1913.

The new centerpiece of the downtown historic district is the long-awaited **Pack Place Education, Arts and Science Center**. Pack Place is dedicated to providing a culturally vibrant Asheville for the people of Western North Carolina and visitors to the area. A constantly varied and changing menu of programs meets the challenge by offering something of interest for everyone. This bustling complex contains four museums, a performing arts theatre, courtyards, permanent exhibitions, a gift shop, restaurant and lobby galleries.

Tickets are required for admission to theater events and to each of the four museums: the **Asheville Art Museum, The Colburn Gem and Mineral Museum, The Health Adventure** and the **YMI Cultural Center**. You can buy a one-day pass that is good for all four, or you can buy single tickets. No admission charge is required for visitors to enter Pack Place and view the historic exhibit "**Here is the Square**," visit the **Craft Gallery** that spotlights regional crafts or shop in the **Museum Gift Store**. The fourth Friday of each month is "Free Day" when you may visit all of the museums with no charge for admission. Call 704-257-4500 for further ticket information and hours.

A landmark in itself, Pack Place also serves as the logical starting point for a number of walking tours of downtown Asheville featuring buildings of architectural and historic significance, including the home of Thomas Wolfe. A popular retreat into the past, this is the Dixieland Boarding House readers will remember from Wolfe's novel *Look Homeward, Angel.*

One of the best day trip excursions is to the **Biltmore Estate and Gardens and Winery**. The architectural style is that of a French chateau designed by Richard Morris Hunt to resemble a chateau in France's Loire Valley. It could easily rival the grandest palace abroad. Built by George Vanderbilt, whose grandfather was a wealthy railroad magnate, the castle-like house contains 250 rooms which took 1,000 artisans (many imported from Europe) five years to build for six people (not including the 100 servants). In fact, the workers built their own housing, which is known today as Biltmore Village and houses shops and restaurants. A railroad was built from the village up to the chateau site to transport materials. The English and Italian gardens were designed by Frederick Law Olmstead, and Biltmore hired

Gifford Pinchot, the great American forester, to plan and redirect the badly eroded forest in the 1880s. Dr. Carl Schenck was brought from Germany to be the chief forester. And it was here that Schenck founded the **Biltmore School of Forestry** that developed the "land use" concept of forestry and conservation.

A favorite visit is Christmas season, when the house is made resplendent with thousands of poinsettias, Christmas trees trimmed with many original ornaments, and musical concerts fill the magnificent halls. The estate is open from 9 a.m. to 5 p.m. year round except Thanksgiving, Christmas and New Year's.

You can tour the main house with its beautiful antique furnishings, priceless paintings and ceiling frescoes that are kept in good repair. But the servant's quarters, where even the butler had his own servant, will give you a better clue as to how life was lived in 1895. Several movies have even been filmed here.

Another enjoyable—as well as tasty—tour is that of the estate's winery. The rolling terrain of the vineyards reminds you of the cotes of Burgundy, and that blue haze dangling over the mountains brings to mind the mists that nestle the hilly vineyards along the Rhine and Mosel. And with the 16th century Biltmore Chateau in the background, it's enough to convince you that you're in Europe rather than a unique corner of North Carolina. The old dairy barn has also been recycled into a lovely open air restaurant—**Deerpark**, where at the right time of the evening you can see herds of deer roaming the land. Then afterward, stop in the Biltmore

*Pack Place Education, Arts and Science Center
is the centerpiece of Asheville's downtown historic district.*

Courtesy Pack Place. Photo by Jon Riley.

Village for a browse through a craft shop of handmade treasures—**New Morning Gallery** at 7 Boston Way. For more information on Asheville, call the **Asheville Area Convention and Visitors Bureau** at 704-258-3858.

BLUE RIDGE PARKWAY AND MOUNT MITCHELL

The Blue Ridge Mountains formed about a billion years ago from "sediment at the bottom of a long-vanished sea." Then just 300 million years back, the "continents collided and our ridges and mountains rose from the depths" to provide a ridge that has been engineered to become one of America's most scenic parkways. The frequent overlooks afford breathtaking panoramas of high peaks, waterfalls and lakes tucked into verdant valleys.

Spring is alive with color with mountain laurel and red rhododendron in awesome abundance. Fall plays the same game with "leaf-lookers," drinking in every ounce of red and gold beauty. An excellent day trip is to **Mount Mitchell State Park** at milepost 355. Mount Mitchell is the highest peak east of the Mississippi River, and you can hike through the park's many nature trails. But if you want to camp here, call 704-675-4611 to reserve one of the nine campsites.

LINVILLE FALLS, LINVILLE CAVERNS, GRANDFATHER MOUNTAIN, OLD HAMPTON STORE

At Linville Falls and Gorge, there are three hiking trail options, from easy to rugged, depending on your energy and time. All are exquisite windows of nature that date

back a half billion years. That was when the great rock folds tipped so far that they broke and pushed older sandstone beds on top of quartz. Then erosion cut through the older rocks leaving openings to expose nature's handiwork. The gorge is the deepest slash in the earth's crust east of the Grand Canyon. And the river tumbles into the gorge from its head to form a 90-foot fall of water. To reach the falls, you'll walk through a half-mile tunnel of towering trees so dense that spatters of sunlight are rare. Waterfalls take on many personalities—these are gushing high-drama ones, particularly at the peak.

This is not a picnic area; you'll have to go further up the parkway for food, but restrooms are available, and the park is open year round, depending on weather.

There are probably undiscovered caves all through the mountains. But **Linville Caverns**, like others, was discovered by accident in 1822, when curious fishermen followed trout disappearing into the side of a mountain. The current trout in this 20-million-year-old limestone cave have become blind, due to low light source. Both Confederate and Union soldiers hid out in this cave during the Civil War, but it wasn't opened to the public until 1939. The knowledgeable tour guide shows the difference between stalagmite and stalactite formations, which is nature's slow sculpting process that makes this phenomenon so eerily attractive to us. Don't expect Carlsbad or Luray splendors, but the cavern, on 3 levels, is an interesting and enjoyable half hour experience. It's open year-round, but check times (704-756-4171).

The **Old Hampton Store** sits just outside the town of Linville. This neat old 1921 general store, restaurant and gristmill has been refurbished only to the point of keeping it from caving in. The store offers a wide assortment of notions that you need, and some that you probably don't—such as horse hoof medication. Churns and washtubs hang from the ceiling, and the back screened door is perpetually in motion. Out back, the gristmill stone grinds cornmeal and grits nearly every afternoon, and these products are sold with apple butter, local jams and old fashioned tin cookware. Kids can buy their marbles by the pound and sturdy clothes are available upstairs.

Best of all, though, is lunch. The store serves the leanest and most delicious barbecue around, and its root beer isn't bad either. Top this off with a slice of terrific carrot or assorted cheesecakes.

GRANDFATHER MOUNTAIN

This famed 6,000-foot mountain can be seen for miles around and looks like a giant sleeping grandfather. It is considered North Carolina's top scenic attraction. This is a perfect day-trip choice that mixes scenery, animal habitats and a museum. You'll want to visit the natural habitats for native black bear, white-tailed deer, cougars and bald and golden eagles. Stop in at the new nature museum that offers state-of-the-art displays along with entertaining movies filmed at Grandfather on native wildlife (especially the red-tailed hawk film). And for those brave enough to cross it, **Mile High Swinging Bridge**, which

Grandfather Mountain near Linville is the highest peak in the Blue Ridge range. A mile-high swinging bridge spans two peaks.

connects Linville's Peak with the Visitor's center, rewards you with a spectacular view.

The museum's restaurant is a good bet for lunch featuring— what else? A dynamite view. You can also picnic on the mountain. Grandfather Mountain is open daily from 8 a.m. to 7 p.m.

One of the most fun Grandfather Mountain experiences is the annual **Highland Games**, the second weekend in July. You don't have to be a Scot to enjoy the bagpipes, dancing, cable toss and watching Border Collies return lost sheep to the herd, as well as other games of skill. Another popular yearly event that comes the fourth Sunday in June is Singing on the Mountain.

BANNER ELK, SKI BEECH, SUGAR MOUNTAIN SKI RESORT, SKI HAWKSNEST, APPALACHIAN SKI MOUNTAIN, VALLE CRUCIS

Remember those Think Snow bumper stickers? Those are from thousands of Georgia, Tennessee, North and South Carolina skiers who listen to weather reports, watch the sky, send up snow prayers and wax skis in hope of bringing on the first winter's snow. And when Mother Nature cooperates, snow guns whirl into action adding and packing ski resort bases. That's when you'll see packed cars with ski racks headed for one of our high country's downhill ski resorts. If you are new to the sport, you can rent equipment at any of the resorts, but Insiders like to save time by renting locally before they go.

Appalachian Ski Mountain, home of the **French-Swiss Ski College** outside Boone, has one of the best teaching schools for beginners. It has eight slopes with a peak elevation of 4,000 feet. Of course, both Beech and Sugar have good ski schools, particularly for very young children, and both offer more challenging slopes. Beech, north of Banner Elk has 14 slopes and a peak elevation of 5,505 feet, making it the highest in the East with a vertical drop of 830 feet. The resort also has a charming Swiss Village-type village appearance with an outdoor ice skating rink encircled with shops and restaurants.

Sugar Mountain, just to the south of Banner Elk on N.C. Highway 184, boasts 18 slopes, peak elevation of 5,300 feet with a vertical drop of 1,200 feet, and needless to say, fairyland views. **Hawksnest** is sometimes less crowded and has seven slopes, a peak of 4,819 feet, and vertical drop of 619 feet, plus night skiing. All of these resorts have chair lifts, rope tows, lockers and restaurants. Beech and Sugar even have nurseries. You can get a ski report by calling **High Country Hosts** at 800-438-7500, also a good

Insiders' Tip

THE NORTH CAROLINA MOUNTAINS ARE A LEAF LOVER'S PARADISE OF SPECTACULAR FALL COLOR FROM MID-SEPTEMBER THROUGH OCTOBER. BOTANISTS HAVE CLASSIFIED 148 DIFFERENT VARIETIES OF TREES HERE.

source of mountain area information.

You can cross-country ski at **Moses Cone Park** on the parkway just outside of Blowing Rock and at other gated-off areas by calling the Ranger's office at 704-295-7591. On **Roan Mountain**, you can ski with cross-country guided trips, including instruction; call 615-772-3303.

ACCOMMODATIONS AND DINING

What skier has not dreamed of that idyllic mountain ski lodge with roaring fireplace and happy apres ski bums sipping hot cider? You and yours can do just that at the **Beech Alpen Inn** (704-387-2252), or bring your family to an on-the-slopes condo at **Sugar Ski and Country Club** (800-634-1320).

On Beech, **Kat's Overlook Pub** is a good place to dine with an enviable mountain view. And a few yards down Beech Mountain is **Fred's General Mercantile Store**. **Fred's Backside Deli** offers good deli food and a smattering of general store vacationer-type needs.

Exceptional dining options in Banner Elk are the **Louisiana Purchase** with to-die-for cajun and creole food, and **Morels** for innovative continental fare.

From Banner Elk, take N.C. Highway 194 east to Valle Crucis. The **Mast Farm Inn** (704-963-5857) serves fabulous, from-scratch country dinners, which are included in the price of a room.

And while you're in Valle Crucis, make it a point to check out the over-100-year-old **Mast Store**. The original post office is still inside, along with a trap door in the

floor where bartered chickens were once deposited. Locals still play checkers with Coke and Pepsi bottle tops beside an original pot-bellied stove. The store's motto is "If we don't have it, you don't need it anyway." Very few browsers leave empty-handed, as the prices are more than reasonable.

BLOWING ROCK, BOONE, GLENDALE SPRINGS, FRESCOES, LAUREL SPRINGS

A lot of towns are dressed up to look quaint these days—Blowing Rock is the genuine thing. In summer, the main street is lined with pyramid-shaped planters spilling over with pink and white begonias. Since the days the rambling hundred-year-old **Green Park Inn** was built over the center of the Continental Divide, the town has taken on an aristocratic appeal.

Window shopping on Main Street is a favorite pursuit with lots of antiques, oriental rug houses and classy mountain wear. Evenings find folks at the auction house, which is a show in itself. The park on Main Street is a gathering place for tennis, people-watching, craft shows, whatever.

The more athletically inclined can enjoy horseback riding along the trails of Moses Cone Estate on the Blue Ridge Parkway. Make reservations with **Blowing Rock Stables** (704-295-7847). The adventurous will enjoy canoeing and white water rafting through Class III to V rapids down the Nolichucky. Call **Wahoo's Adventures** (800-444-RAFT) on U.S. Highway 321 between Blowing Rock and Boone.

Children in North Carolina grow up on trips to **Tweetsie Railroad** on U.S. Highways 321/221 in Blowing Rock. The drawing card is a three-mile adventurous train ride on an original mountain train, complete with interruptions of Indian attacks and settler rescues. The attraction has amusement rides, live entertainment, crafts, shops and picnic tables. It's open daily from May through October, and on weekends in November.

ACCOMMODATIONS AND DINING

The **Green Park Inn** (704-295-3141) is a great place to stay as many of our U.S. presidents will attest. Another romantic B & B is the **Ragged Garden Inn** (704-295-9703), which also has great food. Insiders' favorite restaurant for some of the best food in the mountains is **Best Cellers**.

BOONE

In the heart of Boone lies the beautiful campus of **Appalachian State University**. Boone is also home to the **Appalachian Cultural Museum** where the evolving life-style of mountain people is attractively displayed with artifacts and information on the Appalachia's abundant variety of rare and unusual herbs and plants (some medicinal). The relationship between man and (not versus) environment is the prevailing theme of an eight-minute film accompanied by sweet mountain music.

If you want to shock your system into reality, travel down U.S. Highway 421 to **Bungee Unlimited** (800-523-2322) and take a leap into... It's hard to imagine anyone paying to do that, but jumpers say it is a real adrenaline high.

The Blowing Rock overhangs the Johns River Gorge.

Courtesy N.C. Travel and Tourism. Photo by William Russ.

During the summer (June 21-August 17), make reservations for the outdoor drama *Horn In The West*, now going into its 41st season. The musical drama revolves around life in Appalachia during the days of Daniel Boone. For reservations, call 704-264-2120. Adjacent to *Horn In The West*, you'll find **Hickory Ridge Homestead,** which is an interesting tour of five representative home sites of the 1800s.

ACCOMMODATIONS AND DINING

A comfortable B & B in Boone is **Overlook Lodge.** The place the natives go for a quick snack is the **Appalachian Soda Shop** where Insiders ask for their Carolina Pharmacy Doughnuts. Vacationers like the **Daniel Boone Inn** for lots of food served country-style for the whole family to enjoy.

GLENDALE SPRINGS

It's a toss-up to know whether people go to Glendale Springs for the wonderful gourmet food at the inn or to see the Frescoes. The 1895 **Glendale Springs Inn**, intact with a convivial ghost, is a sophisticated country inn that attracts discriminating visitors from around the country. And Ben Long's controversial frescoes at Episcopal Holy Trinity Chapel, a block away, are among the most highly visited in the state. A number of craft shops have sprung up, which changes the area's once "hidden away" flavor but does not diminish its overall appeal.

LAUREL SPRINGS

Some Hurricane Hugo victims overcame disaster ingeniously. Because Tom and Nancy Burgiss's 200-year-old farm yielded enough "Hugo" lumber to build a dancing barn, the popular **Mountain Music Jamboree** took up new residence here. Folks from near and far come to dance the Texas Two-Step and old-time mountain dances. Staying at the **Burgiss Farm B & B** (910-359-2995) can be restful or exhilarating, and no matter your choice, it's a win-win deal.

Overnight guests are treated to a two-bedroom suite with private hot tub, and private den with fireplace and piped-in, spring-fed water that lulls you to sleep like a trickling brook. The full breakfast offers a unique menu of choices. Dance classes are Monday and Tuesday nights; Texas Two-Step dances are on Friday and live Blue Grass and Old Time Music are on alternating Saturdays.

Photo courtesy Carolina Golf Group.

The yardage book reads "Welcome to the Noose" on the gorgeous,
but tricky, Par 3 #14 at The Neuse Golf Club in Clayton.

Inside
Golf
In North Carolina

Golf and the Carolinas go together like geese and green ponds. A onetime winter recreation for snowbird tourists on their way south, the sport has become big business for the Tar Heel state where almost 11 percent of the populace play the game. Remember, this is the state that graduated Arnold Palmer, Curtis Strange, Jay Haas and Lanny Wadkins among others.

The state's industrial recruiters, for example, use the acres and acres of North Carolina greens and fairways to lure Japanese businesses looking for U.S. plant locations. Travel industry sales people package golf weekends at name North Carolina golf courses such as Pinehurst to boost off-season tourist dollars. Triangle home builders similarly find that "golf course communities" such as Devil's Ridge in southern Wake County make very popular real estate developments. And then, there are all the fat and happy golf writers who comprise a local cottage industry that produces coffee table books and slick magazines detailing the pleasures and pain of North Carolina putts, drives and traps.

For Triangle residents, golf is one of four basic sports groups: there's basketball, golf, basketball and basketball. But, unlike basketball, golf is played year 'round and it's a sport at which you might actually beat Michael Jordan who is known to play in the Triangle. Mild weather almost guarantees at least one good golfing day a week. There are plenty of places to play, despite the lack of any municipal courses in Raleigh, Cary or Chapel Hill. Most importantly, there are gobs of golfers (a gob of golfers is like a gaggle of geese only profane) who play, on the average, about 21 rounds of golf a year.

One Triangle company that is making golf its full time business is the **Carolinas Golf Group**, started in 1989. The company owns—in part or in full—and operates a number of courses in the area such as Devil's Ridge, Lochmere and The Neuse Golf Club. It offers special discount cards for its courses and pro shop merchandise. If you're a frequent golfer, the "golf card" is a good buy. Several are available in the Triangle and the card offers substantial savings for the holder who can buy a certain number of rounds from a number of courses, either in the Triangle or Pinehurst or the coast.

This Insiders' Guide to Triangle Golf is for the golfer who plays the public courses. No, these are not golf courses owned by the public but they are open to the public—for a fee. This is not a list of every course in the area; rather it's a guide to popular and interesting links. The advice is written for the typical weekend duffer, not a semi-pro scratch hustler.

Also, the Guide includes some courses that are within a day's drive of the Triangle. And finally, we mention some of the private club courses in the area because we assume that most of our readers will shortly attain Insider status and be asked to play if not join some of these clubs.

The green fees on these courses vary and often change annually. The typical fee during the week for most Triangle public courses is about $12 to $16 and on the weekend between $17 and $24. Some require you use a cart, which will be an additional cost. Call first to see what the total charges will be.

Triangle Courses

Raleigh and Cary

CHEVIOT HILLS GOLF COURSE
7301 Capital Blvd.   876-9920
This is a veteran course that used to be on the outskirts of north Raleigh but has the city at its clubhouse door today. It is rated about in the middle of area courses, and you can get a view of the fairways by

riding out U.S. Hwy. 1 North. It's one of the better bargains and won't embarrass a beginner. Hole No. 14 is 160 yards and a par 3, and was listed in the *Triangle Report* as one of the Triangle's best holes. Total yardage for the course: 6,475.

DEVIL'S RIDGE GOLF CLUB
5107 Linksland Dr.
Holly Springs   557-6100
The course was on everyone's "hot" list in 1993 and is rated among the best. It was build in 1991 as part of a residential real estate development, so get your eager Realtor to treat you to a round. It is located south of Cary in the one-traffic-light metropolis of Holly Springs. Says one golfer, "I like the layout; it has some water and some interesting holes. You have to think about shot placement, but it's not going to kill you." Hole No. 17 is the signature hole at 388 yards, par 4. Total yardage: 7,002.

HEDINGHAM GOLF CLUB
4801 Harbour Towne Dr.   250-3030
This course is part of the attractive Hedingham planned community in east Raleigh, north of U.S. Hwy. 64, very convenient and close by. It's new and has a well-equipped pro shop and offers a driving range. It is rated above average among the public courses, and it's a good place to find newcomers. Total yardage: 6,638.

LOCHMERE GOLF CLUB
2511 Kildaire Farm Rd.
Cary   851-0611
Lochmere is a favorite in Cary and was a hit when it opened in 1985. It, too, is part of a very

popular residential community and offers very scenic landscape including two lakes; it has more that 40 bunkers and 10 water holes. It was the first home for the One Club World Championships. The clubhouse includes a pro shop and a bar and grill. It has a driving range, and it ranks above average in play. Total yardage: 6,876.

THE NEUSE GOLF CLUB
918 Birkdale Drive
Clayton   550-0550
Running parallel to the Neuse River, this senic golf course opened in December, 1993, in the Clayton development of Glen Laurel. It's signature hole is No. 14, with rocks on the left and water on the right. A well placed tee shot is critical on this 176 yards, par 3 hole. Total yardage: 7,010.

PINE HOLLOW GOLF CLUB
3300 Garner Rd.
Clayton   553-4554
This course has been around for a long time, and it is located east of Raleigh amid rolling fields and tall pines. It has the informal, relaxed air of a men's club, and you can find industrial league players here during the week, and it's a great escape from household, weekend chores, too. The latter is reflected by $30 green fees on the weekend. The course is kept in good shape and it offers a putting green, a driving range and a pro shop with a snack bar. Total yardage: 6,266.

RALEIGH GOLF ASSOCIATION
1527 Tryon Rd.   772-9987
This is another veteran course, perhaps one of the oldest in the Triangle. It was built in the country, south of Raleigh off Tryon Road and is now in the city limits. Described by one player as a "nice member's course" it is unpretentious and plays fast. "It's a good place to start; one tends to graduate from there." The fairways and greens are well-tended, especially Hole No. 13, which is a challenging 434 yards, par 4. The convenience, particularly for residents inside the Beltline, makes it popular during the week when the summer sun stays out. Total yardage: 6,097.

WILDWOOD GREEN GOLF CLUB
3000 Ballybunion Way   846-8376
This was one of the city's older public north Raleigh courses that underwent major surgery during the '80s and emerged as part of a golf course community. It is locally owned and managed and offers a number of membership options including weekday plans for older golfers and junior cards for those under age 21. Hole No. 2 is 377 yards, par 4 and is among the best in the Triangle, "short but scenic." Wildwood Green is rated among the average courses in play and has one of the shorter courses. Total yardage: 5,941.

Durham

HILLANDALE GOLF COURSE
Hillandale Rd.   286-4211
This is the granddaddy of the public courses in the Triangle, and it's the only municipally owned course in these parts. The crowd that hangs out here doesn't put on any social airs, and they have nick-

names like "Dink" and "Zack." There's no charge for the philosophy or golf tales. You might even find a few who will put a friendly wager on a friendly match. The course is kept in excellent condition and has some challenging holes. The pro shop, according to some, is the best in the Triangle. Total yardage: 6,435.

WASHINGTON DUKE INN AND GOLF CLUB

N.C. Hwy. 751 at Science Dr.   681-2288

This is Duke University's course and was a Rees Jones design that opened in the 1960s. It was so popular, says one Triangle golfer, that it "just about got worn out." When the Inn was built, the course was rebuilt and is among one of the highest rated in the Triangle. It has the most accommodations with pro shop, hotel, driving range and 19th hole restaurant. If you're coming to visit Duke University, stay here and work in a round. The club pro, by the way, is the fellow who helped Michael Jordan get started in the game...of golf, that is. Its Hole No. 12 is considered one of the most beautiful in the area. Total yardage: 7,005.

Chapel Hill

FINLEY GOLF CLUB

Mason Farm Rd.   962-2349

This is the University of North Carolina's backyard course; so if you're playing during the week, you may see one of the next NBA stars if not a PGA pro. The course is kept in good shape and Hole No. 16, which was redesigned by Jack

Nicklaus when his son attended UNC, is among the best in the Triangle. There are woods around the hole and the course, and it's convenient to the town of Chapel Hill. The clubhouse has a pro shop, snack bar and there's a driving range and putting green. Total yardage: 6,102.

Private Club Courses

The Triangle also has some of the best private country club courses in the state, too. While these courses are not open to the public, they should be part of every golfer's education about Triangle golf.

There are five courses that rise to the top: Governor's Club and Treyburn in Durham, MacGregor Downs and Prestonwood in Cary and North Ridge in Raleigh.

Governor's Club is a Jack Nicklaus design and opened in 1990, part of a planned community. The setting is against Edwards Mountain and from the ninth tee, you get a spectacular view of the neighborhood. There are five sets of tees, so the course ranges from over 7,085 yards to just under 6,000 yards.

Treyburn, north of Durham's downtown, is equally spectacular. It is part of a vast real estate community developed in part by former governor and senator Terry Sanford. The course was designed by Tom Fazio and opened in 1988 with rave reviews by the golf press. The clubhouse is warm, beautiful and ranked by *Southern Links* as among the region's top five. It also has one of the finest croquet greens around. A number of Duke's and UNC's famous athletes belong here including Mike Giminski and Michael Jordan. It is in the running for a major tournament with a super finishing hole, No. 18, a par 4.

Cary's **MacGregor Downs** is the oldest of these five, going back to 1968. It is considered a great "members' course" and was designed by Willard Byrd. Says golf writer Bruce Phillips of *The News & Observer*, "It's highly rated and one of the best finishing holes in golf, over the lake. When the L&M match play was here, the pro's couldn't get off No. 18. I like it best among the Triangle courses." MacGregor also played host in 1994 to the PING Intercollegiate golf tournament, featuring six of the country's top 10 college teams.

Prestonwood opened in the mid-80s as part of Preston, one of Cary's trademark planned unit developments. The clubhouse is elegant and the course is surrounded by some of the most attractive real estate in the county, with homes going up to $750,000. The Nike Tour will make its Triangle debut here in June '94 and the club pro is former PGA great, Vance Heafner. The club has 27 holes now and Tom Jackson has designed 18 more. Said Heafner in a *Triangle Report* interview, "It's unprecedented anywhere around here—45 holes of golf."

Among the private clubs in Raleigh, **North Ridge**'s 36 holes usually get top honors, although the venerable 1948 Raleigh Country Club over by Wake Medical Center gets good reviews and is notable as one of the last courses designed

by golfing legend Donald J. Ross. North Ridge opened in 1970 and attracted some of the city's new movers and shakers who didn't want to wait to get into the crustier Carolina Country Club. North Ridge's original 18 holes were designed by George Cobb who left his mark on courses at Linville Ridge and Bald Head Island elsewhere in North Carolina. North Ridge is another members' course. Says the *N&O's* Phillips, "It's been home to several LPGA tournaments, and many of the women pro's still come each year for the Rex Classic. It's not as difficult as MacGregor, but both courses are excellent."

Courses Elsewhere

Finally, when Triangle golfers have tired of the local courses, they can tee-up on some of the state's other fairways. This is like falling off Cloud Nine and landing in Heaven.

For instance, it's only an hour's drive to the quaint golfing village of Pinehurst, home of **Pinehurst Resort and Country Club** (800-487-4653). The town dates back to 1895 when James W. Tufts bought 5,000 acres of North Carolina piney woods and hired Frederick Olmsted, the designer of New York's Central Park, to master plan a private village. Tufts then hired Scotchman Donald Ross to build a course in 1899. Olmsted's concentric city plan continues today as the core of a town that Ross developed into the state's acknowledged golf capital and the first home of the PGA's World Golf Hall of Fame.

Queen among the seven courses at the resort is **Pinehurst No. 2**, which will be home to the 1999 U.S. Open Tournament. Guests at the resort can play here, and entire articles have been written just about this one course. If you make the trip, just remember when you line up that first shot that you're playing the same course where Ben Hogan won his first pro tournament in 1940 and golf legends Sam Snead, Byron Nelson and Jack Nicklaus played and won. Makes you want to go right for the flag, doesn't it?

The seven courses at the resort are just the beginning of the feast. There are about two million more courses in and around the towns of Pinehurst and Southern Pines—well, maybe not that many. And most of them wear designer labels with names like Jack Nicklaus, Arnold Palmer, Tom and George Fazio, Dan Maples and Rees Jones.

One Insiders' favorite is **Mid Pines Resort** (800-228-5151) in Southern Pines. This resort has a Donald Ross course that opened in 1921 and was ranked among the top 20 in the state. The greens are small and fairways narrow.

Pine Needles Resort (910-692-7111) in southern Pines is a 1927 Ross course. It is a challenging par 71 and will be host to the 1996 Ladies U.S. Open.

Country Club of North Carolina has two private courses, but guests at Pinehurst Resort can play here. Insiders claim it is among the best in the state—with the best-heeled members. It's kept in immaculate condition.

Rees Jones designed the championship **Talamore** (910-692-5884) course that was nominated for best new public course in the nation in its debut. It offers the unique and often televised feature of llama caddies.

When you travel to the coast, you will find more pieces of golf paradise. At Calabash, there is **Pearl Golf Links** (910-579-8132), designed by Dan Maples. It offers 72 holes of golf and a grand but informal clubhouse. You can gorge yourself on Calabash seafood and then work it off on this public course which also has one of the best driving ranges in the state.

Brandywine Bay Golf and Country Club (919-247-2541) west of Morehead City is set in dense woods and laced with streams and ponds. Originally designed by Bruce Devlin and redesigned by Ellis and Dan Maples, this coastal course plays 6,611 yards from the championship tees, 6,138 yards from the regular men's and 5,196 yards from the women's tees. The resident golf pro, Bill Howe gives lessons by appointment and golfers will find a pro shop, snack bar and putting greens.

Up north, on the Outer Banks, you can get a feel of Scottish moors and winds at **The Village of Nags Head** (919-441-8073) course. You're surrounded by history and hang gliders, and, according to *Golf Digest*, perhaps the "longest, strongest and most irritating 6,100 yards you've ever encountered." But, in the next sentence, the writer raves, "the sheer beauty of the holes along Roanoke Sound will take your breath away."

Lastly, there are the mountain courses and in between, beautiful **Tanglewood** (910-766-5082) in Clemmons, outside Winston-Salem. Tanglewood rivals some of the Pinehurst courses for championship play, and it is among Robert Trent Jones' best known courses. Lee Trevino won the 1974 PGA here and the 1986 Public Links Championship. It's a public course and considered by Insiders to be among the best 25 public courses in the country. The par 5, Hole No. 5, says *Golf* magazine, is one of the "most challenging" in the U.S.

Golfers find summertime happiness in the mountains. **Grandfather Golf and Country Club** is at the center of the courses around Blowing Rock and Linville, N.C. It is an Ellis Maples course and private. The championship course at Grandfather is rated among the top mountain courses in the country, but one of the toughest.

One of the newer courses in the northwest mountains is, despite its name, **Olde Beau** (800-752-1634), about 20 minutes north of Elkin. It is part of a mountain residential community that is being built by some of the same people who built Bermuda Run in Winston-Salem. Billy Satterfield, one of the owners, named the place after—not his sweetheart or his mother—but his bulldog! Another owner in the development is former Wake Forest University basketball star and television sportscaster, Billy Packer. The course is long, 6,713 yards, and the signature hole is No. 15, a par 4 that overlooks the scenic Mitchell River Gorge. As a mountain course, it tends to go up and down, especially on the back nine, but golfers like its character. Arnold Palmer Course Designs helped with the layout and Curtis Strange was on hand for the opening tee off in 1991.

The second hub of mountain golf is in the Highlands area south of Asheville. You will find a number of private clubs here such as **The Cullasaja Club** with a course designed by Arnold Palmer and down the road at Cashiers, there's the **Wade Hampton Club** by Tom Fazio, rated by some to be among the top 10 in the state.

The **High Hampton Inn & Country Club** (800-334-2551) offers some of the most dramatic scenery of any of the mountain courses. It is an 18-hole, par 71 course designed by George W. Cobb. It features bent grass greens, a practice range with a covered hitting area, two putting greens and, during the season, it offers a series of golf schools. The Inn itself, once the home of Confederate General and Governor Wade Hampton, is in the National Register of Historic Places and the resort offers a variety of activities in addition to golf.

WE'LL OPEN THE DOOR TO YOUR NEW HOME.

Whether you're moving across the country, or just across town, The Huntington Mortgage Company can help make your move easier. We offer competitive rates on a wide variety of loans and we're committed to serving your needs. Which means providing personalized attention. Working within your schedule. And being involved from the first step through the last. So if you're house hunting, call us. We'll help you feel at home.

Huntington Mortgage Company

A Smarter Way to Finance

4601 Six Forks Road, Suite 128
Raleigh, N.C. 27609

(919) 781-0744 • 1-800-435-8602

EQUAL HOUSING
LENDER

The Huntington Mortgage Company is a subsidiary of The Huntington National Bank.

Inside
Homes

This section is a guide for those people who plan to make their home in the Triangle or already have a home here. It tells you who will help in relocations, hither and yon. But it doesn't stop there.

The Homes section also lists some of the people who play a part in the selling, building and bettering of a home. There's a list of Triangle Realtors and builders, and we also have drawn a list of helpers, such as landscapers and interior designers. The alphabetical lists are by no means complete, but rather name people and firms who might be mentioned if you were to ask a Triangle Insider about the subject.

This section is divided by location into Raleigh, Cary, Durham and Chapel Hill.

Relocation Assistance

Ah, moving. What fun. There is relief in the Triangle in the form of relocation services.

Families on the move ought to be aware of the relocation services now offered by many of the larger real estate companies. The following list includes some of the Realtors who have such specialists on staff (check also the "Realtors" section that follows):

Ammons Pittman	870-5553
	800-476-6363
Coldwell Banker-Vermilya Waud	
House Hunters Realty	942-4482
Fonville Morisey	800-846-7356
Howard Perry & Walston	800-868-7653
The Prudential Carolinas Realty	847-7599
	800-777-1326
York Realtors	821-7177, 967-9000

Temporary Housing

RESEARCH TRIANGLE
GUEST HOUSES
362-0274

When you're moving to a new location, the first few months can be the toughest, especially if you haven't found a permanent home yet. Bob Jungers and Angie Seagle operate Research Triangle Guest Houses to help newcomers through that transition period. They work with corporations and individuals to find out what your immediate housing needs are, then they match your specifications to vacancies throughout the Triangle area. They can provide apartments, townhomes and condominiums complete with furniture, housewares, etc. They will even help you get your utilities turned on, your cable TV hooked up and your pets cared for. "We try to provide all the comforts of home to help you

153

get acclimated to the new move," says Angie.

SPECIALIZED RELOCATION SERVICES
2607 Lochmore Dr.   787-6631
Raleigh

Toni James-Manus has established a unique relocation service for families with "special needs." If you have a family member with mental retardation, a learning disability, epilepsy, cerebral palsy, visual or hearing impairment, emotional problems or other special needs, she can help you find appropriate public and private schools, residential programs, vocational services, camps, preschools, adult day care, medical care, respite care and parent support groups.

Renting A Home

Renting is really quite simple once you find a place, and we'll tell you some of the best ways to do that. The Triangle apartment market, especially for Raleigh and Cary, has become a landlord's market, with occupancy rates over 90 percent. Most big complexes offer good competitive prices. Expect rents to range from $350 to $700, with the average between $450 to $600 a month. There are a few points to consider if you are renting. Most landlords will ask you to sign a lease, and this is for your protection as well as the landlord's. If you find someone who operates on a handshake, remember, he or she can toss you out just as easily. As a renter in North Carolina, you still have to pay taxes on your personal property. And you may want to consider renter's insur-

ance to cover your apartment's contents. Now, here are some places to look to find apartments, along with some other helpful information.

APARTMENT FINDER
8541-A Glenwood Ave.   781-8990
Raleigh

This is a free, quarterly publication that is available at most large retail centers, banks, hotels and other visitor centers such as RDU Airport. It's a comprehensive guide serving the whole Triangle, and the publishers also operate a free walk-in relocation service at the same address. The magazine gives you a detailed description of the larger apartment complexes and locator maps. It's companion publication, Apartment Finder Monthly, provides a monthly updating of information about apartment communities.

THE APARTMENT BOOK
5613 Creedmoor Rd.   *571-2787*
Raleigh

Veteran publisher Tom Smith started publication of this book and location service in March, 1993, and put the business in a shopping center at Creedmoor Crossing for easy access . The long book can be found at 800 locations throughout the Triangle, usually at big grocery stores next to the other news stands. It's free, and so is the location service, much of which comes over the phone via the company's 800 telephone number from out-of-towners.

CAROLINA APARTMENT LOCATORS
3717 National Dr.   *787-7707*
Suite 207   *800-365-5755*
Raleigh

These people can be very helpful when the market is tight or when you don't have time to look. They can be a great resource, providing a number of services without a fee.

RENTAL RESOURCES
5540 Centerview Dr.   *859-0089*
Suite 411   *800-319-0089*
Raleigh

This innovative firm, designed to assist individuals and corporations in securing rental hous-

ing in the Triangle, began in 1987. It specializes in single family and townhomes, filling a niche left void by apartment communities.

Its Executive Service includes picking up the prospective client, showing currently available accommodations which meet the specified needs, assisting with the leasing process and facilitating school registration for children. The staff will help with the actual moving procedure as well, even including the unpacking of personal goods. Principals, Susan Hasty and Sharon Schovain are dedicated to going that extra mile to ensure a trouble-free move, and their service has proved particularly valuable when international moves are involved.

NEWSPAPERS, REAL ESTATE ADS

The local newspapers are always a good source for current rental properties. Also, check the Triangle's weekly publications (see **MEDIA**). If you're looking just for a room or an apartment, or a house or that little unit in a lonely widow's house a block from campus, these dailies and weeklies are your best bet.

Furniture Rental Companies

AARON RENTS FURNITURE

Raleigh and Cary	878-7811
Durham and Chapel Hill	493-1481

This national furniture rental company has two locations serving the Triangle. It claims to be the nation's largest and has been in business for 30 years, so it's doing something right.

CORT FURNITURE RENTAL

North Raleigh	876-7550
Durham	493-2563
Chapel Hill	929-5075

Cort has been in the Triangle longer than any other rental company and has built up a good reputation for service among area Realtors and apartment complexes. It also offers an option for you to buy what you rent. If you're on a temporary assignment, you may want to check out its package rentals, which include everything from silverware to bed sheets.

Apartment Property Managers

ADAMS-TERRY

1310 Hillsborough St.	832-7783
Raleigh	

This is one of Raleigh's established property management firms, and it handles a number of small properties, too. If you're a student or looking for a modest rent, this is one place you might check.

ALLENTON

3101 Petty Rd., Suite 1000	490-9050
Durham	

This property management company has been in Durham's market for 50 years and also has a Chapel Hill office. It manages houses as well as individual apartments and duplexes.

CALIBRE PROPERTIES

231 Calibre Chase Dr.	828-1344
Raleigh	

Calibre is based in Atlanta, Georgia, and has been in the Raleigh area for several years with some of the city's better luxury units, such as Calibre Chase, Calibre Place, Calibre Oaks, Calibre Springs...you get the picture. Each complex is managed separately. The builders were attentive to things like energy efficiency, too.

CIM
4400 Falls of Neuse Rd.   872-5656
Raleigh
Commercial Investment Management operates a number of apartment complexes, some in Raleigh's suburbs such as Apex and Garner. It also handles houses, duplexes and condominiums.

DRUCKER & FALK
7200 Stonehenge Dr.   870-0777
Raleigh
This company probably is the largest single owner of apartments in the Triangle, with about 6,000 units. Most of the units are in Raleigh and Cary, but it has at least four in Durham, and it covers a large price range as well as locations especially in north, northwest and west Raleigh. This group is well-organized, knows the territory and most of its properties have resident managers who keep up with problems.

KIP-DELL HOMES
2600 Glenwood Ave.   781-3632
Raleigh
This is a local development company, and it manages over 100 single-family homes and 350 apartments in Raleigh, Cary and Garner. Rents go from $200 to $725.

TICON, INC.
3600 University Dr.   493-4331
Durham
This company manages six apartment complexes in the Durham area including one in the planned community of Woodcroft. Rents range from $305 for one-bedroom units, to large duplexes, some with 4 bedrooms, at $650.

H.V. MCCOY & CO.
Chapel Hill   929-0504
This Greensboro-based company manages three Chapel Hill complexes—Franklin Woods, Chambers Ridge and Brookstone—which combined have over 400 apartments. The telephone number above is for Chambers Ridge.

VILLAGE REALTY OF CHAPEL HILL, INC.
1801 E. Franklin St., Ste. 101   967-6043
Chapel Hill
Village Realty is one of the largest property management/rental agencies in the Chapel Hill area. It offers more than 300 rental apartments, duplexes and houses in Chapel Hill and Carrboro as well as in Orange and Chatham counties. According to President Marilyn Cloninger, two-bedroom apartments range from $375 to $600, duplexes rent for about $400 to $450, and homes start at $550. Stop by the office, pick up a free housing booklet, and take a look at its video to get a preview of Village Realty properties.

Apartments

Raleigh

GORMAN CROSSINGS
2101-A Gorman St.   *851-8309*

These apartments are conveniently located near I-40, downtown and NCSU, with many amenities within walking distance. You can choose between a garden apartment or townhouse with extras such as private patios or balconies, fireplaces, central air and heat. All apartments have major appliances, dishwasher, washer/dryer connections, plenty of closet space and are pre-wired for cable TV.

CALIBRE CHASE
231 Calibre Chase Dr.   *828-1344*
(off Six Forks Rd.)

Luxury is the key word here. Fireplaces with Italian tile, built in bookcases, and sunrooms are a few of the amenities found in these unique floor plans. For those in the fast lane, personal services such as housecleaning, dry cleaning and firewood delivery make life a little less hectic. Other Calibre properties found throughout the Triangle area are equally as nice, so if you've got the bucks, check 'em out.

Cary

HIDDEN OAKS
101 Hidden Oaks Dr.   *481-2600*

Elegant but very livable floor plans make Hidden Oaks a great choice for housing in Cary. It's convenient to I-40, RTP and the airport, yet very private and "homey." Recreation amenities are well thought out and the overall European styling is appealing. If Cary is a convenient living spot for you, check out Hidden Oaks—it's nice.

AMBERWOOD AT LOCHMERE
100 Eclipse Dr.   *233-1010*

Conveniently located off U.S. Hwy. 1 South at the Cary Parkway exit, Amberwood offers contemporary luxury in the very pretty environment of Lochmere. There are five floor plans to choose from, offering fireplaces, patios or decks, as well as common amenities that include a pool, Jacuzzi, clubhouse, trails, tennis courts, nearby lakes and a golf course. Corporate apartments are also available with short-term leases.

Durham

OXFORD COMMONS
3800 Merriwether Dr.   *220-7639*

On the north side of Durham, Oxford Commons is convenient to Durham Regional Hospital, Duke and downtown Durham. The one- and two-bedroom apartments feature vaulted ceilings and fireplaces. The clubhouse has a fitness center, hot tubs, pool and tennis courts. Small pets are allowed. Handicapped access and corporate units are available.

PENRITH
N.C. Hwy. 55 and Obie Dr.   *544-3755*

Penrith offers one-, two- and three-bedroom garden apartments and townhomes. Each one is equipped with a washer and dryer, drapes/blinds and fully equipped kitchens. There is an Olympic-size pool, playground, tennis courts and clubhouse with a game room on the grounds. Corporate apartments are available. Penrith is convenient to Research Triangle Park, Duke University and NCCU.

Chapel Hill

WALDEN AT GREENFIELDS
103 Melville Loop   929-8600
These apartments are located just off the U.S. Hwy. 15-501 Bypass, close to the I-40 interchange. They offer convenient access to Chapel Hill, Durham and Research Triangle Park. One- and two-bedroom units are available, and include a washer and dryer, miniblinds, and each has its own patio or a balcony. Many apartments have a fireplace. There is a pool, a pond, a gazebo and a clubhouse on site. Many young professionals and graduate students live at Walden.

THE VILLAGES
1000 Smith Level Rd.   929-1141
Carrboro
The Villages offers ten different floor plans, with one-, two- or three-bedroom units. The complex has a fitness trail, tennis courts, two pools, and volleyball and basketball courts. The complex is convenient to UNC, and to highways U.S. 15-501 and N.C. 54, with quick access to I-40. Many graduate and professional students and young families call these apartments home.

Buying A Home

The task of shopping for or building a new home can be overwhelming, even if you've lived here for years. It's especially confusing and taxing if you're a newcomer, but there is help available. One of the best resources we've found for information on new home communities and home-related products and services is the *NewHome Guide*. Published six times a year, this comprehensive guide to the Triangle's real estate world will go a long way toward getting you started with your search (781-8990). Also, watch for the *N&O's* "Triangle Homes" quarterly for current news about the home market.

Buyers' Agents

The fastest growing trend in real estate—buyers' agents—is now in the Triangle. These agents represent the buyer in the negotiation and purchase of homes and other real estate. Some real estate companies now provide buyer representation exclusively, while other traditional listing companies offer both buyer and seller services.

Buyers' agents are licensed in the full spectrum of real estate transactions and provide Multiple Listing Services as all Realtors do.

FOR HomeBUYERS
8820 Six Forks Rd.   848-4070
Raleigh   800-333-2893
Ann Davis, an experienced real estate agent, established FOR HomeBUYERS in 1991 to serve only

the buyers of property. Home buyers' demand for Ms. Davis' services has quadrupled the number of agents in her office. All agents exclusively negotiate and close deals for buyers. Agents are certified Buyer Representatives. The company has no property listings. FOR HomeBUYERS was the first exclusive buyers real estate agency in the area and serves all of Wake County and the adjacent counties.

HOME BUYERS CHOICE
219 E. Chatham St.   *481-0116*
Cary

Home Buyers Choice in Cary was founded in the Spring of 1993 by Margit Gratzl, an experienced broker with more than 12 years' experience. Within one year the company grew to be a very active

agency with eight full-time, specially trained agents. A full-service relocation department helps clients from other areas to get settled here.

Realtors

There are about 2,000 real estate agents just in the Raleigh-Cary area, a decline from mid-80s numbers. The industry has changed dramatically since the days when most companies were one- or two-man operations clustered around their respective downtowns. Today, a majority of the agents are women, the companies have their offices out near the neighborhoods where the houses are selling and the latest trend is toward large companies, some affiliated with national opera-

tions such as Coldwell Banker and Prudential.

The companies selected for this Guide are recognized in their respective communities as some of the best. They are not the only ones in town, however, and if you want a more complete list, contact the Board of Realtors in the community where you're looking.

Raleigh and Cary

For Raleigh and Cary, the **Raleigh/Wake Board of Realtors'** office is at 1301 Annapolis Drive in Raleigh (834-6739). It also is the location for greater Raleigh's MLS (or Multiple Listing Service), which is computerized and one of the more sophisticated systems in the business (834-0359). MLS members have access to all the homes being offered through real estate companies, which makes house-hunting far less of a chore than it once was. The companies are listed alphabetically. Because Cary and Raleigh are considered part of the same market, most Realtors listed here serve both cities.

AMMONS PITTMAN REALTORS
911 Paverstone Dr.	847-5555
Relocation Office	870-5553
	1-800-476-6363

Jud Ammons is one of the more imaginative developers in the Triangle, and his Greystone Village is Raleigh's first real planned community, similar to the PUDs in Cary. Many of the houses the company lists are ones it has built, but 75

percent are from outside projects. Ammons himself has been active in developing the city's greenway program, especially in the area of acquiring property at no cost to the city. Partner George Pittman is a former president of the Board of Realtors.

CENTURY 21
These are independently owned affiliates of Century 21:
Vicki Berry Realty	
5312 Six forks Rd.	420-0156
Russel Gay & Associates	
5909 Falls of Neuse Rd.	872-5100
Triangle Village Realty	
206-D Colonades Way	859-3500

COLDWELL BANKER-SOUTHERN HOME REALTORS
6900 Six Forks Rd.	846-8892

Formerly Coldwell Banker-Myrick, this agency joined the Coldwell Banker national chain in 1988. New owner Richard Rabon is a builder and a veteran of the Raleigh real estate market. He knows the territory. The company represents a spectrum of properties, from homes under $60,000 to high end country houses.

FONVILLE MORISEY
3600 Glenwood Ave.	
(headquarters)	781-7731
5925 Falls of the Neuse Rd.	872-4450
100 Sawmill Rd.	847-9300
6301 Creedmoor Rd.	781-4452
8100 Creedmoor Rd.	847-2511
2395 Kildaire Farm Rd., Cary	859-0800
1149 Kildaire Farm Rd., Cary	467-3232
1419 Aversboro Rd., Garner	772-7240

Fonville and Morisey are two UNC fraternity brothers who

teamed up in the early '70s in a year that the market dried up. They persevered and today have well over 240 agents and are one of the largest agencies in the Triangle, with new offices to serve Durham and Chapel Hill. They merged with Realmark in Cary and are especially strong in new home developments there as Fonville Morisey Builders Marketing Group, headed by the handsome Audie Barefoot.

Both Fonville and Morisey are active in the Raleigh real estate community; Fonville, for example, is past president of the Board of Realtors. They kept their company in the forefront and were among the first to offer relocation services,

a training school for agents. They also joined Robuck Homes to develop their own projects. Expect these people to be on the cutting edge.

HODGE & KITRELL REALTORS
3200 Wake Forest Rd.   *876-7411*

Joe Hodge has built on his mother Nadine Hodge's business, and in 1991, was president of Raleigh Board of Realtors. Nadine was in the Raleigh-Cary real estate market for years and was one of the first women to establish her own company. Their company's size doesn't keep it from delivering quality service, and the company enjoys a loyal following. It is considered one of the better agencies in the area.

HOWARD PERRY AND WALSTON/ BETTER HOMES AND GARDENS

4112 Blue Ridge Rd.	
(headquarters)	782-5600
7320 Six Forks Rd.	847-6767
6504 Falls of the Neuse Rd.	876-8824
5509 Creedmoor Rd.	781-5556
7417 Hwy. 64 E., Knightdale	266-5500
1130 Kildaire Farm Rd., Cary	467-1882
1004 Vandora Springs Rd. ,	
Garner	772-9410
Relocation Office	1-800-868-7653

HP&W/Better Homes and Gardens is one of the largest residential real estate companies in the Triangle. It has been a trendsetter, and not only in growth. The locations above are just for Wake County; it also has a presence in Durham and Chapel Hill. It is associated with the Better Homes & Gardens national group.

Howard Perry and Walston runs a number of on-site sales offices for developers, as well as for its own projects. It maintains a relocation office, real estate school, property management operation and commercial division. Don Walston is a community leader who has been active in the city's affordable housing programs. But the star in this company is Phyllis Wolborsky, the most prolific real estate salesperson in the Triangle and probably this hemisphere. She even has her own TV ads! If she were an athlete, she'd be a franchise.

POWELL REALTORS

7208 Creedmoor Rd.	848-8881

Tommy Powell is a local Realtor who has been in business for 28 years and opened his own company in 1971. He and his agents have been exclusive representatives for such popular developments as Stonehenge, Coachman's Trail, and now West Lake Village off Leesville Road. The company is small by current standards—less than a dozen people—but it has built a solid customer base in northeast and northwest Raleigh and is affiliated with national relocation services. Powell is a director of the Raleigh Board of Realtors and a member in the Home Builders Association.

PROPERTIES UNLIMITED

N.C. Hwy. 42, Clayton	876-0966

Linda Nelke, a Greenville, N.C. native with 17 years' experience, is the owner of this independent agency that started in Clayton in 1983. She has built a staff of seven agents and belongs to the Johnston County MLS as well as Wake County's. Although Clayton is outside the Triangle, many of its residents now work in Wake County and some even commute daily to Research Triangle Park. Mrs. Nelke's company deals frequently in new homes and is participating in the development of Summerbrook, east of Clayton. She believes that her company moves as much Clayton area property as any agency around.

THE PRUDENTIAL CAROLINAS REALTY

7500 Six Forks Rd.	
Headquarters:	870-0300
Sales:	846-8101
5821 Falls of the Neuse Rd.	876-7030
Crabtree Valley	782-5502
1815 Kildaire Farm Rd., Cary	859-3300
Relocation Office	847-7599
	800-334-8161

"A Limited Edition"

Entering the gates of Regency Park Estates, you will soon discover one of the area's most beautiful neighborhoods.

All homesites are larger than one acre, giving ample room for a large luxury home. There is plenty of space for either a swimming pool or tennis court.

Conveniently located in Cary to schools, recreation, shopping and medical facilities...all within a few minutes from your front door.

Make sure this is one neighborhood you do not miss seeing! Take US#1 South to Tryon Road East (Exit 128A) and follow signs to Regency Park.

Regency Park Estates

(919) 469-8777

On-Site Sales Center Open Daily

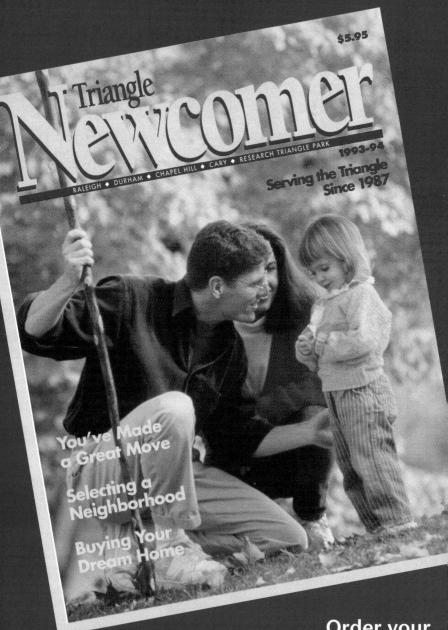

Logan Trading Company

For over 25 years, we have supplied our customers with the essentials as well as the unique items to satisfy any gardener. Located at the historic Seaboard train station, our three-acre site is complete with an award-winning greenhouse, the largest garden book selection in the Southeast and the Seaboard Cafe.

Logan Trading Company, Inc.
707 Semart Drive
Raleigh, NC 27604
(919) 828-5337
Call for directions

BEST SELLERS!

Looking for the most complete new home source in the Triangle? Pick up the best—*NewHome Guide*. Winner of the National Housing Guide of the Year Award three years running, celebrating 12 years as the Triangle's authority in the new home market.

And now, there's *NewHome Builders of 1994*. An annual color publication that showcases the area's new home builders in concise, informative profiles—complete with photographs of new homes crafted by featured builders.

For a free six-month subscription to *NewHome Guide*, or for a complimentary copy of *NewHome Builders of 1994*, call today.

(919) 781-8990 • 1 800-999-5642

FINDING AN APARTMENT HOME

doesn't need to be hard. We're easy to find and we can help you narrow your choices from over 300 apartment communities in the Triangle to the ones that suit your requirements for location, size and price. We also have newcomer information that will make your move as easy as a call to **919-571-2787** or **1-800-849-APTS**.

Centrally located to serve the entire Triangle, the Apartment Book Locator Service is in the Creedmoor Crossings Shopping Center at the intersection of Creedmoor (NC 50) and Millbrook Roads—one mile north of the Crabtree Valley Mall. The shopping center is

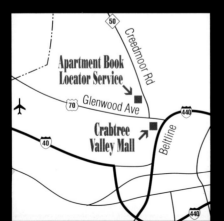

on your left as you come up the hill from Glenwood Avenue. Turn in just before you reach Millbrook. Our address is **5613**.

FREE

THE
Apartment Book®

LOCATOR SERVICE

Great Rooms Like This Take 55 Years To Build.

Realtor Participation Welcome

See One And Take 30 Seconds To Fall In Love.

A Crosland community may not always be the first place people visit. But for more than 15,000 homebuyers since 1937, it was the last. That's because one look is all it takes to see the difference experience makes.

In the Triangle area people have been discovering the beauty and excellence of Crosland homes for 10 years. And with over 40 floorplans and twelve neighborhoods to choose from, Crosland is sure to have the home you want right where you'd like to live. Don't miss your chance to fall in love. Visit a Crosland community today.

John Crosland Company

A DIVISION OF CENTEX HOMES

EQUAL HOUSING OPPORTUNITY

Now that you're all grown up, it's not that simple. At The Prudential Carolinas Realty, we have two Relocation Centers fully staffed to help you. We know how emotional relocation can be. Call us today. The move may not seem as familiar as your own backyard, but we can make you feel more at home with it.

Nancy Harner, Dianne Powell
Relocation Directors

Raleigh Relocation Center
1-919-847-7599
1-800-334-8161

Durham Relocation Center
1-919-383-4663
1-800-438-0012

To Insiders, this is known as Zack Bacon's company. The founder of the company, he remains a key manager in the firm that was acquired by the Prudential Insurance Company. Bacon made many of the early sales with IBM when it moved to RTP and when other corporations came to this area in the late 1960s, and he has been active in real estate and the real estate community ever since. With 32 offices in North and South Carolina, the company is now the largest independently owned and operated real estate company in the Carolinas, and the 15th largest in the country. A leader in financial services, this company is the first to offer in-house mortgage services. It also operates a real estate school and operates the largest relocation department in the area.

RE/MAX PROPERTY ASSOCIATES
1140 Kildaire Farm Rd., Cary	469-4700
811 Spring Forest Rd.	872-0000
5401 Six Forks Rd.	781-5552

If you are looking for experienced agents who really know the area, look here.

RE/MAX PROPERTY CENTER
534 Village Ct., Garner	779-2141

This five-year-old affiliate of the national franchise specializes in Wake and Johnston counties.

SIMPSON AND UNDERWOOD
3700 Computer Dr.	782-6641

Don't be fooled by the single address. Simpson and Underwood is one of the better known names in Raleigh and Cary real estate. The company is well connected to old Raleigh and knows that market. It has gained a reputation for repre-

senting many of the better homes. It's not uncommon to see in its Sunday listings a Hayes-Barton or North Ridge address, prices in the $600,000 range, or the "country estate" where price is not even mentioned.

York Residential

801 Oberlin Rd.
(headquarters and relocation)   821-7177
311 Oberlin Rd.   832-8881
8312 Creedmoor Rd.   846-7100
4400 Falls of the Neuse Rd.   876-5320
1127 Kildaire Farm Rd., Cary   467-1811

This company was established in 1984 as a division of the York companies, a business name that has been in the Triangle building and development market since 1915. It has enjoyed a phenomenal growth rate and continues to expand. It merged in 1988 with The Real Estate Center of Cary, adding to its clout in the western Wake County and Cary market. Division president Ed Willer is a former Board of Realtors president, Realtor of the Year, and also author of one of the best preparatory books for the state licensing exam. He knows the business and puts an emphasis on quality service and customer satisfaction. His sales staff numbers over 100, making the company one of the largest in the Raleigh-Cary market. As the residential arm of the York companies that include commercial brokerage, property management and construction, it offers relocating companies a full range of real estate services.

Durham

For more information on these and other companies, contact the **Durham Board of Realtors** at 3200 Croasdaile Dr.; phone 383-2117. The MLS book covers Durham, Chapel Hill, and even Raleigh area listings. Many of these real estate agents show houses throughout the Triangle, but they may concentrate their expertise on the Durham area.

Century 21

These offices are independently owned affiliates of Century 21:

Haywood Davis Realtors
1011 Broad St.   286-2121
Park West Realty
N.C. Hwy. 54   351-5752
RTA Associates
2515 N.C. Hwy. 54   544-3761

The Chesson Group

21 W. Colony Place, Suite 250   493-0778

Chesson has been handling residential sales for over 20 years and recently added a commercial division to the business. With 30 agents, Chesson can help you find or sell a home, lot or investment property in Durham or Chapel Hill. See also its listing in our section on "Relocation Services."

Darst Realty

3105 Guess Rd.   471-0574

For almost 20 years, owner Glenn A. Darst's firm has specialized in residential, commercial, land and farm sales. Darst's agents are available to help you find properties in Durham, Orange and Person counties.

DISTINCTIVE PROPERTIES

605 Jackson St.   688-9314

Owners Eugene and Signe Brown love historic homes. So it's no surprise that, since 1980, their company has specialized in listing and selling "homes of character," those historic residences in Trinity Park and other older Durham neighborhoods. In fact, the office is located in a renovated 1915 frame house at the corner of Gregson and Jackson streets. If you're looking for an older in-town home, their brokers will be happy to help you.

FONVILLE MORISEY REALTY

1304 N.C. Hwy. 54   493-4434
Chapel Hill Office   942-6000
518 S. Duke St.   688-1341

This Raleigh-based real estate giant now has an ever-growing number of agents to help you find or sell new or old residential properties in Durham, Research Triangle Park, Chapel Hill and also in Chatham County. For more information on the company, see its listing under "Raleigh Realtors."

GRIFFIN ASSOCIATES

3310 Croasdaile Dr.   383-2595

Owner Kim Griffin and five experienced agents can help you find residential, commercial or rental properties in Durham and Chapel Hill. Their property management specialist can even find you a furnished apartment or townhome while you're looking for a permanent residence. Griffin has been in the business for over 15 years.

HOWARD PERRY AND WALSTON/ BETTER HOMES AND GARDENS

5285 N. Roxboro Rd.   479-1020
3518 Westgate Dr.   490-9000

This Raleigh-based real estate giant merged in 1988 with Durham's Allenton Realty, making it the largest real estate outfit in the Triangle (see "Raleigh Realtors" in this section for details).

MARIE AUSTIN REALTY

1204 Broad St.   286-5611

In business nearly 30 years, Marie Austin and her 10 agents primarily handle residential property in Durham city and county and in Orange County.

JON PARKER/COLDWELL BANKER REAL ESTATE

624 1/2 Ninth St.   286-1455

This locally owned Durham-based office specializes in residential resale. It also sells properties in several new subdivisions in Durham and Orange Counties. Jon Parker and his associates manage some rental property as well.

THE PRUDENTIAL CAROLINAS REALTY

701 Morreene Rd.   *383-4663*
      1-800-438-0012

This Durham-based firm handles residential and commercial properties in Durham and Chapel Hill. It offers relocation assistance as well as in-house mortgage services. (See "Raleigh Realtors" for more details.)

SOUTHLAND ASSOCIATES

3104 Croasdaile Dr.   *382-2000*
Northgate Mall   *286-6065*

Established in 1903, Southland has 20+ agents and offers complete real estate services, including residential and commercial sales, leasing and property management. The firm has developed a number of single-family neighborhoods in Durham, including Marydell, American Village, Greyson's Green, Stephen's Wood, Vantage Point and Colony Woods East.

TOMS LEAMING COIE REALTY

2716 Chapel Hill Rd.   *493-8555*

This company specializes in residential real estate, but it also handles some commercial properties. Agents work in both Durham and Orange Counties.

Chapel Hill

For more information on these and other firms, contact the **Chapel Hill Board of Realtors**, 501

W. Franklin St., Chapel Hill, NC 27516; phone 929-4032. The MLS book contains listings for the whole Triangle area, and many Chapel Hill agents show property in Durham, too.

EUNICE BROCK & ASSOCIATES

311 W. Rosemary St.   *933-8500*

Eunice Brock opened her own firm five years ago; she has over 25 years' experience in the local market. Her firm has five other agents, all interested in providing personal service to buyers and sellers.

CHAPEL HILL REALTY

151 E. Rosemary St.   *942-4147*

Since 1954, Chapel Hill Realty has specialized in residential sales. George Meyer and the office's agents are available to assist you in locating a single-family home, townhome or condominium in Chapel Hill as well as other areas of Orange and Chatham Counties. This firm also handles rentals, including furnished apartments, duplexes and homes.

COLDWELL BANKER/VERMILYA WAUD HOUSE HUNTERS REALTY

501 W. Franklin St.   *942-4482*

This agency specializes in residential sales in Chapel Hill and Durham and provides people moving to the area extensive information about their new community and assistance with their move. Relocation Director Marjorie Wiegerink tries to match the buyer's needs with the right broker. The agency has five partners/owners and 17 agents.

FONVILLE MORISEY REALTY

Chapel Hill Office   942-6000
1304 N.C. Hwy. 54   493-6481

This Raleigh-based real estate giant has an ever-growing number of agents handling residential and commercial properties in Durham and Chapel Hill. (See "Durham and Raleigh Realtors and Relocation Services" in this section.)

FRANKLIN STREET REALTY

1720 E. Franklin St.   929-7174

This company is comprised of 13 experiened agents knowledgeable in the Chapel Hill/Carrboro market. It is conveniently located at the corner of Franklin Street and Eastgate Shopping Center, and clients can expect that "hometown" difference with this agency.

THE HOME TEAM

1506 E. Franklin St.   967-6363

The Home Team opened in late 1989 and has 12 experienced agents, all graduates of the Realtor's Institute (GRI) and Certified Residential Specialists (CRS). The Home Team is the only Chapel Hill agency with all its members having earned this professional designation. They can help you with all your residential real estate needs.

HOWARD PERRY AND WALSTON/ BETTER HOMES AND GARDENS

1600 E. Franklin St.   967-9234
Chapel Hill
110 Churton St.   732-6101
Hillsborough

This Raleigh-based real estate giant is one of the largest real-estate outfits in the Triangle today. The Chapel Hill office (with 40+ agents) and Hillsborough office handle both residential and commercial real estate sales. In Chapel Hill, HPW markets new homes in Wexford, Chesley and Herndon Woods, among other neighborhoods. (See "Raleigh Realtors" in this section for more information.)

THE PRUDENTIAL CAROLINAS REALTY

1407 E. Franklin St.   929-2186
                                           800-525-1750

This affiliate office of the national Prudential company is managed by longtime Chapel Hill Realtor A.C. Robbins, who was North Carolina's Realtor of the Year for 1989. The office has 23 agents, and specializes in residential re-sales and property in all price ranges. It also offers relocation services.

RE/MAX

1506 E. Franklin St.   406-9510
                             406-9551/406-9556

The agents of this affiliate of the national Re/Max office are experienced in both the Chapel Hill and the Durham markets. They list and sell residential property and lots for new construction.

TRIPOINTE PROPERTIES

1129 Weaver Dairy Rd.   929-7100
                                           800-752-5006

This firm is located in the Timberlyne shopping center at the north end of town. There are 14 agents in the office, handling a lot of residential resales and new developments, including Fox Hill Farm, Woodland Park and other country properties in Orange and Durham Counties.

WEAVER STREET REALTY
116 E. Main St., Carrboro   *929-5658*

Weaver Street founder Gary Phillips and his partners and associates believe that ecologically sound land development also makes good business sense. In assessing a tract of land, they consider how to preserve fragile plant and wildlife habitats, protect watersheds and provide common open space. (For information on their Morgan Glen development, see **CHAPEL HILL NEIGHBORHOODS.**) Weaver Street handles a variety of residential and commercial properties, but it specializes in home and land sales in western Orange, southern Alamance and northern Chatham Counties. The other branch of the company, Weaver Street Auction Company, also handles estate sales. And you won't want to miss some of the special event auctions held throughout the year.

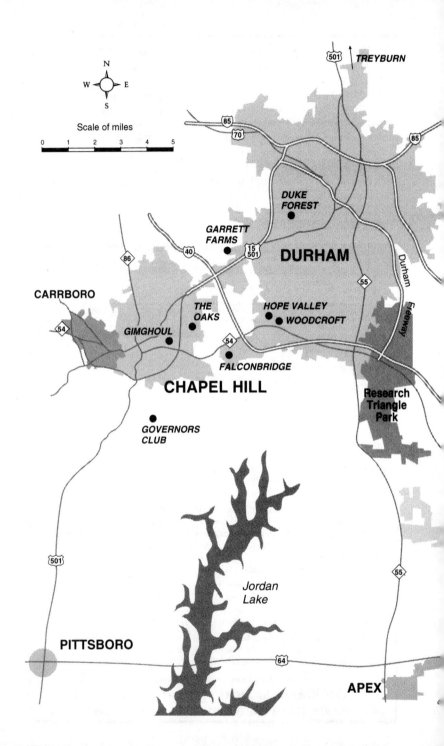

Triangle Neighborhoods

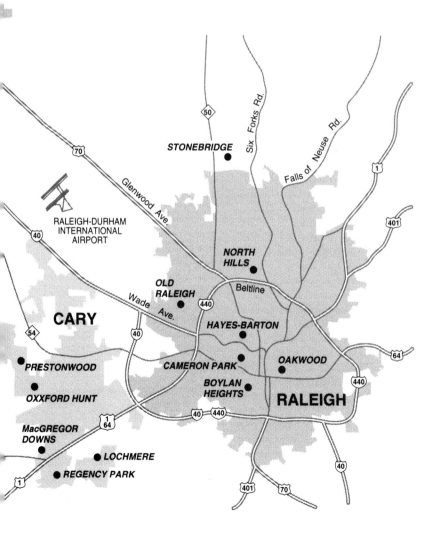

Builders

Raleigh and Cary

The following is a guide to Triangle builders. It is useful for three reasons: one, if you're shopping for a house, you may want to know who built it and most of those listed here are known in the Triangle community, according to one experienced Insider, as "tip top"; two, there are some brave souls who want to build their own home and the builders here are a good place to start; and, three, if you are planning to remodel your existing home, some of the people in our Guide can help—if not with the work, then in finding the tradespeople to do the work.

Another good way to get a list of builders is to call the Home Builders Association of Raleigh-Wake County, 6510 Chapel Hill Rd., 233-2033. In Durham or Chapel Hill, the address is 20 West Colony Place, Suite180, Durham, NC 27705 and the phone number is 493-8899. There are over 400 builders in its membership, and for the asking, Association officials will refer a short list of builders to you depending on location, type of house you want to build, and price range.

Also, you might want to ask if the builder subscribes to Home Owners Warranty Corp (HOW). HOW members carry insurance on their work against major structural defects. Some of the builders in our Guide work primarily on their own projects. Raleigh and Cary builders are combined into one group.

ANDERSON HOMES
4000 Westchase Blvd.   *828-6000*

This company is a real success story, founded by David Servoss in 1980 as a one-man operation and aiming its products at first-time home buyers. The company has built about 2,000 houses since then. An Anderson single-family home will cost between $65,000 and $125,000 and townhouses range from $50,000 to $80,000. It has built in Berkshire Downs on Perry Creek Road in north Raleigh and in Wheeler Park off Lake Wheeler Road south of the city. Its lower-priced new homes often feature amenities such as master suites that are usually found in more expensive houses.

BENCHMARK HOMES
6600 Six Forks Rd.   *847-8924*

Directed by Paul Roseman, Benchmark Homes has a reputation for building custom and specialty homes, perhaps 20 to 30 a year, many in north Raleigh. The houses range in price from $140,000 to $500,000, and Benchmark has been a winner more than once in the annual Parade of Homes. Says one builder of Roseman, "He does a first-rate job."

LACY W. BUFFALOE BUILDERS
5902 Fayetteville Rd.   *779-3310*

Lacy Buffaloe has been in the home-building business for 25 years, putting up homes mostly in southwest and southeast Raleigh, but also in north Raleigh. He builds about 80 homes a year and they sell in the $125,000 to $250,000 range. He has built in MacGregor Downs and more recently in Enchanted Oaks and Nottingham Forest. He caters to the experienced home buyer who knows what he or she wants, such as hardwood floors, raised-panel cabinets, Jacuzzi tubs, etc. As he says, his clients "are willing to pay for what they want."

J.H. CARTER BUILDER
4920 Windy Hill Dr.   *878-6660*

Harold Carter came out of the mortgage banking business and began building homes in 1972. Ninety-five percent of his newest houses have been located within the Beltline, but he has built throughout Wake County. He builds traditional, "nice-looking homes," says a fellow builder, about 16 a year, and few sell for under $200,000. Examples of his custom and speculative houses can be found in the neighborhood where he lives, behind the Blenheim community off Blue Ridge Road.

CAVINESS AND SONS, INC.
715 W. Johnson St.   *833-2711*

As the name suggests, this is a second-generation family of builders. They're noted in Raleigh as builders who will take on the toughest jobs, whether it's restoration work or a difficult custom design where money is not going to be a problem. For example, this firm contracted to restore one of the outbuildings at the historic Joel Lane House.

CREECH CONSTRUCTION CO.
6810 Davis Cr.   *781-2929*

David Creech is a second-generation builder in a company that has been working the Triangle market since 1954. His homes usually are large, around the $185,000 to $250,000 price range, and traditional in style. He has built in developments such as Picardy Pointe in Cary and Shepherd's Vineyard in Apex.

JOHN CROSLAND CO.
A DIVISION OF CENTEX HOMES
3733 National Dr.   *781-1952*

John Crosland Company was started 55 years ago in Charlotte and arrived in the Triangle in 1984. Centex Homes, the nation's largest builder of single-family homes, acquired Crosland in 1987. Crosland builds over 400 homes annually in the Triangle. The general style is transitional, with home starting around $110,000. Crosland neighborhoods are in Cary, North Raleigh, Durham and Knightdale. Crosland, among the most popular builders in the Triangle, was the largest builder in 1992 and 1993.

DECK HOUSE, INC.
2001 Weston Pkwy.   *677-0066*
Cary

This Massachusetts-based company offers assistance in designing a post-and-beam wooden house. It provides the design and supplies; a professional builder does the construction. This company has been in the Triangle for over twenty years; the Cary office opened in 1986. The office itself is a model of the attractive construction concept, and Deck House builds about 10 models a year in the Triangle.

FORTIS HOMES
2700 Wycliff Rd.   782-4790

Fortis, once a subsidiary of the giant Daniel Construction Company of South Carolina, develops, builds and markets its own properties. It arrived in the Triangle in 1977, and this area has become one of its strongest markets. Fortis Homes includes a 10-year warranty and aims at first-time buyers. A good example of its work is Edgehill Farms in Cary where units, from condominiums to single-family houses, began selling between $65,000 to over $100,000. It also has built in The Forest, Brookgreen in Cary and Gralyn in Durham.

HOUSEMAN BUILDERS
5882 Farrington Rd.   872-4444

Michael Houseman operates Concept II, a real estate company and, in 1985, started Houseman Builders. He builds houses that range in price from $80,000 to $200,000, mostly in north Raleigh and developments such as Banbury Woods and Deer Chase. He offers a number of floor plans that vary in style, or he will build to the customer's specifications.

M/I HOMES
4020 Westchase Blvd.   828-1106
Suite 190

M/I, based in Columbus, Ohio, has been in the Triangle since 1987, and has built about 200 homes annually in the Triangle, so it's one of the big players here. The company is careful to build popular models and because of its volume, offers a good house for the money. M/I keeps up with consumer trends and design, so look for open spaces and interesting window designs. Prices range from $90,000 to $350,000. For a sample of its work, check out M/I homes at McArthur Park in Cary or Country Club Downs in Wake Forest.

MPG BUILDERS
2805 Prather   556-1946
Wake Forest

Mike Gilewicz of MPG Builders is a residential and commercial builder based in Wake Forest. The business is family-owned and Mike and Peggy pride themselves in truly serving their clients. They offer affordable quality in custom-built homes and additions, as well as their line of Eagle's Nest Home designs. The Triangle is an exciting place for them to work, and they welcome a chance to talk to anyone interested in building in the area.

PARAMOUNT HOMES
161 W. Chatham St.   460-1889
Cary

Paramount Homes developed Cobblestone and Autumn Hill subdivisions in Raleigh; it is presently building in Prestonwood in Cary and Treyburn in Durham, including the "Hope Plantation" American Wood Council house. Paramount's in-house interior designer is available to assist clients with their custom design and decorating needs.

Staff photo.

The rampant growth in Cary has produced many lovely new neighborhoods.

THE PARKER GROUP

206 N. West St.   *469-5188*
Cary

Lee Parker, Sr., and his son, Lee Parker, Jr., head up this residential construction company. They are known to be custom, quality builders specializing in upscale houses that usually are priced around $180,000 and go up. Current Cary projects include homes in Royal Oaks and Ferren Forest but the company also builds in the Fuquay-Varina area.

PULTE HOMES CORP.

401 Harrison Oaks Blvd.   *677-0122*
Cary

Pulte is one of the nation's largest single-family home builders, based in Bloomfield, Michigan. It arrived in the Triangle in 1986 and has quickly established itself as a successful builder and marketer for its houses. They generally sell in the $140,000 price range, but you will find $400,000 Pulte homes, too. Pulte is one of the prime builders in Durham's Hope Valley Farms, as well as Raleigh's Emerald Chase and Cary's Wellington Park PUD. It has built over 1,200 homes since 1986 and uses its size to carefully research the market for what buyers want. While homes may stick to a traditional look outside, look for more light, bigger closets and master-suite bedrooms and baths.

EDD K. ROBERTS

3924 Browning Pl.   *782-1933*

It's worth a visit to Edd Roberts' office just to see his trophies of big game. Perhaps one of the best known of Raleigh's builders and developers, Roberts, a big man who favors a big beard and cowboy boots, was involved in the boom of north Raleigh growth of the early '70s when he developed North Haven in 1971, Raintree in 1972 and Springdale Gardens in 1976. One of his projects is the far north subdivision, Hawthorne, which features large common areas and deep back yards. Cluster homes in the project go for $140,000, and the larger individual houses sell for $225,000.

ROBUCK HOMES

5800 Faringdon Pl.   *876-9200*

Frank Robuck, Jr., is a third-generation builder and a fourth, Gerri, is carrying on the tradition that began in 1926. During the past two decades, Robuck's company has become one of the Triangle's most successful builders, involved in much of the growth in north Raleigh and beyond, including Apex and Durham. He was Builder of the Year in 1991. More recently, he has teamed with the successful real estate firm of Fonville Morisey in both developing, building and selling residential projects. Crosswinds, off Strickland Road in north Raleigh, is an example of Robuck's work; prices start around $152,000 for homes with three to four bedrooms.

SPARROW RESIDENTIAL INC.

3815 Hillsborough St.   *833-7341*

President Ray Sparrow is probably better known than his company since he has served several terms in the General Assembly as one of Wake County's representatives. Long active in the building business, Sparrow builds small commercial buildings as well as residential projects. He helped lead the way in the '70s toward more energy-efficient homes and also has encouraged area home builders in low-cost housing projects.

STUART HOME CORP.
1140 Kildaire Farm Rd.   *481-2005*
Cary

Begun in 1988, Stuart Home Corp. is a Triangle-wide builder emphasizing Southern Traditional and Transitional design, as well as the Southern Low Country design. Richard Stuart provides constant job supervision to minimize errors, assures strict adherence to completion schedules and sets a standard of quality workmanship in all of his homes. His company is enjoying good success in working with the out-of-town buyer on pre-sales as well as existing inventory, and he benefits from a strong referral base of satisfied customers.

SUNSTAR HOMES
1 Copley Pkwy.   *469-1316*
Morrisville

This company began operating in the Triangle in the 1980s and quickly made a name for itself among real estate agents because its homes continued to sell when the market slowed. Sunstar's emphasis is on quality-control, and David Schmidt, President, says the company created a checklist of 921 items that must be satisfied before the house is turned over to the customer. The company has built homes in Huntington as well as Lochmere.

ROBERT D. SWAIN CO.
125 Edinburgh South   *469-8674*
Cary

Robbie Swain came to the building business via an unusual route—mortgage banking. He learned many lessons there while becoming familiar with the Triangle real estate market, one of which was that the good builders survived hard times. He started his own company in 1983, and builds mostly homes or condominiums in planned communities such as Lockridge. He emphasizes "good management" in explaining his company's success and keeps a close watch himself on projects. Over 75 percent of his project managers are college graduates, and his goal is to stay within the Triangle.

WESTMINSTER HOMES
401 Harrison Oaks Blvd.   *677-0070*
Cary

This company is a subsidiary of the lumber giant, Weyerhauser, and has been building homes for a number of years in the Triangle. The company builds homes for first-time home buyers and offers good prices, some starting in the $80,000 range.

WILLIAMS REALTY & BUILDING CO.
3111 Glenwood Ave.   *781-7107*

John C. Williams, in business since 1953, is considered by some of the competition to be the dean of the local home-building industry with a reputation for erecting some of the Triangle's finest houses. As a member of one of Raleigh's old families himself, he has built many homes that cater to the Country

Club crowd; indeed, he built much of the new Carolina Country Club. One of the city's most exclusive neighborhoods, Williamsborough, was his project. Homes there today sell for $500,000 or more. He built the new brick wall around St. Mary's College. Given his standards, the prices on his new houses reflect the attention to detail.

Chapel Hill and Durham

If you are planning to build a home in Chapel Hill or Durham, check first with the **Home Builders Association of Durham & Chapel Hill** (493-8899). The folks there can provide you with a list of reputable builders as well as answer questions and provide information on the market.

CIMARRON HOMES
20 W. Colony Pl., Suite 120   493-0672
Durham
In the past ten years, Cimarron Homes has earned a solid reputation as a builder that combines experience with the efficiency of advanced computer technology to bring you a home that is attractive, well-designed and affordable. Cimarron prides itself on home design that blends handsome, traditional exteriors with exciting contemporary floor plans, and combines the concepts of space, light, function and energy efficiency with environmentally sound building practices. Past efforts have won high acclaim for the company and its founder, Craig Morrison, includ-

ing 1990 and 1991 Triangle "J" outstanding development awards, the 1990 Builder's Choice award by *Builder Magazine*, and 1990 and 1991 Aurora awards for best affordable housing. Cimarron's newest developments include Buckwater Creek, Crystal Oaks, Fieldstone, Five Oaks-Lakeside, Hidden Hollow, Lenox, Stratton Park, Treyburn, Wingbrook, Woodlake-Candlewood and Woodlake-Dunmore.

CLARIS BUILDING COMPANY
P.O. Box 248   942-7594
Carrboro, NC 27510
Builder Woody Claris specializes in custom-built homes. He and his crews pride themselves on their quality workmanship and their efforts to ensure the satisfaction of their clients. Claris is presently building in The Reserve, Bell Arbor and various other privately owned sites in Orange County.

CYN-MAR DESIGNS, INC.
1408 Christian Ave.   383-9026
Durham
Cyn-Mar has been in the Durham area market for 8 years providing custom-built homes for satisfied customers. In fact, the company attributes much of its success to referrals they have received from those same satisfied customers—a real testimony to the quality of service the company provides. Cyn-Mar is currently building in Hardscrabble Plantation in Hillsborough, Fern Creek and Old Hope Creek in Chapel Hill and Briardale in Durham.

DUFFY REALTY & BUILDING CO.
P.O. Box 15265   471-9707
Durham, NC 27704

Dennis Duffy became owner and president of this 35-year-old family business about five years ago. Always striving for customer satisfaction, the company's success is evident in the repeat business it does. Duffy is currently building in Treyburn, Hardscrabble Plantation, Grand Oak Estates, Pleasant Green Woods, Governors Club, Red Mountain and other privately owned sites in northern Durham County. If you would like to see a sample of its work, the company will soon be starting homes in the Mill Creek subdivision.

ISENHOUR ENTERPRISES, INC.
1506 E. Franklin Street   932-2821
Chapel Hill

If you want to know what to expect from this established design-and-construction firm, just take a look at the quality of The Courtyard shops or the homes at Glenmere and Southbridge on Culbreth School Road. IE homes can be contemporary or traditional. They feature cathedral ceilings, arches, special tile treatments, custom lights, hardwood floors and hand-crafted details like custom mantles and stair railings. You can buy a ready-built home, choose an in-house design or ask for a custom-designed home to meet your own particular needs.

L.E. MEYERS BUILDERS
4528 Hillsborough Rd.   383-1883
Durham

Since 1982, Leon Meyers has been building quality customized homes in Durham and Orange Counties. He'll build from one of your plans or he'll design a plan tailor-made to suit your needs. His homes range from the traditional to the contemporary, and can include both conventional and passive solar heating systems. Meyers also does renovations and additions.

PULLEY & ADAIR CUSTOM BUILDERS
209 Providence Rd.   493-8093
Chapel Hill

This company, owned and operated by Brad Pulley and Mike Adair, is presently building in Oxford Hills, The Oaks, North Haven and Governors Club. Pulley & Adair builds custom homes and has been in business about six years.

BRYANT ROBERTS CONSTRUCTION CO.
411 Andrews Rd., Ofc. 110   383-8518
Durham

Bryant Roberts has been building custom homes in the Durham area for over 22 years. You can see samples of the company's quality workmanship in Chapel Hill developments of Spring Crest and Wexford, and in Durham in Croasdaile, American Village, Sunningdale, Hope Valley Farms, Quail Ridge, Bluffs of Eno and Garrett Farms among others.

SPACE BUILDERS OF CARRBORO
112 E. Main St.   929-7072
Carrboro

This design and construction firm emphasizes custom-designed, energy-efficient homes, many with passive solar features. Space Builders is noted for attention to details and the incorporation of antique, salvaged or hand-crafted doors and trim. As an employee-owned business, the workers have a vested interest in quality construction.

Landscapers

Raleigh and Cary

Some may object to our title, landscaper, but it serves to catch a number of services, including people who can design your yard or the greenery inside.

AMSTERDAM LANDSCAPING
402 Carolina Ave.   *851-4211*

This company's owner, Robert Mulder, has been in business since 1979 and announced in 1987 that he wasn't going to use "standard" pesticides anymore in his landscape work. He says he was worried about his health as well as that of his clients and their pets. Now, he uses what he calls "integrated pest management" that uses traditional practices in keeping the yard and landscape "well-groomed and healthful."

TOM HUNTER
4601 Lake Boone Tr.   *881-0360*

Tom Hunter is a landscape architect who began life as a New York advertising executive, then returned to school at NCSU. He practiced as a partner in one of the city's better-known firms and in 1990 went solo so he could get his hands back in the dirt and into the work he enjoys. Go by his house in Cameron Park to see a sample of his work.

LIBERTY LANDSCAPING
1610 1/2 Old Louisburg Rd.   *833-1128*

Liberty's Mike Fultz, a former *Spectator* columnist, has been in business since 1986 and maintains a staff of 11. The company does no individual homes, and 75 percent of the work is maintenance for commercial centers such as the Triangle Business Center near RDU Airport.

MAC NEWSOM
1912 Stone St.   *839-1188*

Newsom, a former garden columnist for *The Spectator*, does a lot of work with individual home owners. Call him for a consultation appointment.

PATON-ZUCCHINO AND ASSOCIATES
17 Glenwood Ave.   *834-8620*

This group of about 12 landscape architects and staff works very little on individual homes unless they are part of a larger project such as Oxford Park near Raleigh's Five Points. They have done work in Regency Park and the Brookstone PUD.

PLANTS BY GRANT
8109 Ebenezer Church Rd.   *787-0965*

Plants by Grant specializes in the design, sale, leasing and maintenance of interior foliage for commercial spaces. The company also installs Christmas decorations, has a full-service floral division and a gift basket company. Plants by Grant is the largest commercial plant company in North Carolina. Offices are located in Raleigh and Greenville and it does work throughout the

Triangle and eastern North Carolina.

Chapel Hill and Durham

GREENVISION
Pittsboro   *542-4038*

Greenvision is located in Pittsboro and does work throughout the Triangle area. The company provides complete commercial and residential landscaping services.

STONELEDGE LANDSCAPES
Chapel Hill   *942-7180*

Owner Kurt Mattocks is a graduate of NCSU's landscape horticulture program. He uses computer-enhanced design to help plan your landscape and garden, and he will construct retaining walls, patios, walks and irrigation systems, and put in garden lighting.

Interior Design

Now that you've got the outside looking great, you can use the guide below to work on the interior. The list is short, but if these people can't help you, you're just going to have to put up with having an ugly house. By any account, this group contains some of the Triangle's really beautiful people.

Raleigh and Cary

RICHARD BLACK INTERIORS
811 Mordecai Dr.   *828-7700*

Black started his own company around 1982, although he's been in the business much longer.

His office is a restored home near Mordecai Park, and he has seen his clientele grow beyond Raleigh to points as far south as Florida; he's even bringing good taste to Dallas, Texas. No job is too small, he says. "We're just tickled to death for them to come by...as long as they get an appointment first." Black specializes in restoration projects.

HERB HIGHSMITH INTERIORS
107 Glenwood Ave.   *832-6275*

Ask five Raleigh women to draw up a list of top interior designers and Herb Highsmith's name will be on each list. He has many residential customers, and his business is not limited to the Triangle area. He is a veteran who has been in the interior design business for over a decade. Where some designers go overboard, Highsmith is known for keeping his good taste in bounds, which helps explain why he's popular with conservative Raleigh home owners.

LINCOLN AND COMPANY CERAMIC TILE & MARBLE
266-0526

A new business established six years ago in Raleigh, Lincoln and Company is owned by Jim Lincoln, who grew up in the Raleigh area but learned much of his trade from established New York tile and marble layers while living in Manhattan. He does new construction as well as repairs. He has worked with experienced interior designers in the Triangle area. One of his finest examples of work is the all-marble entrance and reception area of Cutter Laboratories in Clayton.

NATIONAL ART INTERIORS

530 Hillsborough St.   *833-9717*

This is the elder statesman of Raleigh interior designers, having started in October 1944. Located on the corner of Hillsborough Street and Glenwood Avenue, this firm is also is one of Raleigh's best-known furniture galleries, with the emphasis on quality and style rather than size of showroom. It tends to be "classic" in its style, and two notable projects, Smedes Hall at Saint Mary's College and First Citizens Bank in New Bern, reflect the company's taste. Much of its work has been for long-time Triangle residents, and it also is a dealer for such lines as Baker, Knoll and Herman Miller.

PERRY AND PLUMMER INTERIORS, INC.

118 St. Mary's St.   821-3101

This is one of the larger designer firms, and both Perry and Plummer are members of the American Society of Interior Designers, with three national awards for their work. They currently have more commercial work than residential, including clients such as advertising agency McKinney Silver and Realtors Howard Perry and Walston. Rodney Perry has been active in the Raleigh market since 1968 and the firm started in 1977. The company also maintains an office in Wilmington, N.C. Professional is the password at this firm.

STEWART WOODARD GALLERIES

412 W. Jones St.   821-7122

Stewart Woodard Galleries not only is one of the Triangle's finer furniture stores, it also offers residential and commercial interior design. Woodard's patron and partner, Alice Eure, is well connected to the North Carolina business establishment through her late husband's (Thad Eure, Jr.) restaurant business (Angus Barn, 42nd St. Oyster Bar) and her father-in-law, former Secretary of State Thad Eure. A tour through the galleries, which opened in the late 70s, will give you a sampler of Woodard's work.

WORKSPACE

108 1/2 E. Hargett St.   821-0944

Workspace is an architectural firm that has made several splashes in the past few years for its commercial interior design work. Its driving force is Norma Burns, who also served two terms on the Raleigh City Council, one of which while she commuted to Harvard University on a design fellowship. She has been active in downtown restoration projects, notably Artspace.

Chapel Hill and Durham

MINTA BELL INTERIOR DESIGN

Eastgate Shopping Center
Chapel Hill   933-9800

Minta Bell works with architects and developers on designing interior spaces as well as with residents on designing the furnishings and finishes for those spaces. She's done everything from individual homes, apartments and condominiums to model homes, whole condominium complexes, and clubhouses, and has over 30 years of experience. Minta Bell is located at Eastgate Shopping Center, on U.S. Hwy. 15-501 Bypass.

CLAUDE M. MAY

1101 West Main Street
Durham   682-9348

The firm of Claude M. May, with Dan Addison, ASID, as its principal designer, has decorated many of Durham's finest homes. It offers comprehensive design and decorating services for its clientele.

Staff photo.

*North Carolina Eye and Ear Hospital is a leading
private eye, ear, nose and throat hospital in Durham.*

Inside
Hospitals and Medical Care

Hospitals

One ingredient to the success of the Research Triangle is the availability of high-quality medical research and teaching facilities such as Duke University Medical Center in Durham and N.C. Memorial Hospital in Chapel Hill. Together with first-rate community hospitals such as Durham Regional Medical Center, Wake Medical Center, and Rex Hospital, Triangle residents have access to some of the finest medical care in the country.

Here's a guide to the basic services and special facilities available at each hospital located in Raleigh, Durham and Chapel Hill. We'll also tell you a little about some of the celebrated diet and fitness centers located in Durham, the Diet Capital of the World.

Raleigh and Cary

Raleigh and Cary residents have access to three general hospitals and three specialty hospitals, not to mention numerous clinics. The focus here will be on the area's hospitals; you may want to check the city section of medical care, too. The hospitals here are all located in Raleigh, although Wake Medical Center is the hub for a county-wide network that includes four addition sites. The newest of these, Western Wake Medical Center in Cary, opened in 1992. The biggest hospital close to Cary is Rex and many residents go there with emergencies, although it is usually the attending physician who decides which hospital he or she will use for operations or other care. All the hospitals are listed alphabetically.

CHARTER NORTHRIDGE
400 Newton Rd.   *847-0008*

This is a for-profit hospital that specializes in the treatment of alcohol and drug abuse for adults and adolescents. It has 85 beds, is located in north Raleigh and also has outpatient programs. Its staff provides assessment, detoxification, specialized treatment for adolescents separate from adults, day and evening programs, individual and group therapy, and family counseling. It also provides counseling for businesses and industries that are concerned about drug abusers in the workplace.

DOROTHEA DIX
820 S. Boylan Ave.   *733-5540*

Dorothea Dix was a crusading Yankee who came South and helped start the state's first programs for the mentally ill. In 1856, the state opened its first hospital for the mentally ill and it was named after the persistent Dorothea Dix.

Today, the hospital occupies several hundred acres of rolling countryside southwest of downtown Raleigh, surrounded by highways and the Beltline, the new Farmers' Market and neighborhoods. Patients at the hospital at one time helped make the institution self-supporting by farming its fields and meadows, which are now coveted by an expanding NCSU and the state Department of Agriculture.

Dix Hospital has seen its patient load dwindle as treatment of the mentally ill in general has de-emphasized institutionalization. With 682 beds, the hospital remains one of the state's largest psychiatric hospitals for adults and adolescents, and it is accredited by the Joint Commission on Accredited Hospitals. It is the largest hospital in Raleigh. It has a full hospital staff with surgery and radiology units and a special child psychiatric outpatient clinic, adolescent education program and adolescent inpatient services.

It often is the subject of news reports because it also provides forensic services and keeps the violent mentally ill until they are able to stand trial. It receives other patients who are referred by the courts for one reason or another. Because it is a state hospital, it also accepts indigent patients and has a policy of billing patients according to their ability to pay.

HOLLY HILL HOSPITAL
3019 Falstaff Rd.   *250-7000*

This is a for-profit psychiatric hospital that was founded here in 1978 and is an affiliate of the giant Hospital Corporation of America. Located off New Bern Avenue near Wake Medical Center, Holly Hill now has 108 beds and offers programs for adults, adolescents, younger children and the elderly. It offers short-term and intermediate care with evaluation and screening service and 24-hour admissions.

It has day programs for both adolescents and adults and lists about 40 local psychiatrists as members of its medical staff. Treatment may include group or individual therapy; family and marriage therapy also is available. It dedicates 29 of its "units" for patients who are 55 years or older, and 25 beds in a separate unit are for young people between 13 and 18. The hospital also operates a speakers' bureau for clubs and organizations interested in learning more about mental illness and its treatment.

RALEIGH COMMUNITY HOSPITAL
3400 Wake Forest Rd.   *954-3000*

Raleigh Community Hospital (RCH) opened its doors in 1978 and has grown with the city's northern growth. It is conveniently located a block north from the Beltline exit onto Wake Forest Road. It is an affiliate of the for-profit Hospital Corporation of America, which owns 82 acute-care hospitals worldwide.

RCH has 230 private and semi-private beds, of which 16 are intensive care beds. It offers general medical and surgical services, adding in 1992 a childbirth center. RCH maintains an emergency room 24 hours a day with a full-time Emergency Medicine Physician.

Other services include radiology, surgery, same-day surgery, cardiac stress testing, pathology, pharmacy, physical therapy, CT and MRI scanners and respiratory therapy. It also has an outpatient program for sports medicine and physical therapy, a sleep study center and psychiatric unit. The staff includes more than 400 area physicians, and the hospital is especially proud of its referral service for its staff physicians.

Several doctors' office buildings are nearby, including a diabetes treatment center. When it

opened, RCH made a splash when it announced that it would serve its patients wine with meals. To many teetotaling Southerners, that was uptown, indeed. The hospital continues to have a relaxed air about it. Visiting hours for family members are generous, between 11 a.m. and 8:30 p.m. Its information packet is the best of the three general hospitals, which probably reflects its for-profit sales philosophy.

REX HOSPITAL
4420 Lake Boone Tr.   *783-3100*

Rex is the city's oldest hospital, and its board of directors always has included the names of Raleigh's power elite. So, it's more than a city hospital; it is Raleigh history as well, tracing its roots to John Rex, a merchant and landowner who left money and land in 1839 to establish a hospital for the capital city. It took city leaders, however, until 1894 before Mr. Rex saw a hospital erected bearing his name on South Street. Since then, Rex has migrated about town and in 1980, moved to its new, $41-million building on a 48-acre site at the intersection of Blue Ridge Road and Lake Boone Trail. It is both the city's oldest and newest hospital and takes pride in its history as a not-for-profit institution.

Rex has 394 beds, all of them private, single rooms including a new birthing center with 40 rooms. Each room has a telephone, bath and individual heating and cooling controls, so there's no reason for you to be too hot or too cold. More importantly, the staff at Rex includes some of the best physicians in the Triangle, and its Cancer Center is as good as you will find, which is reflected in the 40,000 cancer treatments it performs annually. The center has become known statewide and provides chemotherapy, radiation and radiology screening for cancers. It provides psychosocial and nutritional counseling, too. Its Wellness Center has become popular with the fit crowd.

As a full-service hospital, Rex provides care in obstetrics, pediatrics, surgery and the latest in emergency-room care. It also has a same-day surgery unit. Its specialized departments include clinical laboratories, intensive care, cardiac, nursery, physical therapy, radiation and radiology, respiratory therapy and a telemetry unit. It also has a 140-bed convalescent-care center. It is fully accredited with the Joint Commission on Accreditation of Hospitals (JCAHO) and maintains the Wake Blood Plan.

Not content to rest on its laurels, Rex has become a pioneer in today's medical computerization and is in the process of installing one of the most advanced computer systems in the country that will vastly enhance the hospital's resources, from patient monitoring to diagnostics.

WAKE MEDICAL CENTER
3000 New Bern Ave.   250-8000

This is the city's largest general hospital, and as a public hospital, it maintains a high standard of care and serves all citizens regardless of their ability to pay.

It was established in a growing, post-World War II Raleigh when Wake County voters approved a $5-million bond issue to build a second, public hospital. The federal government chipped in $3.2 million and the hospital opened in 1961. The strong public and medical community support for the hospital and its ability to acquire the latest technology has allowed it to offer some of the most advanced care available in the state. It has continued to expand its services, and its site, located on New Bern Avenue near the Beltline in east Raleigh, is a mini-city of medicine today.

Wake maintains 560 beds at the New Bern Avenue site and, with its four division hospitals included, manages over 739 beds total. It has six intensive-care units, 44 outpatient clinics, single-room maternity care and is the county's Trauma Center, treating about 44,000 people yearly. It also has a same-day surgery center and the most technologically advanced intensive care nursery for critically ill newborns in the county. The hospital specializes in the treatment of heart disease, neurological illnesses and injuries and high-risk pregnancies.

The hospital's staff includes 2,800 employees and 654 physicians. It is proud of its technology and equipment. It was, for example, among the first hospital in the area to obtain a CAT scan and MRI machines. Its services include coronary care, open heart and neurosurgery, physical, occupational and respiratory therapy, laboratories and diagnostic testing, outpatient clinics in allergy, dental, dermatology, diabetic, orthopedic, pediatrics and arthritic illnesses, to name a few. It opened a 45-bed Rehabilitation Center in 1990 for people suffering from head and spinal chord injuries.

WMC is fully accredited with the JCAHO and is the hub for a county-wide medical system that includes a **Northern Wake Hospital** in Wake Forest, a **Southern Wake Hospital** in Fuquay-Varina, **Eastern Wake Hospital** in Zebulon and **Western Wake Medical Center** in Cary. Western Wake is a full-service hospital, offering a wide range of services. There is a 24-hour emergency department staffed by board-certified emergency physicians.

Wake Medical Center is a teaching hospital, affiliated with the School of Medicine at UNC-Chapel Hill. The hospital is self-supporting and derives most of its operating income from patient revenues. The board of directors are selected by current board members, but are approved by the elected Wake County Board of Commissioners.

Durham

They don't call Durham the City of Medicine for nothing. The medical industry is the town's top employer, utilizing about a fourth of the work force. It's no wonder. Here there are five major hospitals and a cadre of specialized diagnostic and treatment clinics. Then there are a number of well-known weight-loss and fitness programs, which are discussed in detail in "Durham Medical Care" later in this chapter, earning Durham an international reputation. Here's a brief description of the five hospitals located in Durham.

DUKE UNIVERSITY MEDICAL CENTER
Erwin Rd.   *684-8111*

It all began more than a half century ago when tobacco magnate James Buchanan Duke bequeathed $4 million to the university named for his father for the purpose of constructing a medical school and hospital. Today, Duke University Medical Center is considered one of the best private tertiary-care facilities in the country. With some 3-million square feet of space covering about 140 acres, DUMC offers patient care, physician training and specialized research into the causes and treatment of disease. To give just one example, Duke is a major research and treatment center for pediatric and adult AIDS patients, one of a few sites in the nation conducting clinical trials on AZT, a drug used in the treatment of AIDS.

Duke University Hospital is the facility to which doctors and other hospitals refer patients from all over the world who have complicated, hard-to-treat diseases. At the same time, it is a primary-care hospital for residents of the Durham area.

The original 400-bed facility opened in 1930 is today licensed for over 1,125 beds. The 600-plus bed North Division opened in 1980 includes a 23-room operating suite, a special children's wing, a burn-and-trauma unit, and a helicopter service for the quick transport of critically ill or injured patients.

Connected to the North Division is The Duke Eye Center, the only one of its scope between Baltimore and Miami, providing both patient care and research into the causes of eye disease.

The hospital's South Division includes nine buildings housing inpatients in psychiatry, medicine, surgery and obstetrics/gynecology, as well as outpatient clinics, an ambulatory-surgery program, a rehabilitation unit and the Comprehensive Cancer Center, the only federally supported facility of its magnitude between Washington, D.C., and Birmingham, Alabama.

Most doctors attending at Duke University Hospital are also teachers in the School of Medicine, considered one of the finest in the country. The faculty of over 1,700 clinical and research physicians includes many physicians who are world-renowned in their fields.

DURHAM REGIONAL MEDICAL CENTER

3643 N. Roxboro Rd.
North of I-85   470-4000

Since opening its doors in 1976, this 451-bed facility enjoys a reputation as one of the finest community hospitals in the nation. Currently, a renovation project is underway that will improve access for outpatients and emergency room patients. Surgical capacity will also be enhanced. The hospital has recently added a freestanding surgical center to its spectrum of service.

With 300 medical staff members representing virtually all specialties of medicine, Durham Regional Hospital offers personalized, quality health-care services. Just ask

---

How Do You Find A Good Doctor?

Finding a good doctor can take time. But with the **Physician Locator** service, it's as simple as picking up the phone.

Whether you need a general physician for a routine exam, or a specialist, **Physician Locator** puts you in touch with the right professional in the Durham or Chapel Hill area, and located close to your home or work if possible.

Call Physician Locator

919-470-6525

Durham Regional Hospital

A free service of
Durham Regional Hospital

---

a new mother. Durham Regional delivers almost 3,000 babies each year. Expectant parents are given childbirth classes as well as an orientation tour of the obstetrics facilities before the birth takes place. And many mothers are able to leave the hospital with their newborns on the day they deliver.

Durham Regional Hospital's outpatient services are equally popular. For example, its one-day surgery program features a growing list of operations that do not require an overnight hospital stay. The hospital offers special programs to help patients cope with a variety of problems, from asthma to backaches. There are even wellness classes to help you control your weight and to reduce stress through biofeedback.

Durham Regional Hospital, through its **HomeCare** home health services provides at home services for patients of all ages. The hospital also provides the Lifeline program that allows elderly, frail or handicapped patients to signal the hospital through an electronic device when they need emergency medical service.

In addition to Durham Regional Hospital, its parent corporation, **Durham County Hospital Corporation**, operates other healthcare services.

Lincoln Community Health Center offers a wide variety of medical services on a sliding fee scale. **Oakleigh** (309 Crutchfield Street, 470-6600) offers treatment for chemical dependency for adults and families suffering from alcoholism and drug dependency. **Emergency Medical Services** responds to medical emergencies with **Advanced Life Support** ambulances and can also provide non-emergency, **Basic Life Support** transportation. The **Wheelchair Van Service** is for people confined to wheelchairs or who do not have their own transportation.

VETERANS ADMINISTRATION MEDICAL CENTER
508 Fulton   *286-0411*

This 502-bed general medical and surgical hospital shares many services and physicians with nearby Duke University Medical Center. Through its affiliation with Duke, the VA Hospital participates in accredited residency training programs in psychiatry, internal medicine, general and thoracic surgery, anesthesiology, neurology, neurosurgery and ophthalmology, among other areas. Specialized treatment for veterans is available in such areas as neurosurgery, plastic surgery, open-heart surgery, home dialysis, and nuclear medicine.

NORTH CAROLINA EYE AND EAR HOSPITAL
1110 W. Main   *682-9341*

North Carolina Eye and Ear Hospital (formerly McPherson Hospital) is a leading private eye, ear, nose and throat hospital dating back to 1926. Today it serves more than 52,000 patients a year from all over the Southeast. People with eye, ear, nose and throat ailments can be seen by one of the 12 physician specialists on the staff by making an appointment through the hospital's outpatient clinics.

Your Link To Good Health Has Never Been Easier

UNC Health Link
966-7890

Now you can have the latest health and wellness information delivered right to your mailbox. With your free subscription to *Health Scene*, the Journal of Wellness and Good Health Care, you'll receive timely information on a wide range of health care topics, including:

- Valuable nutrition and wellness ideas
- Important disease prevention and treatment advice
- Tips on how to maintain a healthy lifestyle
- Special features on children's health issues, and more!

Published bimonthly as a community service of UNC Hospitals and the UNC School of Medicine, each issue of Health Scene also contains a wellness events calendar to keep you abreast of the many classes and support groups available at UNC. Call for your free subscription today!

Call UNC HealthLink at 919-966-7890 to receive your free subscription to *Health Scene*.

The hospital also provides training for the staffs at Duke University Medical Center and other area hospitals.

LENOX BAKER
CHILDREN'S HOSPITAL
3000 Erwin Rd.   *684-6669*

This state-supported teaching hospital provides evaluation, treatment and rehabilitation for young patients with cerebral palsy and other types of chronic debilitating medical conditions. While receiving treatment, young patients also learn how to cope with their disabilities and develop to their fullest potential by receiving counseling and physical therapy in addition to medical treatment.

Chapel Hill

UNC HOSPITALS
Manning Dr.   *966-4131*

Built in 1952 as a teaching hospital for UNC, the UNC Hospitals complex has become one of the state's largest medical referral centers, drawing patients each year from throughout the Southeast for specialized diagnostic and treatment services. At the same time, UNCH is the community hospital for residents of Orange and adjacent counties.

The hospital's staff is composed of faculty from the UNC Schools of Medicine and Dentistry, many recognized nationally and worldwide as experts in their fields. Many local doctors in private practice also have admitting privileges here. There are over 700 attending physicians and 500 interns and residents on the medical staff.

UNCH was the first hospital in the nation to have an intensive-care unit and the present Adult and Pediatric Critical Care Centers' services are among the most advanced facilities available. Accident and disaster victims from all over North Carolina use the services provided by the N.C. Jaycee Burn Center, the Comprehensive Hemophilia Diagnosis and Treatment Center, the Trauma Center and Carolina AirCare, the helicopter transport service. UNCH also has an organ-transplant program, the latest in radiological diagnostic equipment, and a lithotripter, the machine that uses sound waves to crush kidney stones without surgery.

The UNC Hospitals (which includes the main facility, the Children's Hospital, the Neuropsychiatric Hospital now under construction and the Lineberger Cancer Center) and its medical staff are recognized as leaders in the care of patients with diseases such as arthritis, cancer, digestive diseases, cystic fibrosis, growth disorders, hemophilia and infertility. UNCH is a major referral center for the care of premature infants and women with high-risk pregnancies.

In addition to providing highly specialized care for patients with complex medical problems, the hospital offers a complete range of high-quality, routine services for families. Expectant parents appreciate the family-centered maternal and infant care, including private delivery rooms with comfortable home-style furnishings and a visitation policy that allows siblings to visit as soon as the baby is born. (Children who participate in an educational program in advance are allowed to be present at the birth.)

UNCH also offered one of the first outpatient surgery programs in the country, making it possible for more patients to avoid the necessity of a costly hospital stay for many types of surgery. The new Ambulatory Care Center that opened in 1993 offers an expanded outpatient surgery service, as well as more convenient and accessible acute and preventive medical care for children and adults. Elderly and home-bound patients can participate in the hospital's Lifeline program, which provides them with an electronic device so they can signal the hospital when they need emergency medical assistance.

Chapel Hill area residents can take advantage of the hospital's Good Life series of wellness classes and workshops covering everything from backaches to first aid training for teens interested in babysitting.

UNC Hospital's staff physicians who specialize in internal medicine, pediatrics, obstetrics and gynecology and family medicine can meet your day-to-day medical needs. Call the hospital for clinic appointment information.

Medical Care

For life-threatening emergencies, dial 9ll.

Having gotten that out of the way, let's talk about medical care in general. Triangle residents have access to a wide range of such care. The medical delivery system has been changing rapidly during the past several years. There is more competition among doctors and dentists than ever before as urgent care centers and Health Maintenance Organizations (HMOs) have arrived on the scene. These new medical care systems have combined with an already large supply of doctors, dentists and health-care specialists who have been drawn to the Triangle because of its nearby, nationally recognized teaching hospitals and the attractiveness of the area itself. So, you shouldn't have a hard time finding a doctor.

Dr. David K. Millward of Raleigh Internal Medicine Associates recommends that everyone should have "a primary care relationship with one physician." This is good advice given today's specialized medical market where you probably see a gynecologist for female problems, a pediatrician for your children, an orthopedist for broken bones, and so on. For your family or "primary care" doctor, however, you want to find a family practitioner or an internist.

But how do you find such a physician? There is no foolproof guide. Most people ask a trusted friend or neighbor to recommend a doctor. If you know a nurse at a local hospital, he or she can be a good, unofficial source (and can sure tell you who NOT to see). If you happen to call a physician who is not taking new patients, ask him or her to recommend someone.

Some people may prefer a group practice that includes not only internists or primary care physicians but also specialists in other areas such as heart, lung, digestive and infectious diseases. Doctors are not as bashful as they once were about advertising their services and a good place to start looking for specialists is the telephone book's Yellow Pages or here in the Insiders' Guide.

Raleigh and Cary

We have combined Raleigh and Cary medical information since the subject spills over city lines; Cary residents, for example, may use Raleigh-based physicians and vice versa. We hope that this information will help you find a family doctor and/or other convenient health care.

The Wake County Medical Society will provide a list of physicians who are members and who are taking new patients. The list is broken down by specialty, e.g., if you want a family physician, the society will give you the names of three doctors and, if you ask, will tell you where they went to school, what insurance programs they belong to, and other details. It rotates the list, and if you specify an area of the Triangle, it will give you names of people only in that area.

The Wake Dental Society has a similar referral system and you can get that information by calling the state society's office and asking

for the number of the current Wake County chapter president. He or she is the one who provides the information.

You can also call the Wake County Information and Referral Center at 856-6700 for general information. The Cary Chamber of Commerce also publishes a list of local physicians and dentists.

Meanwhile, if you sprain your ankle moving in or your child runs a fever before you've found a family physician, you may want to try one of the area's urgent care centers. As one such center advises, "we do not encourage seriously ill or injured patients to come to our facility. These facilities were created to provide you with competent and expedient medical treatment and to counter the high cost of hospital-based medical care." For big emergencies, of course, you can go to the Emergency Room at one of Raleigh's three major hospitals.

Below are contact numbers for health-care sources.

WAKE COUNTY MEDICAL SOCIETY
800 St. Mary's St.
Raleigh, N.C. 27605   821-2227

N.C. DENTAL SOCIETY
1001 Hillsborough St.
Raleigh, N.C. 27605   832-1222

THE ALCHOLISM TREATMENT CENTER
3000 Falstaff Road   250-1500
A Wake County agency, the center provides outpatient services and has 34 beds for inpatient services. If you're a member of AA and want to find a local chapter, the

center can help you. It is a licensed psychiatric hospital with a full nursing staff and certified alcoholism counselors. The center has been open since 1977. It probably sees more patients than any other such facility in the county, and, as a tax-supported agency, it uses a sliding scale fee according to your ability to pay. Services also include family counseling for those who live with alcoholics and drug abusers.

PLANNED PARENTHOOD
100 South Boylan Ave.   *833-7526*

Located at the corner of W. Morgan Street and S. Boylan Avenue near downtown, the local chapter provides family planning programs for individuals as well as organizations such as church youth groups. It also conducts pregnancy tests and some gynecological exams, but performs no abortions. It does make referrals.

CAROLINA BREAST CANCER
DETECTION CENTERS
Cary Professional Center
901 Kildaire Farm Rd.   *467-4191*
North Hills
3821 Merton Dr.   *787-8221*
North Raleigh
6400 Falls of the Neuse Rd.   *876-2848*
West Raleigh
4301 Lake Boone Trail #103   *781-6707*

These centers specialize in the detection of breast cancer. Physicians serving the branches are on staff at Wake Medical Center.

WAKE COUNTY
MENTAL HEALTH CENTER
3010 Falstaff Rd.   *250-3100*

This is also a Wake County agency and maintains a full staff of doctors and nurses. It provides outpatient care and acts as a referral agency to other organizations and schools that treat special children. Regular hours are Monday through Friday, 8:30 a.m. to 5:30 p.m. It also maintains branch offices in Cary, downtown Raleigh area and Wake Forest.

Durham

It is fitting that Durham is called the City of Medicine. After all, the town got its start when Dr. Bartlett Snipes Durham, a physician, gave four acres of land to the North Carolina Railroad Company some 140 years ago (see **INSIDE DURHAM**). And it flourished when the tobacco-enriched Duke family endowed a university that would eventually house one of the most prestigious medical centers in the country. In fact, medicine is Durham's number one industry, employing more than one fourth of the local work force.

If you can't find a doctor in Durham, you aren't going to find one anywhere. There are probably more doctors per capita in this town than in most major cities: More than 1,500 licensed doctors make Durham County's physician-to-patient ratio better than five times the national average.

But how does a newcomer know where to turn for medical care? Probably the best way is to ask your friends, relatives or co-workers for recommendations. If you're unable to come up with a good referral, try one of the sources listed below. (If you'd like information on any of Durham's five hospitals, see **HOSPITALS** at the beginning of this chapter.)

PHYSICIAN AND DENTIST LOCATOR
470-7279

This is a comprehensive physician and dentist referral service available in Durham. Sponsored by **Durham County Hospital Corporation** (see **HOSPITALS** at the beginning of this chapter), this service strives to match you and your needs with the right doctor or dentist. For example, if you want a female gynecologist who has an office near your workplace, it can tell you which physicians will fill the bill.

DUKE FAMILY MEDICINE CENTER
2100 Erwin Rd.   684-6721
(Pickens Bldg.)

This facility, sponsored by Duke University, offers health care for the entire family, including Ob/Gyn, Family Counseling, Substance Abuse Evaluation and Nutrition Counseling.

LINCOLN COMMUNITY HEALTH CENTER
1301 Fayetteville St.   683-1316

Lincoln Community Health Center offers an extensive range of medical services to patients on a sliding-fee basis. Services offered under the sponsorship of **Durham County Hospital Corporation** (see **HOSPITALS** at the beginning of this chapter) include medical care for the whole family, mental health counseling, dental care, health education and home visits.

For other clinics and divisions within either Duke University Medical Center or Durham Regional Hospital, please refer to the **HOSPITALS** section at the beginning of this chapter.

DURHAM URGENT CARE
(4 LOCATIONS)
4125 Chapel Hill Blvd.	*493-0033*
1901 Hillandale Rd.	*383-0003*
5242 N. Roxboro Rd., Bldg. C	*477-0060*
410 Executive Park	*544-0003*

Urgent Care provides walk-in emergency and basic medical

services—no appointment necessary; all locations are open Monday through Friday, 8 a.m. to 9 p.m.; Saturday, 9 a.m. to 6 p.m.; Sunday, 1 p.m. to 6 p.m.

FIRST CARE
1777 Chapel Hill Blvd.
(next to Brendle's) 942-8578
This is one of several urgent care centers located near Durham. This one is actually just outside of Chapel Hill, about 15 minutes from downtown Durham, but the location is convenient to Durham residents. First Care can handle most emergencies and basic medical needs for all ages, with on-site X-ray and lab services. You don't need an appointment; so if you don't have a personal physician, this definitely beats going to the emergency room to get basic care. The facility is open 365 days a year and its hours are Monday and Tuesday, 9 a.m. to 6 p.m.; Wednesday through Friday, 9 a.m. to 9 p.m.; Saturday, 9 a.m. to 5 p.m.; Sunday noon to 5 p.m.

PIEDMONT MEDICAL CLINIC
6005 Russell Rd. 477-3008
Piedmont is another clinic open seven days a week, with no appointments or long waiting. This one is in northern Durham County, a few minutes off Interstate 85. Open Monday through Friday, 9 a.m. to 6 p.m.; Saturday and Sunday, 1 p.m. to 4 p.m.

Diet and Fitness Centers

This city has a number of well-known weight-loss and fitness programs, earning Durham an international reputation as the Diet Capital of the World. Here is a brief description of four of the best known.

KEMPNER RICE DIET CLINIC
1821 Green St. 286-2243
In 1939, Durham physician Walter Kempner designed an eating plan for Duke University Medical Center patients suffering from diabetes, kidney disease, heart disease or high blood pressure.

Today, Kempner's diet is the reason that Durham has become a mecca for the fat and famous, and a spawning ground for dozens of wildly successful and innovative weight-reduction centers.

The Kempner Rice Diet Clinic is Kempner's legacy. Here patients are put on a strict, six-phase eating plan calling for initial emphasis on rice and fruit, eventually followed by steamed vegetables, chicken, fish, eggs and an average weight loss of 15 to 25 pounds in two weeks.

If you hang around this part of Durham long enough, you'll spot the "Ricers," walking energetically around town in their jogging suits, following the Rice Diet Clinic's advice to engage in regular exercise.

To date, some 20,000 patients have been to the Kempner Rice Diet Clinic. And the Rice Diet itself has spawned another major industry for Durham, each year bringing to local weight-loss centers $40 million and 2,000 dieters, including the familiar physiques of Burl Ives and Buddy Hackett.

DUKE UNIVERSITY PREVENTIVE APPROACH TO CARDIOLOGY (DUPAC)

Erwin Rd.   *681-6974*

With an acronym like DUPAC, this may sound like a Duke University political slush fund, but actually it's one of the largest cardiac rehabilitation programs in the country. Started in 1976, DUPAC serves about 1,000 patients a year. The program features a combination of careful medical supervision, diet and exercise. Some Rice Diet Clinic patients are on the DUPAC exercise program.

STRUCTURE HOUSE

3017 Pickett Rd.   *688-7379*

Structure House claims to be the first intensive residential weight-control program in the nation to successfully combine psychology and lifestyle counseling with medicine, nutrition and exercise. Started in 1977, Structure House is the brainchild of Dr. Gerald Musante, the first psychologist in the United States to treat obesity as a psychological, rather than a physical, problem. Patients can enroll in a variety of programs to suit their schedules and needs.

DUKE UNIVERSITY DIET AND FITNESS CENTER

804 Trinity Ave.   *684-6331*

This program, part of Duke's Department of Community and Family Medicine, offers a comprehensive treatment and education plan for individuals with weight management problems. The center emphasizes nutrition, behavior and fitness.

Chapel Hill

Chapel Hill may not offer as many doctors per capita as Durham, but the medical care available here is impressive in both its quality and diversity. You can choose from the outpatient services available at the UNC Hospitals or one of the many private medical practices or clinics in town. There are primary care physicians trained to meet general health-care needs for patients of all ages, and there are specialists for just about anything that ails you.

So how do you go about finding the physician who best suits your needs? The easiest way, of course, is to ask your friends, neighbors or co-workers for their recommendations. Here is a guide to help you get started and give you some idea of the medical services available to the Chapel Hill community. (For more information on UNC Hospitals, see **HOSPITALS** at the beginning of this chapter.)

UNC HOSPITAL SERVICES

Manning Drive   *966-4131*

Many Chapel Hill area residents go to the staff and clinics at UNC Hospitals for their day-to-day medical care. All you have to do is call for an appointment. There are also walk-in clinics for people who do not have a regular doctor and need to see someone right away. Whenever possible, it's still better to call in advance. Here's a brief description of the services that are available:

THE AMBULATORY CARE CENTER
966-7400

The Ambulatory Care Center (or ACC, as its known to Insiders) opened in the fall of 1992 on the corner of Mason Farm Road and South Columbia Street. Many clinics formerly located in the main hospital are now here. There is ample on-site parking. Here are some of the services offered at the ACC.

General Internal Medicine Clinic (966-4615): This clinic offers routine and specialized care for adults.

Surgery Clinics (966-2225): Many of the surgery clinics, including general surgery, ENT and vascular surgery are now located here. Call the main clinic number for more information.

PROFESSIONAL PROFILE
Family Practice

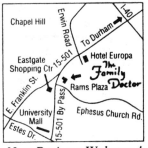

Glenn A. Withrow, M.D., A.B.F.P.
Adona Struve, P.A.-C.
Brent Harrell, P.A.-C.

New Patients Welcome!

The Family Doctor offers convenient health care for the entire family. Located in Ram's Plaza near I-40, *The Family Doctor* is convenient to Chapel Hill, Durham, Research Triangle and much of the Triangle area. The office is open 7 DAYS A WEEK and urgent medical problems are managed without an appointment. If you need a doctor to manage all your health care needs, just call for an appointment with our board certified family physicians. They can admit patients to N. C. Memorial Hospital and can arrange admission to Durham Regional Hospital or Duke Hospitals.

The Family Doctor has modern laboratory and x-ray facilities and twenty-four hour coverage is provided for patients calling after hours. Come by or call *The Family Doctor*. We will be happy to assist you with your health care needs.

151 Ram's Plaza • Chapel Hill, NC • 968-1985/493-1985
Mon. - Sat. 8am-8pm; Sun. 1pm-5pm

Pediatrics (966-1405): Preventive care for infants, children and adolescents is now offered at this location. Acute care (evenings and weekends) remains in the main hospital (see Pediatric Screening Clinic below).

Outpatient Surgical Services (966-7330): There are four operating rooms in the ACC. Most same-day admission-discharge procedures are now performed in this building. Other features of the Ambulatory Care Center include a pharmacy, X-ray facilities, the Peripheral Vascular Lab and an Optical Shop.

THE FAMILY PRACTICE CENTER
966-2491
In this building down Manning Drive from the main hospital complex, you'll find family physicians who can provide general medical care for every member of the family, including obstetrics, pediatrics and minor surgery.

PEDIATRIC CLINIC
966-1405
This is a walk-in clinic open from 8 a.m. to 8:30 p.m. on weekdays.

MEDICINE EVENING AND WEEKEND CLINIC
966-1405
This walk-in clinic is open from 9:30 a.m. to 9:30 p.m. on weekends, and from 4:30 p.m. to 9:30 p.m. on holidays.

FEARRINGTON MEDICAL CENTER
Fearrington Village Market   542-6800
Internal medicine, dermatology and physical therapy are offered at this new UNC Hospitals outpatient facility located at the Fearrington Village Market. Appointments may be scheduled here by calling the number listed.

FIRST CARE
1777 Chapel Hill Blvd.   942-8578
This is one of several urgent-care centers convenient to Chapel Hill. It is open Monday and Tuesday, 9 a.m. to 6 p.m.; Wednesday through Friday, 9 a.m. to 9 p.m.; Saturday, 9 a.m. to 5 p.m.; Sunday, 12 noon to 5 p.m. It can handle most emergencies and basic medical needs for all ages, with on-site X-ray and lab services. You don't need an appointment; you can just walk in.

CHAPEL HILL-CARRBORO COMPREHENSIVE HEALTH SERVICE
400 Roberson St.   942-8741
This health clinic is equipped to treat minor emergencies and offer basic family medical and dental care, on a sliding-fee scale based on family income. It takes walk-ins and appointments.

COMMUNITY WHOLISTIC HEALTH CENTER
103 W. Weaver St.   929-1132
If you are interested in non-Western and non-traditional health care, this may be the place for you. The Community Wholistic Health Center offers a variety of courses on everything from diet to meditation. And it will refer you to health-care providers specializing in alternative therapies. Call for information on classes and referrals.

Playspace in Raleigh's City Market is a wonderland of adventure for young visitors with its seemingly endless variety of activities.

Inside

Kidstuff

Fortunately for families, the Triangle is chock-full of places to go and things to do with kids. There are wonderful museums, parks and other spots perfect for whiling away an afternoon. So, whether a rugged hike through the woods, a quiet hour in a museum or a swing in the sunshine is your idea of recreation, all that and more can be found right here.

We've supplied you with a short list of some of the more popular spots in the Triangle for child-oriented fun, some of which are cross-listed in other sections of this book. (Also, see **ATTRACTIONS, DAY TRIPS AND WEEKENDS** and **SPORTS**, as well as the **PARKS AND RECREATION** chapters of the individual cities and towns of the Triangle for lots more ideas on places to go and things to do.)

Check area newspaper listings for upcoming events, and ask neighbors and friends for more suggestions. Chances are you'll find more than you can do in a month of Sundays.

Museums

Raleigh

N.C. STATE MUSEUM OF NATURAL SCIENCES
102 N. Salisbury St.   *733-7450*

This state-supported museum has lots for kids to see, touch and experience, as well as special programs and activities geared for kids. Some of our favorites include the **Discovery Room, Saturday Storytime** and **Meet the Animals**, a chance to see animals up close and have your questions answered by one of the staff. The museum also has special events on weekends several times a year, such as its "Natural History Halloween" and "State Symbols Day" in August. Admission is free.

N.C. MUSEUM OF HISTORY
109 E. Jones St.   *733-3894*

By the time you read this, the brand new and much larger Museum of History should be open.

It's scheduled for the spring of 1994. Old favorites—Indian artifacts, turn of the century medicine exhibits and more—and lots of new and refurbished exhibits are sure to delight and surprise kids of all ages. Admission is free.

N.C. MUSEUM OF ART
2110 Blue Ridge Rd.   833-1935

The North Carolina Museum of Art has several collections that fascinate children—most notably the Egyptian mummies and the shimmering silver of the Judaica exhibit. There are also changing special shows that are sometimes of interest to younger ones, such as a folk art exhibit a year or two ago. The museum offers classes for children and movies or other entertainment for kids weekdays and some Saturdays each month. The museum also has several Family Festivals each year, which have recently included a **Kwaanza** celebration and a **Rennaissance Christmas Festival**. Admission is free. There is a charge for special classes.

Durham

BENNETT PLACE
4409 Bennett Memorial Rd.   383-4345

Bennett Place is the site of negotiations that led to the largest troop surrender of the Civil War, when Confederate General Joseph Johnston negotiated the surrender of his troops to General William Sherman. Now a state historic site, Bennett Place has exhibits and a video presentation. A highlight of the site's annual calendar is the **Civil War re-enactment**, complete with period costumes and replicas of Civil War era weapons. Admission is free.

DUKE HOMESTEAD & TOBACCO MUSEUM
2828 Duke Homestead Rd.   477-5498

Another state historic site, Duke Homestead is the restored home and tobacco farm of Washington Duke. There is a house, a curing barn, pack house and other outbuildings, all part of the living history program offered here. Staff members recreate late nineteenth century farm life with special programs each fall and spring. There is also a **Mock Tobacco Auction** in October and a **Christmas Open House** with candlelight tours each December. Admission is free.

N.C. MUSEUM OF LIFE AND SCIENCE
433 Murray Ave.   220-5429

Like Topsy, the North Carolina Museum of Life & Science continues to grow. Additions in recent years have brought new or larger exhibits for Aerospace, Small Science (for little ones), natural history and more. There are changing exhibits in the special exhibit rooms—recent favorites have included Dinorama and laser technology. Outside, there are climbing structures, wind chimes, water play, a barnyard area and the ever-popular dinosaur trail. An outdoor maze is lots of fun in warm weather. The musuem has special family day programs throughout the year. The **Halloween Adventure** and the **Santa Train** are popular offerings. You can buy a family membership that gives unlimited admission for a year.

HAYTI HERITAGE CENTER
804 Old Fayetteville St.   *683-1709*

Hayti Heritage Center is housed in an historic church building. It has a gallery featuring African-American art, as well as concerts, plays, programs and events for children and adults. The First Saturday (of most months) family program is a free program designed for school-aged children. Call for information on upcoming events and activities.

Chapel Hill

ACKLAND ART MUSEUM
South Columbia St. at East Franklin St.
UNC Campus   *966-5736*

After renovations several years ago, the Ackland reopened with quite a bit more space for its small but very fine collection. The collection spans the ages, from ancient Greek and Roman pieces to modern paintings and sculpture. There is enough variety in the regular exhibits and the changing special exhibits to keep children interested for a while before ice cream on Franklin Street beckons. The Ackland sponsors a **children's story hour** that links a book's theme with a work of art in the collection two Sunday afternoons each month. The museum has also hosted a display of a lovely hand-built doll house in November and December in recent years. Admission is free.

HORACE WILLIAMS HOUSE
610 East Franklin St.   *942-7818*

Occasionally, the Horace Williams House, the restored home of a former UNC professor, hosts exhibits of interest to children, such as the recent display of dolls from a local collection. Exhibits change monthly. The house is located on a big lawn, perfect for rambling. The Chapel Hill Preservation Society that maintains the house sometimes sponsors family events here, which have included an afternoon of storytelling and a **July Fourth celebration**. Admission is free.

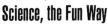

Indoor Entertainment

Raleigh and Cary

DISCOVERY ZONE

Atlantic Ave. and Millbrook Rd.   876-KIDS
Raleigh

Discovery Zone is a giant indoor playground geared for kids ages 12 and younger. It's a treasure trove of activities and fun, especially for preschool and early elementary school-aged kids. There is also a snack bar and a game room here. It's a great place for a birthday party or just a rainy afternoon!

EXHILARAMA

Crossroads Plaza   851-1178
Cary

Exhilarama has almost everything—video games, virtual reality, a play structure, games and more. An Insider's best advice is to bring plenty of money; there's lots to do here. Exhilarama is popular with everybody from college students on dates to families looking for an afternoon of entertainment. Exhilarama can be a little overwhelming for young toddlers; it's recommended for ages 2 and up.

PLAYSPACE

208 Wolfe St.   832-1212
Raleigh

Playspace is the space for little ones. It's a magical place for imagination. Housed here are a pretend bank, a hospital, a grocery store, a dress-up area and a stage, as well as an exploration area designed for infants and toddlers. Play sessions begin on the hour and last for fifty minutes. It's a good idea to arrive a few minutes before the hour in case it is a busy day. Playspace is appropriate for children ages seven and younger, and is closed on Mondays except during the summer and on certain other Monday holidays during the year.

Kindermusik.
Kids of Cary

*Where kids, music, fun and learning
go hand in hand.*

- Music Programs for children
  9 mos.-6 yrs.
- Guitar Instruction 8-12 yrs.
- Birthday Parties with music, art
  or craft themes
- Summer and Winter Camps

**Director/Instructor:
Julia Cobley**

Kindermusik Kids of Cary
Kildaire Plaza • Cary 467-4398

Durham

LITTLE BIG THEATRE
120 Morris St.   383-4931

The Little Big Theater Company, founded by husband and wife team Don and Lisa Bridge, is the Triangle's only theater company just for kids. The company performs almost all year round (taking off some time in the summer), and puts on original versions of familiar stories for kids and their parents. Performances are Wednesdays and Thursdays for school groups (call for reservations) and a 1:00 p.m. show on Saturday for the general public.

MARDI GRAS
N.C. Hwy. 54 at I-40   489-1230

This 24-lane bowling alley and video arcade opened near the end of 1993. It promises to provide a new venue for entertainment for southwest Durhamites and Chapel Hillians. There is food available, and birthday parties and group outings can be scheduled. Bowling fees are cheaper during the day.

PATTERSON'S MILL COUNTRY STORE
Farrington Rd.   493-8149

Patterson's Mill Country Store is in a old house and replicates an old-time general store down to the penny candy in the jars. Shopkeepers John and Elsie Booker also use the store's space to exhibit some fascinating collections; Mrs. Booker, one of the first female pharmacists in the state, has gathered old pharmaceutical items for years. There is also an early 20th century doctor's office housed here as part of this collection. Mr. Booker collected tobacco memorabilia for many years, so there's lots to see in that department as well. In addition to the collections, the Bookers sell crafts, antiques and small gift items such as inexpensive toys and doll house furniture.

Chapel Hill and Carrboro

ARTSCENTER
300-G East Main St.   929-ARTS
Carrboro

The ArtsCenter has classes, Saturday morning "Kids Cabaret" performances, family concerts and summer camp programs. It is a great resource providing almost limitless entertainment and educational services for children and parents. Call for a current schedule of classes and upcoming events.

AUNT LOUISE'S BOOKSHOP FOR CHILDREN

205 West Main St.   942-1183
Carrboro

Besides being one of the only bookstores in the Triangle that is devoted to children's literature, Aunt Louise's offers friendly service and a Saturday morning story hour, so parents can browse while the children listen. There are other shops to look in and places to get a snack close by.

Science, Nature and the Outdoors

Raleigh

DURANT NATURE PARK

8305 Camp Durant Rd.   870-2871

Durant Nature Park is a little gem in the Raleigh Parks and Recreation Department's crown. There are trails to explore, a butterfly and bird garden (best in spring and summer), and many wonderful nature programs for children and families. There are also picnic facilities if you want to make a day of it. One highlight of the park's yearly schedule of programs and events is the **Halloween Trail** each October. Call for more information about the park and its classes and activities.

WILLIAM B. UMSTEAD STATE PARK

1800 Harrison Ave.   677-0062

William B. Umstead and adjoining Reedy Creek State Parks offer 5000-plus acres of trails, fishing, picnic sites, campgrounds and woodlands to explore right in the middle of the Triangle (just minutes from RDU International Airport). There are bridle trails, a self-guided nature trail, boat rentals in warm weather and lots more. Thousands of commuters drive past the park's entrances each day; it's well worth a stop, especially if you need a place to let the kids run loose on a beautiful spring or autumn afternoon. Admission is free.

NCSU ARBORETUM
Beryl Rd. 737-3132

The North Carolina State University Arboretum is a little hard to find and not too large—about eight acres—but it is a delightful place for a quiet stroll. There are Japanese and English-style gardens, self-guided tours to enjoy and places to picnic. If you and the kids need a respite from the high-tech world out there, the NCSU Arboretum may be one solution. Admission is free.

NCSU SCHOOL OF VETINERARY MEDICINE
Hillsborough St. at Blue Ridge Rd.
829-4259

One of Raleigh's best-kept secrets is the fact that the vet school hosts teaching tours of its animal hospital units. The tours offer a firsthand look behind the scenes at the school and may be of interest to many children, especially those enamored with domesticated animals. Call the school for more information or to arrange a visit.

PULLEN PARK
408 Ashe Ave. 831-6468

The highlight of Pullen Park (at least to this Insider) is the carousel. One of only 25 hand-carved Dentzel carousels still in operation, it was restored in 1982. You can ride a horse, an ostrich, a cat or a goat—or perhaps each one, since you'll undoubtedly ride it more than once. There is a also a train and boat ride for little ones, a large playground, picnic areas, paddle boats on the small man-made lake, and if that's not enough, an out-door pool for warm-weather swimming. Admission to the park is free; there are charges for rides and the pool.

Durham

DUKE FOREST
For Information: 684-2421

Duke Forest is over 8,000 acres of woods, part of the research lab for the School of Environmental Sciences (formerly the School of Forestry) at Duke. There are trails to hike and bike, picnic areas, streams and fishin' holes in the forest, which is located in Durham and Orange counties. There are a number of entrances to Duke Forest; the most widely used ones are along N.C. Highway 751 and Erwin and Whitfield roads. The forest is a great spot for a family walk (bring the pup along!) or a solo stroll when you need to clear your head. Admission is free.

DUKE GARDENS
Anderson St.
Duke Campus

The Sarah P. Duke Memorial Gardens are glorious in the springtime, but worth a visit all year long. There are over 20 acres of lawn, flowers and foliage; it's a prime place for families, Duke students and others to picnic or just hang out on a balmy afternoon. There are ponds with goldfish, paths to follow and woodlands to explore. There are outdoor concerts held in the gardens in the spring and fall. Admission is free.

DUKE PRIMATE CENTER
3705 Erwin Rd.   *489-3364*

The world-renowned Duke Primate Center was established to promote the preservation of some endangered species of primates, including lemurs and bush babies. The center is open for tours, which must be scheduled by appointment. It's a fascinating place—a bit of the wild right in the heart of the Triangle. Call for more information or to schedule a tour.

ENO RIVER STATE PARK
Route 2, Box 436-C   *383-1686*
Durham, NC

The Eno River State Park was established in 1973 and runs along a 14-mile stretch of the river. There are a number of access points to the park, including Cole Mill (off the road by the same name) and Cates Ford (at the end of Cole Mill Road), where the park office is located. There are hiking and bridle trails, creeks to fish, picnic spots, and of course, the river itself (for experienced canoers only). Admission is free.

WEST POINT ON THE ENO
5101 N. Roxboro Rd.   *471-1623*

West Point on the Eno is part of the Durham City Parks and Recreation system. There is a reconstructed mill, the 1880s Greek Revival McCown-Mangum house and the Tobacco Barn and Pack House, which is now a photography museum. There are trails to hike, a picnic area and a blacksmith shop, which hosts blacksmithing demonstrations several times a year. The park hosts the annual **Fourth of July Festival** on the Eno, **Hallow-Eno**, a special Halloween celebration, and special programs like moonlight hikes and nature classes for children and adults throughout the year. Admission to the park is free; there is a charge for classes.

Chapel Hill and Carrboro

N.C. BOTANICAL GARDEN
Fordham Blvd.   *962-0522*
(U.S. Hwy. 15-501 Bypass)

The Botanical Garden's 300+ acres are part of the University of North Carolina. There are collections of native plants, grouped in coastal plain, piedmont and mountain areas, herb and wildfower gardens, goldfish ponds and a series of trails to walk throughout the garden property. The annual **Labor Day Open House**, featuring fresh apple cider and a botanical scavenger hunt is a favorite for kids.

COKER ARBORETUM
Cameron Ave. at Raleigh St.

The Coker Arboretum is actually a part of the North Carolina Botanical Garden, but it's several miles away on the UNC campus (just behind the Morehead Planetarium). There are gravel paths to stroll, grass to lay down in and arbors to walk under on sunny days. It's a good place for a picnic.

MOREHEAD PLANETARIUM
East Franklin St.   *962-1236*
Triangle-wide telephone number
for schedule of show times: *549-6863*

The Morehead Planetarium has a changing schedule of shows

throughout the year, from the popular **Star of Bethlehem** program that runs from November to early January to shows on UFOs, the age of the dinosaurs, black holes and much more. The planetarium runs two shows concurrently, one for younger children and one for school-aged children and adults. On Friday evenings, **Sky Rambles** gives a look at the night sky. A small gift shop has a nice selection of astronomy and science-related toys, most less than a couple of dollars. There are also Saturday classes (like model rocket launching) and summer camp programs for kids. In front of the building is a large sundial in the midst of a beautiful rose garden, a favorite place to sit and enjoy the sun and the flowers almost all year long.

MEDIA

*Triangle residents enjoy a variety of convenient choices
of local and national publications*

214

Inside
Media

North Carolina has long been proud of its reputation as a producer of good journalists. Most of its cities have better than average newspapers, and within the past 11 years, the *News & Observer* of Raleigh and the *Charlotte Observer* have won several Pulitzer Prizes. The Triangle television stations are considered some of the best affiliates in the nation, too. The tradition in modern times goes back to Josephus Daniels, a crusading editor who made his capital city newspaper, the *News & Observer*—also known as the *N&O*, The Nuisance and Disturber, and The Old Reliable—a force in state and national politics. But the state also claims such worthies as the Baltimore *Sun's* legendary Gerald W. Johnson and CBS's Edward R. Murrow. Other natives are PBS' Charlie Rose, Clifton Daniel, Tom Wicker, Charles Kuralt, David Brinkley, and Gene Roberts. John Feinstein, David Hartman and Judy Woodruff attended Duke University in Durham and cartoonist Jeff MacNelly, sportswriter Curry Kirkpatrick and broadcaster Jim Lampley are Carolina alums.

Triangle residents are today's beneficiaries of this strong journalism tradition, and this section will give you a guide to the Triangle's newspapers and its other prize-winning media, namely tele-

vision and radio. Readers, viewers and listeners can pick and choose and yet not be overwhelmed by the number of choices. The section does not list every media outlet; it does give you Insiders' tips such as which radio stations carry Wolfpack, Tar Heel and Blue Devil sports.

Raleigh Newspapers

THE NEWS AND OBSERVER
215 S. McDowell St. 829-4500

This is the dominant daily morning newspaper in the Triangle, and many in Chapel Hill and Durham subscribe to the *N&O* in addition to—or instead of—their local newspapers. Owned by the Daniels family, it has a tradition for outspoken opinions dating back to founder Josephus Daniels' campaigns for prohibition and against lynching. A grandson, Frank Daniels, Jr., is publisher today and his son, Frank Daniels III, is executive editor. It takes its nickname, "The Old Reliable," seriously and usually stands up for those who have no voice in the corridors of power.

Because it continues to keep its editorial pages tied to the Daniels' dictum to be a Democratic paper, Republicans and conservatives such as Jesse Helms often use "The Nuisance and Disturber," as they call it, as a convenient whipping post. Its news coverage, separate from its editorial opinions, is tough but fair, and its chief investigative sleuth, Pat Stith, strikes fear in the breasts of bureaucrats no matter what their party affiliation. Former editor Claude Sitton won the Pulitzer Prize for commentary in 1983, and former book editor Michael Skube won it in 1989.

The *N&O's* outlook has become more local and trendy, but it still maintains a statewide and national emphasis on politics and government. With local commentators and veteran reporters such as Ferrel Guillory, Jane Ruffin, Rob Christensen, Steve Riley, Steve Ford, Jim Jenkins, Gene Cherry, and columnists Bob Langford, Barry Saunders and Dennis Rogers, it is the most influential newspaper in the state with a daily circulation over 152,000. Comics include Doonesbury, Peanuts, Outland, Cathy, Calvin & Hobbes, and The Far Side.

Under Frank Daniels III, the newspaper is undergoing a change with more color, graphics and local news. Managing Editor Marion Gregory has strengthened such sections as sports, styles, home and entertainment. The paper has been more encouraging of good writers such as Bill Muller and the irrepressible Mary Miller. If you want to keep up, you'll need to become an *N&O* subscriber.

THE HERALD-SUN/RALEIGH EXTRA
4050 Old Wake Forest Rd.   876-8814
This is the Durham newspaper's attempt to compete in the *N&O's* north Raleigh backyard. It is free and published on Sundays. It adds to the notion that north Raleigh is somehow separate from the rest of the city. For example, it caters to north Raleigh sports, trends, crime and schools, especially the latter. Johnathan Miller covers local politics and is among the more conscientious reporters in the city. Columnist J. L. Shapiro is a fresh, entertaining voice, perhaps because he's not a professional journalist.

THE CAROLINIAN
518 E. Martin St.   834-5558
This weekly aims at the capital city's black community and has its greatest influence there. It has been a voice for Raleigh blacks for decades, but its current principal writer lets his own voice set the agenda more often than not. News coverage is oriented toward black issues and personalities, religious commentary and sensational crime.

NORTH RALEIGH LIVING
5029 Falls of the Neuse Rd.   878-0303
This monthly paper was established in January 1990, by publisher Jan Britton and is written by her husband, Bob. It carries articles and advertising directed to residents of North Raleigh, and changed in 1993 to paid mail subscription. It has an informal, sometimes unprofessional style and takes a definite Republican slant on its news, especially at election time.

Cary Newspapers

THE CARY NEWS
212 E. Chatham St.   *460-2600*

This twice-weekly (Wednesday and Saturday) newspaper has grown with the city and keeps its 10,000 readers focused on Cary. It is owned by the News and Observer Publishing Co. and sometimes serves as a stepping stone for reporters or managers who move up to the larger daily. It does a good job of covering Cary city news and local school news and sports. "Cary Calling," a feature started in 1991, allows area residents to phone in their opinions on suggested topics. The responses are summarized in each weekend edition of the paper; this has become the most popular feature in the newspaper.

Durham Newspapers

THE DURHAM HERALD-SUN
2828 Pickett Rd.
Durham   *419-6900*

It all started back in 1889 when the Durham and Northern Rail Road found itself without any editorial support in its right-of-way battle with the Durham and Clarksville line. At the urging of several alarmed aldermen, the *Durham Daily Sun* was established, eventually taking its place as an afternoon paper. Five years later *The Globe*, another daily, was in financial trouble and had reverted from daily to weekly publication, throwing several printers out of work. Three unemployed printers decided to publish their own paper, calling it *The Morning Herald*. A

month later *The Globe* collapsed and merged with *The Herald*. In 1895, Edward Tyler Rollins bought a half-interest in *The Herald* for $125, making him the business partner of editor Joe H. King, who died in 1919. In 1929, just before the stock market crashed, Rollins purchased *The Sun.*

Today, the Durham Herald Company is in a new building and headed by Rollins' son, E.T. Rollins, Jr. The *The Herald-Sun* emphasizes local news, with state, national and international news coverage provided by the Associated Press wire. In addition to local editorials, you'll find the opinions of nationally syndicated columnists James J. Kilpatrick, Mike Royko, Jack Anderson and Russell Baker. As part of the Great Triangle Newspaper War, *The Herald-Sun* also publishes an Orange County-oriented newspaper, *The Chapel Hill Herald*.

THE CAROLINA TIMES
923 Old Fayetteville St.
Durham 27001   *682-2913*

The Carolina Times, published weekly on Thursdays, emphasizes local, state and national news affecting the black community. The paper was established in 1926 by long time civil rights activist Louis Austin, whose goal was to offer a voice to blacks at a time when they clearly had no say in local, state or national politics. Austin died in 1971, but his objectives continue to be carried out today under the leadership of his daughter, Vivian Austin Edmonds, the current editor and publisher. *The Carolina Times* emphasizes local news, sports and features, but provides state, national and international news from the Associated Press wire service.

Chapel Hill Newspapers

THE CHAPEL HILL HERALD
412 W. Franklin St. 967-6581

Chapel Hill has become a battleground in the great Triangle newspaper wars and the last chapter hasn't been written in the battle for the upscale local readership.

The Chapel Hill Herald, has an impressive local edition. If you subscribe to the Durham paper and you live in the Chapel Hill area, you'll get *The Chapel Hill Herald* edition, with front page coverage of local news, including coverage of adjacent Chatham County.

Inside are local features, national columnists and plenty of scoop on everything from the courthouse to campus.

THE CHAPEL HILL NEWS
505 W. Franklin St. 967-7045

Now owned by the Raleigh *News & Observer,* the local paper in Chapel Hill may be on its way up again. It's been battered by the competition from the larger area dailies in the last few years, and now may survive best under the wing of the larger newspaper.

The Chapel Hill News is distributed as a free paper on Wednesdays, Fridays and Sundays to about 25,000 Chapel Hill-Carrboro households. This Chapel Hill paper aims to keep you up to date on what happened at the Town Council meeting Monday night, as well as goings on down on campus. The newspaper got its start as a weekly in

1923 when Chapel Hill native and former *New York Times* reporter Louis Graves was, as he put it, "seized by an itch" to start a paper of his own. Graves ran *The Chapel Hill Weekly* until 1954 when it was purchased by a corporation formed by George Watts Hill of Durham, and editor/publisher Orville B. Campbell took the helm. In 1972, *The Weekly* became a daily, and was renamed *The Chapel Hill News.*

In its pages today, you'll find coverage of Chapel Hill, Carrboro, the county and the university, as well as state, national and international news from the Associated Press wire service. The editorial page features commentary by local and regional as well as nationally syndicated columnists.

Triangle Publications

CAROLINA PARENT
103 W. Main Street, Ste. 210 489-6512
Durham, NC 27701

This parent and child-oriented publication was begun in 1987 by publishers and editors Barbara Matchar and Gita Schonfeld. In 1993 it was purchased by the Raleigh *News & Observer,* with the papers' founders continuing to edit the publication. It is published monthly (except for combined December-January and June-July issues). The paper features well-written pieces, both humorous and informative, by and for parents. It includes a comprehensive calendar of events of interest to parents and kids in each issue. It is distributed free throughout the Triangle, and has a circulation of over 35,000.

THE INDEPENDENT
2810 Hillsborough Rd.   *286-1972*
Durham, NC 27705

This brave, ambitious weekly hails itself as the state's "news alternative" and it does, indeed, take on some big assignments that others often miss. It was started by Harvard graduate and Nieman Fellow Katherine Fulton. The weekly has settled into a Triangle niche after first trying to be a statewide publication. That niche is a newspaper that's long on crusading opinions and politically correct reporting, and the most entertaining "personals" in the Triangle.

It has scorned local slumlords, state prisons, highway building and General Assembly highhandedness. It also publishes a great entertainment calendar, now called "Audience." Several national journals have cited *The Independent* as one of the best of its kind in the country. And no Insider's week would be complete without reading *The Independent's* wild, brilliant and award winning columnist, Hal Crowther, husband of novelist Lee Smith. Crowther is far and away the state's best newspaper columnist—and the primary reason 150,000 "*Indy*" readers pick it up free at newsstands and racks everywhere on Wednesdays.

THE SPECTATOR
1318 Dale St.   *828-7393*
Raleigh

In 1978, *The Spectator* filled an entertainment void that the once-staid and serious *N&O* missed. The *Spectator's* publisher and editor, the outspoken R. B. "Bernie" Reeves, has no love for the bigger daily and enjoys tweaking the *N&O's* nose whenever possible. *The Spectator* has succeeded, however, not so much by competing with the *N&O*, but by going around it; the weekly specializes in a thorough calendar on shows, restaurants and concerts, as well as opinions and reviews on the Triangle's non-political life, especially movies, music and art, including architecture, the profession of Reeves's late father.

Its "Talk of the Triangle" is a good, gossipy news column and the weekly adds punch to its package with three columnists: conservative political observers Peter Hans and UNC Prof. John Shelton Reed and local history writer Noel Yancy. It also carries Durham cartoonist V.C. Rogers as well as nationally-known cartoonist Jules Feiffer. *The Spectator's* writers, such as Godfrey Cheshire, Kim Devins Weiss and Michael McFee have earned a local following, and the newspaper's no-holds-barred policy on letters to the editor reflects Reeves' indulgence of different points of view.

TRIANGLE BUSINESS JOURNAL
3125 Poplarwood Ct., Ste. 304 878-0010
Raleigh

Started in 1984 by Bernie Reeves, this hustling business weekly is now owned by the Business Journals of N.C. and is published by Charlene Grunwaldt. *Triangle Business* circulates weekly to a select audience of Triangle business people, and its accent is on in-depth trends, personalities and successful companies in the Triangle. It filled what was then a void in business news, and it also publishes the less glamorous but necessary items of record such as land transactions, building permits and, yes, bankruptcies. One very useful calendar is that of business meetings, seminars, university offerings and special events.

Its regular columnists include author Tom Peters and local conservative John Hood. Popular features are Hal Worth's "Biz" column on page one, its TBJ Profile and locally written guest columns. Its positive, upbeat view of business has won it applause from the business community. It's a good place to find out about Triangle business personalities.

There are many other publications providing a variety information to Triangle residents. Here are just a few of special interest to newcomers or visitors to the area:

NewHome Guide
NewHome Neighborhoods
Map Series
NewHome Builders

8541- Glenwood Ave.   781-8990

New Home Guide is published six times a year and is a comprehensive source of information about new home communities and home-related products and services. Published by VSD Communications, the magazine has been recognized as the National Housing guide of the Year for the past four consecutive years and is currently in its 13th year of publication. *NewHome Neighborhoods Map Series* is a companion publication. *NewHome Builders* is an annual publication targeting new

home buyers who wish to learn more about area builders.

Apartment Finder
Apartment Finder Monthly

8541-A Glenwood Ave.   781-8990

Apartment Finder, another VSD Communications product is a 200-plus page, full color, digest-sized quarterly guide to apartments and services for locals and newcomers in search of multifamily housing. *Apartment Finder Monthly* is a companion publication that provides a monthly updating of information about apartment communities. Both publications are free to consumers and are distributed to over 1,200 Triangle locations.

Triangle Report

8541-A Glenwood Ave.   781-8990

Also published by VSD Communications, *Triangle Report* is a slick, thick combination of in-depth business articles and advertorial articles by local companies with the best color photos of Triangle buildings and offices. It regularly looks at banking and finance, real estate, media, telecommunications, health, and transportation. *Triangle Report's Business Properties* is published semi-annually as an insert publication within Triangle Report and features a commercial space inventory survey generated by Triangle Area Office Building Association.

Newcomer Magazine

3101 Poplarwood Ct., Ste. 215   878-6151
Raleigh

This magazine, published annually by Bond Publishing, Inc., has all the information a new resident needs. It includes tips on selecting a neighborhood, home buying, building and decorating, as well as information on public and non-public schools and colleges and universities. Health-care options, leisure activities, retirement and religious options are included along with the Triangle business outlook. Charts and maps direct the newcomer to utilities, financial services, accommodations and radio and television stations. Bond also publishes *Triad Newcomer* and *Charlotte Newcomer* magazines.

TRIANGLE POINTER
88 McClamroch Cr.   688-9468
Chapel Hill

This is a Village Companies' publication and is the Triangle's oldest guide and calendar magazine for lodging, restaurants and entertainment, and a number of other items such as art exhibits, church services, museums and TV. It is free and distributed at area motels. Published weekly, each issue includes a handy guide map to Chapel Hill, Durham, Raleigh and RTP. Mostly advertisements, it has no news copy.

THE INSIDERS' GUIDE TO THE TRIANGLE
Cary   467-4035

You're readin' it! This annual publication, part of a series now being expanded nationwide, offers a subjective view of many aspects of life in the Triangle. Written by local authors, it provides "inside information" in such areas as schools, accommodations, shopping, restaurants, recreation, medi-

cal care, homes, arts and just about anything a newcomer or visitor to the area would want to know. The Guide is published by Becklyn Publishing Group, Inc., which also produces *The Insiders' Guide To Charlotte* and *Down The Road In The Carolinas (Day Trips and Weekend Vacations)*.

Television

While the area's TV stations are located in given cities, they all see themselves as Triangle media and have helped foster the idea that the Triangle is one metropolis probably more than any other institution. Cable connections are available in most parts of the Triangle and bring in a number of outside stations, including Ted Turner's WTBS in Atlanta. The stations based in the Triangle are listed here alphabetically, along with network and channel number. The numbers may be different, however, if you are a cable subscriber.

WKFT-40, IND.
230 Donaldson St.   323-4040
Fayetteville

Sold in 1992, WKFT is an independent broadcaster, which means that it has almost no one save the FCC to answer to. It also means that much of its programming will be limited, both in terms of budget and content. This is the station that carries the NBA Charlotte Hornets' games. The normal times for news—6 p.m. and 11 p.m.—are the times to see "Studs." The programming really is a mixed lot, with some religious shows in the morning, a movie in the early afternoon followed by the usual cartoons, and plenty of syndicated shows such as Murphy Brown.

WLFL-22, FOX

1205 Front St.   *821-2200*
Raleigh

This is one of the newer stations in the Triangle and is an affiliate of Bart Simpson's Fox Network. The station began in 1992 to offer a 10 p.m. live news program and thus focused another camera on local events. It depends mostly on popular re-runs, movies, Arsenio Hall and the Fox network's hits, such as "The Simpson's," "Married with Children" and "In Living Color." It has taken a higher profile in the community as sponsor for events such as the Rex Classic golf tournament and the city's St. Patrick's Day Parade.

WRAL-5, CBS

2619 Western Blvd.   *821-8555*
Raleigh

Although finding the airwaves more competitive these days, WRAL-TV continues to hold its own at the top. This station has the most familiar faces to Triangle viewers and, before it became an affiliate of CBS in 1986, WRAL had established itself not only as the premier station in the Triangle but as one of the best stations in the country. Popular news anchor, Charlie Gaddy, as familiar to Triangle viewers as their favorite uncle, has announced his impending retirement, which will be effective in the summer of '94. Working at WRAL has been shown

to be a proven stepping stone for ambitious broadcasters such as Bobbi Batista who have moved to larger markets.

It has an hour and a half worth of local evening news and reporters such as Mark Roberts, Denece Boyer, Tom Suiter and Duane Pohlman are seasoned Triangle veterans. WRAL goes the extra mile (and spends much more than the extra dollar) to provide coverage on local newsmakers no matter where they go, be it Desert Storm or the ACC tournament. Along with the best local sports coverage, its CBS Sports programming is superb. WRAL was the first, over 10 years ago, to commit to a Weather Center concept and has not one, but three full-time meteorologists and the best weather graphics around. It's the one people turn to and trust for bad-weather coverage (the hint of winter snow, however, seems to set off a Chicken Little alarm).

WRAL and its parent company, Capital Broadcasting, sponsor or televise over 50 nonprofit or community service events each year, making WRAL's civic mindedness renowned among city leaders and charities. The local events include the Labor Day weekend Pops in the Park, Partners Auction, UCP Telethon and the annual Raleigh Christmas Parade.

WRDC-28, NBC

3012 Highwoods   *872-2854*
Raleigh

This is one of the major network stations, and it changed ownership in 1990. It had suffered for years financially, and the new owners made the tough decision to cut the station's local news operations. Reruns have been substituted in the news slots and periodic news breaks give headline news. NBC's continued national success has helped improve the station's prime-time ratings. The station has a fairly new and technologically advanced operation. In the past, it has participated in many local charities and has taken a chance on carrying Raleigh's own version of Wayne's World—The Rob and Bill Show, which has its own loyal following.

WTVD-11, ABC
4111 Liberty St.   *683-1111*
Durham

This station has been challenging for No. 1 since it settled on a solid, veteran North Carolina reporter, Larry Stogner, as its news anchor and Miriam Thomas as co-anchor. The No. 1 ranking goes back and forth between WTVD and WRAL. Thomas has helped bring black viewers to the station with her graceful manners and continued service to the community. When its owner, Capital Cities, purchased ABC, WTVD and WRAL swapped affiliations, and WTVD now is an ABC affiliate.

The station usually gives more attention to political coverage than the competition, and reporters Dave Boliek and Ed Crump and long-time editor Bonnie Moore have good noses for news and scoops. Like its arch rival, WRAL, it broadcasts 90 minutes of suppertime local news and sports, starting at 5 p.m. It has a bureau in Fayetteville, and it provides top coverage on weather news such as the November 1988 tornado and the 1992 Florida hurricane. Capital Cities is making its investment pay off.

WUNC-4, PBS UNC
10 Alexander Dr.   *549-7000*
Research Triangle Park

The state's well-respected university system operates public television in North Carolina. The main studio is in Research Triangle Park. UNC-TV reputedly is one of the best PBS affiliates in the country and has a large following throughout the state, one that usually exceeds fund-raising goals each year. The affiliate has launched several programs that have become national PBS shows, and its local coverage of public affairs includes daily reviews when the General Assembly is in session and a popular Friday, week-in-review of state events starring veteran news people like Ferrel Guillory and Jack Betts.

Unlike many public television operations, it has a seasoned staff and Ted Harrison, the news director, is a North Carolina veteran. In recent years, the station has moved away from sappy, dull local craft shows toward more popular, entertaining programming such as British mysteries and Mark Russell specials. Big Bird and the Sesame Street gang also live here. One gripe: it's almost impossible to get a clear picture without cable or a rooftop antenna.

CABLEVISION

2505 Atlantic Ave.	832-2225
Raleigh	
708 E. Club Blvd.	220-4481
Durham	
1129 Weaver Dairy Rd.	968-4631
Chapel Hill	

Cablevision serves Raleigh-Durham area viewers and offers several levels of service. In 1992, Cablevision also became Chapel Hill's cable company. You can get the networks, ESPN, CNN, TNT, Headline News, USA, BET and some others including local access for about $23 a month. When Raleigh negotiated a new contract with Cablevision, the cable company agreed to help develop local, public studios for grass roots, community-based productions. The Raleigh studio is located in the Civic Center downtown. For information, contact the Civic Center, phone 831-6011. The public access studio in Durham is at the Cablevision office. For Chapel Hill's public access, call 968-4631.

CVI

Cary	467-2800
Garner	772-2553
Wake Forest	556-6011
Wendell	365-9010
Carrboro/Hillsborough	967-7068

CVI stands for Cable Vision Industries and serves Cary and other Wake County communities. Carrboro, Hillsborough and some of Orange County are also served.

Triangle Radio

Like TV, radio tends to serve the entire Triangle market, not just local cities, and some observers believe that there are too many for the market to support. This guide will briefly identify call letters, dial numbers, AM or FM frequency and a short description of the station's programming. Given the nature of the industry, however, a station's format may go from hard rock to country western overnight, so don't be surprised if the music doesn't go round and round the way it's printed here.

WCHL-1360 AM
942-8765

This station bills itself as "non-stop Chapel Hill." It's news, lots of UNC sports, community, and music (adult contemporary) 24 hours a day. It's been around for 35 years.

WCPE-89.7 FM
556-5178

WCPE is the Triangle's premier, 24-hour all-classical music station that is financed by contributions and often staffed by volunteers. It is located outside Wake Forest. The best radio wave in town.

WDCG-105.1 FM
683-2055

The younger, FM sister to the older WDNC in Durham, G-105 plays the hardest, newest rock of the more popular Top 40 rock 'n' roll stations of the Triangle. It is also noted for its popular morning show.

WDNC-620 AM
361-0620

This is Durham's oldest station and once its most popular. It plays hit tunes of yesteryear (swing, Big Band, '50s) and is the station for Duke University's sports network, as well as for the Durham Bulls. For Durham city and county school closings on snow days, listen to it.

WFXC-107.1 FM
941-0700

This Durham station plays contemporary rhythm and blues and has high ratings, especially among black audiences.

WKIX-96.1 FM
851-2711

The former WYLT has changed its name and changed its format from adult contemporary music to hot country hits.

WNND-103.9 FM
481-1039

"The Wind" plays new adult contemporary music. Special programs include Jazz Tracks and Musical Star Streams.

WPTF-680 AM
876-0674

The granddaddy of Triangle radio stations, WPTF features a mostly talk format, including three hours of half-brain-behind-his-back Rush Limbaugh. The Voice of NCSU Wolfpack Sports, "PTF" also is the place to dial for school closings when it snows and Triangle rush-hour traffic reports.

WQDR-94.7 FM
876-6464

The FM sister to WPTF, it once set the standard for album rock but now is country western.

WRAL-101.5 FM
890-6101

Based in Raleigh and consistently at or near the top of the ratings, 101 plays a mix of mostly Top 40 hits, past and present. It also broadcasts school closings on snow days.

WRDU-106.1 FM
876-1061

The hottest kid on the block for true rock 'n' roll, this station goes after a younger audience than WRAL and has a lively morning show.

WTRG-100.7 FM
876-1007

WTRG is the Triangle station for "good times and great oldies." Its popular features include the All Request Lunch Express and Paul Harvey Commentary.

WUNC-91.5 FM
966-5454

This is UNC-Chapel Hill's public radio, home of NPR's indispensable "Morning Edition" and "All Things Considered" as well as medicine man Joe Graedon's Saturday morning call-in show. In between, it plays classical music mostly, with some jazz and a Saturday night folk music line-up.

WZZU-93.9 FM
787-9390

In Raleigh, Z-93 is hip with the younger rock 'n roll crowd and the place that plays UNC-Chapel Hill sports.

Courtesy N.C. Travel and Tourism Division. Photo by William Russ.

One of the 184 marked graves in the Old Town Cemetery in
Historic Hillsborough is that of William Hooper, one of North Carolina's
three signers of the Declaration of Independence.

Inside
Neighbors

The Triangle cities and towns featured in the *Insiders' Guide* have some great neighbors, and this section will introduce you to them. Many of these towns consider themselves part of the "greater Triangle" and indeed, almost all have benefited from the Triangle's recent growth. Companies such as Data General and Glaxo, for example, have built manufacturing operations in one of these neighboring towns to complement their respective research facilities in Research Triangle Park. If small town life or the allure of lower real estate prices is what you want, you might take a look at some of these neighbors.

Even the most distant town is within a 30- to 40-minute commute to the Research Triangle Park, and some have distinct histories and personalities of their own. Pittsboro, for instance, has developed a reputation as a gathering ground for artists and writers who find that Chapel Hill has grown too crowded. Author Doris Betts lives here. In Wake Forest, the one-time home and namesake of the university that now resides in Winston-Salem, you will find the look and flavor of a small college town with its tree-shaded campus and streets. The campus is now occupied by a Baptist seminary.

Even if you decide you're not interested in living in one of these smaller communities, you will find them great places to visit on a weekend drive. Many have annual fairs when they show off their history and wares. They offer the pleasant rhythm of small-town living and easy access to the cultural offerings of the larger Triangle cities. They are listed alphabetically.

Apex

Some real estate Insiders say that Apex may be Wake County's next Cary in terms of growth. Apex, population 4,968, is located off U.S. Highway 1, southwest of Raleigh and almost abutting Cary's town line.

Like many small Southern towns, Apex's history is tied to the growth of the railroads, in this case, the Chatham Railroad Company. The rail tracks still run through the city, but it's now the Seaboard Railway. The land on which the tracks ran was one of the highest points along the line, hence the town's name, Apex. Also because of that, the railroad placed a water and fuel stop at the end of the summit, around which the town began to grow. The community was incorporated in 1873.

Today, Apex finds itself perfectly positioned for future growth. It is only minutes from the Raleigh Beltline and even closer to Cary's office parks such as Regency Park and MacGregor Park. Taking state Highway 55 north, Apex commuters are 15 minutes away from the Research Triangle Park. What has caught the eye of many home buyers is Apex's proximity to Jordan Lake on U.S. Highway 64. The lake has become a mecca for water sports enthusiasts. Companies such as Lufkin (maker of tape measures), Almay Cosmetics and Data General are located here.

The town, however, still retains its main street shops and the old railroad station has become one of the county's most picturesque library branches. There remain a number of older homes in town, and new home building will take off with the new water and sewer system built jointly with Cary. Apex has its own weekly newspaper and a relatively new municipal building.

Fuquay-Varina

Ah, here's another colorful name for your scrapbook. Fuquay-Varina! It's a southern Wake County town of 4,562, located on U.S. Highway 401 about 17 miles from Raleigh's Beltline. It not only has a double name, but two main streets since the two grew up as two communities, one Fuquay Springs and the other Varina, named after the pen name of the postmaster's wife. It joined names in 1963.

The area was long famous for its mineral springs, discovered in 1852 and developed in the earlier part of the 20th century as a tourist and health spa that attracted thousands of visitors, especially on Easter Monday and July Fourth. At one point, the waters were bottled and sold as a curative, and hotels and boarding houses were built to accommodate the guests who came by train. The town was first incorporated in 1909 as Fuquay Springs.

The spring's flow was disrupted when developers began dynamiting nearby, but the waters have since returned, although few come to imbibe today. Instead, city leaders believe that Fuquay-Varina's future lies in the growth coming to the Research Triangle, and town boosters boast of Fuquay's proximity to the Park—20 miles via N.C. Highway 55—and the capital city. Few are friendlier than Mayor Alfred Johnson, who helped lure several manufacturing companies which are impressed by the town's hospitality. Raleigh Insiders also claim that the **Gold Leaf Tea Room** on Main Street serves an excellent lunch and homemade desserts, surrounded by antiques.

Garner

Garner has a population of over 16,000 and is proud of its billing as the "Most Promising Corner In The Triangle." Founded in 1883 as "Garner Station" and rechartered in 1905 as "Garner," the community's National Register Historic District features The Garner Depot, circa 1910. There are 97 other contributing structures that depict the town's early beginnings.

Garner is located immediately south of Raleigh and shares some of its southern city limits with Raleigh at the fork of U.S. Hwy. 401 south and U.S. Hwy. 70. Perhaps because of its proximity to Raleigh and its urban amenities, today's Garner is diversifying as shopping, entertainment and employment opportunities grow at a rapid pace. The town's recent commercial growth began with North Station and South Station Shopping Centers which brought Walmart and restaurants such as Rock Ola Cafe and Goodberry's, and nearby,

Golden Corral Metro and Ragazzi's. A planned 172,000-sq.-ft. Super K Mart Store speaks to the strength of Garner's development as a commercial market.

The completion of the southern link of the Raleigh Beltline and the extension of Interstate 40 have spurred Garner's growth. For example, the I-40 and U.S. Hwy. 70 Interchange has become a prime industrial location, evidenced by its selection for Nabisco's next $400 million bakery and Greenfield Park, an 850-acre Class A business and industrial park. The site hosted

Kerr Drugs' "Land of Fantasy," an annual wonderland of lights enjoyed by 300,000 holiday visitors. Just north along I-40 is the newly announced $20 million expansion of Goodmark Foods.

The road system expansion, including the scheduled opening in November 1994 of Timber Drive, Garner's garden parkway, also provides greater accessibility to the town's growing neighborhoods. At a time when new home prices in Raleigh are averaging over $154,000, Garner's real estate continues to be a bargain.

Part of the Wake County School System, Garner is a "Community Involved In Its Schools." Community leadership through the Garner Educational Foundation has resulted in one of the strongest high school science programs in North Carolina. The town still proudly rallies around its high school sports programs—the football program is one of the best in the state and the girls' softball team has been in the playoffs for eleven straight seasons.

Garner has been a place where many eastern North Carolinians, from small towns themselves, have chosen to settle. It's still a great place to raise a family and offers many opportunities to become involved in the community.

Hillsborough

Despite the phenomenal growth taking place all around it, this bustling county seat of 3,000-

The Garner Depot, circa 1910.

plus inhabitants has retained much of its historic charm. Wood-frame homes dating back to the late 18th century line its small streets. Antique stores, small shops and a 19th century courthouse dominate the central business district, where you'll also find the oldest continuously operating inn in America (see "Chapel Hill" Section in **ACCOMMODATIONS**).

Founded in 1754, Hillsborough was the site of both the Regulator tax revolt and the most successful Tory raid on Colonial forces during the Revolutionary War. It is also said to have been the starting point of Daniel Boone's journey west to Kentucky.

Today Hillsborough is also an antique-lover's paradise, with more than 50 shops in the business district as well as at the Daniel Boone Village antique mall on the outskirts of town. It's about a 15-minute drive north of Chapel Hill, along N.C. Highway 86, or 25 minutes from Durham via Interstate 85.

While Hillsborough has managed to preserve its small-town character so far, it is perhaps more vulnerable to growth pressures today than ever before. Now that the extension of Interstate 40 from Research Triangle Park is complete, this former rural outpost is only about a 20-minute commute to the heart of the Triangle; developers are already looking at Hillsborough as the next suburban frontier.

Knightdale

About six miles east of Raleigh, Knightdale is located off U.S. Highway 64. It traces its history back to 1907, which makes it a relative youngster among most of Wake County's towns, and it's one of the smaller neighbors with a population of 1,884—but growing fast.

It got its start from the railroads when a Mr. Henry Haywood Knight donated land for a depot for the Norfolk and Southern Railroad. One of the town's first landmarks was the Baptist Church, and church activities continue to play an important role in Knightdale's social life. The second biggest social draw is school; the high school is East Wake, the result of a bitter consolidation and compromise between Knightdale and Wendell. The old Knightdale School was believed to have been the first rural school to serve lunches, thanks to the town's Women's Betterment Association, a forerunner to the Extension Homemaker's Club. The EHC remains active in town and holds some of its social functions at the town library, part of the Wake County Library system, located downtown.

The town's role as a bedroom community has replaced its mission as a farming center. Three miles east of town is Wake County's second largest airport, East Raleigh Airport, sometimes known as the "Knightdale Airport."

The downtown retains its main street, although the cantankerous Town Council wants to move City Hall elsewhere. Downtown faces railroad tracks and has among its other buildings, the unusual and artistic Stained Glass Association. It has a farm-supply business, and the town's economy still depends in part on the fate of a good harvest since much good farmland still surrounds the community. The best-known business to Triangle residents probably is Wilder's Nursery, just off main street. The owner, Billy Wilder, is a former mayor. Knightdale Crossing has become the busiest shopping area and meeting place. Located on the south side of U.S. Highway 64, the center has Winn Dixie and Revco Drugs as anchor tenants. Older vintage homes can be found in the downtown area, with large shade trees and quiet streets. But the growth has been in the subdivisions that first began appearing on the town's outskirts, with names such as Barclay Downs and Green Pines that have been around since the '70s. There are a number of newer developments, including Planter's Walk, which is off U.S. Highway 64 near Knightdale Crossing Shopping Center.

Morrisville

Morrisville, another "railroad" town that began as a depot on what is now the Norfolk Southern Railroad, lies between Cary and Research Triangle Park, about eight miles from Raleigh. Morrisville is a rich town because most of its growth has been non-residential, which builds a healthy tax base. The town has moved from a sleepy country village straddling N.C. Highway 54 to a community with industrial parks and planned communities. Its population, however, remains small, about 1,022.

It was named after Jeremiah Morris, who gave in 1852 the land

on which the railroad built a water station. And it was at Morrisville that one of the state's first Confederate companies, the Cedar Fork Rifles, was mustered off to war in 1861.

The boom in RTP growth since 1982 and the development of the 680-acre Huntington planned community have shaken Morrisville awake with a start. Huntington alone doubled the town's population, and companies such as Bristol-Myers, which has a plant located near Huntington's industrial park, have added to the town's job market. The real estate forecast calls for more growth in this western Wake County town.

Pittsboro

Like Hillsborough (see above), this Chatham County seat 16 miles south of Chapel Hill still feels like a small Southern town; after all, it only has about 1,500 residents. Historic homes line its streets. Its inhabitants include a blend of long-time natives and newcomers drawn to the area because of its charm, proximity to UNC and Research Triangle Park, and of course lower land prices and property taxes.

Pittsboro, like Hillsborough, is also becoming a mecca for antique and crafts hunters. If you're driving from Chapel Hill, you'll pass the Fearrington Market, a good place to stop for a casual lunch (see **CHAPEL HILL NEIGHBORHOODS** and "Chapel Hill" Section of **RESTAURANTS**). Also located at the Fearrington development is

Pringle Pottery, a shop featuring hand-thrown stoneware, locally made baskets and hand-dipped candles. As you cross the Haw River at Bynum, you'll see Stone Crow Pottery, located in a rebuilt log cabin and Cooper-Mays Pottery just across the road.

When you arrive in Pittsboro along U.S. Hwy. 15-501, the first thing you'll notice is the courthouse situated squarely in the middle of a traffic circle. Along the main street, you'll find the Pittsboro General Store, a good place to stop for natural foods, wine and cheese. Here you can also pick up a handy map to the many craft and antique shops in the area.

Right in town you'll find Beggars and Choosers, an antique and vintage-clothing and jewelry shop whose goods have been proudly worn by the likes of Joe Namath and Jane Fonda. You'll also want to stop at Edwards Antiques and Collectibles for furniture, quilts and pottery. The best place to eat in town is the Hilltop Restaurant, run by Tom and Cheri Klein, formerly of La Residence (see "Chapel Hill" Section of **RESTAURANTS**). In addition to a Tuesday-through-Friday lunch menu of soups, salads, sandwiches and burgers, it offers excellent seasonal fare including fresh seafood, poultry, pasta and vegetable dishes, and irresistible desserts.

Pittsboro, like the other small towns on the fringe of the Triangle, faces the challenge of balancing growth pressures against the desire to preserve the qualities that make this such a pleasant place to live.

Wake Forest

This lovely old college town is one of the authors' favorite Triangle neighbors, located about 12 miles northeast of Raleigh's outskirts off U.S. Hwy. 1. Its small town charm (population 5,769) and its proximity to the Triangle have been enhanced even more by the recent opening of Falls Lake only a few miles to the west. The challenge to city leaders here is to keep Wake Forest's small-town pace and grace while accommodating the growth that's already chewing at its front steps.

The town's history is intertwined with education, beginning with three private academies that operated nearby in the early 1800s and then the founding of Wake Forest College in 1834 by the state's Baptist Convention. Church members were drawn to the area by the offer to buy a 615-acre farm for $2,500 from Dr. Calvin Jones, a veteran of the War of 1812, who boasted that his neighbors were "without, I believe, a single exception...sober, moral and thriving in their circumstances, and not a few are educated and intelligent." With the growth of the college, the inhabitants continued to thrive and students at the college became some of the state's leading educators.

Students at first were required to spend their afternoons doing farm work in the school's fields, but the regimen was changed to a liberal arts curriculum in 1838, which also was the year the town was established. One family that prospered was that of the Holdings, who founded one of the country's largest cotton brokerages. Other offspring have continued in the family's pharmaceutical business, and one branch founded one of the state's largest banks, First Citizens.

When the college moved to Winston-Salem in 1956 and its buildings were occupied by an older crowd of Southeastern Baptist Theological Seminary students, Wake Forest, in the words of one town historian, became "a much quieter and more sedate place." It also became an attractive residential town, and with the continuing location of manufacturing operations nearby, the town is growing. Because of its history as a college town, it has amenities such as a country club, two libraries, and athletic facilities not usually found in towns of similar size. If you prefer small-town life, check out Wake Forest before it gets any larger.

Wendell

Wendell is named after poet Oliver Wendell Holmes, but residents pronounce the name Wen-DELL, apparently because that's the way the train conductor called out the stop during the town's early years. Its population is 3,182, and it's located about 13 miles east of Raleigh, off U.S. Highway 64.

Incorporated in 1903, the town grew up around the same railroad that ran through Zebulon. Wendell has seen its downtown dwindle, as have many small towns, as the state's farm economy mechanized and better roads carried shop-

pers to bigger cities such as Raleigh. For years, Wendell's economy was tied to tobacco. The weekly newspaper, which keeps a close account of town affairs, reflects that economic dependence in its name, *The Gold Leaf Farmer.*

Today, however, Wendell has prospered from the general Triangle growth and the town has refurbished its downtown with a small, municipal park with a gazebo. Developers are talking about the population doubling with projects such as Deerfield and Maple Court and several manufacturing operations have located close by, bringing jobs and demands for housing.

Eastern Wake Senior Center, a joint public and private venture, has been built to provide a unique social and cultural facility for older adults in the community. It shares space on its two-acre site with a branch of the Wake County Library. Through good and hard times, several Wendell businesses have won a reputation from local as well as outside customers. Two of them are Kannon's Clothing store, started in 1916 by a Lebanese immigrant and continued today by his granddaughters; and Perry's Incorporated, a traditional hardware, guns and farm-supply store where residents like to sit and talk about stalking game or politicians. Theo. Davis Sons printing, located outside the town, is known throughout the state for its quality printing work.

Wendell has yet to experience the boom in residential growth that other Wake County towns have. Some folks like it that way because the older homes in town are a good buy. Timberlake, on the edge of town, is one of the subdivisions with homes in the $100,000 range. Most of them are traditional in style. Deerfield and Maple Court, noted earlier, are two more where home buyers who enjoy small-town life may want to look. Northwinds has homes starting at $70,000.

A favorite attraction in Wendell is St. Eugene's Catholic Church, one of the few in mostly protestant eastern Wake County, which has been there for years and until recently was the parish for Catholics from surrounding counties, too. A new shopping center on Wilson Avenue features a new Food Lion supermarket.

Zebulon

With an address in a town called Zebulon, you can be assured that you'll be asked where you live. In which case, you can reply that Zebulon is located in eastern Wake County, about 17 miles from Raleigh's city limits off U.S. Highway 64. It, too, was born of a railroad, now the Norfolk Southern line, that ran between Raleigh and Wilson. Convict labor was used to build much of the line, and visitors from Raleigh used to come out and watch the work. In 1907, the town was chartered and laid out into "lots, blocks, streets, alleys, avenues and parks" by the Zebulon Company, which took its name from North Carolina Governor Zebulon B. Vance.

The town today has a population of 3,173 and was once a required stopping place on the way to Wilson. N.C. Highway 64 now by-passes the town. While the town's population has shown modest increases over the years, Zebulon's population may show a jump in the next census, given the residential building going on there. The town's most famous son, perhaps, is Clifton Daniel, Jr., *New York Times* journalist and son-in-law of the late President Harry Truman. Truman honored the town in 1958 and again in 1960 when he visited his son-in-law's parents.

The town achieved dubious local fame during the '70s as the only place in the county where a theater showed X-rated movies. Today, it's home to the Carolina Mudcats, a minor league baseball team whose owner built them a field in 1991 and "they came." Whitley's Furniture store also draws Triangle visitors to the town.

One of the loveliest neighborhoods is the two or three blocks of older homes along Gannon Avenue which used to be the main highway through town. The houses, most of them occupied by the descendants of the families who built them, have spacious yards and shade trees and are within walking distance from downtown. Wedgewood, started in the late '60s, is another attractive neighborhood that continues to be developed.

Newer subdivisions include Fox and Hound and Pineview. At the town's outskirts on N.C. Hwy. 97, there is the lovely former Jaycee Park on the Little River that has a small waterfall. A private individual maintains the grounds.

The Texas two-step is popular in the country room at the Longbranch.

Inside
Triangle Night Life

Ah, night life. This section in guide books always quickens the pulse. It tantalizes with the prospect of fast women, hard men and dark, steamy music. A scene from the movies.

If the place advertises all ABC permits, it means it can serve beer, wine and mixed drinks. Also, be aware that North Carolina has a very tough drunk driving law. A few words about the mixed drink law might be helpful. The law requires that restaurants and bars that serve food and mixed drinks must show that half of their sales are for food. Private clubs are not bound by such a standard, but they do have the three-day rule, which says you have to wait three days to become a member once you pay your membership fee. The fee is rarely over $10. A newcomer usually can persuade a nearby member to sponsor him or her for the evening as a guest (guest fees run about $3). If you are a member of a club and want to take some friends, be aware that you'll have to pay guest fees for your non-member friends. Our aim is to help you find your way to a good time, not a hard time. So, put on your high heel sneakers and cruise!

Raleigh

If you were to rate night life like the movies, Raleigh and Cary would be somewhere between PG and PG-13. The universities and colleges certainly give the cities a young and curious audience. The city has attracted the upscale, yuppie strip clubs with names like "Thee Doll House," and there's a gay bar zone on Hargett St. downtown where sad looking pickups stand around in the cold, wind and rain, waiting, waiting, waiting. That's as soft as the fleshy underbelly gets.

In the past few years, Raleigh has gained a reputation as a way station for bands and performers working toward the big time at places like **Charlie Goodnight's Comedy Club**, the **Switch**, the **Longbranch**, the **Brewery**, **Lake Boone Country Club**, and the still rockin' **Fallout Shelter**. Singer Mike Cross was a regular at the now-gone Underground in Cameron Village and Jimmy Buffet once played to sold-out crowds at the old Pier, as did New York's gay Gotham group. Since 1991, Raleigh itself has become the Big Time when **Walnut Creek Amphitheater** opened to headliners like Whitney Houston,

Jimmy Buffet, Rod Stewart, John Denver, the Lollapolooza tours, Reba McIntire, and the Beach Boys.

With the state's anti-pornography law, most of the smut crowd is looking over their shoulders. Which is not to say you can't have a hot time or find a blind pig or maybe even meet Mr. or Ms. Right at one of several popular restaurants and bars. These things do happen in Raleigh. Some of the clubs require memberships—in order to satisfy the mixed drink law—but the fees usually can be obtained at a reasonable rate with a short waiting period of three days.

ALIVE AFTER FIVE

Fayetteville Street Mall   *831-6011*
Civic Center Plaza

This is a pump-primer event sponsored by the city and others to get people downtown and surprise! It works! It happens only in the summer and only on Thursdays, but it has become popular with the younger professionals and working crowd as a place to hear live music, free, and mingle with the svelte and sweaty. The bands are rock 'n roll and R&B.

THE BERKELEY CAFE

217 W. Martin St.   *821-0777*

No, this is not where ex-patriot Californians read beat poetry. It is a small cafe and club facing Nash Square downtown, and the live music won't blow you out in the street. Local folks play here; even the famed local cartoonist Dwane Powell has been known to strum his guitar here. As one critic described

the cafe, it's mostly R&B and rootsy rock acts, "a little bit of Memphis in downtown Raleigh."

BOWTIES

North Raleigh Hilton   *872-2323*
3415 Wake Forest Rd.

Bowties draws some of the prep crowd and has survived the "bar wars" when one hotel was competing with another to attract the singles flock. As one patron put it, "This is not your corner neighborhood bar." It caters to the beach music bunch along with other rock and roll dancing music. What is beach music? It's a holdover from the 1960s and is sung by such groups as The Embers. It took root on the Carolina campuses, especially at UNC fraternity parties, and it's an institution now. Bowties has no live music, but it does have great highballs. It holds 350, so it's a place to meet people. The big screen and four TV monitors for music videos or ACC basketball make it a popular place on game nights. It has a complimentary buffet and all ABC permits.

THE BREWERY

3009 Hillsborough St.   *834-7018*

If your heart is in rock and roll, this is the place for you. It brings in the best of the original R&R groups and has featured the good local bands such as The Connells, Don Dixon and Mitch Easter as well as The Woods and Finger and bands from California and Great Britain. Its proximity to NCSU gives the crowd a student flavor. It serves beer; the cover charge usually is modest, and the crowd—300 is the limit—likes music. It's one of the more popular stops on the rock tour for working bands.

CAPPERS
4217 Six Forks Rd.   *787-8963*

This north Raleigh restaurant, across the street from North Hills Mall, has made a hit among Triangle jazz buffs for its nightly music. It led *The Spectator* magazine's annual "Best List" as the best place for jazz for three years running. Musicians such as Gregg Gelb, Jim Crew and Jim Rhodes are featured six nights a week. It also has a great lunch crowd, seats about 145 and has all ABC permits.

CHAMPIONS—THE AMERICAN SPORTS BAR
Marriott Hotel
4500 Marriott Dr.   *781-2899*

As with Bowties, Champions has been a popular place for singles over the past few years. Like a moveable beast, the swinging crowd will graze for a few months at one place and then try another. Sometimes called "bar wars," the competition among the hotel lounges has been heated at times, but things seem to have settled into peaceful coexistence. Champions has 10 TV monitors and access to satellites, so this is not the place you're going to see N. Y. ballet. The crowd is "sporty," and Monday night is popular with football fans. It's open seven days a week, 12 noon to 1 a.m., and serves dinner. A D.J. spins records Fridays and Saturdays and there's room to dance.

CHARLIE GOODNIGHT'S COMEDY CLUB AND THE NEW BAR
861 W. Morgan St.   *828-5233*

Charlie Goodnight's is the city's first comedy club and is considered one of the best on the East Coast. It has become a fixture for good time entertainment and has plenty of parking off Morgan Street, close to Central Prison so if anyone dies of laughter, it can put the comic away quick. It's been a stop for familiar, and now famous, names like Jay Leno, Richard Jeni, Yakov Smirnoff and the Unknown Comic (the guy with a paper bag over his head).

Charlie Goodnight's restaurant downstairs serves Mexican fare, and the club serves drinks and snacks. The club has all ABC permits, and shows run Tuesday through Saturday with one show a night during the week, two on Friday and three on Saturday. Call for times and reservations. Charge cards accepted.

The New Bar is the new place behind the Comedy Club.

CROWLEY'S OLD FAVORITES
3071 Medlin Dr.   *787-3431*

There are three Crowley's and this is the first one. Another is located on Edwards Mill Rd. and the third is at Stonehenge off Creedmoor Rd. The one on Medlin Dr. attracts some of the young and beautiful and boistrous bunch and the food is good, too. The other two places offer music with their meals. The bar is small enough that it gives you excuses for easy pick-up lines, e.g., "Sorry, I didn't mean to step on your well turned toes, but now that we've met, can I buy you a drink."

EASY STREET
119 E. Hargett St.   755-0404

This is one of the places downtown that has survived, and Easy Street is one new nightspot that ought to survive. It is near Moore Square and the city's art district and has the clientele to match. It serves lunch, but at night, it boogies and rocks with newcomer groups that have wonderful names like Big Root and the Mojo Heads, Bad Bob & the Rockin' Horses, and Death and Taxes. These groups don't play just jazz or rock and roll or R&B; rather, it's jazz fusion, alternative roots rock, renegade R&B or Chicago R&B.

FALLOUT SHELTER
2 S. West St.   832-8855

This is where the guys and gals with spiked hair and black boots go to do a little light dancin'. If there is good heavy metal or "alternative" music in town, it will be blasting in the Shelter. Some of the names who've been on the marquee include Superchunk, Seaweed and the amazing Velocity Girl and Motorolla. It has been described by one patron as "low cover, low ceilings, and low art." On Mondays and Wednesdays, it's Industrial Progressive Dance night, so bring your jackhammers.

FOXY LADY
1817 Capital Blvd.   833-5886

Yes, the Foxy Lady missed out on earlier, more fastidious editions, but it's as much a part of Raleigh's night life as honky tonk bars and beach music. It's the blue collar version of Thee Doll House "adult showclub": it features amateur nights on Tuesdays and Thursdays for the truly desperate. It's been around and has survived long enough to call itself "Raleigh's most established" night club. Don't expect, however, to see many of Raleigh's Establishment types hanging out here.

42ND STREET OYSTER BAR
507 W. Jones St.   831-2811

This downtown restaurant and bar opened in late 1987 and quickly made all the lists in 1988, especially as the new place to be seen among the single set. It has all ABC permits and live music on special days—and an interesting decor, including a bar mural that celebrates the late restaurateur Thad Eure, Jr., and friends. In *The Spectator* magazine's annual poll, the 42nd St. Bar is usually rated the best bar for meeting people and the best place to be seen. If you go on Friday or Saturday night, you will definitely meet people—waiting to get in!

HOOTERS
4206 Wake Forest Rd.   850-9882

Hooters dangles pretty waitresses and a breezy, good time attitude to attract the males who like sports and beer and...shall we say, hooters. As one of the restaurant's founders told a local reporter, "You have to understand we are the alternative to those other restaurants out there now, like the fern bars." Right. It has a basketball hoop outside as well as horseshoes for warm up and its specialty, if you can believe it, is chicken wings. Said one female patron about the attractive waitresses, "It's great. They bait 'em [all the male patrons] and we hook 'em."

LAKE BOONE COUNTRY CLUB
2442 Wycliff Rd.   *571-1093*

This is one of the city's hot spots. The nightclub and sports bar opened New Year's Eve 1991, and brings in live bands as well as plenty of sports fans. There are 26 TVs in the place, including a big screen for those who like their action up close and personal. The location is in a westside shopping center, formerly occupied by Sam's Restaurant, a popular neighborhood steak place. The music is rock 'n roll on Wednesdays, Fridays and Saturdays—presumably not during game time. It serves beer and wine, takes credit cards and grills food.

LONGBRANCH
600 Creekside Dr.   *829-1125*

One of the three or four places in town where you can find name entertainment like, great balls of fire!, Jerry Lee Lewis. It's a membership club with all ABC permits. Despite its name, it features Top 40 acts and "beach music," which is good dancing music popular in the Carolinas back in the '60s that has become institutionalized with the Yuppie set here. The ever popular Embers play here and Three Dog Night has howled here. The Longbranch also has a room for country and western, and country rock groups, so you won't feel out of place in your cowboy boots and

truck. Don't go here looking for heavy metal headbangers, however. It also is one of the singles markets where you can meet the opposite sex and lots of them—it holds 1,000.

OSCAR'S SUPPER CLUB
4000 Atlantic Ave.   *872-7706*

Oscar's Supper Club is available for private parties, wedding receptions and corporate functions any day of the week. It has one of the largest dance floors in the Triangle and is the perfect place for that special event. Sandra Burnett, owner of Sisters' Catering Company, also owns Oscar's, and functions here are catered by Sisters'.

THE PR (PLAYERS RETREAT)
105 Oberlin Rd.   *755-9589*

A Raleigh institution, the PR is a true-blue neighborhood pub or tavern that is rumored to be the oldest such between Washington and Atlanta. Near the NCSU campus, many a State student has grown wise watching the fish behind the bar and debating the finer points of ACC basketball. Pool, darts and video games are available, but the show is in the customers, many of whom are still trying to graduate from the '60s. The Bernie Burger is one of the best hamburgers in town. If you plan to live in Raleigh, you need to visit the PR at least once, like going to the Art Museum, to appreciate the culture. This is a real place, so bring cash and drink beer.

RALEIGHWOOD CINEMA GRILL
6609 Falls of the Neuse   *847-8370*

Raleighwood's logo says it all, "Great Movies, Food & Spirits!"

Basically, the idea is to combine great food, a fun atmosphere and Hollywood's newest movies to create an enjoyable and affordable evening out.

Raleighwood is locally owned and operated by James Keane. The contemporary decor is upbeat, and the wide beverage selection and tempting food is served by a friendly and hospitable staff. The menu has a wide variety of items, including pizza, burgers and salads, and beverages include beer, wine and mixed drinks.

The facilities are available for business meetings, conferences, and private parties. Call for more information.

RED'S BEACH MUSIC
4339 Falls of the Neuse Rd.   876-5333

If you live in North Carolina, you are going to hear beach music, that easy moving rock 'n' roll of the late '50s and early '60s. Red's capitalizes on the nostalgia for the music, and the crowd there will reflect the age of the music. You may even see married people dancing together! It's relaxed and a good place to take the spouse to shake up the metabolism. Red's is a private club and has ABC permits.

WALNUT CREEK AMPHITHEATER
Rock Quarry & Sunnybrook rds. 834-4000

When there's a hot concert in town, this is **the** night life for the Triangle, the Triad and eastern North Carolina. It is the latest in multi-million dollar outdoor amphitheaters built with public and private funds. Walnut Creek has seen tremendous sell-out perfor-

mances over the past three years including Jimmy Buffet, Elton John, Reba McEntire and Rod Stewart among many others. The amphitheater is an important stop on almost all national tours. (See the **ATTRACTIONS** section.)

Cary

What a difference a year makes! Cary now has a topless bar and protestors marching to object. While most night life in suburbia remains G-rated, there are places where you can kick up some...ah, excitement. As you will see, it is a short list. (Most of these places, by the way, are listed in more detail in the "Cary" Section of **TRIANGLE RESTAURANTS**, too.) Here's where Cary insiders get down.

FOX AND HOUND
MacGregor Village   380-0080

Even its proprietor Dane Johnston admits that Cary nightlife is pretty "tame," and he closes at midnight. On Wednesdays and Thursdays, a guitarist plays light and easy music with the good English fare, and things on Thursday get somewhat louder as the musician plays Irish and English ballads with some sing-along college fight songs.

NEWTON'S SOUTHWEST
1837 N. Harrison Ave.   677-1777

The Newtons made a hit with a bit of Texas in north Cary. At the Southwest, the music gets loud and from March 'til October, the feet kick out on a heated, outdoor dance floor called **Pepper's Patio**. It tends to draw a young crowd, which has a "good time," according to the people who do business close by. Wednesday night is Karaoke Sing Along, Friday and Saturday, Rock and Roll.

PURE GOLD
301 N. Harrison Ave.

This is the place that has caused all the rukus even though it's within two blocks of the watchful eyes of City Hall. According to its manager, this is a classy legitimate adult business where some of the female entertainers happen to be topless. Complained Mayor Koka Booth, "It's not required, not needed, not wanted. This is a family community." With all the publicity, however, Pure Gold opened with good crowds and, says the manager, "We're going to do a lot of charity work." Right.

SELDOM BLUES
Waverly Place   *851-2583*

Some might argue this is the only place around that really looks like a night spot because it could fit into the New York City scene in a blink. The live music is jazz and the atmosphere, cool.

Durham

Durham is not really a late-night town. Teens and college students looking for loud music they can dance to will fare better in Chapel Hill and Raleigh. But Durham does have a few nightspots where you'll find mostly jazz, folk or reggae-rock, for a modest cover charge.

DEVINES RESTAURANT AND SPORTS BAR
904 W. Main St.   *682-0228*

This bar, owned by Genne Devine from Boston, has the same flavor as TV's famous Cheers, with a sports theme. Live entertainment is featured two nights a week. The restaurant and bar are open 7 days a week, serving lunches and dinners of salads, appetizers, special grill and sandwich items. Favorites include Coach K's Big B, The Head Coach and All Pro Big Guy. It also caters and offers take out.

HALBY'S
Forest Hills Shopping Center   *489-2811*

Halby's, a sandwich shop and bar, has live music—jazz, blues and rock n' roll—on Friday and Saturday nights. Brother Yusuf Salim & Friends, a favorite of local jazz buffs, appears Thursday evenings.

NINTH STREET BAKERY AND CAFE
754 Ninth St.   *286-0303*

Irish, folk, and acoustic string music are served up here, along with rhythm and blues. Music is on the menu on Friday and Saturday nights, when the cafe's open until 11 p.m.

THE PALACE INTERNATIONAL
117 W. Parrish St.   *687-4922*

Located in downtown Durham, The Palace International is the place to go for reggae, African, Caribbean and salsa music. The Palace is open from 11 a.m. to 3:30 a.m. Monday through Thursday, and from 9 a.m. to 4 a.m. Friday, Saturday and Sunday. The Palace serves snacks, meals, beer, wine and mixed drinks, as well as sodas and fruit juices. There is often live, international music on Thursday, Friday and Saturday nights, with a cover charge.

SHERATON UNIVERSITY CENTER
2800 Middleton Ave.   *383-8575*
Jazz and blues performances are featured in the bar here several nights a week. Shows run 9 p.m. to midnight, and there's no cover.

STEVIE'S
3808 Guess Rd.   *477-8360*
Stevie's is a new night spot in Durham, offering live rock n' roll,

jazz and country music. There is usually music seven nights a week. Recent performers have included Eve Cornelious/Chip Crawford Band, Greg Gelb Swing Band and Cream of Soul.

TALK OF THE TOWN
108 E. Main St.   *682-7747*
Talk of the Town is another new club, specializing in jazz and rhythm and blues. There is live music Thursday through Saturday nights.

Chapel Hill

Being a small town, Chapel Hill doesn't offer a huge number of night spots, but the live music that is available is innovative and occasionally astounding. Here's our guide to a few places that regularly feature live music, usually for a modest cover charge.

THE ARTSCENTER
300-G East Main St., Carrboro   929-ARTS
One of the many activities regularly sponsored by The ArtsCenter is a jazz series. These concerts are held in an acoustically–pleasing auditorium in a painstakingly renovated grocery store on East Main Street. Several times a month, you can catch either a scheduled jazz performance by a well-known musician or an open jam session of local jazz artists. Artists such as Tom Petty, Stanley Jordan and trombonist Steve Turre have also performed here. You're in for a treat for a modest admission price.

CAT'S CRADLE

300 E. Main St.   *967-9053*
Carrboro

The old favorite, Cat's Cradle, has resurfaced at a new location in Carrboro, near the ArtsCenter. Popular with the college crowd for the past 25 years, the Cat's Cradle is open six or seven nights a week and normally features two or three different bands each night it's open. If you call, a recorded message will give you current information on hours and scheduled entertainment.

THE CAVE

452 1/2 W. Franklin St.   *968-9308*

This basement pub below Franklin Street has been around for 30 years. It features everything from banjo pickers and folk rock to rock 'n roll, blues, alternative and acoustic. Every Monday night, women musicians are featured. It's open from 2:30 p.m. until 2:30 a.m. seven days a week and is a great place for a cold beer and a game of pool.

HE'S NOT HERE

112 1/2 Franklin St.   *942-7939*

Despite the name, if he (or she) is young, thirsty and looking for a party, chances are that he (or she) is here and having a good time. A Chapel Hill landmark well known to Insiders, He's Not Here features bands on Friday and Saturday nights, and Karaoke Night for would-be stars on Sunday at 10:00 p.m.

LOCAL 506

506 W. Franklin St.   *9942-5506*

Local 506 has found a niche in the Chapel Hill night scene with its emphasis on local bands. The club can accommodate a dancing crowd when the music is right. There is a cover charge. Live entertainment is usually featured Thursday through Saturday each week.

OMNI EUROPA

Omni Europa Hotel   *968-4900*

Take the glass elevator to the **King's Club** in the elegant Omni Europa Hotel and step into one of Chapel Hill's classiest clubs. Friday and Saturday are Latin nights, with salsa and Caribbean music. There are salsa dance lessons from 8:00 to 9:00 p.m. Dress is casual and the bar is open late Monday through Saturday.

PYEWACKET

The Courtyard   *929-0297*
431 W. Franklin St.

After you've feasted on wholesomely delicious foods, you can sit up near the antique bar and catch jazz, acoustic folk or swing music several nights during the week. Entertainment usually begins about 9:30 p.m.

SKYLIGHT EXCHANGE

405 1/2 W. Rosemary St.   *933-5550*

When Dennis Gavin had to relocate Fair Exchange, his used-book-and-record store in Carrboro, he knew he was going to have to pull some tricks out of his bag to meet the higher rent at his new Chapel Hill address. So, he teamed up with friend John Howell to add a coffeehouse/music club to the book- and record-store business. The place has been packing in music

*Visitors can relax and listen to soft piano music or classical guitar
in the lobby of the Siena Hotel.*

fans ever since. After all, their new home is in an old club space that has long been devoted to live music—such as Rhythm Alley and, before that, the Cat's Cradle. Skylight Exchange features live music—from acoustic folk to rock 'n roll—Thursday through Saturday. During the day and on non-music nights, the Skylight Exchange is always good for a sandwich or light snack, cup of coffee, and several hours of browsing through old paperbacks, records and tapes. Located next to Dip's restaurant (see **Restaurants**), it's open from 8 a.m. to 11 p.m. Monday through Friday and 10 a.m. to midnight Saturday.

SPANKY'S UPSTAIRS

101 E. Franklin St.   *967-2678*

Spanky's is often the place for live music during the week. Local performers play everything from Motown to jazz to acoustic music.

SIENA HOTEL

1505 E. Franklin St.   *929-4000*

If rock isn't your style, the Siena's comfortable Italianate lobby is the ideal spot to hear soft piano music or classical guitar. It's a pleasant place to relax with a glass of wine. Music is usually offered at 6:30 p.m. on weekend nights.

*Big Ed's City Market Restaurant is a favorite gathering place
in downtown Raleigh.*

Inside

Restaurants

Keep two things in mind when you're dining out in the Triangle: one, you're still in the South, and two, the restaurant where you're eating probably was pasture or woods only 20 years ago. Southerners like to eat, and they like good, solid food. As one veteran Piedmont restaurant owner said, "They generally like something that will stick to them; no fancy vegetables like broccoli."

Because the Triangle market has been a fast-growth Sunbelt hot spot, many of the restaurant chains have made the area a pin on their location maps. **Golden Corral**, for instance, started and lives in Raleigh. The bulk of the city's new restaurants are chain operations, whether national or regional in origin. This guide, then, won't waste time telling you about Applebee's, Bennigan's, ChiChi's, T. K. Tripp's, Lone Star or Outback steakhouses, with which you probably are familiar. Rather, it's a guide to special places and aims to direct you to-

ward some of the area's best or unusual or favorite restaurants. Most of them are locally owned and operated. It's not a directory, and the authors declare with fingers uncrossed that none mentioned here is run by a brother-in-law or distant kin.

The dollar signs ($) beside a restaurant entry are an early warning system as to what your bill for an evening meal for two might be, assuming that you don't insist on a bottle of Chateau Lafite-Rothschild with every meal. Remember that lunch at many of the fancier places will be about half the cost of evening fare. If a restaurant has all ABC (Alcoholic Beverage Control) permits, it means the place serves mixed drinks as well as beer and wine. The cost code can be deciphered thus:

Under $20	$
$21 to $35	$$
$36 to $50	$$$
$51 and up	$$$$

Raleigh

Raleigh has come a long way in a short time when it comes to developing a restaurant reputation. As one local wag who grew up on rich, varied New Orleans fare put it, "Raleigh's idea of international dining 25 years ago consisted of Tippy's Taco and the Pizza Hut." The menu has changed dramatically since then and today you can sample a wide variety of foods in the capital city, from northern Italian to hot Szechwan Chinese.

A 1992 city ordinance requires that most restaurants (those that seat more than 50) must have no-smoking sections. The restaurants on the "best" list take credit cards unless stated otherwise. It's always good to check anyway since rules can change overnight. Be advised that on State Fair or football weekends, you may wait 30 to 45 minutes for a table. Raleigh eats out, folks. This section is divided into two parts: first, some of Raleigh's best places and second, some of its special places. So, bless this food, Amen.

Some Of The Best

ANGUS BARN
U.S. Hwy. 70 at Airport Rd.   781-2444
$$$$

This is **the** steak house in town and has been for over 30 years. Because of its location near the airport, it has always been popular with travelers, especially business people, and many a Triangle business deal has been completed over

its tables. The rustic barn decor was something new for the area when it first opened and many came to look. While its reputation was made on its steaks, its success with beef and pork ribs propelled the owners to start the popular Darryl's restaurant chain, which they later sold. Desserts are rich and homemade. Bring a big appetite. It seats hundreds, but reservations are taken and it has all ABC permits.

CAPITAL CITY CLUB
CP&L Building downtown   832-5526
411 Fayetteville St. Mall

It may be unfair to list the Capital City Club because it is a private club, but it's also one of Raleigh's best eating places. It sits 20 stories atop the CP&L building, which also gives diners a splendid view of the city and its greenery. The lunch-time buffet is well prepared and usually includes seafood, red meat and poultry. It's difficult to pick a bad dinner dish, and its after-dinner coffees are show stoppers. The ice cream ball with fudge is conspicuous consumption. If you get an invitation to eat here, accept forthwith. Only the host gets a menu with prices. You don't want to know.

COLONNADE ROOM
Ramada Inn, U.S. Hwy. 70 W.   782-7525
$$

Admittedly, Ramada Inns are not usually known for their food, but this is not your usual Ramada restaurant. One of the owners prepares the recipes, and, over the years, she has developed a strong, loyal following among Triangle diners, boasting three dining awards.

There's usually a crowd at all three meals, and its breakfast sausage (prepared on site) and apple turnovers are locally famous. The luncheon chicken salad is all white meat and the Beef Wellington is a special recipe. The Colonnade Room seats about 90 people and has all ABC permits.

CROSSROADS
5509 Edwards Mill Rd.   787-3840
$$$$

This is one of the fancier restaurants in town, and it sits atop a hill overlooking the lights of Crabtree Valley. Blessed with a spectacular view, its menu and wines are superb, and it is popular among the expense account bunch. One of its best sellers is the mixed-grill seafood entree that includes shrimp, swordfish or tuna. The stuffed jumbo shrimp with crab meat is another favorite, and the beef comes directly from Chicago. All of the desserts, as well as sauces, are made on the premises. It's first come, first served, but Crossroads can be persuaded to make exceptions and take reservations. This restaurant seats over 200 and has all ABC permits.

FIVE POINTS BISTRO
509-101 W. Whitaker Mill Rd.   828-7772
Eckerd Plaza, Five Points
$$$

This restaurant opened in August, 1991, and is a combined mother-daughter effort of Edwina Shaw and daughter Kelly Worth. Both are well-known Raleigh chefs, and Kelly operated her own catering business three years before opening the Bistro. There's a player

piano to add real music to the quiet atmosphere, and a well-appointed bar. The veal marsala and pasta is excellent, as is the pork tenderloin appetizer; Kelly says some of her favorites are the rack of lamb and lobster.

42ND ST. OYSTER BAR
Corner of Jones and West sts.   831-2811
$$$

Built on the site of a long-gone colorful downtown oyster bar, the latest version is another smashing restaurant success for the late restaurateur Thad Eure, Jr., and partner Brad Hurley. Most of the fish is caught by the restaurant's own boats and processed by its own Southport Fish Market on the coast.

The grilled swordfish and tuna are as good as you will get anywhere and the shrimp salad is a meal by itself. The meat dishes rival the city's best, and the menu also has Cajun specials and children's portions. It's a great place to be seen and meet people and frequently rates as the best place in town for "power meals." It has all ABC permits.

GLENWOOD GRILL
2929 Essex Cir.   *782-3102*
Glenwood Village Shopping Ctr.
$$$

This is a hang-out for the young and beautiful as well as many of the Old Raleigh crowd. It is the third restaurant to be in its location, but the owners this time have proved they have staying power. They also are nearby and have had plenty of experience from running the popular Simple Pleasures store and restaurant. They have a flair for presentation, and the grilled seafood and meats are delicious. It has a late-night menu Thursday through Saturday, with live music Friday and Saturday. It has all ABC permits.

HANGCHOW
512 Creekside Dr.   *828-5430*
$$$

The Hangchow arrived in 1973 and has continued to grow. It has been rated as the number one Chinese restaurant by local newspapers, and its success can be measured by its larger quarters. It specializes in northern Chinese dishes, and, like any good Chinese restaurant, has about three million items on the menu for eat-in and take-out. Its large building permits private dining for groups, and the service is quiet and efficient.

IRREGARDLESS CAFE
901 W. Morgan St.   *833-8898*
$$$

A favorite among the university crowd and women's groups, the Irregardless began as a non-meat restaurant in what was then a broken-down location. Musicians performed (and still do), and Raleigh held its breath to see if the place would survive. It survives and prospers, and today serves poultry and seafood, but still caters to vegetarians with a variety of imaginative dishes. Lunch favorites are the super salad, soups and open-faced sandwich. You can call and listen to a recorded mouth-watering, daily description of the evening menu which is changed daily. One of its owners, Arthur Gordon, is the chef, which helps explain its success.

Part of the attraction is its ambience, and the Sunday brunch (10 a.m.-2 p.m.) crowd could pass for a New York City scene. It seats about 90 and has all ABC permits but allows no smoking. The same folks operate the **Museum Cafe** at the N.C. Museum of Art.

JEAN-CLAUDE'S FRENCH CAFE
North Ridge Shopping Ctr.   *872-6224*
$$

One of the author's favorite places, Jean-Claude's offers a French menu in a cafe atmosphere. If you look over the counter, you can see the new owner, Therese Freeman at work, fixing softshell crab or the daily special, which might be duck or fresh salmon. She is, by the way, "100 percent French." The beef stroganoff crepe also is recommended. The desserts are French, and the caramel flan is the best in town. A wine tasting is held once a month. It's popular and relaxed, so get there on time or you may have to stand outside. The new owner has also added banquet facilities.

KAREN'S RESTAURANT & BAR
428 Daniels St.   832-7950
Cameron Village Shopping Ctr.
$$$

The owner, Karen Nowell, has been cooking for years as one of Old Raleigh's preferred caterers. Her restaurant and bar in Cameron Village Shopping Center was a hit from the moment it opened its doors in 1987. The tables have linen cloths and fresh flowers, and there's a wine list to match. There's usually a line for lunch, so get there early. Dinner features beef, veal, poultry and seafood dishes with an emphasis on the seafood. The chef has a light touch. It has all ABC permits and seats about 50.

MARGAUX'S
8111 Creedmoor Rd.
Brennan Station   846-9846
$$$

This French restaurant opened in 1992 and opened to a four stars review in the *News & Observer*. It has continued to be a hot topic on the word-of-mouth circuit. It is way, way out Creedmoor Road in Brennan Station Shopping Center in the land of north Raleigh. The restaurant is operated by two brothers-in-law, Richard Hege, the chef and a top graduate of the Culinary Institute of America, and Steven Horowitz. They turned what had been a sporting goods store into a 110-seat restaurant with a fireplace. Hors d'oeuvres to remember are the chilled seafood platter and the sausage appetizers. The chef's specialties include sole and crab casserole, suckling pig and Carolina quail. The desserts are reportedly among the best in the Triangle (at $4.25, they'd better be!). It has all ABC permits and is closed on Mondays.

VINNIE'S STEAK HOUSE & TAVERN
7440 Six Forks Rd.   847-7319
$$$

This is one of north Raleigh's favorite places and is located in the Peachtree Market, but when you walk in, the smokey, bustling atmosphere could be big-city Chicago or New York. Where other restaurants tried and failed, Vinnie's has succeeded in building a loyal following who want a pleasant, friendly atmosphere and good, well-prepared food. As the name suggests, it features Italian specialties but grills some of the best steaks and chops in town. It's a place where you can go late, too. Watch out for the legislators when they're in town; it's a lobbyist's favorite. It has all ABC permits.

WINSTON'S GRILLE
6401 Falls of the Neuse Rd.   790-0700
$$

Named after Charles Winston, Jr., a member of a celebrated local restaurant family, this restaurant and bar has become one of the places for a power lunch or special dinner. The bar is packed on weekends as the young and single crowd checks out the scene and the "grazing menu," which features such finger tasties as Buffalo-style chicken wings, fried calamari, cajun pasta, steamed oysters and peel-n-eat shrimp. The dinner menu has steaks, cajun shrimp, veal marsala, Cornish hen and duck. The wine list is serious, as is the beer page—over 50 brews listed. If you dare, climb the mile-high pie for dessert, but take a friend. It seats 300, but expect to wait.

Espresso Bar & Restaurant

Lunch 11:30-3:00 Tues-Sat
Brunch 11:30-3:00 Sun
Live entertainment on weekend.

**205 Wolfe Street
City Market
919•832•2201**

Special Places

BALENTINE'S
Cameron Village Shopping Ctr.   832-3741
$

If you plan to live in the Triangle, you need to visit Balentine's at least once. It's a family cafeteria owned and operated by the Balentine family and has become a landmark haven for working moms who want supper out but not a hamburger. There's a distinct Southern flavor, and you can find fried okra, squash, spoonbread like mother made, and corn pudding. The desserts are as good as they look. It also is popular as a banquet facility, but has no ABC permits.

BARISTA JAVA COFFEE HOUSE
City Market, downtown   832-2201
$$

Raleigh needed a place like this, especially for those evenings after the symphony or the theater. It's new and it's a combination coffee house and tea room, the latter dressed in appropriate white cloth table cloths. The owner—and her mother—are not above working the tables and the desserts are made from scratch and rich the way sweets should be. The lunch time sandwiches are fixed with thick slices of homemade bread and the coffee is superb. The tables and teapots are works of art. Expect live music on weekends.

BLACK DOG CAFE
City Market, downtown   828-1994
$$$

This corner lunch and nightspot opened in 1992. It quickly

established itself as one of the hang-outs for the younger set, and the food is light and lively. The pasta and vegetable plates are some of its best lunch fare. It serves a Sunday brunch and draws a good crowd at lunch and on the weekends. The Cafe serves dinner Wednesday-Saturday. It's also a popular starting point for the **Art Walks** downtown.

CAPITAL ROOM
Hudson Belk Store, downtown   832-5852
Fayetteville Street Mall
$

This is another cafeteria that has become an institution for noon-time diners downtown. You can see the editors of the *News & Observer* at one table and the entire North Carolina Supreme Court sitting at the big round table in the room to the right of the ticket register. It features Southern dishes and desserts, but also caters to the diet-conscious professional. Don't be intimidated by the long line; it moves quickly and it's a good place to visit with others.

CAPPERS
319 North Hills Plaza   787-8963
$$$

This restaurant is located across from North Hills Fashion Mall, and it has become a popular lunch stop for north Raleigh business people. In the evening, it's one of the best places in the city for those who like jazz with their food. It started in the 1980s, so it has survived the test of time, and you will find a good selection of seafood here. It seats about 175 and has all ABC permits.

CASA CARBONE'S RISTORANTE ITALIANO
U.S. Hwy. 70 W.   781-8750
Oak Park Shopping Ctr.
$$

It's too long and involved a family story to explain the beginnings of this popular Italian restaurant. It is sufficient to note that the Carbones have been in the business for a long time, and the next generation is taking over. For years their cooking was the standard by which Raleigh measured its Italian food—rated "best" in the Triangle by the *Spectator's* annual reader's poll. Casa Carbone is not too proud to serve pizza—some of the city's best—as well as traditional Italian pasta and veal. This is a family place, so don't worry about taking little ones. It has all ABC permits.

THE CHAR-GRILL
618 Hillsborough St.   821-7636
$

This is an enduring '50s-style, drive-in fixture that keeps the lunch time and late-night crowd standing in line for big burgers, fries and shakes. There are two suburban locations, too, at Olde Raleigh and on Atlantic Ave.

COOPER'S BARBEQUE
109 E. Davie St.   832-7614
$

This downtown, working-man's restaurant serves Raleigh's best pork barbecue—in North Carolina, there's no other kind of barbecue—despite what you might hear elsewhere. It is served in throw-away dishes and comes with fried hushpuppies and crisp pork skin. You can get your pork chopped or sliced. As eastern Carolina barbecue, it has a vinegar sauce, not tomato-based, so don't be surprised. Wash it down with a Pepsi or sweetened tea. You can sit at the counter or at one of the booths, and the person next to you might be the mechanic down the street or a former governor. Cooper's is very democratic that way.

DALAT ORIENTAL RESTAURANT
2109 Avent Ferry Rd.   832-7449
Mission Valley Shopping Ctr.
$

One of the exciting features of Raleigh is its growing diversity, and the variety of oriental foods is a good example. Immigration during the late '70s and '80s established a solid oriental community, of which Dalat is a product. It opened in 1991 serving a Vietnamese menu. The unfried, vegetable Dalat roll and pork dishes are excellent. Try the Dalat pasta salad, too. It seats about 40 and its prices are popular with students. In the same shopping center, you can find Indian fare. Dalat is among a growing number of Indian, Thai, Korean and Japanese restaurants.

EL DORADO
2811 Brentwood Rd.   872-8440
$$

This has become Raleigh's most authentic Mexican restaurant, and Tex-Mex fans swear by it. Indeed, when you walk in the door and see the pool table off to the right with the rolled-up-sleeve crowd in their T-shirts speaking Spanish, you will think you've crossed the Rio Grande. The waiter may or may not understand English, but he will

be polite, nod at your comments and somehow get the right dish to you. On some evenings, you might also listen to a table-side serenade that's as authentic as the enchiladas and Corona beer. Check it out!

EST EST EST TRATORIA
19 W. Hargett St., downtown   832-8899
$$

The address says West Hargett, but you enter the door on Salisbury Street. This brave Italian restaurant went against conventional wisdom by opening downtown and immediately gained a lunch time following. Over the years, it has drawn people back downtown for dinner and features a new menu. The small, intimate atmosphere makes it great for romantics and the elevated bar is a nice place to relax. The excellent pasta is made on premises and service is sometimes slow but always certain. Its cappuccino, espresso and House wines are rated the best in the Triangle.

GREENSHIELD'S BREWERY & PUB
214 E. Martin St.   829-0214
City Market, downtown
$$

For the best beer in town, this is the place. It brews its own and has light and dark varieties. The centerpiece restaurant in the old City Market building, Greenshield's is expanding and has earned a following among the Anglophiles of the Triangle. On certain nights, you will meet up with local rugby teams or dart leagues who are quenching their thirst in a pub that serves pot pies, and fish and chips. The location is superb and the fare reason-

able; it's a great place to take a visiting parent or your NCSU student who has come of age and wants a real beer.

GREGORY'S RESTAURANT
Peachtree Market   847-6230
7420 Six Forks Rd.
$$

This is a popular north Raleigh brunch and lunch place, with glittering glass and tablecloths. You feel like you're in a nice home. North Raleigh residents like it for family parties, and it's where you can visit over a cup of coffee and croissant for as long as you want.

JOE'S PLACE
301 W. Martin St.   832-5260
$

Joe features his mom's cooking and says so on the sign. Always popular with the noontime crowd downtown, even before it became Joe's Place, Joe added a little polish, unsweetened tea and plenty of food on your plate, especially the big sandwiches. He also is open for evening meals.

KANKI JAPANESE HOUSE OF STEAKS
Crabtree Valley Mall   782-9708
(Next to Main Mall Entrance)
North Market Square   876-4157
4500 Old Wake Forest Rd.
$$

It may not be traditional "live entertainment," but the chefs here put on quite a show. The menu is extensive featuring beef, pork and seafood, and the dishes are all prepared at the table with great flair. This is a great place to take the gang from the office or any other fun-loving group looking for good food

and a good time. The North Market location has a Sushi Bar.

MECCA
13 East Martin St., downtown   832-5714
$

The Mecca is an American success story for three generations of the Dombalis family. It is the sterotypical downtown lunchtime restaurant, with fading photographs of fading politicians on the wall and a room upstairs when the wooden booths downstairs are full. The food, however, is solid, good fare—the lightly fried flounder is excellent. Nick buys his produce fresh at the Farmer's Market, and his rice pudding—if and when he makes it—is the best in town.

THE PEDDLER STEAK HOUSE
6005 Glenwood Ave.   787-6980
$$

Small, candlelit and cozy, The Peddler opened in its original location in Oak Park Shopping Center in 1969. If you're a steak lover, you will love this place where you choose your cut of meat right at your table. It also serves lobster, seafood and chicken and has wonderful, fresh homemade desserts. The restaurant is open Monday through Saturday and has two private dining rooms available for meetings.

RATHSKELLER
2412 Hillsborough St.   821-5342
$$

This popular restaurant sits across the street from NCSU and is popular with the faculty as well as local business people. Parking can be a problem, but the meals are worth the effort. Despite its name, the menu is not very German; indeed, it has vegetarian menus and offers daily specials with good, hearty soups. It has all ABC permits.

SIMPLE PLEASURES MARKET & CAFE
Glenwood Village   782-9227
$

This is where you can see beautiful people while you eat beautiful food. Located in one of Raleigh's favorite specialty food stores, the restaurant serves lunch only, but it's open seven days a week with brunch on Saturdays and Sundays. It also caters. The menu is changed daily and is chalked up on the blackboard at the end of the bar. The soups are homemade and zesty, and the light eaters as well as the businessman who wants a real-food beef dish will find accommodating entrees. And when you finish, the chocolate bar in the next room is one of the sweetest in the Triangle.

SUNFLOWER'S SANDWICH SHOP
315 Glenwood Ave.   833-4676
$

This is a bright, corner sandwich shop that serves what may be the best chunky, chicken salad sandwiches in town. You place your order, sit down and your name is called when the food's ready. It's small and open only for lunch, but the noon crowd knows one another, so waiting usually turns into a time to visit. Homemade milkshakes and good cookies are featured. It also caters.

THE UPSTAIRS
Upstairs over Heilig-Levine Furniture
135 S. Wilmington St.   *833-9734*
$

The author's favorite place downtown, the Upstairs (aka Marcus' Upstairs) restaurant and delicatessen has been a fixture in Raleigh's cultural and political life for decades. Many a news leak was sprung at its tables over lunch between capital correspondents and state government leaders. The art crowd, journalists, bureaucrats and politicians continue to swap news here and see who's eating with whom. Patrons memorize Mrs. Levine's daily specials, the best of which is served on Friday—brisket of beef with fried potato cakes, and on Thursday, you can get blintzes. The desserts are scrumptious, especially the bishop's pie—five layers of sin, according to author-hostess Nell Styron.

THE UPPER CRUST
8831 Six Forks Rd.   *847-8088*
Six Forks Station at Strickland Rd.
$

This North Raleigh favorite for casual dining features mouthwatering chicken-salad sandwiches, rich soups, unique salads and de-

lectable desserts served with gourmet coffee, raspberry tea, imported beer or wine. It's open for Sunday brunch, too.

TIPPY'S MEXICAN RESTAURANT
808 W. Hodges St.   *828-0797*
$

To veterans, it's still Tippy's Taco Hut, one of Raleigh's pioneers in international cuisine. The restaurant is bigger and fancier with bullfight scenes on the wall, but the fried beans, chili, tacos and hot enchiladas are as good as when it was a taco hut and served the T-shirt crowd. It's a local survivor and can dish out indigestion with the best Mexican chains in town.

A final word. The above admittedly is a short list, so it's only fair to mention some other places that have survived in what is a notoriously tough business. Survival for a restaurant, after all, is perhaps the best test for local taste. Here, then, is an abbreviated Insider's guide to a few more:

Brothers Pizza Palace on Hillsborough Street has kept NCSU students and families on a budget filled for years. A family-owned, friendly neighborhood place.

Canton Cafe on Hillsborough Street is the city's oldest Chinese restaurant.

Crowley's on Medlin Drive is noted for its rib plate. Its success begat two more, at Stonehenge and Olde Raleigh.

Darryl's, at many locations, is a local phenomenon that capitalized on nostalgic, eclectic decor and

THE
WEATHERVANE

A Southern Season's Comfortable Café

Monday-Saturday 10 am - 11 pm
Sunday, 11 am - 6 pm
Reservations Accepted

Telephone 929-9466
A Southern Season • Eastgate • Chapel Hill

SPANKY'S
101

Fresh Seafood & Chicken Specials
Famous Charbroiled Burgers
Fresh Salads & Pastas
London Broil • Quiche

Serving Lunch, Dinner
Late Night & Sunday Brunch

101 East Franklin Street, Chapel Hill 967-2678
Banquet Reservations 929-5098

four eleven west

Capturing the vitality of
Italy and the Mediterranean
with a casual and imaginative twist.

Serving lunch Monday thru Saturday • Dinner nightly

Seasonal pasta • Wood burning pizza oven • Cappuccino bar

411 West Franklin Street • Chapel Hill, NC • 967-2782 • 96-PASTA

medium priced menus (ribs and sandwiches) to produce some of the longest lines in town. It is no longer locally owned, but people still wait to get in.

Daruma on Hillsborough Street, according to some, is the only authentic Japanese restaurant in town.

Golden Key on Hillsborough Street is one of the city's longest running Greek performances.

IHOP on Hillsborough Street, aka the International House of Pancakes, is where you can go in an emergency since it's open 24 hours and usually has a policeman inside eating.

Plantation Inn on U.S. Highway 1 gives you an idea that what was the best in town 25 years ago is still very good today. It's a traditional favorite of many Raleigh families.

Profile, off Whitaker Mill Road, has a Greek flavor to its Southern cooking, but the owner's irrepressible personality is what draws the fans.

Sadlack's on Hillsborough Street is where you can get great commentary from the cook and observe what's left of hippies and other species.

Swain's Steak House on Milburnie Road near Wake Medical Center cooks one of the best steaks in town and offers much, much more on the menu than beef.

Caterers

In addition to restaurants, here is a listing with brief comments on some of Raleigh's caterers. Since we first started writing, it seems that everyone has become a caterer, so if you have a favorite restaurant, you might check there first to see if it also caters. Most of the larger hotels, for example, now cater, including the Mission Valley Inn, Velvet Cloak, and Marriott.

DON MURRAY'S BARBECUE
2751 Capital Blvd.   872-6270

It does a good job on catering traditional barbecue to small and large groups and will introduce you to an authentic North Carolina pig picking. Among barbecue places, Don Murray's probably is biggest in catering. Coopers, (see previously under **RESTAURANTS**) also caters.

FIVE POINTS BISTRO & BAR
509-101 W. Whitaker Mill Rd.   828-7772
Eckerd Plaza, Five Points

Kelly Worth operated her own catering business three years before opening the Bistro in 1991. Some of her favorites are lobster fajitas, crabcakes and California Thai beef tenderloin salad. Cocktail and dinner parties are specialties.

LADYFINGERS
627 E. Whitaker Mill Rd.   828-2270
Northside Shopping Ctr.

LadyFingers has been catering to private Raleigh social occasions since 1980 and has developed a large corporate following as well. Located in Northside Shopping Center, the storefront offers salads, sandwiches and oven-ready gourmet entres to go, as well as full-service catering. The staff is polite, efficient, and will not only oversee the preparation, but make sure your guests have fresh drinks and full plates. After you've tried LadyFingers, it's hard to go back to doing everything yourself.

MITCHELL'S CATERING & EVENTS
6633 Falls of the Neuse Rd.   847-0135

Mitchell's is big time catering with ice sculpture and the full treatment. When the state celebrated the premier of the TV series "Roanoak" at the N.C. Museum of History with TV stars, the governor and museum patrons, it was Mitchell's that prepared the smoked fish, shrimp, the roast pig and fowl in an appropriate setting.

SISTERS'
Koger Center   782-2837
3300 Woman's Club Dr.

Sisters', the same people who owned the renowned Sisters' Garden of Eating, established in 1976, has become one of the largest privately owned catering companies in the state. Sisters' is the exclusive caterer for two facilities in Raleigh: The Woman's Club and Oscar's Supper club. Sisters' caters to the N.C. film industry and corporate events and is also a wedding reception specialist.

TUXEDO CAFE AND CATERERS
4217 Six Forks Rd.   571-0099
North Hills Mall

The owners were successful enough with their catering that they opened a cafe by the same name in 1992. They serve many corporate clients such as IBM, Exide, and Alcatel for training seminars, business meetings and grand openings. They specialize in French, Italian and Cajun foods. If you call ahead on the way home from work, they can have food waiting for as little as $4 a plate.

THE UPPER CRUST

8831 Six Forks Rd.   *847-8088*
Six Forks Station at Strickland Rd.

This North Raleigh favorite for casual cafe dining offers superb catering, a bakery, wine and gift baskets, served with gourmet coffee, raspberry tea, imported beer or wine.

Cary

Cary's list of restaurants is admittedly short but growing. The city reflects its small town heritage in this respect and the fact that its residents are within a few minutes drive of many of the Triangle's good restaurants. Some of the chain restaurants that have located in this growth hot-spot include local and regional chains like **Ryan's**, **O'Charlie's** and **Courtney's**, and the major fast food dispensers. The restaurants below, however, are the local places where you're likely to find Cary Insiders.

ANGOTTI'S

Maynard Rd. & Walnut St.   *469-5077*
Cary Village Square
$

This popular Italian restaurant got its start on Hillsborough Street in Raleigh, across from NCSU. Now, Cary is its only location and, as an Italian place, it is known for its calzones and pastas. Its menu includes sandwiches and pizza and homemade soups. It has all ABC permits and seats about 90 people.

CHINA PEARL

107-A New Waverly Place   *851-0358*
Shopping Ctr.
$$

This has become Cary's favorite Chinese restaurant, not only for the food but because the host knows his customers and what they want. It is located in one of the Triangle's loveliest shopping centers at Kildaire Farm Road and Tryon Road. Stroll around before or after dinner. It serves Hunan, Szechuan, Mandarin and Cantonese dishes, and it's a family place, so don't hesitate to take the kids. It's busy and has all ABC permits.

COYOTE CAFE

1014 Ryan Rd.   *469-5253*
Cary Village Square
$$

This Mexican restaurant opened in 1989 and offers such specialties as blue corn tacquitos and chicken nogales, as well as salads and white chili, made with northern white beans, and served with jack cheese and sour cream. It is open Wednesday through Sunday for lunch and dinner and is popular with the business bunch. Hands down, it's the best Mexican place in Cary. The crowd comes on Friday.

FOX AND HOUND

MacGregor Shopping Ctr.   380-0080
$$

Given the name of the shopping center, it is required that there be a "public house" on the premises—which the Fox and Hound offers. Proprietor Dane Johnston provides good English fare and for the untutored, suggestions on what dish goes with which wine. And if you have a favorite wine, tell him; he'll special order it for your next meal. He even has port and the beer selection includes Guinness Stout, John Courage Amber Lager, Fuller's London Pride, Bass Ale—you get the taste. The menu is also full of John Bull's favorites: Shepherd's pie, beefsteak and kidney pie, roasted lamb chops, fish and chips. Cheerio! This is a bully handsome pub.

G&M FRENCH CAFE

957 N. Harrison Ave.   469-2288
$$

This cafe opened in late 1987 and has been a hit with its food, wine and atmosphere. The food is not always French, but it is enthusiastically recommended by the customers. A glass of wine comes with weekend specials, which change weekly. The wine is French and the most popular dish is the seafood normandy, with the chicken provencale a close second. It even has a special listing for fondues. Other evening specials include beef bordelaise and roast beef au jus sauce moutards. And yet, it has snails. It also sells coffee blends, sauces and dips, T-shirts, coffee pots and aprons.

MACGREGOR DOWNS COUNTRY CLUB

430 St. Andrews Ln.   467-0146
$$$

Yes, this is a private club, so you can't go there unless you're invited or are a member. If you do get invited, go. It's one of Cary's best eating places and the noontime buffet is generous. The salads are sumptuous. It also is a popular place for business meetings, from banquets announcing new industrial arrivals to two-party lunches. It has all ABC permits and can seat several hundred.

MAXIMILLIAN'S PIZZA GRILLE

1284 Buck Jones Rd.   460-6299
$$

There are not many tables in this place, so come early. It opened in 1991 and has been a hit with Cary eaters, and the lines go out the door on weekends. It describes itself as "a small, intimate cafe with incredible pizzas. Some stone baked. Some actually grilled." It is the place for specialty pizzas, but the pastas, all served with a salad, are impressive as well. The lasagna is made from scratch and the menu has a list of 11 sandwiches made with fresh-baked bread, including grilled sausage of the day, prosciutto, fontina, grilled eggplant, gyro and some favorites like the sub, reuben and turkey. It's closed on Mondays.

MELBA'S COUNTRY KITCHEN

121 E. Chatham St.   467-0929
$
No credit cards accepted

Melba's is what its name indicates. And Melba has been work-

"We Bring the Restaurants to You"™

Too busy or too tired to go out or cook at home?

Let Us Deliver Your Meal!
Call 840-FOOD

Your Favorite Restaurants Are Still At Your Fingertips

In Cary, Raleigh, Durham and soon Chapel Hill.

TAKEOUT TAXI delivers lunch and dinner for dozens
of popular restaurants in the Triangle area. Favorites like
Applebee's, Chili's, Chi-Chi's, Darryl's,
T.G.I. Friday's, Subway, Tripps and many more.

We deliver lunch or dinner promptly
for only a $3.00* fee.

We accept Visa, Mastercard,
American Express and
Discover Card

A gratuity for our drivers/servers is also greatly appreciated.
* Fee is for delivery from one restaurant. Restaurants subject to change.

ing here since 1978. It's a downtown Cary restaurant for working folks and you get two vegetables with your meat. It's a good place for Yankees to get a taste of small town, Southern cooking such as barbecue and hushpuppies or chicken-fried steak, blackeyed peas and onions. The tea is presweetened and you pay in cash.

NEWTON'S SOUTHWEST RESTAURANT & BAR

1837 N. Harrison Ave.   677-1777
$$

This is a 1991 entry to Cary's menu and hot off the Texas grill. Beef is the house specialty, especially certified Angus steaks, barbeque beef ribs, brisket and fresh fish. It also has, as expected, great chili. The restaurant caters to groups and has the space to accommodate. It has all ABC permits and a bar called **The Trophy Room** (with real mounted animals). Hey, this is a Texas place! Although new, Cary boosters believe Newton's is here to stay.

OUTBACK STEAKHOUSE

1289 Kildaire Farm Rd.   460-1770
Saltbox Village
$$-$$$

Although this is a national chain restaurant, its success in Cary has been phenomenal. The "Bloomin' Onion" and other Australian specialties are so popular with customers that a 2-hour wait is not unheard of. Although reservations are not accepted, they give you a beeper so you can shop while you wait! It's open for dinner only.

SELDOM BLUES CAFE

206-B New Waverly Place   851-2583
New Waverly Place Shopping Ctr.
$$-$$$

This southwest Cary cafe is located in New Waverly Place Shopping Center and has the glitz and glitter of a New York City hot spot. It's worth a meal just to see the place. It has a jazz bar as well as a restaurant offering pastas and seafood as specialties, so music is part of the dinner menu, depending on how serious a listener you are.

SERENDIPITY GOURMET-DELI

118 S. Academy St.   469-1655
$
No credit cards accepted

Serendipity opened in the 1970s as a sort of "hippie" place that served anti-establishment foods—it was a quiche pioneer, for example. The gazpacho soup is super, and daily specials usually feature a meatless dish. The chocolate pecan pie is served with real whipped cream and alone is worth the trip. It retains a deli counter and it does a big lunchtime sandwich business; it quits serving at 8 p.m. You can drink Dr. Brown's soda with your meal or wine or beer. It has a small outdoor patio that is pleasant in the spring and fall. It seats about 40 inside.

VINNIE'S STEAK HOUSE & TAVERN WEST

107 Edinburgh S.   380-8210
MacGregor Village Shopping Ctr.
$$$

This has become one of Cary's favorite places and is located in the MacGregor Village Shopping Center, but when you walk in, the atmosphere could be big-city Chicago or New York. Where other restaurants tried and failed, Vinnie's has succeeded in building a loyal following who want a pleasant, friendly atmosphere and good, well-prepared food. As the name suggests, it features Italian specialties but grills some of the best steaks and chops in town. It's the place to take business associates for dinner and it's open late, too. It has all ABC permits.

Caterers

HORWITZ'S DELICATESSEN
MacGregor Village   *467-2007*

This has become one of Cary's most reliable caterers. The same quality that makes Horwitz's one of the best deli's in the Triangle also holds true for its catering platters from smoked fish, gourmet desserts, fat sandwiches and, of course, Jewish delicacies. This deli works with corporate customers as well as mothers of the bride.

LEGENDARY AFFAIRS
311-G Asheville Ave.   *387-8540*

Owner Peggy McCormick bought this eight-year-old Chapel Hill catering company and moved it to Cary a couple of years ago. Specialties include gourmet appetizers and outdoor grilled weddings, but the menu includes everything from biscuits to Beluga. Legendary Affairs will cater an intimate dinner for two or an elaborate reception for 200.

SERENDIPITY GOURMET-DELI
118 S. Academy St.   *469-1655*

One of Cary's better known restaurants also caters, very reasonably. The owners don't pretend to prepare the fanciest spread in town, but they can put together sandwiches, chips and cookies for a competitive price. They do a good business with businesses as well as the traditional wedding and social reception.

Durham

It says something about Durham that two of its most popular restaurants are an upscale restaurant specializing in gourmet creations and a barbecue joint that serves home cookin', Southern style. There are hundreds of dining establishments in this town offering everything from Carolina pit-cooked pork to grilled quail with walnuts. There's no way we can tell you about all of them, so we're presenting some favorites, followed by a quick summary of some notable ones, all in alphabetical order.

ANOTHERTHYME

109 N. Gregson St.   682-5225
$$

Anotherthyme offers a friendly bar where you can get a cocktail made with freshly squeezed juice as well as a choice of wines to suit both your palate and your pocketbook. The regular menu and daily specials include French, Italian, Mexican, Spanish and Chinese entrees featuring vegetables, pasta or seafood, as well as creative appetizers, a colorful array of fresh salads and decadent desserts, all in a subdued decor highlighted by paintings and photographs exhibited by local artists.

Anotherthyme is one of the most popular restaurants in town for those in search of well-prepared, healthy dishes at a reasonable price. Lunch is served Monday through Friday, and dinner is served nightly. Late night snacks and a bar are available until 1 a.m. daily. Dinner reservations are advised.

BAK'S BISTRO

1821 Hillandale Rd.   383-8502
Loehmann's Plaza

Bakatsias Cuisine and Cocktail Bar remodeled and reopened as Bak's Bistro, a casual cafe. It opens at 5:30 p.m. Tuesday-Saturday.

BRUEGGER'S BAGEL BAKERY

626 Ninth St.   286-7897
$

Lox and bagels, pizza bagels, salami and cheese bagels. You can get just about any kind of bagels just about any way you want them. Homemade soups and desserts are

also on the menu, and they're all good. Carry out or sit at a small table in this historic restored bank building. Hours are 7 a.m. to 8 p.m. Monday through Saturday, 8 a.m. to 5 p.m. Sunday.

BULLOCK'S BAR B CUE

3330 Wortham St.   383-3211
(off Hillsborough Rd.)
$
No credit cards accepted

Sooner or later, you'll see everyone at this pig palace, from local politicians to movie people scouting a new location, to the good ole boys (and girls) of Durham. This place offers a no-nonsense decor, veteran waitresses and the most extensive barbecue menu in town. You can get it chopped or sliced, plain or spiced, with the usual sides of hush puppies, slaw, southern-style vegetables (well-done and limp), french fries and, of course, a big glass of sweet tea. If you've still got room after pigging out, there's plenty of home-style desserts.

Bullock's is open Tuesday through Saturday, eat-in or takeout. Don't be put off by the line going out the door; it moves fast.

DARRYL'S 1890

4603 Chapel Hill Blvd.   489-1890
$$

Darryl's expansive menu includes steaks, chicken, seafood, ribs, burgers, sandwiches, salad bar and late-night snacks. Located across from Oak Creek shopping center, Darryl's draws a lunch crowd from Durham and Chapel Hill and is popular in the evenings with the young and the restless. Darryl's opens daily at 11:00 a.m. and serves lunch and dinner.

THE FAIRVIEW AT THE WASHINGTON DUKE

3001 Cameron Ave.   *490-0999*
$$$

The Fairview, in the elegant Washington Duke Inn, is a wonderful place to entertain friends or out-of-town guests. Chef Kenneth Stynes adds Irish flair to the Continental cuisine. Salads, fresh homemade soups, steaks and seafood specialties all melt on the palate. It's also a great spot for a business lunch, and it hass all ABC permits..

FISHMONGER'S SEAFOOD MARKET, CRAB AND OYSTER HOUSE

806 W. Main St.   *682-0128*
$$
No credit cards accepted

Finally, a seafood place that serves fish the way it was meant to be: steamed or broiled to perfection (or fried, if you're on the Calabash diet). It's not fancy. Be prepared to sit yourself down at a picnic table covered with brown paper, roll up your sleeves and dig for those tiny morsels of tender crab meat.

Once primarily a fresh seafood market, Fishmonger's now serves up breakfast, lunch (including seafood salads, fish sandwiches and chowders), as well as dinner, featuring fresh steamed crabs, oysters, shrimp and lobster; broiled fish in season and daily specials. Beer and wine are available. It's the closest you can get to the beach without leaving home.

Across from Brightleaf Square, the restaurant is open Tuesday through Saturday.

HUNAM

910 W. Main St.   *688-2120*
$

If you're looking for a fast Chinese lunch or take-out, this is your place. It serves Cantonese and Szechuan cuisine. Hunam serves lunch and dinner seven day a week.

THE ITALIAN GARDEN/ CATTLEMAN'S STEAK HOUSE

3211 Hillsborough Rd.   *382-3292*
$$

This restaurant now combines an Italian trattoria-style restaurant with a Western restaurant specializing in beef. The menus feature Italian-American cuisine, such as pasta, veal, seafood and chicken dishes, as well as some hefty cuts of meat. There is a cocktail lounge (all ABC permits) and take-out is available. The restaurant opens daily at 11:00 a.m. and serves lunch and dinner.

LONE STAR GRILLE

3630 Chapel Hill Blvd.   *489-0030*
$$

They say Texans like to do things in a big way. So perhaps it follows that if you're going to present authentic Texas cuisine, you may as well go whole hog with the country-western motif. That seems to be the thinking at the Lone Star, where mounted longhorns, raucous country-and-western music and A-1 steak sauce on every table drive the point home. But if you really go for mesquite-grilled steak and seafood you'll be impressed to find that the restaurant burns up to 18 cords of Texas hardwood a month to do it up right. The Lone Star Grille serves lunch Monday through Friday and dinner nightly.Open from 11:30 a.m. to 11:30 p.m. It has all ABC permits

MAGNOLIA GRILL
1002 Ninth St.   286-3609
$$$$

The Magnolia Grill is one of the Triangle's finest places to dine, with its commitment to innovative and absolutely delicious food. Chef-owner Ben Barker cooked at **La Residence** and **The Fearrington House** (see "Chapel Hill" Section of **RESTAURANTS**) before opening Magnolia Grill with several others a few years back. Indeed, Barker was one of 14 chefs nationwide recognized by a panel of food experts, including Julia Child and Craig Claiborne, at the third annual American Chefs' Tribute to James Beard (they particularly liked his grits cakes with fresh morels).

This charming bistro features a daily menu composed of the freshest ingredients of the season. That means you're likely to find anything from pumpkin soup to grilled quail with bleu cheese and walnuts—tantalizing, eclectic fare that defies labeling. Each menu features six to nine appetizers (like asparagus in raspberry-hazelnut vinaigrette), just as many entrees and incredible desserts (like French apple tart with cinnamon creme fraiche).

Magnolia Grill is located at the corner of Knox and Ninth Street in west Durham, the former site of **Wellspring Grocery** (see "Durham" Section of **SHOPPING**). The bar (all ABC permits) opens at 5 p.m., and dinner begins at 6:00 Monday through Saturday. Reservations are essential, especially during American Dance Festival season.

NANA'S
2514 University Dr.   493-8545
$$$

Nana's, named for chef Scott Howell's grandmother, opened in late 1992, and quickly gained acclaim for its new American cuisine. The changing menu features entrees like grilled quail, braised lamb shanks and fresh North Carolina seafood. The atmosphere is pleasant, though the restaurant seating is a bit cramped. Nana's is open for dinner Tuesday through Sunday, and for Sunday brunch from 11 a.m. to 2:30 p.m. Reservations are recommended. It has all ABC permits

NINTH STREET BAKERY AND CAFE
776 Ninth St.   286-0303
$
No credit cards accepted

This whole-grain bakery has evolved into a restaurant, too and it's one of our favorite places to grab a light breakfast or lunch or a cup of cappucino and a chocolate eclair.

The crowd begins most days around 8 a.m. for fresh croissants, Bear Claws, cheese danishes and homemade muffins. The lunch menu includes a zesty homemade soup or salad special, whole-wheat pizza slices and spinach turnovers, as well as sandwiches like the "triple-cheese" (three cheeses with sprouts on a roll) egg salad or pimento cheese. Or you can just order up a bit of brie to spread on a sourdough French roll or demi-baguette. Beverages include fruit juices, SoHo sodas, coffee, teas ranging from Earl Grey to Red Zinger and real hot chocolate with whipped cream and chocolate shavings.

You can carry food out or settle in at one of the small tables to chat with friends, read the newspapers or take in some of the local artwork regularly displayed on the walls. The Bakery is a great meeting place for students, moms and toddlers and people who work in the neighborhood. During American Dance Festival season (see ARTS/Dance), you'll see lots of leotards. The bakery is usually crowded at lunch, but don't fret, it's worth it. Open from 7 a.m. to 7 p.m. Monday through Thursday; 8 a.m. to 11 p.m. Friday and Saturday (often with late-night music entertainment—see "Durham" Section of **NIGHT LIFE**); and 8 a.m. to 3 p.m. Sunday.

PAPAGAYO
501 Douglas St.   *286-1910*
$$

This is one of several highly successful restaurants of the same name in North Carolina. Located in the same building as **MetroSport** health club off Erwin Road, Papagayo is popular with Duke students and Duke Medical Center employees. It's fun to sit by the window or on the sundeck and sip

on your frozen daiquiri, while gazing out over swimmers in the health-club pool below. When you're ready to order, the food won't disappoint. The burritos and chimichangas come with thick spicy sauces laden with cheese and sour cream, and they're filled with a variety of stuffings beyond the usual beef and beans. There's also a nice array of enchiladas, tacos and salads, seafood specialities and domestic and imported beer and wine. The restaurant has all ABC permits and is open for lunch Monday through Friday and for dinner nightly.

PIPER'S DELI
3219 Chapel Hill Rd.   *489-2481*
$

This deli, popular with Duke folk, has the atmosphere of a neighborhood tavern. The prices are modest and the food is homemade. It's worth a visit. Hours are 11 a.m. to 9 p.m. This is an Insiders' lunch favorite.

TAVERNA NIKOS
Brightleaf Square   *682-0043*
$$

Taverna Nikos offers some of the most delicious and authentic Greek food to be found in the Triangle. Moussaka, Spanokotiro-pita and other favorite Greek dishes fill the menu, along with huge salads and hearty soups. The atmosphere is friendly and sometimes even a little loud; it's a great place to come with a group of friends, when you can share platters heaped with food. It has all ABC permits and is open for lunch and for dinner Monday through Saturday.

VILLA DONNA

2610 W. Carver St.   *471-8455*
(off Guess Rd.)
$
No credit cards accepted

Villa Donna's fare is well-prepared Neapolitan cuisine. Beer and wine are available. The restaurant is open Tuesday through Saturday, and its popular pub is open late each evening.

YAMAZUSHI

Hope Valley Rd.   *493-7748*
Woodcroft Shopping Ctr.
Park Terrace Shopping Ctr.   *544-7945*
$$

Yamazushi is one of the few places around where you can get sushi, as well as Japanese cuisine such as Katsudon (deep-fried pork) and stir-fried vegetable dishes. It's open for lunch Tuesday through Friday, and for dinner Tuesday through Sunday. Wine and beer are offered and catering is also available.

Caterers

There are scads of caterers in the Durham area serving everything from picnics and pig pickin's to private parties and weddings. We don't have enough space to tell you about them all, but here, in alphabetical order, are a few to get you started. Also note that many of the restaurants mentioned in these pages also cater.

CLASSIC FOOD SERVICES

1716 Camden Ave.   *688-9663*

Classic Food Services offers a range of catering services, including weddings, luncheons, dinners, cocktail parties, pig pickin's and company dinners.

FOSTER'S MARKET & CATERING COMPANY

2694 Chapel Hill Blvd.   *489-3944*

Sara Foster opened Foster's Market a couple of years ago after a stint with the renowned Martha Stewart, and the market has become a popular source for everything from homegrown fresh vegetables to delicious dinners and desserts to go. It's also a good spot for lunch, afternoon tea or a light snack. Foster's catering service offers creative cuisine for both private and corporate affairs. Call the catering manager for details.

SAGE & SWIFT

3401 University Dr.   *489-0642*

Amy and Joe Sheehy offer full catering service, as well as gourmet take-out for singles, couples and families. Just call and see what's on the menu, make your selection and pick it up on the way home from work.

SAVORY FARE

908 W. Main St.   *683-2185*

Savory Fare proprietor Gary Wein started at the top when he was a Duke University student and offered to cook for then-Duke President (later U.S. Senator Terry Sanford) and his wife. Needless to say Gary's meal was a hit and the Sanfords encouraged him to start a catering business.

Quite a few years later, Gary is still at it, offering everything from simple box lunches to cocktail buffets to elegant six-course dinners, for any number from 10 to 500 or so. His menu reflects the freshest local and regional ingredients he can get his hands on, with an emphasis on French and Italian cuisine.

For clients who don't want to do a completely catered affair, Savory Fare offers small dinner parties to go. You can call in advance, and depending on what's available in Gary's inventory of fresh ingredients, you can order an entire meal for, say, 8 or 10 persons, and come by and pick it up yourself.

Research Triangle Park

You'll be delighted with the fine restaurants within Research Triangle Park. Here's a sample of some dining spots to try.

CARVERY
Meredith Suites at the Park   361-1234
I-40 at N.C. Hwy. 55 (Exit 278)
$

A welcome addition to the breakfast and lunch scene at RTP, the **Carvery** at Meredith Suites offers soups, sandwiches and specials for lunch and a nice place for breakfast meetings. If you do business in and around RTP, you'll enjoy dining at the Carvery.

DELI BOX
10800 Chapel Hill Rd.
Morrisville   467-4163
$

This deli-restaurant has been here since the early stages of the Park's development. It is noted for its sandwiches, cold cuts, cheeses and salads. The Deli Box also caters lunches and buffets.

DEVEREUX
Sheraton Imperial   941-5050
I-40 at Page Rd. (Exit 282)
$$$$

The Sheraton Imperial's finest restaurant offers elegant food, atmosphere and service. The revolving menu features five-course meals offering seafood, poultry, veal and beef entrees as well as hors d'oeuvres and salads, with an emphasis on the freshest seasonal ingredients. You won't want to pass up the incredible desserts created by the pastry chef. Devereux is open for dinner seven days a week. Reservations are advised. It has all ABC permits

GALERIA
Radisson Governors Inn   549-8631
I-40 at Davis Dr. (Exit 280)
$$$$

For many years, this elegant eatery at the **Radisson Governors Inn** was the only place to eat near RTP besides the casual Deli Box and RTP company cafeterias. Its noontime buffet is generous and varied, but it has made its reputation as an evening dining spot. The chef serves some of the best fish and veal in the Triangle, including a selection of low cholesterol gourmet specialities. The Galeria has an extensive wine list and all ABC permits.

PINEY POINT GRILL AND SEAFOOD BAR
Guest Quarters Suite Hotel   361-4660
Meridian Business Campus
I-40 at N.C. Hwy. 55 (Exit 278)
$$$$

Piney Point Grill offers seating at the hotel's bar, in the main dining room, or outdoor dining on the terrace overlooking a lake. While deciding where to sit, sample Piney Point's wine-of-the-week, chosen from one of the 31 wines on its list. If you sit at the bar, you can watch ACC sports on the big-screen TV, eat complimentary hot hors d'oeuvres from 4:30 till 7:00 p.m., or dig into peel-n-eat shrimp sold by the pound.

Both the terrace and main dining room offer the same menu of ribeyes, North Carolina mountain trout, shrimp and salsa, seafood pasta, fresh oysters, and a variety of fresh North Carolina coastal seafood. Be sure to ask about the daily blue-plate special.

Piney Point Grill is open for dinner seven days a week. It has all ABC permits. Reservations are advised.

Chapel Hill

As long as there have been UNC students to feed, there have been restaurants in Chapel Hill. No wonder; in his book *Chapel Hill— An Illustrated History*, James Vickers reports that the meals the university provided for students in the early 1800s rarely consisted of more than coffee and dry cornbread. It was apparently the poor quality and puny quantity of campus food that led to what Vickers calls "increased student-townsfolk interaction, not always congenial."

According to Vickers, it was a Dr. William Hooper who observed that students awaited nightfall, "like beasts of prey," so that they could "go a-prowling and seize upon everything eatable" within a two-mile radius.

You'll have to ask the students if university food has improved much since then. We do know that the quantity and quality of Chapel Hill restaurants has soared. Today the variety of Chapel Hill eateries ranges from those that clearly cater to the student budget and palate to others that have won the acclaim of big-time food critics.

In fact, Chapel Hill seems to have more fine restaurants per capita than either of the two other larger cities of the Triangle. There's no way we could tell you everything you need to know about all of them, but here's a sample of some of the more popular dining spots.

As you'll see from our selections, we like restaurants in all price ranges and styles. We don't think you have to get all dressed up and pay through the nose to get a fine meal in this town, although many times it's well worth it.

ALLEN AND SON PIT-COOKED BARBECUE

6203 Millhouse Rd.   942-7576
$
No credit cards accepted

If you want good smoked barbecue and Brunswick stew, you'll have to drive a few miles north of town to Allen and Son's. You can get barbecue by the plate or by the pound, dine in or take out, Monday through Saturday 7 a.m. to 8 p.m. Full catering service is available.

AURORA

200 N. Greensboro St.   942-2400
Carr Mill Mall, Carrboro
$$$

If you'd like an elegant full-course meal in quiet, comfortable surroundings, Aurora, which received three stars in the Mobil travel guide, is one of your best bets. Here, in the comfortable setting of a restored historic cotton mill, you can enjoy superb Northern Italian cuisine. Select tender veal, lamb, poultry or fresh seafood for the entree, then complement it with one of many handmade pastas. Appetizers, fresh salads, irresistible desserts and fine wine will complete your delightful meal. Lunch is served Monday through Friday, and dinner is served nightly. Dinner reservations are advised. It has all ABC permits

BREADMEN'S

324 W. Rosemary St.   967-7110
$
No credit cards accepted

Breadmen's, long an Insiders' favorite, has moved across the street to larger quarters. Besides good food and character, Breadmen's has two other things going for it. It's the kind of place where, no matter what time of the day it is, you can order breakfast with a friend or alone and take your time reading the newspaper while you drink a bottomless cup of coffee. Besides breakfast anytime, Breadmen's offers the basics: cheeseburgers, sandwiches, salads, and meat and vegetable plates. After an early movie, it's a good place to get a hefty piece of banana bread

with cream cheese or a piece of pie to tide you over until morning. Beer, wine and mixed drinks are also available. The restaurant opens daily at 7:30 a.m.

BRUEGGER'S BAGEL BAKERY

104 W. Franklin St.   967-5248
Eastgate Shopping Ctr.   968-9507
$

This cafe offers just about any kind of bagel, or bagel sandwich you might want: lox and bagels, pizza bagels, salami and cheese bagels and more, like fresh homemade soups and dessert bars. You can take out or eat in. Open 6:30 a.m. to 8 p.m. Monday through Saturday, 8 a.m. to 5 p.m. Sunday.

CARRBORO CAFE

101 E. Weaver St.   929-0010
$

The Carrboro Cafe is part of **Weaver Street Market** at Carr Mill. The Cafe features fresh foods, from delicious salads to grilled fish and Mediterranean pasta dishes, as well as sandwiches and lighter fare at lunchtime. Lunch and dinner are served Monday through Saturday. Sunday brunch is 10 a.m. to 2 p.m.

CHINA CHEF

Eastgate Shopping Ctr.   942-2688
$-$$

China Chef is a welcome addition to Chapel Hill's restaurant scene. Cozy and attractively decorated, China Chef serves well-prepared Chinese food at reasonable prices. Some house specialties include Ivory Shrimp and Chicken with Black Bean Sauce, as well as the more familiar Chinese restaurant dishes. There is a daily special including soup and an egg roll with an entree. Lunch and dinner are served seven days a week, and take-out is available. Wine and beer are offered.

CRACOVIA

220 W. Rosemary St.   929-9162
$$$
MasterCard, VISA

As Cracovia has expanded, it fortunately has retained its charm and good food. It specializes in seasonal Polish, French, German and Scandinavian cuisine, prepared by a European chef. The restaurant is open daily for dinner.

CROOK'S CORNER

610 W. Franklin St.   929-7643
$$$

It is safe to say that there is no restaurant like Crook's anywhere in the Triangle.

First, the food. A changing menu features a wide choice of seasonal entrees, including specialties from South America to North Carolina. This means you can get everything from jambalaya to shrimp and grits, all from the same kitchen.

Crook's has put together ethnically and regionally authentic dishes. The influence of the late Bill Neal, the chef and cookbook author who moved the tastebuds and won the praise of food critics such as Craig Claiborne, is still felt.

Some people call Crook's "haute casual." The first thing you notice about Crook's is the pig on the roof, the work of sculptor Bob Gaston, surrounded by a herd of wooden animal figures, made by

Chatham County folk artist Clyde Jones. You get the picture: Crook's offers fine food served up with a slice of Southern culture. It's always loud, crowded and fun. Dinner is served nightly, and brunch is served on Sunday. Reservations are accepted. It has all ABC permits.

DIP'S COUNTRY KITCHEN

405 W. Rosemary St.   942-5837
$
No credit cards accepted

If you've been looking for The Real Thing southern-style, this is it. Started well over a decade ago by Mildred "Dip" Council, this is the place to get fried chicken or a mess of pork chops, served up with okra, black-eyed peas, collards and cornbread in a no-nonsense restaurant. Dip's slogan is "put a little south in your mouth," and, boy, does she! "Dip" makes up her daily specials with seasonal ingredients in mind, so they are always fresh. Even Yankees who swear they don't take to Southern food like this place because it feels like home without even trying. Dip's serves breakfast, lunch and dinner. Beer and wine are available.

EL RODEO

1404 E. Franklin St.   929-6566
$

This fast and inexpensive Mexican restaurant is heir to the success of the original El Rodeo in Durham. The restaurant features a good variety of dishes, including burritos, chile rellenos and tacquitas, and very moderate prices. As a result, it packs the patrons in for lunch and dinner. El Rodeo is

Staff photo.

*Crook's Corner in Chapel Hill offers fine food
served up with a slice of Southern culture.*

open daily for lunch and dinner and has all ABC permits.

THE FEARRINGTON HOUSE
Fearrington Village Center
Pittsboro   *919-542-2121*
$$$$

Drive about six miles south into Chatham County to Fearrington Village, a planned development (see **CHAPEL HILL NEIGHBORHOODS**) that was once a dairy farm. There, in a plantation-style Southern mansion complete with two-story columns, you'll find this charming restaurant headed by chef Cory Mattson.

The Fearrington House has been noted in *Food and Wine* and *Gourmet* magazines for its "new cuisine of the South"—regional appetizers like soft-shell crab, and entrees such as smoked pork tenderloin with a mustard-apricot glaze and grilled quail in a tomato sauce. Dessert's the house special, chocolate souffle with warm chocolate sauce and whipped cream, fruit tarts and incredible homemade ice creams. Dinner is served as a five-course, *prix fixe* meal (excluding wine). And it's all served in elegant surroundings by a supremely attentive and professional wait staff. The menu changes daily, depending on the availability of seasonal ingredients. Chatham County ABC laws allow for the serving of a fine selection of beer and wine, but no mixed drinks. Set-ups are available for brownbaggers.

The restaurant is open for dinner Tuesday through Sunday. Reservations are required.

FEARRINGTON MARKET & CAFE
Fearrington Village Ctr.   *919-542-5505*
Pittsboro
$-$$

The Cafe serves lunch and dinner, Monday through Friday. A weekend brunch is served from 9:30 a.m. to 3 p.m. You'll enjoy homemade entrees, delicious breads (best bran muffins around), fresh salad platters and deli-style sandwiches in a country-quaint setting. In warm weather, you can sit outdoors and admire the flower beds.

THE FLYING BURRITO
Town and Country Shopping Ctr.   *967-7744*
746 Airport Rd.
$
No credit cards accepted

This place is almost too good to be true. Imagine some of the finest Mexican/Southwestern cuisine in the Triangle along with fresh North Carolina seafood specials? That's what awaits you at the Flying Burrito, tucked alongside the Sav-a-Center on Airport Road.

The Flying Burrito made its reputation hawking some pretty hot stuff to fans at Durham Bulls games. In addition to some of the best smothered burritos around (watch out for the extra-hot green chili sauce), the restaurant offers the real thing in margaritas (made with freshly squeezed lime juice) and a fine selection of Mexican, European and domestic beers.

Arrive early or be prepared to wait in line; this place only seats around 60 and fills up fast. Kids will like the strings of chile pepper lights that adorn the walls, and the coloring books and crayons to use while dinner is cooking.

The restaurant is open Monday through Friday for lunch, and every day for dinner. It has all ABC permits.

FOUR CORNERS
175 E. Franklin St.   *929-4416*
$-$$

As you can tell from the name (borrowed from basketball coach Dean Smith's famed four-corner offense), this downtown eatery aims to please the Carolina crowd (meaning there may be a line out the door on home football and basketball game days). Four Corners' classic menu relies on steaks, hamburgers, sandwiches and salads. It has all ABC permits and opens at 11:30 a.m. daily.

411 WEST ITALIAN CAFE
411 W. Franklin St.   *967-2782*
$$-$$$
No personal checks accepted

411 West opened to rave reviews and good crowds and both the accolades and the steady stream of diners continue. The restaurant's woodburning pizza oven gives an authentic touch to the "pizzettes," or individual pizzas made with top-

pings like four cheeses or prosciutto and peppers. Homemade pasta and fresh seafood are other good choices. Lunch is served Monday through Saturday, and dinner is served seven nights a week. There is a late-night menu and catering is available. No reservations are accepted. It has all ABC permits.

HELLO DELI!
116 Old Durham Rd.   *929-1125*
$

Hello Deli! opened a couple of years ago, and it's a good choice for breakfast, lunch or a casual dinner. It serves a great breakfast, especially on Saturday and Sunday when the Breakfast Bar is open. Hello Deli! serves up a wonderful selection of homemade salads, desserts, soups and appetizers. Everything is fresh, and all of the desserts are baked on site or by local bakers to order. After 3:00 p.m., kids eat free with the purchase of an adult meal.

HENRY'S BISTRO
403 W. Rosemary St.   *967-4720*
$$-$$$

Henry's offers bistro fare "from Paris, Texas, to Dallas, France." Off the beaten path beneath Pantana Bob's on West Rose-

mary Street, Henry's is well worth the extra effort it may take to locate it. The menu changes nightly and features entrees like ribeye au poivre in bourbon gravey, bouillabaisse, sauteed Spanish mackeral and fresh pasta dishes. House salads feature mixed greens, and include unusual selections like cress, radicchio or dandelion leaves, dressed with a walnut vinaigrette.

Chef Henry Samuelson, a veteran of the kitchen at Crook's Corner, offers creative cuisine at very reasonable prices. Early dinner specials are served nightly. Try the delectable flan for dessert. Dinner is served Monday through Sunday.

IL PALIO

Siena Hotel
1505 E. Franklin St.   929-4000
$$$$

The Siena Hotel's gracious Four Diamond restaurant, Il Palio, features Northern Italian and Mediterranean preparations of fresh pasta, seafood, veal, lamb, poultry and beef. Enjoy after-hours cappucino on the private outdoor terrace. Breakfast, lunch and dinner are served daily. There is also a Sunday brunch from 11 a.m. to 2:30 p.m. The restaurant has all ABC permits.

ITALIAN PIZZERIA

508 W. Franklin St.   968-4671
$
No credit cards, no checks accepted

This is an honest-to-goodness, no frills, family-owned New York-style pizza joint. And if you are particularly fond of deep-dish Sicilian pizza, you can't go wrong. What we like about this place is that you can get freshly made slices; so if half your crowd likes regular thin-sliced pizza with pepperoni and the other half likes Sicilian loaded with sausage, everybody can get exactly the quantity and quality he or she wants.

This pizzeria also has Greek salads and great hot sandwiches like the Italian sausage and cheese on a submarine roll. Beer is on tap, service is quick and the price is right. The Pizzeria is open daily.

LA REZ

202 W. Rosemary St.   967-2506
$$$$

La Rez has a long tradition of offering innovative, fine cuisine in the Triangle. Now under the direction of chef Devon Mills (formerly of Magnolia Grill in Durham), La Rez is located in a charmingly remodeled and redecorated home on Rosemary Street and has the sunny look of Provence.

The menu ranges from fresh North Carolina seafood to tender cuts of beef to farm-raised quail, all creatively prepared with a French flair. Mills uses local produce for the seasonal vegetable side dishes and salads. Desserts include La Rez' famous Kaluga, a divine chocolate creation, sorbets and fresh fruit, and berry specialties.

In warm weather, you may dine on the patio overlooking colorful gardens. It's no wonder the restaurant has won accolades in years past from *House and Garden, Food and Wine, Fortune, Bon Appetit, Redbook, Gourmet,* and *The New York Times.* Dinner is served Tuesday

Times. Dinner is served Tuesday through Sunday. Reservations are advised. It has all ABC permits.

LOOKING GLASS CAFE
University Square   929-0296
133 W. Franklin St.
$

This informal eatery is a convenient place to stop for lunch, a snack, or light dinner while shopping in downtown Chapel Hill. The menu has everything from soups and salads to stuffed spuds, deli-style sandwiches, salads, burgers, chili and desserts. Eat in or take out, the cafe opens daily at 11 a.m. Beer is available.

MAGGIE'S MUFFINS
206 W. Main St., Carrboro   933-3898
$

Maggie's Muffins started as a bakery, but it's become a whole lot more. The bakery offers a variety of muffins every day, made with seasonal ingredients. Some favorites offered at any given time might include lemon-ginger, date oat bran, a cholesterol-free muffin, or Maggie's special double-chocolate Jack Daniels muffin. It also sells bagels (fresh each day) and cream cheese, salads, sandwiches and rotisserie chicken. Beverages include natural sodas, and Maggie's Blend of coffee, ground by Broad Street. The bakery is open Monday through Saturday.

MARIAKAKIS RESTAURANT AND BAKERY
U.S. Hwy. 15-501 Bypass   942-1453
$

When it comes to atmosphere, this place has next to none.

But it's one of the few places where you can get home-cooked Greek food like moussaka or souvlaki. It also offers Italian dishes and pizza. We particularly like the garlic bread made with pizza dough. You can dine in or take out. It also has a bakery and gourmet shop up front where you can pick up unusual ingredients, desserts and snacks. The restaurant is open Monday through Saturday from 9 a.m. to 9 p.m. Beer and wine are available.

MARK'S CAFE
454 W. Franklin St.   942-4428
$$-$$$

At Mark's Cafe, chef-owner Mark Moore and his wife Nancy serve such dishes as chicken tortellini dijonaise and grilled salmon complemented by a spicy barbecue sauce, augmented by changing daily special soups and entrees. The atmosphere in the cafe is cozy and comfortable, the service is attentive, and the prices are reasonable. Dinner is served daily and the cafe is open for brunch on Saturday and Sunday from 10 a.m. until 2 p.m. It has all ABC permits.

NEW ORLEANS COOKERY
401 W. Franklin St.   929-3192
$$

Don't let the looks of this tiny restaurant dissuade you. It's more cramped than cozy, and you may have to wait in line, but chef Steve Dominick's Cajun specialties are worth it. The menu included New Orleans' classics—gumbos, jambalayas, muffuletas, authentically prepared. It's open seven days a week for lunch and dinner. Beer and wine are available.

OWEN'S 501 DINER
1500 Fordham Blvd.   933-3505
Eastgate Shopping Center
$$-$$$

Chapel Hill natives, the Owen brothers—Greg, Mark and Peter—opened this new venture in the spring of 1993, and it's quickly become a popular place for breakfast, lunch and dinner. Owen's serves tradtional diner fare like hamburgers, meatloaf and mashed potatoes and other "blue plate specials," as well as more exotic dishes like blackened quail, wild mushroom strudel and seafood bisque. The diner is decorated in mostly black and white, and has a brisk, bustling feel to it. Daily specials and homemade desserts round out the menu. Owen's is open for breakfast, lunch and dinner Tuesday through Saturday. It is closed on Sundays and Mondays, but plans are in the works for a Sunday brunch. It has all ABC permits.

PANTANA BOB'S
300 W. Rosemary St.   942-7575
$$

This place is mostly a bar, a favorite hangout for locals and for the wait staff from other restaurants. Pantana Bob's specializes in casual dining; curry dishes, gourmet burgers and late-night snacks. It's open from 4:30 p.m. to 2 a.m. daily. In warm weather, you can sit on the patio outddoors.

PAPAGAYO
137 E. Franklin St.   967-7145
NCNB Plaza
$$

Like its namesake in Durham (see "Durham" section of **RESTAURANTS**), Papagayo offers Mexican food with delectable sauces. We also like the frozen daiquiris. In the warmer months, it's nice to sit out on the rooftop patio.

Lunch is served Monday through Friday; dinner is served nightly. The bar has all ABC permits and is open until 12:30 a.m. daily.

PASSAGE TO INDIA
1301 E. Franklin St.   967-6622
$$

This was the first Indian restaurant in the Triangle, and it offers a full range of tandoori dishes, authentic appetizers and Indian breads. Catering services are also available. Lunch and dinner are served daily. Beer and wine are available.

PYEWACKET
431 W. Franklin St.   929-0297
The Courtyard
$$

Pyewacket has been a mainstay of the Chapel Hill restaurant scene since 1977. It is known for its vegetarian, pasta and fresh seafood specialties. Oringinal homemade dressings, freshly baked breads and desserts complement Pyewacket's seasonal menus.

You can dine in the lush greenhouse area in the back overlooking the courtyard, or you can choose the outdoor veranda overlooking Franklin Street—a great spot for a cappuccino and some people watching. After dinner, you can enjoy live music in the bar lounge a couple of nights a week.

Desserts here are not to be missed. The restaurant serves lunch Monday through Saturday and dinner every evening with a late nite menu until 1:00 a.m.

THE RATHSKELLER

157-A Franklin St.   942-5158
(in Amber Alley)
$-$$

For over 40 years, "The Rat" has been a major hangout for students, faculty, sports fans and alumni; it's always packed on home football weekends. The restaurant has a good selection of steaks (like its famous "Double Gambler"), sandwiches, lasagna and daily specials. Beer, wine and mixed drinks are available.

"The Rat" is open daily for lunch and dinner.

RUBENS

Omni Europa   968-4900
Europa Dr. and U.S. Hwy. 15-501 Bypass
$$$$

Located in the luxurious Omni Europa Hotel, Rubens is named for the Flemish painter whose art is adapted for the setting. Here you'll find nicely prepared European classics and the lighter nouvelle cuisine, as well as a choice of American steaks and seafood dishes and an international wine list.

Rubens is open daily for lunch and dinner, and serves brunch on Sunday. Reservations are recommended. It has all ABC permits.

SECOND CITY GRILL

Eastgate Shopping Center   942-5844
$$

The Second City Grill is a popular spot with both young singles and those of us who can't claim to be either young or single anymore. Its specialty is Chicago-style pizza, but the Grill also serves hotdogs, burgers, sandwiches and salads. The triangular bar has all ABC permits and is a good spot for a nightcap. The restaurant is open daily from 11 a.m. to 11 p.m.

SLUG'S AT THE PINES

N.C. Hwy. 54 East   929-0428
$$$

A Chapel Hill institution beloved by those who relish a good cut of meat, Slug's features a fine selection of beef, poultry and seafood entrees. It's usually crowded, especially on fall weekends when alumni flock to town. Slug's serves dinner daily, beginning at 5:30 p.m. It has all ABC permits.

SPANKY'S

101 E. Franklin St.   967-2678
$-$$

A downtown landmark, Spanky's is most noteworthy for the wide variety of offerings on its menu. Specialties include burgers, grilled chicken sandwiches, pasta and sautees. Sunday brunch is one of the best in town and it offers a special kid's menu, too. Spanky's is open daily from 11:30 a.m. to 10 p.m., and serves Sunday brunch from 10 a.m. to 2 p.m. Live music several nights a week makes this a popular spot with UNC students, faculty, sports fans and alumni, as well as locals. It has all ABC permits.

SQUID'S

1201 N. Fordham Blvd.   942-8757
U.S. Hwy. 15-501 Bypass
$$

Who would have "thunk" that Chapel Hill connoisseurs would pack a restaurant featuring squid?

If you're hungry and thirsty, you can kill two birds with one stone at the raw bar featuring the Spiked Oyster Shot: an oyster nestled in a shot glass of Stolichnaya vodka, designed to be consumed in one gulp. The bar also offers freshly shucked oysters, peel-your-own shrimp, and littleneck clams.

A main menu of fresh seafood features specialties such as shrimp curry, blackened salmon, smoked salmon manicotti, grilled fresh tuna with fresh fruit salsa, salt and pepper catfish and even squid fradiavlo on linguini. In addition to fish, you'll find steak, poultry, burgers, salads, chowders and an array of desserts. Squid's is open for lunch Monday through Saturday, and dinner nightly and it offers a kid's menu. It has all ABC permits.

THAI PALACE

N.C. Hwy. 54 E.   967-5805
Glenwood Village
$-$$

Thai Palace serves authentic Thai food and offers many vegetarian dishes. It's a pleasant place for a good meal and is open for lunch and dinner daily except Monday.

TRIPODI'S DELICATESSEN

University Mall   933-9407
$
No credit cards accepted

Decent delicatessens are few and far between in the Triangle. This one features homemade Italian sausage, soups, sandwiches and a mouth-watering assortment of homemade desserts. Tripodi's is open from 11 a.m. until 8 p.m., Monday through Saturday.

THE WEATHERVANE CAFE AT A SOUTHERN SEASON

Eastgate Shopping Ctr.   929-9466
$-$$$

A Southern Season has completed a major expansion and The Weathervane offers a delightful place to sit down and sample some of the delicious homemade fare turned out by the kitchen. It serves good deli sandwiches and salads, and is also an incredible place to shop for gourmet foods, wines and gifts (see "Chapel Hill" Section of **SHOPPING**). A Southern Season is open from 10 a.m. until 7 p.m. Monday through Friday, until 5:30 p.m. Saturday and from 1 p.m. until 5:30 p.m. Sunday.

ZORBA'S

105 S. Elliott Rd.   967-5517
Village Plaza
$$

This Greek restaurant features deliciously authentic Greek dishes, huge portions and reasonable prices. The lemon chicken is especially good, and the pastitsio and moussaka melt in your mouth.

The appetizer platter is a good way to sample some of the specialties; it features stuffed grape leaves, spanakopita, gyros and lamb kebabs to share. Zorba's is open for lunch Monday through Saturday, and for dinner Tuesday through Sunday. Beer and wine are available.

Caterers

A LEGENDARY AFFAIR
919-387-8540
Mari Trosclair has been in Chapel Hill for a number of years. She offers fine catering services, from weddings to corporate events.

THE CATERING COMPANY
2 Mariakakis Plaza   929-4775
U.S. Hwy. 15-501 Bypass
One of Chapel Hill's most established caterers, The Catering Company offers imaginative and delicious cuisine for any occasion.

HEAVENLY CINNAMON ROLLS & CATERING SERVICE
1821 Durham-Chapel Hill Blvd.   929-1722
This place does have heavenly cinnamon rolls, but it also has a whole lot more. It offers pasta and

seafood salads, quiches, deli trays, box lunches, dessert trays and more.

HELLO DELI!
116 Old Durham Rd.   929-1125
Owners Bill Fleming and Rick Birgel have been in the catering business for 15 years. Their menu is extensive, offering dozens of creative sandwiches, hot foods, beautiful assorted platters, salads, and delicious desserts. Whatever your needs, they are always happy to work with you to ensure that your event runs smoothly.

MARCEL'S CATERING CAFE
1821 Durham-Chapel Hill Blvd. 967-0066
Marcel's provides gourmet cuisine for any occasion. Whether it's an intimate dinner for two or a corporate event for 50 to 100, Marcel's can provide what you need. Marcel's unique Fried Chicken Salad is a real treat!

TRIPODI'S
University Mall   933-9407
Tripodi's offers full-service catering for weddings, luncheons, cocktail parties and corporate entertaining. Call for its brochure.

Photo by Veryl Berry.

The Triangle has become the location of choice for many retirees
due in large part to its Sunbelt climate.

Inside

Retirement

North Carolina has added population during the past two decades because of its Sunbelt climate and growing job market. Many of these people who now like calling North Carolina home have come here to retire, although they have not become quite the growth industry as in Florida, Arizona and southern California. Some are moving here to be closer to their children who work here and others, especially in places such as Asheville in the west, have started second careers once they've settled in.

When people talk about retirement areas, they usually start with Pinehurst and Southern Pines, south of the Triangle in the Sandhills where golf courses are considered a local crop. The coast, especially the Wilmington area which is only two hours away via Interstate 40 from the Triangle, is another place to take life easy. In recent years, however, the Triangle has become the location of choice for a growing number of retirement communities. Many are "life care" communities, offering independent living for healthy retirees, then providing nursing care on site as residents' health needs require. They are for basically active people who just happen to be of a "certain age,"

as our grandmothers used to say. They offer more manageable housing arrangements and a range of services, from entertainment to lawn care.

This section, then, lists some of these retirement communities as well as retirement-related information.

Retirement Communities

ABBOTSWOOD AT STONEHENGE
7900 Creedmoor Rd.   *847-3202*
Raleigh

This retirement community was started in late 1985 by a group of Raleigh business people. It is designed for the "senior, middle-income adult" and does not require an entrance fee nor a special endowment. Its monthly membership fee covers the rent for the one- or two-bedroom apartments that come with maid service and all utilities except telephone.

The complex contains 120 units and is located on 10 acres off Creedmoor Road in north Raleigh, in the Stonehenge development. The "private quarters" as the apartments are named, have bedrooms, great rooms, kitchens, storage space and, with the two-bedroom unit, two bathrooms. The service at Abbotswood includes a 24-hour security and emergency call system, continental breakfast and dinner, additional storage space and scheduled transportation. Residents also have access to exercise and activity rooms and a library.

There is a Wellness Program that includes a health coordinator on duty Monday through Friday who helps residents keep in touch with their family physician, as needed. There also are special recreation programs. Check with Abbotswood for monthly fees.

INDEPENDENCE VILLAGE

3113 Charles Root Wynd   781-8226
Raleigh

This development opened in 1990 and is 1/2 mile from Rex Hospital, off Duraleigh Road in Raleigh. Within walking distance of Olde Raleigh Shopping Center, it contains 163 units with a choice of studio, one- and two-bedroom units available. It provides meal service along with a crafts room, beauty salon, a library and a billiard room. There is scheduled transportation for residents. For information, call Independence Village's marketing department.

SPRINGMOOR

1500 Sawmill Rd.   848-7000
Raleigh

This is the best-known and most complete of the retirement communities in the Raleigh-Cary area. It was started in the early '80s by developer Judd Ammons, who considers Springmoor his crown jewel among all the projects in which

he has been involved. It is built on 45 wooded acres off Creedmoor Road, three miles north of Crabtree Valley Shopping Mall. The 600 residents are invited to use the walking and jogging trails, as well as the outdoor swimming and tennis complex in the 500-acre Greystone Village community of which Springmoor is a part.

The complex is a mixture of apartments, villas and private homes. The apartments come in one- and two-bedroom sizes, complete with kitchens and living rooms. The villas are somewhat smaller than the homes, but both groups of detached houses have small yards. In the apartment complexes, there are dining rooms, health centers and a nursing wing for those who need 24-hour care.

Springmoor maintains a clinic with a physician on duty and now has a special wing for Alzheimer's disease victims. The security system includes pull-cords in the apartment bathrooms, and if a telephone remains off the hook for more than 30 seconds, a signal will alert the switchboard operator and a security check will ensue.

Residents have access to garden plots, greenhouse, store, bank, post office, beauty salon, crafts center, shop and library. Vespers are held Sunday evenings in the community chapel, and a full entertainment program is offered, including transportation to N.C. Symphony and Friends of the College series and Raleigh Little Theater. The residents, according to one observer, come from all over and include one former North Carolina

first lady, Mrs. Dan Moore. To live here, you must be at least 62 years old. Because there are several options on the cost, it is best to call Springmoor's marketing director for details.

WHITAKER GLEN

501 E. Whitaker Mill Rd.   *755-0337*
Raleigh

This attractive community, started in 1984, is conveniently located close to the old county home not far from Five Points. It is a complex of four buildings, three of them four-story resident buildings. There are 96 units, split between one- and two-bedroom apartments. The support building includes a dining room that serves three meals a day for those residents who choose not to or cannot cook. It also includes a library and exercise rooms. There is a recreational program for residents, too, that has scheduled transportation to shopping centers. Nurses are on duty for those residents who require such care. There are several financial options and interested persons should call the Whitaker Glen marketing office for details.

CAROLINA MEADOWS

100 Carolina Meadows   *942-4014*
Chapel Hill

Carolina Meadows is a not-for-profit, fee-for-service retirement community located minutes from the charm and cultural activities of Chapel Hill. Floor plans range from studio apartments to 1,800-square-foot duplexes with garages.The community prides itself on providing privacy and security along with gracious dining, health care and recreational facilities, including a nine-hole golf course. A 22,000-square-foot recreation building includes a heated pool and Jacuzzi, meeting rooms, library, gift shop, exercise area, beauty/barber shop and an auditorium that seats about 400 people. Current amenities include bocce ball, croquet courts, two tennis courts, a wood-working shop and over 30 acres of natural area.

The **Carolina Meadows Health Center** provides a residential environment to residents at all levels of care. Presently at 50 beds, the Health Center will be expanded to 90 beds by late '94.

Over the next four years, Carolina Meadows plans to add 78 new homes to the existing 308 residences. For more information or to arrange a visit, call or write Carolina Meadows, 100 Carolina Meadows, Chapel Hill, NC 27514.

CAROL WOODS

750 Weaver Dairy Rd.   *968-4511*
Chapel Hill

Opened in 1979, Carol Woods is a not-for-profit, nationally accredited, life care community set in 120 wooded acres at the northeast edge of Chapel Hill. Here, you can choose from 280 individual units and a wide range of floor plans, from a 447-sq.-ft. studio apartment to a 1,538-sq.-ft. garden unit.

Carol Woods offers a comprehensive coordinated health care program. A new health center, scheduled to open in the fall of 1994, will reflect a home-like environment where resident rooms

form clusters or neighborhoods. The existing health center will be converted to assisted living, providing another level of care for residents who need some help with everyday activities.

A life care community, Carol Woods includes utilities (except long-distance telephone and cable TV), maintenance of unit and grounds, housekeeping, one or three meals a day, transportation and health care services in the life occupancy fee. There is a monthly service fee for each unit.

The central area of the community features a dining room, social lounge and library and is connected to the health center and the apartment buildings by enclosed walkways.

Additional activities and amenities include walking paths, an aquatic center with water exercise classes, gardens, croquet, concerts, bridge and a woodworking shop. For more information call, or write Carol Woods, 750 Weaver Dairy Road, Chapel Hill, NC 27514.

THE FOREST AT DUKE

3600-C University Dr.   490-8000
Durham

The Forest At Duke is an "entry-fee (three refund plans) life care community" in Durham. The 42-acre community has 80 cottages and 160 apartments and opened in 1992.

GLENAIRE

901 Kildaire Farm Rd.
Cary   460-8095

Glenaire is Cary's entry in the Triangle retirement competi-

tion. It opened in June of 1993 and is sponsored in part by Raleigh's First Presbyterian Church and is a division of The Presbyterian Homes, Incorporated, which operates a well-known facility in High Point, N.C. The 148 units are designed for people over age 65 who can live by themselves. More units are planned, including 40 that will be devoted to skilled nursing care. An "assisted living" program is also available. Though affiliated with the Presbyterian church, it is open to all denominations. Call or write for more information.

OTHER RETIREMENT COMMUNITIES

There are a number of neighborhoods and developments that are not exclusively for retirees, but do have a large number of retired people in the community. They include **Treyburn** in northern Durham County, **Governor's Club** in Orange County and **Fearrington** in Chatham County.

Other Services

FIFTY PLUS

P.O. Box 51277   493-5900
Durham, NC 27717

This is a monthly tabloid that was produced and owned by The News and Observer Publishing Company, but recently sold to Adventure Publishing, Inc. As the name suggests, it is aimed at those readers who are 50 years old and counting, and it is a good source for information. If your parents, for example, are considering moving here to be closer to their grandchildren, you might want to send them some copies of *Fifty Plus*. It uses larger than normal type and advertises many of the communities and services available to senior citizens including a monthly calendar of such items as AARP meetings, checkers tournaments, bridge games and special trips for seniors.

RSVP

Raleigh	831-6295
Durham	598-9380
Chapel Hill	968-4478

This is one of those wonderful programs where government is at its best. The Retired Senior Volunteer Program in the Triangle is sponsored by the three cities above, and it matches older citizens with volunteer needs in their respective communities. Raleigh's RSVP program, for example, has been around since 1973 and numbers 700 people on its rolls. It serves all of Wake County and volunteers can sign up for traditional duties such as hospital detail, or they might end up as business consultants to nonprofit organizations. One group works the "bread run" gathering day-old rolls and breads from local restaurants to take to local soup kitchens. Some toot their own horns as a dance band for other senior programs including the annual RSVP banquet that honors outstanding volunteers. Don't grow old alone, send in your rsvp for this successful, special program.

WE'RE OUTTA HERE.

For over 15 years, we've done our best to make this your clearest view of our truck. Because, as we see it, having our telephone company's service van parked outside a customer's building is the worst form of advertising there is. At ATCOM, we've set the standard for record-breaking efficiency in our installation and service. Every new phone system is assembled at our company's staging area, so we're in and out of your business quickly with your phones working right the first time. And it's working for everyone all over North Carolina. In fact, we're the business telephone company in North Carolina.

Now, we do slow down long enough to stay on the cutting edge of new, increasingly sophisticated technology. And we work with our customers to provide total system integration with a plan suited just for them. So, if you're moving, expanding, upgrading, or wanting to add voice mail features to your business telephone system, call ATCOM for one simple solution.

See you down the road!

ATCOM inc.
Business Telephone Systems

Raleigh	**Durham**	**Greenville**
(919)832-1345	(919)544-5751	(919)830-9260
Greensboro	**Winston-Salem**	**Charlotte**
(910)665-9294	(910)721-1207	(704)522-7200

Inside

Professional and Miscellaneous Services Directory

Emergencies

AMBULANCE, FIRE POLICE
All locations	911

DRUG INFORMATION CENTER
Raleigh	832-6868
Helpline of Durham	683-8628

EMERGENCY MENTAL HEALTH SERVICES
Raleigh	250-3133
Durham	683-8628
Chapel Hill	929-0479

ENVIRONMENTAL EMERGENCY
National Response Center	800-424-8802
Hazwaste	250-4360

HOPELINE (SUICIDE COUNSELING)
24-hour Crisis Line
Raleigh	828-4300
Durham	683-8628
Chapel Hill	929-0479
Teen Talkline	828-5011

N.C. State Highway Patrol 733-3861

Poison Control Center 800-672-1697

RAPE CRISIS
Raleigh	828-3005
Durham	286-4000
Chapel Hill/Orange County	967-7273/
	967-RAPE

Accounting Services

RALEIGH
Deloitte & Touche	546-8000
Ernst & Young	981-2800
McGladrey & Pullen	781-1055

DURHAM
Andrew Curl, CPA	383-7462
Deloitte & Touche	546-8000

CHAPEL HILL
O. Glenn Spell	968-4626
Carley Walker, CPA	933-2101

295

Agriculture

WAKE COUNTY
Cooperative Extension Service 250-1100

DURHAM COUNTY
Cooperative Extension Service 560-0525

ORANGE COUNTY
Cooperative Extension Service 732-8181

Airlines

American	800-433-7300
	834-4704
Delta	800-221-1212
Atlantic Southeast	800-282-3424
Comair	800-354-9822
Japan	800-525-3663
KLM	800-374-7747
Korea	800-438-5000
Lufthansa	800-645-3880
Northwest	800-225-2525
TWA	800-221-2000
	832-8212
United	800-241-6522
USAir	800-428-4322

RDU International Information
& Paging   840-2123 (Voice & TDD)
Director   840-2100

Alcohol/Drug Assistance

Alcohol/Drug Council of N.C.
Info & Referral Service   800-688-4232

WAKE COUNTY
Alcoholics Anonymous   250-3133
TDD Only   250-1499

PROFESSIONAL PROFILE

Accounting

Carley L. Walker, CPA

Carley L. Walker is a native of Chapel Hill and a graduate of UNC-Chapel Hill.

Professionally active, she is a member of the Board of Directors for the North Carolina Association of Certified Public Accountants; a past president of the Triangle Chapter of NCACPA; and for several years has been a frequent lecturer for the NCACAP on a state-wide level, and for the American Institute of CPAs on a national level.

Her background includes several years as a controller of a multimillion dollar diversified corporation, providing an insider's perspective on the management of small to medium-sized companies.

Her practice offers a very personalized service for individuals and business—with special attention to the needs of small business. Management consultation goes hand in hand with tax planning to give clients the best possible advice and guidance.

600 Franklin Square • 1829 E. Franklin Street • Chapel Hill, N.C. • 933-2101

RALEIGH

Alcoholics Anonymous	783-6144
(24-hour Hotline)	783-6144
Al-Anon	831-5252

DURHAM

Alcoholics Anonymous	286-9499
Al-Anon/Alateen	286-9499
Helpline	683-8628
Narcotics Anonymous	755-5391

CHAPEL HILL

Alcoholics Anonymous	929-1109
Al-Anon & Alateen	929-0155

Animal Care

WAKE COUNTY

Animal Control	250-1745
SPCA of Wake County	772-3202

DURHAM COUNTY

Animal Protection Society	560-0646
Animal Shelter	560-0640

ORANGE COUNTY

Carrboro	968-7709
Chapel Hill	968-2760
Animal Shelter	967-7383

Arts and Culture

RALEIGH/CARY

Raleigh Arts Commission	831-6234
Cary Arts Center	469-4069
Cary Arts Commission	467-2654
Wake Visual Arts Association	828-7834
United Arts Council	839-1498

DURHAM

Carolina Theatre	560-3040
Durham Arts Council	560-2787

CHAPEL HILL/CARRBORO

ArtsCenter Carrboro	929-2787

Automobile Information

WAKE COUNTY

Driver's License Information	733-4241
Garner	662-4366
Raleigh Express Ofc.	676-8957
Capital Blvd.	850-2892
District Dr.	733-4540
Wendell	365-9516
License Tags/Titles	
New Bern Ave.	733-3025
South Hills Mall, Cary	469-1444
North Hills, Raleigh	781-4967

DURHAM COUNTY

Driver's License	
Miami Blvd.	560-6896
N.C. Hwy. 54	560-3378
License Tags/Titles	
N.C. Hwy. 54	544-6607
Northgate	286-4908

ORANGE COUNTY

Drivers License	929-4161
License Tags/Titles	967-7059

Bus Service

Carolina Trailways	834-8410
Greyhound	800-231-2222

RALEIGH

Capital Area Transit	828-7228/833-5701

DURHAM

Durham Area Transit Auth.	688-4587

CHAPEL HILL

Chapel Hill Transit	968-2769

Chambers of Commerce

WAKE COUNTY

Apex Chamber	362-6456
Cary Chamber	467-1016
Fuquay-Varina Chamber	552-4947
Garner Chamber	772-6440
Knightdale Chamber	266-4603
Morrisville Chamber	380-9026

Raleigh Chamber	664-7000
Wake Forest Chamber	556-1519
Wendell Chamber	365-6318
Zebulon Chamber	269-6320

DURHAM COUNTY

Durham Chamber	682-2133

ORANGE COUNTY

Chapel Hill-Carrboro Chamber	967-7075
Hillsboroough Chamber	732-8156

NEIGHBORS

Clayton Chamber	553-6352
Louisburg Chamber	496-3056
Pittsboro Chamber	542-3335
Smithfield Chamber	934-9166

Civic & Fraternal Organizations

Contact Chambers for Listings

Consumer Services

WAKE COUNTY

Better Business Bureau	872-9240
Consumer Credit Counseling	821-1770
Consumer Protection of N.C.	733-7741
N.C. Attorney General's Office of	
Consumer Protection	733-7741

DURHAM COUNTY

Better Business Bureau	688-6143
OMBUDSMAN Hotline	800-662-7952
People's Allience	490-4448

ORANGE COUNTY

Better Business Bureau	967-0296

Convention & Visitors Bureaus

Durham	687-0288
Chapel Hill/Orange Co.	968-2060
Raleigh	834-5900

Crisis Intervention

WAKE COUNTY

American Red Cross	231-1602
Salvation Army	834-6733
Travelers Aid	821-1348
Victim Assistance Program	

DURHAM COUNTY

Contact	683-1595
Helpline of Durham	683-8628
Parents Anonymous	286-7112
Rape Crisis (24-hour)	286-4000

ORANGE COUNTY

American Red Cross	942-4862
HELPLINE	929-0479
Triangle Hospice	942-8597

Employment Services

WAKE COUNTY

Employment Security Comm.	733-3941
Job Information-Raleigh	890-3305
Job Line-Wake	856-6115
Older Worker Program	549-0551
Women's Center	829-3711
Youth Employment-Raleigh	831-6102
Youth Employment-Wake	856-6050

DURHAM COUNTY

Employment Security Comm.	560-6880
EEOC	856-4064
Vocational Rehabilitation	560-6810
Women in Community Service	489-2593

ORANGE COUNTY

Employment Security Comm.	967-0177
Job Corps Information	800-662-7948
Summer Youth Employment	
Program	967-0177
Vocational Rehabilitation	408-0428

Family Services

RALEIGH

Catholic Social Ministries	821-9750
Family Services Center	821-0790

DURHAM

Child/Parent Support Services	286-7112
Day Care Council	688-8661
Social Services Department	560-8000

CHAPEL HILL

Orange Mental Health Ctr.	929-0471
Child-Help Abuse Hotline	800-422-4453

Handicapped Services

RALEIGH

Goodwill Industries	834-0504
Rehabilitation	828-7490
Cued Speech Center	828-1218
Regional Resource Center	733-6714

DURHAM

Disability Hotline	800-638-6810
N.C. Services for the Blind	560-8600
NC. Services for the Deaf & Hard of Hearing	733-5199
Self-Help for Hard of Hearing	489-4821

CHAPEL HILL

Community Access Program	942-5119
Talking Books	800-662-7726
Self Help for Hard of Hearing	968-4862
Chapel Hill Training-Outreach Project	490-5577

Hospitals

WAKE COUNTY

Raleigh Community Hospital	954-3000
Rex	783-3100

Wake Medical Center	250-8000	
Northern Wake Medical Center (Wake Forest)	556-5151	
Southern Wake M.edical Center (Fuquay Varina)	552-2206	
Eastern Wake Medical Center (Zebulon)	269-7406	
Western Wake Medical Center (Cary)	233-2300	

DURHAM COUNTY

Duke Univ. Medical Center	684-8111
Durham Regional	470-4000

ORANGE COUNTY

UNC Hospitals	966-4131

SPECIALTY HOSPITALS

Charter Northridge	847-0008
Holly Hill	250-7000
N.C. Eye and Ear	682-9341

Wake County Alcoholism Treatment Center	250-1500

Legal Assistance

WAKE COUNTY

Legal Aid	828-4647
Legal Services of N.C.	856-2121

DURHAM COUNTY

Dispute Settlement Center	490-6777
Victim/Witness Assistance	560-6840
	or 560-6837
North Central Legal Assistance Program	688-6396

ORANGE COUNTY

American Civil Liberties Union	929-4053
Dispute Settlement Center	929-8800
North State Legal Services	942-7411
	or 942-7712

Libraries

WAKE COUNTY

Athens Drive	856-6868
Cameron Village	856-6710
Cary	460-3350
Chavis Heights	856-6595
Downtown	856-6690
Fuquay-Varina	557-2788
Glenwood towers	856-6596
Halifax Court	856-6594
Knightdale	266-8400
North Regional	870-4000
Richard B. Harrison	856-5720
South Raleigh	856-6598
Southeast Regional	662-2250
Wake Forest	554-8498
Wendell	365-2600
West Poplar	881-1344
Zebulon	269-3610

DURHAM COUNTY

Main	560-0100
Bragtown	560-0210
Mcdougal Terrace	560-0240
North Durham	560-0250
Parkwood	560-0260
Salvation Army boys Club	560-0280
Southwest	560-0290
Stanford L. Warren	560-0270

ORANGE COUNTY

Chapel Hill	968-2777
Orange County	644-3011

Newcomers' Organizations

WAKE COUNTY

Cary Newcomers Club	387-8474
Raleigh Newcomers Club	420-2329
Welcome Wagon	755-5405

DURHAM COUNTY

Welcome Wagon	968-0482
Durham Newcomers Club	286-0952

ORANGE COUNTY

Welcome Wagon	933-9423
(Sponsors Newcomer Club)	

Parks and Recreation

STATE AND COUNTY AREA PARKS

Falls Lake	676-1027
Jordan Lake	362-0586
Kerr Lake	438-7791
Lake Crabtree	460-3390
Lake Wheeler	662-5704
Shelly Lake	420-2331
William B. Umstead Park	787-3033
NC Division of Parks and Recreation	733-7275

WAKE COUNTY

Apex Parks and Rec.	387-3065
Cary Parks and Rec.	469-4061
Garner Parks and Rec.	772-8765
Knightdale Recreation	266-7710
Morrisville Parks and Rec.	
Raleigh Parks and Rec.	890-3285
Wendell Recreation	365-4263

DURHAM COUNTY

Athletics Program	560-4204
AfterSchool/Outreach	560-4616

ORANGE COUNTY

Carrboro Parks and Rec.	968-7703
Chapel HIll Parks and Recreation 24-Hour Information	968-2784

Recycling

WAKE COUNTY

Wake County Solid Waste	856-6186
Wake County "Keep America Beautiful"	856-6778

DURHAM COUNTY

MER Recycling, Inc	598-5795
Reynolds Recycling Station	228-2525
Sun Shares Recycling	596-1870

ORANGE COUNTY

ECOS	932-3050
Recycling Chapel Hill, Carrboro, Orange County	968-2788

Schools-Information

Durham	560-2000
Wake County	850-1600
Chapel Hill/Carrboro	967-8211

Senior Services

LOCAL AARP CHAPTERS:

WAKE COUNTY
Capital City	851-2981
Cary	467-2167

DURHAM COUNTY
Durham County	688-4803

ORANGE COUNTY
Orange County	732-4023

SENIOR CENTERS:

WAKE COUNTY
Eastern Wake Senior Center	365-4248
Garner Senior Center	779-0122
Whitaker Mill Senior Center	856-6444

DURHAM COUNTY
Council for Senior Citizens	688-8247

ORANGE COUNTY
Chapel Hill Senior Center	968-2070
So. Orange Senior Center	968-2080
Carrboro Senior Center	968-2075
Hillsboro Senior Center	732-8181

VOLUNTEER OPPORTUNITIES:

WAKE COUNTY
Community Programs	831-6102
Council on Aging	872-7933
Food Bank of NC	833-9027
Foster Grandparent Program	831-6102
Literacy Council	787-5559
RSVP	831-6295
Radio Reading Service	832-5138
SCORE	856-4739
United Way	833-5739

DURHAM COUNTY
RSVP	598-9380
SCORE	541-2171
Volunteer Center of Durham	688-8977

ORANGE COUNTY
RSVP	968-2054
SCORE	967-7075
Volunteer Center	929-9837

Teen Services

RALEIGH
Teen Talkline	828-5011
Wake Teen Medical Services	828-0035

DURHAM
Helpline	683-8628
Straight Talk	800-660-8336

CHAPEL HILL

Community Service Agency, Straight
Talk   800-660-8336
Drive-A-Teen   929-0479
Youth Employment Service   929-2106

Time, Temperature, Weather

Raleigh   976-2511
Durham   683-9696
Chapel Hill   933-3333

Train Service

Amtrak   833-7594
                              800-872-7245

Veteran's Services

Counseling Services   856-4616
N.C. Div. of Veterans Affairs 560-6672

Volunteer Organizations

WAKE COUNTY
RSVP   831-6295
Samaritans Ministry   839-1019
Volunteer Center   833-5739
Volunteer Referral   831-6102

DURHAM COUNTY
RSVP   598-9380
Volunteer Center of Greater Durham
                              688-8977

ORANGE COUNTY
Volunteer Center of
  Orange County   929-9837
Volunteer Round-Up   929-6380
Volunteer for Youth   942-0005
RSVP   968-2054

Voter Registration

WAKE COUNTY
Apex Community Library   387-2100

Cary Chamber of Commerce   467-1016
Elections Office   856-6240

DURHAM COUNTY
Board of Elections   560-0700

ORANGE COUNTY
League of Women Voters   942-3004
Board of Elections   967-9251
Carrboro   942-8541
Hillsborough   732-8181

Weather

National Weather Service 919-683-8306

Western Union

To find the nearest money transfer
location, call   800-325-6000
Se Habla Espanol   800-325-4045
Credit Card
  Cash Transfers   800-225-5227
Telegram & Mailgram Services
  Up to 50 messages   800-325-6000
  Over 50 messages   800-373-6245

Women's Services

WAKE COUNTY
Coalition for Battered Women
              919-683-8628 or 919-489-1955
N.C. Commission on
  the Status of Women   733-2455
Women's Center of Raleigh   829-3711

DURHAM COUNTY
Coalition for Battered Women 683-8628
Women's Commission   493-2319
Women in Action   482-1431
Women for Sobriety   490-6966

ORANGE COUNTY
Battered Women (Helpline)   929-0479
Women's Center   968-4610

Staff Photo

Brightleaf Square in Durham, proof that you can market retail stores
without neon lights or multi-colored billboards, is now listed
with the National Register of Historic Places.

Inside
Shopping

The Triangle's steady economy has acted like a magnet in pulling national and regional retailers to the area as well as shopping center developers who have glutted the market since 1986. This guide will highlight both the major shopping areas as well as some of the special places where Triangle residents like to spend their time and money. Don't expect this to be a complete listing of every shopping center or store in the area; this isn't the Yellow Pages. And this definitely is not "Shopping in the Triangle on $5 a Day." It's a guide to help you get started and to give you a fast start at finding some of those places you'll need (or want) to know about.

Regional Malls

CARY TOWNE CENTER
Maynard and Walnut Sts.
Cary

This is Cary's largest enclosed mall. It opened in 1979 and was expanded in 1991 by its new owners, Jacobs, Visconsi & Jacobs of Cleveland, Ohio. It is the second largest enclosed mall in Wake County, with about 1 million square feet of retail space. It truly is a re-

gional shopping center with over 100 stores, including anchor tenants **Hudson Belk, Sears, JC Penney, Hecht's,** and **Dillard's**. Merchants who also have stores in other Triangle shopping centers say business here is as good as—and sometimes better than—in their other locations. While many of the stores are members of a chain operation, some are unique to the Triangle, such as the **Disney Store** (although now there's one at Northgate Mall in Durham, too), a retail shop for all of the Disney empire's familiar faces on games, toys and clothing. The chains include **Lerner New York**, a fancy women's clothing store and **Butterfields, etc.**, home furnishings. There is **The Gap** and a **Gap Kids** next door; a **Foot Locker** and a **Lady Foot Locker, The Limited** and **Limited Too.** For the truly vain, try **Glamour Shots**, a photo studio where you undergo a beauty treatment before the cameraman takes your picture, suitable for a Hollywood "wannabe." Other tenants include three book stores, including **B. Dalton**, clothing chains such as **Casual Corner, Eddie Bauer, J. Riggings, County Seat, Lane Bryant**, and those darlings of the daring lingerie, **Victoria's Secret** and **Frederick's of Hollywood**. There are specialty stores such as **Simply Cotton, Bath and Body Works, Cyber Station, Logo Joe's, Kaybee Toys** and **Globetrotter** luggage shop. This list goes on. Like other malls, this one has a food court where you can snack yourself silly. And when you're finished and need to sit down and read, you can pick up all kinds of newspapers and magazines from the **Towne News Center** at the north entrance.

CRABTREE VALLEY MALL
U.S. Hwy. 70 (Glenwood Ave.) at I-440
Raleigh

This is Raleigh's largest enclosed mall and shopping area with over one million square feet of space and over 200 stores, restaurants and services. Crabtree Valley Mall draws approximately 200,000 people a week. **Hudson-Belk, Hecht's** and **Sears** anchor the shopping center. **The Nature Company, The Body Shop, Abercrombie & Fitch, Laura Ashley, Crabtree and Evelyn, The Gap, Eddie Bauer, Luggage and Leather, Lillie Rubin, The Hub Ltd.** men's wear, **Brookstone, Impostors, Aventure Toys** and the **Gift Attic** are a few of the unique stores you will find here. **Varsity Men's Wear** is one of the author's favorite locally owned stores. **The Limited, The Limited Too, Connie Shoes** and **Victoria's Secret** are also available. **Wolf Camera, Babbage's, Electronics Boutique, AT&T Store** and **Radio Shack** round out the up-to-date shopping opportunities. Scheduled to open in the Spring of '94 are **Brooks Brothers** and **Alex & Ivy**.

The Pavilion is filled with a large variety of fast-food merchants as well as specialty shops. Four restaurants, **Capital Room** at Hudson Belk, **Ruby Tuesday's, Mr. Dunderbak's**, and **Kanki** provide additional eating pleasure as you visit Crabtree.

Crabtree Valley Mall • U.S. 70 W. at I-440 • Raleigh, NC • (919) 783-7133

The mall opened in 1972 and is undergoing an extensive renovation and expansion program that includes new Sears and Hecht's stores and will add **Lord & Taylor** to the anchor stores. Additional levels will be added to the south parking decks. One caution: Don't try to hold any secret trysts at Crabtree because you're bound to meet someone you know when you go there.

Although it's not a part of Crabtree, **Kidds Hill Plaza**, which sits across Crabtree Creek and up the hill, has a **Brendle's** discount store and **Food Lion** supermarket.

CROSSROADS PLAZA
U.S. Hwy. I and I-440
Cary

This is Cary's entry into the "power-shopping" market. It opened in 1991. Originally planned as a regional, enclosed upscale mall whose backers went bankrupt, Crossroads settled on its current plan as a sprawling maze of discount giants. The anchor tenants are **Home Quarters**, **Office Max**, **Uptons**, **Service Merchandise**, **Marshalls**, and **Pharmor**. In 1993, it became home to **Exhilarama**, an indoor amusement park that includes virtual reality rides and high-tech entertaiment. Crossroads has some specialty discounters such as **REI**, the membership store for outdoor people, **Toys R' Us**, and **Pet Depot Superstore**. The popular specialty clothing discounter, **Great Mistakes**, is here as well, offering up to 60% off retail for name brand clothing. There are restaurant chains, too, such as **Ryan's**, **Red Lobster**, and a drive-thru **Chick-Fil-A**. The internal traffic pattern is a challenge, but what better place for a power shopper to get lost!

NORTHGATE MALL
Off I-85 at Gregson on W. Club Blvd.
Durham

Durham's first large shopping mall now boasts over 140 stores and services. Its anchor stores are **Hecht's**, moving this fall to a new, larger store in the new wing of the mall, and **Sears**. The mall will soon be welcoming 22 new shops and, in early 1995, a new **Belk Hudson Leggett** will open. Kerr Drugs is in the mall and a **Harris Teeter** grocery store adjoins.

Northgate offers a Food Gallery, that features everything from fresh salads to pizza to homemade desserts. The many specialty shops in the mall include **Morgan Imports**, **The Limited**, **The Disney Store**, **Victoria's Secret**, **Sharon Luggage**, **The Bombay Company**, and a number of unique, locally owned and managed stores. A full-size Italian Carousel is a permanent fixture and a favorite of area children. Northgate provides many services at the Customer Service Center, such as wheelchairs, stroller rental, mall directories, gift wrapping, mall gift certificates and most importantly a smiling person to answer your questions!

NORTH HILLS MALL
Six Forks Rd. and Beltline North Hills
Raleigh

Built in the 1960s, North Hills is Raleigh's original mall. Since that time, it has been updated and now offers a diverse range of shops where you can find just about everything—from clothes and shoes to stereos and sofas. The mall is anchored by **Dillard's** department store and **JC Penney**, but it has found a niche by providing smaller specialty shops such as **Jos. A. Banks Clothiers**, a men's and women's career fashion store, **Victoria's Secret** and **Wrenn-Pharr**. Some of the more elegant notables are **Christian's**, **Montaldo's** and **Nowell's**.

If high fashion is not what you're after, pick up a pair of sweats or running shoes at **DSG Sports** or **Footlocker**. **The Storehouse** is here for furniture, and **The Print Shop** has the perfect accent pieces to with it. And, of course, there's Ruth Green's **Little Art Gallery**, which may be little but commands a big following. Need a break? There are over 15 choices of eating establishments at North Hills Mall & Plaza.

North Hills Plaza is a small shopping center across Lassiter Mill Road from the mall. It is anchored by **Winn-Dixie** and the **U.S. Post Office**, and is geared strongly toward service with merchants such as **Blockbuster Video**, **North Hills Cleaners**, **Montieth Travel** and **N.C. Division of Motor Vehicles**. It has specialty shops as well, such as **Dan Howard's Maternity Outlet**, **Audio Book World** and **Hickory Farms**.

SOUTH SQUARE MALL
U.S. Hwy. 15-501 N./Bus.
(Chapel Hill Blvd.)

The other of Durham's two mega-malls, South Square has 120 stores spanning 790,000 square feet. It's anchored by **Belk-Leggett** department store, **J.C. Penney**, and

Dillard's department store. The mall also includes a fast food center offering everything from pizza and fried chicken to stuffed potatoes and chocolate chip cookies. If you're looking for a poster or print to spruce up your apartment, home or office, check out **Deck the Walls** on the upper level; it also offers custom framing. **The Limited, Express, The Gap** and **Benetton** are popular, especially with local high school and college students.

South Square is located adjacent to the huge **Toys R' Us** toy store (go without your children if you want to come out alive) and **HQ**, the "home quarters" warehouse. Down the road is **Circuit City**, the discount stereo, TV and appliance chain.

If South Square isn't big enough for you, there are three shopping centers nearby: **Parkway Plaza** (4215 University Drive), where you will find a **Pier 1 Imports**, **Regency Plaza** (University Drive and Cosmo Avenue) where you'll find **Service Merchandise** and smaller stores like **Blockbuster Video**, with its huge selection of rental movies, and **Oak Creek Village**.

UNIVERSITY MALL & PLAZA

Featuring over 65 stores, restaurants and services, University Mall and Plaza offers Chapel Hill its most varied array of shopping possibilities. Located on the corner of U.S. Highway 15-501 and South Estes Drive, University Mall and Plaza is anchored by two of the region's most prestigious department stores: **Dillard's** and **Belk Leggett**. A host of apparel and specialty shops ranging from athletic apparel to maps to electronic equipment add to the diversity of University Mall.

Some Insiders' favorites are **Kitchenworks**, an eclectic mix of anything you'd ever want for your kitchen, **Cameron's**, filled with wonderful gifts, jewelry and things that defy description and **The Children's Store** and **The Toy Corner** for quality clothing, toys and games for the wee ones in the family. Other special shops are **Minata** (jewelry and gifts), **The Omni Shop** (maps, books and gifts relating to nature and travel) and **The Country Store** (operated by the Chapel Hill Service League). A customer service center with information on the community, wheelchairs, strollers and diaper-changing facilities is just inside the main entrance near **Kerr Drugs**. Mall hours are Monday-Saturday, 10 a.m. until 9 p.m. and Sunday from 1 p.m. until 6 p.m.

Raleigh

Raleigh has long served as a regional shopping area for eastern North Carolina and it continues to hold that reputation. Raleigh is where people come to buy the fancy shoes and special dress or the delicate dessert and dry wine they can't find in Smalltown, North Carolina. But Raleigh also is where many come for their "big ticket" items at discount prices.

Shopping mores have changed since the times when downtown Fayetteville Street was clogged on Saturdays with farm families buying provisions at Briggs Hardware and ice cream at the "Cali" drug store. Some of the changes have come quite recently. For example, until the 1970s, most city merchants observed the old "blue laws" that prohibited Sunday sales. The advent of national chains changed the habit and today, many stores and most malls have Sunday hours. Saturday remains the big shopping day for most retailers, but not because it's when farm families come to town. It's when the working woman has some time off to go shopping. The working woman also has changed store hours, and few stores close their doors at 5:00 anymore. Others don't open until noon. Several of the supermarkets stay open 24 hours and malls remain open until 9 or 9:30 p.m.

Also, the trend of "off pricing" or discount buying of brand names has made Raleigh a more competitive market during the past five years. Some sophisticates still insist on buying their fashion necessities in Noo Yawk (and telling their friends they did so); and candid residents will concede that Raleigh is a tough place to find Bruno Magli pumps or Neiman Marcus labels. But the adventurous shopper will not be disappointed with Raleigh, and gross retail sales hit $4.4 billion in 1993, second in the state. The figures are proof that the city retains its title as a regional retail center. That trend is growing, too.

Finally, as any Raleigh merchant will tell you, the best way to develop a shopping guide is to go shopping yourself. So, come on down!

Shopping Centers

CAMERON VILLAGE SHOPPING CENTER
Oberlin Rd. and Clark Ave.

Cameron Village is interesting just to visit, since it is contemporary history as well as the city's third largest shopping center. Built during the early '50s, Cameron Village was one of the Southeast's first shopping centers, and it's undergoing a $17-million renovation.

About 1 1/2 miles from downtown, it was an instant hit in 1949, and developer J.W. "Willie" York built residential neighborhoods nearby to provide new customers. It is not an enclosed mall, but canopies keep shoppers from bad weather and the renovations and extensive landscaping have given the Village a brighter look and broader sidewalks.

It is also known for its large number of locally owned, family stores and shops, some into their fourth generation. They include a number of specialty clothing stores such as **Tyler House**, **Burton's**, **Ellisberg's** and **Nowell's**. Others are **Sam Bass Camera**, **Jolly's Jewelers**, **Johnson-Lambe Sporting Goods** (the oldest sports store and reliable supplier of youth uniforms). They keep loyal customers coming back, and new stores such as **Talbot's** and **Lavender and Linen** have brought new clients.

The **Hobby Shop** next to the **Baskin-Robbins** is the best in the city and the place to go for HO gauge model trains. Two good bookstores are located here, too (**Waldenbooks**, and **Village Book and Stationery**), as well as **Jill Flink's** art gallery, which features contemporary and original local artists. **Past and Presents** is a great place to find gifts and home accessories. It features some really unique handcrafted items and collectibles such as Tom Clark gnomes. **Great Expectations** offers designer women's fashions and wonderful accessories and jewelry. Cameron Village also has an **ABC Package Store** (for Yankees, that's a euphemism for a state-run liquor store). **Karen's** restaurant is a fixture, and **Leon's** deli has a homemade macaroni salad that's downright addictive. **Fresh Market**, a specialty food store, augments a **Harris Teeter** supermarket, which will move in 1994 to a larger, super-grocery store across from the Post Office, two blocks north.

Cameron Village also hosts an annual Octoberfest benefit for Hospice. It has the city's most popular library branch, too; check it out.

311

FAYETTEVILLE STREET MALL
Downtown, south of the Capitol

The four or five blocks of Fayetteville Street immediately south of the Capitol building was the heart of Raleigh's retail life until the 1950s and the advent of the shopping center. Shopping downtown declined steadily until the 1970s, when the downtown section of Fayetteville Street was closed and a mall with fountains, trees, flowers and a town clock installed. It is hardly the center of shopping that it once was, but downtown still has some clothing, jewelry, convenience retail and the city's best art district. **Belk's** venerable downtown store is the heart of downtown shopping, and its veteran and helpful sales people are a polite alternative to the often hurried, wait-on-yourself disservice of discount emporiums. **Briggs Hardware** is a historic landmark as well as a place to find the hard-to-find tool, nut or nail. Businesses such as the **Yum Yum Tree** (women's clothing) and **Jem Designs** (jewelry with unique minerals and gemstones cater to the daytime shopper, so don't expect to find much open after 6 p.m. except during the holiday season and except for the restaurants.

CITY MARKET
Downtown, Moore Square

Two blocks east of the Fayetteville Street Mall in the Moore Square Art District is the new City Market complex that is attracting artists and crafts people as well as new customers to downtown. **Artspace**, a large renovated automobile dealership building, is unique and offers artisans both a place to work and to sell their goods. Historic old buildings house unique establishments such as the **Victorian Gift Shoppe, Ltd.** with collectible antiques, **The Robin's Nest** for gourmet foods, candy and gift baskets and numerous other specialty shops. **PlaySpace** provides truly innovative indoor entertainment for children and restaurants such as **Big Ed's City Market Restaurant**,

Greenshield's, The Queen of Hearts Tearoom and Barista Java coffeehouse round out the diverse offerings. Merchants see the City Market as downtown's next specialty shopping area.

Strip Centers

The following alphabetical list is by no means complete; however, it provides a guide to representative strip or neighborhood shopping centers throughout the city. It lists old and new places and some of the special stores that attract shoppers.

CREEDMOOR CROSSING
Creedmoor and Leesville rds.

Creedmoor Crossing is the first of a number of new neighborhood centers that are filling up the intersections along Creedmoor Road (N.C. Hwy. 50), one of the main arteries to residential north Raleigh and the town of Creedmoor and Interstate 85. This small strip center features an anchor food store with one of the Triangle's large chain drug stores, in this case Food Lion and Eckerd. It also is home to **Harmony Farms**, a very well-stocked natural food store, **Simpson's Beef and Seafood** restaurant, and a store called **Classical Clocks**.

GREYSTONE VILLAGE
Leadmine and Sawmill rds.

The quaint stone architecture makes this center stand out. Conveniently located in the heart of rapidly expanding north Raleigh, Greystone Village has a **Save-A-Center** grocery store and **Kerr Drugs**. A number of service-oriented businesses are located here as well, such as Frye Pest Control, **Ashlee's Grooming**, a dry cleaner, a hair salon and a florist among others. Shoppers enjoy stopping by **The Coterie Bakery, Cafe & Deli** for a quick bite, or one of several other restaurants nearby.

NORTH RIDGE
Falls of the Neuse and Spring Forest rds.

North Ridge Shopping Center was built in 1980 at a key intersection, near North Ridge County Club. It is anchored by a major grocery store, **Winn-Dixie** and **Kerr Drugs** and features a number of shops, including **Little Women**, which specializes in petite sizes and accessories and **Thompson-Lynch** lamps, **Bill Touchberry Photography**, one of the largest personal, commercial and industrial photo studios in the area and the **Spa Health Club**. Like most such centers, it has fast-food restaurants sit-

Greystone Village
Shopping Center

We are conveniently located, service oriented and you will recognize us by our distinctive stone architecture.

- Fast Fare
- Kerr Drug
- Frye Pest Control
- Woodworking Shopsmith
- Peck's Tae Kwon Do
- Bare Wall Custom Framing
- The Coterie Bakery, Cafe & Deli
- Save-A-Center
- Imperial Garden
- Casa Doria
- Kelsi Cat Clinic
- Ashlee's Grooming
- Hair Visions Unlimtd
- Pope's Dry Cleaners
- T-Bone Junction
- Raleigh Federal
- Benson's Florist

ting away from the strip and, unlike others, it has a notable, locally owned restaurant, **Jean-Claude's**.

OAK PARK
U.S. Hwy.70 W. and Holly Ridge Rd.

A vintage, late '50s shopping center, Oak Park was built to accommodate its namesake residential development nearby. For merchants, it offers some of the best rents in town and an easy-going, local landlord, Johnny Connell. For shoppers, it has a diverse lineup including **Bernina's World of Sewing**, an auto-parts store and **Hertzberg Furs**, and a pharmacy. **Maus Piano**, which sells Baldwins and provides tuning, has been around since 1934. Oak Park also has several restaurants, including **O'Malley's**, a friendly tavern with the atmosphere of a neighborhood pub, and **The Peddler**, one of the city's better steak houses.

SOUTHGATE PLAZA
Rock Quarry Rd. and I-440

Southgate opened in 1985 and is the first shopping center to be built in predominantly black, southeast Raleigh in decades. It contains a **Winn-Dixie** supermarket plus several clothing stores, a local restaurant, a drug store, beauty shop, cleaners, an ABC Package Store, and a branch of the **Wake County public library**.

TOWER SHOPPING CENTER
U.S. Hwy. 64 and I-440

Built at Raleigh's main gateway to the east, this strip center quickly established itself in the late '70s as a shopping place for east

Raleigh residents as well as commuters from suburbs such as Knightdale and Wendell and cities such as Rocky Mount and Wilson. It caters to the discount shopper and includes a **Food Lion** supermarket and **Kerr Drugs**.

Behind the Tower center is another center. Together, they contain eight theaters, two in the shopping center strip and another six in a complex around back, and fast-food restaurants proliferate in and around the strip. It has service operations like cleaners, animal clinics and shoe repair as well as name-brand stores like **Radio Shack, Advance Auto Parts, The Finish Line, Hamricks, The Rack Room, The Dress Barn** and **Casual Male Big 'n' Tall**.

STONEHENGE MARKETPLACE
Creedmoor Rd.

This is one of the many strip centers along Creedmoor Road, but it's the largest with over 30 retail stores, a post office and several service centers. There is a kiosk and an art gallery and ice cream store. The anchor stores are **Harris Teeter** and **Eckerd Drugs**. It also has **Flythe Cyclery, Radio Shack, Sweetum's Bakery** and on the south side, a **Crowley's** restaurant. Every Tuesday is senior citizens' discount day when Eckerd gives out discount cards.

SIX FORKS STATION
Strickland and Six Forks rds.

This neighborhood strip center has plenty of room for expansion and has a **Food Lion, Eckerd Drugs** and **K-Mart** as major tenants.

315

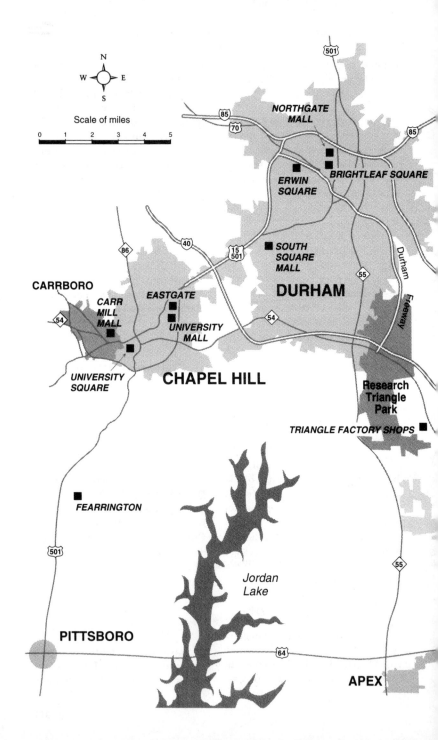

Triangle Shopping

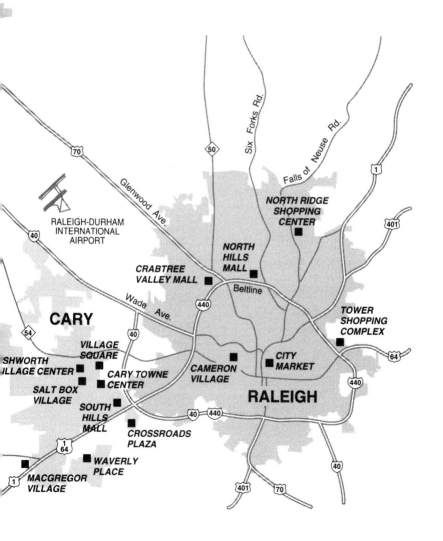

A big attraction has been the six-screen movie complex in the southwest corner. A **Waccamaw** pottery store opened in 1989. You won't go hungry here either with the **Upper Crust Restaurant**, **K & S Cafeteria**, **O'Charley's** and various fast food restaurants.

Special Places

There are certain shops and stores in every community that occupy a special place for special reasons. No, we're not talking about Sam Walton's Wholesale Club, although there is one, on S. Saunders Street at the Interstate 440 intersection. Some of these special places are in shopping centers; others are discovered by chance. Some have been around for a long, long time and others have just opened their doors. What they have in common is an appeal to the shopper who wants to know where Raleigh Insiders shop...the special places.

ALL STAR BIKES

5011 Falls of the Neuse Rd.
Quail Corners Shopping Center   876-9876
3530 Wade Ave.
Ridgewood Shopping Center   833-5070
740 E. Chatham St., Cary
Chatham Sq. Shopping Center   469-1849

This locally owned business has built itself into a four-store chain since opening in 1978 (there's a fourth at Six Forks Celebration Shopping Center). Owner Jeff Hutchinson knows bikes, and his stores are the places to go for information about area bicycle news and races. The stores specialize in all-terrain (or mountain) bikes as well as racing bikes; they offer service on all brands of bikes. All Star sells exercise equipment along with the best selection in town of cycling clothing. It was recognized in 1987 by the national dealers association as one of the top 100 bike shops in the country.

ASKEW-TAYLOR PAINTS

110 Glenwood Ave.   834-4497

There are plenty of prettier paint stores in Raleigh, and there may be some places to get paint cheaper, but none can match the advice and personal service of the Taylors. They carry Benjamin Moore and less expensive Blue Ridge brands. They will work with you on getting a custom color and will tell you whether you can put latex over an oil-based paint. You can park across the street and if you go on Saturday, get there early because they close after noon. They carry all kinds of equipment, such as brushes, rollers, scrapers, etc., and they also are one of the city's biggest dealers in artist supplies.

AUDIO BUYS, INC.

1700 Glenwood Ave.   821-1776

Situated on the corner of Glenwood and Fairview at Raleigh's Five Points, Audio Buys offers quality audio, video and television merchandise, sold and serviced by a knowledgeable staff. For over 11 years, Audio Buys has carried many top brands, including the latest Sony, Canon, JVC, Polk and Harman-Kardan audio and video, usually at prices competitive with the discount chains. The service department, Tech Services, is a full-time, on-premise service department for warranty and repair of audio and video equipment. What has kept Audio Buys in business over the years is a commitment to its customers: answering questions, solving problems, and being willing to help long after the customer buys the merchandise.

ATLANTIC WHIRLPOOLS
8411 Glenwood Ave.   *783-7447*

These folks are experts in designing space for and installing the perfect whirlpool for your bathroom, patio or spa. Bill Mitchell and his staff are great to work with, so go ahead, take the plunge—when winter hits, you'll be glad you did.

AUSSIE-ISLAND SURF SHOP
6325-29 Falls of the Neuse Rd.   *872-6272*

In one of north Raleigh's newer shopping centers (**Sutton Square**), this trendy shop has capitalized on the popularity of California beachwear and skateboard fashions such as Powell Peralta. It is locally owned and really does carry surf equipment such as boards and wet suits, as well as snowboards and ski wear. It's where fashion conscious, "chilled-out" teenagers catch the wave in "radical" clothing.

BEANIE AND CECIL
412 Daniels St.   *821-5455*

Founded in 1992, this store takes its catchy name from the youthful owners, one of whom is the daughter of Jim Goodnight, founder of software success story SAS. The store is a women's boutique with very chic clothes. The owners take custom orders and carry

the FINIS line, usually found in Saks, Bergdorf Goodman and Bendel's. The flannels and cashmeres are from Scotland and the suedes and leathers from Italy.

BOB'S ARMY SURPLUS
1217 S. Saunders St.   *833-8223*

This is a one-of-a-kind shop. Bob has gone uptown somewhat, from the dilapidated wooden shack across the street that looked like surplus itself. He's got a neat, concrete block building, but his prices are still surplus cheap, and he really does carry Army and military surplus, such as Army issue sleeping bags—in good condition—for $45. He has a large selection of military clothes and the usual look-alike, new fashions. Campers and backpackers might check Bob's inventory before buying at the fancy outdoor stores.

BOOKS AT QUAIL CORNERS
5011-B Falls of the Neuse Rd.   *878-5515*

This friendly, family-owned bookstore offers full, personal service by a knowledgeable staff led by Nancy Olson. Its large selection of children's books is enhanced by free weekly children's programs, such as puppet shows, storytelling and music. The store also offers a wide selection of history, travel, women's studies, literature and political books. It frequently sponsors author readings and signings. Books at Quail Corners has been voted "Best Place for Children's Books" in the Triangle since 1988, and it's also home to north Raleigh's unofficial mayor. The owners invite you to browse seven days a week.

BUTTERFIELD'S, ETC.
Crabtree Valley Mall 781-5732

This shop has a great selection of cookware, ceramics, pottery, linens and specialty gourmet items for all of your culinary needs. Gift baskets and special orders are also available. This shop has what you need to get cookin'.

CAMERON PARK BOTANICALS
N.C. Hwy. 64 E. 266-6313

This is a unique store that is located just past the bridge over the Neuse River, and it offers herbal gardening and aroma therapy. For the unwashed, aroma therapy uses certain oils "for physical, emotional and cosmetic purposes" and is a centuries-old art. Bob and Elizabeth Johnson are the proprietors, and they offer classes on growing and using herbs as well as aroma therapy. The store has funny yardbirds, birdfeeders, herbal books, and a greenhouse of plants and pottery.

CARLTON'S FLOWERS
609 Glenwood Ave. 821-3862

You may prefer to deal with a local florist—and there are many good ones in Raleigh—but one look at Carlton's window on Glenwood Avenue will explain why Insiders go here for special occasions or for that special arrangement. **Strother Floral Galleries** in Falls Village in north Raleigh is another florist known for its creativity and is an Insiders' favorite.

DJ'S BOOK & NEWS CENTER
2416 Hillsborough St. 833-2624

DJ's won fame in the 1970s by challenging NCSU's monopoly on textbooks and winning the right to sell such books to students. It doesn't sell textbooks any more, but it is the place around NCSU to go to get out-of-town newspapers and hard to get magazines. DJ's has a store in Crabtree Valley Mall, too.

FAIRGROUNDS FLEA MARKET
Hillsborough St. at Blue Ridge Rd.
832-0361

When Triangle shoppers talk about "the flea market," they probably are talking about the permanent flea market at the State Fairgrounds. It's open weekends, and for a fee, you can set up your stand there, too. It occupies six large buildings with about 175 stalls that sell anything from flashing signs to belt buckles to old furniture. Some things are free...kittens and, occasionally, puppies.

The better bargains are outside in the sun, rain, wind and dust where the amateurs usually set up an umbrella or sell from their station wagons' tailgates. If you're a bargain hunter, the best buys and the hardest bargains come near closing time. The market is one of the best on the East Coast and draws vendors from all over. It opens early and closes at sundown.

STATE FARMERS' MARKET
Lake Wheeler Rd. & I-440 733-7417

This state-operated market is near the southern half of the Beltline interchange and Lake Wheeler Road and provides shoppers from across the state with the garden bounty of area farmers as well as seasonal produce, such as citrus fruits, trucked in from neighboring states. It's open year-round, weekdays, too, and Saturday usually is the big day. It's the place to go in season to get fresh produce...often from the person who grew it: strawberries, blueberries, shelled blackeyed peas, sweet corn, tomatoes, yams, watermelon, you name it. Here you will find your Halloween pumpkin or that perfectly shaped Christmas tree.

In April, Buildings 1 and 2 are in full bloom with flowers and bedding plants. And the Garden Center which features **Fowler's Garden Shop**, is a weekend gardeners paradise.

In the market specialty shops you'll find **Ford's Fancy Fruits "The North Carolina Store,"** and **B.J.'s Candy Garden and The Fudge Factory**—no explanation needed. For those who want their fresh produce or seafood already prepared, **The Farmers Market Restaurant** serves up breakfast and lunch and **N.C. Seafood**, famous for its fried shrimp, serves lunch and dinner.

As the sign leading into the Farmers' Market proclaims, it's "more than fresh vegetables, it's a family adventure." Indeed, for some, going to the Farmers' Market on Saturday morning is almost as uplifting as Sunday church.

FERGUSON'S HARDWARE
2900 Hillsborough St.   *832-3743*
This venerable hardware store continues to hold its own against the giant discount chains. Many consider it the best hardware store in town, and its familiar and experienced clerks dispense "how-to" commentary along with the

merchandise. A good place to find the unusual.

Farther out Hillsborough Street is **Burke Brother's**, across from the Fairgrounds, and another contender for "best in town" honors. It's one place where you can find storm lanterns. If you're in east Raleigh, the neighborhood favorite is **Handy Man** on New Bern Avenue, operated by former City Councillor Ed Walters.

FLYTHE SCHWINN CYCLERY
424 W. Peace St.   *832-5097*
Insiders have several good bike shops to choose from, and Flythe's has carried the standard for years. It is the headquarters for the BMX crowd and carries BMX racers, 10-speeds, all-terrain mountain bikes, and the equipment to go with them. Downstairs is **Endless Grind**, the place for serious skateboarders, and the business of one of the nation's top skateboarders.

FORD'S FANCY FRUITS "THE NORTH CAROLINA STORE"
State Farmers' Market   *821-0851*
Transplanted "Yankees" who want to get a head start on eating "southern" should make Ford's their first stop. With such delicious delicacies as red eye gravy, true grits, possum and everyone's favorite, Bone Suckin' Sauce, this shop offers the largest selection of gourmet foods from North Carolina. There are over 600 specialty products to choose from, including ornaments and books. If you're looking for a gift basket, Ford's is famous for its beautiful fruit gifts and they deliver locally or ship world-

wide. There is a second location in Terminal A at the RDU Airport.

FRAMEWORKS
1520 Dixie Trail   *781-3118*

This custom picture framing business started in 1976 and owner Carolyn Younger says that she can provide you with a frame to fit a miniature or a full-length portrait. The store also sells original artwork, including works by Pat Buckley Moss, a Virginia painter who is noted for her pictures of the Amish. Also popular are Greenwich Workshop and Mill Pond Press prints. The store is one of the larger dealers in the Triangle of the annual duck stamp prints.

CHARLES FRANK, GOLDSMITH
1633 N. Market Sq.   *876-7887*

Charles Frank has been a popular north Raleigh jeweler and jewelry designer for several decades. He carries a wide variety of gemstones and original jewelry and his designs have been prize winners. He has the certified gemologist designation, but it's his reputation that is 18-carat with Triangle customers.

GARDEN MAGIC
1930 Wake Forest Rd.   *821-1997*

This fine store started in 1983 at Five Points and then moved into a renovated 1924 vintage warehouse in 1991 and added a selection of

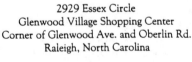

M·HERGET
FINE PAPERS AND GIFTS

Offering Raleigh's Finest Collection of

Custom Stationery • Desk Accessories • Invitations • Fine Pens
Luxurious Linens • Unique Frames • Greeting Cards • Baby Gifts
Monogrammed Silver, Glassware, Lucite, Leather and Luggage

2929 Essex Circle
Glenwood Village Shopping Center
Corner of Glenwood Ave. and Oberlin Rd.
Raleigh, North Carolina

Store Hours:
Monday-Friday 10:00-6:00 • Saturday 10:00-5:30
787-1246 • 787-1297 (FAX)

plants. The owners sell fine quality decorative garden accessories, statuary, teak and iron furniture, planters, English imports, handcrafted brass and copper lanterns, post lights and garden antiques. It's worth a trip to see the water garden and English perennial border in front of the shop's ancient-looking brick wall.

HARMONY FARMS
Creedmoor Crossings 782-0064
2710 Hillsborough St. 832-3237

This natural foods and products shop has grown from being the "hippie hangout" when it first opened on Hillsborough Street years ago to a well-known place for all types who appreciate food and products that are chemical-free and non-exploitative. You can buy whole grains, books, natural health care and beauty items, and the ever-popular Birkenstock shoes.

HAYES BARTON PHARMACY
2000 Fairview Rd. 832-4641

This is a vintage, "old-fashioned" drug store that is the cornerstore for the Five Points shopping area. Surrounded by shops that come and go, the pharmacy serves as a gathering place for neighbors and shopkeepers who brag that the sandwiches are some of Raleigh's best and the gossip unmatched.

M. HERGET STATIONER
Glenwood Village Shopping Center
2929 Essex Circle 787-1246

This is one of Raleigh's trendsetters, whether it's in designer stationery, personalized picture frames, crafted pens or fine imported cotton linens. In business since 1975, it is one of eastern North Carolina's largest dealers of elegant Crane's stationery, and it also sells the black and gold Mont Blanc, Waterman and the newly designed Parker pens. The store is known throughout the gift trade as a place to watch for what's selling, because M. Herget has a knack for bringing to the Triangle what's fashionable and what's fresh with attentive, personal service. And yes, M. Herget is wife to one of the authors, and sells autographed copies of *The Insiders' Guide To The Triangle* at the checkout counter.

HILL'S SPORTING GOODS
1720 N. Blvd. 833-4884

For the duck and deer hunters, as well as the fly and surf fishermen in Raleigh, Hill's has become the place to go for rifles and shotguns and other hunting and fishing supplies. It carries used guns, too, and services what it sells. Some of the brands include Remington, Winchester, Browning, Weatherby, Mannlicher, Colt, Smith & Wesson and Ruger. You can also pick up your fishing and hunting licenses here.

HOBBY SHOP
Cameron Village Shopping Center
2020 Cameron St. 833-1123

This hobby shop deserves a second mention because it's the kind of place that modelers dream about. If you're a child, you can't walk past its display window without stopping. Planes hang from the ceiling, electric trains chug their way around the display area, and notices on the door tell about some special steam-engine excursion or meeting of remote-control fliers. The selection of HO gauge is the best in the Triangle, and the sales people know their products.

HOPPER PIANO
710 W. Peace St.   *755-0185*

There are cheaper places to buy a piano or organ, but Hopper is where you can buy a Steinway. It carries several other brands and offers piano rentals, tuning and, occasionally, a bargain used piano. It's been in business for years and comes recommended by a number of area piano teachers. The sales

people are low-key and experienced, so don't expect to be pressured into the "$10 down, take it home tonight" routine.

IMPOSTORS
Crabtree Valley Mall
U.S. Hwy. 70 at I-440   *782-5777*

If you dream of baubles, bangles and beads, you'll love this place. It carries look-alikes of fine jewelry designs at prices that are hard to believe. Steve and Lori Boole opened this nifty little shop in Crabtree Mall in 1990 and business has been booming ever since. Diamonds, pearls, gold—go ahead and treat yourself—you deserve it.

Crabtree Valley Mall

DEPARTMENT STORES
Hudson Belk
Sears
Hecht's

MEN'S & WOMEN'S APPAREL
Abercrombie & Fitch
American Eagle
Banana Republic
Champs
County Seat
Eddie Bauer
Express/Structure
The Gap
Great Outdoor
  Provision Co.
Merry Go Round
Razzle Dazzle

MEN'S APPAREL
Brooks Brothers
Chess King
Fine's
Hub Ltd.
Big & Tall
J. Riggings
Structure
Varsity Men's Wear
VIP Formal Wear
Y-Knot

WOMEN'S APPAREL
August Max Woman
Catherine's Plus Sizes
Cache'
Casual Corner
Closet
D.A. Kelly's
Express
5-7-9
Lane Bryant
Laura Ashley
Lillie Rubin
Limited
Ormond
Petite Sophisticate
Southport
Stuarts

CHILDREN'S APPAREL
Limited Too
Gap Kids

SPECIALTY APPAREL
Cacique
Dokars
Motherhood Maternity
Moving in Style
Soc Shop
Victoria's Secret
VIP Formal Wear

AUTOMOTIVE
Goodyear Tire &
  Rubber Co.
Sears Automotive Center

BANKS
ATM Machine
First Union National Bank
NationsBank
Wachovia Bank of N.C.

BARBERS & BEAUTY SALONS
Chaz Hair Designers
Hair, Inc.
Hair Secrets
Mitchell's Hair Styling
Valley Style Shop

BOOKS
B. Dalton Books
Barnes and Noble
D.J.'s Book & News
Waldenbooks

CARDS & STATIONERY
Daphne's Hallmark

COMPUTERS & ELECTRONICS
Babbage's
Electronics Boutique
Radio Shack
Software, Etc.

COSMETICS
A Natural Nail
The Body Shop
i Natural
Merle Norman

RESTAURANTS & CAFETERIAS
The Capital Room
Kanki Japanese
  Steak House
Mr. Dunderbak's
Ruby Tuesday

FOOD STORES/ PAVILION
Bella Napoli
Burger King
Frank & Stein Dogs
  and Drafts
Gelato Amare
Hector's
McDonald's
Mr. Barbecue 'n Stuff
Mrs. Fields Cookies
Mrs. Pretzel
Oriental Express
Sbarro
The Steak Escape
Subway
Taco Bell
Teriuaki Sushi 'A'

FOOD STORES/ SPECIALTY
Auntie Anne's Pretzels
Baskin-Robbins
Chick-fil-A
The Coffee Beanery
Cookie Store
Dunkin' Donuts
General Nutrition Center
Gypsy's

DRUGS & VARIETY
G.C. Murphy
Treasury Drug

FLORISTS
Fallons (Mid-1994)

GIFTS
The Attic
Brookstone
Dean's Jewels & Gifts
The Nature Company
Sanrio Surprises
Spencer Gifts
Things Remembered
Tinder Box

HOME FURNISHINGS
Alex & Ivy
Bombay Co.
Butterfield's Etc.
Pier 1 Imports
This End Up

JEWELRY
Accessory Lady
Cabaret
Carlyle & Co.
Cooper's Watchworks
Dean's Jewels & Gifts
Gordon's Jewelers
Impostors
Jewel Box
Osterman Jewelers
Piercing Pagoda
The Pierced Ear
Reeds Jewelers
Silver & Gold
  Connection
To Be Continued
Treasure Isle

LUGGAGE
Luggage & Leather

PAINTINGS & PRINTS
Fast Frame
Village Gallery

PET SHOPS
Sears Pet Store

PHOTOGRAPHY/ PHOTO SERVICES
CPI Photo Finish
Glamour Shots
Kinderfoto
Wolf Camera

PIPES & TOBACCO
Tinder Box

RECORDS & TAPES
Record Bar

SERVICE/PROFESSIONAL
Hakky Shoe Repair
Howard Perry & Walston
MasterPrint
Ticketmaster
U.S. Post Office
Valley Cleaners

SHOES
Athletic Attic
Buster Brown
Connie Shoe Shops
Dolcis
Father & Son
Footlocker
Hanover Shoes
Hofheimer's
Johnston & Murphy
Journeys
Kinney Shoes
Naturalizer
Payless ShoeSource
Roscoe Griffin
Thom McAn

SPECIALTY SHOPS
AT&T Phone Center
The Body Shop
Crabtree & Evelyn, Ltd.
Eye Care Center
Kangaroo & Ewe Too
Leather n' Wood
A Shade Better
Shirtstop
Singer Sewing Center
S. Galeski Optical

SPORTING GOODS
American Eagle Outfitters
Athletic Attic
Champs
Eddie Bauer
Great Outdoor
  Provision Co.
Team Pride

TOYS & GAMES
Bally's Aladdin's Castle
Kay Bee Toys
Toy Adventures
Toys 'R' Us

North Hills Mall & Plaza

DEPARTMENT STORES
Dillard's
JC Penney

MEN'S APPAREL
Aloha II
Dreadz
Esquire Big & Tall
The Gap
Jos. A. Bank Clothiers
Nowell's
Structure
VIP Formalwear
Wrenn Pharr

WOMEN'S FASHIONS
Added Dimensions
Aloha II
Christian's
The Closet
Compagnie International
  Express
Dan Howard's Maternity
  Outlet
Dreadz
Ganto's
The Gap
Jos. A. Bank Clothiers
Lane Bryant
Lerner New York
The Limited
Montaldo's
Victoria's Secret

CHILDREN'S FASHIONS
Limited,Too
Mobley's Shoes

SHOES
Foot Locker
Georgiano's
Glenn's Shoes
Mobley's Shoes
Roscoe Griffin
The Shoe Dept.

SPORTS SPECIALTIES
DSG SPORTS
FOOT LOCKER

Jewelry & Accessories
Afterthoughts
Claire's Boutique
Reed's Jewelers
Zales

**Books, Cards
 & Stationery**
Audio Bookworld
D.J.'s News Center
Lynn's Hallmark
Waldenbooks

**Drug, Grocery
& Variety**
Dollar Tree
Kerr Drugs
Park's Place
Winn Dixie

**Electronics, Music &
Videos**
Blockbuster Video
Carolina Computer
Digital Works
Radio Shack
Record Bar
Tape World

**Home Furnishings,
Gifts & Luggage**
Brass Exchange
The Emporium
The Globetrotter
The Little Art Gallery
NC Museum of History
  Shop
The Print Shop
Storehouse

Specialties
Flower Express
Hungate's Hobbies
  & Crafts
Kay-Bee Toys
Kites Unlimited
Petland
A Shade Better II

Hair & Beauty
A Feminine Touch
Hair Nature's Way
Mitchell's Hairstyling
North Hills Hair Center

Services/Professional
Dr. D.V. Bedsole
Carolina Family Insurance
Carter Glass Insurance
Firestone
First Citizens Bank
Fitting Tailor Shop
Fox Eyecare
Jack Rabbit Photo
Lenscrafters
Monteith Travel (TAI)
NC Div. of Motor Vehicles
North Hills Cleaners
North Hills Exxon
North Hills Optical
North Hills Shoe &
  Luggage Repair
Nutri-System
US Post Office
Wachovia Bank
Wake Paint & Decorating

Restaurants
Cappers
Chick-fil-A
Hickory Hams
K & W Catetria
Tuxedo Cafe & Caterers

Food Specialties
A & W Hot Dogs & More
Andy's Pizza
Bruegger's Bagel Bakery
Chocolate Chip Cookie Co.
Gloria Jean's Coffee Bean
I Can't Believe It's Yogurt
Mutter's Express
Nikki's Chocolates
Pizza Hut Delivery
Scotty's
Taco Bell

GET EVERYTHING YOU WANT OUT OF YOUR VISIT
JUST BY VISITING NORTH HILLS MALL.

NORTH HILLS
MALL & PLAZA
Serious shopping for the fun of it.

KURTAIN KORNER

4524 Old Wake Forest Rd.   *876-7710*
North Market Square

If you're moving into your dream house, or just want to update the one you're in, this is a great place to start. They have window treatments, bedspreads, pillows and more accessories than you can imagine. Your biggest problem will be making a decision—but don't worry, they can help you with that too!

LOGAN'S TRADING POST

The Old Seaboard Train Station
707 Semart Dr.   *828-5337*

Logan's grew to local nursery fame at the old Farmers' Market off Capital Boulevard, but moved in 1990 to its location near Peace College in the Old Seaboard Train Station. It bustles during spring, summer and fall when gardners are at their busiest. You can get seed, seedlings, straw, pots, bulbs—whatever it is you want to plant, fertilize or harvest. Count on meeting someone you know, too.

MAGIC CORNER AND COSTUME SHOP

1213 Hillsborough St.   *834-0925*

Every Insider has to have a little magic and this is the best place to buy it in Raleigh. The owner is a magician himself, and he can make your money disappear if you ask for a demonstration. He added costumes and masks to help business and now it's half of his sales, especially around Halloween.

MAIN AND TAYLOR SHOE SALON

Cameron Village Shopping Ctr.   *821-1556*

There are several department stores such as Montaldo's and Burton's that have excellent shoe departments, but this shoe store that came to Raleigh in 1988 as the shoe concession in the old Boylan Pearce store has brands that mark it as one of the best, Ferragamo and Bruno Magli, to mention two. Owned by South Carolinians who own a successful store in that state's capital, this is a place for the woman who will starve her children to buy good shoes.

325

McKay's Cleaners

7486 Creedmoor Rd.   *846-9201*

Some claim McKay's is the best in town, and it replaces broken buttons, free. There are two other locations: at 8815 Six Forks Road and Olde Raleigh Shopping Center. The staff is conscientious with customers and not afraid to clean wedding, prom or chorus gowns. On Saturdays, McKay's closes at 1 p.m.

Medlin Davis Cleaners

Cameron Village Shopping Ctr.   *828-7254*

This local company has six locations, including three in Cary, which says something about its service over the years since it started in 1948. It boxes your folded shirts, which makes them easy to store. A new generation is running the business now and has made a conscientious effort to keep customers happy by keeping track of your wardrobe.

Michael's Arts and Crafts

Glenwood Ave./U.S. Hwy. 70 W.   *781-1184*
2431 Spring Forest Rd.   *876-3500*

Michael's offers an incredible selection of arts and crafts supplies, as well as hundreds of household items and gift ideas. The two stores sell everything from teddy bears to silk flowers, from closet organizers to sweatshirts you can decorate. Michael's stores also do framing at reasonable prices.

Neomonde Bakery & Deli

3817 Beryl Rd.   *828-1628*

You have to be an Insider to find this place because it's hidden in an industrial sector of town behind the Hillsborough Street Wonder Bread bakery. The Neomonde has grown into one of the largest bakeries of pita bread in the Southeast and the deli is a popular gathering place for lovers of Mideastern food such as kibbi, stuffed grape leaves, and tabouli. Its ladyfinger and napoleon desserts are light and delicious. To accommodate its growing lunchtime trade, it has built a deck outside where you can enjoy a light, healthful lunch and juice.

Noah's Food Store Co-Op

745 W. Johnson St.   *834-5056*

This is Raleigh's oldest ongoing food cooperative where you can buy in bulk and at bargain prices. There are about 1,500 to 2,000 members, and annual membership costs between $10 to $20, depending on your family status. This is a popular place for those who buy organic produce, herbs and spices in bulk, and fresh milk, too. Another plus is that you don't pay for fancy packaging, so bring your own shopping bag. It's open seven days a week, but call for hours. Non-members are welcome, but they pay a 10 percent surcharge. And don't look for meats or booze here.

Nur Grocery

Mission Valley Shopping Center
2250 Avent Ferry Rd.   *828-1523*

For another Middle Eastern and Mediterranean place, you'll want to try this veteran grocery and deli in the Mission Valley Shopping Center. It sells the foods of Egypt (homeland of its owner Mohamed Mousa), Lebanon, Turkey, Syria and Greece. It has feta cheeses and

Basmati rice, stuffed grape leaves and cabbage, and all kinds of vegetables, nuts, oils and pita breads. On weekends, customers come from as far away as Greensboro to shop.

OAK PARK ELECTRONICS
6013 Glenwood Ave. 781-2010

This place has made it despite its interior decorator. The owners, the Kaleel brothers, know TV and other electronics and have earned a reputation for fair dealing and dependable service over the years. They sell Zenith, Sony and GE and service all major brands of TVs, radios, stereos, video recorders and video cameras.

PACKAGING STORE
8111 Creedmoor Rd. 870-1848

This is a good place to remember at Christmas. It packages and ships things for you, and handles "anything from one to 1,000 pounds" including furniture. It sells boxes and packages, if you want to do that part yourself. At Christmas, it has extended hours, including Sundays. The Packaging Store has three more locations, one on Hollyridge Drive and two in Cary.

PET GROOMING

There are a number of pet grooming shops in Raleigh. Two that we like are **Canine Country Club** at 1654 N. Market Drive (876-9539) off Old Wake Forest Road in north Raleigh and **Ashlee's Grooming** (846-6905) in Greystone Village Shopping Center at Sawmill and Leadmine roads. CCC also has dog obedience lessons, and Ashlee's

does show dogs and treats your pooch like its very own pet.

PRINTER'S ALLEY
4112 Pleasant Valley Rd. 781-1777

If you want fabric for your home, this shop is one that Insiders frequent. It is located off Glenwood Avenue near the Walmart shopping center. It has a wide selection and the people who wait on you have good taste and a decorating service, always a help in such matters. The shop advertises over 650 bolts of designer upholstery and drapery fabrics and offers them at discount prices.

RAKE AND HOE
6125 Six Forks Rd. 847-5070

Once at a lonely intersection at Lynn Road and Six Forks, north Raleigh has grown up around this popular garden and nursery center. It's passed the test of time, having started in 1963, and the second generation of Gurganuses are minding the store now. It offers on-site landscape and lawn maintenance plus one of the biggest selections of patio furniture. On staff are certified plantsmen and four NCSU landscape design graduates. Its owner is especially proud of the center's $250,000 expansion that won a design award from the N.C. chapter of AIA.

RALEIGH CREATIVE COSTUMES
616 St. Mary's St. 834-0061

When you need that special costume for a party or you need a script for a play, try this place. It rents costumes and accessories and stocks 1,000 play scripts, from Shakespeare to Shepard. It also has theater supplies for sale, including make-up. It's also a wonderful store to find those special, inexpensive gifts that children always cherish, like an oversized policeman's badge, or a lion tamer's whip, or a fake nose. If you have any imagination at all, you will not be able to leave without a purchase.

RELIABLE LOAN CO.
307 S. Wilmington St.   *832-3461*

This is truly an Insiders' place. It's a pawn shop, operated by the same Raleigh family since 1949. It's one block east of the Fayetteville Street mall downtown, and according to our sources, it's a great place to buy excellent jewelry as well as your fledgling rocker's first Gibson or Stratocaster guitar. It's bigger than it looks from the street and the bargains include audio and television equipment as well as guns and cameras.

SAM BASS CAMERA AND VIDEO
Cameron Village   *832-4438*

Sam Bass has been an institution with shutter-happy Triangle residents for years. No matter what your camera needs, you'll find it here, from family photo cameras to big time commercial machines. Sam Bass also has branched into the video business and has movie-strength video equipment for sale. The sales staff at Sam Bass gets our vote for being one of the most helpful in town.

SCRAP EXCHANGE
Atlantic Ave. Flea Market   *870-7358*

The not-for-profit Scrap Exchange moved its North Raleigh store to the flea market in early '94. This unique place offers scraps to anyone who wants to buy it for such nifty uses as parties, workshops, school classes, birthdays, etc. The materials come from industry and include such items as fabric, nuts and bolts, paper and plastics. You can use the items to make jewelry, castles or crowns and you can get scrap by the truckload. "We bring a truckload of materials on-site and assist children and adults to create their own works of art!" says a store brochure. Besides being fun, it teaches people to reuse as well as recycle and to be creative. A birthday party will cost $60, and wouldn't you know, the kids love the junk.

SILVER THREADS
8847 Six Forks Rd.   *846-2870*
If you are looking for fabrics for yourself and not your couch, then make the trek to north Raleigh's Silver Threads. It's located in Six Forks Station Shopping Center at the intersection of Six Forks and Strickland roads. This shop has an excellent collection of dress fabrics, including materials for bridal and debutante gowns. Pick up some buttons, too. The shop is also a dealer for the Swiss-made Elna sewing machines.

SIMPLE PLEASURES
Glenwood Village Shopping Ctr. 782-9227
Once known as the Raleigh branch of Chapel Hill's successful A Southern Season, Simple Pleasures has become a benchmark on its own since it opened in the mid-70s as a gourmet food store. One of the gathering spots for the city's beautiful people, it has expanded three times and now offers lunch to a talkative noontime crowd. It has one of the best wine and cheese selections in the city as well as a chocolate counter. It has its own baked goods and all kinds of coffees, and it made its reputation with the chablis-and-brie bunch with its made-to-order, wonderfully arranged cheese and fruit plates.

SPORTS EXCHANGE
421 W. Peace St.   *834-0990*
The idea behind the store is attractive, and time will tell if it also is good business. In plain language, it's a used sporting goods store where you can sell those very slightly used exercise machines you bought last January to lose all that holiday weight...or where you can buy such items at a good price. Walk in and look around; you'll see weights and benches, rowing machines, football gear, golf clubs, boating supplies, bicycles, diving and scuba gear.

SRI SHOE WAREHOUSE
6700 Old Wake Forest Rd.   *872-2800*
If you want a good selection at a good price in shoes, then check out this discount store. It has boxes and boxes on shelves, so you wait on yourself, but the beautifully dressed people say that you can find designer names at very good prices.

THE UPPER CRUST
8831 Six Forks Rd.
Six Forks Station   *847-8088*
One foot in the door and you know here's everything you've wanted in a gourmet specialty shop and more. Aromatic coffees, exquisite chocolates, personalized gift baskets, premium wines, imaginative cookbooks and colorful kitchen accessories tempt the shopper. There is a casual dining cafe for tasting the wares and catering is also available (see "Raleigh" Section of **RESTAURANTS**).

WINE 'N THINGS

Stonehenge Market   *847-4986*

For north Raleigh and the Creedmoor Road neighborhoods, this is a favorite wine store. It offers a large selection of imported and domestic wines as well as those funny foreign beers. The "things" in the store's name include mugs, wine glasses and books on wine. For the serious wine drinker, it offers discounts when buying by the case. Don't be bashful about asking for advice.

Home Furnishings and Antiques

North Carolina is the furniture capital of the United States, so it's not surprising that there are good antique dealers in town. There are also several nearby, most notably Boone's in Wilson, which has one of the largest inventories around. The ones here are popular with Raleigh and Triangle residents.

Arthur Danielson, 1101 Wake Forest Road, (828-7739), carries good quality English and American furniture and 17th- and 18th-century ceramics. He also has paintings and porcelain.

Edith Medlin's, 122 Glenwood Avenue (833-1415), has a loyal local following, has been in business for years and is a good place to look for good quality dining room tables and chairs as well as period chests.

Another popular treasure trove is the **Carolina Antique Mall** (833-8227) at Cameron Village Shopping Center. It is located in a downstairs space and is a collection of the choice selections of a number of dealers organized and operated by Carolina Antique Mall, many of them specializing in items such as dolls, toys, medical instruments, as well as porcelain and other fine decorative objects. And don't forget the flea market at the State Fairgrounds.

BELL'S CARPET CREATIONS

2832 Industrial Dr.   *833-5707*

Located off busy Wake Forest Road, Bell's has earned a strong local following for its personal service and fine-quality rugs and carpets. It was started by Victor Bell, who also started Bell's Linens in Cameron Village and who has since sold both businesses. You can find some of the best American-made designer carpets along with traditional, imported Oriental rugs. Bell's personal service and wide selection has continued to make it the Insiders' choice in carpets. Watch for its annual sale.

BRENTWOOD CARPETS

(across from Cheviot Hills Golf Club)
U.S. Hwy. I North   *872-2775*

Since 1974, Brentwood Carpets has provided quality carpeting and flooring for the Triangle area. Brentwood sells and installs carpeting by Armstrong, Mohawk, and Philadelphia, among other leading brands. The company also sells and installs vinyl flooring for residential and commercial use, featuring products by Congoleum, Armstrong, Tarkett, Mannington and Kentile. Brentwood can install a wooden plank or parquet floor for you as well; it represents lines by Bruce and Hartco.

Building Supplies

If you're planning any home repairs or renovations, you'll need to find Yonkers Road on your city map—it runs parallel to the northern loop of the Beltline. There are many lumber and building supply houses around the Triangle, but Yonkers Road has several in a convenient row, including **Lowe's** and the giant **Carolina Builders** which started here. There's also a **House of Lights** located along this strip, and **Ferguson Enterprises** (bathroom fixtures) at 2700-A Yonkers Road (828-7300). If you have a weekend project, get started early because Carolina Builders closes early on Saturday and the other houses attract a crowd.

Capitol City Lumber Company at 4216 Beryl Road (832-6492) is another great resource. It carries a complete stock of millwork and building materials and features Outdoor Wood by Cox.

CHRISTINA MARBLE
1107 New Hope Rd.   231-6060
This is a one-of-a-kind place not only in Raleigh but the whole Southeast. Located east of the city off U.S. Hwy. 64, Christina Marble is named after the daughter of the owner of the David Allen Co., a longtime Raleigh firm known for its work in supplying and installing marble, granite and terrazzo prod-

ucts. The marble company is only a few years old, however, and it uses the latest Italian machinery to cut, polish and finish the large slabs of marble fresh from Italian, Spanish, Portuguese and Mexican quarries. While the bulk of its business is with builders, individuals who want to fashion their own marble tables or countertops can find the real thing here.

FERGUSON ENTERPRISES
2700-A Yonkers Rd.   828-7300
More familiarly known as the "potty place," this store carries Kohler, the Cadillac line of such items. As the Triangle residential market has grown, Ferguson's has grown with it, and its showrooms give you a glimpse of how the once unmentionable water-closet has evolved into a soothing, colorful centerpiece of decadent living. It has a Cary store, too, at 8170 Chapel Hill Road (467-0205) and one in Durham at 319 West Pettigrew Street (682-6211).

Furniture

CAROLINA SOFA FACTORY
7201 Glenwood Ave.   781-8020
This locally owned company opened in 1984 and specializes in living room and den furniture, so don't let the name fool you. It has chairs, love seats, ottomans, and of course, lots and lots of sofas. It carries a number of brands including Stylecraft and the popular KFI sofas. You can choose your own material to custom match your interior design.

CONTEMPORARY BY NATURE

4404 Craftsman Dr. 872-8275

As the name says, this is a contemporary furniture store but featuring mostly solid wood, American pieces, much of it from Vermont. The store opened in 1987 and has gained a following from many of the Triangle's newcomers who are used to something other than Henredon or Thomasville. As many come from Durham and Chapel Hill as from Raleigh and Cary. The store also displays the works of North Carolina artists' on consignment, and its contemporary lighting selection is one of the largest in the area.

JONES BROTHERS FURNITURE

6901 Glenwood Ave. 787-1513

North Carolina is the furniture capital of the country, so there are plenty of good furniture stores in and around the Triangle. Jones Brothers is one of them, and it carries a large selection at competitive prices in some of the country's best-known brands, such as Drexel-Heritage, Henkel-Harris, Hancock-Moore and Hickory Chair. Jones Brothers features Thomasville and Drexel-Heritage galleries as well. The store has a large selection of mirrors, lamps, pictures and other accessories. There is another Jones Brothers located in Smithfield.

LIVIN' ROOMS

4200 Capital Blvd. 878-8454

This is an unusual upholstered furniture operation where you can pick out your own fabric and frame, and Livin' Rooms will build it for you at its Hickory, North Carolina, factory in about a month. Manager Tom Collins will help you pick out a sofa, chair or hide-a-bed frame to go with over 1,000 selections of fabric he can show you. The pieces are built to last; the frames come with a 25-year warranty.

STEWART WOODARD GALLERIES

412 W. Jones St. 821-7122

If you are one of those people who invests in furniture, then you can bank on this store. It carries collectors' items and provides interior design for businesses as well as homes. Installed a few years ago in a renovated downtown building, and backed by the wife of restaurateur Thad Eure, this is where you go if you want to buy swank. The styles cover a wide range, from traditional to contemporary, and the displays are worth a visit. This is one place that's not exaggerating when it calls its showrooms "galleries."

WAYSIDE FURNITURE HOUSE

5425 Hillsborough St. 851-0680
5640 Capital Blvd. 954-0025

Another good, local furniture store that is an Insiders' favorite is Wayside Furniture on Hillsborough Street. There is a second store at 5640 Capital Boulevard, too. Its displays are attractive, reflecting, perhaps, its interior decorating service. It's been in business since 1939 and offers some of the best-known names in furniture such as Heritage, Henredon, Kittinger, Hickory, Council Craftsmen, and Davis Cabinet. It has 27 model rooms and a carpet department and accessories.

WHITLEY GALLERIES
Off U.S. Hwy. 64 East, Zebulon 269-7447

Although this well-respected furniture store is not located in Raleigh proper—it's about 16 miles east of Raleigh in Zebulon—it deserves prominent mention. The showroom for Whitley covers almost a city block and represents over 100 lines of furniture. You can find all styles here and the firm offers an interior design service to help make your choices easier. Delivery is available, too. Whitley Galleries says it's the largest furniture store in North Carolina. So sit on that!

Cary

Cary has plenty of neighborhood shopping centers, two enclosed malls, and a large regional "power" shopping center. According to the Chamber of Commerce, Cary has 24 shopping centers. The biggest attractions are the greatly expanded Cary Towne Center, an enclosed mall that rivals Raleigh's Crabtree Valley Mall in space, and Crossroads Plaza, a collection of large, mostly discount, national operations. Crossroads is typical in that most new stores in Cary are discount chain stores. The following is a list of some of Cary's favorite shopping places that an Insider should know.

Shopping Centers

ASHWORTH VILLAGE CENTER
115 W. Chatham St.
Downtown Cary

This is near the center of old Cary and it is a collection of spe-cialty shops, some of which are described individually elsewhere. You can expect some turnover every year because most of these places are run by real entrepreneurs, starting their very own business for the first time. Here's a list of some of the places: **Rebecca's Gourmet Bakery** serves up specialties to tempt the taste buds; **Chocolate Smiles**; **Stained Glass of Cary; Elegant Stitches** specializes in custom-made garments from a wide selection of fabrics and patterns. A new addition is **Ordinary and Extraordinary**, specializing in antiques.

KROGER PLAZA
Kilmayne Dr.

This is a convenient neighborhood shopping center right off Kildaire Farm Road that opened in 1984 and features, right! a **Kroger** supermarket. But there is more—a book store, Wellington's, which carries current best sellers, plus classics, and hosts book signings and readings; it also has plenty of that rare commodity, personal service. A **Videorama** outlet and two restaurants, **Brother's Pizza** and a Chinese restaurant, can help fill that spare evening. The Kroger grocery is open 24-hours and features a deli and bakery. For a small plaza, this one has a nice mix of interesting shops.

MACGREGOR VILLAGE SHOPPING CENTER
Near U.S. Hwys. 64 and I

This neighborhood shopping center has a great location, close to MacGregor Downs, MacGregor Park and Lochmere. It is best known for some of the restaurants that have located here_ the new **Vinnie's**, **Fox and Hound**, **Hickory Honey Glazed Hams and Cafe**, as well as **Horwitz' Deli**—and it also has a **Kerr Drugs**, **Medlin Davis Cleaners, Land's Florist** and **Wee Creations**, a doll house and miniatures store. **One Step Computer Systems** has become one of the biggest tenants. Since 1991, **Myron Dwoskin's**, an Atlanta-based wallpaper and window decorations franchise operated by Jean and Jim Johnston (who also own Wee Creations and Fox and Hound) has also taken space.

SALTBOX VILLAGE
Kildaire Farm Rd.

This strip shopping center is the home of some of Cary's most unique shops. All Cary Insiders soon find out about **The Fresh Market**, **Possibilities**, a women's clothing boutique, **Advanced Audio, Science Safari** and **Saltbox Valet, a dry cleaners**. **Outback Steakhouse** is also here.

SOUTH HILLS MALL AND PLAZA
U.S. Hwy. I and Buck Jones Rd.

This is Cary's other enclosed mall, and it features a number of outlet stores and specialty shops. It has to be the crafts and country fashion center of the Triangle, with anchor stores like **Jo-Belle's**, a large crafts, gifts and art supplies store, and **Burlington Coat Factory**. It also has **Carolina Wood and Brass, Country Sunshine**, a home furnishing shop, **Life Experiences, Lamps, Etc.** and **Lovely Ladies' Lingerie**. One of the Triangle's better known

dance studios, **Betty Kovach Dance Studio**, is here. Cary boat and ski equipment enthusiasts go to **Overton's,** which is next door. You can also pick up your N.C. automobile plates here.

WAVERLY PLACE
Kildaire Farm and Tryon rds.

This shopping center is worth visiting just to see the planning and architecture. Considered by some planners to be the best looking shopping center in Wake County, Waverly Place opened in 1988, conveniently located near Lochmere and Regency Park. It has multi-levels with fountains and outdoor sculpture and parking lots that compliment rather than dominate its appearance. It sells itself as a convenience, entertainment and fashion center and contains a grocery store; **The Write Stuff,** a stationery store that offers custom calligraphy; and several restaurants such as **China Pearl, Chi-Chi's, 2nd City Grill, Le Coco, Seldom Blues**; and a movie complex.

Special Places

DAVID ANTHONY'S
III W. Chatham St.   467-7600

This is where many Cary Insiders go for their wedding gifts and other home decorations. If you want your gift to look picture-perfect, let David Anthony's staff wrap it for you at no charge. This shop also carries things for the garden and sells "fragrances" for the home and body, which most of us need after a hard day's wedding.

Saltbox Village is home to some of Cary's most unique shops.

ASHWORTH DRUGS
AND HOME HEALTH CENTER
105 W. Chatham St.   *467-1877*

This is the corner drug store that has become, in its 32 years, a place where Cary folks gather. The corner is **the** downtown intersection at Chatham and Academy streets, and the owner, Ralph Ashworth, is a former president of the Cary Chamber of Commerce and Citizen of the Year. It has a soda fountain that serves, according to some, the best hot dogs and milk shakes in town, but Ashworth's is best known for its old-fashioned orangeades, lemonades and cherry cokes. It also provides free delivery.

BLOOMIN' ORCHIDS
402 Church St.
Morrisville   *469-0178*

The owner of Bloomin' Orchids, Nat Carson, is committed to dispelling the notion that orchids are expensive, delicate and hard to grow. Established in 1982 in Cary, in 1990 the facility was expanded and relocated to the present site in Morrisville, just off N.C. Hwy. 54. As the name suggests, this company offers orchid plants for sale or lease, a potting service, and sup-

plies. But that's just the beginning. The best part is that when your orchid quits blooming you can take it back and these friendly folks will care for it until it blooms again!

CHOCOLATE SMILES
SWEET SHOP & FACTORY
115 W. Chatham St.   *469-5282*

If you're a chocolate addict, you can get a fix here. Locally owned, the shop started around 1985 and is part of a collection of specialty stores in the Ashworth Village Center. Smiles makes its own chocolates—from truffles, nuts and chews to fudge. Area companies, wanting a special gift for customers or employees, will buy chocolates made to mold. When it's cooler, Smiles ships chocolate out, especially at Christmas and Valentine's Day. It also has other specialty candies and sells it by the piece or the pound.

ETCETERA CRAFTS
226 E. Chatham St.   *467-7636*

This collection of crafts started in Raleigh and moved to Cary in 1980. It has become one of the Triangle's best known sources for North Carolina crafts, showing the work of 15 potters and 10 quilters, most of them local. Owner Jean Petersen comes from a long line of quilters, so she knows her business. This shop handles crafts on consignment and some jewelry along with mountain toys, stuffed animals and, at Christmas time, lots of handmade ornaments. It also has craft supplies, mainly for quilting.

NOWELL'S FURNITURE
900 E. Chatham St.   *467-9224*

This store helped introduce the Cary and Raleigh area to contemporary and Scandinavian furniture and has been providing "quality home furnishings since 1905," according to its ads. It maintains probably the best inventory of Scandinavian teak imports of any store in the Triangle. If you're looking for something other than colonial Williamsburg, primitive American or French provincial, then you need to visit Nowell's.

ONE STEP COMPUTER SYSTEMS
MacGregor Village   *467-9707*

This is another unusual store and not the kind that is usually found in a neighborhood shopping center. This custom computer shop started in the 1980s and sells not only name brands such as Digital, but will put together a system made just for your business. The idea is to provide customers with a "turnkey solution including hardware, software, training and support." And the store takes care of what it sells you. If you have a small business and are thinking of putting some of the work onto a computer, check with these guys.

SALTBOX VALET
Saltbox Village   *460-6446*

The owner of this new Cary dry cleaning shop not only tries to know all of her customers by name, but replaces missing buttons and does minor mending without being asked and at no additional charge to her customers. This quality of service is rare indeed!

SCIENCE SAFARI
Saltbox Village   *460-6051*

This new entry is located along Kildaire Farm Road in Saltbox Village Shopping Center, and is a great place for children and educators who want to buy something that might even teach them some science! It's a science and nature shop for parents who want their kids to have more than Hulk Hogan or video games with which to stay busy. You can find bug catchers, chemistry sets, microscopes, bird feeders and all sorts of models, including the mandatory dinasaur family. One of the owners has taught classes at area museums and liked it enough to turn her interest into a business. The shop offers classes in science and there's an on-site, rock and mineral cave where customers can explore.

SORRELL'S PAINT AND WALLPAPER
220 W. Chatham St.   *467-1809*
Cary Insiders know to shop at Sorrell's for all their decorating needs. Experienced decorators are on hand to advise you about wallpaper, floor coverings, paints, and window coverings. Since it carries a large selection of each, you're sure to leave Sorrell's satisfied during your next home improvement project.

WELLINGTON'S BOOKS
120 Kilmayne Dr.
Kroger Plaza   *467-0815*
Sarah Goddin owns this fine bookstore. This is the place to come for the best selection of children's and travel books in the area, as well as for the classics and current best sellers. You'll often meet local writers here at author-signing parties. The friendly and knowledgeable staff will be happy to order any book

for you that isn't in stock, and will ship books anywhere.

Durham

There are more than two dozen shopping centers and malls in and around Durham, with new ones cropping up all the time. They offer hundreds of retail outlets, from major department stores and discount houses to small shops and specialized boutiques. Here's our guide to the major malls as well as some other special places to browse and shop.

NINTH STREET
Once upon a time, before the birth of suburbia and malls, shoppers used to patronize small independently owned stores in the retail districts that thrived near their homes. If you have fond recollections of those days, you'll enjoy shopping along Ninth Street.

Ninth Street is neither a shopping center nor a mall. It is a charming commercial block in west Durham that grew up around the Erwin Cotton Mill, a neighborhood that in the past decade has made a comeback. In fact, Ninth Street may be seen as a microcosm of the changes that are taking place all over Durham today. The cotton mill has been converted into chic office spaces and apartments (see **DURHAM NEIGHBORHOODS**) with a brand new mini-shopping center next door. A mom-and-pop drugstore that opened here in the 1920s and an old-time hardware and seed store rub elbows with a Kerr Drugs, a New Age supermarket and an assortment of boutiques and trendy eateries, including an ice cream lover's heaven, a bakery and a bagel bar.

So far, the new has meshed with the old on Ninth Street, as in the rest of the city. But if you want to take a look for yourself, mosey on down to the two blocks of Ninth Street running between Hillsborough Road and West Main Street, within walking distance of Duke University's East Campus. Here's a sample of what you'll find.

We've already mentioned the **Ninth Street Bakery and Cafe** (see "Durham" Section of **RESTAURANTS** and **NIGHT LIFE**) as a great place to get a cup of cappuccino and an assortment of whole-grain goodies. Shops along Ninth Street include **Earth & Spirit,** with gifts from the earth, **Vaguely Reminiscent**, a boutique featuring stylish natural-fiber garments and fun accessories and **Torso**, with clothing for men. An Insiders' favorite is **The Regulator Bookshop**, offering a great selection of hardback and paperback books and the best assortment in town of left-liberal newspapers and magazines and bizarre postcards; and more, including restaurants and movie rentals. Keep on walking and you'll find an exotic ice cream, pastry and chocolate shop called **Francesca's**, where everything is made on the premises. In the old Wachovia Bank Building, you'll now find **Bruegger's Bagel**

Bakery (see "Durham" Section of **RESTAURANTS**). Nearby is **Poindexter Records** and the **Sandy Creek Children's Bookstore**, just off Ninth on Perry Street.

If you've got kids in tow, be sure to check out **The Play House**, a toy store, and of course there is **McDonald's Drug Store**, what one local writer called "the beating heart of Ninth Street." For the last 60 years or so, this family-owned enterprise has been a gathering place for old-timers and newcomers alike. Here you can ask for an old-fashioned soda (or even an egg cream, if you please) while you wait for your prescription to be filled.

Over on the west side of Ninth Street, change has been more dramatic. The developers who renovated the cotton mill also built a new brick mini-shopping center next door. Erwin Square is anchored by **Wellspring Grocery**, an amazing supermarket of natural and gourmet foods, including chemically free meats and whole-grain baked goods. Adjacent to Wellspring is **Eno Traders**, for quality outdoor clothing and gear and a **Kerr Drug** store.

Shopping Centers

ERWIN SQUARE, II

Because of its size and location—adjacent to historic Ninth Street—the expansion of the Erwin Square complex has been quite controversial. The plans call for a total of 300,000 square feet of office, commercial and housing space on 37 acres once occupied by the Burlington Industries textile plant.

The brainchild of Durham developers Clay Hamner and Terry Sanford, Jr., the site takes advantage of a prime location between West Main Street, Ninth Street, Hillsborough Road and the Durham Freeway. The phase-one construction of a 10-story, $34-million office building—First Union Plaza—is complete, offering about 255,000 square feet of space. Several shops and restaurants are located at Erwin Square, including **Jewelsmith**, **K. Peterson** for leathergoods and other luxuries, **Tiong Tan**, Durham's acclaimed couturier, and **Parizade** restaurant.

BRIGHTLEAF SQUARE

In 1980 a couple of local businessmen saw potential beauty and bucks in the twin giant American Tobacco Company warehouses at the corner of Gregson and West Main streets. They worked painstakingly to preserve and display the all-heart-pine beams, 20-inch-thick brick walls and ornate chimneys. Several years later, what had become a symbol of economic decline was resurrected as an upscale shopping center for a variety of specialty stores that would draw renewed interest in Durham's downtown.

Brightleaf is proof that you can market retail stores without neon lights or multi-colored billboards. Thanks to the developers' sensitivity to the architectural significance of these buildings, they are now listed with the National Register of Historic Places.

A brick courtyard separating the two former warehouses has become a place for outdoor art and drama productions. This is where a conglomeration of community artisans staged the street opera *Carmen*, an event of which even *The New York Times* had to take note.

Inside are a series of specialty shops anchored by **Fowler's Gourmet**—offering one of the best assortments in town of high-quality meats, cheeses, cold cuts and an incredible assortment of wines.

At Brightleaf Square, you'll find **Casey & Co.** for fine stationery and flowers, a **CD Superstore** (the largest in the area) and **Torso** men's clothing store. **Horizon and Tyndall Galleries** offer fine art, and there are several antique stores including **Lafayette Antiques, James Kennedy Antiques** and **Wentworths & Leggett Old Rare Books.** Food is plentiful as well with **El Rodeo, Taverna Nicos** and **Satisfactions** (see "Durham" Section of **RESTAURANTS**). You will find women's clothing at **Collections**, and for custom jewelry and more, try **Goldworks.**

Across the street is **Morgan Imports**—where you can find a reasonably priced gift for anyone for any occasion (and a great place to buy Christmas ornaments all year long), and **Rosie's Redux**, for fine consignments.

WOODCROFT SHOPPING CENTER
Hope Valley Rd. and N.C. Hwy. 54
(near I-40)

There are many shopping centers in Durham about the size of Woodcroft: 20 stores anchored by a chain supermarket, a bank and a fast-food eatery. But we're making a fuss over this one because it was done with style and sensitivity to its location. There are no screaming lights, towering billboards, or overwhelming structures at Woodcroft. The entire mall is done in earth-toned brick. Each store has its name presented in about the same-sized, off-white electrically illuminated letters. The awnings are uniform evergreen. Even the McDonald's has class and, by the way, no golden arches.

The reason may be that Woodcroft has a captive shopping audience located conveniently next door in the planned residential development by the same name (see **DURHAM NEIGHBORHOODS**). These businesses don't have to assault passersby with neon messages because their neighbors already know they are there and patronize them regularly. We call it good design and good planning that didn't seem to put a significant dent in the developers' profit margin.

HOMESTEAD MARKET
N.C. Hwy 54 and Fayetteville Rd.

Just down the road from Woodcroft is the Homestead Market shopping center, anchored by a **Harris Teeter** supermarket, **Kerr Drugs** and **Rose's**. Other stores and shops include **The Book Zoo**, with a great children's book selection, a jewelers, an optical shop and more. You can also take your driver's license exam or get your driver's license renewed here.

LOEHMANN'S PLAZA
1821 Hillandale Rd.

The Plaza offers several dozen stores including the anchor store **Loehmann's**, where you can

get great discounts on women's designer clothes, and a number of small shops. Loehmann's Plaza also features **Bak's Bistro** (see "Durham" Section of **RESTAURANTS**), a casual cafe.

OAK CREEK VILLAGE
U.S. Hwy. 15-501   493-3922
4422 Chapel Hill Blvd.

Oak Creek features **T.J. Maxx**, the designer-label discount clothing store, **Phil's Shoes, DSG Sporting Goods** and **Dress Barn**. Other stores include a pet store, waterbed store, cellular phone outlet and more. Restaurants at Oak Creek include **Tripp's**, popular with singles, **Chili's Grill & Bar** and **Subway** sandwiches.

WILLOWDAILE SHOPPING CENTER
Guess Rd. and Horton Rd.

This north Durham shopping center features the **Willowdaile Cinema 8**, a mega-movie house capable of showing eight films at one time, as well as a grocery store and other shops.

Antiques

WILLOW PARK MALL
U.S. Hwy. 15-501 South
(Durham-Chapel Hill Blvd.)

Here you'll find dozens of antique dealers and **Fargo-Hanna Rugs** under one roof. It's an antique lover's paradise. Need we say more?

THE PERSIAN CARPET
5634 Chapel Hill Blvd.   968-0366

Located midway between Chapel Hill and Durham, at the

intersection of I-40 and U.S. Hwy. 15-501, this shop offers a broad selection of fine antique and new Persian, Chinese, Indian, Rumanian and Turkish carpets. The Persian Carpet also buys, repairs and appraises rugs.

Automobiles

The stretch of U.S. Highway 15-501 between Durham and Chapel Hill has become a retail corridor for automobile dealers. You will find well-known dealerships such as UzzleCadillac-Oldsmobile, Durham Lincoln Mercury, Performance Acura and RPM Nissan to name a few.

Books

THE BOOK EXCHANGE
107 W. Chapel Hill St.   *682-4662*
While you're downtown, check out The Book Exchange, which bills itself as "the South's largest and most complete bookstore" (we don't doubt it). If you're a book junkie you may not get out of here without a carton full, for there are two stories stocked to the rafters with new and used hardback and paperback titles you thought you'd never be able to find: out-of-print scholarly works, used textbooks and a complete line of Bibles. And if you don't find it, this store will order it for you.

True to its name, The Book Exchange will buy, sell and exchange titles with you. At the beginning of each semester students from Duke and N.C. Central are lined up out the door waiting to trade in their old textbooks or buy new ones for the coming months. The store is open from 8:45 a.m. to 6 p.m. Monday through Saturday.

Garden Shops

STONE BROTHERS AND BYRD
700 Washington St.
(near the Durham Bull's Park)   682-1311

If you want to be a Triangle Insider, you're going to have to learn to talk gardening. And if you're going to live in this sunny climate, you're probably going to find yourself turning over a few spades of dirt and liking it. Stone Brothers and Byrd's is one of the oldest and best-stocked feed and seed centers in town and worth a visit just to browse through the seed packets and tools.

Chapel Hill

From boutiques to malls, Chapel Hill offers just the range of shopping choices you would expect to find in a growing, upscale university community. We don't have enough pages to tell you about them all, but here's a quick guide to Franklin Street, the major shopping centers and malls, and a few other unique places to browse and shop.

DOWNTOWN/FRANKLIN STREET

This is Chapel Hill's main thoroughfare, the first place UNC students and visitors hit when they wander off campus. As a result, Franklin Street has its fair share of places for cheap eats, Carolina paraphernalia and basic collegiate clothing. Though many Franklin Street businesses are designed with the college community in mind, they also have plenty to offer the over-25 crowd as well.

September of 1992 brought a dramatic change to Franklin Street when fire destroyed the Intimate Bookshop, long a favorite with returning alumnae. The store has been rebuilt on the existing site with a new look on the outside, but proprietor Wallace Kuralt (brother of CBS newsman Charles) promises that the new wooden floors creak just like the originals.

The downtown area has three cinema houses with six screens. The **Varsity I and II** offer first runs and foreign films and **The Ram Triple** on Rosemary Street also shows first runs. **Chelsea Theatre** owner Bruce Stone recently reopened a scaled-down version of the old Carolina Theatre in the back of the original theatre building (now housing The Gap in front). Ice cream and frozen yogurt aficionados have lots of choices: **Swensen's, Ben and Jerry's, The Yogurt Pump** and **Yogurt Oasis** are among the Franklin Street vendors of frozen confections. If you crave a shake or an ice cream soda, try the homemade ones at the lunch counter at **Sutton's** drug store.

There are a number of clothing stores on Franklin, including the aforementioned **The Gap, The Lodge,** with updated prep-style clothing, **Anjana's,** and **Barr-ee Station,** which specializes in catalog clothing like J. Crew and Tweeds at discounted prices. For a bit older crowd, there's **Julian's** and **The Hub** with top-quality menswear, and **The Little Shop,** where lots of university women shop for career and formal clothing.

The west end of Franklin Street is becoming more of a specialty shopping district each year, as new stores and restaurants open for business, and existing ones expand and remodel. In a funky vein, **Time After Time** on West Franklin sells vintage clothing. Close by is **Modern Times**, the only place that sells local designer Lisa Heyward's creations. Newcomers to the block are **Uniquities**, with accessories and Betsy Johnson and Nicole Miller attire, and the **Mast General Store**, which offers two floors packed with outdoor equipment and attire, men's and women's casual clothing and gifts and toys for adults and children. Another shop you'll want to visit is **Hill Country Woodworks**. Here you will find handmade contemporary furniture in solid cherry and walnut, individually built and

Serving the Triangle community since 1946

❊

specializing in weddings, receptions and corporate functions.

1-800-368-5058
929-1119 • fax (919) 967-6086
124 E. Franklin St. • Chapel Hill

signed by the craftsmen. The shop also carries accessories and attendant furniture from other craftsmen, artists, importers and small workshops.

West Franklin is also home to a number of second-hand bookstores (see "Books/Records and Video" section). They're all great places for an hour's browse.

CARRBORO'S MAIN STREET

If you continue west on Franklin Street, you will eventually run into Carrboro's Main Street. Just as you enter Carrboro, you'll see **Nice Price Books** (see "Books/Records and Video" section) in the white and hot pink little house. On your right, just before the railroad tracks, you'll find **Surplus Sid's**, a good source for military gear, rain slickers and odds and ends. Just beyond the railroad tracks is Carr Mill Mall (more on that later).

Keep heading west and at the corner of Main Street and Greensboro you'll find **Cliff's Meat Market**, a good old independently owned butcher shop offering an assortment of quality meats and fresh seafood. Cliff does a booming business during the holiday seasons.

Continuing west, don't miss one of our favorite shops, **The PTA Thrift Shop**, where you'll find unbelievable bargains among the castoffs of Chapel Hill's well-dressed contributors; proceeds go to the Chapel Hill-Carrboro schools via the PTA.

Just up Main Street from The PTA, look for the newly reopened **Aunt Louise's Bookshop for Chil-**

dren and the **NC Crafts Gallery,** showing ceramic pieces, jewelry, woodwork and more, all made in the Tar Heel state.

Shopping Centers

CARR MILL MALL
Carrboro

Some year's ago, Carrboro's long dormant cotton mill was converted into an upscale shopping village. Rather than see Julian Carr's old mill demolished, local citizens and businesses banded together to see it preserved and transformed. Today it is one of the area's more unique shopping centers, thanks to the careful restoration of the original brick exterior, heart-pine interior and other fine architectural details of the original structure. The Carr Mill site now houses more than two dozen businesses including **Aurora Restaurant** (see "Chapel Hill" Section of **RESTAURANTS**), the fashionable **Talbot's** clothing store, and other fine specialty shops like **Benchmark Furnishings, Mandarin Gazebo** (a gift shop), **O'Neill's** (for menswear), **The Velveteen Rabbit** children's store and **A New Attitude,** a women's clothing store. The mall is anchored by **Harris Teeter Supermarket** and **Revco** on one side and **Weaver Street Market** (see below) on the other.

THE COURTYARD
West Franklin Street

You won't believe that this chic shopping complex tucked into Chapel Hill's West Franklin Street was once a milk processing plant. Today The Courtyard features

Pyewacket, a natural foods eatery (see "Chapel Hill" Section of **RESTAURANTS**); **The Stock Exchange,** an upscale consignment clothing store for women, **Pipes by George,** and **Panacherie,** another clothing store, a hair salon and a number of offices.

UNIVERSITY SQUARE
West Franklin Street

This small shopping center is located on West Franklin Street, just a few steps away from the UNC campus. It offers a diverse mix of shops and restaurants, geared to a wide range of tastes and budgets. You can find quick fried chicken and biscuits at **Time Out,** or designer clothes at **Fine Feathers,** with a lot in between. There's **The Painted Bird** that sells imported clothing for women and children and Central and South American crafts, **Shoes at the Square** with fine footwear for women and **Peacock Alley** that purveys fine gifts and accessories for the home. Browse at **T'boli,** and **The Whistlestop,** both great sources for inexpensive and always unusual gift ideas. Stop at **The Looking Glass Cafe** (see "Chapel Hill" Section of **RESTAURANTS**) for a bite of lunch, and when you tire of shopping, try **Swensen's** (mentioned under Franklin Street) for a big dish of ice cream.

EASTGATE SHOPPING CENTER
East Franklin Street and U.S. Hwy. 15-501

Undergoing a renaissance of sorts these last few years, Eastgate has many noteworthy features setting it apart from the run-of-the-mill shopping center. First, there's the expanded and remodeled **A Southern Season**, offering a dazzling assortment of fine wines, coffees, nuts, cheeses, crackers, chocolates and other gourmet goodies, as well as **The Weathervane** cafe. Next to A Southern Season, **Steinway Gallery** offers everything from art prints to oil paintings. The framing is done onsite and most framing jobs can be completed in a day or two. Owners Bill and Pat Steinway are both former artists, as is the rest of the staff, so they're glad to offer artistic advice. Other Eastgate attractions are **The Intimate Bookshop**, **The Potted Plant**, for a wide array of house plants, and **Workbench**, a locally owned store from the largest contemporary furniture chain in the country.

There's also **The Bentwood**, for contemporary furniture and accessories for the home, Joe Rowand's **Somerhill Art Gallery**, and **Black Mountain**, for handwrought gold and silver jewelry, **The Paw-Paw Patch** and **Womancraft** are great for gifts, and **Harrison Antiques** and **Minta Bell Interior Design** can help you furnish and decorate your home. **Blockbuster Video**, **Eckerd**, an enlarged and remodeled **Food Lion**, **Lynn's Hallmark** and **The Piece Goods** fabric shop are some other tenants. Good places to eat at Eastgate include **The Weathervane**, **Sal's** (for family dining) and **China Chef**.

VILLAGE PLAZA
Elliott Rd.

The Village Plaza, located on Elliott Road, is anchored by **Well-spring** grocery, which expanded here from its first location in Durham (see "Durham" section of Shopping). **Penguin's Cafe** is located inside the store. There is a mini-mall here, with **Knit-a-Bit**, **The Cotton Boll** for fine fabrics, **The Design Workshop**, **Lacock's Shoes**, **Shaw Business Machines** and other shops and services. **Viking Travel** and the remodeled art deco **Plaza Triple Theater** is here, and several restaurants (**Red, Hot & Blue** and **Zorba's**). Across the street is the **Galleria** with specialty shops such as the **Purple Puddle I and II**, **The World Traveller** for books, maps and travel items, **Silk Quarters** for elegant women's apparel and **Mina's**, a salon for women and men. The **Chapel Hill Senior Center** is adjacent to the Galleria shops.

GLENWOOD SQUARE
N.C. Hwy. 54 East

This shopping center is distinct in its charming brick design with a clock tower. Glenwood Square houses a **Harris Teeter** supermarket, **Subway** sandwich shop, **Thai Palace** restaurant (see "Chapel Hill" Section of **RESTAURANTS**), **Kerr Drugs**, an optical shop, a dry cleaner, and dentist and veterinarian offices.

GLEN LENNOX
N.C. Hwy. 54 East

Glen Lennox was one of Chapel Hill's first shopping centers, and is home to **Pace**, a lovely gift shop popular with old Chapel Hillians, **Imperial China** restaurant, a bank, a travel agent and more.

RAM'S PLAZA

U.S. Hwy. 15-501

Across U.S. Hwy. 15-501 from Eastgate, Ram's Plaza features some interesting places to shop like **Livin' E-Z**, now one of the largest furniture retailers in the Triangle, specializing in contemporary designs for home and office. **Rolane** offers an array of men's and women's clothing (from socks and underwear to coats) at discount prices. **Dance Design** is the place to go for dancewear and for costumes for parties and Halloween. There's also a florist, a women's fitness center, a tanning salon and several other businesses. Just behind Ram's Plaza is the relocated **Yarnell-Hoffer**, a locally owned hardware store, that stocks almost anything you need to fix up your home.

COLE PARK

In Chatham County, just south of Chapel Hill, Cole Park serves the growing population in this developing area. The shopping center contains a **Lowe's** grocery, **Revco** drugstore, **Lisa's**—a card and

gift shop, hardware and video stores and more.

Six miles south of Chapel Hill in rural Chatham County lies a village complete with its own quaint post office, a pasture with grazing Belted Galloway cows, a market/cafe, an inn and a four-diamond restaurant (see "Chapel Hill" Sections of ACCOMMODATIONS and RESTAURANTS). Amidst this pastoral setting, you'll find a collection of truly unique shops, including a greatly expanded **Pringle's** for pottery and gifts, **A Stone's Throw** for jewelry and gemstones, **Dovecote** garden shop, **A.L. Carlsen** gift shop and **McIntyre's Books**. McIntyre's often hosts readings by local and regional authors; call for a schedule.

WILLOW CREEK

U.S. Hwy. 15-501 Bypass

Off the U.S. Hwy. 15-501 Bypass in Carrboro, Willow Creek features a **Food Lion**, **Kerr Drugs**, **Carolina Soccer/Lacrosse Supply** for sporting goods, and a number of other shops and restaurants. Just down the road is **Carrboro Plaza**, with a **Sav-a-Center**, **Rose's**, a video store, and several small shops and places to eat.

TIMBERLYNE
Weaver Dairy Rd.

This growing shopping center on Weaver Dairy Road features a **Food Lion, Kerr Drugs, Tsing Tao** restaurant, **For Baby's Sake** (second-hand children's clothes), **Johnson-Strowd-Ward Furniture, Bishop's Custom Kitchens** showroom, **Timberlyne Hardware, Visart Video, Chelsea Theatres** and other shops, deli's and casual restaurants. **Small World Travel** and the **Post Office** have branches here. A new seven-theatre movie complex opened in the July, 1993, bringing the number of movie screens in Chapel Hill to eighteen!

SOUTH SQUARE MALL
U.S. Hwy. 15-501

If you crave the overwhelming offerings of a mega mall, you'll have to leave Chapel Hill. About 10 minutes away on U.S. Hwy. 15-501 North is the closest large mall, South Square in Durham (See "Durham" Section of **SHOPPING**).

Antiques

WHITEHALL AT THE VILLA
1213 E. Franklin St.   *942-3179*

Located in the fascinating restored Villa Teo building, the former Whitehall Shop features 18th- and 19th-century English, French and American furniture. Whitehall also sells unique accessories and collectibles, fabrics, and wallcoverings. The owners can also provide full appraisal services and estate liquidation. Open Monday through Saturday, 10 a.m. to 5 p.m.

COUNTRYSIDE ANTIQUES
U.S. Hwy. 15-501 S.   *968-8375*

Located in a frame house a few miles south of Fearrington Village, this shop specializes in American antiques. Pottery, porcelain, and cut- and pressed-glass are also sold here.

THE PERSIAN CARPET
5634 Chapel Hill Blvd.   *968-0366*

Located midway between Chapel Hill and Durham on U.S. Hwy. 15-501, this shop offers a broad selection of fine antique and new Chinese, Persian, Indian, Romanian and Turkish carpets. The Persian Carpet also buys, repairs and appraises rugs. Open 10 a.m. to 5 p.m. Monday through Saturday and 1 to 5 p.m. on Sunday.

Books, Records and Video

INTIMATE BOOKSHOP

Eastgate Shopping Center   *929-0414*

Books, books and more books. The Intimate has been a staple for the readers in the Triangle area for decades, starting with the original store on Franklin Street, and expanding to the Greatstore located in Eastgate. After the Franklin Street store burned in a fall 1992 fire, the Greatstore carried on the legacy. The downtown store reopened in the fall of 1993.

USED BOOKS AND RECORDS

What's a university town without a supply of used books and records? Chapel Hill and Carrboro offer plenty. **The Book Shop** on West Franklin Street features a variety of second-hand hardbacks and paperbacks, including many limited editions and collectors' items. The **Avid Reader** is across from Pyewacket, and **Nice Price Books**, located on Carrboro's Main Street in the old Byrds Shopping Center (adjacent to the new ArtsCenter) also has a large selection of hardbacks and paperbacks, but prices tend to be lower, typically half the list price of the item. Nice Price also has an amazing collection of comic books and magazines and some records. For an excellent selection of used records in good condition, go straight to the **Skylight Exchange**, a book/record store and coffeehouse on West Rosemary Street next to Tijuana Fats and Dip's (see "Chapel Hill" Section of **RESTAURANTS**).

VISART VIDEO

300 E. Main Street
Carrboro   *932-1945*
The Village Plaza
Chapel Hill   *929-4584*
Timberlyne Shopping Center
Chapel Hill   *929-7634*

Three locations to find great selections of current as well as older, foreign or more obscure videos to rent. Start the popcorn popper!

Home Furnishings

THE BENTWOOD
Eastgate Shopping Center

Formerly located in University Mall, The Bentwood sells contemporary furniture and gifts. Very few—if any—pastels are in evidence, and if you are looking for the perfect octagonal black dishware to complement your red, white and black placemats, you probably will find it here. One Insider's favorite pastime is to lounge, albeit briefly, in one of The Bentwood's black leather chairs for sale.

LIVIN' E-Z
Rams Plaza   967-7060

Livin' E-Z sells furniture for today's home, like futons (available in hundreds of fabrics), and frames, upholstered pieces, desks, dining room tables and chairs and furnishings for the bedroom. The store imports furniture from a couple of dozen different countries; its pieces offer style as well as utility. Livin' E-Z guarantees your satisfaction with the furniture it sells or it wll give you a refund. Many items are available for immediate delivery or pick-up.

Specialty Food

FARMERS' MARKET
Carrboro

While you're in Carrboro, you won't want to miss the Farmers' Market. In fact, it's worth scheduling your Saturday shopping around it. For over 10 years, the Farmers' Market has given local growers and craftspersons a place to display and sell their goods. Every Saturday morning from April through November, they set up in the parking lot across Main Street from Carr Mill, offering plants, home-baked goods, herbs, flowers, berries, fruits and fresh and exotic vegetables, and sometimes even kittens and puppies looking for a home. Get there early; they are often cleaned out by noon. There is a smaller version of the Farmers' Market on Tuesday mornings at Cedar Falls Park on Weaver Dairy Road.

WEAVER STREET MARKET
101 E. Weaver St.
Carr Mill Annex, Carrboro

Time was when you could walk into your neighborhood grocery and find fresh, locally produced fruits, vegetables, fish and whole grains. Today, Weaver Street Market offers all of the above and much more. Like Wellspring Grocery in Chapel Hill and Durham (see "Durham" Section of **SHOPPING**), Weaver Street Market features a wide variety of gourmet and health products, with an emphasis on organic and locally grown food. In addition it sells organic meat and poultry, beer, wine, coffee and even non-homogenized milk with the cream still on top. The Market is becoming more than a grocery store; it's evolving into a local community meeting place. The cafe is a pleasant place to sit down and enjoy soup, salad, a sandwich, coffee and a cookie.

The market is open from 9 a.m. to 9 p.m. Monday through Friday, 8 a.m. to 8 p.m. Saturday, and 10 a.m. to 7 p.m. Sunday.

The Raleigh Ice Caps ice hockey team has won the hearts of Triangle fans since its debut in 1991.

Inside
Sports

North Carolina is a sports crazy state, and the Triangle is the core of that craziness. Consider that within the confines of the Triangle, there are not one, not two, but three NCAA Division I universities: archrivals University of North Carolina and North Carolina State University, and as if that weren't enough, those famous Duke University teams with their now nationally infamous "Dookie" fans. And these aren't limp-wristed, kiss-your-sister schools. They play to win, and depending on the sport and year, they will bring home some national championships, especially in basketball and soccer.

Where New York City, Boston, Chicago and Los Angeles fans have their professional teams, Triangle residents choose up sides over Atlantic Coast Conference (ACC) college powers. Indeed, if you haven't already, you need to pick an ACC team if you want to be socially acceptable in the Triangle. You don't have to be an alumnus; that's only a minor detail, although it is helpful. It's not considered good form, however, if you are an ACC alumnus and you don't support the ole *Alma Mater*—unless, of course, you went to Clemson. Having your own ACC team will give you a dependable topic of discussion at any business meeting, neighborhood party or church social. This is the only place in the United States, according to someone, where people during basketball season spend more time talking about sports than the weather or sex!

Consider the time, for example, when Gov. James B. Hunt, Jr., was holding an emergency meeting in his Capitol office on the state's 1977 energy crisis. It was the first afternoon of the fabled ACC Basketball Tournament and North Carolina's Wake Forest University Deacons had just been upset by one of the out-of-state teams, a game to which Hunt had been intermittently listening. The emergency committee gave its report, which was mostly glum news. Hunt sat pensive for several quiet minutes, finally shook his head in resignation and looked up at the somber faces opposite him and said: "Poor old Wake Forest, they just don't have any luck, do they." As governor of North Carolina, he knew better than the crisis committee members what really was bothering his constituents.

Since 1991, the conference stretches down the Atlantic coast all the way to Florida, namely Tallahassee, whose Florida State University Seminoles have been polished up, semi-civilized and made members of the ACC. The purpose of this section is to introduce you to some of this madness and share with you some Insider sports tips. The emphasis here is on watching sports, not playing; if you're interested in playing, check the Guide's city section chapters on recreation.

Raleigh and Cary

NCSU

Ticket office: Box 8503   515-2106
Raleigh, NC 27695

The powerhouse in the Raleigh-Cary corner of Triangle sports is North Carolina State University (aka State, NCSU, the Pack), the sprawling campus between Hillsborough Street and Western Boulevard in Raleigh. It has a rich sports tradition and when it's winning, you can feel it in Raleigh's mood. Its teams, nicknamed the Wolfpack, have produced athletes such as Roman Gabriel, long time quarterback for the Los Angeles Rams; Eric Kramer with Detroit; Mike Quick, receiver for the Philadelphia Eagles; running back Ted Brown and Outland Trophy Winner Jim Richter; baseball pitchers Mike Caldwell, Tim Stoddard and Dan Plesac, and in tennis, John Sadri, who, in his senior year, lost to one John McEnroe for the NCAA singles championship.

FOOTBALL

Carter-Finley Stadium
Blue Ridge Rd.

Football gets the academic year off to a pulse-pumping start, and after seven bum years, the Pack returned to winning ways under former Furman Coach Dick Sheridan. Sheridan resigned before the 1993 season and assistant Mike O'Cain was elevated to the head coach job. In his first season, he put the Pack in the Hall of Fame Bowl. Sheridan took the Pack to the 1989 Peach Bowl, the 1991 All American Bowl, the 1992 heart-stopping Peach Bowl, and the fogged-in Gator Bowl following the 1992 season. Indeed, there's no better bowl team for excitement and play than the Wolfpack.

The last time the team won an ACC championship was 1979. Notre Dame's Lou Holtz once coached here, and Insiders remember when he ordered the arrest of a professor who was jogging around the practice field and whom Holtz suspected of spying for Maryland. The professor was released after much embarrassment, and Holtz added further chagrin by losing the game. Sheridan gave Pack fans reason to cheer again and fans believe Mike O'Cain will carry on the winning tradition.

Home games are played at 53,500-seat **Carter-Finley Stadium** next to the State Fairgrounds, off Blue Ridge Road. Game tickets are $20 at the gate; season tickets in 1993 were $120. Some consider the ritual tailgate feast before the game the best part of the contest, and North Carolinians have raised the custom to culinary heights. Some bring linen table cloths, dry wine and candles. Consider yourself a baptized Insider to Triangle sports when you go to the home game that falls during State Fair Week because you'll never be in a bigger crowd (estimated at 170,000 in '92) while you're in North Carolina.

BASKETBALL
Reynolds Coliseum
Main Campus

Some people will tell you that Baptists are the largest single religious group in North Carolina, but that's not true. It's basketball fans. And NCSU fans are some of the most fervent, especially those who call themselves "ABC" fans—Anybody But Carolina. State fans demonstrated their faith in sacrificial bonfires in 1983 when the late Jim Valvano's "Team of Destiny" rallied from a lukewarm season record to first win the ACC Tournament, which was the only way it could have earned an NCAA Tournament bid. Then, after one last-second upset after another, the team found itself in the final game with Akeem the Dream's slamming-jamming University of Houston team. The Cardiac Pack won that one, too, on the last shot in the final seconds. End of sermon.

The Pack also won the NCAA championship in 1974 after beating UCLA and Bill Walton in three overtimes in what some consider the best NCAA tournament game ever. Valvano was replaced by popular NCSU alum Les Robinson, 20-11 in 1990-91 (his first year), but 12-18 in 1991-92. A string of unfortunate events led to a disappointing 8-19 record in 1992-93 and continued to haunt the '93-'94 team , but Robinson is too nice a guy not to win a national championship, so stay tuned.

Season tickets for 16 home games cost about $200; they're $15 at the door but only $10 for most non-conference games. Don't expect to get any tickets at the door when other ACC teams are in town. **Reynolds Coliseum**, a vintage structure built on the championship seasons compiled by Everett Case, holds 12,400 and you can see the action from just about any seat.

Men's football and basketball are the only profit producers for State's athletic program, but officials expect that the next program to make money will be women's basketball. The **Lady Wolfpack** also plays in Reynolds, and the team's coach, Kay Yow, is recognized as one of the best in the country. It was her USA basketball team that brought home the Olympic gold medal in 1988 from Seoul when the men couldn't. Tickets to the Lady Wolfpack games are $5 a game; $25 for the season.

OTHER SPORTS

NCSU's other sports also put championship athletes on the field. The Pack's **baseball** team made it to the NCAA tournament in 1986, 1988 and 1993. The team plays at **Doak Field** on Sullivan Drive. Team coach is alumnus Ray Tanner, who replaced Sam Esposito, a former White Sox star who coached at State for 20 years. The Pack plays about 30 games a year and non-conference games are free.

State's **swimmers** have racked up 14 of the last 17 ACC titles and an NCAA champ in 1993; one alum, Duncan Goodhew, a Brit, won a gold medal for his country in the '84 Olympics. Three other Pack swimmers have won Olympic gold in past games. The team swims at the Carmichael Gym complex.

NCSU **wrestlers** have been repeat ACC champs, and N. F. Terkay and Scott Turner were NCAA national champions in '88 and '93. The team's most celebrated graduate is Tab Thacker, the 450-lb. 1983 NCAA champion who now wrestles with movie star heavies such as Goldie Hawn and Burt Reynolds.

In **track**, State's 400-meter relay team was the 1984 national champion, as was the team's triple jumper in '93. The track team defended its ACC championship throughout most of the '80s and was runner-up in 1991. Laurie Gomez was the 1991 NCAA champion in the 5,000-meter race. Meets are held at Derr Field, which NCSU generously shares with the greater Raleigh community as one of the city's favorite jogging and running fields.

Soccer is another sport where NCSU's women have shared ranking honors with the men. Both teams are usually ranked among the nation's top 20 and the men's team made it to the Final Four in 1990. The women's team in 1988 was runner-up to the national champs, UNC. Hey, the kids are good!

RALEIGH RELAYS
Derr Field, NCSU

The open meet is sponsored by NCSU on the last weekend in March. It is not an ACC event, and track-and-field competitors come from all over, including those from private clubs. It has grown so fast that organizers have made it a two-day event. Over 56 teams competed in 1989, and as one of the first of the season, it attracts many world class athletes anxious to test the competition. Admission is free. For information, call NCSU Sports Information, 515-2102.

CAROLINA MUDCATS BASEBALL
Zebulon   *269-CATS*

Steve Bryant is a fellow who heard a voice say, "Build it and they will come." He did and they did. Bryant, who is a billboard advertising executive, wanted Raleigh to have its own baseball team once again and although he was kept out of the city by the arcane 30-mile rule (he had to be at least 30 miles from the Durham Bulls, the Triangle's other pro team), Bryant built his stadium in a field outside Zebulon, a town made for AA baseball. The stadium opened in mid-season 1991 and has averaged an amazing 4,900 fans per game, many from eastern North Carolina, and is tops in attendance in the league.

The Mudcats' logo is a grinning catfish and the Mudcat baseball hat reputedly is the hottest cap in the league among collectors. The Mudcats are a farm team to the Pittsburgh Pirates and have put 10 graduates, including pitcher Tim Wakefield and third baseman John Wehner, into the Big Leagues.

Tickets range from $3.50 to $5.50—one of the best sports bargains in the county. You can get the usual baseball fare at the concession stand as well as a catfish—yes,

"Muddy the Mudcat" is symbolic of the family atmosphere
at the Carolina Mudcats games.

catfish—sandwich! So, take yourself out to the ballpark and eat a mascot.

GREAT RALEIGH ROAD RACE

This is Raleigh's biggest single participant sporting event with as many as 4,000 runners and joggers lining up for the starting gun on Wilmington Street next to Memorial Auditorium for a 10K (about 6.2 miles) race. It's the highlight of a whole weekend of activities, including the city's Artsplosure. The race is scheduled in April when the weather usually is great for running. It attracts world-class runners, but there is no purse. The course winds its way through downtown and then up Hillsborough Street—and that's UP, too, folks—past NCSU and then back to the downtown, finishing at the Civic Center. The route is usually lined the whole way with cheering, jeering and envious bystanders. It attracts some name runners and is a sanctioned event, but the bulk of the crowd is formed of those men, women, boys and girls whom you see plugging along the Triangle's byways and sidewalks year-round. The early registration fee is about $5; more, if you want a commemorative T-shirt.

CAPITAL CITY CRITERIUM
Carolina Velo Club

This, folks, is a bicycle race that goes very, very fast. Started around 1979, it quickly has become one of the East Coast's premier races and has attained the distinction of a "national classic." It usually runs the last weekend in April. Part of its

success can be attributed to the prize money: about $5,000 for the winner. The race attracts over 400 racers who compete at different levels in about eight or nine races. The main money race is about 50 miles long and follows a tight, one-mile figure 8 course through downtown Raleigh. The Criterium always takes place on a Sunday and is directed by the Carolina Velo Club. Each year the crowd of spectators gets bigger.

ICE HOCKEY
Raleigh Ice Caps   *755-0022*
Dorton Arena, State Fairgrounds

The latest addition to the pros on the Triangle sports scene is our Raleigh Icecaps team, which amazed and attracted everyone in its debut '91 season. The team had 14 sellouts in a town that has more ice in tea than rinks in winter! It has a 34-game home schedule in the East Coast Hockey League, which starts in late October. Coach Kurt Kleinendorst, a former U.S. Olympian and NHL player, is a great coach as well as a community-minded and family-oriented guy, which helps create the kind of atmosphere that president Pete Bach wants here in Raleigh. Look for the blue and silver team colors and go out and see some hockey at Dorton Arena—it's a fast-paced, exciting game to watch and the Icecaps, after making the playoffs in 1992 and 1993, are a contender. Tickets are $8 for adults and $5 for senior citizens, students and children. Season tickets for all 34 home games cost $205. Melt 'em, Icecaps!

RACQUETBALL
Raleigh Racquet Club   876-0847
Falls of the Neuse Rd.

The club sponsors two regional tournaments a year: one, the Raleigh Seniors Tournament, usually in early September; and the Junior Classic in October. The seniors features some of the best club pros and amateurs in the state, aged 40 and over. The juniors are age 18 and under. Club legend has it that John McEnroe once played on center court during his pre-stardom, semi-pro years. Center court stadium seats about 2,000, and the club has the best facilities in the Triangle with 29 courts, eight of them covered in winter.

NIKE GOLF TOUR
Prestonwood Golf Club   467-9601
300 Prestonwood Pkwy.
Cary

This is Cary's newest pro sporting event, and the June '94 tournament will bring in some of the PGA's up and coming pros and older ones who are trying to get back on the tour. It's like the minor leagues for golf and will feature a purse of about $35,000.

WRASSLIN'
Dorton Arena   733-2626
State Fairgrounds

If professional wrestling is your sport or therapy, then check with Dorton Arena for the best in Wednesday night Mid-Atlantic Championship Wrestling. Matches are scheduled once or twice a month, and they tend to be "extravaganzas," with some of your favorite body slammers and all 'round baddies and goodies. Call the day of the match to get ticket prices and information. Prices vary, depending on who's wrasslin', but it can cost up to $15.

Half of the show is watching the crowd, and if you've never attended one of these character-building events and believe that they are third-rate entertainment, remember that one of the most popular

selling look-alike dolls at Christmas a few years back was one of Hulk Hogan.

CARY ROAD RACE

This race, sponsored by the *Cary News* and conducted by the Cary Parks and Recreation Department, is usually held in April and attracts hundreds of runners each year. The race started in 1978. Runners tackle either a 5K or 10K course that winds through Cary. For more information, call the Recreation Department at 469-4062.

RUGBY

The Raleigh Rugby Club has expanded in recent years, fueled by local talent as well as by international members new to the Triangle area. The club won the 1991 North Carolina Union Championship, which placed it in contention for the National Championship. NCSU was the 1991 collegiate champion. Team members have taken to going to the World Cups abroad. New and experienced players are always welcome. Have good medical insurance. For information, call Jim Kellenberger (919-833-9678).

SOCCER

Now in its second season, the **Raleigh Flyers** soccer team plays in the U.S. Interregional Soccer League. Led by manager/coach Roland Paiva, matches are played at Broughton High School. This is great family fun and a good chance to see some exciting, hard-hitting soccer played by future MSL stars.

Durham

DUKE UNIVERSITY
Ticket office: *681-2583*

Duke is the bumblebee of ACC sports. Just as the blimpy bee isn't supposed to fly, a school that's sometimes called the "Harvard of the South" (or calls Harvard the Duke of the North) isn't supposed to have big-time sports. After all, Duke is a small school compared to its Triangle neighbors in Raleigh and Chapel Hill. The undergraduate enrollment is about 5,700. It's a private school with high academic

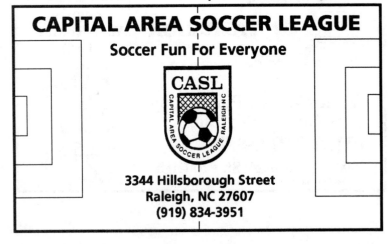

Photo courtesy Raleigh Flyers.

The Raleigh Flyers are attracting new Triangle fans to the sport of soccer.

standards. Its SAT scores average around 1300; all normally fatal signs when you're out recruiting 270-pound tackles or seven-foot basketball centers.

Yet, the bee flies and Duke teams soar—like the 1990-91 and 1991-92 Blue Devil basketball teams, which won back-to-back national championships. They won it all against teams like undefeated (well, almost) UNLV, Kansas, Kentucky and Michigan. Duke went to the Final Four five years in a row and was the first team since UCLA to repeat. (If you lost money betting on Duke in the 1989-90 championship game, you can recoup it by wagering that Duke will graduate more of its players than UNLV will. Indeed, Duke has been No. 1 or 2 in recent years in the percentage of its athletes who graduate and recently landed on the cover of Parade magazine for its success in promoting good grades and great athletes.)

FOOTBALL
Wallace Wade Stadium
Main Campus

Blue Devil teams have been national powers in football since the '30s, when the famous 1938 Iron Dukes under Football Hall of Famer Wallace Wade went undefeated, untied and unscored on but lost the Rose Bowl, 7-3, to Southern Cal. in the last 40 seconds. The Blue Devils are one of only a handful of schools who have played in all four of the major football bowls: Rose, Cotton, Orange and Sugar. Former Blue Devil stars include quarterbacks Sonny Jurgensen, Ben Bennett, and Dave Brown, line-

backer Mike Curtis and George McFee of the Chicago Bears and Mike Junkin of Cleveland.

After the dream season of 1989 that included a bowl game, Coach Steve Spurrier, Coach of the Year in 1988, left for Florida's warmer climes. Coach Barry Wilson resigned in 1993 and Coach Fred Goldsmith has taken the helm beginning with the '94 season.

The availability of tickets for non-alumni is the silver lining in this Duke Blue cloud. On almost any sunny autumn Saturday afternoon or evening that the Blue Devils are playing at **Wallace Wade Stadium** (except the Carolina game), you can get a ticket at the gate. The price is $16 cash; season tickets in '93 were $90. The stadium seats about 34,000, and with Duke's wide-open passing offense, "Airball," you can count on an exciting game.

BASKETBALL
Cameron Indoor Stadium
Main Campus

Tickets to the basketball games are another matter, which is not surprising because Duke's basketball teams have been one of the best shows in the nation for the past decade. And **Cameron Indoor** is absolutely one of the best spots to watch college basketball in the country. If you can get a ticket—go! In 1978, 1986, 1990, 1991, 1992, and 1994 the team went to the NCAA's Final Championship game for the national title and, in between, it's been as regular as a Christian Laettner dunk shot in making the NCAA tournament. The team won it all in 1991 and 1992, proving that good students can also be champion athletes.

Duke stars who moved into the NBA include heartthrob Laettner, Bobby Hurley, Danny Ferry, Johnny Dawkins, Mike Gminski, Gene Banks, Jeff Mullen and Jack Marin, with more to come. Dick Grote was a star at both basketball and baseball.

At Cameron Indoor Stadium (which seats 9,314), you get two shows for the price of one: you get to watch the basketball team and you get to see the notorious Duke student fans—Dookies. A third of the crowd usually is comprised of Dookies, and long before TV broadcasters like Al McGuire and Dick Vitale compared them to Attila's hordes, the students were entertaining visiting teams with all sorts of digs, barbs and sarcasms. When one of NCSU's stars was arrested for mugging a pizza delivery boy, the athlete was greeted in his first game at Cameron Stadium by Dookies hurling Domino's Pizza box tops onto the court. Every time balding former Maryland coach Lefty Driesell, a Duke alum, showed up, you could count on a squad of skin heads in shower caps to sit behind him. To paraphrase Rodney Dangerfield, Dookies have no respect.

The best way to get basketball tickets is to send your child to Duke and then borrow his or her tickets. If that's too costly, you can join the Iron Dukes club (minimum $100 contribution), which supports Duke athletics, but that's still no guarantee. Tickets cost $18, and for the season, about $311. (No, it's not true that if you can spell Coach Mike Krzyzewski's last name, you get in free.)

OTHER SPORTS

Duke's national athletic prowess doesn't stop with basketball and football. Its **soccer** team usually is ranked among the top 20, and it won the 1986 NCAA national championship. In the final game in 1982, it lost after a record eight overtimes. For free, you can watch some of the best soccer in college at the Duke soccer field in the spring.

The Blue Devils also are ranked in **lacrosse**, and the men's and women's tennis teams are frequent ACC champs and the **women's volleyball** team won the ACC championship thrice in recent years. **Track** teams have included the likes of Dave Sime, once one of the world's fastest runners.

The school sponsors 23 NCAA sports altogether, and all are free except for football and basketball.

DUKE CHILDREN'S CLASSIC
P.O. Box 2975   *493-0495*
Duke Medical Center
Durham, NC 27710

This yearly special event has become one of the Triangle's biggest spectator attractions since its inception in 1974. That was when a Duke Medical Center pediatrician asked his friend, singer Perry Como, to help establish a celebrity-amateur golf tournament to raise money for the pediatrics department. Como did that and more, and today, the Med Center can count on the Classic to raise almost $500,000 annually.

The Classic today also includes tennis and running, plus entertainment and a sumptuous banquet. The Classic will be May 21-22 in 1994 and tickets for participants usually are sold out before Christmas. It's a weekend event that works like this: Some 210 amateurs and celebrities pay a handsome fee to play golf or tennis together, or run with the likes of Jim Ryan, who has made the last several Classics. Celebrities at past events have included former President Gerald Ford, Bob Hope, Frank Sinatra, Dinah Shore, Glen Campbell, Pat Boone and, of course, always Como, the permanent chairman. If you sign up for tennis, you may have Stan Smith as a partner, or Arnold Palmer if you're golfing.

The weekend starts with a pool party Friday, where you can meet the stars; sports follow on Saturday and Sunday, with a Saturday evening banquet and show. The entry fee for participants isn't cheap—$2,700—but that includes two nights at the hotel. Corporate entry fees start at $5,000. If you just want to go out and watch the celebrities at play, there will be no charge in 1994 in celebration of the event's 20th anniversary. And if you just want to see the Saturday night show, tickets run from about $12.50 to $25. It's all for a good cause.

DURHAM BULLS

Durham Athletic Park
Corner of Morris and Corporation sts.
Tickets: 956-BULL
Office: 688-8211

The Durham Bulls have been a Triangle tradition since the first Bulls' team took the field in 1902. Ninety years and several leagues later, the Bulls are a worldwide phenomenon. A good bit of that success is due to the 1988 movie "Bull Durham," in which stars Kevin Costner and Susan Sarandon brought stardom to the Bulls and their home, **Durham Athletic Park**, as well.

The 1993 season was to be the last in the venerable old "DAP" before moving to a new ballpark just off the Durham Freeway but construction delays will mean one more great year in the DAP. To commemorate this second "final season," the Bulls will be rolling out the red carpet for a season-long celebration of the 56 years the stadium has served as home to the team.

The Bulls' organization is planning events such as "Turn Back the Clock" nights that will mark different eras in Bulls' history with reunions of former players and period costume contests for fans. So, y'all come.

Since 1980, the Bulls have been the advanced Class A affiliate for the National League Champion Atlanta Braves and have played a large role in the team's recent success. More than 30 former Bulls have logged time in the big leagues in the past 13 years, including nine current members of the Braves. Steve Avery, Ron Gant, David Justice, Jeff Blauser, Mark Lemke, Mike Stanton, Kent Mercker, Brian Hunter and Javy Lopez all spent time in a Bulls uniform before advancing to Atlanta. The Bulls are charter members of the Carolina League, one of the top talent-producing leagues in all of minor league baseball. Stars such as Dwight Gooden, Darryl Strawberry, Barry Bonds, Fred McGriff and World Series MVP Pat Borders sharpened their skills in the Carolina League.

Fan support of the Durham Bulls is also phenomenal, as the Bulls continue to rank in the upper echelons of minor league attendance, drawing more fans than even some AA and AAA clubs. And at the bargain prices of $6 for reserved seats and $3 for general admission, it's no wonder that Bulls fans return again and again to watch some baseball and partake of great ballpark food at the El Toro Grill. An evening with the Bulls is always cause for excitement.

NORTH CAROLINA CENTRAL UNIVERSITY
Fayetteville and Lawson sts.   560-6574
Durham

NCCU, Durham's other university, is a member of the Central Intercollegiate Athletic Association and offers a number of sporting events to Triangle residents. The school is best known, perhaps, for its track teams, coached by now-retired Leroy Walker, who was the U.S. track coach at the Montreal Olympics. There are 14 schools—including St. Augustine's and Shaw in Raleigh—in its conference, which has produced dozens of players in the pro ranks. To get to the campus off Interstate 40, take the Alston Avenue exit and turn south, drive

about four blocks, and there you are.

FOOTBALL
O'Kelly Stadium, Main Campus

Like the bigger ACC schools, football is one of the Eagles' biggest spectator sports, and season tickets go for about $40 for five home games. **O'Kelly Stadium** seats about 15,000. The team went to the NCAA quarterfinals in 1988, has been a contender in the conference in recent years, and past NCCU stars include John Baker of the Pittsburgh Steelers (now sheriff of Wake County) and John Brown, one of the first black pros, who played for the old Los Angeles Dons.

BASKETBALL
McDougald Gym, Main Campus

In 1990, when Duke lost the championship to UNLV, Durham did not go without an NCAA national title—the Eagles brought home the NCAA Division 2 basketball championship title instead! Not bad for a school that hadn't had a winning season for 20 years until 1985! Season tickets for NCCU basketball cost about $60, and games are played in the 4,800-seat McDougald Gym.

NCCU's basketball history includes John D. McLendon's then-dramatic fast-break teams of the 1930s and one of the game's first 7-foot players. Former stars include Sam Jones of the Boston Celtics.

OTHER SPORTS

NCCU's **track** teams under Leroy Walker brought national attention to the Durham school, especially the Eagles' famed "six-pack" of sprinters who helped win the NCAA Division 2 national championship in the '70s. The team continues to get respect at national meets such as the Penn Relays.

In women's sports, NCCU's **volleyball** team made it to the NCAA playoffs in 1988 and its basketball team is an annual contender for conference honors. Outside of football and basketball, admission to Eagles' sporting events is free.

Chapel Hill

UNIVERSITY OF NORTH CAROLINA
Dean Smith Student Activity Center
("The Dean Dome")   962-2296
Manning Drive

UNC, also known as Carolina, the Tar Heels, the 'Heels, and Chapel Hill, has the kind of athletic tradition that engenders its opponents to become "ABC" fans—Anybody But Carolina. This reaction also can be blamed in part on Carolina fans' sincere belief that God probably is a Tar Heel which, they say, explains why the sky is Carolina blue. This attitude is not moderated by the fact that many among the state's ruling Establishment attended Carolina, and they often take the view attributed to Harvard's fans who, when watching a setback on the playing fields, chant: "That's all right, that's okay; you'll still have to work for us some day." But most of all, Carolina's athletic tradition is a winning one, which is why many of the state's college-unbound, from tobacco pickers to textile workers, root for the Tar Heels and are as

dyed-in-the-wool loyalists as Kenan family members.

The 1992-93 men's basketball team won the national championship and the women's team won it all in the 1993-94 season, continuing the tradition that spans a wide range of NCAA sports. In 1982, for example, the school posted national championships in three different sports: basketball, lacrosse and women's soccer. UNC women have one of the best all-around sports programs in the country.

FOOTBALL
Kenan Stadium, Main Campus

You have to act fast to buy season tickets for UNC football games. They go fast. Look for ticket sales in the spring when the billboards around the Triangle start warning you about "Carolina Fever, Catch It!" Individual tickets are $18 and about $108 for the season.

The football tradition is strong at Carolina with names like Charlie "Choo Choo" Justice among its great running backs. The team fell on hard times in 1988, going 1-10 under coach Mack Brown. It has rebounded, and was the spoiler in 1990 by keeping national champ Georgia Tech from having an unblemished record. The 1992 Tar Heels were 8-3 and won the Peach Bowl and the '93 team was Gator Bowl bound.

The tradition of the Tar Heel program can be measured in part by some of its graduates, including N.Y. Giants all-pro linebacker Lawrence Taylor and fullback Kelvin Bryant. Other Carolina greats include Buddy Curry, "Famous"

*Center Eric Montross helped lead the 1992-93 Tar Heels
to the NCAA National Championship.*

Amos Lawrence and Natrone Means.

If you go to a Carolina football game, plan on making a day of it since pre-game parties and tailgating are part of the ritual. Don't get alarmed when you start running into bumper-to-bumper traffic as you approach Chapel Hill. It's that way every home game. Parking in Chapel Hill on game day is like looking for a lost contact lens in a dark movie theater. Plan ahead. In 1992, it also became illegal to park on sidewalks during game days. Parking there will result in a ticketed or towed car after the game. If you don't know where the stadium is, just follow the crowd. **Kenan Stadium** seats 52,000.

Coolers are not allowed in the stadium, but fans manage somehow to sip more than branch water once inside. Because tickets are retained by families year after year, you may see the same folks at the games, which makes the afternoon a neighborly get together. In North Carolina, it still can get pretty hot in September and October, so the dress is casual but neat. (The bare-chested people in cutoffs and drinking out of brown paper bags probably are Clemson fans.)

BASKETBALL
The Dean Dome, Manning Drive

This is **the** spectator sport in the Triangle. Under Coach Dean Smith—the guy after whom the 22,000-seat **Dean Dome** is named—Carolina basketball has written a record as legendary as that of Knute Rockne's Notre Dame football teams including two NCAA cham-

pionships. Every Insider knows, for instance, about the famous game with Duke in the early 70s when Carolina was behind by a seemingly insurmountable seven points with only 17 seconds to go. Dookies began to celebrate, only to watch in amazement along with a regional television audience as Smith used the clock, strategy and luck to pull out a victory. That ending came to typify Carolina's never-quit style of play.

Smith, a Kansas transplant, has led a U.S. Olympic team—with a number of Carolina players—to the gold medal. The victory was evidence, said true-blue Carolina fans, that the Tar Heels were not only the best in the ACC, but the best in the world. For years, before the ACC adopted the shot clock, Smith frustrated opponents with his fabled "four-corners" offense, which guard Phil Ford, now an assistant coach, developed to perfection.

The team in 1986 moved into its new home, the **Dean Smith Student Activity Center**, almost tripling the number of seats. Yet, the season remains a sellout. UNC box office officials agree tickets are rarely available. However, if you don't mind going to pre-season games against non-ACC opponents, your chances for tickets aren't that bad. Check the sports sections of various media for tickets to these games. When such tickets are available, they cost about $17. So valuable are Carolina basketball tickets considered, they sometimes have been singled out in wills and as part of divorce settlements. Students comprise about a third of the crowd and provide Carolina basketball teams with plenty of back-up at home games. Joining the Rams Club improves, but doesn't guarantee, your chances at obtaining basketball tickets.

If you're wondering why there's such a fuss over Carolina basketball, just look at the list of some of the pros who wore Tar Heel blue: Michael Jordan, James Worthy, Michael Jordan, Bobby Jones, Michael Jordan, Mitch Kuptchak, Phil Ford, Walter Davis, Brad Daugherty, Sam Perkins, and, of course, Michael Jordan.

Finally, the Heels are winners and behave accordingly as evident in the 1993 NCAA championships that brought UNC its third national title, defeating the highly touted "fab five" from Michigan. Who can forget the last minute "time-out" called by Michigan's Chris Weber? Not Tar Heel fans— one of Chapel Hill's most popular late-night eateries, Time Out Chicken, now offers a Chris Weber special and prominantly displays a photo of the infamous event.

Smith tries to pick smart players, and he is proud that his teams have one of the highest graduation records among Division I basketball. Like UCLA's legendary John Wooden, Smith demands teamwork and, until 1982 when he won the NCAA Championship with a team that included Jordan, Worthy, Perkins and Jimmy Black, he was often accused of blowing chance after chance at national titles because of holding too tight a rein on his players. But it's the smart and smooth play that makes Carolina basketball so artful a show to watch.

It's not just men's basketball that has fans in a fever these days. Disappointment over the early exit from the NCAA Tournament by the 1993-94 men's team turned to celebration when the Lady Heels sank a last second three-point shot to win the women's NCAA National Championship.

OTHER SPORTS

Carolina is a competitor in a long list of other NCAA sports, most of which charge no admission to watch. The school has become during the past 10 years as much a national power in **lacrosse**—1987 NCAA champs—as it is in basketball. It swaps national championships and number one ranking with Johns Hopkins and Syracuse regularly.

Likewise, **women's soccer** at Carolina simply is the best in the country; the team was '88, '89, '90, '92 and '93 national champs and won three national championships in a row before losing in '87. What other team has done that?

The **women's basketball** team usually is among the top three in the ACC. **Track and field, wrestling**—UNC had a NCAA champ in '93—and **baseball** round out the school's other spectator sports. Carolina placed third in the nation in **golf**.

Baseball fans, when Yankee owner George Steinbrenner's daughter was a Carolina student, used to get treated to a spring warm-up between Tar Heel teams and Yankee players. Games are played at Boshamer Stadium on campus.

From The Chamber...

Welcome To Cary!

Cary is a warm, comfortable community where professionals can reside in the heart of the Research Triangle area and still escape at the end of the day by enjoying an ample choice of leisure activities. Having planned for growth rather than reacted to it, numerous parks, swim clubs and golf courses exist to enhance everyday life and provide a healthy environment for growing families. Shopping abounds in Cary offering everything from clothing to camping equipment. Cary's elementary and secondary schools continue to rank among the State's best. Located near 10 major colleges and universities, Cary considers higher education another one of its priorities.

Although it has all the amenities of a big city, Cary continues to offer a small-town flair. Its population has more than doubled in the past decade, yet traditional values continually carve a pattern of growth. Through it all, Cary's stringent commitment to planned growth and economic development continues to make it one of the top-rated places to live in the nation.

The Cary Chamber of Commerce stands ready to assist you at any time. For information contact Howard Johnson, President, at the Cary Chamber of Commerce, 307 North Academy Street, P. O. Box 4351, Cary, North Carolina 27519-4351, Telephone #(919)467-1016 Fax #(919)469-2375.

Sincerely,

Howard S. Johnson
President
Cary Chamber of Commerce

Inside
Cary

Cary has made a name for itself in the past 30 years as one of the state's fastest growing towns and one of the Triangle's prime residential nesting places. It's the third largest town in the Triangle as the 20th Century looms and one wag has suggested that the Triangle may have to change its name to Research Rectangle if Cary continues to grow at its current pace. The 1990 Census showed a population of 43,858 and city planners estimate a 1994 population of nearly 60,000. Say "Cary" and people think of planned neighborhoods, comfortable homes, neat lawns, well-wheeled commuters, devoted band supporters and soccer games on Sunday. Cary is this and more. But what was Cary before it was, well, Cary?

Unlike some ersatz post-World War II suburbs, Cary has a past. It's been around for more than 100 years on the state's legislative books. Citizens are especially proud of its record for establishing the first public school in the state, the Cary Academy for which Academy Street is named.

Before it was a town, it was the busy home and gathering place for business friends and family of A. Francis (Frank) Page. He was founder of the town and father to five sons, one of whom was to become one of the state's more famous sons—writer and diplomat Walter Hines Page. Indeed, some citizens then and later believed Cary should have been named Page, after Frank. It was he who, in the mid-1850s set up a sawmill, store and inn along the main road between Raleigh and the university in Chapel Hill. He also ran the post office and began rearing his family there. But it was the coming of the railroads in 1868 and the junction they formed at Page's place that literally put it on the map. That same year, he sold some of his lots: one 70-acre parcel went for $140 and a 10-acre piece sold for the grand sum of $50.

In 1871, the General Assembly incorporated the various enterprises and railroad crossing as the town of "Carey" a misspelling on the town clerk's part which was later corrected. The name was selected to honor one Samuel F. Cary, a famed Ohio temperance orator who reportedly stayed at Page's inn on one of his speaking tours in the south and greatly impressed the host. The selection must have been a brave choice for the times. Cary was not only a teetotaling Yankee outsider, he also had been a general in the Union Army, not a recommendation for honors in the South of 1871. Despite this lack of North Carolina lineage, the choice of the name has turned out to be fitting because Cary, in the 1990s, has become a favorite among many new Triangle residents who have moved here from the north.

Cary no longer is a bedroom community and boosters bristle today at the suggestion. It is home to several industries including SAS, one of the fastest growing software companies in the country, Bahlsen cookie company's U.S. headquarters, several IBM operations and MCI's regional operation. To appreciate Cary's growth, consider that in the first quarter of 1993, Cary led all cities, including Raleigh and Charlotte, in the number of new housing starts. Look for Cary to continue to make history in the '90s.

Line drawing by Jerry Miller.

The new Cary Chamber of Commerce.

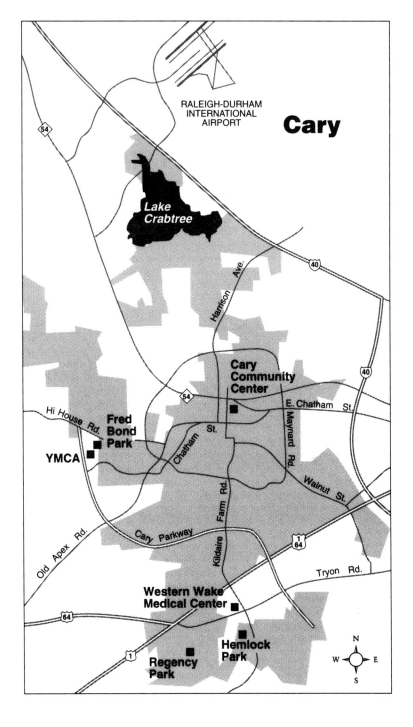

RALEIGH-DURHAM
INTERNATIONAL
AIRPORT

Cary

54

*Lake
Crabtree*

40

Harrison Ave.

Cary
Community
Center

54

E. Chatham St.

Hi House Rd.

Fred
Bond
Park

YMCA

Chatham St.

E. Maynard Rd.

Walnut St.

40

Old Apex Rd.

Cary Parkway

Kildaire Farm Rd.

1
64

Tryon Rd.

Western Wake
Medical Center

64

Hemlock
Park

1

Regency
Park

N
W   E
S

Inside

Cary Government Services and Utilities

The following is a short guide to some of the services that you will want and need to know as a Cary resident. The list also has helpful information about other utilities and items such as driver's licensing and automobile plates. Cary and Apex have their own phone book so be sure to obtain a copy along with the greater Raleigh telephone directory.

Utilities

Cable TV

Cable television service in Cary is provided by CVI. It is located at 1006 Maynard Road, 467-2800.

Electricity

Call Carolina Power and Light for electrical service. It is located at 1020 W. Chatham Street, 783-5400.

Gas

Public Service Company of N.C., Inc., is located at 223 East Chatham Street, 469-9461.

Telephone

To order your telephone service for the Cary area, call Southern Bell at 780-2355.

Trash

The Town of Cary provides trash pick-up, call 469-4096 if you have questions. For more information on Cary's recycling efforts, call 469-4387.

Water

If you are a new customer, call the Town of Cary's Utility Department at 469-4051. If you have billing questions, call 469-4050.

Emergencies

Call the 911 number for fire, police, sheriff or rescue emergencies and be sure to talk clearly, give your name and the location of the emergency.

Government and Civic Services

Automobile Information
Driver's License   733-4540
Auto Plates   469-1444
Bus Service
Capital Area Transit 828-7228
Cary Arts Center   469-4069
Cary Chamber of Commerce
114 Chatham St.   467-1016
Cary Parks & Recreation
469-4061
Cary Community Center
404 N. Academy St. 460-4965
Cary Public Library
310 Academy St.   460-3350

Child and Family Services
856-5300
Pet Licenses
Cary Town Hall   469-4000
United Arts Council   839-1498
Wake County Health Department
250-4400
Wake Social Services   856-7000
Voting
Wake Board of Elections
856-6240

Community Service Numbers

The 1994-95 edition of the local Southern Bell phone book includes a great listing of human services numbers ranging from crisis hotlines, family planning, mental and physical health services, to senior citizen's, veteran's and women's services. This list includes public agencies and nonprofit organizations.

Staff photo.

The Cary Family YMCA on Cary Parkway is the center of neighborhood activity.

Inside
Cary Neighborhoods

Cary has grown so fast in the past 25 years that many of its neighborhoods are still new and growing. Remember, this is a town of nearly 60,000 that counted fewer than 1,500 people in the 1950 Census! Today, several of the larger neighborhoods alone will contain that many residents and more.

Many of the newer neighborhoods are Planned Unit Developments or PUDs, and they are built as complete communities. They contain a mixture of housing, from apartments to single-family homes on conventional lots. Some even include neighborhood shopping centers and office and industrial sections. Most also have their own recreation centers and complexes. In and around Cary, there are over 20 such PUDs.

The Guide lists some of the established as well as some of the newer neighborhoods of Cary. Our list is not inclusive; rather, it is a sampler and highlights some of the places that have gained special attention. They are spread all around, and all have convenient access to the Research Triangle Park or the Beltline around Raleigh. Indeed, some of the newest neighborhoods are growing up along Harrison Avenue, between I-40 and downtown.

Cary has not suffered the market glut of other Triangle communities and it has been the strongest housing market by far for most real estate companies. Because of Cary's reputation as a prime residential area, prices reflect its popularity. It's hard to find any new homes for less than $70,000, and most start at $125,000 or more. One developer found that his PUD's typical resident stayed only three and a half years and then moved to new quarters. That's not much time to develop a settled down feeling. But these planned communities are designed to help newcomers get to know their neighbors in a hurry. Some you will meet on the jogging or walking paths that may run past your back yard; you'll meet others at homeowner's associations or at the community's clubhouse, swimming pool or tennis courts. Most of the latter have regular activities scheduled that are often a good way to meet the neighbors. In today's mobile culture, it's nice to know that your neighborhood is designed to be neighborly.

Downtown

This is the older part of town, and it retains much of Cary's small town flavor. The intersection of Chatham and Academy streets, a stone's throw from the Seaboard Railroad line, is the "x" that marks what's left of downtown. The **Town Hall** and **Chamber of Commerce** are nearby, as is **Ashworth's Pharmacy** on the corner where you can get a first-rate milkshake. The library and **Cary Elementary School** (where once stood the famed Cary Academy) are within walking distance, as is Russell Hills, one of the downtown subdivisions. Older homes in downtown's residential area, some in the process of restoration, come in a mixture of styles that one finds in most small towns of the 1950s. Prices vary, depending on the house, but it's one place where you might find a $70,000 bargain, although the larger homes with the spacious yards will sell for $200,000.

Greenwood Forest

This is one of Cary's first large subdivisions, once on the southeast outskirts of town, but now right in the middle. It is bounded by the slanting Walnut Street from the northeast and the curving East Maynard that wraps around its southern border. It is a typical 1950s, early 60s neighborhood (no sidewalks) and has a mixture of homes and, according to one veteran resident, a mix of neighbors from lawyers, doctors and academics to blue collar tradespeople. Its entrance streets have modest signs announcing "Greenwood Forest," and its residents gather for Fourth of July picnics, so it has a sense of place about it. **Cary High School** is nearby—some would say within walking distance—as are the town's two largest shopping centers, **Cary Village Square** and **Cary Towne Mall**. Prices on these conventional homes start at $85,000 and go up to $130,000. Other neighborhoods of this vintage and price range are **Tanglewood, Pirate's** and **Walnut Hills**.

MacGregor Downs

If there is one subdivision that lit the fuse that led to Cary's growth explosion, this is the one. Developed in the late 1960s by one of Raleigh's old families, the Gregory Pooles, MacGregor Downs quickly became a showplace. And even if you couldn't possibly afford its big lots or large homes, your Realtor still wanted you to see it. It gave Cary, more than ever, the reputation as a place for nice residential living. This is, in trendy parlance, a "power neighborhood" where the home tells visitors that its occupants are people of means and accomplishments; NCSU's successful ex-football coach, Lou Holtz, lived here.

MacGregor Downs boasts a lake, a championship golf course and private country club, and a tournament-caliber tennis complex as well as a swimming pool. Most of the golf course lots have been developed, but there are still a few available. On property closer to the club and tennis complex town houses and condominiums are built. The latter start at $140,000 and don't be surprised to see homes selling for over $400,000.

An adjacent but separate neighborhood is **MacGregor West**. It is especially upper-end in price range, starting around $300,000 and reflects the sumptuous amenities that newer homes offer today, such as master bedroom suites and bathrooms that Caesar would find extravagant. The MacGregor West mini-estates, those homes sitting on two to three acre lots, go as high as $1.5 million.

Kildaire Farms

This was Cary's first PUD and was hailed with lavish press during the 1970s when it was first announced. It was named after the 927-acre farm owned by the Kilgore family, who established the Triangle's Pine State Creamery. It is located at Kildaire Farm Road and Cary Parkway. About 2,600 residential units fill the PUD. It includes a 230-acre greenway system winding throughout the community, with jogging trails and bike paths.

The **Kildaire Farms Racquet and Swim Club** has 13 lighted tennis courts and an 8,500-square-foot swimming pool. There's a modest membership fee for Kildaire Farm

residents and, unlike most PUDs, non-residents may also join. For more information, call 467-4313. The **Cary Athletic Club** is also located here.

The development moved slowly during its first stages, but in 1984, it was purchased by the Harlon Group, an aggressive, out-of-state real estate development group that went bust. During the 1990s, Kildaire Farms regained its balance and appeal. Traffic along Kildaire Farm Road has improved with completion of road widening projects and portions of Cary Parkway. Prices vary, depending on the project. For example: homes in **Royal Ridge** go over $250,000 and **Fox Chase** homes start at around $120,000, while some town homes are being marketed for around $55,000.

Regency Park

Located off the intersection of U.S. Highway 1 South and U.S. Highway 64, Regency Park is Cary's southern-most PUD. Approved in the late '70s, Regency Park did not begin developing until the '80s, but when it did, it established itself as one of the Triangle's classiest developments. It also marked a change from previous PUDs in that it did not focus entirely on residential projects; it also contains some of the Triangle's best office buildings. It has helped change Cary's image from that of a bedroom community to a professional work center. Then, IBM's location in two of the buildings quickly marked Regency Park as someplace special. The residential area is made up of single family detached homes, cluster homes, town homes and estate lots large enough to accommodate a swimming pool. Planned along with the homes are greenways, volleyball courts, a lake with fishing and a health spa.

Lochmere

The 1,000-acre Lochmere development began in 1981 and became a textbook successful PUD. It offers a variety of neighborhoods and is located on the southern end of Kildaire Farm Road, east of U.S. Highway 1, not far from Regency Park. It was planned several years ago by the developers of MacGregor Downs, but building didn't take off until the economic recovery that began in late 1982. Lochmere has two man-made lakes big enough for sailing, canoeing and fishing. In the center is its world-class golf course at the **Lochmere Golf Club**, whose membership was quickly sold out. A swimming and tennis complex is also available to residents, along with jogging trails, including a path around the larger lake. There are at least seven neighborhoods within the development and they have names like **Fairways**, **Lochwood**, **Lochview**, **Windsong**,

The Greens, **Williamsburgh Commons** and **Lockridge**. Homes adjoining the golf course start at $150,000, while The Greens homes start at about $220,000 and lakeside lots alone sell for $110,000. **Birkhaven** homes start at $290,000. Condominium prices start at about $90,000 and the larger homes in Williamsburgh Commons and The Greens sell for prices between $140,000 and $180,000.

Preston

Preston is the Triangle's largest golf course community and was the state's top-selling country club community in 1993. Located off High House Road, only 10 minutes from the Research Triangle Park and RDU Airport, Preston is at the heart of the area's booming residential market. Thoughtful planning that emphasizes beauty, privacy and convenience, has allowed the community to respond to the tremendous growth of the area.

More than 20 neighborhoods make up this development, offering a diversity of homestyles and a variety of price ranges—from $160,000 to $750,000. The newest neighborhood, **Preston Village**, boasts a two-acre Great Lawn, athletic field, putting greens, sheltered picnic areas, gazebos overlooking the lake and a huge play area designed for kids of all ages. Generous amenities are something Preston residents have come to expect.

The centerpiece of the community is Prestonwood Country Club which is undergoing a major expansion. A new clubhouse complex and ballroom, expanded Olympic pool (with poolside dining), a new fitness center, and additional composition tennis courts are among the changes. The championship golf course has recently been expanded to 45 holes. If you're looking for convenience, comfortable living and fun for the entire family—Preston has it all.

The Highlands

This development, started in 1987, is a neighbor to Lochmere and was started by the same firm, MacGregor Development Co. It contains 343 homes, most of which are single-family detached homes. Like Lochmere, it has a swim and tennis club, and members in each development's club have access to the other club. Houses sell for around $170,000 and up.

The neighborhood is about 15 minutes from RDU and downtown Raleigh and NCSU if you take the back roads (Apex-Macedonia and Holly Springs roads). Over 35 percent of the land is devoted to open space.

Oxxford Hunt

This is another residential community of about 450 homes and apartments in west Cary, located off Chatham Street. It has a mix of housing, from single family homes to condominiums and apartments. The landscaping is fully developed like so many Cary neighborhoods, new and old, and prices are more moderate, from $125,000 and up for the single family homes. Expect to see kids riding their bicycles here. Residents have access to jogging trails, tennis club and swimming pool, and it is close to **Fred Bond Park**.

The Parkway

This Planned Unit Development stretches along Cary Parkway and has become one of Cary's more popular addresses. It is located in west Cary and contains 20 separate neighborhoods with names like **Arlington Ridge**, **Candlewood** and **MacArthur Park**. As a PUD, it offers a variety of prices and includes rental units as well.

It is adjacent to two parks including 42-acre Bond Park, the town's largest. Its proximity to the **Prestonwood Country Club** and golf course have also been selling points. It also includes the new **Cary YMCA** complex, which has a pool and tennis courts. It is new and still building, so, if you like new neighborhoods where you can be a founding member, this may be the place for you.

Fred Bond Park in Cary is a favorite with the younger set.

Inside
Cary Parks and Recreation

Like other Triangle cities and towns, Cary enjoys a Sunbelt climate, so its residents have time to play year-round. You will see people running, playing tennis or golf, 12 months of the year. So, plan on maximizing your leisure time in Cary.

Here's a brief guide to some of the town's parks and recreation programs. Keep in mind that Cary is a late bloomer—only 3,500 people lived there in 1960—and its recreation programs are straining to take care of the town's current 60,000 people. That same growth, however, includes a silver lining in the name of PUDs or Planned Unit Developments. Cary has over 20 PUDs currently, which tend to offer their own recreational amenities to residents. Kildaire Farms, for example, has its own swimming pool with team swimming, a tennis complex and a nearby private racquetball club. The community is laced with jogging and walking trails that connect neighborhoods and include exercise stations along the way. Lochmere and Preston offer a similar menu of activities and have cham-

pionship golf courses in the middle of their neighborhoods.

The Guide focuses on the town's public programs. The town's **Parks and Recreation Department** is located at the Town Hall, 316 Academy St., 469-4061. Working hours are 8 a.m. to 5 p.m.

The town also has a very active YMCA on Cary Parkway that maintains its own youth and adult programs. Also, because Cary is so close to Raleigh, many of its residents belong to Raleigh clubs and organizations, such as the famed YMCA on Hillsborough Street or the Raleigh Racquet Club (swimming and serious tennis). Many of Raleigh's recreation programs are open to Cary residents, too, for a slight fee, such as the Pullen Park Acquatic Center—Cary has no public swimming pool. So, don't forget to check out the section on Raleigh's recreation. The listings are by activity and appear in alphabetical order.

Be sure to enjoy Summerfest at Regency Park and Cary's Lazy Daze, perhaps the town's biggest festival, both events described in our ATTRACTIONS section.

383

Parks

Cary has 13 public parks with six more on the planning boards. Listed below are some of special interest including two state parks that are nearby, **Reedy Creek** and **Umstead State Park**. Also, there is a Wake County park surrounding Lake Crabtree, which is one of the County's flood control lakes in north Cary. It has pleasant jogging trails and limited boating. And again, don't forget to check the Raleigh section because many Cary residents are closer to some Raleigh parks than some Raleigh residents. Lake Wheeler is one such example.

FRED BOND PARK
High House Rd.   *469-4100*
This 310-acre park, named after Cary's long-time mayor, is the town's showpiece. It has picnic shelters, three softball fields, a lake for fishing, boat rentals, fitness trail, amphitheater, playground and concessions. You can rent pedal boats, sailboats or fishing boats for a modest fee. The park is home to several annual events such as the Easter Egg Hunt and July 4th celebration.

HEMLOCK BLUFFS
Kildaire Farm Rd.   *469-4100*
This is a nature preserve in southern Cary, located between Tryon and Penny Roads. It contains about 150 acres and, as the name suggests, its featured attraction is a grove of Canadian hemlocks and a series of trails winding around the cool 90-foot bluffs. The

preserve is not for picknicking or camping, but for walking and observing. The state purchased the heart of the park and the town and private donors have added to it; the town maintains the park today, a good example of public-private sector cooperation.

Park tours are available on weekends, and guides will tell you that hemlocks used to be common in this part of the country 10,000 years ago. But time flies, and so did the hemlocks, except in special places like Hemlock Bluffs, which the good citizens of Cary and North Carolina have preserved for your hiking pleasure.

ANNIE JONES PARK
1414 Tarbert Dr.   *469-4061*
This park is located in southwest Cary off Cary Parkway. It has five tennis courts, four of which are lighted. There is a lighted ballfield, basketball courts and a comfort station.

ROBERT GODBOLD PARK
Northwest Maynard Rd.
This is one of the town's northernmost parks, not far from Northwoods Elementary School off Harrison Avenue. It is loaded with facilities, including four lighted tennis courts, two outdoor lighted basketball courts, playground equipment, volleyball courts, exercise trail, playfield and bathrooms.

LAKE CRABTREE COUNTY PARK
Off Aviation Parkway
This is a Wake County park located in Cary. It's a popular, 71-

acre park surrounding 500-acre Lake Crabtree, which you can see off I-40. It became locally famous in 1991-92 when the "Cary Flasher" made several appearances here along the jogging trails, but he was caught, and walkers and joggers returned to observing Mother Nature. The lake is not deep, from three to 10 feet, but it is stocked with bass, bluegill and catfish. Sailboats are available for rent at $6 an hour—there's a $10 deposit, too. Canoes and rowboats are cheaper. There are picnic shelters for rent, a playground and, when completed, six miles of trails. Enter off Aviation Parkway.

UMSTEAD STATE PARK
1800 N. Harrison Ave. 677-0062

This state park is really two-in-one, namely William B. Umstead and Reedy Creek State Parks. Both parks are connected and offer 5,214 acres of parkland right in the middle of the Triangle, next to Raleigh-Durham Airport. There are two entrances to the park, the Umstead entrance off U.S. Hwy. 70 and the Reedy Creek entrance, which is nearest to Cary, at the north end of Harrison Avenue, off Interstate 40. You cannot drive through, however.

The park has nature trails, fishing and rental boats, 28 campsites and four large campsites for

group camping such as church youth groups or Scouts. In the spring, go for a Sunday walk in the Reedy Creek section down by the creek where you will see the rhododendron bloom.

Sports

BASEBALL AND SOFTBALL

The Cary Parks and Recreation Department (469-4063) operates seven different leagues of youth baseball, starting with T-ball for 6-7 year olds, and going up to senior league players, ages 17-18. The coaches are volunteers and the emphasis is on sportsmanship. Registration is held in early March, usually on a Saturday. Fees are determined annually, so call for information. The girls' softball program has four leagues: ponytail (ages 8-10) through senior league (16 to 19). Registration times and places are the same as for the baseball leagues, as are the fees. In addition to the youth leagues, the town operates adult softball leagues for women and men. It also coordinates a slow-pitch church league and a coed league in the fall. There is also a men's fall league.

For information on registration times and places, call 469-4063. Games are played in one of five town parks with baseball fields, Annie Jones Park, Fred Bond Park, Lions, Ritter or Lexie Lane Park. Also check with the **Cary Softball Club** for older, more competitive AAU play.

BASKETBALL

The Cary Parks and Recreation Department (469-4063) sponsors boys and girls leagues, starting at age 9 and going through age 18. There are four boys' leagues and three for girls. Registration takes place in early October, and practice and games are held at the **Cary Community Center** at 404 N. Academy St. Costs are usually the same as in youth baseball. There are two adult basketball leagues, one in the fall and one in the winter for men age 35 or older. The **Cary YMCA** offers seven basketball leagues for children (K-12) and men. They play at the YMCA and at Kingswood Elementary. For more information call 469-9622.

DANCING

There are a number of dance groups in the Triangle area. To get more information, consult the Wake County Library's referral services or the **ARTS** section of this book. In Cary, there is a Plus Level square dance group, the **TNT Twirlers**, who meet weekly on Wednesdays at 8 p.m. While it is not a town-sponsored group, The Parks and Recreation Department (469-4063) provides contact information. Shag and Two-Step adult dance lessons are offered on a continuing basis at the **Cary Community Center** (460-4965).

DAY CAMP

The town offers a summer day camp for children, ages 6

through 11. It meets weekdays from 7:45 a.m. until 5:15 p.m. Activities include arts and crafts, drama, field trips, games, music and sports. There are four, one-week sessions, starting in mid-June and going through the first week in August. Call **The Cary Parks and Recreation Department** (469-4063) for fee and registration information. The **Cary YMCA** has two summer day camps for K-5. **Camp Rising Sun** meets at the Y and **Camp Outer Limits** meets at the West Cary Middle School. **Kindercamp** for ages 3-5 meets at the Y two half days a week. Call 469-9622 for more information.

FOOTBALL

The town can provide you with information on the youth football program, but it is operated by the **Cary Booster Club** (467-5827). It has three different divisions separated by age and weight. Youths can begin play as young as seven or as old as 15, provided they don't weigh more than 125 pounds. Registration is on the first two Saturdays in August at the Booster Club office at 411 West Chatham Street. Fees are determined annually.

GOLF

Like Raleigh, Cary has no municipally-owned golf course. Shame! Golfers do not want for courses, however. There are reportedly 18 courses open to the public in and around Raleigh and Cary. For a short list, see the "Raleigh" section in **GOLF**. Cary also has perhaps three of the best private club courses in the Triangle. They are:

LOCHMERE
2511 Kildaire Farm Rd.   *851-0611*

This is a championship course and is owned in part by the

former pro at MacGregor Downs. It is an 18-hole course and memberships sold briskly once they went on the market. The club is not limited to Lochmere residents, but you will need to call to find out membership costs and rules. Meanwhile, if you are invited to play as a guest, don't hesitate to tee off.

MacGregor Downs
430 St. Andrews Ln.   *467-0146*

This is the oldest of Cary's three members-only courses and it's considered one of the best in the Triangle. There is a lake around which the course winds. It is an 18-hole course and the site of tournaments. Memberships will cost more than Lochmere because the club is not limited to golf, but includes tennis, swimming and dining facilities. Again, if you're invited by a member to play here, accept.

Prestonwood
300 Prestonwood Pkwy.   *467-2566*

This is the newest of Cary's private courses and it boasts a name pro: Vance Haefner. It also has been the site of some of the Jordan League golf matches around the region and in 1994, a Nike League Tournament. It is a 45-hole championship course and club memberships are available to residents, corporations and non-residents of Preston. The clubhouse is magnificent.

Ice Skating

The Ice House
1410 Buck Jones Rd.   *467-6000*

This ice skating rink, located on Buck Jones Road behind the Ford dealership, opened late in 1986 and has been a big hit, especially with those cold-blooded Yankees addicted to ice hockey. For the locals, it's a novel experience to see people using ice for something other than to cool tea. The managers cater to families and offer lessons as well as ice hockey league play for adults and children. The rink has a well-stocked game room and snack bar for the hungry. You can rent skates for $1.50, and admission is $4 for adults, $3 for students and $2.50 for children. Ice House is open to the public seven days a week. Check for specific hours and for information on lessons or league play.

Racquetball

Cary Athletic Club
302-A Pebble Creek Drive   *467-5405*

The club has six courts, a Nautilus room and exercise classes. It is conveniently located near the Kildaire Farms tennis and swimming pool complex. Memberships are open to the public; they also have corporate memberships.

Running, Jogging

As noted earlier, many of the PUDs have their own jogging and running trails. The town also is developing its own greenway network. The system is designed to connect existing facilities such as schools with parks to churches and lakes. Existing trails total about nine miles and include the **Tarbert-Gatehouse Trail, Pirate's Cove, Maynard Oaks, Black Creek** and **Higgins Greenway**.

Cary is home to the **Cary Road Race**, sponsored by the *Cary News*. The race usually is scheduled in April and features a 5K and 10K course. It is one of the earlier races in the year, and serves as a good warm-up for some of the longer runs.

SOCCER

CAPITAL AREA SOCCER LEAGUE
3344 Hillsborough St.   834-3951
Cary is part of the Capital Area Soccer League (CASL), which is the largest program in the Southeast, with over 510 youth teams and 42 adult teams and over 8,000 participants. CASL runs fall and spring seasons for boys' and girls' teams. Children can start at age 6. Forms are available at local sports stores or the permanent CASL office in Raleigh. There is a fee per individual; children must buy their own uniforms and shoes.

SWIMMING

Amazingly, Cary has no municipal swimming pool, so most of the swimming is done at the many private swimming clubs connected to residential developments. Many of these clubs will accept members from outside their particular development. Some to check are **Kildaire Farms** (467-4314), and **Scottish Hills Recreation Club** (469-8109).

The **Cary YMCA** offers an extensive summer swimming program. Swimming priviliges are included in Y Memberships, but you can also join for just summer swimming. Call (469-9622) for further information.

Silver Lake, near Swift Creek, is a favorite swimming hole for Cary and Raleigh residents, and it has developed into one of the area's most popular public swimming parks. It features a 400-ft.-long waterslide, white sand beach, pedal boats, snack bar and picnic areas. It gladly accommodates groups.

TENNIS

In addition to the many private tennis clubs in Cary's planned communities, the town also maintains 14 tennis courts, of which 13 are lighted. Reservations are permitted during certain times of the year by calling the recreation office (467-4063). The department sponsors tennis lessons for a fee from May through August. There are four seasons for team tennis, too, with four levels of play. The town sponsors two tournaments: the **Polar Doubles** in January or February and **Cary Town Championships** in September. A popular league is the **"Ladies Morning Tennis Team"** play.

WALKING

You can go walking through your neighborhood or around the town's parks, but there's a special walking tour of Cary's historical places that will help you learn about the town and provide you with a little exercise, too. You can pick up a tour folder from the Chamber of Commerce on Chatham Street.

389

Line drawing by Jerry Miller.

First Baptist Church is the oldest southern Baptist church in Cary.

CARY WORSHIP

Inside
Cary Worship

If there is one element in Cary that has kept up with its growth, it's the churches. The town has over 38 listed by the Chamber of Commerce. Despite the influx of newcomers from outside the South, the largest number of churchgoers in Cary probably are Baptist. The Triangle area, however, is large enough now that most recognized faiths are represented in the community. The focus in this Guide is on some of the mainline and special churches; for additional information, check the Cary Chamber of Commerce's "Community Profile" and also the **RALEIGH WORSHIP** section in this book. Churches are listed alphabetically.

BETHEL BAPTIST
1111 West Chatham St. 467-6789
This is one of the larger independent Baptist congregations in Cary. The pastor is Bobby G. Jordan.

CARY PRESBYTERIAN
614 Griffis St. 467-8700
This is the oldest of the mainline Presbyterian congregations and one of the largest. It also operates a nursery and kindergarten. The Rev. J. David Wiseman is minister.

CHRIST THE KING LUTHERAN
600 Walnut St. 467-8989
The dean of the Lutheran congregations, this church has a preschool, too. Its pastor is the Rev. John Nagle.

FIRST BAPTIST CHURCH
218 S. Academy St. 467-6356
A pillar of downtown, First Baptist is the oldest and perhaps largest Southern Baptist church in Cary. Its programs include a preschool and kindergarten. It also has a Korean Mission for Korean Baptists in the Triangle. The pastor is the Rev. Harvey Duke.

FIRST UNITED METHODIST CHURCH
117 S. Academy St. 467-1861
This the oldest of Cary's United Methodist congregations and one of the town's biggest with over 2,000 members. Its minister is the Rev. Doug Jessee and it operates a preschool and kindergarten.

GREENWOOD FOREST BAPTIST CHURCH
110 E. Maynard Rd. 467-0481
Another large, Southern Baptist Church, Greenwood Forest's minister is the Rev. Luther Brewer. It, too, maintains a kindergarten and nursery.

Christ Among Us

WHITE PLAINS
UNITED METHODIST CHURCH

White Plains is an enthusiastic church family featuring dynamic corporate worship, excellent and varied music, and faith-building ministries for persons of all ages and stages of life. There is a congregation-wide commitment to make a transforming difference in all persons whose lives we are privileged to touch.

Christ, who has made a place for us here, invites you to find your church home among us as a friend and fellow disciple!

Sunday Morning
Worship Services
8:30 and 11:00AM

Sunday School
9:45AM

313 S.E. Maynard Road
Cary, NC 27511
919-467-9394

PEACE PRESBYTERIAN CHURCH
2850 S.W. Cary Pkwy.   *467-5977*

This congregation of 175 families belongs to the Presbyterian Church of America and started in Cary in 1979. The church has an active Bible study program and a number of its members are "home schoolers" who teach their children at home. The music program includes handbells and starts choristers at age three. The minister is Stephen D. Bostrom.

ST. MICHAEL'S CATHOLIC CHURCH
790 E. Maynard Rd.   *467-6026*

Like most Catholic parishes in the Triangle, this one is bulging. It is the only Catholic parish in Cary, and its priest is Father Kevin Fahey. It operates an early childhood center at the church.

ST. PAUL'S EPISCOPAL CHURCH
221 Union St.   *467-1477*

Like St. Michael's, St. Paul's is one of a kind in Cary with a congregation of about 500. The Rev. Charles Hocking is rector.

SYNAGOGUE BETH SHALOM
P.O. Box 5161   *481-1880*

This synagogue is Cary's one and only, and members meet in temporary space. The congregation consists of over 70 families who are members of the reformed movement. Started in 1983, it has an active Sunday School. The rabbi is Mike Moskowitz.

WHITE PLAINS UNITED METHODIST
313 E. Maynard Rd.   *467-9394*

This church was founded in 1961 and has become home to some

Peace Presbyterian Church PCA
Cary, N.C.

PEACE PRESBYTERIAN
"Growing in Grace & Peace."

2850 SW Cary Parkway • 467-5977
Corner of Cary Parkway & W. Chatham St.

830 families. It has active music and missions programs—members of the congregation in recent years have traveled to Jamaica. In its "children's center," it has one of the Triangle's few preschool programs that includes handicapped and "special needs" children with other children. Two ministers serve the church; the senior minister is Rev. W. Edward Privette.

Courtesy White Plains United Methodist.

Worshipers participate in the Christmas service at White Plains United Methodist church.

393

CHAMBER OF COMMERCE
CHAPEL HILL
CARRBORO

Dear Friends and Neighbors,

Chapel Hill is a university town. In Chapel Hill you will find the university (with a teaching hospital), a bunch of small shops, and lots of neighborhoods.

We enjoy all the benefits of being a university town. Chapel Hill was recently recognized by a major sports magazine as the best college town in America. The University of North Carolina provides many cultural, athletic, and educational opportunities for all.

Our population is just over 40,000, of which half are students. The citizenry is well educated and pro-education. Parental involvement in public education is tremendous. SAT scores and graduation rates of our students are among the highest in North Carolina.

Chapel Hill's beauty is protected by a billboard ban and quality appearance standards. We protect our trees, and there are lots of them.

We place great emphasis on our neighborhoods and our quality of life. Our close proximity to Raleigh, Durham, and Cary makes the amenities of the Triangle easily available to Chapel Hill citizens.

As you consider a place to live, give us a look. We don't think you will be disappointed.

Sincerely,

Joel K. Harper
President

TEL. 919.967.7075 ◆ FAX. 919.968.6874

P.O. BOX 2897 ◆ CHAPEL HILL ◆ NORTH CAROLINA 27515-2897

Inside
Chapel Hill

Chapel Hill is not your ordinary small Southern town. First of all, there is nothing ordinary about the people who live here: there are more Ph.D.'s per capita living in Chapel Hill than just about any other place on the planet.

Secondly, it's not all that Southern. Believe it or not, a higher percentage of the population here reads *The New Yorker* magazine than in the Big Apple. That's not to say that everyone who lives here comes from New York; they come from everywhere, many of them to study or teach at the University of North Carolina, to work in the Research Triangle Park, or to retire in the hospitable climate.

Come to think of it, Chapel Hill is not really very small, as North Carolina towns go. While the downtown still feels like a village, the town's population and borders have expanded considerably; today there are 40,000 residents, with another 20,000-plus students when the university is in session.

Finally, although Chapel Hill is geographically situated in the conservative Bible Belt, it has long been considered an oasis for liberals, and one of the most tolerant communities in the state. Perhaps that's why our notoriously conservative U.S. Senator Jesse Helms is said to have once suggested that instead of wasting tax dollars on a state zoo, we simply build a fence around Chapel Hill.

So it is that the "Southern part of heaven" has grown into a most unusual and appealing community. Chapel Hill is the home of UNC—the first state-owned university in the nation. In fact, in most parts of North Carolina, the words Chapel Hill and UNC are synonymous and, therefore, used interchangeably. For instance, if you sit at a lunch counter in any small town around the state and loudly express your fondness for the politics of Ted Kennedy, someone will undoubtedly raise an eyebrow and observe that you "must have gone to Chapel Hill." That doesn't mean they think you went shopping here; it means they are assuming you must have picked up your liberal views while attending the University of North Carolina in Chapel Hill.

It's not clear just when UNC and Chapel Hill picked up their reputations for being scandalously tolerant. Some would say it goes back to that fateful day in April 1865, when General Atkins of the Union forces then occupying Chapel Hill paid a visit to the home of University President Swain. It was there that the Yankee General met Swain's young daughter, Eleanor, and fell instantly in love. The two were married in August while students hung the General and the President in effigy. Later, someone recalling the disgrace scribbled on a classroom blackboard, "This old University . . . has busted and gone to hell."

If Chapel Hill's identity is inescapably intertwined with UNC's, it is because, like twins, their births occurred simultaneously. Legend has it that the location of both UNC and Chapel Hill was sealed one warm summer day in 1792 when a committee entrusted with selecting a site for the first state university embarked on its search mission.

They stopped to rest in the shade of a great tulip poplar, not far from the New Hope Chapel. Refreshed by a picnic lunch and a few rounds of "exhilarating" spirits, the group agreed this was the perfect spot for their university. It was beautiful, served by pure water from a nearby spring and, most importantly, "inaccessible to vice" (or so they thought). More likely than not, the site was really chosen because the property had been donated to the cause by some wealthy benefactors. At any rate, on October 12, 1793, a formal ceremony was held for laying the cornerstone of Old East, the university's first building. That same day, taking advantage of the crowd that had assembled, an auctioneer offered 22 large lots for sale in what would soon become the surrounding town.

Prior to the opening of the university, Chapel Hill was nothing

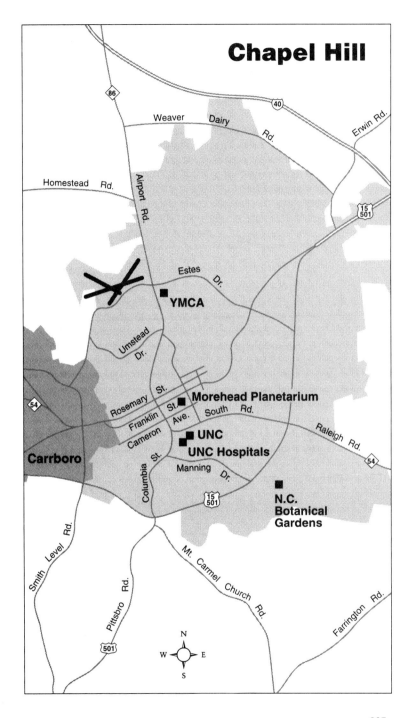

Chapel Hill

86

Weaver Dairy Rd.

40

Erwin Rd.

Homestead Rd.

Airport Rd.

15 501

Estes Dr.

■ **YMCA**

Umstead Dr.

Rosemary St.

Franklin St. ■ **Morehead Planetarium**

54

Cameron Ave. South Rd.

Raleigh Rd.

■ **UNC**
UNC Hospitals

54

Columbia St.

Carrboro

Manning Dr.

15 501

■ **N.C.**
Botanical
Gardens

Smith Level Rd.

Pittsboro Rd.

Mt. Carmel Church Rd.

Farrington Rd.

501

N
W E
S

more than a muddy crossroads in the wilderness, a hamlet of Scottish and English families who had arrived in the mid-1700s. The community took its name from the New Hope Chapel located on a hill overlooking a valley to the east. The hamlet contained perhaps a half-dozen houses, a blacksmith shop and an inn. The town of less than 1,000 inhabitants was incorporated in 1851 and elected its first mayor in 1879.

Meanwhile, west of Chapel Hill, another community had sprung up around the only railroad station that served the university. One student, on a train he thought was destined for the UNC campus, wrote of finding that he had been dropped off "in the middle of nowhere."

Eventually a settlement grew up around the railroad depot, consisting of a flour mill, a blacksmith shop and a cotton mill built in 1898 by Chapel Hillian Tom Lloyd. The community was known as West End, then West Chapel Hill and later Venable, for former UNC President Francis P. Venable. Finally after Lloyd's mill was purchased by the Julian Carr family of Durham, the town took the name of Carrboro, as it is still known today.

Although they grew up side by side, Chapel Hill and Carrboro were for years distinct communities. Chapel Hill evolved as a university village and a haven for liberal intellectuals, while Carrboro's population was made up of blue collar workers employed to service the university and the cotton mill. When Carr Mill shut down after the Great Depression, the town became more of a small bedroom community for people who worked at the university or its hospital. Right up through the 1970s, Chapel Hill and Carrboro maintained their distinct identities, one as the university village, the other as a small historic town. With the continuing surge of growth in the county, the two towns have grown together; however, merger of the two municipalities is not on the current agenda.

Downtown Chapel Hill still has a "village" feel, but a boom in residential construction in the last decade has brought many new citizens to the community. Meanwhile Carrboro has become one of the fastest growing municipalities in the Triangle and one of the most densely developed communities in the state. Its population of about 11,000 is expected to double by the end of the century. Vacant farmland and mill houses are rapidly being replaced by apartments and condominiums. The old cotton mill has been converted into a quaint shopping mall housing local businesses.

The interest in Chapel Hill and Carrboro can be linked to several factors. First, they offer the charm of small-town life with the sophistication of a university community tied to a booming metropolis. Second, they are accessible to a number of desirable jobs nearby in Research Triangle Park. And finally, with the recent extension of Interstate 40, Chapel Hill and Carrboro are within convenient commuting distance to Raleigh. It's impossible to maintain the charm of village life while attracting thousands of newcomers each year. And that is the challenge facing local officials here today.

Residents of Chapel Hill and Carrboro, like their counterparts in the other cities of the Triangle, worry that runaway development will destroy what is unique about their communities. They may have a reputation for tolerance, but one thing they cannot stand is unsightly development, hence some rather restrictive zoning laws. Today citizens and elected officials are continuing to work together to ensure the preservation of those qualities that make their towns such attractive places to live and work. In the following pages we will introduce you to life in the bustling communities of Chapel Hill and Carrboro. We'll give you a tour of some of their neighborhoods, acquaint you with the school systems, and introduce you to recreational facilities, parks, and places of worship. You will find additional information about Chapel Hill and Carrboro in our special sections covering everything from **AIRPORTS** to **SHOPPING**.

The Orange County Court Building is also home
to the Franklin Street branch of the U. S. Post Office.

Inside

Chapel Hill Government Services and Utilities

When you're new in town, it can take forever to sort out the local do's and don'ts. Here's a handy guide that we hope will make it a little easier for you to get set up in Chapel Hill or Carrboro. For more information, call the **Chapel Hill Town Hall** at 968-2757, the **Carrboro Town Hall** at 942-8541 or the **Chapel Hill-Carrboro Chamber of Commerce** at 967-7075. Ask the folks at the Chapel Hill Town Hall for a copy of their guide "*Information for New Residents of Chapel Hill, Town Services and Policies.*"

EMERGENCY CALLS
DIAL 911
NON-EMERGENCY CALLS
(CHAPEL HILL)

Police	968-2760
Fire	968-2781
Ambulance	929-8109

ABC Laws

In Chapel Hill and Carrboro, as in most areas of the Triangle, you buy your liquor at the ABC stores operated by the state Alcoholic Beverage Commission. ABC stores are located in Eastgate Shopping Center (off U.S. Highway 15-501) in Chapel Hill and in Carrboro Plaza off N.C. Highway 54 in Carrboro; there is also an ABC store on U.S. Highway 15-501 South just south of Chapel Hill in Chatham County. The stores are open from 9 a.m. to 9 p.m. Monday through Saturday. You can buy beer and wine at most supermarkets and convenience stores, seven days a week depending on the store's hours. However, remember that alcoholic beverages are not sold on Sunday until after

12:00 noon (a recent change from the former hour of 1 p.m.). Mixed drinks are available at most luncheon and dinner restaurants in Chapel Hill and Carrboro.

State laws prohibit the establishment of facilities designed only for imbibing spirits; therefore, places that serve alcohol must also serve food to chase the drinks down. And don't be surprised if, when you venture outside of the cities of the Triangle, there are a few remaining places you cannot purchase liquor, beer or wine at all. In each county and municipality, it's up to the voters to decide if booze will be available, and in what fashion. For example, in rural Chatham County just south of Chapel Hill, you can sip beer and wine in several restaurants, but you can't get a legal drink of whiskey. You can, however, buy your bottled liquor at the local ABC stores. In some parts of North Carolina, the only way you can get any spirits at all is to find the nearest bootlegger and be prepared to pay premium prices for store-bought goods bootlegged from the next county.

We've also got some pretty stiff drunk-driving laws now. As of October 1993, if you get pulled over by a state trooper and blow 0.08 or more on the breathalyzer test, you're in a heap of trouble. (You're also probably pretty drunk.) You can lose your license, go straight to jail (do not collect $200) and be required to perform some community service. In addition, under the "dram shop" provision of the law, restaurant owners or even hosts and hostesses of private parties can be held liable if someone drinking at their place gets into an automobile accident involving property damage, personal injury or death. The minimum drinking age in North Carolina for beer, wine and liquor is 21.

Automobile Insurance, Licenses, Registration And Tags

Out-of-state licenses and plates are valid for 30 days after North Carolina residency is established. But get yours switched as soon as possible because our friendly state troopers will pull you over just to check if you've been here more than 30 days. For your new license, go to the **North Carolina Driver's License Examiner's Office** at Carrboro Plaza Shopping Center on N.C. Highway 54 West. You will be asked to take written, road sign recognition and vision tests. Study the book you get there; it's not as easy as you might think. In some cases, a driving test may be required. The office is open from 8 a.m. to 5 p.m. Monday through Friday. Fees range from $10 to $20, depending on classification, and must be paid in cash. Licenses are good for four years and expire on the driver's birthday. Call 929-4161 for more information.

If you need a new license plate, go to the **North Carolina Motor Vehicle License Plate Agency** at University Mall in Chapel Hill (967-7059). Before your auto can be registered, you must provide a title to the vehicle, your insurance company's name and a policy number, an odometer reading and photo identification. Automobile owners can also expect to receive a personal property tax bill on the car within a few months of registering the auto. Safety inspections must be done, in most cases, within 10 days after initial plates are purchased and then on an annual basis. This can be done at most service stations.

Government

Chapel Hill, Carrboro and Orange County are run by the council-manager form of government. The governing bodies consist of the Town Council and Mayor in Chapel Hill; the Board of Aldermen and the Mayor in Carrboro, and the Board of County Commissioners and the Manager in Orange County. The county seat is Hillsborough. Orange County residents elect two state senators and two representatives to the General Assembly. Chapel Hill and Carrboro are located in the 4th U.S. Congressional District (See **"Voting"** section below).

Maps

One of the first things you will want when you get to town is a decent map to help you figure out where you are. Good maps of Chapel Hill, Carrboro and the school districts are available from the Chapel Hill-Carrboro Chamber of Commerce at W. Franklin Street in downtown Chapel Hill. Call 967-7075.

Pet Regulations

Chapel Hill ordinances require dog leashes, tags and rabies vaccination. All dogs must be leashed, in a vehicle or in an enclosure when off the dog owner's property. Dogs and cats older than 4 months must have a current rabies vaccination. And dogs older than 3 months are required to have current dog tags ($3 for spayed or under 9 months, $5 for all others). For more information call the animal control office at 968-2760.

Taxes

Chapel Hill, Carrboro and Orange County do not tax personal income, but all residents must list personal and real estate property for taxation each January, by mail or at the Orange County courthouse. If you live within the town limits of Chapel Hill and Carrboro, you will pay property tax to those municipalities in addition to the property tax you pay to the county. North Carolina's sales tax is 6 percent. Two percent of this is returned to the county and municipalities.

Transportation

Chapel Hill Transit provides bus and shared-ride service throughout Chapel Hill. Buses run regularly 7 a.m. to 6:30 p.m. weekdays, with less frequent service in the evening and on weekends. Buses also run less often when the university is not in session. Printed schedules are available at local stores and banks. Call 968-2769 for fares and further information. In some areas where buses do not run, residents can call Chapel Hill Transit at 968-2772 and request a ride to the nearest bus stop for the price of regular bus fare. This service, called "shared-ride feeder service," is available in a number of areas in town. A special **"E-Z Rider"** service is provided for people who have mobility handicaps or are unable to use regular bus service.

TRI-A-RIDE, the Triangle's regional ride-sharing program, provides information for commuters wishing to organize or join a carpool or vanpool. For more information call 549-9999.

Utilities

You can usually expect to have your gas, electricity, water and sewer service turned on the same day (or, at the latest, the next day after you apply) if you call or go to the appropriate office first thing in the morning. But Murphy's Law being what it is, we wouldn't put this chore off until Friday morning, because if your service isn't on by 5 p.m. you will have to wait until Monday. Phone service can take at least two or three days and more if you've never had local service before.

CABLE TV

Carolina Cable, 1129 Weaver Dairy Road, Chapel Hill (968-4631) services Chapel Hill and parts of Hillsborough. Carrboro is served by **CVI** (967-7068).

ELECTRICITY

For electric power service, apply at **Duke Power Company** on Homestead Road, west of N.C. Highway 86/Airport Road (967-8231). Renters should expect to pay a deposit. Allow a minimum of 24 hours for service to be connected. **Piedmont Electric**, on N.C. Highway 86 south of Hillsborough, serves most of rural Orange County. A deposit may be required. Call 732-2123.

GAS

Apply for service at **Public Service Company**, 200 Elliott Road (942-5104). Renters will be asked to show proof of their address and pay a deposit based on the number of rooms.

TELEPHONE

Apply for service by calling **Southern Bell** at 780-2355. You may be asked to pay a deposit, and you should allow at least two or three more working days if you are moving into a new residence that has not had phone service before.

WATER AND SEWER

Apply to **Orange Water and Sewer Authority (OWASA)** at 968-4421. Renters should expect to pay a deposit.

Voting

To register to vote you must be a U.S. citizen, a non-felon, at least 18 years of age by the date of the upcoming election, and a resident of North Carolina and your precinct for 30 days prior to the next election. You can register year-round at the **Chapel Hill Town Hall** (8 a.m. to 5 p.m.), the **Carrboro Town Hall**, the **Chapel Hill Public Library** (call first, 968-2777), and the **Board of Elections** (967-9251) and the **Orange County Library** (732-8181), both in Hillsborough. For more information, call the **County Board of Elections** at 967-9251. Registration books close 21 working days before an election.

State and county elections are held every even year; city and school board elections every odd year. Primaries are held in May. The Mayors of Chapel Hill and Carrboro are elected for two-year terms; the council members of each town, members of the Chapel Hill-Carrboro school board, and County Commissioners hold four-year overlapping terms. Members of the Orange County school board hold six-year overlapping terms.

Members of the General Assembly serve two-year terms. North Carolina's two U.S. Senators are elected to staggered six-year terms. Senator Jesse Helms' seat was re-elected in 1990. Lauch Faircloth was elected to North Carolina's other Senate seat in 1992. Representative David Price currently serves Orange County and the 4th District in the U.S. House of Representatives. Members serve two-year terms.

Community Service Numbers

The Southern Bell phone book includes a great listing of community services numbers (see the customer guide index in the front of the phone book). They range from crisis hotlines, family planning, and mental and physical health services, to senior citizens, veterans' and women's services. This list includes public agencies and nonprofit organizations and was compiled by the **Interfaith Council for Social Service**.

405

Photo by Nancy Kitchener.

In addition to its natural beauty, the convenient location makes Franklin Street a favorite neighborhood for UNC faculty and administrators.

Inside
Chapel Hill-Carrboro Neighborhoods

Chapel Hill has come a long way from that autumn day in 1793 when an auctioneer offered the first 22 lots for sale in the new university village. Today, this growing town of 40,000 residents and more than 20,000 students is considered one of the most desirable addresses in the Southeast.

It's not hard to understand why so many people want to live here. Despite the pressures of new commercial and residential development, Chapel Hill still exudes the charm of a historic university village. Add to that some of the best public schools in the state and access to Research Triangle Park, Raleigh and Durham, and it is no wonder Chapel Hill has become a haven for young families, professionals and retirees.

The demand for housing translates into some of the highest home prices in the Triangle, although Raleigh and Durham are quickly catching up. In 1992, the average sales price of a home in Orange County was $138,950. Large older homes or custom-built new homes in some of the finer neighborhoods can easily cost $250,000 or more. And although it's been more of a buyer's market of late, if you see an attractive listing in the newspaper, don't be surprised to find several other bidders vying to make a deal on the same house.

Real estate prices in Carrboro are generally somewhat lower than in Chapel Hill. There you can still find single-family homes in the $100,000 to $150,000 range for a three- to four-bedroom new home, which can be hard to locate in Chapel Hill proper. And some folks are choosing to build on land in the rolling countryside to the north and south where an acre sells for anywhere from $12,000 to $40,000+, depending on how close it is to town.

Both Chapel Hill and Carrboro also offer a wide range of condominiums and townhomes, from $30,000 for a small one-bedroom unit to $175,000 and up for a luxury apartment. After a glut of townhomes on the market several years ago, they are now a hot item again, generally selling quickly to retirees, small families and singles.

In the following pages we'll show you a sample of neighborhoods in Chapel Hill and Carrboro. We'll start with some of the most desirable ones in the heart of both communities, then head for newer areas surrounding them. For further information and help in choosing a home, condominium or apartment, call a local real estate agency listed in our **TRIANGLE HOMES** section.

CHAPEL HILL NEIGHBORHOODS

HISTORIC DISTRICTS

One way to get around Chapel Hill's traffic and parking problems is to live and work right in town. Chapel Hill has two Historic Districts. The first, **Franklin-Rosemary District**, established in 1976, includes sections of the town's main thoroughfares, Franklin Street (Chapel Hill's main business street, named for Ben) and Rosemary Street, a block to the north. (It is said that Rosemary Street was so named to honor a Lady Rose who lived at one end and a Lady Mary who lived at the other.)

The second, the **Cameron-McCauley Historic District** was established in 1990, takes in an area ranging from just south of West Franklin Street to the University Drive area, and encompasses such landmarks as the **Carolina Inn**. Both districts are within walking distance of the campus and many restaurants and stores. These are two of the most convenient neighbor-

hoods for university faculty and medical center personnel, if the often large and gracious homes are not out of one's price range.

Here's where you'll find rambling, brick or wood-frame colonials, many built in the 1920s and '30s. Expect to pay $200,000 for a home that needs work, and $300,000 or more for one that's been remodeled and updated. Also in this area is a unique neighborhood centering around **Cobb Terrace**, a narrow winding circular road, featuring a mix of larger colonials and more modest wood-frame homes and cottages on smaller lots.

GIMGHOUL

Believe it or not, Chapel Hill even has its own mysterious castle, for which this striking neighborhood is named. **Gimghoul Castle**, located at the east end of Gimghoul Road, owes its existence to the romantic fantasies of a former law student, Edward Wray Martin (class of 1891). Seems that Martin, a devoted reader of Arthurian legends, liked to walk in this hilly wooded area and look out over what was then a great plain, where he envisioned a castle rising from a sea of pines and oaks. He apparently told his friends of his dreams. In 1915 two students who belonged to the Secret Order of the Gimghouls, persuaded their fellow members to purchase 94 acres here to build a castle for their lodge. In 1924, a local architect and UNC graduate was hired to design a building to be "medieval and mysterious-looking." Masons from Valdese in the western North Carolina mountains filled the bill; the ivy-covered stone castle continues to be the meeting place of the Secret Order of the Gimghouls to this day.

Nearby is **Dromgoole's Tomb**, a rock marked by blotches of iron oxide resembling blood stains, alluding to a legendary and apparently mythical duel in which a UNC student named Peter Dromgoole is said to have shed his blood (others say it was his foe's blood that was spilled) in a fight over the affections of his sweetheart, Miss Fanny.

Gimghoul is indeed a storybook neighborhood with its low stone walls and winding, narrow lanes barely wide enough for a car. As in the Historic District to the north, homes here are 2,000 square feet or more and tend to be 50- to 60-year-old wood-frame and brick colonials. Some are situated on large, well-landscaped yards; others are nestled on the top or sides of bluffs looking into the woods of adjacent **Battle Park**, where the **Forest Theatre**, an outdoor rock amphitheater, occasionally hosts dramatic productions and outdoor weddings.

Homes in this historic neighborhood generally sell for $250,000 or more, depending on size and condition. But don't hold your breath; homeowners tend to hang on to these gems until they die or get divorced, and when they finally do hit the market they are sold almost immediately.

GLENDALE

If you like the idea of owning a home adjacent to **Battle Park**, but you favor more contemporary architectural styles, Glendale is for you. Located between Franklin Street and the northern perimeter of the park are magnificent contemporary homes built into the sides of hardwood-covered bluffs overlooking the woods. Here you'll see a variety of contemporary styles including ranches and split-levels on hillside lots large enough to convey the feeling that you are in the wooded countryside, rather than a few minutes from downtown Chapel Hill. Here homes built in the 1960s sell for $185,000 to $275,000.

GREENWOOD

Just southeast of Glendale and Battle Park and still a pleasant walk to campus is Greenwood, featuring a mix of traditional and more contemporary homes. Prices here are in the $175,000 up to the $400,000 range for the large custom homes built in the last several years.

WESTWOOD

Until 1950, the town of Chapel Hill was composed of 850 acres. Another 289 acres were annexed east of town that year and in 1951 the town took in 61 acres, which today make up the neighborhoods of Westwood and Forest Hills to its south.

Westwood is located along a winding, hilly drive across Columbia Street from the **UNC Hospitals**. Here you'll find large two- and three-story traditional homes of brick or wood, many built in the 1950s. They feature hardwood floors, high ceilings, sweeping porches and spacious yards framed by low stone walls.

Home prices go up from about $200,000 for a fixer-upper to $350,000 plus for a recently remodeled home.

FOREST HILLS

Next to Westwood is another neighborhood of generally smaller homes of a similar vintage. Here you'll see a variety of home styles and sizes from modest wood-frame cottages to larger traditionals and a sprinkling of newer homes. Prices are in the $150,000 to $250,000 range.

FRANKLIN HILLS

This new in-town development off East Franklin Street boasts stately two- and three-story homes with plenty of custom features: gourmet kitchens, formal dining rooms, jacuzzis, vaulted ceilings, winding stairwells, porches, upper balconies, and more. Expect to pay $300,000 to $400,000.

KINGS MILL ROAD

Heading east of Chapel Hill, off the U.S. Highway 15-501 bypass are two 1950s neighborhoods known as Glen Lennox and Kings Mill Road. In **Glen Lennox**, you'll find mostly frame and brick ranches, selling for $100,000 to $150,000. In **King's Mill**, adjacent to the **N.C. Botanical Gardens**, homes are larger and prices are higher, usually $150,000 to $200,000 and up.

THE OAKS AND THE OAKS II AND III

East of Glen Lennox is this newer neighborhood surrounding the **Chapel Hill Country Club** and its golf course. It features a mix of traditional and contemporary homes. In the Oaks II and III, you'll find sprawling custom homes of brick, stone, stucco and wood on spacious lots with greenway views. Most feature large living rooms, spacious master suites, cathedral ceilings, arched windows, detailed woodwork and two- or three-car garages. Some homes in the Oaks II and III are in the Durham County school system. Expect to pay $350,000 and up, with asking prices in the neighborhood reaching up to $1 million. Some lots in the Oaks are available, beginning at about $100,000.

MT. BOLUS/WINDING RIDGE

Heading north of town off Airport Road you'll turn east into another neighborhood with a legendary name. Mt. Bolus is the magnificent hill rising above Bolin Creek. It was named for Joseph Caldwell, the first official UNC president whom the students affectionately called Diabolus (devil), or Bolus for short. Seems that Caldwell was unusually vigilant in tracking down and subduing the more mischievous students of his day. Today **Mt. Bolus** offers a mixture of traditional, ranch and contemporary homes clinging to the sides of steep hard-wood shaded bluffs.

Just south of Mt. Bolus Road is a new neighborhood called **Winding Ridge**. It features several spacious homes with an abundance of custom detail such as oak panelling, granite kitchen counters and wine cellars. These neighborhoods offer lots of privacy and wooded views, all just minutes from UNC and downtown. Prices vary with the size and location of each home, but generally range from $250,000 to $400,000. Lots are available for $50-$60,000.

HIDDEN HILLS, ESTES HILLS, COKER HILLS AND COKER HILLS WEST

These family neighborhoods are located in the wedge-shaped area between East Franklin Street and Airport Road. They feature a variety of ranch, contemporary and colonial homes, some built in the 1960s, others in the 1980s. They are on mid-size to large lots and are convenient to both elementary and middle schools. Prices range from $15,000 to $400,000.

OLD FOREST CREEK

Just off Piney Mountain Road, this newer development runs along Rock Creek within walking distance of Estes Hills Elementary and Phillips Middle schools. Larger traditional and contemporary homes here feature wood, stucco

and stone exteriors; cathedral ceilings; formal dining rooms and spacious master bedrooms. All are within walking distance of town and UNC. Prices are in the $220,000 to $300,000 range.

IRONWOODS/NORTH HAVEN AT IRONWOODS

Just 2.5 miles north of town off Estes Drive, these developments offer wooded lots and spacious traditional and contemporary homes with custom features. Prices begin around $185,000, and a few lots in the $40-50,000 range are still available for custom building.

LAKE FOREST

What's special about this neighborhood is that it has its own private lake, **Eastwood Lake**, large enough for fishing and boating. Like the neighborhoods to the south, Lake Forest offers a variety of housing styles from New England and American colonials to ranches, split levels and other contemporaries, most built in the 1960s and 70s. Prices range from $180,000 to $600,000-plus for a large property with a pool and its own dock on the lake.

BOOKER CREEK

Northeast of Lake Forest is Booker Creek, a neighborhood featuring one- and two-story traditional homes. Most homes in Booker Creek are 1,800 to 2,500 square feet, and prices range from $165,000 to $200,000.

COUNTRYSIDE

Heading north, just above **Cedar Falls Park**, is Countryside, a neighborhood of one- and two-story homes ranging in size from 1,500 to 2,200 square feet. These homes sell for about $140,000 to $185,000.

CEDAR HILLS AND TIMBERLYNE

Just north and west of Countryside along Weaver Dairy Road are two neighborhoods offering traditional and contemporary homes from 1,800 to 3,000 square feet. These neighborhoods are popular with families, and homes here sell for $185,000 to $300,000 and up for a large house with many custom features.

STONERIDGE AND SEDGEFIELD

Further north of Chapel Hill, on the other side of Interstate 40, are two developments of gracious contemporary and traditional homes with the privacy afforded by wooded lots of one acre or more. **Stoneridge** also has a private racquet and swim club in the neighborhood. This location provides easy access to Research Triangle Park, Durham, Raleigh and RDU Airport. Prices range from $200,000 to $500,000 and up.

SOUTHBRIDGE

Just south of Chapel Hill, across from Culbreth Middle School, is a newer development featuring two-story traditional and transitional homes on hilly terrain. This

is a popular neighborhood for medical and university faculty due to its proximity to UNC. Homes sell for $140,000 to $250,000, and new homes are still being constructed.

CULBRETH PARK/TANDLER

These are two new, planned developments in Chapel Hill, designed to provide affordable housing in a tight marketplace. **Culbreth Park** is next to the school of the same name, and **Tandler** is closer to the UNC campus off Merritt Mill Road. Home prices range from $85,000 to $135,000, depending on whether the buyer is eligible for a subsidy based on family income level. See a realtor for more information.

MORGAN CREEK HILLS, FARRINGTON HILLS AND LAUREL HILL

These three neighborhoods offer a mix of home styles on large, wooded lots in the rolling countryside off Mount Carmel Church Road south of town. Homes here start at about $200,000 and go as high as $350,000 or more.

DOGWOOD ACRES

A few miles south of town, between U.S. Highway 15-501 and Smith Level Road is this older neighborhood of small cottages and ranch-style homes. Although Dogwood Acres is not in the Chapel Hill city limits, it is within the boundaries of the Chapel Hill-Carrboro school district. One of the more affordable neighborhoods in town,

Photo by Veryl Barry.

In addition to single family dwellings, both Chapel Hill and Carrboro offer a wide variety of condominiums and townhomes.

Dogwood Acres is a good place to look for a first home. Homes start at about $95,000.

HERITAGE HILLS

Like Dogwood Acres, Heritage Hills is south of the town limits but within the Chapel Hill-Carrboro school district. Homes here are 15 to 20 years old and start at about $110,000. Heritage Hills offers a private swimming pool and tennis courts.

DOWNING CREEK/DOWNING WOODS

The Downing Creek and Downing Woods neighborhoods are located off N.C. Highway 54 east of Chapel Hill. The neighborhoods offer homeowners homesites amid buffered forests, custom-built transitional homes and a private swim/tennis club. Though the address is Chapel Hill, these neighborhoods are in the Durham Public Schools district. Homes are convenient to Chapel Hill, Research Triangle Park and Interstate 40, and are priced from $185,000 to $300,000.

FALCONBRIDGE

Located midway between Chapel Hill and Durham on N.C. Highway 54, Falconbridge offers townhomes and single-family residences convenient to the cultural, educational and employment opportunities afforded by both towns. It's also minutes from Jordan Lake and Research Triangle Park and is served by Durham Public Schools.

Falconbridge offers traditional and contemporary single-family homes ($160,000 to $275,000) and 231 townhomes (starting at about $110,000). There is a private clubhouse with tennis courts and a swimming pool. Lots of about one-third of an acre are available for $45,000 to $50,00.

Carrboro Neighborhoods

WEBBWOOD

Just north of downtown Carrboro off N. Greensboro Street is Webbwood, a neighborhood featuring a blend of modest traditional and contemporary homes built in the 1970s. Prices start around $110,000.

SPRING VALLEY

If you drive through Webbwood, you will come to a brand new development called Spring Valley, featuring two-story rustic-contemporary homes, many with a view of a man-made pond. Homes here start at about $120,000-$130,000.

BARRINGTON HILLS

Travel north of Webbwood out Old Highway 86 and you'll come to Barrington Hills. Here you'll find modest contemporary homes built in the late 1970s, starting at over $115,000.

BOLIN FOREST/ QUARTERPATH TRACE

Just south of Webbwood are Bolin Forest, a neighborhood of two- and three-bedroom homes ranging from about $120,000 to $185,000, and Quarterpath Trace. Homes here are three- to four-bedrooms, and prices range from $165,000 to $200,000.

PLANTATION ACRES

Wedged between North Greensboro Street and Old Highway 86 is Plantation Acres, a family neighborhood of ranch-style homes built in the 1960s. Most are three-bedroom houses, that sell for $90,000 to $135,000.

WINDWOOD

West of downtown Carrboro is Windwood, another neighborhood of ranch homes built in the 1960s. These are smaller houses selling in a similar price range.

WEATHERHILL

These award-winning cluster and patio homes are adjacent to the **Chapel Hill Tennis Club**. In the $120,000 to $150,000 range, these are some of the more affordable of the single-family homes built in the area in the last five to ten years.

MORGAN GLEN

Not long ago, a 112-acre farm west of Carrboro went on the market. It was the largest tract of undi-vided land within Carrboro's zoning jurisdiction. Several developers thought it would carve up nicely into 60 or more lots. But Gary Phillips and the partners of **Weaver Street Realty and Auction Company** were worried that a dense residential development would harm the fragile ecosystem of the creek, endanger wildlife and pose a serious threat to the quality of University Lake, the area's water supply. So they took an option on the land with the idea of turning it into a model development to demonstrate that land stewardship and profit don't have to be mutually exclusive principles.

The result is Morgan Glen, a pastoral residential development including eleven 10-acre tracts, with restrictions against further subdivision. A 150-foot swath along Morgan Creek was given to the **Triangle Land Conservancy** for a perpetual wildlife conservation easement. All property owners have access to the creek which runs through the development. And the easement allows wildlife to coexist with people on the property. A few 10-acre lots are available for $100,000 to $150,000; houses are selling for $300,000 to $450,000.

Chatham County Neighborhoods

FEARRINGTON

Fearrington is located about eight miles south of Chapel Hill in rural Chatham County. When completed, this planned development on a former dairy farm will house an estimated 5,000 people, about the size of the largest town in Chatham County.

Fearrington features rustic-contemporary homes and condo-miniums clustered around greenways, tennis courts, a four-star restaurant (see **"Chapel Hill"** section of **RESTAURANTS**) and a market area. The **Fearrington Village Center** includes a cafe, book-store, pottery shop, gardening store and jewelry store, among others (see "Chapel Hill" section in **SHOPPING**), as well as a country inn (see **ACCOMMODATIONS**).

Fearrington is very popular with retirees to the area, but is home to young families as well. Children living here attend Chatham County schools. Home prices start at about $130,000 and can be more than double that for the larger homes now under construction in the newest phases of the development, such as Camden Park.

The lower property taxes and often lower home prices of Chatham County have helped Fearrington and other smaller developments in this area prosper. You can find a three-bedroom home in one north Chatham community for $88,000. There are also still many two- to ten-acre tracts to build on. For more information on home and land sales in Chatham County, follow the real estate listings in *The Chapel Hill News,* as well as *The Chatham Record* in Pittsboro.

THE GOVERNORS CLUB

One of several exclusive golfing communities going up around the Triangle, the Governors Club is situated on 1,600 rolling acres adjacent to Jordan Lake on scenic Edwards Mountain, about four miles south of Chapel Hill. Among its many features is an 18-hole golf course designed by Jack Nicklaus, horse trails and footpaths, a private swim and tennis club and a full-service country club.

Developers of the Governors Club have attracted both retirees and professionals and executives with families. Plans call for about 700 single-family homes, golf villas, townhouses, patio homes and "club cottages" with home prices starting at around $290,000. Lots are available for custom building, and the country club memberships go for $16,000.

New Development

There is plenty of new development around Chapel Hill and Carrboro, offering condominiums, townhomes and single family homes for a wide range of prices. Here's a list of some newer neighborhoods in and around town.

SINGLE FAMILY HOMES

You can still find new homes in the Carrboro area at the lower end of the price spectrum and **Fairoaks**, off North Greensboro Street, is a good example. Three-bedroom homes here are priced in the $105,00 to $125,000 range.

Most new development in Chapel Hill is presently on the north side of town. In **Laurel Springs**, homes of 2,000 to 3,000-plus square feet sell for $175,000 to $275,000. Off Homestead Road close to Chapel Hill High School and Seawell Elementary is **The Highlands** and **Wexford**, one of the newest developments. Here, large transitional homes are priced in the $210,000 to $325,000 range. And in the new neighborhoods of **Chesley** and **Chandler's Green** along Weaver Dairy Road, large, elegant homes in the $295,000 to $500,000 range are under construction.

On the south side of Chapel Hill near Southbridge (mentioned above), Cazwell Properties has built some attractive two- to four-bedroom homes in **Glenmere**, priced from $165,000. And east of town is **Colony Woods East**, where three- and four-bedroom models start around $180,000.

In Chatham County, development has begun at **ArborLea**, where three- to five-acre tracts of land are available for custom building. And, off Mann's Chapel Road, the new **Highland Forest** neighborhood has new homes for sale in the $140,000 to $160,000 range.

Townhomes And Condos

On the east side of Chapel Hill you'll find townhomes in the $90,000 to $110,000 range at **Colony Lake**, and over $100,000 at **The Meadows**. On the northeast edge of Carrboro, ranging from $30,000 to $175,000 in price.

Photo courtesy N.C. Travel and Tourism Division.

Sailing and windsurfing are popular activities on nearby Lake Jordan.

Inside

Chapel Hill-Carrboro Parks and Recreation

Both Chapel Hill and neighboring Carrboro have their own parks and recreation departments, providing acres of park land and a wide variety of activities for Orange County residents of all ages. Together the two departments provide 10 ball fields, 21 lighted tennis courts, three gymnasiums and two swimming pools.

The Chapel Hill Parks and Recreation Department oversees nine parks, two playgrounds, a pair of community centers and one separate athletic field. It also offers an amazing assortment of activities including adult volleyball as well as youth and adult tennis, swimming, basketball, baseball, softball and lacrosse. You can sign up for outdoor programs and trips involving rock climbing, kayaking or skiing, or take classes in everything from martial arts to pottery. The department sponsors special activities for senior citizens and handicapped persons.

In addition, Carrboro's own Recreation and Parks Department has plenty of similar activities. It maintains more than 72 acres of park land at six locations, providing ball fields, basketball courts, playgrounds, tennis courts, nature trails and a lake. And, like Chapel Hill's recreation department, it offers a wide range of athletic programs for both youth and adults including basketball, softball, baseball, volleyball and football. You can sign up for classes and workshops on all sorts of activities, like aerobic dancing, tennis, basketry and stained-glass classes, or you can participate in the annual fishing rodeo or kite-flying field day. In Chapel Hill and Carrboro, some activities are free but most require a nominal charge or registration fee.

Along with all the activities and facilities sponsored by the parks and recreation departments, Chapel Hill-Carrboro area residents are also served by private programs and clubs such as Rainbow Soccer (for kids) and Sunset Soccer (for adults), the YMCA, and a number of swim and tennis clubs and health spas.

Here's a handy guide to help you sort it all out. First we'll list the facilities at each of the parks in

419

Chapel Hill and Carrboro, followed by an index to specific recreational activities, classes and programs available through both public and private sponsors. For a schedule of activities and more information, contact the Chapel Hill Parks and Recreation Department at 968-2784 or the Carrboro Recreation and Parks Department at 968-7703.

Chapel Hill Parks

HARGRAVES PARK

This park has three lighted tennis courts, athletic fields, basketball goals, play equipment, recreation center, outdoor pool, picnic and play areas. Volleyball courts are on the drawing board.

UMSTEAD PARK

Not to be confused with Umstead State Park located between Raleigh and Durham, this town park is located on Umstead Drive in Chapel Hill. One lighted tennis court, athletic fields, basketball court, nature and fitness trails, recreation center, picnic shelter, play areas and a volleyball court are available.

OAKWOOD PARK

This park has one lighted tennis court, picnic facilities and a wonderful play area designed for kids to really have fun!

CEDAR FALLS PARK

This facility offers six lighted tennis courts, ball fields, nature trails, picnic and play areas. Fitness trails and a basketball court are planned. The park is convenient to

Booker Creek, Chesley, Chandler's Green and Countryside/Cedar Falls. (See **NEIGHBORHOODS**.)

EPHESUS PARK

Six lighted tennis courts, ball fields, basketball goals, picnic and play areas are available here and nature and fitness trails are planned.

PHILLIPS PARK

This park features four lighted tennis courts with a picnic area on the drawing board. It is located adjacent to Phillips Middle School.

JONES PARK

Jones Park offers nature trails, picnic and play areas and is tucked away off South Columbia Street near UNC Hospitals.

WESTWOOD PARK

This picnic and play area is located off Dogwood Circle in Westwood. (See **NEIGHBORHOODS**.)

Carrboro Parks

CARRBORO COMMUNITY PARK

Open from sunrise to sunset, this park includes a lake, tennis courts, lighted softball and football fields, and lighted outdoor basketball courts, a baseball field, nature trails, picnic spots and play areas. It is located off N.C. Highway 54 just west of town.

WILSON PARK

Lighted tennis courts and softball field, picnic and play areas are available at this facility located off North Greensboro Street.

BREWER'S LANE MINI PARK

This park features basketball courts, picnic and play areas.

CARRBORO ELEMENTARY SCHOOL PARK

A youth baseball field, basketball court, playground and multipurpose area are offered here.

SIMPSON STREET TRIANGLE

This is a delightful place for a picnic and swings are available for the young and the young at heart.

HENRY W. BALDWIN PARK

This adventure playground has a multi-purpose area and a small picnic shelter.

Sports

BASEBALL AND SOFTBALL

Both Chapel Hill and Carrboro sponsor youth and adult baseball and softball leagues. Girls ages 7 through 15 play in softball leagues; boys play baseball. For Chapel Hill adults, there are separate competitive and recreational co-rec softball leagues. There is co-rec (co-ed) softball in Carrboro. For further information, call the parks and recreation departments in either location.

BASKETBALL

Newcomers may find it difficult adjusting to the basketball fever that suddenly strikes otherwise perfectly healthy adults here sometime after Thanksgiving. After you've lived here awhile, you too will probably succumb, planting yourself in front of the TV regularly, with your hand in a bag of potato chips and your heart in your mouth as you watch **your team** experience the thrill of victory or the agony of defeat.

One way to keep your mind and body from completely deteriorating between the months of November and April is to get out of the recliner and go down to the gym and shoot a few. The Chapel Hill Parks and Recreation Department offers two men's basketball leagues. The "recreational" league is for men 18 years and older; but don't worry, former college players are not allowed. Then there's the "competitive open" league for the same age group; the action is a bit fiercer here.

There are also youth leagues in both Chapel Hill and Carrboro. For information on teams and registration, call the Chapel Hill and Carrboro parks and recreation departments.

If you just want to practice your jump shot or play a few pick-up games, there are basketball hoops and willing participants available all over town. You can play at any one of the following locations in Chapel Hill: Hargraves, Umstead and Ephesus parks, and the Lincoln and Community Center sites. In Carrboro there are basketball courts at the following sites: Community Park, Brewer Lane Mini-Park, and Carrboro Elementary School Park.

BIKING

Bicycle enthusiasts may be interested in joining the **Carolina**

Tarwheels, a Durham-based cycling club that sponsors special bike trips and activities throughout the Triangle. For information, contact the Carolina Tarwheels at 942-8186 or 929-9012.

BOCCE BALL

Believe it or not, they've been playing this Italian game of lawn bowling in the Chapel Hill area for a dozen years now. Bocce ball is played on a court next to the Community Center on Plant Road every Tuesday and Friday morning starting around 9:00 a.m. You can start pick-up games anytime; balls are available at the Community Center. There are also two more bocce courts located at the Fearrington development, about eight miles south of Chapel Hill on U.S. 15-501.

CANOEING AND KAYAKING

The Haw River, about 10 minutes south of Chapel Hill, is a great place to put in a canoe or kayak and spend a day shooting rapids or dodging rocks, depending on the level of the water. The Haw is best in the early spring or after a good rain. The **Trail Shop** in Chapel Hill rents canoes and gives lessons. For information, call 929-7626.

The Chapel Hill Parks and Recreation Department usually sponsors a couple of trips a year, including canoeing flatwater among the virgin cypress at Merchants Millpond down east and rafting through rapids on the French Broad river in the western N.C. mountains. For information, call the department.

In addition, there is the **Carolina Canoe Club**, which sponsors trips for canoeists and kayakers of varying skill levels. Call 688-6917.

GOLF

There are four places to play golf in Chapel Hill: the (private) **Chapel Hill Country Club**, the (new and private) **Governors Club**, the (public) **Finley Golf Course**, and the (public) **Twin Lakes Golf Course**, just south of town in Chatham County. You can take private lessons at Finley; call 962-2349 for details. Twin Lakes Golf course, located on Manns Chapel Road off U.S. Highway 15-501 South offers play from 7:30 a.m. till dark on the weekends and from 8 a.m. during the week.

HEALTH CLUBS

The **YMCA** and three private health clubs provide a range of exercise facilities for residents of Chapel Hill and Carrboro.

The Gym in Carrboro (933-9249) offers nautilus equipment, sauna, whirlpool, weights and aerobic classes. **The Club for Women Only** in Rams Plaza (929-8860) offers nautilus equipment, sauna, whirlpool, aerobics and a pool. The Chapel Hill-Carrboro YMCA on Airport Road (942-5156) offers nautilus equipment, racquet sports, sauna, whirlpool, a gym, aerobics classes, a pool, massage and tanning. And **the Spa Health Club** on Elliott Road (967-9263) has nautilus, sauna, whirlpool, aerobics classes, a pool and tanning facilities.

Photo by Veryl Barry.

Fishing is a popular pasttime on area lakes.

HORSESHOES

That most Southern of sports, horseshoes, still thrives in small towns, including Carrboro. Carrboro's Parks and Recreation Department sponsors horseshoe tournaments, with men's, women's and youth divisions, several times a year. Call 968-7703 for information on the next scheduled tournament.

LACROSSE

Lacrosse has seen an increase in popularity in Chapel Hill in the last several years, due in part to the successful record of the UNC lacrosse team. Culbreth and Phillips Middle Schools and Chapel Hill High now field competitive teams, and Chapel Hill Parks and Recreation Department has begun offering a summer lacrosse clinic for boys in 7th through 9th grades. Call for more information (968-2784).

SOCCER

Thanks to Kip Ward, long-time soccer enthusiast, former UNC player and coach, Chapel Hill has a thriving co-ed soccer program with activities for all ages and skill levels. In 1972, Ward founded **Rainbow Soccer**, a private, nonprofit organization that has been growing ever since. Though Ward himself no longer runs the program, it continues to expand each year.

If you or your child want to play in a Rainbow Soccer league, all you have to do is sign up and pay the registration fee. This is a "non-competitive" league. The goal is to have fun, learn the game and play your best; everybody gets to play and gets plenty of encouragement.

Co-ed leagues—divided by age in two-year increments—are available for preschoolers (ages three and four) all the way through ninth graders. The adult league, called **Sunset Soccer**, includes anyone beyond the ninth grade. There are also two all-girls leagues, for grades 1 through 4 and 5 through 9.

Rainbow Soccer leagues play during the fall and spring seasons. Practice is twice a week and games are on the weekends. Rainbow Soccer also sponsors special summer day camps for youths up to age 15 and for coaches and goalkeepers. For more information, call 967-8797.

If your kids are interested in highly competitive play, they should try out for the **Central Carolina Youth Soccer Association** teams. For additional information, call: **Carolina Soccer/Lacrosse Supply**, Willow Creek Shopping Center, Carrboro at 929-8507.

SWIMMING

In Chapel Hill, you can swim year-round in the indoor pool at the Community Center. The pool is open for lap swimmers only from 6 to 9 a.m., 11:30 a.m. to 1 p.m. and 5 to 6:30 p.m. weekdays. On weekends, lap-swim times are 11:30 a.m. to 1:30 p.m. and 6:30 to 8 p.m. There are special times for water exercise for the back, parents and tots, senior citizens, masters swimming, community swim team and open swims. Fees range from 75 cents for children 6-17, to $1.25 for 18-61, $1.00 for age 62 and up; kids 5 and under swim free. Year-round season passes are available for

$62.00 for youths, and up to $219.00 for a family (two-four members) pass. Passes run from Memorial Day to Memorial Day, and may be prorated.

There is an outdoor pool open during the summer at Hargraves Park, with lap swimming from 9 to 10 a.m. weekdays and noon to 1 p.m. on weekends. Open swim is 11 a.m. to 1 p.m., 3 to 5:30 p.m. and 7 to 8 p.m. weekdays; it is 1 to 8 p.m. on weekends. Pool passes are valid at either pool.

Indoor pools are also available at three private membership facilities: The **YMCA** on Airport Road (942-5156), **the Spa Health Club** on Elliott Road (967-9263) and **The Club for Women Only** at Rams Plaza (942-0955).

TENNIS

Tennis lessons are available for youths ages 8 to 17, and for adults through Chapel Hill's Parks and Recreation Department. Chapel Hill also has a youth tennis league and a men's and women's singles league. Further information is available from the Chapel Hill Parks and Recreation Department at 968-2784. Tennis may be played at public courts at the following locations: in Chapel Hill— Hargraves, Umstead, Oakwood, Cedar Falls, Ephesus Park and Phillips Parks; in Carrboro—Community and Wilson Parks.

Members and guests can play at the **Chapel Hill Tennis Club** (929-5248). There are also private courts at the **Stoneridge Racquet and Swim Club**, the **Chapel Hill Country Club**, the **Faculty-Staff Recreation Association** facility (owned by UNC with membership open to permanent UNC faculty and staff) and several other private swim and tennis clubs in town.

VOLLEYBALL

Co-rec (men's and women's) volleyball leagues are open to players at all competitive levels, ages 18 and up. Teams play regularly at Culbreth Junior High School from August to November. Registration is on a team basis. Call the Chapel Hill Parks and Recreation Department for more information.

WINDSURFING

A few years ago the U.S. Army Corps of Engineers dammed up the Haw River to form Jordan Lake. In doing so, the Corps destroyed the best whitewater section the Haw had to offer, but it also inadvertently created an inland windsurfer's paradise.

There are so many wide open spaces on the lake that just about anywhere is a good place to practice windsurfing. You can rent a sailboard and get information about lessons at **The Trail Shop** on West Franklin Street in Chapel Hill. Call 929-7626 for information and directions to the best windsurfing spots. The Chapel Hill Parks and Recreation Department also sponsors classes on windsurfing.

Photo by Nancy Kitchener.

G 92

UNIVERSITY OF N.C.
AT CHAPEL HILL

First state university
to open its doors. 1795.
Chartered in 1789 under
the Constitution of 1776.

*The Chapel Hill public school system is heavily populated by the sons and
daughters of academics and professionals from the University of North Carolina.*

Inside

Chapel Hill-Carrboro Schools and Child Care

Chapel Hill and Carrboro are served by one of the best public school systems in the state. There are also several fine private schools in and around the area. In this section, we'll tell you a bit about both, as well as offer you some help in finding child care services for your preschooler, or after-school care for your school-age child.

The Public Schools

Although Chapel Hill and Carrboro are separate towns run by two different mayors and town councils, they share one superb school system. The Chapel Hill-Carrboro school system boasts the highest average California Achievement Test scores and the lowest drop-out rate in the state. Eighty-five percent of the system's graduates go on to continue their education.

If you think about it, it's not surprising that these schools enjoy such an excellent track record. Chapel Hill and Carrboro schools benefit from both the wealth and education levels of local residents. The system has one of the highest per-pupil expenditures in the state, over $5,000 annually. And you can only imagine what it means to have a public school system heavily populated by the sons and daughters of academics and professionals.

The combination of a well-endowed tax base and parents who are concerned about excellence also means that the system can afford to spend money on special programs. Chapel Hill-Carrboro schools educate a larger-than-average percentage of "exceptional" students, particularly in programs for the academically gifted and learning-disabled. Resource programs begin in the third grade, with programs for the "highly gifted" offered in grades 5 and 6.

Honors courses are available in the language arts, math and sciences in grades 6 to 8, with advanced placement classes available at the high school level. Phillips Middle School is currently operating a model math and science program using computers and lab experiences to increase both faculty and student achievement in those areas. And Chapel Hill High School offers an impressive array of athletic and extracurricular activities, including 13 team sports from lacrosse and soccer to tennis, golf, football and basketball.

The Chapel Hill-Carrboro schools provide for over 7,300 students in six elementary schools (K-5), two middle schools (6-8) and one senior high school (9-12). There is also a special school at UNC Hospitals for young inpatients unable to attend school. A third middle school is under construction and scheduled to open in the fall of 1994. A site on Weaver Dairy Road has been chosen for a second high school; it is expected to open in 1996. The districts are drawn with the intention that no one school's student population deviates by more than about five percent from the system's 26 percent minority enrollment.

Keep in mind that the boundaries of the Chapel Hill-Carrboro school district are not the same as the Chapel Hill and Carrboro town limits. That means it's possible to live outside of either town and avoid paying city property taxes but still be within the Chapel Hill-Carrboro school system. For example, you can live in Dogwood Acres or Heritage Hills two or three miles south of the Chapel Hill town limits, or in Stoneridge or Sedgefield one or two miles north of town, and still send your kids to the Chapel Hill-Carrboro public schools.

But if you live way out in the countryside to the north, your child will attend Orange County schools in Hillsborough, about 10 miles away. And if you live in rural Chatham County to the south your child will attend Chatham County schools.

If you're still deciding where you are going to live, we recommend you visit the schools, talk to the principals and observe a few classes before closing a deal on your new home.

Dr. Neil Pederson is the superintendent of the Chapel Hill-Carrboro school system. For more information, call the Administrative Offices at Lincoln Center on Merritt Mill Road at 967-8211.

Here's a guide to what schools go with each neighborhood:

Northwood, Timberlyne, Cedar Hills, Ironwoods, Homestead Road area: Seawell Elementary, Phillips Middle and Chapel Hill Senior High School.

Staff Photo.

*Chapel Hill High School offers an impressive array
of athletics and extracurricular activities.*

Countryside, Lake Forest, Booker Creek, Coker Hills, Coker Hills West, Estes Hills, Hidden Hills and Mt. Bolus: Estes Hills Elementary, Phillips Middle and Chapel Hill Senior High.

Historic District and Glendale: Glenwood Elementary, Phillips Middle and Chapel Hill Senior High.

Gimghoul, Greenwood, Glen Lennox, The Oaks I, Westwood, Forest Hills: Glenwood Elementary, Culbreth Middle and Chapel Hill Senior High.

Southbridge, Morgan Creek Hills, Farrington Hills, Laurel Hill, Dogwood Acres, Heritage Hills: Frank Porter Graham Elementary, Culbreth Middle and Chapel Hill Senior High.

Webbwood, Bolin Forest, Spring Valley, Plantation Acres: Carr-boro Elementary, Phillips Middle and Chapel Hill Senior High.

Windwood: Carrboro Elementary, Culbreth Middle and Chapel Hill Senior High.

Briarcliff, Colony Woods, Ridgewood: Ephesus Elementary, Culbreth Middle and Chapel Hill Senior High.

Stoneridge, Sedgefield, Chandler's Green, Chesley: Ephesus Elementary, Phillips Middle and Chapel Hill Senior High.

Private and Parochial Schools

Chapel Hill and Carrboro are served by several private and parochial schools. Below we'll tell you a little about each one and how much it will cost to send your child there, based on the latest tuition information available. More detailed descriptions of the Carolina Friends School, Durham Academy and St. Mary's School appear in our **DURHAM SCHOOLS** section.

CAROLINA FRIENDS SCHOOL
425 students, Pre thru 12
Friends School Rd.   929-1800
Rt.1, Box 183
Durham 27705

This non-denominational school, founded in 1963 by the Quakers, is located on 45 acres of wooded countryside equidistant from Durham, Chapel Hill and Hillsborough. 1993-94 tuition ranges from $3,350 for pre-school to $5,950 for upper school.

DURHAM ACADEMY
1000 students, Pre thru 8 and 9 thru 12
(Pre thru 8) 3116 Academy Rd.   489-9118
Durham, NC 27707
(9 thru 12) 3601 Ridge Rd.   489-6569
Durham, NC 27705

Founded in 1933, Durham Academy is the oldest primary through secondary private school in the area. It is located in Durham, about a 20-minute drive from Chapel Hill. 1993-94 tuition is $4,925 for pre-school, and ranges from $6,475 to $7,255 for the primary through high school grades.

THE EMERSON WALDORF SCHOOL
150 students, Pre thru 8
6211 New Jericho Rd.   967-1858

The Emerson Waldorf School is located on 25 wooded acres off N.C. 86 north of Chapel Hill. As one of the 600 worldwide Waldorf schools, it is part of the world's fastest-growing independent school movement. The mission of the Emerson Waldorf School is "to offer the children and the larger community a transformative education, based on a developmen-

431

tal approach to children, so that our children can, out of freedom, take responsibility for the future."

A typical day at Emerson Waldorf begins with a two-hour "main lesson," which focuses on a single theme. That subject may remain the same for several weeks. Meanwhile, all history, spelling, mathematics and science problems are related in some way to the main lesson subject. In addition to the basics, Waldorf students study foreign languages, music, handwork and a variety of other electives offered by specialty teachers.

Tuition for 1994-95 is $2,875 for the kindergarten, $4,710 for grades one through four, and $4,920 for grades five through eight. Tuition assistance is available for those in need.

MONTESSORI SCHOOL

66 students, Pre thru 3
1165 Weaver Dairy Road   929-3339
Chapel Hill, NC 27514

Founded in 1979, the school practices the methods of Marie Montessori, an Italian educator and physician who believed that children learn naturally if placed in an environment consisting of "learning games" suited to their individual abilities and interests.

The three- and four-year-olds attend until 11:45 a.m., five-year-olds until 2:00 p.m. and 6 to 9 year olds until 2:30 p.m. There are about 20 students in each of the preschool classes and 30 students enrolled in grades 1 to 3. Tuition ranges from $2,700-$3,075 a year.

ST. MARY'S SCHOOL

170 students, Pre thru 12
St. Mary's Rd.   732-7200
Hillsborough, NC 27278

St. Mary's was named for its scenic location adjacent to a historic Anglican church between Durham and Hillsborough. It is a non-sectarian, college-preparatory school for Grades K-12. 1993-94 tuition ranges from $2,290 for pre-Kindergarten to $2,875 for grades K to 8 and $3,606 for the upper grades 9 to 12.

ST. THOMAS MORE SCHOOL

385 students, pre thru 6
U.S. Hwy. 15-501 Bypass   929-1546
Chapel Hill, NC 27514

This school was built in 1964 as an outgrowth of St. Thomas More Catholic Church parish. The school's enrollment is open to non-Catholics as well. The school's philosophy is "to help our students to integrate religious truths and values with life in contemporary society and our world of technology, to foster . . . a positive self-image and a spirit of inquiry and discovery . . . to provide our students with fundamental knowledge and usable skills to prepare them for life work and develop a sensitivity to cultural and aesthetic experiences . . . and to extend the interest and concern of our students beyond themselves into the total community. . . ."

Students from Pre-K to Grade 6 are served, and there is an after-school program as well. 1993-94 tuition for Pre-K is $1,602. Tuition for grades 1 to 6 is $1,721 for members of the parish and $2,306 for non-members. Rates are lower for each additional child.

Child Care Providers

Affordable after-school care is available at all six public elementary schools. For more information contact the Administrative Offices at Lincoln Center on Merritt Mill Road, 967-8211.

Some of the private schools we described also offer after-school care. For more information, contact the school.

There are at least two dozen preschools and many more day care providers in Chapel Hill and Carrboro. The best way to learn about which facility is right for your needs is to ask for recommendations from friends and neighbors, then go observe.

Or you can contact **Child Care Networks**, a private, nonprofit organization that assists people in matching their child care needs with the right facility or provider. Child Care Networks makes referrals to local child care centers, preschools and in-home caregivers for anyone who lives or works in Orange or Chatham counties. It also recruits new child care providers and offers training and support for day care centers and day care homes. It can advise you on what to look for in quality child care. For more information, contact Child Care Networks at Carr Mill Mall in Carrboro, 942-0184.

The following are full day care and preschool programs in the Chapel Hill-Carrboro area:

AMITY UNITED METHODIST NURSERY SCHOOL
825 Estes Dr.   929-6149

BINKLEY PRESCHOOL
1712 Willow Dr.   968-1427

CARRBORO UNITED METHODIST DAY CARE
200 Hillsborough Rd.
Carrboro   929-5143

CHAPEL HILL COOPERATIVE
106 Purefoy Rd.   942-3955

CHAPEL HILL DAY CARE CENTER
211 W. Cameron Ave.   929-3585

FAMILY PRESCHOOL
632 Laurel Hill Rd.   967-9684

HOLY FAMILY DAY CARE
200 Hayes Rd.   929-5004

KINDERCARE
210 N. Elliott Rd.   942-7223

LA PETITE ACADEMY
110 Kingston Dr.   929-9148

LITTLE HEELS PRE-SCHOOL
1702 Legion Rd.   933-2103

ORANGE METHODIST PRESCHOOL
1220 Airport Rd.   942-2825

UNIVERSITY METHODIST PRESCHOOL
150 E. Franklin St.   967-8867

UNIVERSITY PRESBYTERIAN PRESCHOOL
209 E. Franklin St.   929-8658

VICTORY VILLAGE DAY CARE CENTER
Mason Farm Rd.   929-2662

Photo by Nancy Kitchener.

*The Chapel of the Cross has always been
one of the most socially conscientious churches in Chapel Hill.*

Inside

Chapel Hill Worship

The town of Chapel Hill takes its name from the New Hope Chapel, which in the mid-1700s was located on a hill overlooking a valley to the east. Given that it owes its identity to that humble chapel, it's not surprising that the town offers many and varied places of worship. There are dozens of religious institutions in Chapel Hill and Carrboro, offering spiritual sustenance to just about everyone from Southern Baptists to Jehovah's Witnesses. However, space prevents us from expounding on the blessings of them all. Instead we offer you a glimpse at a cross section of the community's spiritual side. For a listing of all churches, consult the Yellow Pages.

Baptist

BINKLEY MEMORIAL BAPTIST CHURCH

1712 Willow Dr.   *942-4964*

Like most Southern towns, Chapel Hill and Carrboro have plenty of Baptist churches, running the gamut from Southern to American to Freewill Baptist affiliations. Binkley and its congregation are known for their progressive outlook. Binkley has been affiliated with both the Southern and the American Baptist churches. The senior minister is Dr. Linda Jordan. Binkley also has a highly regarded preschool program. (See listing under "Child Care Providers" in **SCHOOLS**.)

FIRST BAPTIST CHURCH

106 N. Roberson St.   *942-2509*

Chapel Hill's largest black church was established in 1865. The church's longevity in the community is also reflected in the durability of its pastors. The Reverend J.R. Manley has been its pastor for over 45 years. Church school starts at 9:30 a.m., and morning worship is at 11 a.m. The church is affiliated with the National Baptist, Southern Baptist and American Baptist conventions. It is also the location of one of the school system's **Head Start** preschool programs.

Catholic

ST. THOMAS MORE

742 Gimghoul Rd.   *942-1040*

Established in 1930, St. Thomas More has grown dramatically in the last 10 years. As the only Catholic parish in town, it now boasts more than 1,200 members. There is a

Saturday evening Mass (5:30 p.m.), and Sunday Masses at 8 a.m., 9:30 a.m. and 11:15 a.m., and at 5 p.m. Daily services are held at 5 p.m. Monday through Friday. The parish is affiliated with St. Thomas More School, Pre-K-6. (See **CHAPEL HILL SCHOOLS.**) Mass is also celebrated at the Newman Center on Pittsboro Street, adjacent to the UNC campus. It is held daily at 12:15 p.m., at 5:15 p.m. on Saturday and at 9 and 11 a.m. on Sunday. Call 929-3730 for information on the Newman Center.

Episcopal

CHAPEL OF THE CROSS
304 E. Franklin St.   *929-2193*

After the New Hope Chapel (for which the town is named) disappeared during the American Revolution, no organized Episcopal congregation existed until 1842. At that time, the Rev. William Mercer Green, then chaplain for UNC, presided over the organization of the Church of the Atonement. This 15-member parish met in each other's homes until the chapel was constructed of handmade bricks in 1848. The building was then consecrated as The Chapel of the Holy Cross. The tiny church survived and eventually prospered, adding other parish buildings and constructing the present church next to the existing chapel in 1925.

The Chapel of the Cross has always been one of the most socially conscientious churches in town. The Rev. Pauli Murray, the first black woman to be ordained to the Epis-

copal priesthood, celebrated her first Eucharist at Chapel of the Cross. The church has fostered and housed many service programs, including **Habitat for Humanity, Meals on Wheels, AA and Narcotics Anonymous** meetings, and **English as a Second Language** classes. The child care center at the church, a half-day program, is very popular. (See "Child Care Providers" in CHAPEL HILL **SCHOOLS.**) The ministers are Rev. Stephen Elkins-Williams, Rector and Rev. Stephen Stanley, Associate for Campus Ministry and UNC Episcopal Chaplain.

Interdenominational

COMMUNITY CHURCH OF CHAPEL HILL
106 Purefoy Rd.   *942-2050*

Founded in 1957, the Community Church is an inter-faith congregation that is concerned with issues of peace, justice and spirituality. Sunday services are held at 11 a.m. Rev. W.W. Olney is the pastor. A weekday cooperative preschool is held at the church; call 942-3955 for information.

Lutheran

HOLY TRINITY
300 E. Rosemary St.   *942-2678*

Holy Trinity, the first Lutheran church in town, was established in 1946. It is located in the Historic District, one block from downtown. Services are held at 8:30 and 10 a.m. Pastors are Rev. Louis Bauer and Rev. Larry Hartsell, the campus pastor.

Jewish

HILLEL FOUNDATION
(JEWISH STUDENT CENTER)
210 W. Cameron Ave.   *942-4057*
Though there are two synagogues in Durham (Beth-El and
Judea Reform), the Hillel Foundation is the only Jewish center in
Chapel Hill; it serves the needs of
members of the UNC community,
with High Holy Day services,
Shabbat, Jewish university classes,
parties, dances, discussion groups,
and occasional dinners and breakfasts. Call for information and a
schedule.

Methodist

CARRBORO UNITED METHODIST
200 Hillsborough Rd.   *942-1223*
Established in 1910,
Carrboro United Methodist has a
growing congregation, presided
over by the Rev. David Harvin.
Church school is at 9:45 a.m. and
the service is at 11 a.m. The church
sponsors a daily **Dial-a-Devotion**
(call 942-4818). It also houses a day
care center (929-5143).

UNIVERSITY METHODIST
150 E. Franklin St.   *929-7191*
The Rev. William Gattis presides over this large congregation,
with over 1,500 members. Services
are held at 8:45 and 11 a.m. There
is a half-day preschool at the church
(967-8867).

Presbyterian

UNIVERSITY PRESBYTERIAN
209 E. Franklin St.   *929-2102*
The largest Presbyterian
church in town, University Presbyterian has more than 1,000 members. There are two Sunday services.
The church also is the site of a
parents' morning out program and
a preschool and half-day kindergarten. The Rev. Dr. Robert Dunham
is the pastor.

CHURCH OF THE RECONCILIATION
110 N. Elliott Rd.   *929-2127*
This Presbyterian commu-
nity is characterized by its progressive congregation. Sunday services
are held at 10 a.m. The **Sycamore
Preschool** is located at the church.

United Church of Christ

UNITED CHURCH OF CHAPEL HILL
211 W. Cameron Ave.   *942-3540*
United Church was the
founder of the Inter-Faith Council
and has been a strong participant
in its activities. In fact, the **Family
Assistance** program and the administrative offices of this group are
housed at the church. Through **US-
USSR Bridges for Peace**, United
Church has participated in numerous exchanges with Soviet citizens
and in the past few years has been
very active in the Habitat home-
building program. The Reverends
Jill and Richard Edens are ministers at the church. It is also the site
of the **Chapel Hill Day Care Center**.

From The Chamber...

Greater Durham
CHAMBER OF COMMERCE

Welcome...

... to North Carolina's famed Research Triangle. Recently ranked by Money Magazine as the "fifth best place to live in the United States" and Fortune Magazine as the "#1 Best City for Business in the United States", the Research Triangle area is an exciting place in which to live and work.

As you review this comprehensive publication, I think you will agree that the Triangle region has a lot going for it. Whether you're a new resident or a visitor for just a few days, we hope you'll enjoy discovering this vibrant area and all it has to offer.

Please call on the Durham Chamber of Commerce if we can be of assistance to you.

Sincerely,

Robert H. Booth
President/CEO

CITY OF INDUSTRY, EDUCATION, MEDICINE AND RESEARCH
Peoples Security Insurance Building • Suite 1400
919/682-2133 • P.O. Box 3829, Durham, N.C. 27702 • FAX 688-8351

Inside
Durham

Time was, almost 150 years ago, Durham was not much more than a whistle stop on the North Carolina Railroad's east-west line. In the last decade, Durham has been one of the fastest growing communities in North Carolina.

The forces that built this town—tobacco, textiles, medicine, education—also shaped its uniquely diverse character. Durham's population is about evenly divided between blacks and whites. Once heavily populated by blue-collar cigarette and textile workers, it is as much a home today for doctors and dancers, high-tech execs and entrepreneurs.

To understand how all this came about, you have to know a little local history. It all started at the corner of Peabody and Corcoran streets where Bartlett Snipes Durham, a local physician, built his country estate and called it, some would say prophetically, "Pandora's Box." In 1852, Dr. Durham offered four acres of his homesite to the North Carolina Railroad Company for a depot along its Goldsboro-to-Charlotte line. Thus was born the hamlet known as Durham Station, Durham Depot, Durhamville and later as just plain Durham. Durham's official birth date is April 26, 1853, when its first post office opened. By 1860, three stores, two saloons and a carpentry shop had sprung up on what was still an agricultural landscape inhabited by fewer than 100 persons. Dr. Durham's homesite was then owned by R. F. Morris, whose small tobacco factory nearby would add another significant chapter to the community's development.

Durham played a relatively minor role in the Civil War until the very end, when Confederate General Joseph Johnston surrendered to Union General William Sherman in 1865 at a nearby farm owned by James Bennett. The event marked the end of the Civil War in the Carolinas, Georgia and Florida. Ironically, it also launched the beginning of Durham's prosperity.

While Sherman and Johnston were taking care of business out on the Bennett farm, the boys in blue and gray were swapping war stories and smoking the peace pipe down at the Durham depot. Seems that soldiers from both sides had gotten a bit restless, broken into the nearby tobacco factory, then owned by John R. Green, and made off with what turned out to be the finest Bright Leaf weed any of them had ever smoked. When the honorable terms of surrender were finally consummated, the troops took their tobacco and went home.

It wasn't long before orders for Green's tobacco began pouring in to the Durham post office from as far away as Maine and Texas. To meet the sudden demand, Green cranked up production on a brand of tobacco he named "Bull Durham" after the picture of a bull on the jar of Coleman's Mustard manufactured in Durham, England. Pretty soon the image of that bull was appearing in advertisements on walls and rooftops around the world, even on one of the Great Pyramids of Egypt. An ad painted behind the New York Yankees' dugout inspired a new baseball term—"bullpen." Durham was on the map and the "Bull City" shifted into high gear.

The demand for Durham tobacco prompted other entrepreneurs to get into the business, including Washington Duke and his sons Brodie, Ben and James. With the introduction of the cigarette rolling machine, the Dukes became the leading cigarette makers in the nation. Their powerful American Tobacco Co. was later broken up by antitrust legislation into Liggett & Myers, P. Lorillard and R.J. Reynolds.

Thanks to tobacco, Durham's population grew to more than 2,000 by the mid-1870s. Tobacco profits provided the capital for other ventures, including cotton and flour mills, banks, trucking firms and more railroads. Notable enterprises included Erwin Mills, the first in the South and one of the largest in the nation to manufacture denim, and Durham Hosiery, the largest maker of stockings in the world.

The history of Durham's earliest commercial and industrial ventures has been carefully preserved. In 1977, Durham became the first North Carolina city to have its large downtown district placed on the National Register of Historic Places.

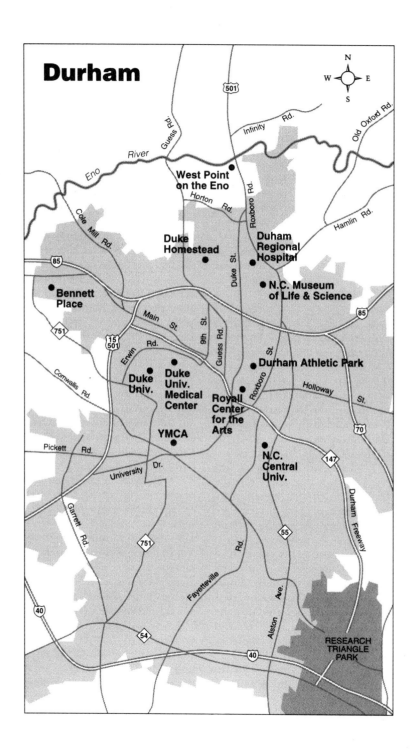

Durham

N W E S

501

Infinity Rd.

Old Oxford Rd.

Eno River

Guess Rd.

West Point on the Eno

Horton Rd.

Roxboro Rd.

Hamlin Rd.

Cole Mill Rd.

85

Duke Homestead

Duke St.

Duham Regional Hospital

Bennett Place

N.C. Museum of Life & Science

85

751

Main St.

9th St.

Guess Rd.

15 501

Erwin Rd.

Duke Univ.

Duke Univ. Medical Center

Durham Athletic Park

Roxboro St.

Holloway

St.

70

Cornwallis Rd.

Royall Center for the Arts

YMCA

147

Pickett Rd.

University Dr.

N.C. Central Univ.

Garrett Rd.

751

55

Durham Freeway

40

Fayetteville Rd.

Alston Ave.

54

40

RESEARCH TRIANGLE PARK

The tobacco that built the city also had a hand in shaping what would be Durham's next major industries: education and medicine. Tobacco magnate James Buchanan Duke thought it would be a good idea to endow Trinity College. With the aid of an $85,000 gift from James' daddy and land donated from tobacco-textile executive Julian Shakespeare Carr, Trinity College moved to Durham from Randolph County in 1892. In 1924, James B. Duke gave the college $40 million. As you might expect, it was warmly received; the college was promptly renamed Duke University.

Today Duke University is Durham's largest private employer and one of the top private colleges and medical research facilities in the nation. Duke's reputation, as well as its proximity to three other universities and Research Triangle Park, helped to eventually establish Durham as an ideal location for high-tech research companies.

There are many other success stories in Durham. While the Dukes were striking it rich in tobacco, Durham's black leaders were also thriving. Beginning around 1905, West Parrish Street turned from an industrial to a commercial district when the black-owned-and-operated North Carolina Mutual and Provident Association purchased several lots there. After the insurance company prospered and attracted other businesses, the block became known as the "Black Wall Street." The company, now known as North Carolina Mutual Life, remains the largest black-managed financial institution in the world.

Meanwhile, North Carolina Central University, founded in 1910 as a religious training school, went on to become the first state-funded liberal arts college for blacks and is now part of the University of North Carolina system. Little did Dr. Bartlett Durham realize when he opened "Pandora's Box" to the railroads and tobacco merchants, that a muddy, country whistlestop would evolve into the eclectic "New South" city that it is today.

Durham's population has exploded from the 100 or so who gravitated to the train depot in the 1860s to its current population of 130,000 in the city. Durham County is among the fastest growing areas of the state, with about 200,000 residents. The evidence of this phenomenal growth is everywhere. New subdivisions have gone up throughout Durham County in the last several years. A number of new schools have been built to meet increasing enrollment in the county.

With the influx of new businesses and industries have come changes in the nature of Durham's work force. Tobacco and textiles were once the leading industries. Not so today, as the top employers include Duke University and its Medical Center, as well as some of the new large research facilities in and around Research Triangle Park.

So it is that tobacco warehouses and cotton mills have been converted to chic shops, condominiums and office spaces. Plans are in the works for others to accommodate apartments for senior citizens and studios for artists, dancers and craftspersons.

But sudden changes have also meant growing pains. A part of Durham's black community was razed to make way for a cross-town expressway. Some downtown businesses have lost out to the competition of nearby suburban malls. However, local leaders are hoping new developments—such as the downtown civic center complex and arts center—will bring businesses back downtown again.

At the same time, rapid growth has meant that roads are becoming snarled, strip development is transforming the rural landscape and real estate speculation is fast driving the price of a home out of reach for many who grew up here. Like their counterparts in the other cities of the Triangle, Durhamites are determined to tame this growth surge so that it does not destroy the very characteristics that make so many people want to live here.

The following pages will detail some of Durham's many and varied charms. We'll show you around a few of the city's special neighborhoods, inform you about the schools and churches, and provide you with the scoop on Durham's recreational activities and parks. You will find additional information about Durham in our special sections on everything from **AIRPORTS** to **SHOPPING**. If that doesn't satisfy your curiosity, check with the **Durham Convention and Visitor's Bureau** (687-0288 or 1-800-446-8604) or drop by their new **Visitor's Center** at 101 E. Morgan.

Courtesy Durham Chamber of Commerce.

Durham's North Carolina Mutual Life remains the largest black-managed financial institution in the world.

Photo by Nancy Kitchener.

Road crews work night and day to keep up with Triangle growth.

Inside

Durham Government Services and Utilities

When you first move into a new community, the number of things you don't know about who's who and what's where are overwhelming. Here's a quick guide that we hope will make it a little easier for you to get set up in Durham. For more information, call **Durham City Government** at 560-4100, the **Durham County Government** at 560-0220 or the **Greater Durham Chamber of Commerce** at 682-2133.

ABC Laws

In Durham, as in most of the rest of the Triangle, you buy your liquor at the ABC stores operated by the state Alcoholic Beverage Commission. ABC stores are open from 9 a.m. to 9 p.m. Monday through Saturday. You can buy beer and wine at most supermarkets and convenience stores seven days a week, but keep in mind that alcoholic beverages may not be purchased on Sunday until 12:00 noon.

Liquor by the drink is available at many restaurants in Durham. State laws prohibit the establishment of facilities designed only for imbibing spirits, which simply

means that places that serve drinks have to serve food to go along with it.

Don't be surprised if, when you venture outside of the cities of the Triangle, you find you can get neither liquor nor beer and wine. In each county and municipality, it's up to the voters to decide if booze will be available and in what fashion. In some parts of North Carolina the only way you can buy the stuff is to inquire about the nearest bootlegger and be prepared to pay premium prices for store-bought-but-bootlegged goods.

The State Legislature strengthened the already stiff drunk-driving law in the 1993 session. If you get pulled over by a state trooper and blow 0.08 on the breathalyzer test you're in big trouble. You can lose your license, go straight to jail (do not pass Go) or be required to perform some community service activities. In addition, under the "dram shop" provision of the law, restaurant owners or even hosts of private parties can be held liable if someone drinking at their place gets into a messy automobile accident involving property

445

damage, personal injury or death. You must be at least 21 years of age to purchase beer, wine and liquor.

Automobile Insurance, Licenses, Registration and Tags

Out-of-state licenses are valid for 30 days after North Carolina residency is established. And you better believe the State Highway Patrol is serious about this. Even if you've just gotten here, it's worth getting your North Carolina license right away.

Before an auto can be registered, the applicant must show "proof of financial responsibility," or documentation of liability insurance coverage. Out-of-state plates are valid for 30 days after state residency is established. For new plates, which are $20.00, go to the **Motor Vehicles License Service** at Northgate Shopping Mall (286-4908) or on N.C. Highway 54 (540-6607). Safety inspections must be done, in most cases, within 10 days after initial plates are purchased and then once a year thereafter. This can be done at many service stations.

For your new license, go to the State Highway Patrol station on Miami Boulevard (560-6896) or the examiner's office at Homestead Market Shopping (560-3378). You will be asked to take written, road sign recognition and vision tests. Study the book they give you; it's not as easy as you might think. In some cases a driving test may also be required. Fees range from $10 to $20.

Government

Durham is the only municipality in the county. The city operates on a council-manager form of government with an elected mayor and 12 council members elected at-large and from wards.

The county is governed by a five-member board of commissioners and administered by a county manager.

Durhamites elect two state senators and three representatives to the General Assembly. They reside in the 2nd U.S. Congressional District.

Maps

Probably one of the first things you will want to do when you get to town is figure out where you are. City and county maps are available from the Durham Chamber of Commerce, at 300 West Morgan Street (682-2133).

ASK DUKE POWER WHY
THE HOUSE ON THE TOP
IS A SMARTER MOVE.

They'll show you the energy-efficient features that really make a difference. The Comfort Machine® is just one of them. It's Duke Power's high-efficiency heat pump. The more temperate the climate, the better it works. So the Comfort Machine's perfect for the Carolinas' mild weather.

If you plan on building or purchasing a new house, ask your builder or Realtor about The MAX®, an all-electric home featuring the Comfort Machine. The MAX is designed to meet Duke Power's strict energy-efficient guidelines. So it's also sure to meet your strong desire for lower power bills.

Before heading off on the house hunt, save yourself a lot of energy and call Duke Power at (800) 786-3853. They know some tips you can't afford to live without.

Pet Regulations

When you list your personal and real estate property holdings with the city and county tax offices, you will be asked if you own a dog. If you admit that you do, you will be assessed a small fee. Dogs are also required to have all the appropriate shots.

Taxes

Durham City and County do not tax personal income, but all residents must list personal and real-estate property for taxation during January, by mail or at the **Durham County Judicial Building** on East Main Street downtown (560-0380).

What tax rate you pay depends on exactly where you live. If you live anywhere inside the city limits, you have to pay a city property tax in addition to the county property tax. Check with a real-estate agent, map or the county tax office to determine exactly what rate applies to you. The rates are set each summer.

In addition to property taxes, North Carolina levies a 4 percent tax on retail sales, exchange and rentals. And by option, Durham County levies and retains an additional 2 percent sales tax, giving a 6% sales tax rate.

Transportation

Durham is served by DATA (**Durham Area Transit Authority**), an intra-city bus system. Call 688-4587 for route, rate and schedule information.

TRI-A-RIDE, the Triangle's regional ride-sharing program, provides information for commuters wishing to join or organize a carpool or vanpool. Call 549-9999.

Utilities

For all utilities except telephone service, renters have to go to the appropriate office, apply in person and pay a deposit. If you own your home, there is usually no deposit.

Usually, if you make your application in the morning, you can expect your power, gas and water service to be turned on the same day. It's best not to wait until Friday morning, however, because if anything goes wrong you won't have service until Monday. For telephone service, plan on it taking up to five days.

Cable TV

Apply for service with **Cablevision of Durham** at 708 East Club Boulevard or call 220-4481.

Electricity

For electric service apply at **Duke Power Company**, 101 East Main Street (382-3200). Renters should expect to pay a deposit of $50 to $100.

Gas

Apply for service at **Public Service Company of North Carolina**, 3001 Harvard Avenue (682-5661). Renters must apply in person, show proof that they live at the address for which service is requested, and pay a deposit of $35 to $100, based on the number of rooms. Homeowners can apply by phone and do not have to pay any deposit.

Telephone

Apply by calling **GTE** at 683-9641. But plan ahead, it can take four or five days before your service is turned on.

Water and Sewer

Apply to the **Water and Sewer Customer Service**, first floor, City Hall, 101 City Hall Plaza downtown (560-4411). Renters must pay a deposit. There is no deposit for homeowners. You can usually expect same-day service if you apply first thing in the morning.

Voting

To register to vote, you must be a U.S. citizen, a non-felon, at least 18 years old by the date of the next election and a resident of North Carolina and your precinct for 30 days prior to the next election. You can register at the **Durham County Public Library** (560-0100)

and its branches, or at the **Durham County Board of Elections** in the County Judicial Building on Main Street downtown, from 8:30 a.m. to 5 p.m. Monday through Friday.

State and county elections are held every even year. City elections are held every odd year. Primaries are held in May. The Mayor is elected to a two-year term; city council members to four-year staggered terms. County commissioners hold office for two years at a time. And state senators and representatives serve two-year terms.

North Carolina's two U.S. Senators are elected to staggered six-year terms. U.S. Senator Jesse Helms was re-elected in 1990. Lauch Faircloth became North Carolina's newest Senator in 1992.

A U.S. representative is elected for a two-year term, in even election years. Durham is part of the 2nd Congressional District, and is served in Congress by Representative Tim Valentine.

Good Numbers To Know

The current edition of the local GTE phone book includes a great listing of community service numbers ranging from crisis hotlines, family planning, mental and physical health services, to senior citizens, veterans and women's services. This list includes public agencies and nonprofit organizations and was compiled by the Durham County Library.

*Forest Hills is one of the most exclusive and most picturesque
of Durham's older neighborhoods.*

Inside

Durham Neighborhoods

When Yankees began invading the Triangle in the late 1970s, it seemed they all wanted to live in North Raleigh, even though Durham was a shorter commute to their jobs in Research Triangle Park. Apparently, the only thing anybody knew about Durham was that it used to be some kind of cigarette manufacturing center.

Gradually, Durham has been discovered, and it's a great place to live.

Thanks to Durham's recent popularity, home prices have gone up significantly in recent years, placing the cost of housing here slightly above the national average. The average cost of a home in Durham is now about $113,500, generally selling for less than in Raleigh and Chapel Hill.

Durham is also convenient. It's 15 minutes to Research Triangle Park, 15 minutes to Chapel Hill and 25 minutes to downtown Raleigh. And although it has many of the educational and cultural resources of a big city, Durham's neighborhoods still have a small-town feel.

Durham offers homes, apartments and condominiums to suit just about any lifestyle and pocketbook. Thanks to a building boom in recent years, there's a good selection of homes in a variety of price ranges.

Durham has more than 60 identifiable neighborhoods, with many charming older sections developed in the first half of this century. Here's a sample of what some of them have to offer. Our "tour" starts in-town, heading next to the southwestern suburbs and finally, northward. At the end of this section, we are also including a listing of newer developments, their price ranges and locations. For further information and help in choosing a home, apartment or condominium, see one of the local real estate agents listed in our **HOMES** section.

Neighborhoods

TRINITY PARK

Durham's older in-town neighborhoods have enjoyed a comeback, thanks in part to those young, urban you-know-who's and their yearning for historic charm. The oldest and one of the most popular in-town locales is Trinity

451

Park, the community that sprang up at the turn of the century around Trinity College, now Duke University's east campus.

Here you'll find medium to large (1,600 to 3,000 square feet) one-, two- and three-story homes on small city lots conveniently located between Duke University and downtown. High ceilings, hardwood floors, fireplaces, front porches and ornate trim reflect the period between 1900 and 1949. A few homes contain apartments and condominiums, but most remain single-family residences, selling for over $125,000.

Trinity Park is within walking distance of Duke's east campus and a short bus ride to the west campus. It is convenient to jogging trails, good city parks and good neighborhood schools.

The neighborhood thrives today because its residents—university professors, students, young professionals and older Durham natives—have banded together to protect their common interest in preserving the past. In 1974, they formed the Trinity Park Association and prevented the city from axing some old oak trees to widen a street. The organization, which has been a model for other in-town neighborhood associations, also raised $26,000 to purchase vacant land for a "tot lot" and community park and formed a successful babysitting cooperative for residents. The only problem with Trinity Park is that there are more people who want to live here than there are available homes. It's a seller's mar-

ket and homes tend to go quickly for the asking price.

WATTS HOSPITAL

If you can't snap up a home in Trinity Park, there are plenty of other in-town neighborhoods that are also enjoying a resurgence. Directly to the north of Trinity Park is an area known as Watts Hospital, named for the facility that was once the focal point of the neighborhood. Today the old Watts Hospital building houses the North Carolina School of Science and Mathematics, a special public high school for students who are particularly talented in those fields (see **DURHAM SCHOOLS**).

What's nice about the Watts Hospital-Hillandale-Club Boulevard neighborhood is that it is so diverse. Here you'll find young singles, families and senior citizens from modest to more-than-middle-class means. That's because of the varied housing stock, from small cottages to sprawling family homes.

The homes are newer (1940s and 50s) and the lots are much larger than in Trinity Park. The main streets are shaded by some of the most majestic willow oaks in Durham. Oval Park is a pleasant recreational retreat here for kids and adults. Most homes sell for $100,000 and up.

DUKE PARK

Like Watts Hospital, Duke Park is demographically and architecturally diverse. Located east of

Trinity Park and just south of Interstate 85, it features a variety of homes built from the 1940s to '60s and selling for prices similar to the Watts Hospital area. Like Trinity Park, Duke Park has an active neighborhood association and babysitting co-op. And it's served by an oak-shaded community park, complete with a swimming pool.

DUKE FOREST

Duke Forest was built in the 1930s adjacent to Duke University's own woodlands in southern Durham to provide comfortable housing for faculty and administration. Today, residents include "civilians" as well.

Here you'll find architectural styles ranging from the traditional homes of the 1930s to today's wood-and-glass contemporaries. Prices range from $125,000 to over $250,000.

FOREST HILLS

One of the most exclusive and picturesque of the old city neighborhoods, Forest Hills features gracious homes on winding, tree-shaded lanes adjacent to an expansive park.

Large homes constructed in the 1930s and '40s of brick, stone and wood are nestled on carefully landscaped, one-acre lots; they sell for anywhere from $150,000 for a bungalow to $375,000 and more for a stately brick mansion. Once an 18-hole golf course, **Forest Hills Park** now features tennis courts, a swim-

ming pool, softball fields, open fields for frisbee and other weekend sports, and a seemingly endless greenway flanked by gigantic willow oaks.

MOREHEAD HILL

In the 1880s, some of Durham's industrialists and financiers began building their homes in a neighborhood developing adjacent to Forest Hills around the hilltop residence of Eugene Morehead. Unfortunately, during the last 20 years, the construction of the East-West Expressway saw the demolition of many fine homes. To this day, Morehead Hill remains a small island of wide tree-lined boulevards and well-landscaped yards. Its homes date from the turn of the century to more contemporary energy-efficient solar models.

LAKEWOOD

Of all the neighborhoods that grew up around the turn of the century, Lakewood was the most popular, thanks to the now defunct Lakewood Park, a rollicking amusement park known as "the Coney Island of the South." Today, Lakewood is a shopping center surrounded by bungalow homes dating from the 1890s to the 1930s. Prices range from $70,000 to $95,000.

ROCKWOOD

Rockwood is a lesser known hilly, winding, tree-shaded neighborhood, located just south of Forest Hills. Contemporary homes are interspersed with those built in the 1940s. Rockwood also has a neighborhood park. Home prices start around $110,000.

OLD NORTH DURHAM

If you want historic charm for a more reasonable price and you have the time and energy to tackle a restoration job, Old North Durham may be your best bet. Here some of the city's most elegant and spacious homes, once fallen into disrepair, are now being returned to their earlier splendor. Built in the same period and with the same elegance as the homes in Trinity Park, these homes can be bought for considerably less.

A very active homeowners association in Old North Durham is helping draw new people into the neighborhood to participate in its renaissance.

EAST DURHAM

Like Old North Durham, East Durham—the neighborhood due east of downtown—holds some amazing housing bargains, although these homes are not nearly as grand. East Durham grew up around cotton mills, whose owners built wood-frame rental dwellings for their employees. Today, many of those homes are still in good shape. Several years ago, a 1920s vintage one-story, two-bedroom home, requiring little more than a fresh coat of paint, could be bought

for $25,000. You won't be able to find that kind of deal today, but there are still many bargains available. East Durham may just be the most eclectic neighborhood in town. Its residents are black and white, blue collar and white collar, old-timers and young professionals, all of whom seem to co-exist peacefully.

SOUTHEAST DURHAM

The predominantly black community of southeast Durham began with the late 19th century development of the Hayti neighborhood along Fayetteville Street. The area prospered as local black businessmen invested profits from the North Carolina Mutual Life insurance company, the largest black-managed financial institution in the world.

The neighborhood expanded first to the west into an area known as St. Theresa, named for a Roman Catholic church. Then in the 1920s and '30s it evolved southward into neighborhoods now known as Lincoln Hospital and Dunstan. By 1940, College View grew up around North Carolina Central University, the first state-supported liberal arts college for blacks.

While much of Hayti was leveled by the construction of the East-West Expressway, attractive, moderately priced homes still exist in College View, a middle-class neighborhood along Fayetteville Street and around NCCU.

MAP OUT YOUR STRATEGY
WITH DURHAM'S PREMIERE HOME BUILDER

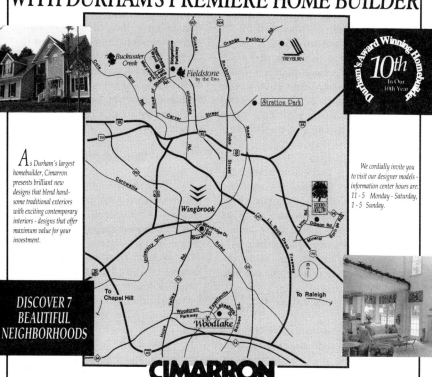

As Durham's largest homebuilder, Cimarron presents brilliant new designs that blend handsome traditional exteriors with exciting contemporary interiors - designs that offer maximum value for your investment.

We cordially invite you to visit our designer models - information center hours are: 11 - 5 Monday - Saturday, 1 - 5 Sunday.

DISCOVER 7 BEAUTIFUL NEIGHBORHOODS

CIMARRON
Homes

Treyburn
$169,000 - $230,000
Treyburn Marketing Company
620-0002

Buckwater Creek
$120,000 - $160,000
Prudential Carolinas Realty
479-4918

Lenox
$120,000 - $150,000
383-4489

Hidden Hollow
$71,950 - $102,950
Prudential Carolinas Realty
598-1034

Stratton Park
$65,500 - $80,600
Prudential Carolinas Realty
471-2941

Wingbrook
$120,000 - $160,000
Prudential Carolinas Realty
490-1295

Woodlake Candlewood
$90,000 - $130,000
Fonville Morrisey
544-6098

Dunmore
$120,000 - $160,000
Fonville Morrisey
544-6098

Throughout The Years Cimarron Has Been Awarded: Best Affordable Home • Builders Choice Award • Home Builder of the Year

ROLLING HILLS

The largest downtown development occurring today is the **Heritage Square Shopping Center** and the adjacent Rolling Hills residential complex, both located on 28 acres of the section of Hayti that was once razed in the name of "urban renewal." The complex was developed by the nonprofit Rolling Hills Associates with $250,000 from the City of Durham, a $450,000 federal grant and a loan from the National Co-op Bank.

Rolling Hills offers 159 townhomes and patio homes for $60,000 to $75,000. Across the street, the Heritage Square shopping center has nine stores that are owned by a group of shareholders in the community, giving the neighborhood a financial stake in the future and success of the complex.

HOPE VALLEY

Here is where you'll find a variety of residences ranging from nicely landscaped middle-class suburban ranches priced at $150,00 to $200,000 to some of the most colossal older homes in Durham. (Flanking the Hope Valley Country Club's 18-hole golf course, tennis courts and swimming pool are Old English Tudors and Colonial mansions with price tags that start at $275,000.)

But spread along Hope Valley Road and its side streets are the more affordable dwellings that are home to many Durhamites. Of special note is Green Mill, an all-solar subdivision off Hope Valley Road, where homes sell for $175,000 to $325,000 (see "Durham Builders" section in **HOMES**).

Hope Valley is the gateway to Durham's southwestern suburbs. Conveniently located midway between Research Triangle Park and Chapel Hill, the area has experienced an unprecedented building boom in recent years. Here you'll find brick ranches, colonials, split levels and solar contemporaries at a variety of prices.

WOODCROFT

Perhaps the most successful newer development in southwest Durham is Woodcroft, a $300-million planned community and shopping center on 750 acres. Begun in 1981, Woodcroft offers some 2,500 residential units. The area is almost fully developed, and available lots and new homes are scarce, although many homes are available for resale.

Woodcroft features a series of distinct "neighborhoods" offering a variety of housing options from $70,000 condos and $90,000 townhomes to single-family homes selling for $125,000 to $250,000. Each mini-subdivision is surrounded by woods or open space. And all residents have access to jogging trails, athletic fields and a community club, complete with a swimming pool and tennis courts. There is also a shopping center that serves the Woodcroft community and adjacent neighborhoods (see "Durham" section of **SHOPPING**).

PARKWOOD

One of the oldest residential subdivisions in southern Durham, Parkwood offers a range of appealing family homes in a neighborhood setting, priced in the $90,000 to $135,000 range. Located on N.C. Highway 54 near Interstate 40, it's convenient to Durham and Chapel Hill and only minutes from Research Triangle Park. An elementary school and a branch of the Durham Library are located in Parkwood.

FALCONBRIDGE

Located midway between Chapel Hill and Durham on N.C. Highway 54, Falconbridge offers townhomes and single-family residences convenient to the cultural, educational and employment opportunities afforded by both towns. It's also minutes from Jordan Lake and Research Triangle Park and it's within the Durham Public Schools system.

Falconbridge's traditional and contemporary single-family homes sell for $140,000 to $250,000 and townhomes start at $79,000. There is a clubhouse with tennis courts and swimming pool in Falconbridge. Lots of about one-third of an acre are available for $42,500 to $45,500.

WILLOWHAVEN

Like the southwest suburbs, developments north of town offer varied housing styles from traditional to contemporary, on family-size lots larger than you'll find in the city. Since the 1950s, Willowhaven has been developed on one-and-a-half-acre lots around the Willowhaven Country Club.

CROASDAILE

Ten years after Willowhaven was developed, Croasdaile followed a similar pattern, focusing around its own championship, 18-hole golf course and country club. Homes in Croasdaile usually sell for $200,000 up, with a few in the $500,000 plus range.

The new Croasdaile Farm section offers homesites of one half to over two acres ($47,000 to $135,000, choose your own builder) and luxury townhomes from $300,000.

TREYBURN

Situated on 5,300 rustic acres along the Little River north of Durham, Treyburn is the largest development in the Durham area.

When completed in 8 or 10 years, it will be a residential-industrial-commercial complex about the size of Research Triangle Park. The developers say it will eventually house 10,000 residents in 4,400 condominiums, apartments and single-family homes "oriented to provide golf, waterfront or open space views." About a third of the acreage will be set aside for open space and recreational use, including three golf courses. One of the Fazio-designed courses is open and in great shape, the gorgeous 39,000-square-foot clubhouse is complete, and the

457

tennis facility is ranked one of the finest in the country.

A number of families already call Treyburn home, and a 369-unit residential retirement community and condos adjacent to the clubhouse are planned. Meanwhile, homesites are selling for $65,000 for a half-acre lot to $175,000 for two acres on the waterfront. Homes sell for anywhere from $200,000 to over $1 million. Many of Treyburn's residents and club members are prominent community and state movers and shakers, as well as retirees moving to the area.

Treyburn is expected to be a boon to the Durham area, and should attract enough light industries, research facilities and office spaces to provide 65,000 jobs and add $1.6 billion to the tax base.

MILAN WOODS

Located in northeast Durham, off U.S. Highway 70 at the Geer Street exit, Milan Woods has in the past been selected by a panel of Triangle real estate agents as "the most attractive community," and "the best home value" in its price range. Milan Woods offers affordably priced ($85,00 to $130,000) transitional and traditional homes on wooded homesites. Milan Woods is minutes from Research Triangle Park, Duke, Treyburn, Raleigh-Durham Airport and downtown Durham.

New Developments

Housing developments have been springing up all around Durham in the last few years. Here's a brief listing of what's available, along with price ranges and locations.

PLANNED COMMUNITIES

In addition to the planned communities of Rolling Hills, Woodcroft and Treyburn (mentioned above), there are two others worth exploring. **Spring Hill**, located along N.C. Highway 54 convenient to Research Triangle Park, offers condominiums (from $60,000), townhomes (from $105,000) and single-family homes (from $130,000). The **Villages of Cornwallis** is located east of town along Cornwallis Road near N.C. Highway 55, and offers condominiums (from $60,000), townhomes (from $75,000) and single-family homes (from $95,000).

SINGLE-FAMILY HOMES

There are dozens of newer single-family developments ringing Durham. On the south side of town you'll find three- and four-bedroom homes in the $150,000-plus range in **Fairfield**, and for $175,000 and up in **Bent Creek** and **Marydell**. A new community worth taking a look at is **Hope Valley Farms** off N.C. Highway 751 (Hope Valley Road), just north of Interstate 40, with large lots, attractive prices and quality construction. Also in southern Durham you can purchase smaller, less expensive homes in the $85,000 range in **Folkestone, Forest Edge** (off Hope Valley Road), **Lassiter Place, Nottingham Forest,**

Wimbledon Forest and **The Woodlands**. On the east side of Durham, near the new Forest View Elementary School are **Montvale, Lochn'ora** and **Garrett Farms,** with homes in the $175,000 to $225,000 price range.

On the northern side of Durham, many homes are generally less expensive than in southwest Durham. Here you'll find single-family residences selling from $75,000 in **Greenwood, Meadow Heights, Milan Woods** and **Scarsdale Village.** Key Homes has built some $65,000 homes in **Scotland Manor.** More expensive four-bedroom homes are available in **Waterford** (from $165,000). And northeast of town, off U.S. Highway 70, Americraft Builders has three- and four-bedroom homes for $90,000 and up in **Stirrup Creek.**

Other developments north of Durham include **Black Horse Run, Hardscrabble Plantation, Horton Hills** and **Vantage Point.**

Town Homes and Condominiums

There are several major condominium and townhome complexes in and around Durham offering size and floor plans to suit just about any taste. They include townhomes with 1,800 to 2,200 square feet as well as two- and three-bedroom units with 1,200 to 1,400 square feet. On the lower priced end ($60,000 to $90,000) are the condos and townhomes available in **Beech Hill, Breckenridge, Five Oaks-Lakeside, Park Place, Falconbridge, Wimbledon Forest** and **Woodstream Glen. Innisfree** in southwest Durham offers two and three-bedroom units from $130,000.

Staff photo.

This lovely apartment complex near Duke University is one of many luxurious choices in Durham.

Staff photo.

*Northgate Park, one of 53 parks maintained by the city of Durham,
is a favorite with young people.*

Inside

Durham Parks and Recreation

If Durham is lacking in nightlife, it more than makes up for it with the daytime activities available at public and private facilities all over town.

With a more than $4 million annual budget, the city's Parks and Recreation Department oversees more than 1,300 acres of park land throughout the county, including 53 parks within the city limits. The department's 12 recreation centers offer a full range of individual and team sports for children and adults, including baseball, basketball, boxing, soccer, softball, racquetball, handball, swimming, tennis and volleyball. In addition there are a variety of arts, dance and crafts classes and other special programs for all ages, including senior citizens and the handicapped.

Durham has 18 lighted athletic fields. A dozen parks provide 72 hard-surfaced tennis courts, 68 of them with lights. There are four public swimming pools and another nine available at private membership clubs.

What's more, there are plenty of hiking, biking, jogging and horse trails as well as fishing and boating opportunities and public and private golf courses.

Here's a handy guide to how and where you can participate in some of these activities. Those facilities operated by the Parks and Recreation Department are noted. For more information, contact the **City of Durham Parks and Recreation Department**, 101 City Hall Plaza, Durham, NC 27701 (560-4355). (For information on camping, fishing and water sport activities at nearby recreational areas, see **ATTRACTIONS**.)

DURHAM YMCA

2119 Chapel Hill Rd. 493-4502

The Durham YMCA is a complete fitness center, offering separate men's and women's free-weight rooms, universal-weight rooms, saunas and steam rooms. The Y features an indoor 25-meter pool, two full-size indoor basketball courts and four indoor racquetball courts.

Behind the main facility is a 1/5 mile graded outdoor track. The Y offers men's, women's, coed and senior aerobics classes for all levels. Child care is available for those taking classes. Call for more information.

SPORTS

BASEBALL

Little League Baseball is played at five city parks: Lakeview, Red Maple, Long Meadow, Oval Drive and Lake Michie Recreation Area. Contact the Parks and Recreation Department for information on how to register your child for one of the 65 youth teams.

BASKETBALL

You can probably find a good in-your-face pickup game at any one of the 50 full-size outdoor courts (30 of them lighted) located at city parks, or at the gyms at the Edison-Johnson or W.D. Hill recreation centers. Courts are located at the following city parks: Old Farm, Lakeview, Red Maple, Sherwood, East Main Street, Lyon/Ramseur, East End, Long Meadow, East Durham, Birchwood, C.R. Wood, Burton, Hillside, Elmira Avenue, Unity Village, Southern Boundaries, White Oak, Rockwood, Forest Hills, Lyon, Morreene, Crest Street, West Durham, Oval Drive and Whippoorwill. There is a lighted court at Walltown Center. There are half-courts at Rocky Creek, Carroll Street and Albany/Sovereign parks.

Contact the Parks and Recreation Department for information about youth- and adult-league play.

BIKING

Durham's Trails and Greenways Commission has been a little slow getting started, but it is working on providing hiking, biking and jogging trails throughout the city.

Bike trails marked with green and white signs will run from Durham Academy to Duke University to North Carolina Central University. There are plenty of paved secondary roads ideal for biking through the surrounding countryside. For more information, contact the **Durham Trails and Greenways Commission**, 101 City Hall Plaza, Durham, NC 27701 (560-4137).

Bicycle enthusiasts may be interested in joining the **Carolina Tarwheels**, a Durham and Chapel Hill cycling club that sponsors special bike trips and activities throughout the Triangle. For information, contact Carolina Tarwheels at 489-8936 or 490-0035.

CANOEING

If you're interested in exploring the flat and white water in Durham and across the state, contact the **Carolina Canoe Club** for an outing schedule. It sponsors trips for canoeists of varying skill levels. Call 688-6917. **River Runners' Emporium** at 201 Albemarle Street, can also assist you with canoeing information at 688-8001.

EAGLE WATCHING

The northern section of Jordan Lake is home to the largest collection of bald eagles in the eastern United States. You can spot them from several bridges passing over the water, but the best vantage point is from a special observation deck built by the **New Hope Audubon Society**. This site is located along N.C. Highway 751 south of Durham, six miles south of Interstate 40. Turn right after the "Wildlife Observation Site" sign, park your car and enjoy a pleasant 15-minute walk through the woods to the deck. Best observation times are dawn and dusk.

GOLF

Durham's mild climate means you can golf year-round. There are four public courses and four private ones—all of them 18 holes. The public facilities are: **Duke University Golf Course (Washington Duke)** at N.C. Highway 751 and Science Drive (684-2817), **Hillandale Golf Course** at Hillandale Road (286-4211), **Lakeshore Golf Course** at Lumley Road (596-2401) and **Lake Winds Golf Course** at U.S. Highway 501 North (471-4653).

Championship courses are available to members and their guests at the country clubs serving some of Durham's most prestigious neighborhoods: **Croasdaile**,

Willowhaven and **Treyburn** north of town, and **Hope Valley** to the southwest.

Every spring Croasdaile, the Washington Duke Golf Course and Perry Como host the **Duke Children's Classic**, a three-day golf/tennis benefit for Duke University Medical Center's pediatric department. Celebrities abound, drawing some 20,000 spectators.

HIKING AND JOGGING

The Durham Trails and Greenways Commission has plans for 170 miles of hiking, jogging and biking trails throughout the city.

As of this writing, only one 1.2-mile trail is open, running between Rock Quarry Park on Stadium Drive and Northgate Park on East Club Boulevard. The Quarry Trail will eventually join at its southern end with the Pearl Mill Trail, providing a connection to downtown and eventually a network of trails and greenways throughout Durham.

Meanwhile, some local developers have been persuaded to set aside land for hiking and jogging trails through their new residential neighborhoods. Woodcroft in southwest Durham (see **NEIGHBORHOODS**) already has a network of paved trails in place.

For getting away from it all, the best hiking opportunities are at **Duke Forest** (684-2421), **Lake Michie** (477-3906), **Eno River State Park** (383-1686) and **West Point on the Eno** city park (471-1623, see details below). Call for information and maps. For additional information on day and overnight hiking trips in the Triangle or across the state, contact the **Sierra Club**; members meet the second Wednesday of every month at the Durham Friends' Meeting House, 404 Alexander Avenue.

Horseback Riding

You can go horseback riding in some of the same places recommended for hiking. In addition, riding and stables are available at the following private facilities: **B-Bar Stables** on Bivins Road (471-2153) and **Quail Roost Stables** on U.S. Highway 501 North (477-8932).

Lake Michie

This small lake about 10 miles north of Durham is an ideal place for a summer outing. You can fish, rent canoes and paddle boats, and camp overnight. Call 477-3906 for information on boating and fishing, and 560-4355 for camping.

Racquet Sports

Racquetball and handball can be played at two facilities run by the city's Parks and Recreation Department: the Edison Johnson Center at 600 West Murray Avenue and Duke Park at 1530 Acadia St.

Courts for racquet sports are also available at the following private facilities: **MetroSport**, 501 Douglas Street (286-7529) and the **YMCA**, 2119 Chapel Hill Road (493-4502).

For information on tennis clubs and public tennis courts, see "Tennis" in this section.

Senior Citizen Activities

The Parks and Recreation Department provides a variety of activities of interest to senior citizens, including exercise classes, square dances, field trips and social clubs.

Among the most popular activities are the **Seniors Achieving Fitness** classes, offered free at the following locations: East Durham Center, E.D. Mickle Center, Lyon Park Center, Walltown Center, West Durham Center, Grace Lutheran Church, J.F.K. Towers, J.J. Henderson Towers, Northgate Presbyterian Church and Oldham Memorial Towers.

Free **square-dance classes** are offered at J.F.K. Towers and J.J. Henderson Towers. And senior citizen clubs meet twice monthly at the following locations: West Durham Center, E.D. Mickle Center, T.A. Grady Center, Walltown Center, Edison Johnson Center, East Durham Center, Lakewood Baptist Church and W.D. Hill Center.

Soccer

The city's Parks and Recreation Department oversees 38 soccer teams for youth and nine for adults. Seven playing fields (five of them lighted) are available at the following parks: Old Farm, Rock Quarry, Northgate, C.R. Wood, Southern Boundaries, Weaver Meadow and Erwin.

If your son or daughter wants to be a soccer star, contact the **Central Carolina Youth Soccer Association** for tryouts. The CCYSA is a nonprofit organization that provides opportunities for children to play highly competitive soccer in contests all across the state. The teams are comprised of kids from the Durham and Chapel Hill areas. For additional information, write: CCYSA, 3505 Rugby Road, Durham 27707.

SOFTBALL

The city Parks and Recreation folks supervise about 300 youth and adult softball teams playing at the following parks: Old Farm, Rock Quarry, Sherwood, Long Meadow, Edgemont, East Durham, Birchwood, Hillside, Elmira Avenue, Campus Hills, Southern Boundaries, Lyon, Wrightwood, Morreene, Walltown and Whippoorwill. Call the Parks and Recreation Department for registration information.

SWIMMING

Public pools are available at four city parks: Duke Park at 1503 Acadia Street (560-4306), Forest Hills at 1639 University Drive (560-4286), Hillside at 1300 South Roxboro Road (560-4290) and Long Meadow at Liberty Street (560-4202).

If you are a member or guest, you can also swim at one of the following private membership clubs: Croasdaile Country Club at Farm Gate Avenue (383-1591), Eno Valley Swim and Racquet Club at Rippling Stream (477-9042), Hollow Rock Racquet and Swim Club on Erwin Road (489-1550), Hope Valley Country Club at Dover Road (489-6565), MetroSport at 501 Douglas Street (286-7529), Poplar Swim Club (383-3830), Spa Health Club at Willowdaile Shopping Center (471-3964), Willowhaven Country Club at 253 Country Club Drive (383-5511) and the YMCA at 2119 Chapel Hill Road (493-4502).

A number of housing developments have private swimming facilities for residents. They include Five Oaks at 519 Pine Cone Drive (493-1495), Woodcroft at Hope Valley Road (489-7705) in southwest Durham, and Treyburn in north Durham. (See **DURHAM NEIGHBORHOODS**)

Don't forget to check out the swimming holes on the Eno River.

There's also a **Masters Swimming Program** that is very active in the Triangle area. (In fact, members of this program have been National Champions.)

TENNIS

If you can't find a place to play tennis in Durham, you're not trying very hard. There are 72 hard-surface courts (all but four are lighted) at these city parks: Rock Quarry, Northgate, Sherwood, East End, W. E. Hill, Elmira Avenue, Southern Boundaries, Garrett Road, Forest Hills, Morreene, Oval Drive and Whippoorwill.

Or you may want to join one of the following private facilities:

The original West Point Mill collapsed in 1973, but was reconstructed with materials from other grist mills.

Croasdaile Country Club (383-1427), Eno Valley Swim and Racquet Club (477-9042), Hollow Rock Racquet and Swim Club (489-1550), Hope Valley Country Club (489-6565) and Willowhaven Country Club (383-5511). Tennis classes are available through the Parks and Recreation Department. Under a city program, instructors have also provided classes at some public housing complexes.

VOLLEYBALL

There are more than 100 volleyball teams for youth and adults competing through the Parks and Recreation Department. For times and registration information, contact the department.

WINDSURFING

Thanks to Durham's proximity to both Falls and Jordan Lakes (see **TRIANGLE ATTRACTIONS**), windsurfing has become very popular in the area. For more information, contact the **Triangle Board Sailing Club** at 596-8185.

West Point On The Eno

Of all Durham's city parks, West Point on the Eno is the most unique. This 40-acre setting represents the joint efforts of a group of citizens (The Friends of West Point) and the city to restore and preserve a part of the 19th-century community that existed before Durham.

West Point was a thriving community of about 300 families, with a post office, general store, blacksmith shop, saw mill and cotton gin. Its inhabitants depended on water power generated by the West Point Mill, which operated continuously along the river from 1778 to 1942. The original mill building collapsed in 1973, but was later reconstructed with materials from other grist mills. Today you can visit the park and see corn and wheat grinding demonstrations; the cornmeal and flour produced are bagged and sold in the park's mill country store.

You will also see a traditional timber-frame blacksmith shop, a tobacco barn typical of the sort used to produce brightleaf tobacco for cigarettes, and the restored Greek Revival country house of longtime mill owner John Cabe McCown.

Every year, West Point on the Eno is the site of a **Fourth of July folk life celebration** attracting musicians, artists and craftspersons from all over North Carolina.

West Point is part of the 1,600-acre **Eno River State Park,** a water-oriented wilderness where you can hike for miles, enjoy primitive walk-in camping and go fishing, canoeing or rafting. For more information on West Point, call 471-1623, and for details on Eno River State Park, call 383-1686.

Staff Photo

The North Carolina School of Science and Mathematics, a public high school for students gifted in science and math, is located in Durham.

Inside

Durham Schools

There is no shortage of educational opportunities for your child in Durham. The area is served by the newly merged Durham Public Schools and about a dozen private and parochial schools. The North Carolina School of Science and Mathematics, a state residential school for gifted high school students, is also located in Durham. The only real problem is trying to figure out which schools will best meet your family's needs.

The Public Schools

In the Durham Public Schools system, students attend neighborhood schools generally based on geographic zones. Some redistricting will occur in the next year as the school administration, under the leadership of new Superintendent Owen Phillips, works to balance the number of enrollees and the racial diversity of students attending each school.

The Durham Public Schools offer excellent educational and recreational opportunities and have a reputation for innovative programs and tough academic standards. Graduation requirements exceed state standards and include computer education and more math and science courses. And the system enforces the state's toughest academic standards on student athletes.

The student-teacher ratio is slightly lower than the statewide average. A significant number of the system's teachers have master's degrees. More than seventy-five percent of Durham high school graduates go on to continue their education.

Strong funding for the school district translates into a variety of innovative programs. For example, the school system expanded the state's definition of "academically gifted" with a local program for elementary students who are gifted in the arts and communication.

In addition, the system employs special academic programs for gifted, handicapped and learning-disabled students in grades K-12. It also provides advanced courses such as Latin and foreign languages in the middle schools, an extensive cultural arts program, and sophisticated audio-visual facilities, including cable television instruction to supplement classroom work.

469

A vocational education program offers instruction in 65 different courses, one of the most comprehensive in the state. Programs for academically gifted students begin in kindergarten and continue through advanced placement courses in senior high. The system also provides one of the best individualized services in the state for students with learning disabilities or with physical, emotional, speech, hearing, visual or mental handicaps. A special developmental reading program is available for grades 1 to 5 followed by a supplemental program in basic skills for grades 6 to 8. A number of other programs, including elementary physical education, computer instruction and cultural arts, have been state and national models.

The Durham Public Schools are spread out over 42 campuses serving 27,000 students. There are 27 elementary (K-5), nine middle (6-8), and six senior high (9-12) schools as well as a school program for hospitalized students.

Here's a quick reference for the schools that presently serve the in-town neighborhoods we described in our **DURHAM NEIGHBORHOODS** section. Since the Durham school system is in the midst of redistricting controversy, changes are imminent.

Trinity Park: George Watts Elementary, Brogden Middle and Durham High.

Watts Hospital: Watts Street is served by George Watts Elementary, West Club Boulevard by E.K. Powe El-

ementary and East Club Boulevard by Club Boulevard Elementary. Brogden Middle and Durham High serve the entire area.

Duke Park: Club Boulevard Elementary, Brogden Middle and Durham High.

Old North Durham: Club Boulevard or East End Elementary, Brogden Middle and Durham High.

Duke Forest: Lakewood Elementary, Rogers-Herr Middle and Hillside High.

Forest Hills: Morehead or Lakewood Elementary, Rogers-Herr Middle and Hillside High.

Morehead Hills: Morehead Elementary, Brogden or Rogers-Herr Middle and Durham or Hillside High.

Rockwood: Lakewood Elementary, Rogers-Herr Middle and Hillside High.

If you are in the suburbs of Durham, here's a quick guide to how the elementary schools (K-5) presently feed into the middle (6-8) and senior high (9-12) schools.

In northern Durham County, Grades K-2 attend Mangum Primary School, and grades 3-5 attend Little River Elementary School. Students then attend Carrington Middle (6-8) and Northern High School (9-12).

In the suburbs immediately north of town, students in K-5 attend one of the following elementary schools: Eno Valley, Glenn, Hillandale, Holt or Merrick-Moore. Grades 6-8 then go to either Carrington or Chewning Middle Schools. They go to Northern or Riverview High Schools.

In the southern suburbs, students in K-5 attend one of the following elementary schools: Bethesda, Hope Valley, Lowe's Grove, Oak Grove, Parkwood, Pearsontown or Southwest. They go on to Githens, Lowes Grove or Neal Middle Schools. Most students in the southwest go to Jordan High School (though some Githens students were transferred to Riverview in fall 1992), while southeastern kids go to Southern High.

To learn more about the schools serving your neighborhood, plan to visit some of the facilities, talk to the principals and observe a few classes.

For more information on the Durham Public Schools, contact: **Public Information Officer**, Durham Public Schools, P.O. Box 30002, Durham, NC 27702, (560-2000).

NORTH CAROLINA SCHOOL OF SCIENCE AND MATHEMATICS
1219 Broad St.   *286-3366*
Durham, NC 27705

This unique school opened in 1980 as the nation's first public residential high school for students with a strong interest and potential in science and mathematics. The school provides exceptional opportunities for 400 high school students from all socioeconomic backgrounds across North Carolina, chosen for their academic achieve-

ment and talent. Students live on the 27-acre campus of the former Watts Hospital and School of Nursing, now on the National Register of Historic Sites.

Private and Parochial Schools

In addition to its two public school systems, the Durham community also offers a wide choice of private and parochial schools. We are listing them here with the latest available information on tuition rates. Again, we advise that you visit these facilities, meet the principals and observe a few classes and activities before making a decision.

CAROLINA FRIENDS SCHOOL
425 STUDENTS, PRE THRU 12.
Friends School Rd.   *383-6602*
Rt. 1, Box 183
Durham, NC 27705

This non-denominational school, founded in 1963 by the Quakers, is located on 45 acres of wooded countryside equidistant from Durham, Chapel Hill and Hillsborough. The Friends School features a decidedly open and progressive approach to education: students are grouped by common interests and abilities rather than age or grade level. There are no letter or number grades; instead, students receive written evaluations and "credit" or "no credit." There is a lower school for six- to ten-year-olds, a middle school for ages 10 to 14 and an upper school for those 14 to 18. Children enter the Earth class at age six and after a year or so are placed in Fire or Water classes until they are ready for middle school.

While reading, writing and math are continually stressed, students also focus on annual themes, such as "the human body" or "ecology." Independent study, community service projects, field trips and sports are also part of the curriculum. While 90 percent of the students go on to college, programs are available for the non-college-bound as well.

1993 tuition ranges from approximately $2,800 for preschoolers to $5,600 for upper school students. Some financial aid is available.

CFS also has "early schools" for three- to five-year-olds in two locations: 404 Alexander Street in Durham and 531 Raleigh Road in Chapel Hill.

CRESSET CHRISTIAN ACADEMY
240 STUDENTS, PRE THRU 12
3707 Garrett Rd.   489-7258
Durham, NC 27707

Cresset Christian Academy adopts the "historic, Christian view of life as presented in the Bible." In addition to math, language, science and social studies, all students in grades 7-12 are required to take one Bible course each year. 1993 tuition ranges from approximately $2,600 for K-5 to $2,900 for grades 6-12.

DURHAM ACADEMY
1,000 STUDENTS
PRE THRU 8 AND 9 THRU 12
3116 Academy Rd.   498-9118
Durham, NC 27707 (Pre thru 8)
3601 Ridge Rd.   489-6569
Durham, NC 27705 (9 thru 12)

Founded in 1933, Durham Academy is the oldest primary-through-secondary private school in the area. Admission is based on the student's potential to satisfactorily perform college-preparatory work. Enrichment courses include computers, wind ensemble, chorus, dance, drama, studio art, typing, economics and comparative religions. Independent study, internships and volunteer service concludes the 12th year. Juniors and

seniors may take a semester of independent study. Many of these kids go on to the Ivy Leagues. 1993 tuition ranged from $4,500 for preschool to $5,925 - $6,985 for primary through high school grades.

DUKE SCHOOL FOR CHILDREN
170 STUDENTS, PRE THRU 8
Erwin Rd,   286-1866
Durham, NC 27705

Founded in 1947, the Duke School for Children is run by a parent-owned corporation. Activities take place in two separate, passive solar, energy-efficient buildings separated by a courtyard and amphitheater. A new middle school (Grades 6-8) is now open. 1993 tuition ranged from approximately $2800 for three-year-old preschoolers to $4,200 for sixth

graders. Limited financial aid is available.

FIVE OAKS SCHOOL
25 STUDENTS PRESCHOOL
15 STUDENTS, 1 THRU 8
4124 Farrington Rd.   489-7777
Durham, NC 27707

Five Oaks was founded in 1982 by the Seventh Day Adventist Church. It is located in southwest Durham, about 10 minutes from Chapel Hill. Tuition for the 1993 school year ranged from $100 a week for preschoolers ages 3 to 6 to $200 a month for grades 1-8.

HILL LEARNING DEVELOPMENT CENTER
3130 Pickett Rd.   489-7464

The Hill LDC, affiliated with Durham Academy, offers a reme-

The Hand Bell Choir at Cresset Christian Acaademy.

dial program for children with learning disabilities or achievement difficulties in grades K-12. The LDC program provides private instruction for children enrolled in schools in Durham and the surrounding counties in conjunction with their regular classroom work.

IMMACULATA SCHOOL
150 STUDENTS, PRE THRU 8
721 Burch Ave.   682-5847
Durham, NC 27705

This is a Catholic school founded in 1909 to provide a unique learning program in a Christian environment. Class instruction, small groups and independent study are geared to meet the needs of both slower and more advanced students. 1993 tuition for Catholic members of the parish was about $1,900 per year, for non-Catholics it was about $2,600 annually.

LIBERTY CHRISTIAN SCHOOL
100 STUDENTS, K THRU 12
1606 Liberty St.   683-5522
Durham, NC 27703

Liberty Christian School was founded in 1982 "to bring each student to a saving knowledge and relationship with Jesus Christ, to train the student in a way of life in keeping with Scripture, and to prepare the student for a life of service while providing excellent academic training." The school requires Bible study, daily devotions and weekly chapel services. 1993 tuition was approximately $1,500.

MONTESSORI COMMUNITY SCHOOL
4512 Pope Rd.   493-8541

This school has a toddler program (half, 3/4 or full day) and an elementary program up through grade 3. Tuition for the half-day preschool is $2,400; elementary school tuition is $3,800.

ST. MARY'S SCHOOL
175 STUDENTS, PRE THRU 12
St. Mary's Rd.   688-3469
Hillsborough, NC 27278

Named for its scenic location adjacent to a historic Anglican church between Durham and Hillsborough, but not affiliated with any religion, St. Mary's was established "to provide academic excellence in the basic areas of learning in a college preparatory environment." 1993 tuition ranged from $2,300 for preschool to $3,700 for the upper grades.

STANLEY H. KAPLAN EDUCATIONAL CENTER, LTD.
2634 Chapel Hill Blvd., Suite 112
     489-8720 or 489-2348

If you've got a son or daughter planning to go to college or graduate school, take note. This is the oldest and largest standardized test preparation service in the United States. Classes are designed to prepare students for the SAT, LSAT (for law school), MCAT (medical school), GMAT (business school) and other standardized admission tests. In addition, there are speed-reading classes for students and executives.

Child-Care Providers

The public schools in the Durham area offer before- and after-school care if enough parents at the school request it. For a nominal fee, children can be dropped off at 6:30 or 7 a.m. and picked up at 5:30 or 6 p.m. Call the school to inquire or request the service. In addition, some of the private schools also offer before-school care. (See the private-school listings above.)

What's more, after-school care is provided at six neighborhood centers run by the Durham Parks and Recreation Department: Lyon Park, T.A. Grady, East Durham, W.I. Patterson, Walltown and E.D. Mickle. And a special after-school program for pre-teens is available at the Y.E. Smith and East End elementary schools. For more information on these after-school programs, contact the Durham Parks and Recreation Department, 101 City Hall Plaza, Durham, NC 27701, (560-4355).

Moreover, there are at least 85 day-care providers in the Durham area. They include Montessori schools, church-affiliated centers, national chains and small independent operators. Day-care centers in Durham charge $60 to $135 a week. Child care in private homes usually costs $50 to $100 a week.

North Carolina has recently enacted new minimal standards for child-care facilities. All providers must be registered with the North Carolina Office of Child Day Care

(733-4801), so you should always ask for their registration number. If you want to check out a center's record, you can go to the state office in Raleigh and look in its files to see if there have been any complaints.

State standards also set the following adult-to-provider ratios: infants up to one year old (1:7), two years (1:12), three years (1:15), four years (1:20) and five and older (1:25). These are much looser than federal standards.

The best way to learn about which day-care center or home is right for you is by asking around. If you are new to the area, that may mean quizzing people in your church, neighborhood or workplace. Or you can contact the Durham Day Care Council. It will answer your questions and try to help you match your needs with an appropriate day-care center or home. The Council publishes a map showing exactly where each facility is located, accompanied by a list of centers and their hours. For more information, contact the **Durham Day Care Council,** 119 Orange Street, or call 688-8661 for general information or the **Totline** at 688-9550, 9 a.m. to 1 p.m. Monday through Friday for specific referrals.

THE NORTH CAROLINA SCHOOL OF SCIENCE AND MATHEMATICS OPENED IN 1980 AS THE NATION'S FIRST PUBLIC RESIDENTIAL HIGH SCHOOL FOR STUDENTS WITH A STRONG INTEREST AND POTENTIAL IN SCIENCE AND MATH.

Insiders' Tip

The architectural style of Duke University Chapel is English gothic, and the tower is patterned after the Bell Harry Tower of Canterbury Cathedral.

Inside
Durham Worship

Durham is part of the Bible belt, so as you might expect there are dozens of places of worship to choose from, covering every conceivable religious and spiritual interest from southern Baptist to orthodox Jew. We're not about to mention every place of worship here (try the Yellow Pages for that), but we will offer you a glimpse of what some of the more popular or special ones are like.

Baptist

GREY STONE BAPTIST CHURCH
2601 Hillsborough Rd.   *286-2281*

With nearly 3,000 members, this Southern Baptist Church constitutes the largest congregation in Durham. Established in 1894, Grey Stone has been in its present location, near Ninth Street in west Durham, for more than half a century. It's no wonder this church is so popular. There are enough activities going on here to keep every member of the family occupied.

The Family Life Center includes basketball, volleyball and racquet ball courts, a weight room, game room and gymnasium. Youth programs include camping, sports and a summer beach trip. There are weekly church suppers, activi-

ties for senior citizens and a "Single Again" club for divorced members. Grey Stone even has its own full orchestra. In addition, the church operates a year-round child-care center for ages two through five.

If you can't make it to church Sunday morning, you can catch the 11 a.m. service on radio station WTIK (channel 1310).

FIRST BAPTIST CHURCH
414 Cleveland St.   *688-7308*

With nearly 2,000 members, this church represents the second largest Southern Baptist congregation in town. Established in 1845, First Baptist has been in its present location more than 45 years. Each Sunday, there is 9:45 a.m. Sunday school, 11 a.m. worship, and 7 p.m. evening worship. Weekly church suppers are held Wednesday evenings. And there is a half-day preschool (ages two to four) from September through May.

WHITE ROCK BAPTIST CHURCH
3400 Fayetteville St.   *688-8136*

Established in 1866, White Rock is one of the largest predominantly black churches in Durham.

Other large Southern Baptist congregations include those of

Bethesda Baptist Church (Miami Boulevard) and Guess Road Baptist Church.

Catholic

IMMACULATE CONCEPTION
810 W. Chapel Hill St.   682-3449

Years ago, there were few Catholics in the area. But thanks to an influx of newcomers, there are now four Catholic churches, including Immaculate Conception, with one of the largest congregations in town. One of Durham's oldest churches, Immaculate Conception was established in the early 1900s. The parish has more than 1,200 families. There are three Masses every Sunday morning, and one every Saturday evening. In addition, the church operates preschool, after-school and summer-camp programs.

The other Catholic churches are Holy Cross (on N.C. Highway 55), which serves a predominantly black community located near N.C. Central University, Holy Infant, which has enjoyed a sudden surge in membership thanks to a blessed location near Research Triangle Park, and St. Matthews in northern Durham County.

Episcopal

ST. PHILLIPS
403 E. Main St.   682-5708

St. Phillips is the oldest and probably the largest Episcopal church in town. Established in 1880, it now has about 750 members under the spiritual leadership of the Rev. Dr. C. Thomas Midyette III. There are three Sunday morning services from September through May, and two during the summer months. In addition there is a 10 a.m. Thursday service year-round.

St. Joseph's (1902 West Main Street) is the second oldest Episcopal church in Durham. And St. Luke's Episcopal (1737 Hillandale Road) is reputed to have one of the best preschool/kindergarten programs in Durham. St. Titus Episcopal Church (400 Moline Avenue) serves a predominantly black community. St. Stephen's (82 Kimberly Drive) has services at 8 and 10 a.m., with Christian Education classes at 9:30. It is located in Durham's Hope Valley neighborhood.

Interdenominational

DUKE UNIVERSITY CHAPEL
Main Campus   684-2572

Never mind that when tourists inquire as to where Duke students worship they are often directed toward the basketball stadium; Duke Chapel's reputation as the most stunning church facility in Durham is well intact. The 1,800-seat Gothic Revival structure was built to fulfill James B. Duke's dream of "a great towering church which will dominate all the surrounding buildings." The 210-foot tower, patterned after Canterbury Cathedral, contains a 50-bell, four-octave carillon. Inside, the double doors are flanked by portal figures of churchmen Savonarola, Martin Luther, Thomas Cooke and John Wesley, as well as Thomas Jefferson and, of course, Robert E. Lee . The vaulted interior is lighted with 77 stained glass windows.

Jewish

According to local lore, Jews migrated to Durham from New York when James B. Duke needed highly skilled cigarette rollers for his emerging tobacco empire. Unfortunately, not long after the Jewish craftsmen arrived, many of their jobs were displaced by cigarette-rolling machines. Nevertheless, the Jewish community has prospered and continues to grow. There are two synagogues in town: one is conservative and orthodox, the other reformed.

BETH-EL SYNAGOGUE AND CENTER
1004 Watts St.   *682-1238*
Established a century ago, this conservative and orthodox synagogue is 260-members strong and growing, under the leadership of Rabbi Steven Sager. Services are 8 p.m. every Friday and 10 a.m. on Saturday. Beth-El also operates a nursery school for two- to four-year-olds during the school year.

JUDEA REFORM CONGREGATION
2115 Cornwallis Rd.   *489-7062*
More than 15 years old, the Judea Reform Congregation now has more than 300 members, under Rabbi John S. Friedman. Services

are Friday evening and Saturday morning.

Lutheran

ST. PAUL'S LUTHERAN CHURCH IN AMERICA
1200 Cornwallis Rd.   *489-3214*
The largest Lutheran church in Durham, St. Paul's congregation numbers more than 500 and is growing. There are two Sunday morning services year-round.

The second largest Lutheran Church in America congregation in the area is **Christus Victor** located on N.C. Highway 54 at Parkwood (near Research Triangle Park). **Grace Lutheran** (Buchanan Street) is the only Missouri Synod congregation in town. And **Abiding Savior**, an American Lutheran of Christ Church (Alston Avenue), serves the predominantly black East Durham community.

Presbyterian

FIRST PRESBYTERIAN
305 E. Main St.   *682-5511*
Durham's oldest and largest Presbyterian church is located downtown. Built more than a century ago, First Presbyterian boasts a congregation of more than 650 today. Services are 11 a.m. every Sunday. There are active youth and adult fellowship programs as well as a year-round, all-day preschool program.

Staff photo.

Yates Baptist Church on Chapel Hill Road in Durham
is affiliated with the Southern Baptist Convention.

Quaker

FRIENDS MEETING HOUSE
404 Alexander Ave.   *286-4958*

Associated with the Carolina Friends School, this is the only Friends Meeting in Durham. It is located near Duke Gardens.

United Methodist

TRINITY UNITED METHODIST CHURCH
215 N. Church St.   *683-1386*

This was the first Methodist church in Durham, built in 1832 in a school house in Orange Grove about a mile east of town. The current Gothic stone building, located across the street from City Hall, was reconstructed following a fire in 1923. With nearly 1,000 members, it is among the largest Methodist congregations in Durham. There are two services on Sunday morning.

DUKE MEMORIAL UNITED METHODIST CHURCH
504 W. Chapel Hill Blvd.   *683-3467*

Duke Memorial was established over 100 years ago. Today, with more than 1,500 members, it is the largest of the 23 Methodist churches in town. Duke Memorial also operates a preschool from September through May.

From The Chamber...

"Building the economy, strengthening business and creating an even better way of life."

Welcome to the Capital City!

The largest of the Triangle communities, Raleigh is not only the capital of North Carolina, but is also the Wake County seat. This government presence, combined with the diversity of the industry base, adds to the stability of the economy in the Raleigh area. In fact, our unemployment rate has been below 4% for the last ten years.

As the state capital, Raleigh boasts numerous cultural amenities, including the North Carolina Theatre and the North Carolina Symphony. State museums include the North Carolina Museum of Art, the North Carolina Museum of Natural Science, and the North Carolina Museum of History.

Located just minutes from Research Triangle Park - the nation's largest planned research and development park - Raleigh is surrounded by eleven other Wake County municipalities and is the home of seven colleges and universities, including North Carolina State University. Also nearby is the Raleigh-Durham International Airport.

Recreational opportunities are plentiful in Raleigh/Wake County with 49 major parks, semi-professional baseball, hockey and tennis teams, and six lakes. Walnut Creek Amphitheatre, located in Southeast Raleigh, offers concerts throughout the spring, summer and fall, and seats 20,000 people.

The Raleigh-Durham area has received many accolades recently as a great place to live and to do business, including: "#1 City for Business Innovation" by *Fortune* magazine, "#5 Best Place to Live" by *Money* magazine, and "#6 Quality of Place to Live" by the *Places Rated Almanac*.

Whether you are a visitor or a newcomer to the area, we welcome you, and hope that you will take the opportunity to see for yourself why so many people are choosing to call Raleigh, North Carolina home.

Sincerely,

Harvey A. Schmitt
President and CEO

THE GREATER
RALEIGH
CHAMBER OF COMMERCE ...

800 S. Salisbury Street • Raleigh, NC 27601 or PO Box 2978 • Raleigh, NC 27602 • Telephone (919) 664-7000 • Fax (919) 664-7099

Inside
Raleigh

Raleigh is the capital city of North Carolina, with a population of 230,418 in 1993, and has become one of the "hot spots" in America as a place for good living. It was a planned city from its beginning, which distinguishes it from other colonial capitals. Its residents retain a strong interest in urban planning today as it undergoes some of its most dramatic expansion. From atop one of its tallest buildings, the growth surprisingly is hidden among verdant, rolling terrain and under the shade of hardwoods and tall pines.

The city takes its name from the 16th-century English gentleman and explorer, Sir Walter Raleigh. It was Sir Walter, according to romantic lore, who spread his cloak before Queen Elizabeth to spare her feet a mud puddle. Unfortunately for Sir Walter, Elizabeth was not around in 1618 to spare his head when James I asked for it. It was also Sir Walter who lost a colony on North Carolina's coast in 1587 and, despite three years at Oxford, had trouble spelling his name, using Rawleyghe in his youth, then Ralegh and sometimes Raleigh. Such a checkered reputation, however, did not deter admiring North Carolinians in 1792 from naming their new capital after him. They spelled it Raleigh, and today's residents pronounce it Raw-lee or Rah-lee, depending on their lineage.

The selection of the new capital city's site in Wake County was a political decision. Members of the state's General Assembly were tired of meeting in various cities and were anxious for an "unalterable seat of government." They purchased 1,000 acres of "woodland and old field" from Revolutionary War veteran and state Sen. Joel Lane for 1,378 pounds (under $3,000). A planned city was mapped and lots were auctioned to raise money for the new Capitol building. The parcels sold for $60 to $263. Regrettably, prices have risen somewhat since then, but politics have remained in the lifeblood and fiber of the city.

The city in its early years was dependent on the legislature for many of its public works and conduct. The city's commissioners, for instance, were instructed in 1801 to fine merchants who did business on the Sabbath; in 1803, city fathers were empowered to keep hogs from running at large; in 1820, they were given authority to establish a fire department, and in 1825, they were urged to keep infectious diseases from spreading. Members of today's General Assembly continue the tradition of giving advice to Raleigh and its residents. In turn, Raleigh residents are fond of the saying, "The Legislature is in session, let us pray."

The city grew and shrank in spurts during the years until the Civil War. Its first railroad puffed into town in 1840 and its population doubled during the decade, totaling 4,518 by 1850. Not surprisingly, its commerce centered around state government, and one of its largest private businesses was based on the state's printing contract and book binding. The best beds in town for travelers were at the Yarborough House, sometimes called the legislature's "third house" because of the off-hours business conducted there. The city had taken the slogan "City of Oaks," and it was under such a tree on North Street that Whig presidential candidate Henry Clay wrote the "Raleigh letter" opposing annexation of Texas.

The Civil War left its mark on Raleigh as it did other Southern capitals. It was in Raleigh that the scourge of the South, Gen. William Tecumseh Sherman, was quartered with 60,000 restless Union troops when news of President Lincoln's assassination arrived. Luckily, the city escaped any vengeful wrath, thanks to Sherman's rein on his soldiers, but his good deed failed to improve his reputation among Raleigh residents. Indeed, the story persists to this day that Sherman's brief occupation of the governor's mansion so tainted the place that no respectable North Carolina governor would set foot in it. The empty house finally burned, and in its place today stands the city's graceful Memorial Auditorium, home of the North Carolina Symphony.

By 1910, Raleigh's population was 19,218 and it had become a flourishing education center as well as seat of government. St. Mary's School for Girls, begun in 1842, had been joined by two of the nation's first colleges for blacks, Shaw University (1875) and St. Augustine's Normal and Collegiate Institute (1867), as well as by Peace College for women (1872). The Baptist Female Seminary, which is today's Meredith College, was founded in 1889, the same year as the North Carolina College of Agriculture and Mechanical Arts, now the renowned North Carolina State University (whose current enrollment is over 24,000). Champions for the new state college banded together in the Watauga Club, which remains a loose collection of some of the state's power elite and still champions state education issues. Membership includes every former governor and always the editor of the Raleigh *News and Observer*. The editor's place in the club is in deference to one of the club's founders, Josephus Daniels, editor, cabinet officer, ambassador and perhaps the city's most famous citizen before World War II.

The city turned on electric street lights in 1885 and at least 1,900 people were gossiping over

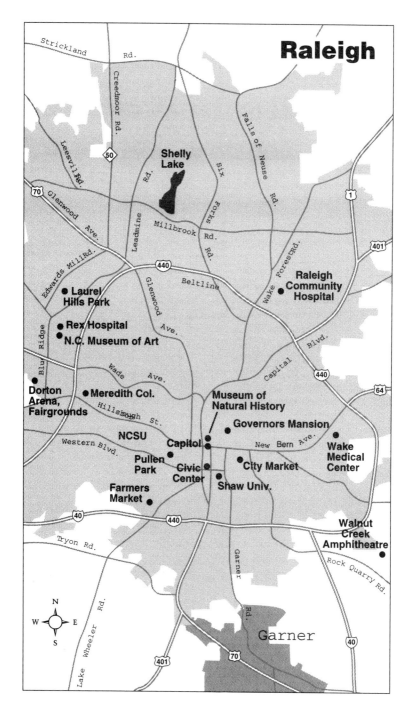

Raleigh

Strickland Rd.

Creedmoor Rd.

Leesvil Rd.

50

70 Glenwood Ave.

Leadmine Rd.

Shelly Lake

Six Forks Rd.

Falls of Neuse Rd.

1

Millbrook Rd.

Edwards Mill Rd.

440

Beltline

Glenwood Ave.

Wake Forest Rd.

Raleigh Community Hospital

401

● Laurel Hills Park

Blue Ridge

● Rex Hospital

● N.C. Museum of Art

Wade Ave.

Capital Blvd.

440

64

● Dorton Arena, Fairgrounds

● Meredith Col.

Hillsbough St.

Museum of Natural History

● Governors Mansion

Western Blvd.

NCSU

● Capitol

New Bern Ave.

● Wake Medical Center

● Pullen Park

● Civic Center

● City Market

● Shaw Univ.

● Farmers Market

40

440

Tryon Rd.

Garner Rd.

Walnut Creek Amphitheatre ●

Rock Quarry Rd.

N W E S

Lake Wheeler Rd.

Garner

401

70

40

the telephone by 1910. A count of manufacturers the same year produced a list of six cotton mills and 33 other manufacturing operations. Interestingly, it wasn't until the 1981-82 recession that Raleigh's last textile mills closed down.

Suburbia came early to Raleigh with the pre-World War I subdividing of the Boylan Plantation into Boylan Heights and the promotion of Cameron Park as a place to enjoy quiet country pleasures in the shadow of city lights. Both are considered downtown neighborhoods today.

The city roared through the 1920s, posting a population in 1930 of 37,379, a 10-year increase of 53 percent. It was in 1920 that the city's first families first displayed their Southern belles in a Debutantes Ball, sponsored by the Terpsichorean Club. An invitation to the ball and its summer of parties can cost today's parents over $8,000.

When the state decided to sell its Raleigh fairgrounds in 1925, it asked the newly formed Raleigh Board of Realtors to sell the property while it moved to more spacious ground farther west. There were sale restrictions on the auction. For example, if you bought a lot on the city's main western boulevard, Hillsborough Street, you agreed to build a suitably grand home on the property—one that cost at least $7,500! The farther away from Hillsborough Street, the less demanding the restrictions. On Brooks Street, you could get by with a $5,000 home and east of Chamberlain Street, $2,500. The area is today called Fairmont after the fair-

grounds. In its center is the Raleigh Little Theater and park grounds, which include the city's Rose Garden and amphitheater. If you look hard enough, you will see that they sit in what used to be the old fairgrounds racetrack.

The Great Depression lived up to its name in Raleigh, despite the city's government payroll. Housing starts dwindled and no major commercial building was erected before 1942. Even fancy, new neighborhoods such as Hayes-Barton, named after Sir Walter's English home, did not escape foreclosures. A young realtor of the times recalled being offered by a banker friend the chance to live in one of Hayes-Barton's largest, newest homes rent free. He would have to pay only the utilities. The bank had foreclosed on the home, then had second thoughts when the vacant house deteriorated. The young realtor was sorely tempted until he discovered that the house's heating bill alone was more than his annual salary. (The same home sold for over $800,000 a few years ago.)

The New Deal brought public housing to town along with public works, among them Halifax Court, Chavis Heights and the Raleigh Little Theater. World War II brought the city a full employment economy, and the city's growth has been on an incline ever since. FHA and VA loans financed whole neighborhoods following the war as Raleigh builders such as E.N. Richards and J.W. "Willie" York put up small, but affordable $6,000 homes with 4 percent mortgage rates. York went on to build the region's first shop-

Courtesy N.C. Travel and Tourism Division. Photo by William Russ.

The Joel Lane House dates from the 1760s and was the center of a large plantation that was chosen as the site of the state's capital.

Courtesy N.C. Travel and Tourism Division. Photo by Mary Johnson.

The State Capitol, completed in 1840 and restored in 1976, is a National Historic Landmark.

ping center, Cameron Village, about a mile from the downtown business district, which was seen as a "crazy, wild" venture. It also proved very successful.

But the major event of the 1950s didn't even take place in Raleigh. It was Gov. Luther Hodges' hope to develop an alternative to the state's traditional, low-wage industrial base of textiles, furniture and apparel. His alternative became the Research Triangle Park, located between the neighboring cities of Durham and Chapel Hill. Through Hodges' influence, the National Institute for Environmental Health Sciences agreed to put research facilities there, but it was IBM's move to the Park in 1965 that certified the Park to other companies with a corporate seal of approval.

City government moved to meet new challenges, including the explosive issue of civil rights. Mayor W.G. Enloe used his office in 1963 to encourage better community relations and the shedding of institutional segregation. Amazingly, within a year of Enloe's initiative, most of Jim Crow's noxious feathers had been plucked and the era of separate black and white restaurants, hotels, parks, etc., faded. The city also moved to a city manager form of government as its population went from 93,931 in 1960 to 122,830 in 1970. A highway beltline across its northern half gave Raleigh a new profile on road maps and accelerated north Raleigh growth.

The 1973 municipal elections were a turning point in city politics. A summer flood along Crabtree Creek raised neighborhood concerns about too rapid development and lack of comprehensive planning. Candidates were divided into pro-neighborhood or pro-development camps, and the neighborhood coalition swept all

Fayetteville Street Mall, a pedestrian mall lined with trees and fountains, is the center of downtown activity throughout the year.

but one council seat and elected the city's first black mayor, Clarence Lightner.

In 1975, Raleigh won the "All America City" designation and began showing up on surveys as one of the top 10 best places to live in the country—No. 5, thank you, on *Money Magazine's* 1993 survey. Smug Raleigh residents were not surprised. When the nation's 1976 Bicentennial arrived, citizens were ready to dance in the streets. After all, the garbage got picked up three times a week, the tap water tasted good, rush hour traffic was only a half-hour, the schools were progressive, utility bills were manageable, the Symphony was not above playing a Strauss waltz, the airport was only 20 minutes away and, most importantly to some, tickets to ACC basketball games, even the fabled ACC Tournament, could be obtained without selling your spouse into bondage.

When G. Smedes York, scion of "old Raleigh," became a two-term mayor in 1977 and united development and neighborhood groups, the city surged as the fastest growing place in the state. The 1980 census showed 149,771 residents while North Carolina passed Massachusetts and became the 10th most populous state. By 1985, Raleigh passed Greensboro as North Carolina's second largest city, behind Charlotte, and the 1990 Census counted a population of 207,951. The 1981-82 recession, the worst for the nation since Depression days, found Raleigh with an unemployment rate only slightly over 5 percent and a local economy almost immune to hard times. The southern half of the Beltline was completed in the next few years.

The boom that followed left veteran developers shaking their heads in amazement. Office space, which had been growing at about 350,000 square feet a year until 1983, jumped in one year to 700,000 square feet. In the last half of the decade, however, the building boom tapered off, especially in apartment and commercial development as the market tried to catch up with an abundant supply. A 1988 school bond issue was adopted overwhelmingly.

The coming of the American Airlines regional hub has been the biggest of recent economic boosts. American now connects the Triangle with such exotic destinations as Paris, France, and Cancun, Mexico, and in the spring of 1994, London, England.

The July, 1991, opening of the Walnut Creek Amphitheater in southeast Raleigh put the city on the "big time" concert tour. A year-round, acquatic center opened in 1992 in Pullen Park as the city celebrated its 200th birthday under five-term, likeable Hizzonner Mayor Avery Upchurch who stepped down in 1993.

The city's Fayetteville Street Mall and the City Market with its Art District of seven galleries have been a magnet for a downtown renaissance that includes two new skyscrapers, while the city's northern boundary has the profile of a giant amoeba, absorbing old subdivisions and growing new ones. Indeed, suburban north Raleigh is seen sometimes as a separate country, peopled by Yankees, IBMers and others who "talk funny," vote Republican and seldom cross the Beltline border into "old Raleigh" or, God forbid, downtown. Some have never even eaten barbecue.

The different accents, food, politics and customs are testimony,

however, to Raleigh's arrival as a city. One suspects that the urbane and adventurous Sir Walter in 1994 would find his namesake city not too provincial. Not too sophisticated. Not too busy. Not too slow. Not too hot. Not too cold. Not too big. Not too small. But just right.

PROFESSIONAL PROFILE

Have you ever thought about buying or selling a home without any hassles? With 80% of Joe's listings selling in 10 days or less and at greater than 98% of the list price, it's no wonder Joe Luck is becoming a household name in the Triangle. Whether you are moving in or out of the Triangle, moving up to a larger home, or buying your first home, Joe can offer you professional advice and service, without the pressure.

Joe has lived in the Triangle since 1984 and has an extensive knowledge of the area. Joe can help with information about schools, the best places to eat, Triangle nightlife and even where to take the pets for grooming.

Call Joe for a free, no obligation estimate of your house, or to talk to him about buying or selling in the Triangle area. Work with a leader!

Joe Luck
Fonville Morisey Realty
Multimillion Dollar Producer

Home: (919)-839-1760
Voice Mail: (919)-839-4653
Pager: (919)-737-2296
Car Phone: (919)-280-1456
Office: (919)-781-4452
Fax: (919)-781-1253

Robust growth in population and building keeps Raleigh utility companies busy.

Inside

Raleigh Government Services and Utilities

Raleigh, like Carl Sandburg's Chicago, is a city that works. Your garbage gets picked up on time, thrice a week. The streets are built and repaired on schedule. You turn on the kitchen faucet and get clean, drinkable water. You call the police and they come within minutes. Firemen make routine neighborhood visits to give you free advice on home hazards. In the fall, there's even a leaf pickup service.

This does not mean Raleigh is problem-free; like most Sunbelt hotspots, it suffers from growing pains, and north Beltline traffic, in particular, can be a headache. Older neighborhoods battle continuously to keep the Transportation Department from putting thoroughfares through their living rooms. But the problems that overwhelm large cities are managed here, and the scandal-free, city-manager form of government during the past four decades has been dull but diligent in its duties. Most city employees provide service with a smile, and they act on your complaints through a handy "Feedback" form that goes out with water bills.

Moreover, after a while, you begin to take for granted what citizens in New York City pray for. The following is a short guide to some of the services that you want—and need—to know as a Raleigh resident. The list also has helpful information about other utilities and items, such as driver's licensing and automobile plates and decals.

Utilities

TELEPHONE

To get new telephone service for your home, call 780-2355. Business customers, call 780-2800. If you're out of state, you call your local operator to obtain a toll-free 800-number. Remember, Ma Bell ain't like she used to be, so you'll need to either buy your own phone or make arrangements with **Southern Bell** to rent one. Assuming that your residence doesn't need wiring or phone jacks, count on three days before service is started. For other information, check the phone book. By the way, Raleigh's area code is (919) and Southern Bell's local street address (you have to search to find it in the phone book) is 5715 Glenwood Avenue.

WATER AND SEWER

If you need to have your water hooked up, call **City Hall** at 890-3245. For repairs to your water meter, call 831-6900. Your water and sewer charges are combined on your bill, which is sent monthly. If you have questions about your water bills, call 890-3245. City Hall is located at 222 W. Hargett Street, across from Nash Square.

ELECTRIC POWER

Raleigh and Cary are served by **Carolina Power and Light Co.**, more familiarly known as CP&L and headquartered at 411 Fayetteville Street on the Raleigh downtown mall. For newcomers, a deposit may be required. For service, call 783-5400.

NATURAL GAS

The gas company for Raleigh and Cary has the high-sounding name of **Public Service Co. of North Carolina**, even though it's a private company. It is a public-spirited company, has clever billboards and provides the cheapest form of heat. For service, call 833-6641. Its office is located at 1720 Hillsborough Street, Raleigh.

CABLE TELEVISION

Cable TV service in Raleigh is provided by a subsidiary of Time Warner, **Cablevision of Raleigh**, located at 2505 Atlantic Avenue. Call 832-2225 to arrange for service. If you are outside the city, you may be served by **Cablevision Industries (CVI)**. CVI may be reached

in Wake Forest at 556-6011, in Cary at 467-2800, in Wendell at 365-9010 or at 772-2553 in Garner.

Automobile Information

Driver's License

There are several offices in Raleigh where you can get a North Carolina driver's license. If you're moving to North Carolina, you have a 60-day grace period in which to get a license. If you already have a license, you will be asked to take a written test and a visual test of road signs. The tests are not difficult, but it helps to first read over the booklet North Carolina provides. Take cash ($10) to the office; personal checks are not accepted. Licenses are good for four years and expire on your birthday. Telephone first to get information about the office closest to you and to obtain a copy of the driver's handbook; call 733-4241.

Auto Plates

Raleigh and Cary residents need to register to get North Carolina auto license plates within 30 days of moving to the state. Many new residents wait until the new year and get away with it, but they take a risk. Plates cost $20 plus a $5 transit fee in Wake, Durham and Orange counties, and the state only requires one per vehicle and uses a staggered date system that permits motorists to obtain plates and renewal decals by mail. For an extra $20, the state also permits "vanity" plates so you can put your name, message (keep it clean!) or favorite

number on your plate. Now, the bad news: newcomers also have to obtain a N.C. title ($35) for their car and registration, which ranges from $40 to $100. The Division of Motor Vehicles (DMV) is headquartered in Raleigh at 1100 New Bern Avenue, and there are several offices where tags can be purchased. The main DMV telephone number is 733-3025. Call early.

Raleigh Auto Tax

Raleigh collects $15 per vehicle from Raleigh residents annually, with most of the money going for the city's mass transit program. The county collects the fee when it sends out property tax bills or you can go by City Hall at 222 W. Hargett Street downtown. For information, call 890-3200.

Dog and Cat Regulations

Raleigh pet owners are required to purchase tags for their dogs and cats and, like auto decals, you can obtain these through the mail. The tags are issued once you show evidence that your pet has had a rabies shot. Spayed animals are cheaper than non-spayed to encourage residents to help reduce the stray dog and cat population. The pet tags must be renewed annually and can be obtained at **City Hall**, 222 W. Hargett Street; call 890-3200. For stray dogs or cats to be picked up, call 831-6311. The city also has a leash law for dogs, although your pooch is not likely to get picked up unless it becomes a nuisance. If your dog does get collared, you can retrieve him from the **SPCA** kennel on U.S. Highway 70 South in Garner.

RALEIGH BUS SERVICE

Raleigh's municipal bus system serves the city and some outlying areas such as Cary and Garner in peak hours and goes by the acronym of **CAT** (Capital Area Transit). In a medium-size city where most people have automobiles, the CAT system serves mostly those with lower incomes and diehard mass transit stoics. The system doesn't make change, so have the exact fare of 50 cents. The buses are safe, clean and rarely crowded. Unfortunately, there can be a long wait between rides and the routes are limited. Once a year, the system is jammed during State Fair week when every vehicle that rolls is used to ferry people to and from the Fairgrounds. It's a bargain, and you escape the traffic jam. For CAT information, call 828-7228 or 833-5701.

RECYCLING INFORMATION

Raleigh is in the throes of changing its throwaway behavior. By the end of 1991, all homeowners had curb side recycling service, twice a month. The city collects aluminum, newspapers, plastic milk jugs and soft drink bottles, and glass. Check with your neighbors to learn which week and which day is your pickup day (i.e., first and third Mondays), and call the city's **Sanitation Division** (831-6522) to obtain your green recycling container.

The city also manages eight drop-off sites for apartment dwellers and those not currently served by curb side pickup. The sites are: **Jaycee Park** at Wade Avenue, **St. Raphael's Catholic Church** on Falls of the Neuse Road, **Colony Shopping Center** on Six Forks Road, **True Value Home Center** on New Bern Avenue, and **Watson's Flea Market** on Old Garner Road at the I-440 Beltline, **Brennan Station Shopping Center** at Strickland and Creedmoor roads; **Mission Valley Shopping Center**; and **North Boulevard Plaza** at the "Mini City." Reynolds Aluminum also operates a center at which you can take your aluminum cans for reimbursement, and BFI has opened a recycling facility, **The Recyclery**, at Eastridge Commerce Park off U.S. Highway 64 East at which tours are conducted. The city also offers certain days per year when it accepts hazardous wastes such as engine oil, old paints, pesticides and pet flea collars at designated drop-off sites.

SENIOR CITIZEN SERVICES

As a capital city, Raleigh has a number of statewide services to help retired and senior citizens. Check the **Dept. of Human Resources' Division of Aging** for more information (1985 Umstead Drive, 733-3983). The city of Raleigh also has a very active life for senior citizens, starting with its **RSVP** program, (831-6295). This is a good way for you to meet some very interesting people and do some very interesting good deeds such as reading news accounts over the **Radio Reading Service** for blind listeners. RSVP also sponsors the **Foster Grandparents Program** that pairs

Photo courtesy Raleigh Chamber of Commerce.

The Raleigh Municipal Building.

older citizens with youngsters who need good role models. Says one older witness for the program, "Since I joined the program, my limp has gone away and my blood pressure has dropped and I've grown younger." Now what other program can make such claims?

If you like dancing and card playing, there's a regular group that meets at the city's **Golden Years Association** at Pullen Park's Activity Center. Yes, there's a **Meals on Wheels** program in Wake County, too (833-1749).

There are two AARP chapters in Raleigh and the **Council on Aging** is another good place to start for information on services as well as nursing homes. For a listing of community services and telephone numbers of the preceding, check the front of the telephone book (pp. 20-21) under Community Services numbers. Also, see the section on **RETIREMENT** in this Guide.

TAXES

Neither Raleigh nor Cary has a city income tax. The state does have an income tax that has a 7 percent cap. The state's sales tax is 4 cents, but counties have the option to tack on 2 more cents and all do, so the rate is 6 cents per dollar of merchandise. Local governments (cities and counties) raise money primarily through the property tax. This tax is levied against real estate as well as personal property, so renters have to pay personal property taxes (on such items as automobiles) as homeowners do. If you live in the county, you pay only the county property tax. If you live in Raleigh, you pay both the city and the county property tax. A Raleigh resident with a house assessed at $100,000 can expect to pay a combined property tax bill of $1,311 annually. Property is re-evaluated every eight years and the most recent valuation happened in 1992, so you're safe for another six years.

VOTER REGISTRATION

Don't forget to register to vote. Wake County makes it easy for you; you can register at your local library by simply showing some identification that includes your permanent, local address. The deputy registrar at the library will swear you in, tell you where to vote and send in the form to the county Board of Elections which is located downtown. You will receive a postcard from the Board confirming that you are a registered voter and the location of your polling place. You must be registered, however, 30 days before an election. The **Wake County Board of Elections** is located at 339 S. Salisbury Street, 856-6240.

Insiders' Tip

YOU MUST BE REGISTERED TO VOTE **30** DAYS BEFORE AN ELECTION. WAKE COUNTY MAKES IT EASY FOR YOU; YOU CAN REGISTER AT YOUR LOCAL LIBRARY IF YOU HAVE IDENTIFICATION THAT INCLUDES YOUR PERMANENT LOCAL ADDRESS.

Here is a quick-reference listing of numbers that may come in handy:

EMERGENCIES
DIAL 911

Call the 911 number for police, fire or ambulance emergencies and be sure to talk clearly, giving your name and the location of the emergency.

CITY GOVERNMENT AND CIVIC SERVICES

Arts Commission	831-6234
Better Business Bureau	872-9240
Capital Area Transit	828-7228
	or 833-5701
Chamber of Commerce	664-7000
Convention and Visitors Bureau	834-5900
Housing Authority	831-6416
Merchants Bureau	833-5521
Parks and Recreation	890-3285
Public Works Dept.	890-3415
Revenue Collector	890-3200

COUNTY SERVICES

Wake Blood Plan	781-0011
Wake County Board of Elections	856-6240
Wake County Dept. of Social Services	856-7000
Wake County SPCA 503 U.S. Hwy. 70 E.	772-3203

STATE SERVICES

Driver's License Bureau	733-4241
	or 733-2069
Employment Security Commission	733-3941
N.C. Dept. of Human Resources	733-4261

COMMUNITY SERVICE NUMBERS

The local Southern Bell phone book includes a great listing of human services numbers ranging from crisis hotlines, family planning, mental and physical health services to senior citizens, veterans and women's services. This list includes public agencies and nonprofit organizations.

Photo by Nancy Kitchener.

Raleigh's comfortable affluence is broad-based, and one lovely neighborhood simply leads to another filled with homes like this one in Wood Valley.

Inside
Raleigh
Neighborhoods

Raleigh is a city of neighborhoods, most of them stuffed with comfortable homes of conservative design.

The neighborhoods reflect the city's history as a place of moderate and broad affluence. There is no great wealth such as that of the Duke family of Durham or the Reynolds of Winston-Salem. There are no grand mansions in the Capital City, except for the wonderfully Victorian gingerbread Governor's Mansion downtown and the small but beautiful Tatton Hall on Oberlin Road across the street from White Memorial Presbyterian Church. Happily, the city also has no great slums, either. It has its share of shabby housing, and there is a long wait to get in one of the city's 2,100-plus public housing units. But Raleigh's comfortable affluence is broad-based, and visitors often are struck by how one lovely neighborhood simply leads to another.

The housing boom that began at the end of 1982 has brought more contemporary styles to the city, such as California cluster homes, and it also has left the city

with more large, luxury homes that sell for $250,000 and up. Such prices 10 years earlier would have signified to most Raleigh residents that a Yankee spendthrift or a new money showoff was in town; today, it's not that unusual.

There certainly is a more open attitude toward home building and the emphasis today is on "neighborhood amenities," from jogging trails to Olympic-size swimming pools to tennis complexes to soccer fields. And neighborhoods today are planned as part of an overall community.

If you divide the city into quarters with the Capitol building at the center, you will find that most of the recent growth has been in the northwest and northeast quadrants. The city's southeast, predominantly black neighborhoods have shared in the growth and have expanded more since the completion of the southern half of the city's Beltline in 1984. The growth area in the future is the northeast where land is available and new sewer lines and pump stations have opened 33,000 acres to new development.

This Guide is by no means an index of all the city's neighborhoods. Rather, it is a select list of some of the city's storied places and those whose names have come to represent a certain kind of neighborhood. And for newcomers, we've included some of the newer neighborhoods. The median price, by the way, for a new home in Wake County in October 1993, was $110,000.

To find out what schools serve your neighborhood, consult the section on schools and child care. If your favorite neighborhood is not here, blame the hard-nosed editor who demanded a short list or send us your suggestions.

Biltmore Hills

This is one of the city's first predominantly black subdivisions that was built in the late '50s and '60s. It is southeast of downtown, lying between Rock Quarry Road to the east and Old Garner Road to the west, and is split by the Beltline. The homes are modest brick houses with some two-story homes in the newer section south of the Beltline. It is a well-organized neighborhood and has been home to some of the city's black leadership. Activities have focused around **Fuller Elementary School** which, at one time, was the school where Gov. James B. Hunt, Jr.'s, primary-grade child attended. It also contains **Biltmore Hills Park**. The **Southgate Plaza Shopping Center**, the first in southeast Raleigh in years, serves the neighborhood. Houses sell between $60,000 and $65,000.

Boylan Heights

This is another, older frontline neighborhood, located within walking distance of the downtown complex. It was part of the **Boylan Plantation** and, as the name implies, occupies high ground. It has a mixture of very low income housing on its periphery and lovely, larger homes at its core. Like historic Oakwood, Boylan Heights began to enjoy a renewed popularity during the mid '70s when buyers could get 2,000- and 3,000- sq.-ft. homes in reasonable condition for $30,000 to $40,000. They now sell for $70,000 and up, a bargain by Raleigh standards. An active neighborhood group encourages yard beautification and lobbies for city attention. The new Western Boulevard Extension will remove much of the commuter traffic that pours through the neighborhood today, which can only improve Boylan Heights' reputation. It is bounded by the large Central Prison complex to the west, the Norfolk Southern Railroad to the north and east, and the Dorothea Dix Hospital complex to the south.

Brentwood

This area includes a number of neighborhoods, most of them with Brentwood in their names and located north of the Beltline and west of U.S. Highway 1. They were some of the first subdivisions spawned by the circumferential highway and the city's growth north, and have come to represent '60s suburbia. It's hard to live there and not have a car. The homes are affordable brick, single-story or split-level, and residents generally have been families with growing children. The yards are neat and homeowners rally to neighborhood campaigns. Brentwood parents show up often at school board meetings, although many of the children have grown up and probably are driving BMWs and living in condos now. Median sales price for homes is about $85,000.

Brookhaven

Brookhaven is another of the 1960s suburbs outside of the Beltline and northwest, beyond Crabtree Valley Mall, off Glenwood Avenue. You used to think you had to go to the country before you got to Brookhaven. Not anymore. It has been the jumping off place for much of the city's northwest growth that has gone north up Creedmoor Road and west out Leesville Road.

For years, Brookhaven residents lived outside the city limits, but today it is protected by a neighborhood overlay zoning district, reserved for older Raleigh neighborhoods. Like a more recent version of Country Club Hills, its lots are spacious and its homes well built. Most show a conventional design and were made for families with more than 2.5 children. One homeowner who bought his home new in the early '60s marveled a few years ago that his monthly mortgage payment was only $115 while new home buyers in houses of comparable size were facing $1000-plus

payments. In Brookhaven's older section, homes will sell for slightly less than in the newer sections; the median price is around $150,000 and goes up.

Cameron Park

This is one of the author's favorite Raleigh neighborhoods, but not just because he lives there. It has big, old trees throughout and three neighborhood parks around which streets wind and curve, and in which residents play, picnic and walk the dog. Cameron Park has been called the Georgetown of Raleigh and was one of the city's first suburbs, started in 1910. It is located one mile west of the Capitol and is bounded by Hillsborough Street to the south, St. Mary's College and St. Mary's Street on the east, Oberlin Road and NCSU on the west, and Clark Avenue and Cameron Village Shopping Center to the north.

The residents are a mixture of academics, professionals, government managers, business people, artists, journalists, students and retirees—most of them willing to speak their mind and many in public office. It also claims more architects and designers per square foot than any place in the state, many of whom teach in NCSU's famed Design School. It's a real neighborhood where people sit on their front porch and visit.

The NCSU track field, Pullen Park and the YMCA are nearby, so there are plenty of joggers about. Cameron Village is within walking distance, as are **Wiley Elementary** and **Broughton High** schools. Homes range from some of the most contemporary in town to traditional, white-columned Southern manses, but most are comfortable structures with plenty of room. The bargains are gone and homes today sell routinely for $180,000 and several for over $300,000. But Cameron Park's worth it.

Country Club Hills

As its name implies, Country Club Hills surrounds much of the golf course at the **Carolina Country Club** on Glenwood Avenue. The development is marked by large lots and hilly terrain, which has invited some unconventional designs. It has a '50s look about it with lower profile, ranch-style homes, although most are large and there are many conventional, two-story homes, too. The neighborhood has retained a woodland flavor, helped in part by its lack of sidewalks and a street matrix that is winding and twisting and as puzzling as a Greek maze. Its streets are named after North Carolina counties such as Transylvania, Pasquotank and Perquimans. Its location off Glenwood Avenue puts it close to both the Beltline and Crabtree Valley Mall as well as one of the main thoroughfares downtown. Many of its residents custom-built their homes and it is not a hotbed for sales; expect prices to be around $250,000.

Eaglechase

As land became more and more precious in north and northwest Raleigh, developer Jud Ammons looked east, where he has started Eaglechase, off Poole Road. It is has been very popular with first-home buyers and, for the money, it's one of the best buys in the Raleigh market. You can find three- and four-bedroom homes with two baths with median prices at $105,000. The community is nicely

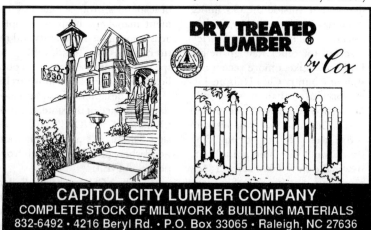

landscaped with protective earthen berms at the entrances and along Poole Road. There is a swim club and other amenities.

Foxcroft

Foxcroft is one of the few "equestrian" neighborhoods near Raleigh, and it has been there since the 1960s when it was developed by C.O. Weaver, the man who began the North Boulevard Plaza more familiarly known as "Mini City" on U.S. Highway 1. The area is located east of the city—it's not in the city limits, by the way—north of U.S. Highway 64 and east of New Hope Church Road. Foxcroft was developed for people who wanted enough room to include their horses and, even with land prices 10 times what they were when it began, some residents still do keep horses, including one Arabian owner whose spread would be a showplace no matter where it was located. Homes vary in size and style, going back to the single-story ranch house popular in the 1960s and including some very contemporary designs built in the 1980s. Foxcroft, once it started, grew slowly during the 1970s, but after 1982, more new homes appeared. Median prices are around $220,000.

Greystone

This subdivision lies outside the Beltline to the northwest. Greystone began in 1980 and reflects the trend towards planned communities. Instead of dividing a piece of property into lots and selling to individual home builders, Greystone's developers planned an entire community with a series of neighborhoods, many with theme styles, and integrated with various types of housing such as townhouses and condominiums, not just single-family homes.

And unlike many suburban developments that aim at the young or middle-aged family, Greystone hits the entire age market and even includes a retirement village for older residents. It features a child-care center in the middle of the community, recognizing the prevalence of two-income families today. Emphasis is also placed on amenities like two recreational lakes stocked with fish and the option to join a swim and tennis club. Walkways are provided throughout the development, including paths around the lakes. Prices vary, but they are aimed at the great market of middle-income buyers: from $80,000 to $200,000.

Hawthorne

Hawthorne is the latest in a series of housing developments by veteran local builder and big game hunter Edd K. Roberts, who has been a moving force in Raleigh's growth since the early 1970s. Among other projects, Roberts developed North Haven, Raintree, Springdale Gardens, Woods of Tiffany, Broadlands and several apartment complexes.

To get to Hawthorne, drive six and one-half miles on

Creedmoor Road from Crabtree Valley Mall, turn left on Norwood Road and go another two and one-quarter miles. It's a 385-acre development of bluffs, streams and rolling countryside that will contain 385 homes, either on quarter-acre lots or in clusters with sixth-acre lots. The lots will have deep back yards and homeowners will share 13 parks and three miles of jogging trails, which include exercise stations. Land also has been set aside for a swimming and tennis complex. It was built in three stages, and houses range in price from $175,000 to $225,000.

Hayes-Barton

Named after Sir Walter Raleigh's home place in England, Hayes-Barton has become the home for many of the city's Establishment since its development in the 1920s and '30s. It is where the late Josephus Daniels' family compound is located, including Josephus' home, now a Masonic building. A few streets over is U.S. Sen. Jesse Helms' house. The neighborhood is located close to downtown and is roughly bounded by Glenwood Avenue to the east and St. Mary's Street to the west, both of which curve around and intersect in the north. Wade Avenue serves as its southern boundary.

This area is filled with large homes, some on spacious lots, as well as many of modest size. One of the grander houses is reputed to be a small model of Mt. Vernon, while another favors Sir Walter's stone English manor. A winding stream runs down Cowper Drive, the center of a small park that leads to the neighborhood's entrance off Glenwood Avenue. So desirable is a Hayes-Barton address that several builders in the past two or three years have bought smaller old homes, torn them down and rebuilt new, bigger ones, albeit somewhat squeezed onto the lots.

Nearby is the venerable **Colony Theater**, now the **Rialto**, which shows classics as well as better European films. Residents also gather for sandwiches at the **Hayes-Barton Pharmacy**, the center of the neighborhood's small shopping area whose small Piggly Wiggly supermarket is known for its fresh turkeys at Thanksgiving and Christmas. The hub of the Old Raleigh Establishment, the **Carolina Country Club**, is conveniently nearby on Glenwood Avenue. House prices are all over the lot: from $150,000 on the periphery to up, up, up. There are some that sell for $1 million. Naturally.

Hedingham

This is the premier, planned community in northeast Raleigh, an example of what might be expected as this part of the city develops. It sits on 553 acres between New Hope Road and the Neuse River and has access to U.S. Highway 64 East. Fred Smith, local attorney-turned-developer, began building the project in 1989. It contains a variety of homes and apartments that are priced accordingly and is expected to have over 2,400 units when completed. The centerpiece is the golf course development, **Hedingham on the Neuse**, that wraps lots around a championship 18-hole course. The community has 62 acres of greenways and a riverfront park, not to mention the usual amenities that go with a golf course, such as clubhouse, grill room, swim and racquet club, and basketball and volleyball courts. Homes start at the amazingly low price of $90,000 and go up to $200,000.

Hymettus Woods

This inside-the-Beltline neighborhood represents a phenomenon in the real estate market in the last half of the '80s that has been dubbed "infill." Developers buy up small parcels of property inside the Beltline and build large, expensive homes on small lots. George M. Womble III has put 14 lots on less than five acres adjacent to **Hymettus Park** which occupies the corner of Wade Avenue and Dixie Trail. The homes are custom homes with attention to detail, and most of the homeowners are people who have moved from an older, established neighborhood. The entrance is off Wade Avenue. Price tags start at $450,000 and go up to $700,000.

Lake Boone Place

This is another of the new, expensive, inside-the-Beltline neighborhoods, and it takes its name from the small lake that used

to sit where Lake Boone Trail ends at Cambridge Road. All that's left of the lake is the small creek that fed it. Close to **Glenwood Village Shopping Center** and Glenwood Avenue, its location is a principal attraction: you're five minutes from **Crabtree Shopping Mall**, three minutes from the Beltline, not far from **Rex Hospital** and 10 minutes from downtown. The homes, many incorporating "transitional" styles (traditional exteriors with more contemporary interiors), start at $375,000.

Madonna Acres

This east Raleigh subdivision is where a number of the city's black leaders live, including its first black mayor, Clarence Lightner. It was developed from the old Delany Farm adjacent to **St. Augustine's University** and is sometimes referred to as Delany Drive. The developer was John Winters, the city's first black city councilman who has had a distinguished career as state Senator and state Utilities Commissioner. It has about 35 homes on 12 acres and was first developed in the late 1950s. Winters built all but two of the custom homes. Median price for recent sales is about $85,000.

Mordecai

Pronounced Mord'e-kee, this downtown neighbor to the better known Oakwood has many of the same advantages. It is within walking distance to state government complex jobs, **Peace College** and a neighborhood grocery and shopping area. It also contains some solid homes, including the restored **Mordecai House and Park** which, together, are one of the city's historical treasures. They belonged to one of the city's early families. Bordered by one of Raleigh's old gateway roads, its faded history can be read in the tourist and motel signs that still hang outside a few of its larger, converted homes on Wake Forest Road. Mordecai does not have Oakwood's uniformity of architectural styles and many of its homes are hardly vintage. One of the city's oldest public housing projects, **Halifax Court** also is nearby. Yet, Mordecai's sturdy homes are survivors and it's a place for bargain hunting home buyers, $80,000 and up.

North Hills

Although there also is a specific, respectable neighborhood called North Hills, many Raleigh residents consider North Hills to be that vast, sprawling, growing world north of the Beltline. There are also **North Hills Terrace**, **North Glen**, **North Ridge**, **North Bend**, and **Northclift**. Here, North Hills encompasses the broad stretch of north Raleigh suburbs roughly bounded by Wake Forest Road and Falls of the Neuse Road to the east and North Hills Drive to the west. It has financed many a Realtor's beach home or mountain retreat, and it contains one pleasant subdivision after another. Its thoroughfares, like Old Wake Forest, Six Forks, Millbrook and Spring Forest have

become major roads whose pulses are taken daily by helicopter traffic observers.

Mostly developed since 1960, the area surged when IBM announced its plans in 1965 to build its Research Triangle Park operations. Indeed, some neighborhoods were peopled almost entirely by Big Blue's commuters. There are numerous shopping centers, anchored by **North Hills Mall,** which has undergone a face lift. North Hills homes vary in size and look, although most reflect the conventional styles of the '60s and '70s. Some are ranch style, others brick colonial, but all of them stand alone as single-family homes. Trees abound and the city's **Optimist Park Pool** near Six Forks Road and Millbrook Road serves the area. It's a place where people stay busy and eat out a lot. Realtors consider the area a good value for the real estate dollar and homes sell between $90,000 and $150,000.

North Ridge

The neighborhood that sits like a crown on north Raleigh is North Ridge. It surrounds **North Ridge County Club**, which is the city's only real competition to the Carolina Country Club. North Ridge Country Club has a more inclusive membership policy and it attracts many in the New Establishment—those who come from outside the Old Raleigh family connections and often are connected instead to the Triangle's corporate establishment. It's less stuffy and younger. The

Photo courtesy Raleigh Convention and Visitors Bureau.

Historic Oakwood, Raleigh's nineteenth century Victorian neighborhood, is listed in the National Register of Historic Places.

homes surrounding the club also reflect this new power, money and vigor. They are big and impressive and many show the touch of an architect, so it's not stamped by any particular style. It's not the kind of place where one will see too many Saturday yard sales. The residents connected to the larger corporations are inclined to move every three years, but they are active while they're here. If you want to suffer "sticker shock," this is where you go; some of the older homes may sell for under $200,000, but a $300,000 price tag doesn't raise eyebrows anymore.

Oakwood

Oakwood is one of the city's oldest neighborhoods and one that has pulled itself back into demand by its bootstraps. It is located downtown, behind the **Governor's Mansion**, roughly bounded by Person, Franklin and Edenton streets and historic **Oakwood Cemetery** where some of Raleigh's most famous citizens are buried. Oakwood is where the bankers and burghers and railroad managers who prospered in the years after the Civil War built Victorian, mostly frame, homes with spacious rooms and high ceilings.

Like many downtown neighborhoods, Oakwood declined during the migration to the suburbs during the 1950s and '60s. It began to make a comeback after the '73 recession and oil embargo when young couples couldn't afford new subdivision prices and wanted to walk to downtown jobs. They bought the old houses for as little as $10,000 and restored them to splendid, colorful single-family homes. To show off their handiwork and the glory of times past, residents established an annual **Historic Oakwood Christmas Tour**—a good introduction to Raleigh's history for newcomers.

If you want a new home, look at **Oakwood Green**, a new development on 3.5 acres within the boundaries of Oakwood (prices between $125,000 and $150,000). For the larger older homes, prices now easily go over $100,000, but bargains still come on the market for masochists willing to scrape wallpaper, refinish floors and restore supporting beams.

Olde Raleigh

This is anything but old Raleigh. It's one of the most lavish new developments in the city, between Duraleigh Road and Edwards Mill Road in northwest Raleigh, not far from **Rex Hospital**. It is being developed by road contractor C. C. Mangum, and it has 137 single-family lots, three small lakes and guarded, electronic gates. The brick and iron fence that encloses the property is built to stay and will certainly keep out the small-budget buyers. The streets already are paved, mallards paddle on the lakes and cast-iron mail boxes line the "wynds," as the streets are called. The project also includes two "village office" complexes and "village shoppes" at the south end where Duraleigh and Edwards Mill roads intersect. Lots sell for about $90,000

and the median price for new houses is $429,000. If you take Sunday drives, go see it before it fills up and they close the gates.

Robert's Park

This 15-acre southeast neighborhood has an interesting history and was once owned by the Gatling family. Located east of the **National Cemetery** off Tarboro Road, the area was once filled with the big top tents of the Ringling Brothers circus when it came to town. The city's first semipro baseball park also was nearby. It takes its name from a nearby park, and is home to a number of the area's black hierarchy, such as Cecil Goins, the state's first black federal marshal. It also has its own community association. The city's best-known black developer, John Winters, built some of the homes here, most of which went up in the 1960s. Prices range from $100,000 to $150,000.

Springdale Estates

Springdale Estates is one of three Springdale neighborhoods in northwest Raleigh, located on either side of Leesville Road in rolling, wooded countryside outside the city limits. It began development in the 1970s and, typical of the period, includes homes on large, acre lots. It has a lake in the middle, and it's one neighborhood where you will find contemporary designs mixed in with traditional and colonial styles. The neighborhood is well established and has been a success-

ful place for Realtors in terms of resale. It's close to **Raleigh-Durham Airport** and the **Research Triangle Park**. Prices here average around $180,000.

Stonebridge

Further north of Stonehenge is Stonebridge, with its entrance off Six Forks Road. It was started in the 1970s and was once considered the far suburbs, but north Raleigh has grown up around it with new shopping centers and parks like **Camp Durant**. It will include about 600 homes when completed. Like most of the newer subdivisions, the roads wind and curve through the neighborhood and builders have retained many of the trees. The houses are traditional in style, but large: three and four bedrooms are the norm with 2 baths or more. Expect to pay $190,000 for homes in this neighborhood.

Stonehenge

Located on both sides of Creedmoor Road, Stonehenge has been one of the favorite north Raleigh communities among real estate agents because the houses sell so easily. It was started in 1976, but has continued to grow and add new neighborhoods such as **Bridgeport**, in authentic Williamsburg style, as well as townhouses and apartments. It is close to many of the new, neighborhood shopping centers such as **Stonehenge Market** and close to **Stonehenge Office Park**. The homes are traditional in appear-

Raleigh's older neighborhoods are filled with beautifully restored homes.

ance and located on acre lots in the older sections. Homes are spacious, usually two-story with driveways and/or garages. **Seven Oaks Recreation Center** is part of the Stonehenge community, and includes 12 acres of lighted tennis, basketball and volleyball courts as well as a competitive-size swimming pool. It's been a popular address for families, although many of the children who used to play in the street are now off to college or driving on the streets. Prices for the single family detached homes generally start around $150,000.

Trego

Named after a Montana village that the developer once visited, Trego (pronounced tree-go) has been called a neighborhood of "executive housing" by one Triangle publication. It began in 1982, and is located off Honeycutt Road in north Raleigh. It contains 33 lots on about 85 acres. The houses are large: minimum square footage is 2,000 square feet, but most contain upwards of 3,500. The architecture ranges from Georgian to contemporary houses that blend in with the wooded terrain. Residents are mostly corporate executives, doctors, lawyers and other professionals, many of whom moved to the Triangle from elsewhere. Median sale price is $550,000.

Wildwood Green

This is a northwest Raleigh community being built around one of Raleigh's old private golf courses located off Strickland Road and not far from Creedmoor Road. It is being developed and sold by Howard, Perry and Walston Realtors, one of the city's largest and most respected firms. And the firm has spent enough money to have it done right. The amenities do not stop with the 18-hole championship fairways and greens; they also include swimming and tennis, as do most of the newer communities. The homes are being custom built and the average price in 1993 was $270,000.

Williamsborough and Drewry Hills

Some have called these two developments the "new Hayes-Barton" because they are favored by the same crowd. The homes, however, are much newer and have been built for today's modern conveniences, including some with swimming pools. Both are entered off Lassiter Mill Road and, while parts of Drewry Hills are 1950s, most of the homes have been built since then. The larger, Williamsborough houses caused much sightseeing when built in the 1970s, especially when a couple of them had to be picked up and moved because of a lawsuit. While there are a few contemporary styles, the traditional and Williamsburg homes prevail. At Christmas, the windows light up with proper white candles—no red or blue ones, please.

These neighborhoods are within the Beltline, but near **North Hills Mall**. One of the city's

greenways along Crabtree Creek forms the southern boundary, and the old **Lassiter Mill Dam** attracts city fishermen. Housing prices may not go as high as those in Hayes-Barton, but most will start higher. Older parts of Drewry Hills have homes that sell for $120,000, and Williamsborough has prices that go up over $500,000.

Wyndfield

One of the first of the far out subdivisions, Wyndfield (pronounced Windfield—the "y" is to let you know that it's a distinctive neighborhood) is not large in size, but its homes are. Located west of Six Forks Road, it's actually closer to **Falls Lake** than Raleigh, and isn't in the city limits. Many of the origi-

nal homes were built in the '70s for the owners, so they have a personal touch.

Residents prize their spacious lots, narrow streets and quiet isolation. Swimming pools are not unusual, and several cars, including a 4-wheel-drive Jeep or Bronco, in the garage or driveway are expected, since few places are within walking distance. There are some neighborhood tennis courts, and residents are close to the boating, fishing and recreation at Falls Lake. Once an outpost of affluent living, Wyndfield today is one among a number of similar subdivisions with names such as **Coachman's Trail**, **Martindale**, **Trappers Creek** and **Trotters Ridge**. Home prices start at over $200,000 and quickly escalate.

Staff photo.

PlaySpace at Raleigh's City Market is an innovative indoor playground.

Inside

Raleigh Parks and Recreation

Given its Sunbelt climate and geography, Raleigh offers a generous spread of parklands and recreation programs. The city won a national gold medal in 1990 for having one of the best programs in the nation and was declared a Tree City USA in 1993 for the fifth year in a row. This section is designed to guide you to those recreational programs in which you or your family can participate. Other sections in this Guide will detail spectator sports as well as attractions. So, if you want to participate, read on.

Tennis addicts, for example, can play year-round, and the city even sponsors a Frostbite Doubles Tournament in December. The city's Optimist Park Swimming Pool wears an inflatable dome during winter to accommodate competitive swimmers, and the Pullen Park Aquatic Center opened in 1992 as one of the region's premier indoor swimming pools. The city also was featured in *National Geographic* for its aggressive greenway program that connects the city's neighbor-

hoods and its suburbs with a network of 34 miles of trails and paths.

Indeed, as leisure time has become more important to all Americans, Raleigh residents have voted consistently for tax and bond issues that have increased parklands to 4,800 acres, 50 parks and thousands of recreational activities. With justification, Raleigh calls itself "the park with a city in it."

This section will not list every park in the system, but it will single out those with special attractions, such as **Pullen Park**—home to both a celebrated **Denzel Carousel** and its own miniature train. Also listed is an entertainment jewel, **Walnut Creek Amphitheater**, with 20,000 seats and a five-field softball complex that opened in 1992 to rave reviews. Raleigh has a neighborhood parks network, so there should be one near your house. The city also has three "Leisure Lines," telephone numbers that bring you up-to-date information about the parks program and its activities. Call 831-6575 (athletics),

517

831-6577 (events), or 831-6579 (other) for their taped messages.

There also is a weekly update on cable television. The city maintains an active recreation program for all ages and sizes. And there also are some programs—the most notable being the **Capital Area Soccer League** (CASL)—that are independent of municipal administration but an integral part of metropolitan recreation. In addition to special parks, this Guide lists items by activity, such as tennis, swimming, golf, etc. For more information about city programs, call 831-6640 or write **Raleigh Parks and Recreation**, P.O. Box 590, Raleigh, NC 27602.

Of special note, **Laurel Hills Park** in west Raleigh (Glen Eden Drive and Edwards Mill Road) opened in 1992 and offers a unique playground for all children including the handicapped.

Parks

PULLEN
408 Ashe Ave.

This is the granddaddy of the city's parks with 65 acres that lie between the NCSU campus and the state's School for the Blind, off Western Boulevard. A train ride through the park and over its lake offers a great view of the amenities, including children's boat rides and even pedal boats on the lake.

The crown of the park is its **Denzel Carousel,** which has been restored to its original grandeur with great skill and hundreds of thousands of dollars. Put your child on a carved masterpiece and watch him or her go round and round. It's also a great place to picnic and has several covered pavilions that may be reserved for large groups.

A $4 million indoor aquatics center opened in 1992 and is connected to a **Special Programs Center** offering classes and activities such as senior citizen dancing. A concession stand offers the usual hot dogs, soda pops and cotton candy. Six tennis courts and, across the railroad tracks, two ball fields and the city's **Theater in the Park** are located here. There is also an **Arts Center**.

JAYCEE
Oberlin Rd. and Wade Ave.

This is another inside-the-Beltline park, and it also houses many of the city's Parks and Recreation managers, so it's a good place to know about. It has two tennis courts and a community center that stays busy with basketball, aerobics, volleyball and other activities. There are four ball fields, a playground, a jogging trail with exercise stations and the ever popular **Raleigh Beach**, home to the city's outdoor volleyball addicts. The city's most popular drop site for recycled aluminum, glass and paper products is located here, too.

LIONS
516 Dennis Ave.

Inside the Beltline in northeast Raleigh, Lions Park is one field after another and where many of the city's football and baseball games are played. It, too, has a community center in which basketball and organized table tennis are played. Its special attraction is the **BMX bicycle course**.

SHELLEY-SERTOMA
1400 Millbrook Rd.

The park has a lake with canoes, row boats, sail and pedal boats for rent. Fishing also is permitted. But Shelley-Sertoma is best known as a starting or stopping point on one of the more popular sections of the Greenway system, and the **Sertoma Center** has become the *de facto* arts center in the city's park system and hosts any number of study programs.

It houses a first-class photography lab for city-sponsored programs. You may find an art show of watercolors, quilts, pottery or oils during the week. On the second Sunday of each month, you may enjoy a harpsichord or flute concert or even a jazz band. It also has begun to stage plays. For information on scheduled events, call 420-2331.

DURANT
Durant Rd.

This is among the city's largest parks and was a former Boy Scout camp. It was a wise acquisition since much of the city's growth is to the north where Durant sits. It is being developed as a nature park and has a large nature study center. It is home for the city's popular summer day camp, **Ronocca**, as well as **Camp Friendly**, a special nine-week day camp for handicapped children. For information, call 870-2872.

Photo courtesy Raleigh Convention and Visitors Bureau.

The Denzel carousel at Pullen Park has been restored to its original grandeur with great skill and hundreds of throusands of dollars.

LAKE WHEELER
6404 Lake Wheeler Rd.

The biggest of the city's parks, Wheeler lies just south of the city limits and serves also as one of the city's main reservoirs. It's aimed at the water-sports crowd and has swimming, boating, water-skiing and fishing. Fishing boats are available for rent. It is the base of the **NCSU Sailing Club**, and also home to the annual **Tar Heel Regatta** in June when the large, deafening powerboats come from all over to race over Lake Wheeler's 650 acres of water.

WALNUT CREEK
Rock Quarry and Sunnybrook rds.
Amphitheatre   *831-6400*
Softball Complex   *250-2726*

This 280-acre park and its outdoor amphitheater has quickly established itself as the concert mecca for eastern North Carolina with such acts as Whitney Houston, Jimmy Buffet, the Beach Boys, Paul Simon—the list goes on. The theater seats 20,000 people, 7,000 under the roof, the rest under the stars on the grass. The park's softball "wheel" opened in 1992 with five fields under lights and a network of trails and picnic areas. Another five-field wheel will be built here in the future. (See **ATTRACTIONS.**)

Sports

BASEBALL

RALEIGH PARKS AND RECREATION
Jaycee Park Center   *831-6836*

There are five youth leagues operated by the city Recreation Department, starting with T-ball for seven- and eight-year-olds and including Little League. The senior, or Palomino, league is for students, age 17 to 18. Tryouts are held in March, and a mid-summer city tournament ends each season. Games are played on 13 fields throughout the city, and local businesses underwrite team expenses for uniforms.

SALVATION ARMY
902 Wake Forest Rd.   *832-6918*

The Salvation Army operates its own youth athletic program including baseball. Athletic Director Chris Davis keeps busy year round between baseball, basketball and soccer. In baseball, the emphasis is on fundamentals, so there's no tournament and each child—they have boys and girls—must play during the games. Registration starts in March and the season ends before school is out in June. It costs $40 to register and there are 30 teams in the age group 5 to 10 (T-ball, coach-pitch and machine pitch), and five teams for Little League-age children. Games are played on the three fields at the Salvation Army Center on Wake Forest Road and the older teams play at the nearby Peace College field.

BASKETBALL

RALEIGH PARKS AND RECREATION
831-6836

The city runs an active youth league 12-game schedule in the fall, plus a tournament for city champions. It's a competitive league with lots of teams. Players, ages 10-18 in the youth programs, sign up at their respective neighborhood recreation centers. Call for the nearest one to you. Registration is in October, practice in November, and play starts in late December. Most facilities also have free time for pickup games, but call first.

The city also operates an adult league that follows a 16-game schedule with registration starting in October. Play begins in November.

SALVATION ARMY
902 Wake Forest Rd.   *832-6918*

The Salvation Army's basketball league fields 32 teams for ages 5 to 10, which are divided into three leagues. Every child gets to play and parents are recruited as coaches. Registration costs $40 and begins in

October, followed by November-December practices, and league play in January on Friday nights and Saturday mornings at the Army's center. Games are scheduled throughout the day.

YMCA
1601 Hillsborough St.   *832-6601*
Old Garner Rd.   *833-1256*

The Hillsborough Street YMCA sponsors six youth leagues in the fall and two members-only adult leagues, one in the summer and one in winter. It's an open registration for the youth league and costs about $48 for members. There's a league for kindergarteners. (This is North Carolina—we start 'em young!) Other leagues go by school grades, starting with third graders and stopping at 12th grade for boys and 8th grade for girls. About 500 participate, and each child gets to play, with emphasis on the fundamentals. Sign-ups start in November, practice in December, and play begins in January and runs to March. Most games are played at the Y, but some have moved to public school gyms.

The adult leagues are competitive and sometimes include past ACC stars. Eight teams play in the summer and 12 teams in winter. Cost is about $25 over and above membership fees.

The Old Garner Road YMCA in east Raleigh operates four boys leagues, for ages 13 to 15 and in 1993, one of their leagues won an AAU national championship. Registration is open and nominal, about $12, and fields about four teams per league. The season starts in November and play begins in January. The YMCA rents space for two adult leagues, one connected with CP&L and the other with local churches.

BIKING

The city adopted a comprehensive bicycle plan in 1991 and has an active bicycle lobby pushing for designated bikeways. There are about 34 miles of greenway trails currently available to bikers. For an excellent $3 bike map of the city's bikeways, contact Stacy Barbour at the Planning Department in City Hall, 890-3125. There are plenty of sport bikers, and they come in two varieties: BMX and 10-speed touring cyclists. **Lions Park** at 1800 Watkins Street is the center for BMX racing. Teams compete there on Sundays most of the year, and on Wednesdays during the summer. Bikers come from all over and races are organized through the **Capital City BMX Association**. For information and race times, call Lions Park at 831-6995.

Ten-speedsters are seen on city byways in their black racing shorts and helmets, particularly in April and training for the **Capital City Criterium**. This popular race goes round and round downtown Raleigh for 50 kilometers on the last weekend in April. For more information on other 10-speed events, call Jeff Hutchinson at **All Star Bike Shops**, 833-5070.

FOOTBALL

RALEIGH PARKS AND RECREATION
831-6836

The city operates the only football league in town outside of the schools, but it is active and has three divisions for ages 7 to 13. There are weight limitations to make things even. About 23 teams, or about eight per division, compete over six fields in the Parks system. Registration starts in July, and games begin in September, running to mid-November, when a Superbowl champion in each division is crowned.

GOLF (DISC GOLF, TOO)

In a state that boasts the **Golf Hall of Fame**, the Capital City has no publicly owned golf course. Shame! It does have a number of excellent private-club courses as well as private courses open to the public. The private-club courses, in case you're invited, include **North Ridge Country Club, Raleigh Country Club, Carolina Country Club** and **Wildwood**. There also is **Hedingham,** which is open to the public and is part of the Hedingham planned community. The other courses open to the public are all out of the city and include: **Wilmar Golf Club** on Route 5, Knightdale, 266-1800; **Eagle Crest Golf Course** near Garner, 772-6104; **Pine Hollow** near Clayton, 553-4554 and **Raleigh Golf Association** on 1527 Tryon Road, 772-9987. Check Cary, too, which has three private courses. The city does maintain two disc golf (**Frisbee golf**) courses at Kentwood Park and Cedar Hills Park.

HORSEBACK RIDING

There is no publicly owned riding stable in Raleigh, although the State Fairgrounds maintains one of the best show-horse arenas and schedules in the state. **MacNairs County Acres Stables** probably is the best known of the private stables and offers lessons and boarding. Call 851-1118 for information. Other stables include **Raleigh Riding Academy** in north Raleigh, 571-1412; **Triton Stables**, 847-4123; and **Wakefield Farms** in Wake Forest, 556-1856.

HEALTH CLUBS

Like the rest of the country, health and fitness centers boomed

like junk bonds in Raleigh during the '80s and, like the bonds, the weaker ones busted before the end of the decade. There are still plenty to go around including franchise operations like **Gold's Gym** or **Spa Health Club**, and established local operations such as **Raleigh Athletic Club** at Celebration at Six Forks, the **Imperial Athletic Club** in Research Triangle Park, **Fitness USA** on Front Street and **The Club For Women Only** with locations in Raleigh and Cary. Both the **YMCA** and the **YWCA** have extensive programs, including indoor pools.

YWCA OF WAKE COUNTY, INC.
1012 Oberlin Rd.   828-3205

The face of the YWCA has changed, and it's not just for women anymore. The Raleigh YWCA has a pool, nautilus equipment and aerobics classes, as well as other fitness and recreation programs. The basic membership fee is $20; an additional monthly or annual fee gives you access to the use of the particular facilities that you plan to use. Call for more information and a copy of the YWCA's schedule.

ICE SKATING

There's no ice skating rink in Raleigh, but there's one in Cary, the **Ice House**, on Buck Jones Road. Along with open skating, the Ice House hosts area club hockey teams. (See **CARY PARKS AND RECREATION** for more.)

JOGGING, RUNNING, WALKING

If you're a jogger, you probably will want to map out your own course, but you'll have company because Raleigh is a running town. Its premier **Great Raleigh Road Race**, for instance, draws up to 5,000 runners and joggers annually. The city also has worked with the **Raleigh Roadrunners Association** to build a course near Lake Johnson.

Two of the more popular courses are the paths around Shelley Lake in northwest Raleigh and NCSU's track stadium on the main campus near Pullen Road. The city's award-winning **Capital Area Greenway** system is one of the best in the country, and it laces the city like a spider web, generally running beside the city's creeks and streams. The master plan shows a 200-plus mile system of which 34 miles are completed now. The Shelley Lake to Sawmill Road Trail is the most popular, followed by the Lake Johnson and Buckeye paths. Motorized vehicles are not allowed. Some of the trails are paved and are shared by bicyclists, but other parts are strictly for walking or jogging. A packet of maps and a description of the system is available at the city Planning Department for a small fee. Call 890-3125.

The city's Parks and Recreation Department also cosponsors the **5K Run for the Oaks** in early summer, as well as other youth races. It also can put you in touch with the people who coach the city's formidable **Junior Striders**, who are comprised of elementary and junior high age-children. For information, call 890-3285. Finally, a number of the newer planned communities have met the demand for jogging and walking by installing their own walking trails.

RACQUETBALL

Despite all the interest in racquetball, the city still has no public courts. Again, shame! If you want to play, you'll have to join a club or the **YMCA** on Hillsborough Street. The YMCA has the best courts; they're solid and give you a lively bounce, but you have to share them with handball players. Other places where you will find strong racquetball crowds are **Fitness USA**, 1207 Front Street (832-5555), **Raleigh Athletic Club** at Celebration at Six Forks, (847-8189) and the **Imperial Athletic Club** at 4700 Emperor Boulevard in RTP (941-9010). These places attract a younger, "upwardly mobile" crowd and include body-building rooms where the svelte Pepsi generation ogles each others' pectorals.

SOCCER

CAPITAL AREA SOCCER LEAGUE (CASL)
3344 Hillsborough St.   834-3951

This is **The** league for soccer players, be they boys, girls or grown-ups. Last season, over 8,000 participated. It is a nonprofit league but run separately from municipal or school programs, and has been the training program for some of the area's best players. It sponsors several Classic or Select teams and you'd better have plenty of suitcases if your child gets on one of

these teams because they travel. Play begins with five-year-olds and, in the youth leagues, goes up to age 19. There are over 40 adult teams. The 118-acre **WRAL Soccer Center** on Perry Creek Road off U.S. Highway 1 North has 32 fields in use. A new complex in Morrisville has eight fields.

CASL has two seasons, fall and spring, with eight games in the fall and eight in spring. Say goodbye to your weekends.

SALVATION ARMY
902 Wake Forest Rd.   832-6918

The Salvation Army has added soccer to its athletic program and it organized 18 teams in 1993, boys and girls, ages 5 to 8. There's a $40 registration fee, and sign-ups begin in August. Play starts in September. Each child must play during the game and children come from all over Wake County. Games are played at the center's three fields on Saturday mornings.

SOFTBALL

The city doesn't have the only game in town, but it has most of the fields. City officials can put you in touch with the **Raleigh Amateur Softball Association** and, among others, a very active church league and some company team leagues. Altogether, the city coordinates play among six leagues including medium pitch, slow pitch,

RALEIGH'S CAPITAL AREA GREENWAY SYSTEM IS ONE OF THE BEST IN THE COUNTRY, LACING THE CITY LIKE A SPIDER WEB, GENERALLY RUNNING BESIDE THE CITY'S CREEKS AND STREAMS. THE MASTER PLAN SHOWS A 200-PLUS MILE SYSTEM OF WHICH 34 MILES ARE NOW COMPLETE.

Insiders' Tip

coed, and 40-years-and-older leagues. It also sponsors a "pigtail league" for girls between the ages of 10 and 15. Registration for most leagues begins in mid-February and play starts in April. The "pigtail" season is somewhat later. Call the city's Athletic Office, 831-6836, for information.

SWIMMING

CANDLER SWIM & GYM CLUB

1013 Jones Franklin Rd.   *851-3935*

There are a number of private clubs in Raleigh, but Candler is one of the oldest and best known, and you can find out about competitive teams, here. Its founder is a former Olympian and the quality of his diving program and swim teams has won the club national attention. It has an olympic-size diving tower and a 25-meter pool. It was the site for the very successful 1987 **Olympic Festival** diving competition.

RALEIGH PARKS AND RECREATION

831-6852

The city runs an active aquatics program, from teaching babies how to swim to hosting some of the region's top swimming competitions. The centerpieces of its swim program are the $4 million indoor **Pullen Park Aquatics Center**, which opened in 1992, and the **Optimist Park** pools, which are open year-round, too. The Pullen Center is home to a number of area swim clubs and has a diving board. Optimist includes a diving pool, a shallow baby's pool and a competitive, 50-meter olympic-size swimming pool. The city has pools at the following locations: **Biltmore Hills**, **Chavis Park**, **Lake Johnson**, **Longview**, **Millbrook Exchange**, **Optimist Park**, **Pullen Park** and **Ridge Road**. Some of the pools are purposely located near public schools, namely Lake Johnson near Athens Drive High School, Longview near Enloe High School, Optimist Park near Sanderson High School and Ridge Road near Martin Junior High, so that the schools can take advantage of swim programs. The city offers season passes if you plan to swim often; otherwise, there is an admission charge for everyone over the age of six. Diving lessons are taught, as well as **American Red Cross** courses. For information on swim clubs and teams, call Jim Parker at the above number.

SILVER LAKE

5300 Tryon Rd.   *851-1683*
Group Rates   *851-7782*

This favorite swimming hole for Cary and Raleigh residents is east of Cary and has developed into one of the area's popular privately operated swimming parks open to the public. It features a 400-foot-long waterslide, white sand beach, pedal boats, snack bar and picnic areas. It welcomes groups.

YMCA

1601 Hillsborough St.   *832-6601*
Old Garner Rd.   *833-1256*

Both YMCA's sponsor competitive coed swim teams, and also have pools for instructional and lap swimming for members. Competitive swimming at the Hillsborough

Street YMCA is a year-long program but can be taken on a month-by-month basis. Swim classes are available for toddlers, too.

YWCA OF WAKE COUNTY, INC.
1012 Oberlin Rd.   *828-3205*
   The YWCA offers swimming programs and classes for children and adults. The pool is available for members' use for lap swimming and recreational swimming. The basic membership fee at the YWCA is $20; call for additional information on fees and types of memberships that include the use of the pool.

TENNIS

RALEIGH PARKS AND RECREATION
Millbrook Exchange Park   *872-4129*
1905 Spring Forest Rd.
   Raleigh was caught napping when the tennis boom hit in the mid '70s, but it has recovered since then and maintains 90 courts today—83 of which are lighted. Operation Central for city tennis programs is the **Millbrook Exchange Park**, which has 15 courts and hosts city tournaments. The old clay courts have been converted and all courts today are hard surface. There is plenty of league play, and tournaments go into December.
   Play at all parks is free unless you sign up for a tournament or league or reserve courts at Millbrook Exchange. League play, by the way, is a good way to meet people.

RALEIGH RACQUET CLUB
5516 Falls of the Neuse Rd.   *876-0847*
   This is a private membership club with clubhouse and swimming

pool attached. It is also home to some of the best tennis in town, and features composition (soft surface) as well as hard-surface courts, over two dozen total including eight indoor courts. It also has a stadium court, and its tournaments attract some of the stars of tomorrow—John McEnroe passed this way as a youngster. The **Raleigh Edge** stars played their first season here. In addition, the club hosts the **Rex Classic** and other charity tournaments. Marshall Happer, the head of the pro tennis association, helped start the club and stops by when he's in town.

VOLLEYBALL

RALEIGH PARKS AND RECREATION
                                          831-6836
   The city sponsors several leagues at different park centers and cosponsors, with the **Inland Beach Volleyball Association,** tournaments at **Raleigh Beach** in Jaycee Park on Wade Avenue. Lions Park has a power volleyball league with six-person teams, that begins registration in August. Other centers with volleyball programs include **Millbrook Exchange, Biltmore Hills, Chavis Center, Robert Park** and **Jaycee Park**. The city is looking at the Green Road Park to add another outdoor program. For a taste of California, two-man ball under the sun or under the lights, stop by Raleigh Beach on the weekend or during warm summer nights. It's where some of the East Coast's champion teams work out.

Inside

Wake County Schools and Child Care

Raleigh and Cary have good public schools today, thanks to some gutsy political decisions made in the 1970s to consolidate city and county school systems. Students consistently score above national norms, and individual schools within the system have earned national recognition for their programs. Raleigh and Cary both are part of a consolidated, Wake County Public School System so there are no individual city or town systems. Furthermore, the Wake School system includes a series of "magnet" schools that draw students from all over the county. What this means, in effect, is that where you live may not determine where your child will go to school. There still are neighborhood schools—indeed, most are neighborhood schools—and there are a number of private schools from which to choose, although some of the city's public schools enjoy academic reputations better than or equal to the private institutions.

This section will review the public school system and will highlight some of the individual public and private schools. School assignments are based on the home ad-

dress of the students' parent or guardian. To find out what schools serve specific neighborhoods, call 850-1931.

The Wake County system enrolls about 73,450 students in kindergarten through 12th grade, making it the second largest in the state and in the top 50 in the nation. It employs over 4,800 teachers, counselors and librarians and the teacher-student ratio averages about 1 to 23.

In North Carolina, the state provides the bulk of public school funds, and local revenues supplement the base. The property tax is the county's principal source of supplemental school revenue.

Dr. Robert Wentz is superintendent for the system. A veteran teacher and administrator, he was selected by the board in 1989 and was named as one of the country's top 100 educators in 1987. The system contains 94 schools, of which 14 are senior high schools. It has a 70 to 30 ratio between white and minority students. Although the system offers a "school of choice" plan with 30 "magnet" schools, you must first register your child at his

529

or her base school and then apply for admission. Magnet schools offer a range of options:

1. **Gifted and Talented** (GT) K-8 schools offer a basic program in English, math, science and social studies, and a variety of electives that emphasize the basics but also include computer studies, foreign languages and fine arts. There are 15 located throughout the county. There is one high school designated as a **GT magnet**, Enloe High School in east Raleigh. It offers students a chance to concentrate in special fields such as mathematics, biology, chemistry, the humanities, art, music and drama.

2. **Classical Studies** schools emphasize the basic courses and basic education skills such as homework. The two classical schools are Bugg and Root, both in Raleigh.

3. **International Studies** are offered at two elementary schools and, besides the basic courses, offer electives in foreign languages and study of world cultures.

4. The **Language/Communication** magnet is located at Joyner Elementary and, as expected, concentrates on skills in language arts.

5. **Year-Round** programs are offered in four elementary magnets and in one middle school. Application must be made to attend the year-round schools and slots are filled through a lottery. Year-round schools do not serve a base population, so you can't guarantee attendance by where you buy your home. The school year is divided into four nine-week quarters with students in school nine weeks and off three weeks for a total of 180 days in class. Parents choose between 4 tracks of attendance which provide different vacation schedules. The philosophy behind year-round school is that it makes better use of the facilities, and students retain more of what they've learned.

6. **Extended-day** magnets are located at three elementary schools in Raleigh and provide before- and after-school supervision. In short, it's day care for students and offers instruction in arts, sports, music, industrial arts, etc., rather than babysitting. It does cost extra: $120 per month for the first child in 1993.

There are differences between schools even though they are in one county-wide system. Neighborhood schools that draw from the more affluent neighborhoods continue to enjoy more financial support from parent-teacher associations, for example, and standardized test scores tend to be higher. The present Board of Education has put more emphasis on basic education after a half-dozen years of consolidation and program innovation by two controversial superintendents, both of whom left under fire.

For example, the board initiated a tougher policy for student athletes. They now must make passing grades if they are to play sports. Similarly, in 1988, the board adopted a tougher attendance policy. It also requires more credits in the basics such as English, mathematics, science and history, including U.S. history and world civilization. The state also requires all students to pass a competency test of basic skills before they are awarded a diploma. The board, however, has attracted national attention with experimental programs such as the Writing to Read Program, which uses IBM computers to help students develop writing skills at an early age and become familiar with computers. All middle schools (junior high) also have computer labs and courses for students to learn about computers.

The high schools that serve Raleigh and Cary students offer a broad range of courses, including foreign languages and higher mathematics. The latest California Achievement Test results (1993) showed the system well above the national average in the grades tested (3rd, 6th and 8th). In reading, the scores in percentiles for the three grade levels were 75, 69 and 70 respectively; in math, 79, 80, and 74; and in language, 72, 68 and 66. If the scores were limited just to the Raleigh and Cary schools instead of all of Wake County, the tests probably would have been higher.

Moreover, through the magnet program, parents can select schools that emphasize a curriculum that best fits their child's talents. As befits a large system, the schools offer special programs for handicapped children, including educable mentally retarded and seriously emotionally- and learning-disabled children. **Project Enlight-**

enment is an acclaimed service of the system that offers family therapy as well as individual therapy for young children, parents and teachers. Because of rapid growth in the county, the system's biggest headache now is building new classrooms so it can retire the ugly mobile versions from the overcrowded campuses throughout the county.

Also, parents should be aware that North Carolina operates two nationally recognized residential state schools for gifted students in the arts and sciences. The **North Carolina School of the Arts** is located in Winston-Salem and the newer **North Carolina School for Science and Math** is in nearby Durham (see **DURHAM SCHOOLS** for more details).

Public Schools

Here is a close-up of a few selected, individual schools:

BROUGHTON HIGH SCHOOL
Raleigh's Broughton High School is among the oldest in the Wake system, having opened its doors in 1929. The Romanesque, three-story, stone building was one of the largest schools in the state when it was built. Enrollment is about 1,625 in grades 9 to 12.

The federal Department of Education in 1984 recognized Broughton as one of the top 114 high schools in the nation, and its principal, Diane Payne, is a veteran who served in the same capacity at the Enloe magnet high school. Broughton was featured in a *U.S.*

News and World Report article in 1984, which noted that 75 percent of its graduates go on to four-year colleges and five percent attend trade or vocational schools. It was also the recipient of a unique program for public schools: endowed teaching chairs made possible by a $100,000 gift of Broughton alumnus, Richard Jenrette, chairman of the Equitable Insurance Co.

Broughton also has a vigorous extracurricular program; the girls and boys basketball and baseball teams have won three state championships and runner-up honors in recent years, and the show chorus program is rated among the best in the nation.

ENLOE HIGH SCHOOL

This east Raleigh high school has an enrollment of about 1,975 and was selected to be a "magnet" high school, grades 9 to 12, pulling gifted and talented students from all over the county. It offers courses not offered in the regular high school program and allows students to concentrate in special fields of study through an eight-period day and multiple periods in specified courses. Among all state high schools, it frequently has the highest number of merit scholar finalists except for the N.C. School for Science and Math in Durham.

Principal Bobby Allen arrived in 1993 and directs a school whose English program received national recognition in 1986 and received an award of excellence from the U.S. Department of Education in 1983. It also won a grant from the Carnegie Foundation for the Advancement of Teaching. The school offers eight foreign languages. It has two dance studios, two art studios, a piano lab, a TV studio and two computer labs.

CARY HIGH SCHOOL

The current Cary High School was built in 1960 and has an enrollment of about 1,700 in grades 9 to 12. The principal is Donna Hargens. The school has a long history dating back to the town's famous Cary Academy, and many town residents still take pride in their local public schools. CHS, too, sends a large percentage of its graduates on to higher education, over 80 percent, and in one recent class, six graduates were awarded NCSU's prestigious Caldwell Scholarships. Its test scores are among the highest in the Wake system, and the school is famous for its music program. The Cary Band has marched in the Rose Bowl Parade and presidential inaugural parades, and even performed abroad. It became the host for one of the state's noted music events, **Cary Band Day**, which started in 1960.

Like Broughton, Enloe and six other high schools, CHS participates in the Community Schools Program, which means it holds classes at night and opens its facilities for civic and recreational activities. The school also has been a wrestling powerhouse among Triangle schools, and its team was '93 state champs.

MILLBROOK HIGH SCHOOL

This is one of three high schools located in suburban north

Raleigh, and it had an enrollment of 1,963 for 1993. Principal Joann Patton oversees a faculty that offers a strong academic curriculum that helps send most graduates on to college. The school offers sciences, including advanced physics, advanced anatomy, four foreign languages, computer science and advanced placement in nine courses.

Millbrook's busy extra curricular activities, including strong football and basketball programs, have helped the students cope, and Dr. Patton has brought fresh leadership.

FRED OLDS ELEMENTARY SCHOOL

The extended-day magnet program offered here has become popular with single-parent families and those in which both parents work. Located in west Raleigh near NCSU, the school draws about 425 students from throughout the county to its extended-day program, which begins at 7 a.m. and ends at 6 p.m. Students spend their extra time at school in the following activities: arts and crafts, industrial arts, physical education, music, and homework, and special interests and clubs such as Girl Scouts. Cost for the program is $120 per month for the first child, with reduced charges for additional children. Joyner and Combs elementary schools also offer extended-day magnet programs.

LEESVILLE ROAD HIGH SCHOOL

Leesville, the Triangle's newest addition to the high school system, opened its doors in August of 1993. It is part of a K-12 campus and will graduate its first senior class in

1995. First year enrollment was approximately 1,200 students, and full enrollment is expected to exceed 1,800. Richard J. Murphy serves as principal.

MORRISVILLE ELEMENTARY SCHOOL

When the Morrisville Elementary School near Cary opened in 1991 it was the largest year-round school in the nation. It offers four tracks of year-round classes to students from Morrisville, Cary, Apex and north Raleigh. The school offers an after-school program in co-operation with the Cary Family YMCA and has some of the highest test scores in the county.

WEST LAKE ELEMENTARY AND MIDDLE SCHOOLS

The demand for year-round schools caused these two new schools to be designated as year-round magnets in 1992-93. A high school has been proposed at the same site.

Private Schools

Like most of the South, the Triangle's private and parochial school tradition is not as pronounced as it is in the northeastern part of the United States and large Midwestern cities such as Chicago and Detroit. There are only two K-8, Catholic elementary-middle schools and one 9-12 high school, for example. All but one of the private schools are day schools only. There was a surge in private school growth when public schools were first integrated, but after the city and county public school systems were merged, the flight to private schools subsided. The private school tradition, nonetheless, is a long one, dating back to Raleigh's early decades when Saint Mary's College—grades 11-12 and the first two years of college—was founded in 1842. Some of the private schools and their programs are:

SAINT MARY'S COLLEGE
1900 Hillsborough St.   *828-2521*

Yes, Saint Mary's is a female-only, junior college, but it also teaches the last two years of high school and, beginning with the 1994-95 school year it will offer grades 9 and 10 for day students. So, girls can attend six years of school here, and many will. In the old days, two years of college seemed sufficient for Southern ladies, but today, 95 percent of Saint Mary's college graduates continue on for a four-year college degree. Its alum-

nae are loyal and prominent. It is the only private secondary school in town that boards students. The student-teacher ratio is 10 to 1, and the campus is one of Raleigh's beautiful landmarks.

Affiliated with the Episcopal Church, it holds chapel services which, however, do not harm the girls' reputation for active social lives. Tuition for high school students is slightly more than for college students. For boarders, 1994-95 tuition is $14,910, and for day students, $7,595.

RAVENSCROFT SCHOOL
7409 Falls of the Neuse Rd.   *847-0900*

Ravenscroft School, one of the best-known of the non-public schools in the area, is a coed, college-preparatory day school with a preschool through twelfth grade program. The school was founded in 1862 by members of Christ Episcopal Church and named for the first Episcopal bishop of North Carolina. While the school is no longer affiliated with any denomination, it maintains its Judeo-Christian heritage and strives to help students understand basic values and pursue ideals of integrity, service, compassion, and sportsmanship.

The School upholds rigorous academic standards in keeping with its college-preparatory goals. Of the 53 graduates in the class of 1992, for example, 100 percent were accepted to college or university. They had an average SAT of 1118.

The school is located on an attractive, wood-fringed 123-acre campus in North Raleigh and enrolls approximately 850 students. The tuition ranges from about $3,800 for kindergarten to $6,900 for grades 7-12.

CARDINAL GIBBONS HIGH SCHOOL
2401 Western Blvd.　　　*834-1625*

This is Raleigh's only Catholic high school, and it is coed. It includes grades 9 through 12 and has an enrollment of about 280. It provides a college-preparatory curriculum, and about 94 percent of its approximately 70 seniors go on to college. The average SAT score for seniors is over 1000, well above the state average of 833.

No uniforms are required, but, as expected, there is a dress code and students must take religious instruction in all grade levels. There are about 24 full-time teachers, some of whom are Sisters. Tuition for Catholic families in 1993-94 is about $2,700 and for non-parishioners, $4,000.

St. Timothy's Lower School
4523 Six Forks Rd.
Admissions: 781-0531
School Office: 787-3011

St. Timothy's Lower School, an Episcopal coed school, is the oldest accredited non-public school in North Carolina. It was established in 1958 by the Rev. and Mrs. George Hale with the authorization of the vestry of St. Timothy's Episcopal Church. The school strives to instill Christian principles in a program of academic excellence and to promote the self-esteem of each student so that the early school years are positive ones.

The instructional program is organized to challenge the individual to perform to his or her ability level. A six to one student-teacher ratio helps in the development of close student-adult relationships.

As part of an ambitious expansion program, to be completed in two phases by 1996, fifth-graders from St. Timothy's Lower School will join sixth graders from the Middle School in a new facility. It is believed this will help students make a smoother transition from elementary to junior high school.

Tuition ranges from over $3,600 for Pre-K to $4,500 for fifth grade. All books and fees are included in the tuition.

Hale High School
3400 White Oak Dr.   782-3331

St. Timothy's and Hale are actually two schools that began as one. Hale High School was built in 1973 on 18 acres in one of Raleigh's loveliest neighborhoods, and named for St. Timothy's founder, Rev. George Hale. Like St. Timothy's, the school is founded on Christian principles and maintains academic excellence with emphasis on college preparatory. Last year's ninth grade California Achievement Test (CAT) scores averaged in the 96th percentile. Hale goes through grade 12 and classes are kept to 18 students.

Raleigh Christian Academy
2110 Trawick Rd.   872-2215

Sponsored by the First Free Will Baptist Church, this school began in 1977. It is rooted in the Bible and the belief that the "public school system is not teaching the basic skills as it once did." It believes in discipline and teaches the "Genesis account of the creation of man as opposed to the theory of evolution of man." Boys wear pants and girls wear dresses, and no "weird fingernail polish." It has all grade levels, from kindergarten to 12th as well as a day care program that takes infants as young as six weeks old. Enrollment is around 650. At

A Tradition of Excellence

St. Timothy's Lower School
St. Timothy's Middle School • Hale High School

Classic curriculum including art, computer, drama,
foreign languages, music & physical education.

Two beautiful campuses located in the North Hills area

Co-ed Episcopal school

Maximum class size sixteen

100% of students accepted to college

Competitive athletic program

North Carolina's oldest accredited non-public school by
Southern Association of Colleges and Schools

Providing academic excellence in a nurturing environment
pre-kindergarten through high school.

Established in 1958

St. Timothy's Lower & Middle and Hale High

PO Box 17787 • Raleigh, NC 27619

(919) 781-0531 (lower school)

(919) 782-3331 (middle & upper school)

the elementary school level, day care starts at 7 a.m., and ends at 6 p.m. Tuition for high school is about $1,900; for elementary school, $1,700.

FRIENDSHIP CHRISTIAN SCHOOL
5510 Falls of the Neuse Rd. 872-2133

Friendship is another Baptist-affiliated K-12 school for boys and girls. It was started in 1970 as a day care and kindergarten and continued to grow over the years to its current 450 enrollment. Its senior class in 1992 totaled 30 students; the average classroom contains 20 students. It follows a traditional teaching format, has a conservative dress code and takes a fundamentalist view of Bible study that is required at each grade level. Tuition for senior high is about $2,000; for elementary school, $1,900.

CATHEDRAL SCHOOL
204 Hillsborough St. 832-4711

Cathedral School, proud of its tradition of academic excellence, is ideally located in the heart of historic Raleigh and enrolls about 260 pupils. Cathedral students experience Raleigh's history firsthand, visiting cultural, historical, and scientific facilities, all within walking distance. The school, a Catholic faith community since 1909, encourages students from all denominations and ethnic backgrounds to pursue academic excellence within the framework of Christian principles. This school offers a four-year-old program, a K-8 curriculum and a supervised after-school program.

OUR LADY OF LOURDES
2710 Overbrook Dr. 782-1670

This is the other Catholic elementary-middle school serving the Raleigh and Cary area. It goes through the 8th grade, and many of the students continue at Cardinal Gibbons. The school requires uniforms. Lourdes has about 260 K-8 students and uses lay teachers.

MONTESSORI SCHOOL OF RALEIGH
7005 Leadmine Rd. 848-1545

Started in 1975, the school takes children from 21 months old and goes through the 5th grade. Enrollment is about 220, and teachers follow the Montessori method, which emphasizes individual development at the child's own speed and meeting the needs of each child. Parental involvement in the school is expected, though not required. Classes average about 25 students, but have two teachers. Day care service for before- and after-school hours is available. Call for tuition information.

NORTH RALEIGH COUNTRY DAY SCHOOL
10200 Strickland Rd. 847-3120

This school, along with two other related schools—**Millbrook Country Day** (787-7568), and **Cary Country Day School** (467-6991)—is a member of an association of private schools begun in 1963 for younger children. All have excellent reputations and are known for providing educational extras such as computer instruction, swim lessons in on-campus pools, and complete before- and after-school day care programs. All the teachers here hold degrees. Summer camp programs are also provided at all four locations. The Raleigh Country Day School (the largest with 200 students) offers instruction for children from age two through first grade; the others either through kindergarten or third grade; call each campus for information on monthly tuition costs.

THE ACHIEVEMENT SCHOOL
400 Cedarview Ct.   *782-5082*

This is a local private school founded by Leon Silber, a consultant who once advised the state on its own learning disability program. In 1979, he started the school, believing he could do more with his own school in helping children with learning disabilities such as dyslexia. The school offers children in grades 1-12 a highly structured program with close personal and positive teaching. The teacher-pupil ratio is 1 to 4 and the school's total enrollment ranges between 60-80. The school is accredited and offers half- and full-day instruction in a wide range of courses including the basics, language and mathematics. Call the school for tuition information.

RALEIGH PRESCHOOL
1215 Ridge Rd.   *828-5351*

This is a 40-year-old co-op, which means that parents have to help with some of the chores. It began as a preschool when North Carolina had no kindergarten in its public schools. Many of Raleigh's current civic leaders enrolled their children here when they were young families on a tight budget; it's not unusual to hear such couples say today, "Oh, we met at Raleigh Preschool." It is accredited by the National Association for the Education of Young People, and children can start here at the age of 18 months. The parents voted in 1992 to expand through the third grade, and with this change, enrollment is expected to reach around 200.

Day Care

North Carolina has the highest percentage of working women in the nation, and because many of these women are mothers, day care for children has long been part of the state's social fabric. The Triangle also has a higher-than-state average of working women, many in professional ranks, and it is fair to say there is a shortage of good day care, especially for infants. The Triangle has a number of private and quasi-public day care operations, and several Triangle businesses—such as Cary software house

SAS—provide day care for employees' children as part of the company's benefit package. It's a growing trend, according to Stephanie Fanjul of **Workplace Options**, a day care consulting firm familiar with the Triangle market. A good rule to follow is to start with your local church or synagogue because many operate some form of day care or know of others who do. The following list is a guide to some of the better or more established programs, and it lists preschools as well as full day care operations.

CHILD CARE RESOURCE CENTER
3901 Barrett Dr., Ste. 104   571-1420

This is not a day care center but rather a nonprofit information center that helps families find day care suitable to them and their budgets. Its main purpose is to coordinate information about child care resources and referral services to the general public and to promote quality of child care. It provides a very useful map and chart, for example, that identifies 125 day care providers in Wake County and their respective services, e.g., hours, size, age of children accepted, etc. Before you start looking for a day care center to fit your particular needs, call the center.

DISCOVERY CHILD CARE CENTER
1120 Sawmill Rd.   846-1164

Discovery Child Care Center is one of the area programs that has begun to supply community oriented care—most children who attend Discovery live within a three- to four-mile radius of the Center.

Located within the Greystone neighborhood (see **RALEIGH NEIGHBORHOODS**), the Center provides full-day and preschool care for infants (six weeks) through four-year-olds and after-school programs for children up to fifth grade. The Center offers after-school pickup from Lynn Road, Stough, York and Jeffries Grove elementary schools. It opened a Poole Road location in east Raleigh in 1989. Hours are from 7 a.m. until 6 p.m. Call for tuition.

KIDS CLUB AND HEALTH CENTER
Cary Pkwy. and YMCA Dr. 460-9233

This child care center and its sister center in north Raleigh, the **Growing Child** at 321 Spring Forest Road, are strictly for "mildly ill" children who require temporary care during the day while their parents are at work. Opened in the fall of 1989, Kids Club has spaces for up to 31 children, ranging in age from four months to 12 years. Licensed by the state, it's staffed by child care professionals and registered and licensed nurses. Parents with sick children must call the center on the day they need care to discuss the child's illness with a nurse and to reserve a space. The center is owned and operated by Raleigh pediatrician Dr. James Poole.

Mother's Time Out

This service is offered almost exclusively by churches in the area, and it gives mothers a daytime respite from their children for a reasonable fee. Most programs are for a few hours and serve the children some kind of refreshment. The "time out" usually comes one or two days a week. Popular programs include:

BENSON MEMORIAL UNITED METHODIST CHURCH
4706 Creedmoor Rd.   781-3310

FIRST BAPTIST CHURCH
99 N. Salisbury St.   832-4650

Preschools

These are primarily half-day programs, although some include kindergarten classes. They teach, rather than babysit. Children begin at age two, although some are taken at age one. **Raleigh Preschool**, one of the older programs, is an independent parent cooperative, which means parents are required to help during the day and can be expected to cut the grass, trim hedges and paint from time to time. **White Memorial Presbyterian Church, St. Michael's Episcopal Church** and **Temple Beth Or** are among other established programs with solid reputations.

RALEIGH PRESCHOOL
1215 Ridge Rd.   828-5351

ST. MICHAEL'S PRESCHOOL
1520 Canterbury Rd.   787-5167

TEMPLE BETH OR
5315 Creedmoor Rd.   787-3619

WHITE MEMORIAL PRESBYTERIAN
1704 Oberlin Rd.   834-4637

RALEIGH CHILD CARE
2035 Lake Wheeler Rd.   834-8762
1201 Kent Rd.   851-4457

After-School Programs

These are programs for the older child who is in school, but who needs an activity to keep him or her busy until mom or dad gets home. There are three primary providers in the Raleigh-Cary area: the public schools' extended-day program, the YMCA and YWCA, and the different city recreation programs. Contact information can be found elsewhere in this Guide under schools or recreation.

Full-Day Programs

There are several kinds of providers for full day care service, which usually takes infants from six weeks old to kindergarten-aged children. The small mom-and-pop provider is at one end of the spectrum, yet regulations and insurance rates are putting many such programs out of business. At the other end are the for-profit chain operations such as **Kinder-Care,** which has eight locations (two in Cary), **La Petite Academies** (six locations), **Young World** and **Children's World.** They can be found in the Yellow Pages under "Child Care."

In between are single-site providers, many of which, again, are in churches. Two of the best are **First Baptist Church** in downtown Raleigh and **Pullen Memorial Baptist Church's Method Day Care,** which also was one of the city's first desegregated programs. Some of the other churches with established programs for two-year-olds and up are **West Raleigh Presbyterian,**

Edenton Street Methodist and **First Cosmopolitan Baptist Church.**

    Learning Together is operated on contract with Wake County School System and Department of Social Services, and it serves gifted and learning-disabled children. **Tammy Lynn Center** is a nonprofit school for the handicapped. Three of the city's housing projects have day care centers. They are: Chavis Heights, Walnut Terrace and Halifax Court.

**EDENTON STREET
METHODIST CHURCH**
228 W. Edenton St.   832-2029

**ERNEST MYATT PRESBYTERIAN
CHILD DEVELOPMENT CENTER**
4926 Fayetteville Rd.   779-0316

FIRST BAPTIST CHURCH
99 N. Salisbury St.   832-4650

**FIRST COSMOPOLITAN
BAPTIST CHURCH**
1515 Cross Link Rd.   833-3283

**HILLCREST BAPTIST CHILD
DEVELOPMENT CENTER**
3800 Hillcrest Rd.   231-6389

**HUDSON MEMORIAL
CHILDREN'S MINISTRIES**
4921 Six Forks Rd.   787-1086

LEARNING TOGETHER
568 Lenoir St.   856-5200

MACGREGOR CREATIVE SCHOOL
203 Gregson Dr., Cary   469-2046

**NEW HOPE BAPTIST
LEARNING CENTER**
4301 Louisburg Rd.   876-5850

**PULLEN MEMORIAL
BAPTIST CHURCH**
1801 Hillsborough St.   828-2926

TAMMY LYNN CENTER
739 Chappell Dr.   832-3909

WEST RALEIGH PRESBYTERIAN
Horne Street   833-3492

Capitol Square in downtown Raleigh is surrounded by historic churches.

Inside
Raleigh Worship

Unlike Charlotte, Raleigh does not claim to have more churches per capita than any other city, but Raleigh has plenty from which to choose. A good place to start is Capitol Square downtown, which bears out Alexis de Tocqueville's observation that the churches in America, while separate from the state, keep close watch on government. There sits the Capitol, and hardly 100 steps away in any direction, you will find four churches: the First Baptist (mostly white), the First Presbyterian, another First Baptist (mostly black), and Christ Episcopal. Then, two blocks away is Church of the Good Shepherd (Episcopal), Sacred Heart Cathedral (Catholic) and Edenton Street United Methodist.

The churches in Raleigh that have grown rapidly have been the Southern Baptists—no surprise—and the Catholics—surprise!—although most mainline churches also have shared in the Triangle's population boom. Raleigh and Cary are close enough that it is not unusual to find residents in one attending a church in the other. For small congregations such as the Friends or the Unitarians or Christian Science, one church or meeting place usually suffices for both municipalities.

There are too many churches to mention by name, so this Guide will limit itself to a slice of the city's religious life. Most are mainline, formal congregations. To find the Greek Orthodox, or Church of the Latter-Day Saints (Mormons), or Jehovah's Witnesses, check the Yellow Pages. You are in the South, so if you want to wash your sins away in the river, you probably can find a congregation that does that. The Yellow Pages also lists charismatic churches (those whose members sometimes speak in tongues). Raleigh has no resident televangelists. Snakehandlers—especially after one in the western part of the state was bitten and died—also have been in short supply.

Call first for time of worship. During the summer, many churches will change their schedules. During the remainder of the year, most mainline Protestant churches hold at least one Sunday service at 11 a.m.; Catholics services will vary but the early mass is normally at 8 a.m.

Baptist

FIRST BAPTIST CHURCH
101 S. Wilmington St.   *832-1649*

One of the oldest—175 years—and largest of the predominately black churches, First Baptist sits across from the southeast corner of the Capitol, downtown. Its pastors have been active in the Raleigh black community as well as the community at large, including City Councillor Brad Thompson. Its congregation numbers over 600 members, a number of whom are part of the city's civic leadership. The church maintains an active youth, music and religious education. A big day in the church year is its anniversary Sunday, which is celebrated the first Sunday in March and usually draws a big crowd.

FIRST BAPTIST CHURCH
99 Salisbury St.   *832-4485*

This is one of the city's largest Southern Baptist congregations. It is a busy, active church and includes many city leaders among its congregation, such as Agriculture Commissioner Jim Graham. Dr. R. Wayne Stacy, a professor of the New Testament, is pastor. The church remains a member of the Southern Baptist Convention, but as one member adds, "just barely," which means it is more moderate than the denominational fundamentalists who now control the SBC. The church maintains many needed services including a popular infant and toddlers day care.

FIRST COSMOPOLITAN BAPTIST
1515 Cross Link Rd.   *833-3283*

Another of the city's large black Baptist churches is First Cosmopolitan, which sits just outside the Beltline in east Raleigh. The Rev. W.B. Lewis has been active in city affairs and leads a congregation of about 800 members. The church is about 90 years old and operates a day care program for over 50 preschool children. It also has a special program to help older children with their homework.

FOREST HILLS BAPTIST CHURCH
3110 Clark Ave.   *828-6161*

Forest Hills is a Southern Baptist Church with a rich heritage for ministering to a wide variety of persons. As one of the largest congregations in the city, Forest Hills offers programs for families, single adults, college students, internationals, senior adults, youth, children and preschoolers. The ministry staff offers many creative programs to meet the demands of such a diverse congregation. Dr. John Lewis is interim pastor. Worship services are Sunday mornings at 8:30 and 11 a.m., and Wednesday evenings at 6 p.m. Bible study is each Sunday at 9:30 a.m. Specialized ministries are held each Sunday evening at 6 p.m.

GREYSTONE BAPTIST CHURCH
7509 Leadmine Rd.   *847-1333*

Michael Jamison is pastor of this Southern Baptist congregation that was founded in 1983 as a mission of First Baptist Church.

Jamison, a native of western North Carolina, describes his congregation as "open and involved" and says the church reflects that attitude. It numbers about 590, about 25 percent having come from non-Baptist backgrounds. Eight Girl Scout troops meet here, as do a number of homeowner associations. There are two Sunday services, and a van taxies members from nearby Springmoor retirement complex. The median age of the congregation is in the mid-30s.

HAYES-BARTON BAPTIST CHURCH
1800 Glenwood Ave. 833-4617

This is a Southern Baptist congregation and one of the largest in the city, 1,900 members. In the heart of the Establishment neighborhood, it has many influential citizens as members; Senator Jesse Helms attends church here when he's home from Washington. Hayes-Barton offers a wide range of Bible and church programs. Pastor George Balentine oversees an active program, including a mission for the deaf. It also sponsors Girl, Cub and Boy Scout troops.

MID-WAY BAPTIST CHURCH
6910 Fayetteville Rd. 772-5864

An independent Baptist church, Mid-Way is one of the largest in the area with 1,600 members. While it has a Raleigh address, it really lies outside the city limits. It was started over 20 years ago with 15 people. James L. Upchurch has been the pastor from the beginning and saw the church rise over what was once a hog pen. It considers its preschool and singles classes

some of its stronger programs. The main Sunday service starts at 10:30 a.m.

MT. OLIVET BAPTIST CHURCH
3500 Edwards Mill Rd. 787-1910

Mt. Olivet is in the middle of the city's northwest growth area and has grown with it, especially with Southern Baptist minister Tom Vestal, who has been there since 1978 and has helped double the church's membership. The congregation today numbers around 450 and services are broadcast on the public cable channel weekly. Vestal also has gained notice in the local press for speaking out for conservative political causes and has been active in voter registration among Protestant conservatives.

PROVIDENCE BAPTIST CHURCH
6339 Glenwood Ave. 571-1171

This Southern Baptist congregation has made a reputation for outgrowing its buildings, and its current home, dedicated in 1992, was once one of the city's largest hotels. It has a strong Bible-study program and a prayer room that is open 24 hours a day. Pastor David Horner preaches in what was once a convention hall, backed up by a choir with full orchestra. Sunday School classes are held in the old bar room. The church also oversees a busy missionary effort.

PULLEN MEMORIAL
BAPTIST CHURCH
1801 Hillsborough St. 828-0897

When Southern Baptists around here brag about their independent congregations, they often point to Pullen Memorial as a case in point. It was regular sport at the state conventions for fundamentalists to try to throw Pullen's liberal congregation out of the Baptist ranks. They succeeded in 1992 over the issue of homosexual unions sanctioned by Pullen, which remains at the forefront of social change. It is next to the NCSU campus and attracts a college crowd, including students and faculty. It has active outreach programs and led the way among churches with an integrated day care center. Minister Mahan Siler oversees a diverse congregation of about 600 and a strong music program.

Catholic

SACRED HEART CATHEDRAL
226 Hillsborough St.   *832-6030*

Catholic life has been growing in Raleigh since 1821, and has boomed during the past 25 years when many Catholic families moved into the city from the northeast. Built in the 1920s, the Cathedral sits on the corner of Hillsborough and McDowell streets and is the parish to about 450 households. Cathedral School, K-8, has a student body of 250. The rector is Father Tim O'Connor. Three masses are said on Sunday morning. There is also a Spanish mass. The Cathedral is the smallest cathedral in the contiguous United States.

CHURCH OF ST. JOSEPH
630 Peartree Ln.   *231-6364*

Located near Wake Medical Center, this relatively young church serves the black Catholic commu-

nity of east Raleigh. It was established in 1968 and has a parish of about 160 families. Its pastor is the Rev. JaVan Saxon. The church has had a significant impact upon the black community and is the worship place of many of the city's black leaders. The church offers Sunday School for all grade levels and a continuing religious education program for adults. On the first Sunday of each month, it celebrates a Share Sunday by donating food and cash offerings to the city's outreach programs.

OUR LADY OF LOURDES
2718 Overbrook Dr.   *782-1973*

Our Lady of Lourdes began in 1954, and has 1,320 families. It also maintains a K-8 school. The church building, which can be seen off Anderson Drive, was completed in 1976 and is one of the more contemporary in Raleigh with glass and gleaming white exterior. Members are proud of their summer Bible program and adult education. The parish celebrated the feast of Our Lady of Lourdes this year with a successful Mardi Gras. The pastor is Rev. Jeffrey A. Ingham, who oversees an assistant, a full-time youth minister and a music minister.

ST. RAPHAEL
5801 Falls of the Neuse Rd.   *876-1581*

An offshoot of Our Lady of Lourdes, St. Raphael has become the biggest Catholic parish in town with 2,100 families and well over 6,000 total parishioners. Pastor J. Paul Byron directs a staff that includes an associate pastor, music director, religious and youth education directors. Its parish center is used by many groups such as the Italian-American Club, which has been known to hold sumptuous cooking contests. The parish also holds an annual Colonial Fair and auction in September to raise money. It has an active CYO as well as a program for divorced and separated parishioners. It celebrates three masses Sunday, the last at 11:30 p.m. It sponsors Cub, Boy and Girl Scout troops.

Episcopal

CHRIST EPISCOPAL CHURCH
120 E. Edenton St.   834-6259

As noted earlier, this is one of the foundation churches of the city, organized in 1821 and located across the street from the Capitol. It carries almost two centuries of history in its parish records. The congregation in 1993 selected Rev. Winston Charles as rector and he has two assistants. The congregation contains some of the city's influential families, such as Justice Sarah Parker. The church building is historic and its stained glass windows are beautiful. The Sunday Schools are lively, the music is some of the best in town, and the church's outreach programs include missions to Appalachia, volunteers to help the illiterate to read, a Wednesday night AA chapter and classes for new parents.

ST. MARK'S
1725 New Hope Rd.   231-6767

For years, St. Mark's was one of the smaller Episcopal congrega-

tions in the area but one of the most enthusiastic and loyal, even sporting its own bumper stickers. It is the kind of parish that you expect to find near a college campus, although it is across town from most of the city's campuses and outside the Beltline. Its minister is the Rev. Jane Gurry, the first woman deacon in the diocese who has returned to become the first woman rector of her own parish. One member describes the congregation as an "involved" membership and notes that the church holds communion at every service. Its 300-member congregation has worshiped at this location since 1987.

ST. MICHAEL'S
1520 Canterbury Rd.   782-0731

St. Michael's is one of the largest Episcopal parishes in its diocese with 2,400 members, many of them newcomers and young families. The Rev. Lawrence K. Brown was the associate minister before becoming the church's second rector since it was started in the mid-1950s. The church's contemporary building displays a high, steep, slate roof that is held up by huge laminated wooden beams, giving the nave a dramatic openness and allowing the grand pipe organ room to play. The church yard includes a columbarium among the trees to the north. It has a busy preschool and kindergarten as well as an excellent choir and music director. To relieve some of the pressures of its bulging congregation, the church has sponsored a new mission in north Raleigh.

Jewish

BETH MEYER SYNAGOGUE
504 Newton Rd.   *848-1420*

This synagogue is the oldest of the three Jewish congregations in Raleigh. Beth Meyer, with about 320 families, moved from Cameron Park to Newton Road in 1983 with a procession that carried the Torah scrolls on foot the eight-mile distance. Rabbi Dan Ornstein assumed responsibilities in 1989. The congregation is conservative in practice. Beth Meyer worship service is held at 8 p.m. Friday and 9:30 a.m. Saturdays.

TEMPLE BETH OR
5315 Creedmoor Rd.   *781-4895*

Like Beth Meyer, Temple Beth Or was downtown before it moved to the present location on Creedmoor Road. Its new synagogue is a very contemporary, award-winning design and worth a visit just to see. The Bema was rescued from a temple in Chicago which was being torn down. Beth Or is reform, has about 300 families and has been under the leadership of Rabbi Lucy Dinner since the summer of '93. Worship service is held on Friday at 8:00 p.m.

Lutheran

HOLY TRINITY
2723 Clark Ave.   *828-1687*

This is a congregation of the Lutheran Church of America and numbers about 1,200, making it one of the largest in the Triangle. It was organized in 1912 and has helped start St. Philip's and Christ the King Lutheran as well as two new missions. Close to NCSU, it considers itself a "home congregation away from home" for Lutheran students, and pastors Stephen P. Gerhard and Paul Abbe have help from the Rev. Beverly D. Alexander, who serves as the church's campus pastor. The busy days are Sunday (which has two services plus Sunday School) and Wednesday, which is choir night. It sponsors a Boy Scout troop and an AA chapter.

Methodist

ASBURY UNITED METHODIST
6612 Creedmoor Rd.   *847-2818*

One of the fastest growing Methodist churches in the state, Asbury is located along one of the city's growth arteries outside the Beltline. Started in 1979, its minister is Jerry Smith, who pastors, with a full-time staff of four, to about 1,150 members. In November 1988, the church was struck by a tornado, and members worshiped in Greystone Baptist while their church was rebuilt. The church rebounded with a rush and boasts 150 teenagers in the junior and senior high groups. Its newness means opportunity for members to participate in church life. Not surprisingly, it caters to young families and operates a preschool program as well as an after-school program for working families. It also has a day camp in the summer. And like almost all churches its size, it maintains a nursery during services.

Photo by Nancy Kitchener.

Temple Beth Or, home to one of Raleigh's three Jewish congregations, has won architectural awards for its contemporary design.

EDENTON STREET UNITED METHODIST

228 W. Edenton St.   *832-7535*

Considered the "mother" church for Raleigh's Methodists, Edenton Street traces its history back to 1811, and with a membership of 2,900, it is one of the city's largest congregations of any faith. Its brick building with tall spire is kept in good repair, and, including the parking lot and other church buildings, Edenton Street occupies almost an entire city block. The Rev. William C. Simpson, Jr., is the senior minister and has carried on the church's leadership in such fields as urban ministries. Music lovers throughout the city also have long enjoyed the church's tradition in music, the pipe organ and the Raleigh Oratorio's seasonal concerts, many of them favorite sacred works such as Handel's "Messiah" or Verdi's "Requiem." As one church official noted about church members, many of whom live in the suburbs, "They all have to drive past other churches to get here, so they must want to come here."

HIGHLAND UNITED METHODIST

1901 Ridge Rd.   *787-4240*

Started in 1954, Highland has about 1,900 members and a congregation that is filled with many of the people who work in Research Triangle Park and NCSU, giving it a definite "high tech" flavor. Minister Charles M. Smith has an associate pastor, Vickie Pruett. The church attracts many members because of its music program, which includes a hand bell choir. There's a large preschool program for two-to five-year-olds and an after-school program for grades K-5, along with a pretty good church softball and basketball team. One member describes the congregation as mostly "under 55" and active. Sunday School is as large as the church service. Many members come from Cary or north Raleigh since the church is near a Beltline exit.

Presbyterian

DAVIE STREET PRESBYTERIAN

300 E. Davie St.   *834-8855*

This Presbyterian church is a downtown congregation that contains some of the city's prominent black families, including House Speaker Dan Blue, D-Wake, and former Mayor Clarence Lightner. It was founded in 1872 and numbers about 140 members. Its minister is J.W. Brown, who cites the church's outreach programs for youth and older parishioners as strong points.

FIRST PRESBYTERIAN

111 W. Morgan St.   *821-5750*

This oldest Presbyterian church in town continues to have a lively role in the city's life. Its new pastor, Louisianan Dr. Edwin W. Stock, Jr., succeeded the popular Scotchman Albert G. Edwards, and continues preaching the church's televised Sunday sermon on WYED (Channel 17). The church began in 1816 and today counts a membership that is slightly over 1,700. One of its popular services is sandwiched between two bargain lunchtime meals on Wednesday; the first is at noon, the second at 1 p.m.

Over 300 visitors of all faiths dine and pray. The church also has a special program for elderly members and attracts 60 men to a Wednesday 7 a.m. breakfast and Bible study. Despite its age, the church, according to one member, "baptizes a lot of babies."

HUDSON MEMORIAL PRESBYTERIAN
4921 Six Forks Rd.   *787-1086*

Started in 1957, this north Raleigh congregation met first in nearby schools. It has grown and expanded to 1,400 members and, says minister Robert E. Fields, "We are quite strategically located one mile north of the Beltline on a major thoroughfare connecting the northwest quadrant of Raleigh to the downtown area. It is an area where most newcomers will likely begin looking for a home." The church has several Sunday services and supports a preschool program and mother's morning out on Tuesdays and Thursdays. It also provides a mother's day out, Monday through Friday, an active music program, and after-school care from 3 to 6 p.m.

WEST RALEIGH PRESBYTERIAN
27 Horne St.   *828-5468*

This is a university church, a block away from the NCSU campus, whose 350 members include many faculty and students from not only NCSU but Peace College and Meredith as well. Dr. P. Joseph Ward is the minister. The church has many outreach programs serving the community. Active junior and senior high youth members number about 25 and the church's day care center serves 97 children between ages two and four.

WHITE MEMORIAL PRESBYTERIAN
1704 Oberlin Rd.   *834-3424*

White Memorial has the largest Presbyterian membership in the city—4,010. Located on the edge of Hayes-Barton, an important part of its mission centers on community ministry. It has an interim minister while it searches for a successor to the popular Edwin Pickard who packed the congregation for 26 years into the typically austere, brick church. Its slender, white spire can be seen for miles. The church maintains a full range of programs, including a well-known preschool and kindergarten with veteran teachers for children two to five years old. The church's steady growth culminated in a major expansion that added a three-story building to the church's cramped quarters in 1986.

*Sir Paul Girolami Research Center on the Glaxo campus
in Research Triangle Park, home to the company's worldwide research center
in the area of cancer and metabolic disease.*

Inside
Research Triangle Park

Insiders in the Triangle scene generally agree that the establishment of a vast research complex midway between the University of North Carolina, N.C. State University and Duke University was a good idea. But getting a consensus on just whose idea it was is another matter.

Our research leads us to conclude that the development of the now world-famous Research Triangle Park grew from the dreams of more than one creative individual.

There was the late Dr. Howard W. Odom, founder in 1924 of UNC's Institute for Research in Social Science; he envisioned an academic center for research in the social sciences and human relations. Beginning in 1952, Odom wrote a series of proposals for the establishment of research institutes that would involve programs affiliated with the Consolidated University of North Carolina.

At about the same time that Odom was envisioning an academic center, Greensboro builder Romeo H. Guest was dreaming of ways to attract research and industrial development to the area. It was Guest who in 1953 coined the name—Research Triangle—to describe the triangular-shaped area lying between the state's three major research universities.

Guest was concerned that the influx of northern industries was slowing down. As a graduate of MIT in Cambridge, Massachusetts, he was familiar with the now famous research and industrial complex growing up along Boston's Route 128. Guest believed that the development of similar research facilities here would eventually spawn new industrial growth.

In 1955, Guest talked with then-Governor Luther H. Hodges about the idea. The Governor went for it, and the rest is history. By the spring of that year, Hodges appointed a committee composed of prominent bankers, business executives, industrialists and university heavyweights. The committee eventually established a nonprofit organization known today as the Research Triangle Foundation.

The Foundation was entrusted with the task of acquiring land and finding appropriate tenants for the park. Its first executive director was Dr. George L. Simpson, a UNC sociology professor and former colleague of Dr. Odom.

Plans were soon made that forged the dreams of both Odom and Guest: there would be a vast research-industrial complex, including a separate Research Triangle Institute to be owned by the three universities.

By 1958, the Research Triangle Foundation had raised enough money to begin purchasing and developing the land that would soon be known as Research Triangle Park. The following year, the Chemstrand Corporation purchased a 100-acre site to build the Park's first research campus, now known as the Monsanto Triangle Park Development Center.

Things moved along slowly but steadily after that, with about one new tenant added each year, until 1965 when both the National Institute of Environmental Health Sciences and IBM Corporation announced plans to construct major facilities here.

IBM put Research Triangle Park on the map. The number of companies located here has grown since 1965 from six to almost 60. Today the park employs over 34,000 people working out of 13 million square feet of office space. By the year 2010, more than 50,000 people are expected to be employed in the Park.

The Research Triangle Foundation is now developing the Park's southernmost section, including 2,700 acres of building sites, most of them located in northern Wake County. The area includes about 40 building sites, ranging from 8 to 116 acres. Plans for the new section include five man-made lakes, a jogging trail and a greenway system.

With over 60 major companies situated here and plenty of room to grow, Research Triangle Park is the largest planned research park in the United States. Park occupants must be organizations engaged in "research, development and scientifically oriented production." While IBM and the microelectronics industry gave RTP its first big boost, the Park is now home to research giants from other fields including biotechnology, telecommunications, medicine and environmental science. The roster of tenants includes the research facilities of some of the largest corporations in the world: Burroughs Wellcome, Northrop, Data General, Northern Telecom, Union Carbide, General Electric, Glaxo, Sumitomo Electric, Ciba Geigy, Reichold and DuPont among others.

What's more, the Triangle Universities' Center for Advanced Studies, Inc. (TUCASI), a joint activity of UNC, Duke and N.C. State will sponsor development of advanced studies on its 120-acre campus at the center of the Park. Its tenants include the National Humanities Center, for the study of history, literature, philosophy and other humanities. Also included in plans for TUCASI are the Microelectronics Center of North Carolina, the N.C. Biotechnology Center and the N.C. Science and Technology Research Center.

The federal government has several major research centers at RTP, including the National Institute of Environmental Health Sciences, National Center for Health

Statistics, the U.S. Forest Services' Forestry Sciences Laboratory, and the U.S. Environmental Protection Agency (EPA).

Despite the unprecedented influx of such mammoth research facilities, RTP retains its pleasant campus atmosphere, thanks to restrictive covenants requiring tenants to purchase large tracts of land and limit their buildings to no more than 15 percent of their tract.

However, the Park's impact on surrounding areas has not always been equally wholesome. RTP and the extension of Interstate 40 connecting each of the points of the Triangle, have driven real estate prices sky high. What was once inexpensive, rolling farmland has largely been converted into $100,000-an-acre-and-up office complexes, accompanied by a string of hotels, fast-food restaurants and shopping centers.

The amount of business and industry that RTP has lured to the area has no doubt exceeded Romeo Guest's wildest expectations. But at the same time, its impact has dramatically altered the agricultural way of life in this region that Dr. Howard Odum wanted to preserve.

In a way, RTP and the intense development accompanying it, symbolize both the tremendous opportunities and problems that growth has brought to the entire Triangle. The area enjoys one of the highest growth rates and lowest unemployment rates in the nation. The cost of living is still relatively reasonable, compared to some of the metropolitan centers of the Northeast, West and Southwest. But at the same time some of the rural qualities that make this such an attractive place to live and work are being threatened. How to balance positive opportunities for growth against long-term social and environmental costs is the dilemma facing local planners and elected officials throughout the area. How these challenges are addressed in the next few years will determine the quality of life throughout the Research Triangle area for the future.

If you'd like more detailed information on Research Triangle Park and the companies located here, contact the Research Triangle Foundation, P.O. Box 1225, Research Triangle Park, NC 27709, 549-8181.

Staff photo.

Research Triangle Park is headquarters for research and develovment
as well as the manufacturing of telephone equipment and switching systems
for Northern Telecom.

Inside
Research Triangle Park Corporations

AIRCO SPECIAL GASES ELECTRONIC DEVELOPMENT FACILITY
30 EMPLOYEES
11 Triangle Dr.   549-0633

Airco conducts development of gasses and blending techniques in support of semiconductor development and fabrication.

ALCAN-SUMITOMO ELECTRIC, INC.
30 EMPLOYEES
74 T. W. Alexander Dr.   549-8361

Development of Cable Optic Ground Wire is the focus here.

AMERICAN ASSOCIATION OF TEXTILE CHEMISTS AND COLORISTS
23 EMPLOYEES
1 Davis Dr.   549-8141

This Association is the world's largest technical and scientific textile membership society.

BASF CORPORATION
AGRICULTURAL CHEMICALS
200 EMPLOYEES
26 Davis Dr.   248-6500

RTP is the Agricultural Chemicals Headquarters and Research Center for BASF.

BECTON, DICKINSON AND COMPANY RESEARCH CENTER
180 EMPLOYEES
21 Davis Dr.   549-8641

B-D conducts basic and applied research related to medical devices and health-care products at this location.

BNR (BELL NORTHERN RESEARCH)
1500 EMPLOYEES
35 Davis Dr.

This lab undertakes research and development for digital central office switching systems.

BATTELLE
8 EMPLOYEES
200 Park Dr., Suite 211   549-8291

Battelle administers the Scientific Services Program, subcontracting services with independent, university and company-affiliated researchers.

STATISTICS AND DATA ANALYSIS SECTION
100 Park Dr., Suite 207   549-8970

This section provides statistics, data management, health and environmental risk assessments.

BURROUGHS WELLCOME COMPANY
2,019 EMPLOYEES

South Campus	3030 Cornwallis Rd.
North Campus	3025 Cornwallis Rd.
	248-3000

RTP is the corporate headquarters for this pharmaceutical giant. Also in this location are the pharmaceutical research and development laboratories.

BURROUGHS WELLCOME FUND
5 EMPLOYEES

3030 Cornwallis Rd.   *248-4136*

Financial awards in specific areas of medical research are provided by this fund.

CHEMICAL INDUSTRY INSTITUTE OF TOXICOLOGY
150 EMPLOYEES

6 Davis Dr.   *541-2070*

This independent nonprofit research corporation is dedicated to developing an improved scientific basis for understanding and assessing potential adverse effects of chemicals, pharmaceuticals and consumer products on human health.

CIBA-GEIGY BIOTECHNOLOGY
RESEARCH CENTER
110 EMPLOYEES

3054 Cornwallis Rd.   *541-8500*

Biotechnical research and development to come up with more productive crops and more effective means of crop protection is conducted here.

COMPUCHEM CORPORATION
480 EMPLOYEES

3308 Chapel Hill/Nelson Hwy. 406-1600

CompuChem provides testing services for the measurement of toxic chemicals and hazardous wastes in the environment and uri-

Burroughs Wellcome & Company in Research Triangle Park.

nalysis testing services for the detection of drug abuse.

COMPUTER SCIENCES CORPORATION
200 EMPLOYEES
79 W. T. Alexander Dr.
4401 Bldg.   541-9287
This company provides software development and maintenance, scientific modeling and government contract support.

DATA GENERAL CORPORATION
500 EMPLOYEES
62 T.W. Alexander Dr.   549-8421
This facility houses the Systems Software Development, the Software Qualifications and Support and the Customer Documentation divisions of Data General.

DU PONT ELECTRONICS TECHNOLOGY CENTER
250 EMPLOYEES
14 T. W. Alexander Dr.   248-5000
Research, development, applications engineering and sales support associated with materials and systems for the electronics industry are the focus here.

ENVIRONMENTAL HEALTH, RESEARCH AND TESTING, INC.
70 EMPLOYEES
P. O. Box 12199
RTP, NC 27709   544-1792
This company conducts research and testing of environmental chemicals suspected to be carcinogenic or mutagenic agents.

ERICSSON GE MOBILE COMMUNICATIONS, INC.
10 EMPLOYEES
1 Triangle Dr.   549-7530
Mobile telephone communications research and development is conducted here.

FOUNDATIONS FOR EDUCATIONAL DEVELOPMENT, INC.
200 Park Dr., Suite 111A   549-8947
This foundation provides research, planning, development, public relations and other services for educational entities or private enterprise.

GLAXO, INC.
6,000 EMPLOYEES
5 Moore Dr.   248-2100
The corporate headquarters and research facilities of this pharmaceutical company are located in RTP and a manufacturing plant is located in nearby Zebulon.

GTE-GOVERNMENT SYSTEMS CORPORATION
160 EMPLOYEES
400 Park Plaza   549-1111
This engineering organization is responsible for the development of communications and command & control systems, including hardware design, software development and systems integration.

HARRIS MICROELECTRONICS CENTER
347 EMPLOYEES
3026 Cornwallis Rd.   549-3100
Harris designs and fabricates AVLSI (Advanced very large-scale integration) circuits for U.S. mili-

tary systems and commercial applications.

INSTRUMENT SOCIETY OF AMERICA
120 EMPLOYEES

67 T. W. Alexander Dr.   *549-8411*

This is headquarters of an international society of engineers, scientists, technicians, managers and educators. The Society develops publications, standards and educational programs in instrumentation and automatic control.

INTERNATIONAL BUSINESS
MACHINES CORPORATION (IBM)
10,000 EMPLOYEES

3039 Cornwallis Rd.   *543-5221*

This facility undertakes development, assembly and programming in the telecommunications products area.

KOBE DEVELOPMENT CORPORATION
18 EMPLOYEES

79 T. W. Alexander Dr.
4401 Bldg.   *549-0544*

Principal activities include research and development of electronic materials and devices and new business development through investment.

LITESPEC, INC.
84 EMPLOYEES

76 T.W. Alexander Dr.   *541-8400*

Litespec manufactures optical fiber.

MCMAHAN ELECTRO-OPTICS, INC.

79 T. W. Alexander Dr.   *549-7575*

This company contracts research and development in laser,

electro-optic, unconventional imaging and applied physics technologies.

MCNC (MICROELECTRONICS
CENTER OF NORTH CAROLINA)
245 EMPLOYEES

3021 Cornwallis Rd.   *248-1800*

This private, non-profit corporation supports advanced education, research and technology programs in partnership with the state's universities, research institutes and industry.

NSI TECHNOLOGY SERVICES
CORPORATION
340 EMPLOYEES

2 Triangle Dr.   *549-0611*

NSI provides technical support services to various agencies of the U.S. government and to industry.

NATIONAL CENTER FOR HEALTH
STATISTICS
131 EMPLOYEES

12 Davis Dr.   *541-4873*

This center prepares health data and undertakes computer operations and data processing research.

NATIONAL HUMANITIES CENTER
19 EMPLOYEES

7 T. W. Alexander Dr.   *549-0661*

This is an institute for research and advanced studies in history, literature, philosophy and other fields of the humanities.

NATIONAL INSTITUTE OF ENVIRONMENTAL HEALTH SCIENCES
900 EMPLOYEES
Headquarters
South Campus   111 T. W. Alexander Dr.
East Campus   79 T. W. Alexander Dr.
North Campus   104 T. W. Alexander Dr.
(Information Services Branch)   541-3426

NIEHS conducts biomedical research on the effects of chemical, physical and biological environmental agents on human health and well being.

NATIONAL TOXICOLOGY PROGRAM
111 T. W. Alexander Dr.   541-3991

This program conducts toxicology and test-methods development research and provides information to research and regulatory agencies.

NORTH CAROLINA BIOTECHNOLOGY CENTER
39 EMPLOYEES
79 T. W. Alexander Dr.
4501 Bldg.   541-9366

This nonprofit organization works through the state's universities, industry and government to assure that North Carolina gains long-term economic benefits from the development and commercialization of biotechnology.

NORTH CAROLINA STATE EDUCATION ASSISTANCE AUTHORITY
50 EMPLOYEES
10 T. W. Alexander Dr.   549-8614

The Authority plans, finances and administers student financial assistance programs of a statewide or inter-institutional nature.

NORTHERN TELECOM INC.
8,600 EMPLOYEES
4001 E. Chapel Hill/Nelson Hwy. 992-5000

This is headquarters for the company's Integrated Network Systems Group, which is concerned with development, marketing and assembly of digital switching systems for central office telephone exchanges.

RADIAN CORPORATION
220 EMPLOYEES
3200 E. Chapel Hill/Nelson Hwy. 541-9100

Radian provides environmental services, mainly to the U.S. government.

REICHHOLD CHEMICALS, INC.
430 EMPLOYEES
2400 Ellis Rd.   800-448-3482

This is corporate headquarters and home for the research and development laboratories for Reichhold.

RESEARCH TRIANGLE FOUNDATION
8 EMPLOYEES
2 Hanes Dr.   549-8181

This trusteeship is owner and developer of Research Triangle Park, working in conjunction with the three major universities in the Triangle.

RESEARCH TRIANGLE INSTITUTE
1,800 EMPLOYEES
3040 Cornwallis Rd.   541-6000

The Institute provides contract research in the physical, life and social sciences.

RHONE-POULENC AG COMPANY
570 EMPLOYEES
2 T. W. Alexander Dr.   *549-2000*

This company conducts research and development, engineering and marketing of agricultural products.

SCIENCE AND TECHNOLOGY RESEARCH CENTER
16 EMPLOYEES
2 Davis Dr.   *549-0671*

The Center provides specialized information to government, industry, research and educational institutions using computer-indexed databases.

SEMICONDUCTOR RESEARCH CORPORATION
36 EMPLOYEES
79 T. W. Alexander Dr.
4401 Bldg.   *541-9400*

The goal of this not-for-profit cooperative is to plan, promote, coordinate and sponsor semiconductor research at universities.

SCR COMPETITIVENESS FOUNDATION
79 T. W. Alexander Dr.
4401 Bldg.   *541-9400*

This foundation works through educational institutions to advance U.S. competitiveness in microelectronics.

SIGMA XI, THE SCIENTIFIC RESEARCH SOCIETY
35 EMPLOYEES
99 T. W. Alexander Dr.   *549-4691*

The Society works to encourage scientific research and public understanding of science and technology and science education.

SOUTHEASTERN EDUCATIONAL IMPROVEMENT LABORATORY
30 EMPLOYEES
200 Park Dr., Suite 200   *549-8216*

Educational research, policy analysis and dissemination of information in the six southeastern states are the activities of this group.

SUMITOMO ELECTRIC FIBER OPTICS CORPORATION
400 EMPLOYEES
78 T. W. Alexander Dr.   *541-8100*

This company develops and manufactures fiber optic cable and sells fiber-optics apparatus and engineering services.

TRIANGLE RESEARCH COLLABORATIVE, INC. (TRC)
100 Park Dr., Suite 115   *549-9093*

Products for time-and-motion study applications are developed here. TRC offers customized system integration and software-development services also.

WITH OVER 60 MAJOR COMPANIES SITUATED HERE AND PLENTY OF ROOM TO GROW, RESEARCH TRIANGLE PARK IS THE LARGEST PLANNED RESEARCH PARK IN THE UNITED STATES.

TRIANGLE UNIVERSITIES CENTER FOR ADVANCED STUDIES, INC. (TUCASI)

2 Hanes Dr.   *549-8181*

This corporation facilitates the planning and execution of nonprofit research and educational programs for the three major universities in the Triangle.

TROXLER ELECTRONIC LABORATORIES, INC.
125 EMPLOYEES

3008 Cornwallis Rd.   *549-8661*

Troxler develops, manufactures and distributes instruments and systems for measuring physical properties and characteristics of engineering materials.

UAI TECHNOLOGY, INC.
55 EMPLOYEES

68 T. W. Alexander Dr.   *541-9339*

This company produces databases, software, consulting and education in the corporate cash-management field, personal financial-planning software and research studies for financial institutions.

UNDERWRITERS LABORATORIES, INC.
449 EMPLOYEES

12 Laboratory Dr.   *549-1400*

Product testing for public safety is conducted in these labs.

U.S. DEPARTMENT OF AGRICULTURE-FOREST SERVICE
46 EMPLOYEES

3041 Cornwallis Rd.   *549-4000*

The Southeastern Forest Experiment Station provides basic and applied forest research.

U.S. ENVIRONMENTAL PROTECTION AGENCY
1,250 EMPLOYEES

79 T. W. Alexander Dr.   *541-3014*

This agency conducts research, develops and standardizes techniques for monitoring, and develops and evaluates technologies for controlling air pollutants.

UNIVERSITY OF NORTH CAROLINA CENTER FOR PUBLIC TELEVISION
209 EMPLOYEES

10 T. W. Alexander Dr.   *549-7000*

This is headquarters for North Carolina's 10-station statewide public television network.

UNIVERSITY OF NORTH CAROLINA EDUCATIONAL COMPUTING SERVICE
18 EMPLOYEES

2 Davis Dr.
Science and Technology Bldg.   *549-0671*

Computing service and technical support for the UNC system, plus many state, community and private colleges is provided here.

Inside

Research Triangle Park Support Services

Because of its proximity to Raleigh, Durham and Chapel Hill, you will find many of the support and service-oriented companies that serve RTP listed in other sections of the Guide. (See chapters on **ACCOMMODATIONS, RESTAURANTS** and **SHOPPING.**) Following are a few of the services you will find especially convenient if you do business in the Park.

FEDERAL EXPRESS
2311 Englert Dr.   *1-800-238-5355*
This full-service Federal Express office receives packages until 8:30 p.m. Monday through Friday and until 5 p.m. on Saturdays.

CAROLINA ASSOCIATION OF TRANSLATORS AND INTERPRETERS
RTP   *851-1901*
CATI connects Triangle-area translators and interpreters

The sprawling campuses in Research Triangle Park provide wonderful outdoor escapes for office dwellers.

with the businesses who need their services. Organized in Raleigh in 1985, this organization is a chapter of the American Translators Association and serves both North and South Carolina. CATI also distributes a Translation Services Directory, including an annually updated compilation of local translators and their specialties. Call for more information.

RESEARCH TRIANGLE FOUNDATION
2 Hanes Dr.
P.O. Box 1225
RTP, NC 27709   549-8181
This trusteeship is owner and developer of Research Triangle Park, in conjunction with the three major universities in the Triangle. If you would like information on RTP or its resident companies, you can find it here.

U. S. POST OFFICE (27709)
6 Park Plaza   549-9903
For the prestige of an RTP address, this full-service post office is conveniently located to serve the Park. The hours of operation for the post office windows are 8:30 a.m. to 5:30 p.m., Monday through Friday.

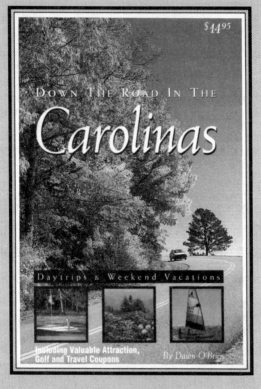

ORDER FORM

Mail to : Becklyn Publishing Group, Inc.
Post Office Box 14154
Research Triangle Park, NC 27709

Name ―――――――――――――――――――――――――――

Address ――――――――――――――――――――――――――

City, State, Zip ―――――――――――――――――――――

Quantity	Title	Price	Shipping	Total
	Insiders' Guide To Charlotte	14.95	3.00	
	Insiders' Guide To Wilmington	12.95	3.00	
	Insiders' Guide To Crystal Coast	12.95	3.00	
	Insiders' Guide To The Outer Banks	12,95	3.00	
	Insiders' Guide To Charleston	12.95	3.00	
	Insiders' Guide To Myrtle Beach	12.95	3.00	
	Insiders' Guide To Richmond	12.95	3.00	
	Insiders' Guide To Virginia Beach	12.95	3.00	
	Insiders' Guide To VA's Blue Ridge	12.95	3.00	
	Insiders' Guide To Williamsburg	12.95	3.00	
	Insiders' Guide To Washington, D.C.	12.95	3.00	
	Insiders' Guide To Civil War Sites	12.95	3.00	
	Insiders' Guide To Orlando	12.95	3.00	
	Down The Road In The Carolinas	14.95	3.00	

Sub Total

N.C. residents add 6% sales tax

Grand Total

or
Call toll free at

1-800-777-4843   We accept M/C and Visa

When ordering by mail, please enclose payment in full (check, cash or money order) with order form. Allow 3-4 weeks delivery.

ALSO FROM
THE INSIDERS' GUIDE SERIES

NORTH CAROLINA

THE INSIDERS' GUIDE TO THE CAPE FEAR COAST & WILMINGTON
THE INSIDERS' GUIDE TO THE CRYSTAL COAST & NEW BERN
THE INSIDERS' GUIDE TO THE OUTER BANKS
THE INSIDERS' GUIDE TO CHARLOTTE

SOUTH CAROLINA

THE INSIDERS'GUIDE TO CHARLESTON
THE INSIDERS' GUIDE TO MYRTLE BEACH

VIRGINIA

THE INSIDERS' GUIDE TO THE BLUE RIDGE
THE INSIDERS' GUIDE TO GREATER RICHMOND
THE INSIDERS' GUIDE TO VIRGINIA BEACH/NORFOLK
THE INSIDERS' GUIDE TO WILLIAMSBURG

FLORIDA

THE INSIDERS' GUIDE TO ORLANDO

OTHER

THE INSIDERS' GUIDE TO METRO WASHINGTON, DC
THE INSIDERS' GUIDE TO CIVIL WAR SITES (EASTERN THEATER)

COMING IN 1994...

INSIDERS' GUIDE TO MISSISSIPPI
INSIDERS' GUIDE TO SARASOTA/BRADENTON
INSIDERS' GUIDE TO FLORIDA'S GREAT NORTHWEST
INSIDERS' GUIDE TO LEXINGTON AND KENTUCKY'S BLUEGRASS
INSIDERS' GUIDE TO LOUISVILLE
INSIDERS' GUIDE TO TWIN CITIES (MINNEAPOLIS/ST. PAUL)
INSIDERS GUIDE TO BOULDER
INSIDERS' GUIDE TO DENVER

COMING IN 1995...

THE INSIDERS' GUIDE TO WESTERN NORTH CAROLINA
THE INSIDERS' GUIDE TO ATLANTA

PLUS...additional titles to be announced!

Index of Advertisers

Index

Symbols

A

574 •

G

H

MORE PRODUCT INFORMATION

Please send information on the following areas and advertisers:

❏ **Raleigh**   ❏ **Cary**   ❏ **Durham**   ❏ **Chapel Hill**

Projected Moving Date: _____

❏ Accommodations
❏ Apartments and Rental Property
   Monthly Rent: _____ to _____
❏ Banking and Financial Services
❏ Builders
   Price Range: _____ to _____
❏ Chamber of Commerce
❏ Child Care
❏ Developments
   Amenities desired: ❏ Pool
   ❏ Tennis   ❏ Golf Course

❏ Employment Services
❏ Private Schools
❏ Publications
   ❏ Apartment Finder
   ❏ Apartment Locator
   ❏ New Home Guide
   ❏ Newcomer Magazine
❏ Realtors
❏ Shopping

Please print clearly

Name _____

Title _____

Company _____

Address _____

City, State, Zip _____

Phone ( )_____ FAX ( )_____

Are you a:
   ❏ Resident   ❏ Newcomer   ❏ Visitor   ❏ Planning to relocate

How did you obtain this book?
Purchased in: ❏ AAA   ❏ *News & Observer*
                 ❏ Bookstore   ❏ Publisher
                 ❏ Chamber of Commerce ❏ Other/Retail Store

Received as a gift from: ❏ Employer   ❏ Friend/Relative
                           ❏ Other   ❏ Realtor
                           ❏ Welcoming Service

Suggestions for future editions: _____

The Insiders' Guide to The Triangle

Please take a moment to fill out our reader survey and you will receive a coupon good for **$5.00 off** the purchase of your next *Insiders' Guide*. We would love to hear from you and will also enter you in our Grand Prize drawing in appreciation of your time. Thanks!

$500 GRAND PRIZE
IN ENTERTAINMENT AND DINING GIFT CERTIFICATES

$100 SECOND PRIZE
IN ENTERTAINMENT AND DINING GIFT CERTIFICATES

FIVE $25 THIRD PRIZES
IN ENTERTAINMENT AND DINING GIFT CERTIFICATES

UNLIMITED $5.00 FOURTH PRIZES
COUPON GOOD TOWARD PURCHASE OF NEXT INSIDERS' GUIDE.

EVERYONE'S A WINNER!

BECKLYN
Publishing Group, Inc.

NO POSTAGE
NECESSARY
IF MAILED
IN THE
UNITED STATES

BUSINESS REPLY MAIL
FIRST-CLASS MAIL PERMIT NO. 4450 Raleigh, NC

POSTAGE WILL BE PAID BY THE ADDRESSEE

Becklyn Publishing Group, Inc.
Post Office Box 14154
Research Triangle Park
North Carolina 27709-9988